Harland Wm. Whitmore, Jr.

Aggregate Economic Choice

With 40 Figures

Springer-Verlag
Berlin Heidelberg New York Tokyo

Prof. Harland Wm. Whitmore, Jr.
University of Cincinnati, Department of Economics
1220 Crosley Tower ML #371, Cincinnati, OH 45221, USA

ISBN 3-540-16162-7 Springer-Verlag Berlin Heidelberg New York Tokyo
ISBN 0-387-16162-7 Springer-Verlag New York Heidelberg Berlin Tokyo

Library of Congress Cataloging in Publication Data.
Whitmore, Harland William, 1934– Aggregate economic choice. Bibliography: p. 1. Macroeconomics – Mathematical models. 2. Consumption (Economics) – Mathematical models. I. Title. HB172.5.W47 1986 339'.0724 85-30318 ISBN 0-387-16162-7 (U.S.)

Printing and bookbinding: Offsetdruckerei Julius Beltz, Hemsbach/Bergstr.
2142/3140 543210

Acknowledgement

I am indebted to my colleagues Haynes Goddard, Saul Pleeter, Wolfgang Mayer and especially Lloyd Valentine who read part or all of this manuscript and provided valuable comments and advice. Sue Burns painstakingly typed several drafts of the entire manuscript and Phyllis Trosper typed the final draft. My thanks to both of them for their excellent typing and their patience.

Contents

1. - Conventional Macro Models and Aggregate Economic Choice

Frequent references to economic analysis as the "theory of choice" notwithstanding, macroeconomists generally take a severely limited view of the degree of choice available to private economic agents. Portrayed as price takers buffeted by the dictates of a policy authority, private agents in conventional macro models directly decide only the quantities of labor, privately-produced goods and nonmonetary financial assets. A fictitious auctioneer announces all wages, prices, and interest rates while an outside policy authority determines the levels of government-produced goods, taxes, and the stock of nominal money. Furthermore because existing models typically prohibit private agents from engaging in transactions until the auctioneer has set all wages and prices at their "market clearing" levels, they cannot explain the existence of involuntary unemployment if wages and prices are free to vary. Consequently several assumptions underlying conventional macro models drastically reduce their ability to explain important aggregate economic phenomena.

Although Brunner, Cukierman and Meltzer [1983], Sweeney [1974], Fair [1974, 1984], Siven [1979], Iwai [1981], and Nagatani [1981] present disequilibrium macromodels in which economic agents themselves deliberately set wages and prices, only Brunner et al., Sweeney, and Fair include financial markets in their analyses. But they employ explicit optimizing models to explain only the behavior of the household and/or nonfinancial business sectors and only in the commodity and labor markets. Their financial market specifications ignore the special role of money, the diversity of nonmonetary financial assets, and the optimizing behavior of the private depository institutions.

Studies by Brunner and Meltzer [1971, 1976] do incorporate commercial bank behavior and alternative financial assets. However these models are subject to the same criticisms outlined above with respect to the standard treatment of the pricing mechanism. Also the recent exchange among Friedman and Froewiss [1977, 1981], vanLoo [1980], and Brunner and Meltzer [1981] indicates that some confusion has arisen as to whether the "banks' desired portfolio" and "the stock of money supplied by banks" in the Brunner-Meltzer models represent only the plans of the banks themselves or market equilibrium curves that also incorporate the plans of the non-bank sector. Brunner and Meltzer contend they represent the latter, in which case their models do not portray bank behavior as explicitly as might appear on the surface.

As typically envisioned by the macroanalyst, the policy authority's role involves either effectuating what are presumed to be desired changes or preventing undesired changes in production, employment, prices and interest rates by manipulating one or more policy parameters. In the standard framework, if a given policy parameter (government spending, for instance) is found to be "ineffective" as a stabilization device, it becomes immaterial to the rest of economic activity. Under these conditions the policy parameter is not only left unexplained by other variables but it also fails to help explain them. In the eyes of at least some macroeconomists both monetary and fiscal measures have indeed lost credibility as reliable policy instruments. For instance, "monetarists" and "new classical" economists assert that discretionary fiscal and monetary actions serve poorly as stabilization devices. If these assertions are correct, then the standard "optimal control" approach provides no basis for establishing optimal levels of government spending, taxes, or the nominal money stock.

Whether or not one accepts the "invariance proposition" that predictable changes in policy variables produce no real effects, standard macroeconomic analysis views monetary and fiscal variables strictly as stabilization tools. By bestowing upon the policy authority the responsibility for selecting the levels of government production and taxes, for instance, macroeconomists have ignored the utility which the private sector derives from the services provided by the government. In the conventional framework, government spending on goods and services provides the private sector with earned income but nothing else. At least in democratic societies, however, the citizennary itself ultimately decides the optimal levels of government production and taxes. Furthermore to the extent that the central bank responds to "political pressures" it too behaves in accordance with what it interprets to be the wishes of the people. This suggests that the private sector itself cognitively chooses the optimal levels of government production, taxes and the monetary base in conjunction with its choices in the private markets.

Grossman and Lucas [1974] recognize the productivity of government spending, but the remainder of their model conforms to the standard intermediate macro model. Building upon notions put forward by Buchanan and Tullok [1962], Atkinson and Stiglitz [1980] and Negishi

[1979] offer positive theories of public-goods production, but not within a complete aggregate framework.

The purpose of the present study is to develop a dynamic model of aggregate economic behavior which ventures substantially beyond the current literature in terms of integrating positive theories of wage and price formation, government activity, and the monetary aggregates into a single internally consistent model of national income determination and aggregate economic choice. Real private economic agents deliberately set all wages, prices and interest rates in this model. The private sector, in cooperation with an accommodating government and central bank dedicated to serving the public rather than to controlling it, ultimately chooses as well the optimal levels of public goods, taxes and all financial assets. In the open-economy version the domestic private depository institutions also set the exchange rate between the domestic and foreign units of account.

The model developed here contains five centralized decision-making units: households, nonfinancial businesses, private depository institutions, the government, and the central bank. In Part IV these optimizing agents interact not only with each other, but also with a foreign sector. Each sector is viewed as an optimizing agent. Households maximize utility, the business sectors maximize the present values of the income streams to their owners, the government minimizes the cost of providing "public goods" (whatever goods the community has decided shall be produced by the government and distributed to the households free of charge), and the central bank maximizes its own income.

Based upon the technology and costs facing it, the government sector presents to the households a menu of alternative levels of public goods and the corresponding tax levels necessary to finance their production. The community then selects the optimal level of public goods production in light of its preferences, the taxes must incur to obtain the public goods, and the prices and opportunities prevailing in the financial, labor, and commodity markets. Once the private sector selects the level of public goods it wants, the government attempts to produce those goods at minimum cost. This differs from the conventional approach which views government spending as merely generating income to factors of production and ignores any direct benefit to the community from the public goods themselves. One might legitimately question the ease with which a democratic government laden with bureaucracy can respond to the wishes of its people.

Nevertheless in a democracy the community itself ultimately decides the activities of its government.

The central bank modeled here is not permitted to engage in open-market operations or to adjust reserve requirements. Permitting it to do so would allow it to manipulate unilaterally bank reserves and/or the stock of money in accordance with the conventional "monetary authority" view of central banking. Instead, the central bank passively lends high-powered money to private depository institutions upon demand. In the process it sets the "discount" rate at the level that maximizes its own income. In this manner, additional high-powered money automatically enters the economy provided the private sector is willing to pay a higher discount rate to obtain it. Should the private sector decide instead to reduce the volume of base money it holds, the central bank will automatically absorb the unwanted funds. But it will simultaneously lower the discount rate in order to induce the private sector to keep some of the base money it no longer wanted. Therefore, behaving as a profit-maximizer and thus violating a central tenet of modern central banking theory, the central bank in the present model automatically accommodates the needs of the private sector as it simultaneously "leans against the wind".

The financial markets are fully developed in the present study. Because money serves as the medium of exchange, it reduces transactions time and hence conserves real resources. Therefore money represents more than merely an alternative form of storing value. The present analysis explicitly incorporates this attribute of money. In addition, in the present study the levels of money and bank reserves are mutually determined through the interactions of the households, the nonfinancial businesses, the private depository institutions, the government and the central bank. Checkable deposits and currency explicitly reduce the transactions time incurred by the nonfinancial sectors. Excess reserves provide a similar function for depository institutions. Also, the present model offers a complete description of the private depository institutions as distinct optimizing units charged with setting bond prices and interest rates on personal loans and checkable deposits. Furthermore the effects of the choices of other sectors upon this sector as well as the implications of this sector's decisions upon the remaining sectors are fully integrated into a single consistent framework. For instance, the private depository institutions base their interest rate and financial asset price announcements upon the discount rate charged by the central bank; their estimate of the market demands for checkable deposits, loans, and their equity shares; and upon the government's supply of bonds. These announcements by the depository institutions in turn affect the amounts of currency and checkable deposits that the nonfinancial sectors decide to hold. Consequently both the money stock and the volume of the monetary base emerge as endogenously determined variables which are mutually consistent with every other choice confronting the aggregate economy.

All economic activities of a particular sector are derived from a common microtheoretic foundation in this study. For instance, the household sector's market demands for current consumption goods, physical capital, loans, checkable deposits, equity shares issued by the business sectors, as well as its supply of labor and its demand for public goods are derived simultaneously from a single utility maximizing model of household sector behavior. This approach contrasts sharply with the customary partial-equilibrium microfoundations which: treat household income as a parameter in deriving the consumption function; set personal saving equal to zero in deriving that sector's supply of labor function; and ignore spending, saving and work decisions in deriving a theory of household portfolio selection.

Furthermore because every price is called out by some economic agent in this model, each price represents the solution to an optimizing problem facing the economic agent announcing that price. For instance, the private nonfinancial business sector deliberately sets the hourly wage, the price of consumption goods, the price of capital goods, and the market price of its equity shares in conformance with its attempt to maximize the present value of the income stream to its current owners. With a similar objective in mind, the private financial institutions set the interest rates on checkable deposits and loans as well as the market prices for their own equity shares and government bonds. In the model of the large open economy, the domestic private financial sector also sets the exchange rate in accordance with these interest rates and prices. Trading takes place at announced prices even if they do not happen to "clear" their respective markets. Consequently, after the wages, prices and interest rates have been announced for the current period, producers may experience unanticipated changes in inventories, private depository institutions may find themselves issuing more or fewer checkable deposits than they anticipated, and households may find that some among their number are unemployed even though others are working overtime.

This treatment is consistent with Franklin Fisher's [1983] assertion that disequilibrium theory must be grounded in the optimizing behavior of economic agents who are able to perceive when markets do not clear and who act on that information.

> Without this, we cannot hope to provide a theory of what happens when arbitrage opportunities appear, for the essence of the appearence of such opportunities is that agents see and act on them. A theory that wishes to show how such actions cause the disappearence of these opportunities and a restoration of equilibrium cannot content itself with supposing that they never exist. [1983, p.11]

Consequently, Fisher rejects the conventional notion that some prices move so rapidly that they can be treated as if they were always set by an auctioneer at their market-clearing levels.

The method followed in the present study represents a workable compromise between two other approaches. The first, and until recently the most widely adopted one, views macroeconomic relationships as possessing a life of their own, separate and distinct from their micro counterparts. According to this view, aggregation over many diverse individuals yields macro relationships connected only loosely to the optimizing behavior of individuals. Therefore, this "ad hoc" approach to macro model building largely keeps micro analysis behind the scenes, drawing upon it occasionally to identify potentially relevant variables for inclusion in a particular macro function.

The second alternative, associated with Negishi [1979], Iwai [1981], Hahn [1978], Grandmont [1977] and Siven [1979], among others, diametrically opposes the first. It regards microeconomic analysis of a disaggregated decentralized economy as essential to an understanding of macroeconomic phenomena, such as the existence of involuntary unemployment under endogenously determined wages and prices. This "decentralized" approach relies upon differences in individual tastes, expectations, and constraints in explaining aggregate economic behavior. To this point, however, the associated analysis has been highly abstract and severly limited in scope. None of the studies mentioned in this paragraph, for instance, adequately incorporates the financial markets.

Weintraub [1979] questions an underlying assumption employed in the "decentralized" models. In particular he disagrees with the position that the appropriateness of applying micro principles (i.e. optimization theory) is dependent upon the level of aggregation involved. The reason micro models have not been appropriate for analyzing macro phenomena, he argues, is that until recently micro models were almost exclusively Walrasian general equilibrium models, i.e. models of "coordination success." But macro phenomena fundamentally involve "coordination failures". According to Weintraub, highly aggregated choice theoretic models that incorporate such notions as "imperfect information, transactions costs, and expectations adjustments" could provide the appropriate microfoundations for macro phenomena. It is in this spirit that the present highly aggregated disequilibrium model is formulated.

In his Nobel lecture, Tobin [1982] recants earlier statements (see Tobin [1969]) in which he advocated viewing private wealth holders in macroeconomic models as facing a "wealth constraint". According to this constraint the net value of the sum of a wealth holder's net demands for assets minus the sum of his net ex ante supplies of liabilities at a given moment must equal the value of his actual net wealth at that moment.

Tobin now argues that economic agents instead face "budget restrictions" linking their decisions to save on the income account during a particular period with their plans to accumulate assets and/or retire liabilities on the capital account between the dates delineating that period. Consequently, Tobin now views private economic agents in macro models as facing a restriction comparable to the government's budget constraint, which Christ [1968] popularized more than a decade earlier. Budget restrictions, which have also been adopted by Turnovsky [1977], provide a natural link between an agent's decisions on the income and product accounts. Consequently they will be employed throughout the present study.

For decades economists have recognized that the expectations of economic agents constitute an important factor shaping macroeconomic behavior. But recent macroeconomic analysis seems to focus almost exclusively upon expectations formation, leaving the economic aspects of these models to crude ad hoc specifications. For the most part, contemporary models incorporate rational expectations, claiming that except for a well-behaved disturbance term economic agents possess perfect foresight. These agents are presumed to know the structure of the economy and to possess all available information.

Expectations also play an important role in the present study. The production, pricing, spending, and financial-market decisions of every sector depend heavily upon the conjectures which these respective agents form at the beginning of the current period. However, expectations are not presumed to be formed "rationally" in this study; instead, I treat the agents' conjectures as exogenous. In this sense they are placed on equal footing with household preferences, which are universally treated as exogenous. As Hahn [1978] argues, "... [I]t is not obvious that one is justified in treating preferences as given and quite unjustified in treating conjectures as given." Thus while contemporary macroeconomic models attempt to explain expectations in light of exogenously determined government spending, taxes and the money supply, the present study attempts, among other things, to do the opposite.

Before proceeding to more specific features of this study, the reader should be reminded that, unlike conventional macroeconomic analysis, the purpose of this study is not to analyze the effectiveness of alternative stabilization devices available to policy authority. No policy prescriptions for controlling the economy will be found within these pages. Instead, my purpose is simply to delineate the fundamental factors influencing aggregate economic choice in a democratic society.

An Overview of the Book

Because the complete model is fairly complicated, it will be constructed in four stages. The first two stages constitute the simplified model. After a brief presentation of the complete model's skeleton in Chapter 2, the first stage of construction begins in Chapter 3. The economy is viewed as consisting of only two sectors (households and nonfinancial businesses) participating in four markets (labor, consumer goods, currency, and equity shares issued by the nonfinancial business sector). This stage highlights wage and price setting behavior, the productivity of money, and trading at prices that fail to "clear" the respective markets. The relationship between movements in commodity inventories and money balances among sectors is also developed. Chapter 3 presents the theory of the household sector and Chapter 4 contains the theory of the non-financial business sector. Chapter 5 defines national product and explores the dynamic properties of the simple model.

In the second stage, contained in Chapter 6, the government sector is added, allowing the household sector to select the optimal combination of taxes and public-goods production. For simplicity, government borrowing is precluded. The government simply meets any unanticipated deficit by issuing additional currency and uses any unanticipated surplus to withdraw currency from the economy. This stage highlights the factors influencing the household sector's choices between public and private goods.

The third stage constitutes the complete model of a closed economy. It is presented, sector by sector, in Chapters 7-12. Chapter 7 outlines the positive theory of government sector behavior modified to permit government borrowing and to accommodate checkable deposits held by the government at depository institutions. Chapter 8 modifies the earlier analysis of household behavior to permit not only capital goods and checkable deposits to be owned by households, but also to permit consumer borrowing from depository institutions. Chapter 9 introduces physical capital into the production function of the nonfinancial business sector and also allows that sector to hold deposit balances. Chapter 10 offers a positive theory of the economic behavior of private depository institutions. In Chapters 7-10 the analysis is intended to be strictly descriptive. However in Chapter 11 it becomes prescriptive in that it offers an alternative model of a central bank dedicated to serving the public, rather than to controlling the economy's stock of money, interest rates, or prices.

In Chapter 12 the components depicted in Chapters 7-11 are integrated into a single mutually consistent model of collective economic choice for a closed economy. National income and product are defined in terms of this framework, and a dynamic analysis is performed to highlight the short-run influences upon and joint determination of: national income, prices, the monetary base, the volume of public goods, taxes, and the money supply. The model's long-run properties are also briefly explored in this chapter.

In Chapter 13 the economy is opened to trade and financial transactions with the rest of the world. This constitutes the fourth and final stage of the model's development. The chapter begins by broading the economic activity of the sectors other than the domestic private financial institutions to include foreign trade and capital flows. Then a formal model of the domestic depository institutions is developed in which those institutions set the market exchange rate at the level they deem optimal in light of the other interest rates and prices they must set and in light of their overall objective to maximize their own present value. The various components of the model are then integrated into a single model of a large open economy and the impacts of various foreign-induced shocks upon the domestic economy are examined. Chapter 14 offers a brief summary and conclusion.

References

Anderson, W.H.L., 1979,National Income Theory and Its Price Theoretic Foundations (McGraw-Hill, New York)

Atkinson, A. and J. Stiglitz, 1980, Lectures on Public Economics (McGraw-Hill, New York)

Brunner, K., A. Cukierman and A. Meltzer, 1983, Money and Economic Activity, Inventories and Business Cycles , Journal of Monetary Economics, May, 281-319

Brunner, K. and A. Meltzer, 1972, Money, Debt and Economic Activity, Journal of Political Economy 80, Sept./Oct., 951-977

________, 1976, An Aggregate Theory for a Closed Economy, in J. Stein, ed., Monetarism (North-Holland, New York)

________, 1981, Time Deposits in the Brunner-Meltzer Model of Asset Markets, Journal of Monetary Economics 7, Jan., 129-139

Christ, C., 1968, A Simple Macroeconomic Model with a Government Budget Restraint, Journal of Political Economy 76, Jan-Feb., 53-67

Fair, R., 1974, A Model of Macroeconomic Activity, Vol. 1: The Theoretical Model (Ballinger, Cambridge)

_______, 1984, Specification, Estimation, and Analysis of Macro-econometric Models, (Harvard, Cambridge Mass.)

Fisher, F., 1983, Disequilibrium Foundations of Equilibrium Economics (Cambridge Univ. Press, Cambridge)

Friedman, B. and K. Froewiss, 1977,Bank Behavior in the Brunner-Meltzer Model, Journal of Monetary Economics 3, April, 163-178

_______, 1981, More on Bank Behavior: Reply to vanLoo, Journal of Monetary Economics 7, Jan., 125-128

Grossman, H. and R. Lucas, 1974, The Macro-Economic Effects of Productive Public Expenditures, The Manchester School 42, 162-170

Hahn, F., 1978, On Non-Walrasian Equilibria, Review of Economic Studies 45, 1-17

Iwai, K., 1981, Disequilibrium Dynamics, Cowles Foundation Monograph 27 (Yale University Press, New Haven)

vanLoo, P., 1980, Time Deposit Supply in the Brunner-Meltzer Model, Journal of Monetary Economics 6, Jan., 129-139

Nagatani, K., 1981, Macroeconomic Dynamics (Cambridge University Press, Cambridge)

Negishi, T., 1979, Microeconomic Foundations of Keynesian Macro-economics (North Holland, New York)

Sargent,T., 1979, Macroeconomic Theory (Academic Press, New York)

Siven, C., 1979, A Study in the Theory of Inflation and Unemployment (North Holland, New York)

Sweeney, R.J., 1974, A Macro Theory with Micro Foundations (South-Western Publishing, Cincinnati)

Tobin, J., 1969, A General Equilibrium Approach to Monetary Theory, Journal of Money, Credit and Banking, Feb., 15-29

_______, 1982, Money and Finance in the Macroeconomic Process, Nobel Lecture printed in: Journal of Money, Credit and Banking 14, May, 171-204

Turnovsky, S., 1977, Macroeconomic Analysis and Stabilization Policy (Cambridge Univ. Press, Cambridge)

Weintraub, E.R., 1979, Microfoundations: The Compatibility of Microeconomics and Macroeconomics (Cambridge Univ. Press, Cambridge)

2. - The Basic Structure

The complete model of the closed economy developed in this study contains five centralized decision-making units interacting in nine markets. The non-financial markets include those for labor, consumption goods (nondurables), and capital goods. Separate financial markets exist for checkable deposits, advances, IOU's issued by the household sector, government bonds, equity shares issued by the private nonfinancial business sector, and equity shares issured by the private financial sector. Together these markets simultaneously comprise a market for high-powered money. The model also contains non-market mechanisms through which the household sector produces some of its own services and selects the optimal volume of public goods to be produced by the government. Figure 2.1 provides a visual overview of the closed economy as described in this study.

The model is specified in discrete time with each sector formulating its plans at time t (representing the beginning of the "current" period) so as to optimize an objective function within a two-period time horizon. All stocks of physical and financial assets held at time t are taken as given by everyone. No sector suffers from "portfolio imbalance" with respect to its balance sheet at time t. Assets held at t will yield returns during the current period. Assets acquired anytime during the current period, i.e. before time t+1 (which represents the beginning of "next" period), will not begin to yield returns until next period. Because of the two-period time horizon, each sector plans at time t to sell all assets and retire all liabilities by time t+2, marking the close of next period. Of course when t+1 actually arrives, each sector will face a new two-period time horizon possibly extending beyond t+2. Therefore, by t+1 each sector will be free to alter the plans it made at t with respect to its desired balance sheet for t+2.

In spite of incorrect assertions by May [1970] and others that some sectors' budget constraints take a different form under continous time than they do under discrete time (see Whitmore[1980]), the economic content of the analysis presented below would not be affected if it were placed in a continous framework. Certain macroeconomic models--especially those employing rational expectations to determine the time path of prices--indeed may be simpler to work with within continous time. However in the present study this is not the case. For in the present model prices are announced at the beginning of the current period by real economic agents. Athough these price setters may have a notion as to the prices they will announce next period, the price takers do not know their plans. Furthermore, at the end of the current period the price setters themselves are free to revise their earlier plans and announce an entirely different set of prices in light of new information available to them. Since prices do not adjust instantaneously to clear the respective markets, continuous time affords no inherent advantages over discrete time.

The length of calendar time elapsing between the beginning and the end of each of the current and next periods is left unspecified in this model. The length may differ for each decision-making unit. Furthermore, within a given optimizing model, the current and next periods do not necessarily refer to equal calendar time. In the analytical sense, used here, the current period merely represents the length of time before a variable changes (or is anticipated to change). The next period merely represents all time remaining between the end of the current period and the decision-maker's time horizon. Consequently in the analytical sense, the assumption of a two-period time horizon simply compresses all future time that can be contemplated by the decision-maker beyond the current period into a single next period. Since each decision-maker is permitted to revise its plans at the end of every current period, the two-period planning horizon is not very restrictive.

Besides its initial balance sheet, which it takes as given, each domestic sector formulates its plans at time t with respect to a desired balance sheet for time t+1 as well as with respect to a planned balance sheet for time t+2; the latter contains no assets and no liabilities. On the income account, each sector is free to plan at time t to save or dissave during each of the current and next periods. However its plans on the income account must be consistent with its plans on the capital account. In particular, if every item in both the initial balance sheet at time t and the planned balance sheet for time t+1 is valued in terms of the price at which the decision-maker expects it will be traded during the current period, then the value of the assets minus the value of the liabilities in the balance sheet planned for time t+1 must exceed the value of the assets minus the value of the liabilities in the actual balance sheet at time t by exactly the amount that the sector plans to save on the income account during the current period. Furthermore, if every item in the balance sheet planned for time t+1 is valued in terms of the market price which the sector expects will prevail next period, then (since the balance sheet planned for time t+2 contains no assets or liabilities) the value of the liabilities minus the value of the assets in the balance sheet planned for time t+1 must equal exactly the amount which the sector plans at time t to save on the income account next period. In effect, both of these budget constraints stipulate that, for a given vector of prices, saving out of income is both necessary and sufficient for net wealth accumulation.

Because prices are announced by price setters rather than by fictitious auctioneers in this study, the chapters which integrate the activities of two or more sectors into a single dynamic aggregate model (see Chapters 5,6,12, and 13) produce recursive, rather than simultaneous, systems. In models employing fictitious auctioneers, both demanders and suppliers are viewed as price takers. The prevailing price and quantity produced and sold in a given market are jointly determined as the solution to the simultaneous market demand and supply functions. In the present setting however, each price-setter announces its current-period price at the beginning of the period based upon its estimate of the market demand (or supply) of the good or service in question. The price-takers then react to this information by deciding the amount they would like to buy or sell at the announced price. Actual sales for a period are not established until the end of the period and are determined by the particular trading rules in that market. In the markets for checkable deposits and equity shares, for instance, the price-setter presumably stands ready throughout the period to meet the market demand (or supply). In the markets for labor and loans, on the other hand, the price-setter is not obligated to purchase more labor or to grant more loans than it intended when it announced the market price or interest rate at the beginning of the period.

The following paragraphs discuss the economic activities of the various decision-making units in greater detail.

Government Sector

The government sector begins the current period with a given number of bonds outstanding. It also holds a given volume of checkable deposits at private depository institutions as well as a given stock of physical capital. At time t the government already knows not only the volume of goods the community wants it to produce during the current period, but also its current period tax revenues. Furthermore the

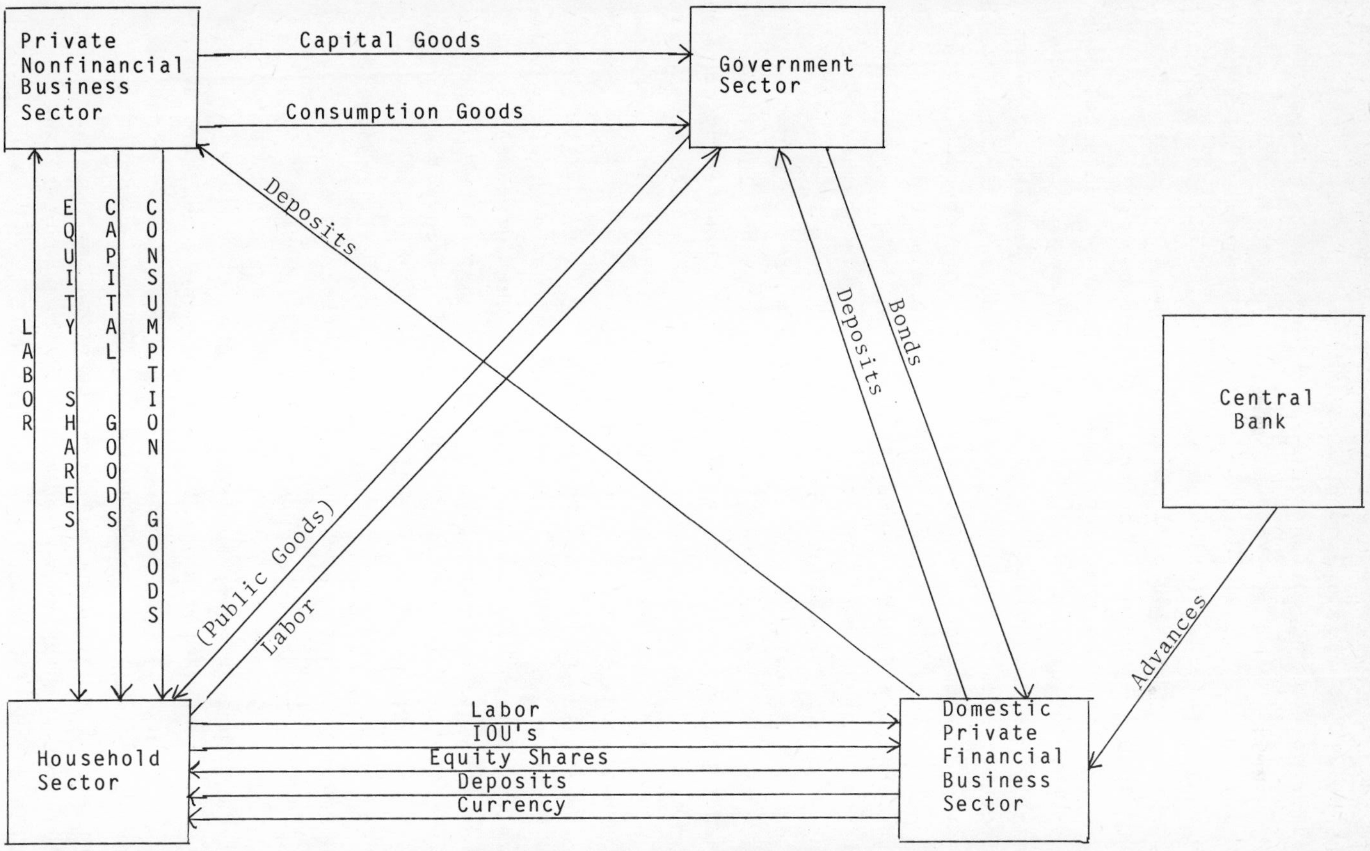

Figure 2.1 - The Five Domestic Sectors and the Markets in which they Participate in the Closed-Economy Model

government has already hired a given number of people by time t to work during the current period at an hourly money wage which has already been established for the current period. However, the government has yet to decide at time t the average number of hours it will have its employees work during the current period. Therefore, its current period wage bill remains variable at time t. During the current period, the government also will purchase consumption goods from the private nonfinancial business sector. These goods will be combined with the services of current labor and the stock of physical capital the government holds at time t to produce the volume of government-produced goods desired by the community. The government's current production of the good "national defense," for instance, involves its strategic and tactical deployment of people along with weapons, ammunition, food, and other materials which have been purchased from the private business sector.

As it formulates next period's minimum tax requirements, the government must plan as though it will sell all assets and retire all liabilities by time t+2. For if it were permitted to plan to carry outstanding debt beyond time t+2, it could reduce the level of taxes the community must pay for a given volume of government-produced goods next period without forcing the community to reckon with the private goods it must sacrifice eventually in order to retire the debt which the government plans to carry forward beyond time t+2.

One implication of attempting to minimize the taxes which the community must pay to obtain any given level of goods produced by the government next period is that the government must produce the current level of government-produced goods at minimum cost. For by reducing the cost of producing this period's goods, the government will need to borrow less (or will be able to retire more debt) during the current period. The less it borrows (or the more debt it retires) during the current period, the less it must pay out in principal and interest next period. The less it pays out in principal and interest next period, the less it must collect in taxes next period to provide the community with a given volume of government-produced goods.

Although its work force and stock of physical capital are fixed when it decides how best to produce a given amount of goods in the current period, similar constraints do not face the government as it contemplates at time t how it will produce goods next period. It is free to vary the number of employees and the quantity of physical capital with which it will begin next period.

In the course of purchasing consuption goods during either the current or next period the government will incur transactions costs. That is, some workers will have to devote at least some of their time to procurement. By holding a ready reserve of checkable deposits at the beginning of the period in question, the government presumably will be able to conserve transactions time and hence procurement costs. Naturally, the productivity of these checkable deposits varies directly with their purchasing power over consumption goods. The government's initial real checking deposit balance is given at time t. However the government is free to decide the level of deposits with which it will begin next period.

Although the U.S. federal government also maintains a deposit account at the central bank and even pays its bills from that account, it typically waits until it is ready to spend the funds before transferring them to the central bank from its accounts at the private financial institutions. The intermediate step involving the temporary transferral of funds to the central bank before spending them is ignored here.

Household Sector

The household sector begins the current period with given amounts of physical capital, checkable deposits, currency, equity shares issued by private depository institutions and equity shares issued by private non-financial businesses. At time t the sector also has a given amount of debt outstanding in the form of personal loans which must be repaid to the private depository institutions during the current period.

As the current period opens, a given number of people in the household sector already have been hired by the government, the nonfinancial businesses, or the depository institutions to work during the current period. Presumably the households have no nonpecuniary preferences among potential employers. Last period, as it assessed its labor needs for the current period, each employer presumably planned that each person it hired would work the standard number of hours, h, during the current period. The households presumably placed equal confidence in each potential employer's ability to assess correctly its labor needs for the current period. They felt that no matter who employed them for the current period they all would work h hours. But even though every potential employer guaranteed the same hourly money wage for the current period, none guaranteed that its employees would work h hours during the current period. Some employers may ask their employees to work less. In order to be able to formulate a single household labor supply function (rather than three separate ones), the households presumably, despite possible current or past experience to the contrary, continue to show unfailing confidence in each potential employer's ability to correctly anticipate its labor requirements for next period. Therefore even though they may be working overtime or only part-time in the current period, the households, in deciding how many people will (re)enter the labor force this period in order to find (retain) a job for the next period, will expect that no matter who (re)hires them for the next period they will all work h hours.

Households receive wage, interest, and dividend income during the current period. The amount they save out of this income is the residual after deducting current taxes, interest on outstanding personal debt, and expenditures on consumption goods. This saving may take the form of accumulations in physical capital, equity shares, currency and checkable deposits as well as the net retirement of personal debt obligations between the beginning and end of the period.

At time t the households formulate their plans so as to maximize present utility, which is a positive, increasing function of current and future public-goods as well as of current and future services produced within the household sector itself. Services produced within the sector are generated by applying "leisure" time (i.e. time <u>not</u> spent either working outside the household sector or engaging in transactions) to consumption goods and to capital goods purchased from the nonfinancial business sector. By reducing transactions time, household checkable deposits release real resources which can be used to provide other household services. Once again, the marginal productivity of these balances depends upon their purchasing power. Although the households take their real checkable deposits at the beginning of the current period as given, they do formulate a demand for these deposits for the end of the period in light of the anticipated marginal product of those balances next period and the opportunity costs of accumulating the balances during the current period.

Besides accumulating money during the current period, the households may also purchase equity shares issued by either the financial or nonfinancial business sectors. At time t, however, the returns next period on shares to be held at time t+1 are not known. The conventional approach for dealing with this uncertainty is to apply expected utility theory. However since two separate assets are involved whose future returns are unknown, the optimizing conditions associated with conventional utility maximization contain double integrals. This fact coupled with the wide range of nonfinancial and financial decisions facing the households in the present study, causes the standard expected utility approach to become exceedingly cumbersome.

Alternatively, in this study the households formulate only a subjective point estimate at time t as to the next period return from each type of equity share they plan to hold by time t+1. But even though they do not formulate complete subjective density functions covering all possible returns, they do recognize that their subjective estimates may not materialize. Presumably the households are concerned with the ability of equity shares to serve as stores of value. Since the shares carry limited liability, the maximum potential dollar loss to the shareholders next period is represented by the dollar value of the shares they plan at time t to hold by t+1. The households presumably become "dissatisfied" or "uneasy" with the prospect that their equity shares may depreciate in nominal value next period. The degree to which they feel this way depends not only upon their assessment of the ability of these shares to serve as a store of value, but also upon the purchasing-power loss which the maximum potential dollar loss would represent next period. In particualr, their uneasiness at time t with the prospect of holding a particular type of equity at time t+1 presumably increases at an increasing rate with the anticipated purchasing power that would be lost if the equity shares were to depreciate in value next period. Given the current market price of a share of equity issued by one of the private business sectors, household disutility then will grow at an increasing rate either as the households add shares to their portfolios over the period or as they revise downward their notion about next period's price of consumer goods.

Nonfinancial Business Sector

At the beginning of the current period, the nonfinancial business sector holds initial stocks of physical capital and checkable deposits as well as a beginning inventory of consumption goods. A given number of its equity shares are outstanding at time t. Only those shares outstanding at time t yield dividends to their owners during the current period. Trading in existing shares among households at time t presumably does not take place. Any new shares sold by the nonfinancial business sector to the households during the current period will not yield income to the household sector until next period. The income of the nonfinancial business sector stems from producing and selling consumption goods and capital goods to the government and household sectors.

The objective of the nonfinancial business sector is to maximize its persent value. It formulates its plans for the current period and the next in a manner that maximizes the dollar amount which the owners of existing shares at time t would have to place in their next best alternative at the moment in order to duplicate period by period the income which the nonfinancial business sector contemplates distributing to shareholders in each of the two periods.

At the beginning of the current period, the nonfinancial business sector announces the current period market price of its own equity shares. The price it sets will depend upon its estimate of the function determining the household sector's demand for holding nonfinancial business sector shares by time t+1 as well as upon whether the nonfinancial business sector desires to have more or fewer equity shares outstanding by time t+1 than it does at time t. Suppose the sector were to set the current market price of its shares at a level which it estimates will lead to additonal shares outstanding by time t+1. Next-period income must be the same for owners holding "new" shares or "old" shares at time t+1. Therefore, owners of existing shares at time t (and therefore of "old" shares at time t+1) will be hurt next period if the nonfinancial business sector sells additional shares during the current period and uses the proceeds from their sale in a manner that reduces next period's income <u>per share</u> without a compensating increase in current income per share to the current owners. Consequently, the objective of the nonfinancial business sector is to maximize the present value of the income stream per share to its owners at time t.

Maximizing the present value of income per share for the two periods is tantamount to maximizing the shadow price of the existing shares at time t. For it represents not only the maximum amount someone would be willing to pay at time t for the right to receive one share's worth of income during the two periods (provided that person were privy to the information held by the nonfinancial business sector), but also the minimum amount which an owner of a share at time t would ask for that share at time t (provided that owner had the same information). Since a market in existing shares is abstracted from in the present analysis, the present value of income per share must remain a shadow price.

Since the nonfinancial business sector itself produces all the intermediate goods it requires for the production of consumption and capital goods in the closed-economy models, its only current expense is its wage bill. Although the number of its employees for the current period as well as the hourly money wage at which they will work during the current period have already been established by time t, the nonfinancial business sector is free to decide the number of hours its employees will work during the period. As the dominant employer in the labor market, the nonfinancial business sector also must decide the hourly money wage it will announce at which it will hire people this period to work next period. It sets this money wage at the level which it estimates will attract the optimal number of workers in light of its estimates of the number of people who will be hired by the gpovernment and the private depository institutions.

Consequently, in a manner consistent with its objective of maximizing its present value, the nonfinancial business sector at time t decides: (a) the number of hours during it will use its current employees, (b) the hourly wage it will announce at the beginning of the current period which it will guaranteee to pay every person it hires (retains) during the current period to work next period, (c) the current-period price it will announce for consumption goods, (d) the current period price it will announce for capital goods, (e) the stock of physical capital it will hold at time t+1 to use in production next period, (f) its current production of consumption goods, (g) its current production of capital goods, (h) the volume of checkable deposits it will hold at t+1, and (i) the current period market price of its own equity shares. In making these decisions at time t, the sector must rely upon its estimates of the household sector's supply of labor function, the government sector's demand function for capital goods, and the household sector's demand function for its equity shares.

Private Financial Sector

The private financial sector also has a given number of equity shares outstanding at the beginning of the current period. Its objective is to maximize the shadow price of those shares through its operations in the financial markets. This sector epitomizes the financial intermediary by serving as the only purchaser of government bonds who then offers its own liabilities in the form of interest bearing checkable deposits. It also lends to the household sector.

In order to undertake the various transactions associated with its lending activities and with the activities of its depositors, the private financial sector presumably requires the services of labor. Excess reserves enable it to conserve on the amount of labor it must use, just as money serves to conserve transactions time for the household, government and nonfinancial business sectors.

As a simplifying assumption in the ensuing analysis, only the households and (possibly the depository institutions) hold currency at the beginning of the period and only they may plan to hold currency by the close of any period. Nevertheless, the government and nonfinancial business sectors are free to withdraw currency from the private financial institutions during the period in order to make purchases which, for one reason or another, are more easily accomplished with currency than by check. If the government or the nonfinancial business sectors receive currency as payment, presumably they will redeposit the currency at the depository institutions before the close of the period. As a result of these (and other) activities, the private depository institutions may experience temporary intraperiod cash drains. To the extent that they hold excess reserves at the beginning of the period, they are able to meet temporary withdrawals without being forced to temporarily sell an income earning asset to obtain the funds to meet the cash drain. To the extent that they avoid intraperiod transactions of this type, they are able to conserve labor time and thereby reduce current expenses.

Therefore, in accordance with its objective of maximizing its present value, the private financial sector at time t decides: (a) the interest rate it will announce this period that it will pay next period on checkable deposits held by time t+1, (b) the interest rate it will announce this period that it will collect next period on loans it grants before time t+1, (c) the price at which it will stand ready during the current period to trade government bonds, (d) the market price it will announce for its own equity shares for the currrent period, and (e) the optimal level of advances from the central bank at time t+1. In making these decisions, the sector relies on its estimates of; the market demand function for checkable deposits, the household sector's demand function for loans (ex ante supply of IOU's), the supply function for government bonds, the demand function for government bonds, the demand function for its own equity shares, and the discount rate which the central bank will announce this period.

Central Bank

Because the central bank in this study does not attempt to manipulate the monetary base, the rate of interest, or the stock of money, it neither engages in open market operations nor alters the required reserve ratio on checkable deposits. Instead, it merely lends as many reserves to private depository institutions as they wish to borrow at the discount rate it sets. As the analysis of Chapter 11 clearly demonstrates, by setting the rental rate at the level which maximizes its own income, the central bank not only accomodates the needs of the private sector but also helps automatically to "lean against the wind."

Chapter 12 combines the analysis of Chapters 7-11 into a single internally consistent model of aggregate economic choice for a closed economy. After defining the trading rules as well as national income and product, technological improvements are assumed to take place in the production functions of the government, private nonfinancial business and household sectors respectively. In each case, the short-run effects upon production, prices, employment and interest rates are examined in detail.

The Open-Economy Model

Figure 2.2 provides a summary of the interactions among sectors in the open version of the aggregate model developed in Chapter 13. The household sector purchases goods from the foreign sector as well as from the domestic nonfinancial business sector. But its participation in the labor and financial markets remain essentially the same as in the closed-economy version of this sector presented in Chapter 8. The government sector's behavior differs from that outlined in Chapter 7 only to the extent that it also purchases goods from abroad to use in the production of government-produced goods. Because the government's range of asset choice is narrower than the household sector's, I also allow the government to demand checkable deposits denominated in the foreign unit of account in order to facilitate its anticipated purchases of foreign goods. Since the government does not set the market price of the bonds in this model, the fact that some of its IOU's are now purchased by the foreign sector does not directly affect its own behavior. But the domestic bond market is linked to the foreign sector nevertheless.

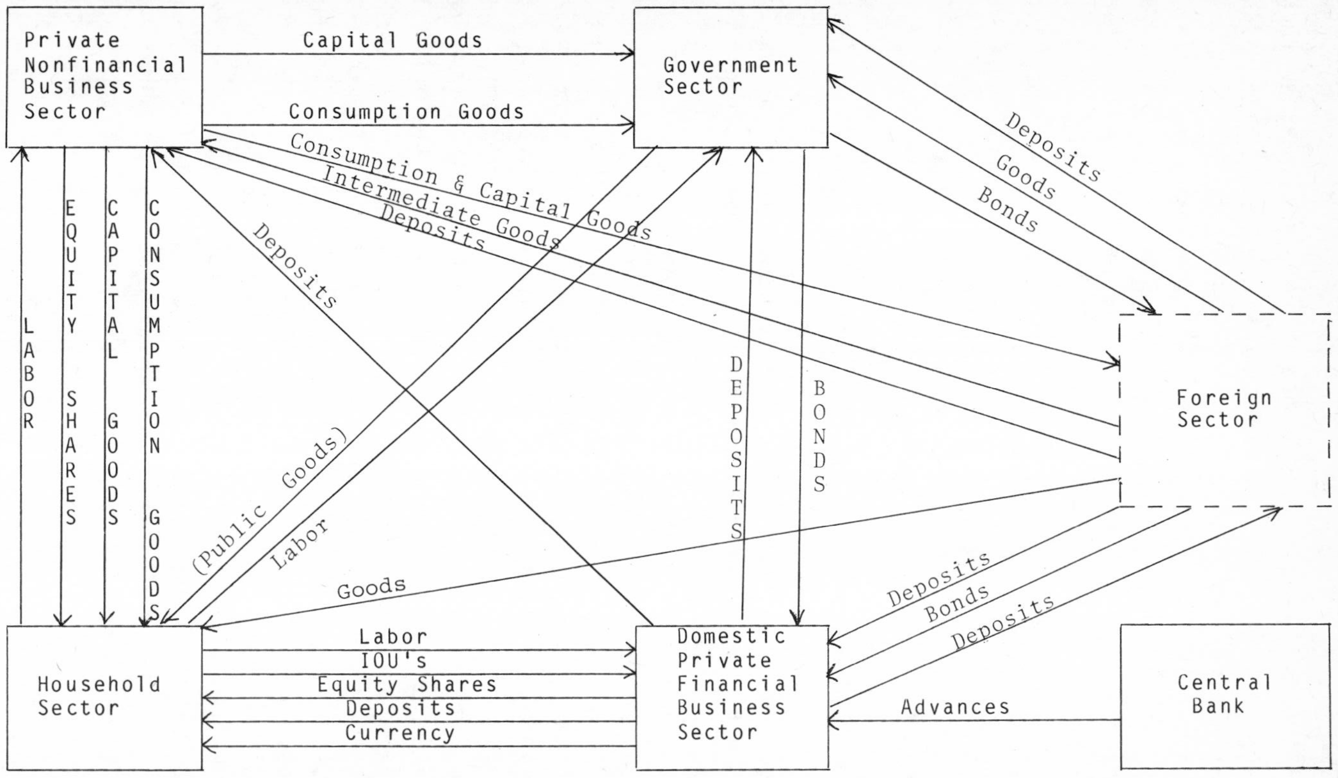

Figure 2.2 - The Five Domestic Sectors, the Foreign Sector and the Markets in which they Participate in the Open-Economy Model

The private nonfinancial business sector is linked to the foreign sector in Chapter 13 through the domestic and foreign product markets as well as through the market for checkable deposits denominated in foreign exchange. In particular, the domestic business sector sells both of its products to foreign buyers as well as to other domestic units. Consequently, as it sets the prices on its products, it must anticipate the foreign demand for its products as well as the domestic demand. In addition, the domestic private business sector also purchases foreign-produced goods as an intermediate good in the production of its own products. This introduces an additonal factor into the production function of this sector. To facilitate its purchases of foreign goods, the sector is also viewed as demanding checkable deposits denominated in foreign exchange. The central bank in the open model provides precisely the same function it provides in the closed version. It does not attempt to intervene into the foreign exchange market and hence has no reason to hold foreign currency.

The decision-making confronting the domestic private financial business sector becomes somewhat more complicated in the open version. The lion's share of Chapter 13 is devoted to extending the analysis that appears in Chapter 10. For one thing, the private financial sector must anticipate the foreign sector's demand for domestic bonds as it sets the market price of those bonds. For another, since it issues its own checkable deposits liabilities to the foreign sector as well as to other domestic sector's, the private financial institutions must estimate the foreign sector's demand as part of the estimated total demand for its deposit liabilities. In addition, the domestic private financial sector is permitted to purchase bonds issued by the foreign sector. More importantly, however, as the dominant financial sector, the domestic depository institutions also sets the exchange rate betweeen domestic and foreign units of account. Consequently, the sector must estimate the net flow demand for foreign exchange at each potential exchange rate. Furthermore, the sector must stand ready during the period to meet the net transactions in foreign exchange during the period. The domestic depository institutions therefore hold an initial inventory of foreign exchange (in the form of checkable deposits at foreign institutions) at time t and must also decide at that time the amount of foreign exchange they deem optimal to hold by the end of the period. In terms of "calendar" time, the length of time between time t and time t+1 may be extremely short--possibly only a few seconds.

After respecifying the econmic behavior of each of the setors individually, Chapter 13 then contains an attempt to integrate the economic behavior of all six sectors into a single unified framework for a large open economy. Then the short-run responses are examined for exogenous changes in the interes rate on checkable deposits at foreign depository institutions and in the price of foreign-produced goods respectively.

According to the conventional approach to macroeconomic analysis, a policy authority manipulates government spending, taxes, and the stock of money in an effort to promote changes it deems desirable in the aggregate economy. The present study does not provide any ready-made policy prescriptions for controlling the economy. Its purpose instead is to explain how a democratic society, aided by accommodating public institutions, chooses its optimal combination of: government-produced goods, privately-produced goods, current market goods, and future goods. In the course of making these decisions, it simultaneously determines the levels of national income, employment, interest rates, prices, and the stock of money.

Although one might legitimately question the ease with which a democratic government heavily laden with bureaucracy can respond in practice to the wishes of its people, the approach followed here appears to reflect more accurately than the standard one the priciple behind this form of government. At the very least it indicates that the community's desired level of public goods depends not only upon the taxes it must incur to obtain them, but also upon the costs and opportunities in the financial, labor, and private commodity markets. Consequently, the present approach illustrates the myriad of economic factors which might influence the popularity of a proposal, say, calling for an expansion of government-produced goods.

In the next section of this study, Chapters 3-5 offer a simplified model of collective economic choice involving only the household and nonfinancial business sectors. The implications of adding an accommodative government sector are then explored in Chapter 6.

References

May, J., 1970, Period Analysis and Continuous Analysis in Patinkin's Macroeconomic Model, Journal of Economic Theory 2, March, 1-9.

Whitmore, H., 1980, Unbalanced Government Budgets, Private Asset Holdings, and the Traditional Comparative Static Multipliers, Journal of Macroeconomics 2, Spring, 129-157.

3. The Household Sector in the Simple Model

The simple national income model developed in Chapters 3-5 contains two centralized decision-making units participating in four markets. The household sector, discussed in the present chapter, purchases commodities and equity shares from the nonfinancial business sector. The business sector presented in Chapter 4, buys labor services from the households. Currency, the only type of money in this simple framework, is exchanged in all three of the commodity, equity, and labor markets. Consequently these three markets taken together simultaneously constitute a market for currency. Chapter 5 combines the household and business sectors into a simple model of national income determination with the prices of labor, commodities, and equity, set by the business sector.

The government sector is introduced in Chapter 6. The government buys privately-produced goods from the business sector, buys labor services from the households, and produces the level of government-produced goods demanded by the households. The government also levies taxes and issues currency to pay for the goods it produces. The second half of Chapter 6 extends the simple national income model presented in Chapter 5 to include the activities of the government sector. In this extended model, the households choose for themselves the level of government spending and taxes in light of other economic factors.

Formal Model of the Household Sector

Budget Constraints

The household sector's balance sheet at time t (i.e. its "initial" balance sheet) contains equity shares acquired earlier from the business sector and currency. Let Sn_t represent the number of equity shares it holds and let p^n_t represent either the actual price or the price at which the household sector anticipates these shares can be traded during the current period. (Price p^n_t is announced by the business sector at time t.) Then the current market value of the household sector's equity shares is denoted by $p^n_t Sn_t$. With Cu^h_t representing the number of dollars households hold as initial money balances at t, the household sector's initial balance sheet may be represented as:

Household's Initial Balance Sheet
(at Time t)

Assets	Liabilities
Cu^h_t	0
$p^n_t \cdot Sn_t$	
	Net Wealth
	NW^h_t

where NW^h_t, the household sector's net wealth at time t, equals Cu^h_t + $p^n_t Sn_t$. The household sector is constrained by the composition of its initial balance sheet as well as by its net wealth. At time t it cannot plan a new portfolio for that moment containing different amounts of currency or equity shares. It takes these initial amounts as given. The possibility of so-called "portfolio imbalance" with respect to the beginning-of-period balance sheet does not exist.

During the current period the households will receive income in the form of wages and dividends from the business sector. As the current period opens, a given number of people, N_t, presumably have already been hired to work during the current period at a wage rate, w_t, that was announced earlier by the business sector. Current labor income therefore equals the product $w_t h_t N_t$, where h_t denotes the average number of hours that the business sector decides its employees will work during the current period.

Current dividends per share, π^n_t, are announced at the beginning of the current period by the business sector. These dividends are paid on all shares the household sector holds at time t and only on those shares. Any shares which the households purchase from the business sector during the current period will not begin to yield dividends until next period. Also, any shares the households sell back to the business sector during the current period will continue to yield dividends to the households during the current period. Consequently, current dividend income received by the household sector may be represented by $\pi^n_t Sn_t$ with current personal (and disposable) income denoted by $w_t h_t N_t + \pi^n_t Sn_t$.

Although the households regard their initial portfolio as given, they are permitted to plan to accumulate net wealth during the current period by saving a portion of their current income. By definition, current personal saving equals current disposable income minus current consumption. Let c^h_t depict the household sector's (real) demand for current consumption goods and let p^c_t denote the current-period price of commodities announced by the business sector at time t. Then at time t ex ante current personal saving is represented by $w_t h_t N_t + \pi^n_t Sn_t - p^c_t c^h_t$.

Let Cu^{nd}_{t+1} represent the number of dollars of currency which the households plan at time t to hold by the end of the current period. Let Sn^d_{t+1} denote the number of equity shares which they plan at time t to hold by time t+1. Then the balance sheet which the households plan at time t for time t+1, expressed in terms of current period prices, may be presented as:

Household Sector's Planned Balance Sheet at Time t
for Time t+1 (in Current Period Prices)

Assets	Liabilities
Cu^{hd}_{t+1}	0
$p^n_t Sn^d_{t+1}$	
	Net Wealth
	NW^{hd}_{t+1}

where net wealth planned for time t+1, NW^{hd}_{t+1}, equals $Cu^{hd}_{t+1} + p^n_t Sn^d_{t+1}$.

When valued in terms of the prices at which they can be traded during the current period, the net value of the assets which the household sector plans to hold at time t+1, $Cu^{hd}_{t+1} + p^n_t Sn^d_{t+1}$, must exceed the net value of the household sector's initial assets, $Cu^h_t + p^n_t Sn_t$, by precisely the dollar amount which the sector plans to save out of current income during the current period. This budget constraint exists simply because, at a given set of asset prices, (i) current savings must be the source that finances any net accumulation of wealth and (ii) every dollar of current saving is necessarily applied to the purchase of some asset. (In the models presented later saving may also be used to retire outstanding liabilities.) Obviously current-period asset prices are the relevant ones; only they reveal the number of assets which the households can purchase with their current saving. Therefore, according to the budget constraint facing the household sector with respect to the current period, the following equation must hold:

$$w_t h_t N_t + \pi^n_t Sn_t - p^c_t c^h_t = Cu^{hd}_{t+1} + p^n_t Sn^d_{t+1} - (Cu^h_t + p^n_t Sn_t) \qquad (3.1)$$

The households also formulate plans at time t with respect to next period. At the beginning of the current period the business sector calls out the hourly wage, w_{t+1}, which it promises to pay next period's employees. To simplify the analysis, assume that the firms base their wage announcement upon the supposition that everyone will work the standard number of hours, h, next period. Although it does not guarantee that everyone will indeed work h hours, the business sector nevertheless announces its intention that everyone will do so. On the basis of this information, the household sector must decide at time t how many people, N^s_{t+1}, it would like to have employed by the end of the current period. If the household sector places full confidence in the business sector's ability to correctly assess its labor requirements, the households will also plan that the people who are employed next period will work an average of h hours. In that case the household sector anticipates at time t that next period's wage income is represented by $w_{t+1}hN^s_{t+1}$.

Let π^{nh}_{t+1} represent the income per share which households expect at time t to receive next period from their equity holdings. Then their expected total income next period is represented by $w_{t+1}hN^s_{t+1}$ + $\pi^{nh}_{t+1}Sn^d_{t+1}$. If p^{ch}_{t+1} depicts the households expectation at time t as to price of consumption goods next period and if c^h_{t+1} denotes the households sector's real demand at time t for consumption goods next period, then at time t the amount that the sector plans to save out of next period's income is denoted by $w_{t+1}hN^s_{t+1}$ + $\pi^{nh}_{t+1}Sn^d_{t+1}$. If p^{ch}_{t+1} depicts the households' expectation at time t as to the price of consumption goods next period and if c^h_{t+1} denotes the household sector's real demand at time t for consumption goods next period, then at time t the amount that the sector plans to save out of next period's income is denoted by $w_{t+1}hN^s_{t+1}$ + $\pi^{nh}_{t+1}Sn^d_{t+1}$ - $p^{ch}_{t+1}c^h_{t+1}$. This amount must be consistent with the sector's plans on the asset accounts.

In particular assume for simplicity that at time t the households expect that next period a market will no longer exist for equity shares. Presumably the households recognize that the business sector's time horizon also extends only to time t+2. Consequently, everyone presumably expects at time t that any shares held or acquired beyond time t+1 will earn no additional income beyond the anticipated π^{nh}_{t+1} to be paid next period on those shares held at time t+1. As a result π^{nh}_{t+1} represents not just next period's anticipated dividends per share, but the total payment on each share the households hold at time t+1. Since π^{nh}_{t+1} represents the expected total payment next period from equity shares whose present market value is p^n_t, then $\pi^{nh}_{t+1} = p^n_t(1+r^e)$, where r^e_t denotes the expected nominal rate of return on equity.

At time t the households presumably expect that the market value of equity shares next period will equal zero. Therefore, when valued in terms of next period's anticipated prices, the household sector's planned balance sheet for t+1 becomes:

Households' Planned Balance Sheet at Time t
for Time t+1 (in Next Period's Anticipated Prices)

Assets	Liabilities
Cu^{hd}_{t+1}	0
	Net Wealth
	NW^{d*}_{t+1}

As viewed at time t and valued in terms of next period's prices, the market value of the household sector's portfolio at time t+1 equals only the amount of currency it plans to hold at time t+1, namely Cu^{hd}_{t+1}. Furthermore, since at time t the households cannot see beyond t+2, assume that the households plan at time t to hold no assets by time t+2. Therefore as it formulates its plans at time t, the household sector's planned net wealth for time t+2 equals zero. Consequently as the current period opens, the household sector plans on the capital account to reduce its assets next period by the number of dollars of currency with which it plans to begin that period.

Since the plans on the income and capital accounts must be

mutually consistent, the household sector's budget constraint for next period (as viewed at time t) is given by:

$$w_{t+1}hN^{s}_{t+1} + \pi^{nh}_{t+1}Sn^{d}_{t+1} - p^{ch}_{t+1}c^{h}_{t+1} = - Cu^{hd}_{t+1} \qquad (3.2)$$

where h in the first term represents the average number of hours which the households anticipate they will be asked to work next period. Rewriting (3.2) as:

$$p^{ch}_{t+1}c^{h}_{t+1} = w_{t+1}hN^{s}_{t+1} + \pi^{nh}_{t+1}Sn^{d}_{t+1} + Cu^{hd}_{t+1} \qquad (3.3)$$

emphasizes the fact that the dollar amount which the households anticipate at time t that they will be able to spend next period equals the sum of its anticipated wage income next period, its anticipated equity income next period and the currency it plans to hold at the beginning of the next period. Of course, the real values of the three dollar amounts on the right hand side of (3.3) are not known to the household sector at time t simply because the business sector will not decide next period's commodity price, p^{c}_{t+1}, until time t+1. Since it presumably does not have all the detailed information available to the business sector, the household sector's conjecture at time t as to p^{c}_{t+1} may differ from what the business sector plans at time t to announce at t+1. By time t+1 the business sector may also change its mind about p^{c}_{t+1} as well

But uncertainty also surrounds the nominal values of two of these three potential sources of next period's spending power. In particular, even though the business sector presumably announces at time t the wage rate, w_{t+1} it promises to pay all people it hires (or retains) as workers next period, the households at time t have no guarantee either that everyone who decides he would like to work next period will indeed find a job or that next period's employees will indeed work (on the average) the standard h hours. Also, the business sector will not announce next period's equity income until time t+1. Therefore, at time t, the only source of next period's nominal spending power which is entirely under the control of the household sector is the amount of currency it decides to hold at time t+1.

Depending upon the assumptions one makes as to how the household sector formulates its expectations with respect to the future values of p^{c}_{t+1}, h and π^{n}_{t+1}, the households' uncertainty as to the future real purchasing power of each of the above three sources may not coincide with the uncertainty of their nominal values. For instance, if one were to assume that households' expectations about p^c_{t+1} and π^n_{t+1} are highly positively correlated, then households may feel less unsure at time t about the real purchasing power of future equity income from a share held at time t+1 than they do about the real purchasing power of the dollar of currency held at time t+1 even though the nominal value of the latter is certain while the nominal value of the former is not. For simplicity, household expectations as to the future values of p^c_{t+1} and π^n_{t+1} are treated as exogenous variables in the present model. Furthermore I arbitrarily assume that the household sector's sense of "security" at time t with respect to its plans to purchase a given amount of c^h_{t+1} next period grows with the portion it plans to finance out of currency held at time t+1.

Because money is useful in undertaking transactions, uncertainty as to future nominal (or real) values is not necessary to establish a demand for this asset by the household sector in this study. However, in later chapters the households will also choose between two assets that yield only market incomes. In order to permit the households to decide to hold some of both of these assets--not just the one yielding the higher market return--these two assets must somehow be qualitatively different in the mind of the household sector. The notion that the households regard the anticipated future nominal income of one of the assets as less certain than that associated with the other and that this uncertainty matters will provide a basis for the households to demand both assets. To aid the reader's understanding of the role that uncertainty plays in these later chapters, it is introduced here while the model of the household sector is still quite simple.

Present Utility Function

In a manner consistent with the two budget restrictions derived above, the household sector formulates its plans at time t for the next two periods so as to maximize its feeling of well-being at time t, i.e. its present utility. Present utility presumably increases as the amounts of commodities it plans to purchase from the business sector in each of the current and next periods increases. But some of the goods and services which the households consume are produced within the household sector itself. Consequently present utility also presumably rises as the planned quantities of household production in each of the current and next periods increases. In addition, I assume that present utility is also an increasing function of the household sector's sense of security at time t associated with its plans to purchase a given amount of c^h_{t+1} next period.

The customary approach to solving problems of economic choice under uncertainty entails assigning subjective probabilities as well as utility indicies to each of the possible outcomes of the random variables. The decision-maker is then viewed as attempting to maximize expected utility, defined as the weighted average of the utility indices with the corresponding probabilities serving as the weights. The expected utility approach has been applied successfully to a number of problems involving choices among "risky" assets. But when more than one continous stochastic variable is involved (as will be the case in the more complicated versions of the present model) comparative statics analysis becomes rather messy, since the second-order conditions then involve linear combinations of products of double or multiple integrals. Also the range of choices facing the household sector in the present model is broader than found in the standard expected utility problem. For instance, even in the simple version presented in this chapter, the household sector must decide not only the composition of its planned portfolio for the end of the period but also the amounts of current comsumption, future labor income, and future household production. Furthermore, rather than yielding a fixed market return, one of the financial assets in the present model, namely currency, yields an endogenously determined implicit return from the households' point of view. Because of these complexities, and for other reasons, the alternative approach outlined above will be followed here. (See Blatt [1983] for a full-scale critique of the expected utility approach.)

The present approach recognizes the qualitative difference between currency, on the one hand, and equity shares and labor, on the other, in terms of the degree of uncertainty of their future nominal returns (or values) without actually specifying the subjective probability densities associated with the returns from equity shares and labor.

Finally, in this study present utility presumably dimishes as the amount of transactions time which the household sector plans to incur in either the current or next period increases. Transactions time in any period is assumed to be an increasing function of the number of commodities which the households purchase from the business sector that period but a decreasing function of the average real currency balances they hold during the period. Since assets are measured in this model only at the beginning of each period, the beginning-of-period real balance of currency will serve as a proxy for its average balance during the period. In the persent model, then, currency serves a dual function in the eyes of the household sector. It not only provides a means of accumulating financial wealth whose future nominal value is already known at time t, but because it serves as the medium of exchange it also helps conserve the household sector's time.

As is well known, the existence of a generally accepted means of payment conserves real resources (household time, in this case) even if it is not held between transactions. For if an economic agent, person A, wanted to buy good X in a barter economy, he would first need to find someone who has good X and is willing to accept what person A holds in exchange. But in a money economy, person A will be willing to sell the good he has for money which he can then use to buy good X from someone else. In a money economy, an economic agent does not need to spend time searching for a "double coincidence of wants" in order to effect an exchange of one good for another.

But, if an agent decides to hold the medium of exchange between transactions he can save even more time. For if the agent does not hold money between transactions, then every purchase entails two exchanges. In the example cited above, since the agent held no money prior to the time he wanted to buy good X, he first had to sell another good in order to obtain the money with which to buy good X. But if he already holds money when he is ready to buy good X, the agent can avoid making another exchange prior to purchasing good X. Therefore by holding money between transactions an agent is able to reduce by as much as one-half the number of exchanges associated with his purchases.

The formal specification of the function depicting present utility will be kept as simple as possible in order to accommodate the broad range of choices facing the household sector. In particular this function as well as the transactions time functions which enter it are presumed to display additive separability. In a micro setting involving a large number of close substitutes and complements this approach would be questionable. For under these circumstances a change in the amount consumed of one good undoubtedly affects the marginal utilities of other goods as well. In the present context however the variables entering the utility function represent broad categories of goods or services or qualities whose substitutability or complementarity are considerably weaker. Therefore the assumption of additive separability appears to be defensible in the present case.

As discussed informally above, the household sector's present utility basically depends upon: the volume of commodities it plans to purchase from the business sector in both the current and next periods, the volume of services which the households plan to produce themselves in each of the two periods, the amount of transactions time the sector plans to incur in each of the two periods, and the sense of "security" or "safety" it associates at time t with a given anticipated purchasing power over goods next period. Each of these arguments now will be discussed more formally, beginning with the ones pertaining to the current period.

The household sector's present utility with respect to commodities purchased from the business sector during the current period, c^h_t, current household production, μ, and current transactions time, τ, will be represented as the sum of three additively separable concave functions:

$$U = \tilde{U}_1(c^h_t) + \tilde{U}_2(\mu) + \tilde{U}_3(\tau) \qquad (3.4)$$

where $\tilde{U}_1(.),\ \tilde{U}_2(.) > 0;\ \tilde{U}_3(.) < 0$

$\tilde{U}'_1,\ \tilde{U}'_2 > 0;\ \tilde{U}'_3 < 0$

and $\tilde{U}''_1,\ \tilde{U}''_2 > 0;\ \tilde{U}''_3 = 0.$

The household sector's own current period production of household services presumably depends only upon the amount of "free time" available to the households in the current period. Let h* represent the total number of hours in the current period and let N represent the population of the household sector. Then h*N denotes total time available to that sector. However, part of this time must be diverted to providing labor services to the business sector this period. Recalling that h_t depicts the average number of hours which the N_t people who are employed by the business sector this period will work this period, h_tN_t represents total time working outside the household sector this period.

The household sector's current period production function is assumed to be an increasing, strictly concave function of $h^*N - h_tN_t$, the number of "free" hours available to the household sector to produce its own goods and services this period. Let (3.5) represent this production function:

$$\mu = \mu(h^*N - h_t N_t) \tag{3.5}$$

with $\mu(\ )$, $\mu' > 0$ and $\mu'' < 0$.

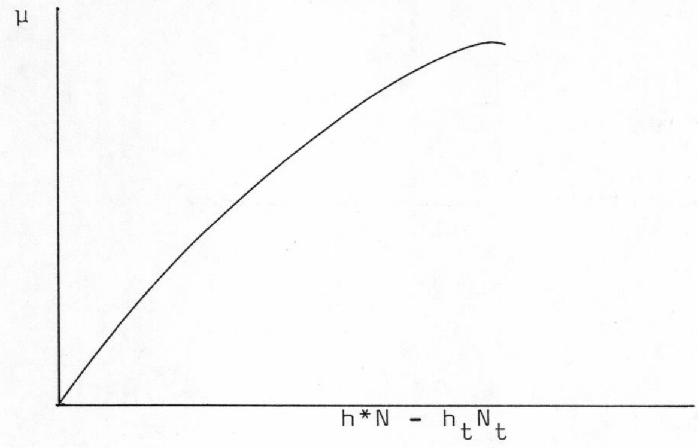

Figure 3.1 - Current Household Production Function

Current period transactions time is presumably small relative to the total number of hours $h^*N - h_t N_t$ available to the households. Therefore, transactions time presumably does not significantly affect the volume of services the households produce internally. As a result, transactions time is not subtracted from total available time in the above production function for household services. But even though transactons time may be small relative to total time, the household sector nevertheless holds money balances in order to reduce transactions time. Specifically, assume that transactions time for the current period is represented by the following strictly convex function:

$$\tau \equiv \tau_1(c^h{}_t) + \tau_2(Cu^h{}_t/p^c{}_t) > 0 \tag{3.6}$$

where $\tau_1(\ ) > 0$, $\tau_2(\ ) < 0$; $\tau_1' > 0, \tau_2' < 0$; and τ_1'', $\tau_2'' > 0$.

(This specification is a simplified version of the one found in Saving [1971].)

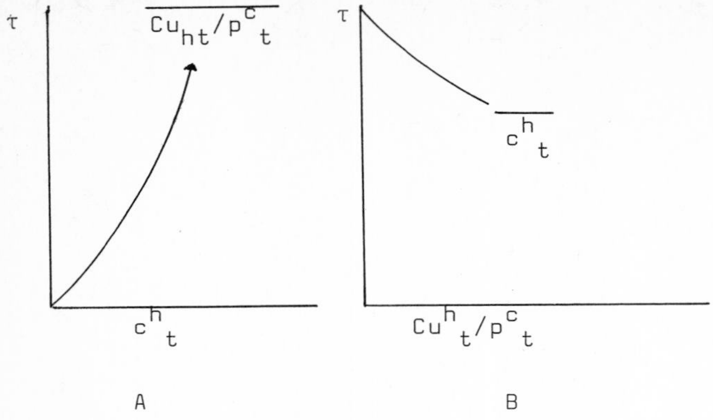

Figure 3.2 - Current Transactions Time as a Function of c^h_t (Panel A) and Cu^h_t/p^c_t (Panel B)

Substituting (3.5) and (3.6) into (3.4) yields:

$$\tilde{U}=\tilde{U}_1(c^h_t)+\tilde{U}_2\ (\mu(h^*N-h_tN_t))+\tilde{U}^3(\tau_1(c^h_t)+\ \tau_2(Cu^h_t/p^c)) \tag{3.7}$$

Combining terms, U may be written as:

$$\tilde{U}=U_1(c^h_t)+U_2(h^*N-h_tN_t)+U_3(Cu^h_t/p^c_t). \tag{3.8}$$

where $U_1(.) = \tilde{U}_1(.)+\tilde{U}_3(\tau_1(c^h_t))$

$U_2(.) = \tilde{U}_2(\mu(.))$

$U_3(.) = \tilde{U}_3(\tau_2(Cu^h_t/p^c_t))$

The first term on the right hand side of (3.8) represents the present utility associated with current commodities purchased from the business sector net of the disutility stemming from the transactons time associated with those purchases. Since $\tilde{U}_3(.)$ is a negative (decreasing) linear function and since $\tau_1(.)$ is a positive strictly convex function, $\tilde{U}_3(\tau_1(.))$ is strictly concave (but negative). Since $\tilde{U}_1(.)$ is also strictly concave, so is $U_1(.)$, which we assume is also positive.

Because the second term, $U_2(.)$, is a positive increasing strictly concave function of another positive increasing strictly concave function, it is also positive, increasing and strictly concave. This term represents the effect on present utility from a given amount of time available for production within the household sector in the current period.

The third term, $U_3(.)$, is a negative, decreasing linear function of a negative decreasing strictly convex function. Therefore $U_3(.)$ is positive, increasing and strictly concave. It shows the present utility stemming from the ability of beginning-of-period real cash balances, Cu^h_t/p^c_t, to reduce current transactions time and therefore reduce the present disutility associated with those transactions.

Assume that present utility is also an additively separable function of the commodities, c^h_{t+1}, which the households plan to purchase from the business sector next period, the services, μ^*, which the households plan to produce within the household sector next period, the amount of time, τ^*, devoted to transactions next period and the degree of security it attaches to a given amount of purchasing power over goods next period:

$$\hat{U}=\hat{U}_1(c^h_{t+1})+\hat{U}_2(\mu^*)+\hat{U}_3(\tau^*)+\hat{U}_4(.) \tag{3.9}$$

where $\hat{U}_1(.),\hat{U}_2(.),\hat{U}_4(.) > 0;\hat{U}_3(.)<0$

$\hat{U}'_1, \hat{U}'_2, \hat{U}'_4 > 0;\ \hat{U}'_3 < 0$

and $\hat{U}''_1,\hat{U}''_2,\hat{U}''_4 < 0;\ \hat{U}''_3 = 0.$

In a manner consistent with that used to specify the households' current production function, suppose next period's planned production of household services, μ^*, is given according to the following strictly concave function:

$$\mu^* = \mu^*(h^*N - hN^s_{t+1}) \tag{3.10}$$

where $\mu^*(.) > 0$, $\mu^{*\prime} > 0$ and $\mu^{*\prime\prime} < 0$. The symbol h^* denotes the total number of "hours" contained in next period and N represents the anticipated population of the household sector next period (assumed, for simplicity, to equal current population). As a result, h^*N depicts the total time available to the households next period. As mentioned above, the household sector presumably anticipates that on the average people working for the business sector next period will work the "standard" h hours. Since N^s_{t+1} represents the number of people that the household sector plans to have working for business next period, the planned amount of time available next period for household production is denoted by $h^*N - hN^s_{t+1}$.

A function analogous to the one that specifies current transactions time is used to represent the amount of time the households expect to devote to transactons next period. In particular, assume the following function exists:

$$\tau^* = \tau^*_1(c^h_{t+1}) + \tau^*_2(Cu^{hd}_{t+1}/p^{ch}_{t+1}) \qquad (3.11)$$

where $\tau^*_1(.)$, $\tau^{*'}_1$, $\tau^{*''}_1 > 0$; $\tau^*_2(.)$, $\tau^{*'}_2 < 0$; $\tau^{*''}_2 > 0$.

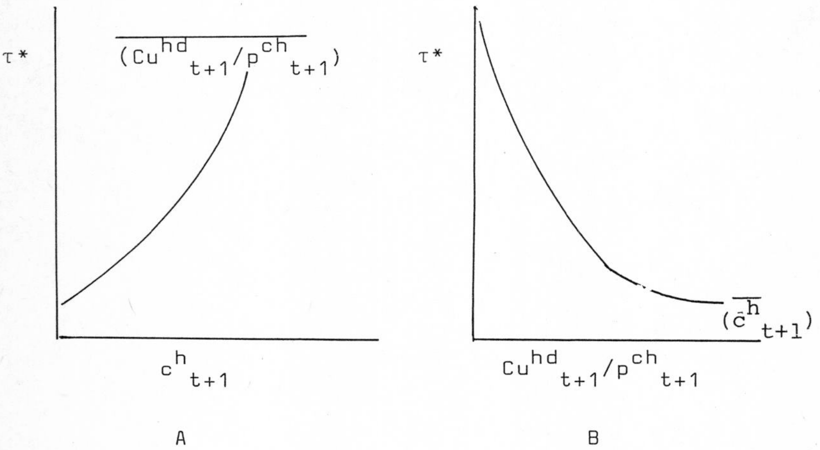

Figure 3.3 - Anticipated Future Transactions Costs as a Function of c^h_{t+1} (Panel A) and as a Function of $Cu^{hd}_{t+1}/p^{ch}_{t+1}$ (Panel B)

Substituting (3.10) and (3.11) into (3.9) yields:

$$\hat{U}=\hat{U}_1(c^h_{t+1}) + \hat{U}_2(\mu^*(h^*N-hN^s_{t+1}) + \hat{U}_3(\tau^*_1(c^h_{t+1}) + \tau_2^*(Cu^{hd}_{t+1}/p^{ch}_{t+1})) + \hat{U}_4(Cu^{hd}_{t+1}/p^{ch}_{t+1}) \qquad (3.12)$$

The term $\hat{U}_4(Cu^{hd}_{t+1}/p^{ch}_{t+1})$, with $\hat{U}_4(.)$, $\hat{U}'_4 > 0$ and $\hat{U}''_4 < 0$, summarizes the dual assumption that (a) present utility is an increasing strictly concave function of the degree of security which the sector attaches to a given amount of real purchasing power over commodities next period and (b) that this degree of security is an increasing strictly concave function of the real money balance component of this given amount of real purchasing power over commodities. In terms of (3.3), which is repeated here for the reader's convenience (this time in real terms),

$$c^h_{t+1} = \frac{w_{t+1}hN^s_{t+1}}{p^{ch}_{t+1}} + \frac{\pi^{nh}_{t+1}}{p^{ch}_{t+1}} Sn^d_{t+1} + \frac{Ch^d_{t+1}}{p^{ch}_{t+1}} \tag{3.3}$$

the underlying notion states that for a given level of c^h_{t+1} (ignoring household production and transactions costs) present utility will increase at a decreasing rate as $Cu^{hd}_{t+1}/p^{ch}_{t+1}$ rises. The reason is that as these planned real balances increase, the households' feeling of security as to actually being able to consume c^h_{t+1} rises at a decreasing rate), causing present utility to increase (also at a decreasing rate). More formally, let ψ represent the degree of security associated with the level of $Cu^{hd}_{t+1}/p^{ch}_{t+1}$ for a given c^h_{t+1} in equation (3.3). Then $\psi(Cu^{hd}_{t+1}/p^{ch}_{t+1}) > 0$, $\psi' > 0$ and $\psi'' < 0$. Assuming present utility, $\hat{U}_4(\;)$, derived from ψ is also an increasing strictly concave function, then $\hat{U}_4(\psi(Cu^{hd}_{t+1}/p^{ch}_{t+1})) \equiv \hat{U}_4(Cu^{hd}_{t+1}/p^{ch}_{t+1})$ is also an increasing strictly concave function.

Expression (3.12) may be simplified as

$$\hat{U} = U_4(c^h_{t+1}) + U_5(h{*}N-hN^s_{t+1}) + U_6(Cu^{hd}_{t+1}/p^{ch}_{t+1}) \tag{3.13}$$

where $U_4(.) \equiv \hat{U}_1(.) + \hat{U}_3(\tau^*_1(.))$

$U_5(.) \equiv \hat{U}_2(\mu^*(.))$

$U_6(.) \equiv \hat{U}_3(\tau^*_2(.)) + \hat{U}_4(.)$

The term $U_4(.)$ represents present utility associated with future consumption net of the disutility associated with the transactions time attached to that consumption. Given that $\hat{U}_1(.)$ is strictly concave, that $\tau^*_1(.)$ is strictly convex and that $\hat{U}_3(.)$ is negative and linear, $U_4(.)$ is strictly concave. By assumption, $U_4(.)$ is positive. The second term in (3.13), $U_5(.)$, simply represents the present utility derived from future time available for household production. Since $\hat{U}_2(.)$ and $\mu^*(.)$ are presumed to be strictly concave, so is $U_5(.)$. Finally, $U_6(.)$ denotes the present utility associated with the amount of currency (deflated by next period's anticipated price level) which the households plan to hold at the beginning of next period. This utility stems from the ability of these real balances (a) to conserve future transactons time and (b) to provide a secure source of purchasing power over commodities in the future. Since $\hat{U}_4(.)$ is strictly concave, $\tau^*_2(.)$ negative and strictly convex, and $\hat{U}_3(.)$ negative and linear, $U_6(.)$ is positive and strictly concave.

Combining the "current period" and "next period" components, present utility, U, may be represented as $U = \tilde{U}+\hat{U}$. From (3.8) and (3.13), we have:

$$U=U_1(c^h{}_t)+U_2(h^*N-h_tN_t) + U_3(Cu^{hd}{}_t/p^c{}_t))+U_4(c^h{}_{t+1}) + \qquad (3.14)$$

$$U_5(h^*N - hN^s{}_{t+1}) + U_6(Cu^{hd}{}_{t+1}/p^{ch}{}_{t+1})$$

The objective of the household sector at time t is to maximize the right hand side of (3.14) with respect to $c^h{}_t$, $c^h{}_{t+1}$, $N^s{}_{t+1}$, $Cu^{hd}{}_{t+1}$ and $Sn^d{}_{t+1}$ subject to restrictions (3.1) and (3.3). Solving (3.1) for $Sn^d{}_{t+1}$ and substituting into (3.3) yields the following expression for $c^h{}_{t+1}$:

$$c^h{}_{t=1} = \frac{w_{t+1}hN^s{}_{t+1}}{p^{ch}{}_{t+1}} + \frac{(\pi^{nh}{}_{t+1})}{p^n{}_tp^{ch}{}_{t+1}}[(p^n_t+\pi^n_t)Sn_t+w_th_tN_t+Cu^h_t-p^c_tc^h_t]$$

$$+ (1 - \frac{\pi^{nh}{}_{t+1}}{p^n{}_t})(Cu^{hd}{}_{t+1}/p^{ch}{}_{t+1}) \qquad (3.15)$$

Finally, substituting the right hand side of (3.15) for $c^h{}_{t+1}$ in (3.14) produces the following unconstrained objective function:

$$U = U_1(c^h{}_t) + U_2(h^*N -h_tN_t) + U_3(Cu^h{}_t/p^c{}_t)$$

$$+ U_4 \left(\frac{w_{t+1}hN^s{}_{t+1}}{p^{ch}{}_{t+1}} + \frac{[\pi^{nh}{}_{t+1}]}{p^n{}_tp^{ch}{}_{t+1}}[(p^n + \pi^n{}_t)Sn_t+w_th_tN_t+Cu^h_t-p^c_tc^h_t]\right.$$

$$\left.+ (1 - \frac{\pi^{nh}{}_{t+1}}{p^n{}_t})(Cu^{hd}{}_{t+1}/p^{ch}{}_{t+1})\right) \qquad (3.16)$$

$$+U_5(h^*N - hN^s{}_{t+1}) + U_6(Cu^{hd}{}_{t+1}/p^{ch}{}_{t+1}).$$

which the household sector presumably attempts to maximize with respect to c^h_t, N^s_{t+1} and Cu^{hd}_{t+1}. Its optimal behavior with respect to c^h_{t+1} and Sn^d_{t+1} is found by substituting the solution to (3.16) into equations (3.15) and (3.1) respectively.

Each choice variable in (3.16) is constrained to be nonnegative. Therefore, if the optimal value of a choice variable is zero, the partial derivative of (3.16) with respect to that variable must be less than or equal to zero. On the other hand, if the solution assigns a positive value to the choice variable, the partial derivative with respect to that variable must equal zero. These are the first-order necessary conditions. The following analysis concentrates exclusively on the first-order conditions associated with an interior solution.

First-Order Necessary Conditions

Partially differentiating (3.16) with respect to commodities purchased in the current period, c^h_t, produces first-order condition (3.17) for an interior solution

$$U'_1 - \frac{\pi^{nh}_{t+1} p^c_t}{p^n_t p^{ch}_{t+1}} U'_4 = 0 \qquad (3.17)$$

This condition is derived holding constant the decision variables N^s_{t+1} and Cu^{hd}_{t+1} but allowing c^h_t (and implicitly c^h_{t+1} and Sn^d_{t+1}) to vary. Consequently the partial derivative of (3.16) pertains to an increase in current consumption financed through a reduction in current saving in the form of a smaller number of equity shares purchased in the current period. The reduced current saving enables the household sector to purchase fewer goods next period. Since π^{nh}_{t+1} represents the household sector's anticipated total return next period from an equity share held at the end of the current period, the ratio π^{nh}_{t+1}/p^n_t has the dimension of $(1 + r^a_t)$ where r^a_t represents the anticipated nominal rate of return per share. The ratio of the current price of commoditites to their anticipated future price, p^c_t/p^{ch}_{t+1}, may be viewed as the reciprocal of $1 + \dot{p}^a_t$ where $\dot{p}^a_t$ depicts the anticipated rate of inflation of commodity prices. Therefore the ratio $\pi^{nh}_{t+1}p^c_t/p^n_t p^{ch}_{t+1}$ in (3.17) may be viewed as $(1 + r^a_t)/(1 + \dot{p}^a_t)$ or $(1 + R^a_t)$ where R^a_t denotes the anticipated real rate of return next period on an equity share held at the end of the current period. In the present context, $1 + R^a_t$ represents, ceteris paribus, the amount by which the households must plan to reduce future real consumption, c^h_{t+1}, for each additional unit of real current consumption, c^h_t, they undertake. Condition (3.17) merely repeats a standard result of intertemporal utility maximization, namely, that the household sector will continue to increase current consumption until the increase in persent utility U'_1 derived from a unit increase in c^h_t just equals the reduction in present utility $-U'_4$, associated with the sacrifice of $1 + R^a_t$ units of c^h_{t+1}.

If we were to view the household sector as attempting to maximize (3.14) (rather than (3.16)) subject to the constraint formed by substituting (3.1) into (3.3), the first-order condition (3.17) may be represented according to the following familiar diagram:

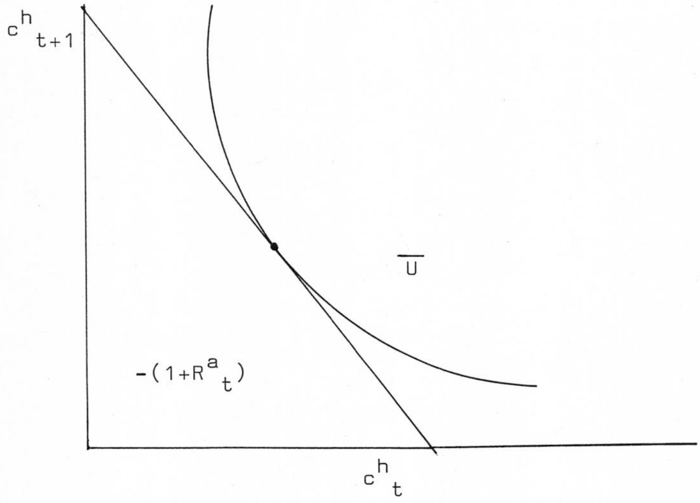

Figure 3.4 - The Subjective Rate of Substitution (U'_1/U'_4) Equals the Market Rate of Substitution $(1+R^a_t)$ of c^h_t for c^h_{t+1}.

The partial derivative of (3.16) with respect to the number of people, N^s_{t+1}, that the household sector wants at time t to have employed by businesses next period yields (3.18):

$$U'_4 \frac{w_{t+1}h}{p^{ch}_{t+1}} - U'_5 h = 0 \tag{3.18}$$

The term $(w_{t+1}h/p^{ch}_{t+1})$ represents the extra number of units of c^h_{t+1}

that the sector will be able to purchase next period if one additional individual becomes employed next period. $U'_4(w_{t+1}h/p^{ch}_{t+1})$ denotes the extra present utility dervied from the prospect of that much more c^h_{t+1}. In the term U'_5h, letter h represents the drop in the number of hours which the households can devote to household production if one more person becomes employed next period so that $-U'_5h$ represents the fall in present utility stemming from the loss in future household production if one more person becomes employed. According to (3.18) then, the household sector will continue to send more people into the labor force in the current period to find jobs for the next period until the increase in the present utility from the extra consumption goods the households can buy next period with the extra wages from the last person employed just equals the drop in present utility from the resulting reduction next period in household production.

If the household sector were viewed as maximizing (3.14), rather than (3.16), subject to the constraint (3.15), then the first-order conditions associated with the partial derivatives of c^h_{t+1} and N^s_{t+1} would reduce to condition (3.18). Consequently, condition (3.18) may be represented by the following diagram:

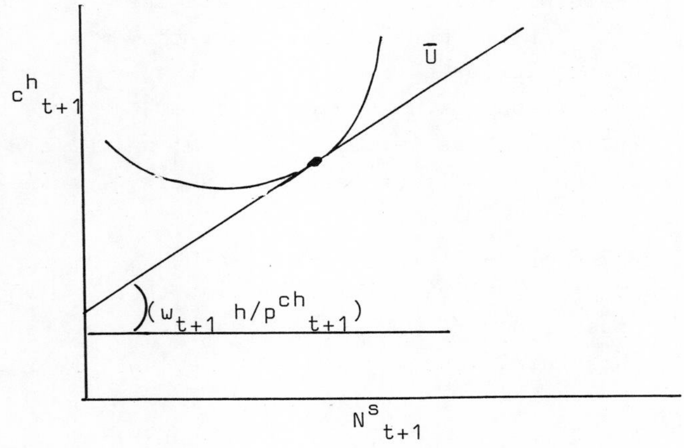

Figure 3.5 - The Utility Maximizing Household Sector Equates Its Subjective Rate of Substitution of Future Labor for Future Consumption with the Market Rate of Substitution.

The partial derivative of present utility, denoted by (3.16), with respect to the amount of currency, Cu^{hd}_{t+1}, the households plan to hold at the end of the current period results in condition (3.19):

$$U'_4 \left(1 - \frac{\pi^{nh}_{t+1}}{p^n_t}\right) \frac{1}{p^{ch}_{t+1}} + U'_6 \frac{1}{p^{ch}_{t+1}} = 0 \tag{3.19}$$

Since current consumption and current income are held constant, just as they were in condition (3.18), current household saving also remains unchanged in equation (3.19). However, unlike the situation connected with condition (3.18), in the present case the composition of current saving is allowed to vary. The expression $(1 - \pi^{nh}_{t+1}/p^n_t)(1/p^{ch}_{t+1})$ represents the drop in future real purchasing power over commodities resulting from diverting a dollar of current saving from purchasing equity shares to accumulating currency. Consequently $U'_4(1-\pi^{nh}_{t+1}/p^n_t)(1/p^{ch}_{t+1})$ denotes the reduction in present utility due to the reduction in future consumption caused by saving an extra dollar as currency rather than as equity shares during the current period. The term $U'_6(1/p^{ch}_{t+1})$ represents the increase in present utility associated with the extra convenience and safety of principal afforded by holding a unit of currency rather than a dollar's worth of equity shares at time t+1. Assuming the households demand a positive amount of currency, they will continue to add to these planned end-of-period holdings until the marginal utility of these balances just equals the marginal utility of the future consumption goods they must sacrifice by holding an additional dollar as currency rather than as equity shares at the beginning of next period. Given that Cu^{hd}_{t+1} is positive, condition (3.19) also stipulates (provided both U'_4 and U'_6 are positive) that the anticipated nominal rate of return on equity shares must be positive.

Viewing the household sector as maximizing (3.14) subject to (3.15) and partially differentiating with respect to c^h_{t+1} and Cu^{hd}_{t+1} yields two first order conditions which can be combined to form equation (3.19). Therefore, equation (3.19) may be represented by Figure 3.6:

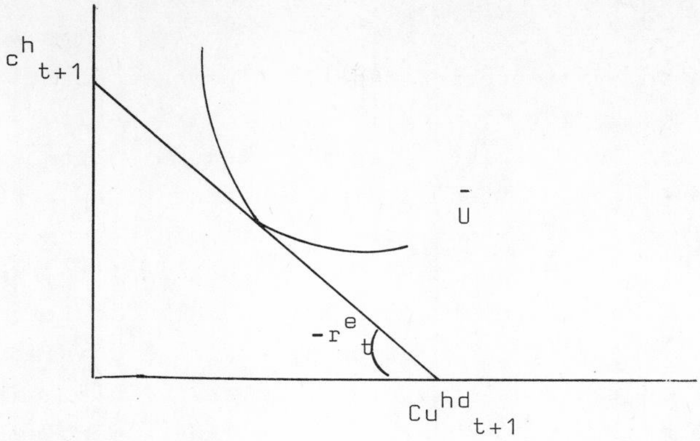

Figure 3.6 - The Utility-Maximizing Household Sector Equates Its Subjective Rate of Substitution to the Market Rate of Substitution ($\pi^{nh}_{t+1}/p^{ch}_{t+1} - 1 = r^e_t$) of Cu^{hd}_{t+1} for c^h_{t+1}.

Household Sector's Demand and Supply Functions

The properties of the household sector's demand and supply functions may be obtained by totally differentiating first-order conditions (3.17)-(3.19) and then solving the new system for the changes in c^h_t, N^s_{t+1} and Cu^{hd}_{t+1} with respect to changes in the various parameters facing the sector at time t. The corresponding net effects upon Sn^d_{t+1} and c^h_{t+1} are then found by substituting the effects upon c^h_t, N^s_{t+1} and Cu^{hd}_{t+1} into equations (3.1) and (3.3) respectively. Since the household sector's planned demand for c^h_{t+1} at time t is unobservable, we will not delineate the net effects on that variable.

Each parametric change produces several effects simultaneously. These effects can be explained easily in terms of the first-order conditions. In interpreting these effects, however, it is useful to keep in mind that each first order condition holds two of the three decision variables c^h_t, N^s_{t+1} and Cu^{hd}_{t+1} constant. Each condition denotes the effect on utility due to a change in the third decision variable accompanied by a corresponding change in future consumption, c^h_{t+1}, and/or the household sector's end-of-period demand for equity shares. The effects for an increase in the current price of commodities will be considered first.

Current commodity price, p^c_t

As is well known, an increase in p^c_t (holding constant all other parameters including the anticipated levels of next period's commodity and equity prices and next period's equity income) produces both a substitution and an income effect. The substitution effect arises because the rise in p^c_t raises the real rate of return on equity, $\pi^{nh}_{t+1}p^c_t/p^n_t p^{ch}_{t+1}$. From condition (3.17) this rise in the real rate of return causes the households to substitute some additional future consumption for some current consumption by saving a greater portion of current income as acquisitions of equity shares. This shift toward more future consumption presumably lowers the marginal utility associated with that consumption, thereby affecting the household sector's other decisions. In particular, condition (3.18) indicates that as U'_4 falls, the marginal utility of the extra goods the households could buy next period by sending an extra person into the labor force also falls. This reduces the household sector's supply of workers. In addition, condition (3.19) shows that as U'_4 falls, the loss in utility from shifting a dollar of saving from equity shares to currency acquisition also becomes smaller. This stimulates the household sector's end-of-period demand for currency. If only the substitution effects prevailed, we might find households saving more during the current period both through currency and equity shares, as well as supplying less labor in response to a rise in p^c_t.

However, an increase in p^c_t also produces an income effect. From the objective function (3.16) it is clear that, holding constant the decision variables c^h_t, Cu^{hd}_{t+1}, an increase in p^c_t reduces the amount that the sector can save during the current period (via equity) and therefore reduces the amount of commodities it can buy next period. This is tantamount to a loss in current income. The resulting drop in future consumption raises its marginal utility, U'_4. From conditions (3.17)-(3.19) respectively, this rise in U'_4 induces the household sector to demand fewer consumption goods in the current period, to supply fewer workers to the labor market by time t+1 and to reduce its end-of-period demand for currency. The income effect reinforces the substitution effect only in the case of current consumption. Consequently, even though c^h_t falls, the net effects upon the remaining decision variables are indeterminate without making additional assumptions.

From the budget constraint depicted in equation (3.1):

$$0 = c^h_t + p^c_t \frac{\partial c^h_t}{\partial p^c_t} + \frac{\partial Cu^{hd}_{t+1}}{\partial p^c_t} + \frac{\partial (p^n_t Sn^d_{t+1})}{\partial p^c_t} \qquad (3.20)$$

$$\qquad\qquad (-) \qquad\qquad (?) \qquad\qquad (?)$$

The analysis in the next chapter, pertaining to the behavior of the nonfinancial business sector, reveals that the business sector will set p^c_t in the elastic range of the function it estimates to be the household sector's demand for current commodities. If this price also happens to fall on the elastic portion of the actual demand function, then the sum of the first two terms on the right hand side will be negative. Under these conditions, then, an increase in p^c_t causes the dollar amount to current ex ante saving to rise so that $\partial Cu^{hd}_{t+1}/\partial p^c_t + \partial(p^n_t Sn^d_{t+1})/\partial p^c_t > 0$. If one were willing to assume, in addition, that both currency and equity shares are gross substitutes for current consumption, then both of these last two partials would be positive. However, neither one is necessarily positive a priori. If the household sector does save more during the current period, an increase in p^c_t also has the net effect of increasing planned consumption next period, causing U'_4 and therefore N^s_{t+1} to fall. But the anticipated drop in next period's wage income will be smaller than the increase in next period's non-wage income in order to permit the additional consumption that period.

Next period's money wage, w_{t+1}.

An increase in the hourly wage rate, w_{t+1} which the nonfinancial sector announces at t that it will pay its workers next period produces the familiar substitution and income effects.

The rise in w_{t+1} raises next period's return to work, inducing the household sector to send more people into the labor force to work next period. The added labor income induces the sector to plan to buy more consumption goods next period thereby lowering U'_4. As U'_4 falls the households are induced to increase its end-of-period demand for currency. Therefore, if we consider only the substitution effect of a change in w_{t+1}, a rise in w_{t+1} induces the households to increase the amount of currency they accumulate during the current period but to reduce total current saving (via equity shares) in order to finance an increase in current consumption. At the same time, the sector will plan to send more people into the labor force by the end of the period.

But the rise in w_{t+1} also raises next period's wage income even if the sector were not to increase its supply of labor. For given levels of c^h_t, N^s_{t+1} and Cu^{hd}_{t+1}, then, an increase in w_{t+1} allows the sector to plan to purchase more consumption goods next period. Thus, the rise in w_{t+1} is equivalent to an increase in income. As the sector decides to purchase more consumption goods next period in response to the increase in w_{t+1}, the marginal utility of that consumption falls. As U'_4 falls, the households are encouraged to reduce their supply of labor, N^s_{t+1}, but to increase current consumption and their end-of-period demand for currency. Since the households plan to increase current consumption in the face of this 'income effect' even though their current income has not changed, they necessarily plan to save less (even though their planned accumulation of currency rises) during the current period. Consequently the volume of equity they plan to hold at time t+1 is smaller.

But because the households plan to spend more on consumption goods as a result of the income effect, their reduction in N^s_{t+1} must be less than in proportion to the rise in w_{t+1}. The amount $w_{t+1}hN^s_{t+1}$ must be larger after the rise in w_{t+1} or the planned increase in consumption next period simply could not materialize.

To summarize, both the income and substitution effects arising from an increase in w_{t+1} cause the household sector to increase its demands for current and future consumption and its end-of-period demand for currency. Both effects also cause the household sector to reduce its end-of-period demand for equity shares. In addition, although the income and substitution effects upon N^s_{t+1} are in opposit directions, the household sector nevertheless plans that next period's wage income, $w_{t+1}hN^s_{t+1}$, will be greater after the rise in w_{t+1}. From the household sector's budget constraint for the current period:

$$0 \equiv \underset{(+)}{\frac{\partial p^c_t c^h_t}{\partial w_{t+1}}} + \underset{(+)}{\frac{\partial Cu^{hd}_{t+1}}{\partial w_{t+1}}} + \underset{(-)}{\frac{\partial (p^n_t Sn^d_{t+1})}{\partial w_{t+1}}} \tag{3.21}$$

The effects on the household sector's supply of labor function may be summarized follows:

$$\frac{\partial N^s_{t+1}}{\partial w_{t+1}} \gtrless 0, \text{ but } N^s_{t+1} + w_{t+1}\frac{\partial N^s_{t+1}}{w_{t+1}} > 0. \tag{3.22}$$

Equity price, p^n_t.

In terms of the present model, a change in p^n_t produces two substitution effects and an income effect.

First of all, an increase in p^n_t reduces, ceteris paribus, the anticipated real rate of return on equity shares. This is the opposite of the substitution effect associated with an increase in p^c_t. As a result, the sector plans to save less during the current period (i.e. to spend more on current consumption). The reduction in saving partially takes the form of a reduction in its end-of-period demand for equity shares. The shift away from future consumption raises the marginal utility associated with that consumption thereby increasing the loss in utility associated with the reduction in future consumption caused by saving in the form of currency rather than equity shares. Consequently, the household sector decides to save less in the form of currency as well. In addition the rise in U'_4 (due to the reduced demand for future consumption) raises the marginal utility of the extra goods available to the households from an additional unit of labor; the sector's supply of labor will tend to rise.

The second subtitution effect associated with the rise in p^n_t reduces the number of future consumption goods the household sector must sacrifice if it decides to save a dollar during the current period as currency acquisition. Therefore, the sector will tend to increase its end-of-period demand for currency but reduce its end-of-period demand for equity shares. The former tends to offset the first substitution effect on the demand for equity. In any case, as a result of the second substitution effect, the sector will plan to consume less next period, since it will be saving more in the form of the asset whose market income is zero. This in turn raises U'_4. causing the household sector to reduce current consumption and to increase its supply of workers to the business sector.

The net effect of the two substitution effects, then, is to reduce the household sector's end-of-period demand for equity shares and to increase its supply of labor. The sector will also plan to reduce next period's consumption. The net effects upon current consumption and its end-of-period demand for currency are indeterminate.

In addition to the two substitution effects, an increase in p^n_t also produces a negative income effect, provided the sector plans to purchase additional equity shares during the current period, i.e. to the extent that $(Sn^d_{t+1}-Sn_t) > 0$. Consequently in spite of the often-discussed positive 'wealth effect' due to the rise in the market value of its existing shares, p^n_t, the household sector is indeed worse-off as a result of the rise in p^n_t if it plans to save by accumulating equity shares during the current period. This means that for given levels of c^h_t, Cu^{hd}_{t+1} and N^s_{t+1}, the sector must plan to purchase fewer consumption goods next period because it is unable to buy as many equity shares. This raises U'_4 thereby reducing the sector's demand for current consumption and its end-of-period demand for currency; but its supply of labor will rise. Since the income effect causes the sector's end-of-period demand for equity to fall but its supply of labor to rise, the income effect reinforces the two substitution effects for these two cases. The remaining signs are still indeterminate.

From the household sector's current-period budget constraint, however, the following relationship must hold:

$$o = p^c_t \frac{\partial c^h_t}{\partial p^n_t} + \frac{\partial Cu^{hd}_{t+1}}{\partial p^n_t} + (Sn^d_{t+1} - Sn_t) + p^n_t \frac{\partial Sn^d_{t+1}}{\partial p^n_t} \tag{3.23}$$

According to the above discussion, if the household sector plans to save via equity shares during the current period, the fourth term on the right hand side of (3.23) is negative. In the next chapter we will find that the business sector will set p^n_t in the elastic range of its estimate of the household sector's demand curve for its equity shares. If p^n_t also happens to fall in the elastic portion of the household sector's actual demand (where "demand" is expressed in terms of the number of shares the sector plans to purchase during the period), then the sum of the last two terms on the right hand side of (3.23) will be negative. As a result, an increase in p^n_t will cause the amount the households either spend on current consumption or add to currency holdings to rise:

$$p^c_t \frac{\partial c^h_t}{\partial p^n_t} + \frac{\partial Cu^{hd}_{t+1}}{\partial p^n_t} > 0. \tag{3.24}$$

Current income and initial wealth

An increase in current labor income, $w_t h_t N_t$, current equity income per share, π^n_t, the number of equity shares held by the households at time t, Sn_t, or the number of dollars held as currency at time t, Cu^h_t, produces positive "income" or "wealth" effects upon the household sector's current demand functions. In particular, an increase in any one of these variables implies that if the sector were to purchase the same number of current consumption goods, to plan to have the same number of people working next period, and to hold the same amount of currency at the end of the current period, it would be able to consume more goods next period because it would be able to accumulate more equity shares in the current period. This causes the marginal utility to future consumption to diminish which tends to cause c^h_t and Cu^{hd}_{t+1} to rise and N^s_{t+1} to fall.

From the budget constraint facing the household sector,

$$1 = \underset{(+)}{\frac{\partial(p^c_t c^h_t)}{\partial x}} + \underset{(+)}{\frac{\partial Cu^{hd}_{t+1}}{\partial x}} + \underset{(+)}{\frac{\partial(p^n_t Sn^d_{t+1})}{\partial x}} \qquad (3.25)$$

where x represents any one of $w_t h_t N_t$, π^n_t, Sn_t or Cu^h_t.

Unlike the "mean-variance" approach to the demand for financial assets, an increase in current income in the current framework does not imply that the demand for the "risky" asset will fall. Consequently, the approach taken here, while simpler than the "expected utility" approach, nevertheless yields the desirable properties of that approach with respect to the possibility that both the "safe" and "risky" assets are "normal".

Anticipated future commodity prices and equity income.

An anticipated increase in future commodity prices reduces the anticipated real return on equity shares thereby reducing the opportunity cost of current consumption in terms of future consumption. By itself, this causes the households to substitute present for future consumption on the margin. The repurcussion upon the number of people the households plan to have employed next period is positive; by working more in the future, households can save less today and therefore spend more on present consumption. However, the repercussion on the household sector's demand for currency for the end of the period is negative; since the sector plans to consume less next period, it has less need for currency at the start of that period.

But, an anticipated increase in p^{ch}_{t+1} also reduces next period's anticipated real wage. Ceteris paribus, this causes the households to plan to send fewer people into the labor force, causing anticipated future wage income to fall. This increases the tendency for the households to save during the current period (in the form of equity shares) and to consume less currently. However, since planned future consumption tends to be lower, the end-of-period demand for currency will tend to fall. Consequently the two substitution effects associated with an increase in p^{ch}_{t+1} have opposite influences upon c^{h}_{t}, Sn^{d}_{t+1} and N^{s}_{t+1}, but reinforcing effects upon c^{h}_{t+1} and Cu^{hd}_{t+1}.

The increase in p^{ch}_{t+1} also produces an income effect. In particular, since future goods are now expected to cost more, the households in effect have experienced a reduction in future income. This causes them to plan to reduce future consumption, to send more people into the labor force, to spend less on current consumption, to reduce the end-of-period demand for currency and, therefore, to increase their end-of-period demand for equity shares.

In addition, an increase in p^{ch}_{t+1} reduces the anticipated future purchasing power of currency held at the end of the current period. This raises the marginal utility of an extra unit of nominal currency since the reduction in real balances raises the marginal product of an additional unit of nominal currency in reducing transactions costs. Furthermore, for a given amount of planned future real consumption, the reduction in the purchasing power of the end-of-period demand for nominal currency raises the marginal utility derived from the extra safety of nominal purchasing power provided by an additional unit of currency. Consequently, the effect of an increase in p^{ch}_{t+1} upon the purchasing power of the household sector's planned end-of-period currency holdings causes it to plan to accumulate more (nominal) currency during the current period, to reduce current consumption, to send more people into the labor force, and to purchase fewer consumption goods next period.

The net effect of an increase in the anticipated future price of commodities upon current consumption, the demand for currency, the demand for equity shares and the supply of labor is indeterminate in every case.

An anticipated increase in future equity income per share, π^{nh}_{t+1}, increases the opportunity costs of current consumption and of end-of-period currency accumulation in terms of future consumption goods. As a result, households will tend to cut back on current consumption and their demand for currency, meaning that they will tend to save more during the current period in the form of equity share acquisitions. The extra future income from the extra current saving causes the marginal utility of future consumption to fall, therby reducing the number of people which the households plan to have working for the business sector next period.

However the increase in π^{nh}_{t+1} also means that even if the households were to hold the same number of equity shares at the end of the current period they would be able to consume more next period. By itself, this causes the households to reduce their supply of labor. It also causes them to increase their demand for currency because the marginal utility of the safety and convenience of money grows with the rise in planned future consumption. In addition this income effect causes current consumption to increase, meaning that the end-of-period demand for equity shares tends to fall. Only in the case of the supply of labor are the income and substitution effects reinforcing for a rise in π^{nh}_{t+1}.

Summarizing the discussion to this point, the household sector's demand and supply functions may be expressed as:

$$c^h_t = c^h_t(\underset{-}{p^c_t}, \underset{+}{w_{t+1}}, p^n_t, \underset{+}{w_t h_t N_t}, \underset{+}{\pi^n_t}, \underset{+}{Sn_t}, \underset{+}{Cu^h_t}, p^{ch}_{t+1}, \pi^{nh}_{t+1}) \quad (3.26)$$

$$Cu^{hd}_{t+1} = Cu^{hd}_{t+1}(p^c_t, w_{t+1}, p^n_t, \underset{+}{w_t h_t N_t}, \underset{+}{\pi^n_t}, \underset{+}{Sn_t}, \underset{+}{Cu^h_t}, p^{ch}_{t+1}, \pi^{nh}_{t+1}) \quad (3.27)$$

$$Sn^d_{t+1} = Sn^d_{t+1}(p^c_t, \underset{-}{w_{t+1}}, \underset{-}{p^n_t}, \underset{+}{w_t h_t N_t}, \underset{+}{\pi n_t}, \underset{+}{S^n_t}, \underset{+}{Cu^h_t}, p^{ch}_{t+1}, \pi^{nh}_{t+1}) \quad (3.28)$$

$$N^s_{t+1} = N^s_{t+1}(p^c_t, w_{t+1}, \underset{+}{p^n_t}, \underset{-}{w_t h_t N_t}, \underset{-}{\pi^n_t}, \underset{-}{Sn_t}, \underset{-}{Cu^h_t}, p^{ch}_{t+1}, \underset{-}{\pi^{nh}_{t+1}}) \quad (3.29)$$

The partials of these functions satisfy restrictions (3.20)-(3.25) listed above as well as the following conditions:

$$0 \equiv p^c_t \frac{\partial c^h_t}{\partial p^{ch}_{t+1}} + \frac{\partial Cu^d_{t+1}}{\partial p^{ch}_{t+1}} + p^n_t \frac{\partial Sn^d_{t+1}}{\partial p^{ch}_{t+1}} \quad (3.30)$$

$$0 \equiv p^c \frac{\partial c^h_t}{\partial \pi^{nh}_{t+1}} + \frac{\partial Cu^d_{t+1}}{\partial \pi^{nh}_{t+1}} + p^n_t \frac{\partial Sn^d_{t+1}}{\partial \pi^{nh}_{t+1}} \quad (3.31)$$

The fact that a number of signs in (3.26)-(3.29) are unknown even in this extremely simple model of household behavior means that those interested in predicting household behavior - namely the business sector (who must anticipate the households' demand functions for commodities and equity shares as well as their supply of labor function) and the policy authority - have precious little a priori information upon which to base their predictions. The results of this chapter also indicate that even if we were to model the formation of households' expectations of next period's commodity prices or next period's equity income, the effects of a change in these expectations upon household behavior would nevertheless remain indeterminate.

However, according to the above results, firms can rest assured that (a) the partials of c^h_t and Sn^t_{t+1} are negative with respect to their respective prices, (b) these demands are both positively related to current income and to the initial household balances of equity shares and currency and (c) the households will adjust their labor supply in response to a higher money wage in a manner that will tend to increase the business sector's wage bill next period. In the model of the business sector developed in the next chapter, the firms incorporate this information in their estimates of the c^h_t, Sn^d_{t+1} and the N^s_{t+1} functions as they attempt at time t to decide the optimal levels of p^c_t, p^n_t, w_{t+1}, h_t and π^n_t.

References

Anderson, W.H. Locke, 1979, National Income Theory and Its Price Theoretic Foundations (McGraw-Hill, New York).

Blatt, J.M., 1983, Dynamic Economic Systems (M.E. Sharpe, Inc., Armonk).

Deaton, Angus and Muellbauer, John, 1980, Economics and Consumer Behavior (Cambridge University Press, New York).

Green, H.A. John, 1976, Consumer Theory (Academic Press, Inc., New York).

Saving, T.R., 1971, "Transactions Costs and the Demand for Money," American Economic Review, June, 407-420.

4. The Nonfinancial Business Sector in the Simple Model

The nonfinancial business sector presumably formulates its plans at time t so as to maximize its present value. Because the number of its equity shares outstanding at time t is given, this objective is tantamount to maximizing the price which those people who hold its shares at time t could receive for their shares if they were to sell them at time t. But, since all households are viewed as belonging to a single decision-making unit, any trading in existing shares at time t among households presumably fails to affect aggregate behavior. Consequently in this model the price of an existing share at time t remains a shadow price.

The reader should not confuse the shadow price of an equity share at time t with the current market price of an equity share. The latter refers to the price the business sector announces at time t at which it stands ready to trade equity shares <u>during</u> the current period. Any new shares acquired by the household sector in this manner during the current period will not begin to pay dividends until next period. Furthermore, any shares that households sell back to the business sector in the current period will continue to pay dividends to households this period (but not next period). On the other hand, any internal exchanges of existing shares among households at time t (at the shadow price) would entitle the new owners to dividends in both the current and next periods.

The business sector maximizes the present value of an existing share (and therefore the present value of all existing shares) by maximizing the present value of the dividends per share it plans to distribute during the "current" and "next" periods. For if both actual and potential shareholders (within the household sector) at time t were to know the business sector's plans as to the stream of current and future dividends per share (and if both were to place full confidence in this information), then the present value of the income per share calculated by the business sector would also represent the shadow price of an outstanding share at time t. No shareholder would be willing to accept less and no potential shareholder would be willing to pay more.

The income which the business sector plans at time t to earn during the current period equals the value of its planned current production less its current expenses. Its planned level of current (net) business saving, by definition, is the portion of this net income which it plans to retain rather than distribute to existing shareholders. The sector will plan at time t to retain a dollar of net income during the current period only if by doing so it will be able to increase the present value of the future dividends per share by at least that amount. Standard Modigliani-Miller arguments purporting to show that it does not matter how much net income firms retain during the period are based on the untenable assertion that <u>every</u> dollar retained during the current period necessarily increases the present value of future dividends by exactly one dollar.

Let Cu^n_t denote the nonfinancial business sector's initial stock of currency at time t, let Q_t depict the initial (real) inventory of consumption goods and let Sn_t, as before, represent the number of nonfinancial business sector equity shares outstanding at time t. Suppose the business sector holds no other assets and has no outstanding liabilities at time t.

At time t, the business sector must decide whether to liquidate (i.e. sell its initial inventory and distribute the proceeds as well as its initial currency holdings to the shareholders) or to remain in business as a "going concern". Presumably the option it elects is the one that maximizes its present value. As a going concern, its net income in any period is defined as the market value of its production in that period minus its operating costs, i.e. its value added. The value of its production equals its sales revenue plus the value of its additions to inventories that period.

Let $R^e\{.\}$ represent expected current period revenue. To simplify the analysis, suppose that the business sector plans that if it remains in business it will want to hold a zero inventory of consumption goods at the end of the current period. Under these conditions, the planned value of current production may be expressed as $R^e\{.\} - p^c_t Q_t$ where p^c_t is the current market price of consumption goods which the business sector must decide (and announce) at time t.

Sometime prior to time t (presumably at the beginning of last period) the business sector announced an hourly money wage, w_t, that it would pay during the current period to those people whom it employed by time t to work during the current period. Let N_t represent the number of people who are employed by the business sector at time t to work during the current period. Let h_t represent the average number of hours which the business sector must decide at time t that these people will work during the current period. Then the current wage bill is given by $w_t h_t N_t$, which constitutes the only componenet of current operating costs in this simple model.

Let y^n_t denote the current nominal net income that the business sector anticipates at time t. Then, in light of the above discussion, y^n_t may be expressed according to (4.1):

$$y^n_t \equiv R^e\{.\} - p^c_tQ - w_th_tN_t. \qquad (4.1)$$

Current dividends, $\pi^n_t \cdot Sn_t$ (where π^n_t represents current dividends per share), will be announced by the business sector at the beginning of the current period. These dividends equal the anticipated level of y_t minus the business sector's planned net business saving (i.e. its planned additions to retained earnings), s^{nd}_t, for the current period:

$$\pi^n_tSn_t = y^n_t - s^{nd}_t. \qquad (4.2)$$

As it formulates its plans at time t, the business sector is constrained by the fact that the amount of currency it accumulates during the period will necessarily equal the sum of the value of the inventories it sells during the period plus the value of its net sales of equity shares during the period plus the amount it saves on the income account during the current period. More formally, let Cn^{nd}_{t+1} denote the amount of currency the business sector plans to hold at the end of the current period, let Sn^{de}_{t+1} represent the number of equity shares it plans to have outstanding by the end of the current period (i.e. the anticipated household sector demand for equity shares for time t+1), and let p^n_t denote the current market price of equity shares which the business sector announces at time t. Then the business sector faces the following current period "budget constraint":

$$Cu^{nd}_{t+1} - Cu^n_t = p^c_tQ_t + p^n_t(Sn^{de}_{t+1} - Sn_t) + s^{nd}_t \qquad (4.3)$$

or

$$s^{nd}_t = (Cu^{nd}_{t+1} - Cu_t) - p^c_tQ_t - p^n_t(Sn^{de}_{t+1} - Sn_t). \qquad (4.4)$$

Substituting the right hand sides of (4.1) and (4.4) into (4.2) yields the following expressison for current dividends:

$$\pi^n_tSn_t = R^e\{.\} - w_th_tN_t - (Cu^{nd}_{t+1}-Cu^n_t) + p^n_t(Sn^{de}_{t+1}-Sn_t) \qquad (4.5)$$

with current dividends per share to those holding shares at time t expressed as:

$$\pi^n_t = \frac{1}{Sn_t} [R^e\{.\} - w_t h_t N_t - (Cu^{nd}_{t+1} - Cu^n_t) - p^c_t Q_t - p^n_t (Sn^{de}_{t+1} - Sn_t)] \quad (4.6)$$

As it formulates its plans at time t, the business sector faces similar decisions with respect to next period's income and capital accounts. Let $R^{e*}\{.\}$ represent the sector's expected sales revenue for next period. Since at time t the sector's time horizon occurs at the end of next period, assume that the sector plans at time t to hold no assets and to have no liabilities outstanding by time t+2. Among other things, this implies that its planned inventory of consumption goods at the end of next period equals zero. Since we have already assumed that the planned inventory of consumption goods for the beginning of next period also equals zero, this means that the planned value of next period's sales revenue equals the planned value of next period's production.

The net income which the business sector expects at time t to receive next period, y^n_{t+1}, is defined as the planned value of next period's production, $R^e\{.\}$, minus next period's expected wage bill. Let w_{t+1} denote the hourly money wage which the business sector announces at time t and guarantees it will pay its employees next period. Let N^d_{t+1} represent the number of people the business sector plans at time t to employ next period. Since the business sector presumably plans that everyone it hires (or continues to employ) next period will work the standard h hours next period, the business sector's anticipated wage bill for next period is denoted by $w_{t+1}hN^d_{t+1}$. Therefore, at time t, the businss sector's anticipated net income for next period, y^n_{t+1}, may be expressed as:

$$y^n_{t+1} = R^{e*}\{.\} - w_{t+1}hN^d_{t+1}. \quad (4.7)$$

As it formulates its plans for next period, the business sector faces a constraint similar to (4.4). In particular, the amount of currency it plans to accumulate during that period necessarily equals the sum of (a) the value of its planned net reduction in inventories next period, (b) the value of its planned net sales of equity shares during that period, and (c) the amount it plans to save on the income account next period. But, as mentioned above, its planned reduction in inventories next period equals zero. Furthermore, since the sector's time horizon extends only to time t+2, it does not anticipate at time t that a market will exist for its shares next period. Any new shares the sector might issue next period would not yield an income to the purchaser until after time t+2. Since at time t the sector does not plan to generate any income beyond time t+2, it does not expect that anyone will be interested in buying any of its shares next period. Furthermore, the sector will be unwilling at time t to contemplate buying back next period any shares it plans to have outstanding at time t+1. The reason is that it will have to pay dividends next period on all shares outstanding at time t+1 whether it buys back these shares next period or not. Therefore at time t the amount of currency the business sector plans to accumulate next period must equal the amount it plans to save on the income account next period.

But, at time t the sector does not plan to hold any currency at time t+2. Therefore its planned accumulation of currency for next period is represented by $(0 - Cu^{nd}_{t+1})$, or simply, $-Cu^{nd}_{t+1}$. Therefore, at time t the sector must plan to dissave next period, i.e., to distribute dividends, $\pi_{t+1}Sn^{de}_{t+1}$, to its owners in excess of next period's income, y^{n}_{t+1}. In other words, at time t the business sector presumably plans to distribute to its owners next period all the income it earns that period plus the currency with which it plans to begin that period. This relationship is shown by first defining next period's (ex ante) dividends in equation (4.8):

$$\pi^{n}_{t+1}Sn^{de}_{t+1} = y^{n}_{t+1} - s^{d*}_{t+1} \tag{4.8}$$

where π^{n}_{t+1} represents anticipated dividends per share next period and s^{d*}_{t+1} denotes next period's ex ante net business saving. The next period budget constraint (as viewed at time t) is then depicted in (4.9):

$$-Cn^{d}_{t+1} = s^{d*}_{t+1} \tag{4.9}$$

Substituting the right hand side of (4.7) and the left hand side of (4.9) into (4.8) produces the desired expression for next period's dividends per share:

$$\pi^{n}_{t+1} = \frac{1}{Sn^{de}_{t+1}}\left[R^{e*}\{.\} - w_{t+1}hN^{d}_{t+1} + Cu^{nd}_{t+1}\right] \tag{4.10}$$

The business sector's objective at time t is to maximize the present value of the anticipated stream of dividends per share as denoted by expressions (4.6) and (4.10).

In the general case, the present value of an income stream from a particular asset refers to the amount which the owners of that asset would have to place in their next best alternative at time t in order to duplicate the anticipated income each period from the asset in question. (If the present value exceeds the market price, a potential owner should purchase it since he would have to put a greater amount in an alternative asset at time t to obtain the same income stream.) In the present model, currency represents the only market alternative to holding equity shares for the household sector. Since currency yields no explicit return, the households would have to put π^n_t dollars into currency at time t in order to receive π^n_t dollars from that asset during the current period. Also, households would have to place π^n_{t+1} dollars in currency at time t in order to duplicate the dividends per share which the firms are contemplating distributing next period. (After holding π^n_{t+1} dollars in currency for one full period it will still only represent π^n_{t+1} dollars.)

The nonfinancial business sector presumably does not know the implicit return which the households anticipate receiving from their curency balances. Therefore, the present value of the income stream associated with expressions (4.6) and (4.10) is simply the sum of those two items. Letting p^n_o represent the shadow price of an equity share at time t, the business sector's objective at time t is to maximize p^n_o, where:

$$p^n_o = \pi^n_t + \pi^n_{t+1} = \frac{1}{Sn_t} [R^e\{.\} - w_t h_t N_t - (Cu^{nd}_{t+1} - Cu^n_t) + p^n_t (Sn^{de}_{t+1} - Sn_t)]$$

$$+ \frac{1}{Sn^{de}_{t+1}} [R^{e*}\{\cdot\} - w_{t+1} hN^d_{t+1} + Cu^{nd}_{t+1}] \qquad (4.11)$$

<u>The Anticipated Current Revenue Function</u>

At time t the business sector presumably bases its anticipations as to its curent period sales revenue upon its estimate of the household sector's current demand function for commodities. Let equation (4.12) represent its estimate of this function:

$$c^{de}_t = c^{de}_t (\underset{-}{p^c_t}, \underset{+}{v_c}) \qquad (4.12)$$

Where v_c represents a vector of shift parameters which the business sector estimates will affect the position of the household sector's demand for consumption goods during the current period.

Taking the total differential of (4.12), dividing all terms by the non-zero partial derivative, c^{de}_1, and so solving for p^c_t yields (4.13):

$$dp^c_t = \frac{1}{c^{de}_1} dc^{de}_t - \frac{c^{de}_2}{c^{de}_1} dv_c \tag{4.13}$$

Therefore, we may express p^c_t according to the following "inverse" function:

$$p^c_t = p^c_t \,(\underset{-}{c^{de}_t}, \underset{+}{v_c}) \tag{4.14}$$

Equation (4.14) represents the maximum commodity price that firms estimate they will be able to sell a given quantity, c^{de}_t, of consumption goods during the current period. Multiplying the right hand side of (4.14) by c^{de}_t yields the business sector's estimated current revenue function (4.15):

$$\begin{aligned} R^e &= p^c_t \,(c^{de}_t, v_c).c^{de}_t \\ &= R^e\{\underset{?}{c^{de}}, \underset{+}{v_c}\}. \end{aligned} \tag{4.15}$$

As is well known, if the business sector sets p^c_t in the range for which the estimated demand is price elastic, then R^e_1, marginal revenue, is positive. In fact, as will be shown below, a necessary condition for maximizing p^n_o implies that R^e_1 is positive. Assuming that (4.14) is linear in c^{de}, marginal revenue diminishes as c^{de}_t increases.

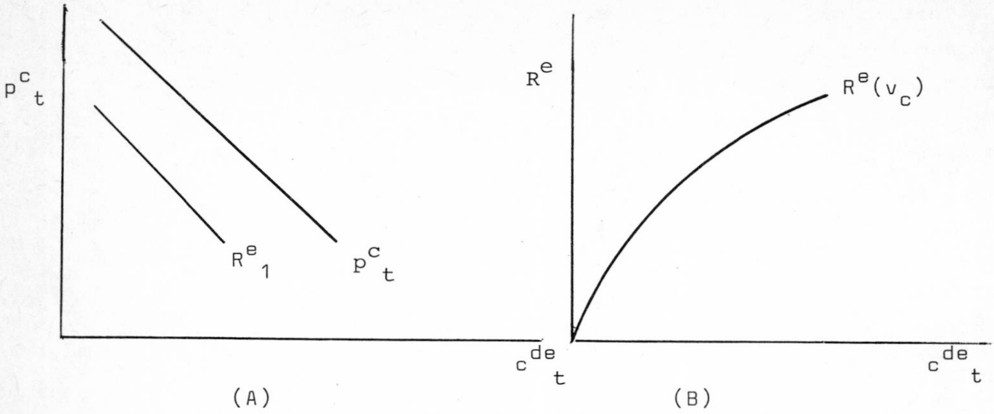

Figure 4.1 - The (A) Estimated Current Commodity Demand, Marginal Revenue, and (B) Estimated Current Revenue Functions.

Since the number of goods the business sector plans to sell during the current period equals the amount it plans to produce in the current period minus its planned accumulations to inventories over the period, current expected sales may be expressed by (4.16):

$$c^{de}_t = q(.) + Q_t \tag{4.16}$$

where q(.) represents current production and where Q_t, once again, represents initial inventories (and the anticipated current period sales from inventories).

Current production of consumption goods is presumed to be an increasing strictly concave function, q(.), of current labor time devoted to production. As noted above, h_tN_t represents the total number of hours of labor services employed by the business sector during the current period. Since the business sector is assumed to be completely integrated, labor constitutes the only factor it purchases from other sectors. But the initial inventory, Q_t, also potentially affects current production, both adversely and favorably. To the extent that real resources are required to store and handle these inventories, Q_t adversely affects current production. But to the extent that initial inventories smooth the production process, they potentially conserve labor time. For simplicity, we abstract from these effects.

However, labor must perform other duties besides producing consumption goods in the present model. Specifically, I assume that the business sector must devote some current labor time not only to making payments to its current employees but also to searching for new employees for next period (or to providing "working conditions" that encourage current employees to continue working for the buisness sector next period).

Although the amount of time which firms devote to transactions may be small relative to the total number of hours of labor utilized during the current period, the cost of this transactions time is not necessarily insignificant from the firms' point of view. In the present model, the business sector's currency holdings at the beginning of the current period serve to reduce the business sector's anticipated current transactions time. These currency holdings provide a ready reserve from which to make payments to labor during the current period without having either to wait for revenues from current sales or to issue intraperiod IOU's (i.e., loans which are repid before the end of the current period). Assume that current transactions time for the business sector is represented by the following strictly convex function:

$$\tau = \tau(h_t N_t, \ Cu^n{}_t, w_t) \tag{4.17}$$

with $\tau(.)>$; $\tau_1, \tau_3 > 0$; $\tau_2 < 0$; $\tau_{11}, \tau_{22}, \tau_{33} > 0$;
$\tau_{12}, \tau_{23} < 0$; $\tau_{13} > 0$.

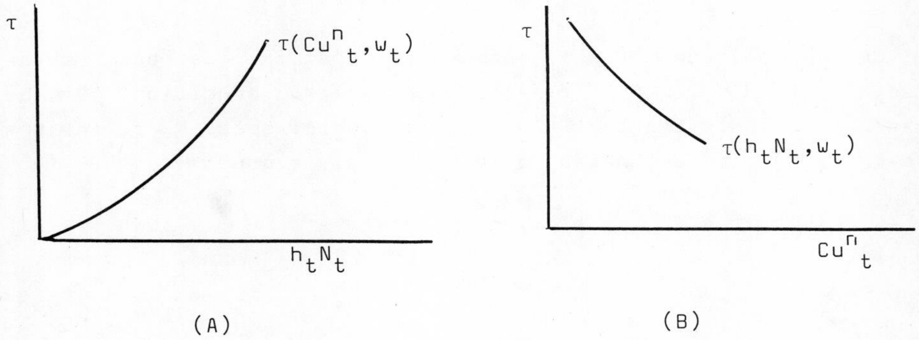

Figure 4.2- Current Business Sector Transactions Time as (A) an Increasing Function of Total Labor Time and as (B) a Decreasing Function of Initial Currency Holdings.

Expression (4.17) asserts that the anticipated ability of a given amount of initial currency, Cu^n_t, to conserve current transactions time diminishes as the volume of transactions, $h_t N_t$, rises and as the wage rate rises, since the latter reduces the purchasing power of the currency over labor services.

The amount of time, τ, which the business sector anticipates at time t that it will have to devote this period either to searching for employees for next period or to providing "working conditions" that encourage current workers to remain employed next period, presumably depends not only upon the number of people, N^d_{t+1}, which the business sector plans to employ for next period, but also upon the number of people, N^{se}_{t+1}, it estimates will be looking for jobs for next period. Specifically assume that current search time by the business sector is a positive function that increases at an increasing rate as the number of people it wants to employ next period rises. Assume also that current search time diminishes (at a decreasing rate) as the number of people it estimates will be willing to work next period rises.

Assume that the business sector's estimate at time t of the household sector's supply of labor for next period, N^{se}_{t+1}, is given by the following linear function:

$$N^{se}_{t+1} = b_0 + \underset{(?)}{b_1 w_{t+1}} + b_2 v_n; \text{ with } \frac{w_{t+1}\,\partial N^{se}_{t+1}}{N^{se}_{t+1}\,\partial w^{t+1}} > -1 \tag{4.18}$$

where v_n denotes a vector of shift parameters that the business sector estimates affects N^s_{t+1}. A first-order necessary condition, to be presented below, indicates that the business sector sets w_{t+1} in the range in which N^s_{t+1} is estimated to be positively sloped:

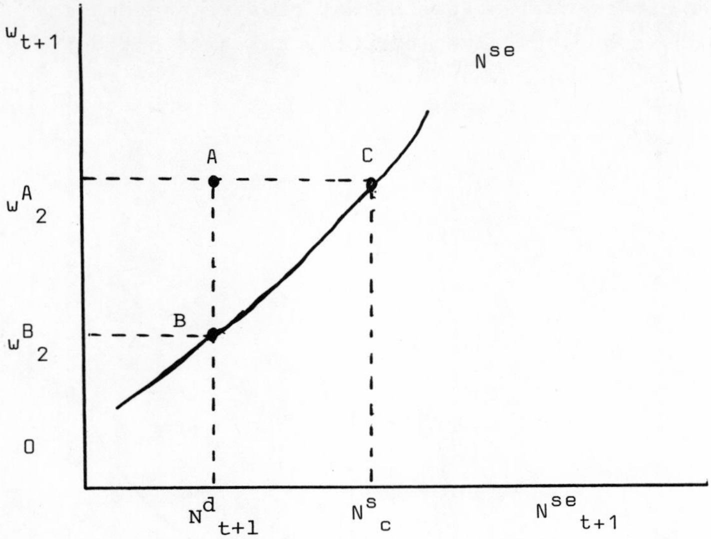

Figure 4.3 - The Business Sector's Estimate of the Household Sector's Labor Supply Function

Let N^d_{t+1} represent the number of people the business sector plans at time t to employ next period. Presumably as the business sector raises the wage rate it announces at time t (that it will pay per "hour" next period) above the minimum level that it estimates is necessary to attract the desired number of workers, it thereby reduces the costs (i.e., the labor time it must expend) it anticipates will be required to search for and recruit the desired number of workers. For instance, if the sector sets the wage rate at w^A_2 in Figure 4.3, it estimates that N^s_c people will be willing to work next period. Given that the sector wants to hire only N^d_{t+1} people for next period, the wage bill it expects to incur next period, $w^A_2hN^d_{t+1}$, exceeds the minimum wage in expects it would have to incur, $w^B_2hN_{t+1}$, in order to eventually enlist N^d_{t+1} people by time t+1. The business sector will be willing nevertheless to commit itself to this higher wage bill next period provided the higher announced wage is expected to reduce current search and recruiting costs enough to at least offset the reduction in the firms' present value associated with the higher wage bill. The reduction in current recruiting costs presumably stem from the anticipated excess supply of workers that will respond to the money wage w^A_2.

Specifically, assume current-period anticipated search costs, γ, are given by the following positive, strictly convex function:

$$\gamma = \gamma(N^d_{t+1}, N^{se}_{t+1}(w_{t+1}, v_n)) \tag{4.19}$$

where $\gamma(.) > 0$; $\gamma_1 > 0$; $\gamma_2 < 0$; $\gamma_{11}, \gamma_{22} > 0$; $\gamma_{12} < 0$;

with $N^d_{t+1} \leq N^{se}_{t+1}(.)$.

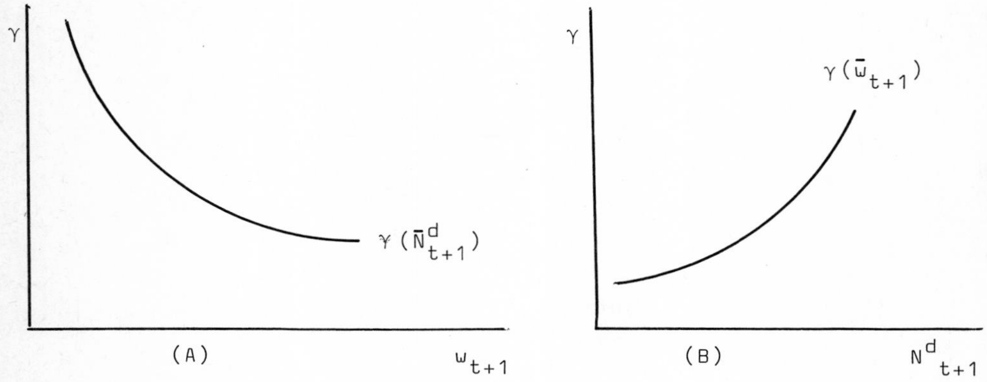

Figure 4.4 - Anticipated Current Search Costs as (A) a Decreasing Function of the Announced Wage Rate for Next Period and (B) as an Increasing Function of the Number of People that Businesses Want to Employ Next Period.

In light of current transactions costs, as depicted in (4.17), and current search costs, as specified in (4.19), the number of hours which the business sector anticipates it will apply to production of consumption goods in the current period is therefore represented by $h_tN_t - \tau(.) - \gamma(.)$. Substituting this expression into the current production function q(.) yields expression (4.20):

$$q = q(h_tN_t - \tau(h_tN_t, Cu^n_t, w_t) - \gamma(N^d_{t+1}, N^{se}(w_{t+1}, v_n))) \tag{4.20}$$

$$= \hat{q}(h_tN_t, Cu^n_t, w_t, N^d_{t+1}, w_{t+1}, v_n)$$

where $q(.) > 0, q' > 0$ and $q'' < 0$. Expression (4.20) is strictly concave in the choice variables h_t, N^d_{t+1}, and w_{t+1}. Assuming that a unit of labor raises current transactions time by less than one unit (i.e., assuming $(1-\tau_1) > 0$), then the marginal product, $\hat{q}_1$, of labor <u>net</u> of transactions costs associated with using that labor, is positive. Beginning cash balances reduce transactions time and raise current output, $\hat{q}_2 > 0$. The higher the current money wage, the lower the purchasing power of cash balances and the greater the level of transactions time and the smaller the level of current output; the partial derivative of current output with respect to w_t, $\hat{q}_3$, is negative. Ceteris paribus, as the sector raises its demand for workers for next period, it increases current search time and reduces curzent production: $\hat{q}_4 < 0$. But as the sector raises w_{t+1}, it reduces search time (provided $N^{se}{}_1 > 0$), raising current output; $\hat{q}_5 > 0$. An estimated shift in N^{se} so that the sector anticipates that more people will be willing to work at each wage also reduces search time and raises current output; $\hat{q}_6 > 0$.

All own second-order partial derivatives in (4.20) are negative, as shown by the following symmetric matrix of second-order partials:

$$\begin{bmatrix}
\hat{q}_{11} & \hat{q}_{12} & \hat{q}_{13} & \hat{q}_{14} & \hat{q}_{15} & \hat{q}_{16} \\
(-) & (?) & (?) & (+) & (-) & (-) \\
\vdots & \hat{q}_{22} & \hat{q}_{23} & \hat{q}_{24} & \hat{q}_{25} & \hat{q}_{26} \\
 & (-) & (+) & (+) & (-) & (-) \\
 & \vdots & \hat{q}_{33} & \hat{q}_{34} & \hat{q}_{35} & \hat{q}_{36} \\
 & & (-) & (+) & (+) & (+) \\
 & & \vdots & \hat{q}_{44} & \hat{q}_{45} & \hat{q}_{46} \\
 & & & (-) & (+) & (+) \\
 & & & \vdots & \hat{q}_{55} & \hat{q}_{56} \\
 & & & & (-) & (-) \\
 & & & & \vdots & \hat{q}_{66} \\
 & & & & & (-)
\end{bmatrix}$$

The above matrix is negative definite. Only the signs of $\hat{q}_{12}(\hat{q}_{21})$ and $\hat{q}_{13}(\hat{q}_{31})$ are unknown. The partial derivative $\hat{q}_{12}$ is given by $\hat{q}_{12}=(1-\tau_1)\cdot q''(-\tau_2)+q'(-\tau_{12})$. The negative first term in this sum indicates that as current money balances increase they release more labor to the production of consumption goods thereby reducing the marginal product of labor. The positive second term shows that as current money balances increase they reduce the extra transactions time that an additional unit of labor creates thereby raising the net marginal product of a given amount of labor services. In the remainder of this study, I assume the second term dominates, i.e. that $\hat{q}_{12} > 0$. The partial derivative $\hat{q}_{13}$ is given by $\hat{q}_{13} = (1-\tau_1)q''.(-\tau_3) + q'(-\tau_{13})$. The positive first term indicates that an increase in the current wage rate increases current transactions time, which reduces the quantity of labor which can be applied to the production of consumption goods, thereby raising the marginal product of that labor. The negative second term shows that an increase in w_t increases the extra transactions time associated with a marginal increase in labor services, thereby reducing the net marginal product of a given amount of labor services. In what follows, I assume the second term dominates so that $\hat{q}_{13} < 0$.

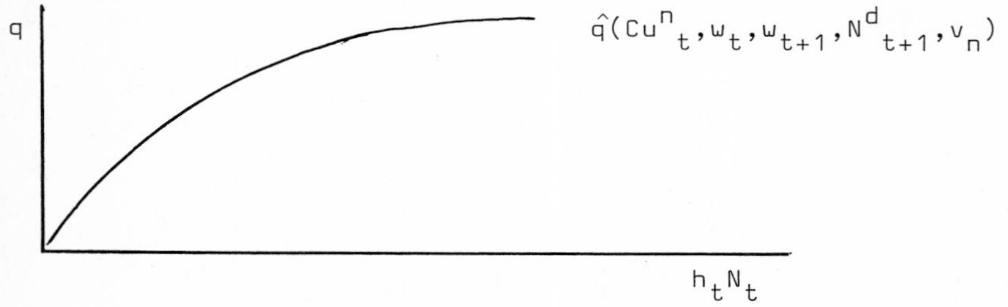

Figure 4.5 - Current Production Function for Commodities.

Returning to the earlier specifications of the business sector's current revene function (4.15):

$$R^e = R^e\{c^{de}_t, v_c\} \tag{4.15}$$

and current expected sales (4.16):

$$c^{de}_t = q(.) + Q_t \tag{4.16}$$

we see that by substituting (4.20) for q(.) in (4.16) and then substituting (4.16) for c^{de}_t in (4.15) yields expression (4.21) as the current-period revenue function:

$$R^e = R^e\{q(h_tN_t - \tau_1(h_tN_t) - \tau_2(Cu^n_t, w_t) - \gamma(N^d_{t+1}, N^{se}(w_{t+1}, v_n)) + Q_t, v^c\}$$

$$= R^e\{\hat{q}(h_tN_t, Cu^n_t, w_t, N^d_{t+1}, w_{t+1}, v_n)) + Q_t, v_c\} \quad (4.21)$$

Next Period's Anticipated Revenue Function

Since the business sector anticipates at time t that it will hold no inventories either at the beginning or at the end of next period, its anticipated production next period, q*, must correspond to next period's expected (real) sales, c^{de}_{t+1}. Suppose that the sector anticipates future commodity demand to be a diminishing linear function of the commodity price that the sector plans to announce at the beginning of <u>next</u> period:

$$c^{de}_{t+1} = \underset{(-)}{d_1} p^{cd}_{t+1} + v^*_c \quad (4.22)$$

where v^*_c represents a vector of shift parameters. Solving (4.22) for p^{ce}_{t+1}, the business sector's estimated revenue next period, R^e, may be expressed as:

$$R^{*e} = \left(-\frac{v^*_c}{d_1} + \frac{1}{d_1} c^{de*}_{t+1}\right) \cdot c^{de*}_{t+1} \quad (4.23)$$

$$= R^{*e}\{c^{de*}_{t+1}, v^*_c\}$$

By definition, if the sector plans to set p^{ce}_{t+1} in the elastic range of the estimated demand function, then $R^{*e}_1 > 0$. Since (4.22) is linear, $R^{*e}_{11} < 0$. Also, since anticipated future production, q*, equals anticipated future real sales, c^{de*}_{t+1}, the revenue function (4.23) may be re-written as:

$$R^{*e} = R^{*e}\{q^*(.), v^*_c\}. \quad (4.24)$$

The specification of next period's anticipted production function is necessary to complete the specification of next period's anticipated revenue function. In a manner consistent with the current-period production function, assume that future production is a prositve, increasing linear function of the amount of labor time that the sector plans to devote to commodity production next period. As viewed from time t, total labor time next period will be divided between commodity production and transaction associated with making payments to next period's labor. In other words, at time t the business sector presumably does not anticipate engaging in search next period.

Suppose the following strictly-convex function represents next period's anticipated transactions time for the business sector:

$$\tau^* = \tau^*(hN^d_{t+1}, Cu^{nd}_{t+1}, w_{t+1}) \tag{4.25}$$

where $\tau^*(.)>0$; τ^*_1, $\tau^*_3>0$; $\tau^*_2<0$; $\tau^*_{13}>0$; τ^*_{12}, $\tau^*_{23}<0$ and all own second-order partials are positive. Function $*(.)$ states that next period's transactions time increases at an increasing rate as the number of workers, N^d_{t+1}, the sector plans to employ next period grows. The sector can reduce next period's transactions costs at a decreasing rate by adding to the amount of currency it plans to hold at the beginning of next period. However the ability of these cash balances to conserve transactions time diminishes as the sector raises next period's hourly money wage, w_{t+1}; an increase in w_{t+1}, ceteris paribus, reduces the purchasing power of Cu^{nd}_{t+1} over the labor services the sector plans to buy next period.

In light of the above discussion, next period's anticipated production function may be written as the strictly concave function (4.26):

$$\begin{aligned} q^* &= q^*(hN^d_{t+1} - (hN^d_{t+1}, Cu^{nd}_{t+1}, w_{t+1})) \qquad (4.26) \\ &= \hat{q}^*(N^d_{t+1}, Cu^{nd}_{t+1}, w_{t+1} \end{aligned}$$

where $q^*(.)>0$, $q^{*\prime}>0$, and $q^{*\prime\prime}<0$. Assuming that $\tau_1<1$, a unit increase in labor time next period adds less than one unit to transactions time, making the net marginal physical product of a unit of N^d_{t+1} (i.e., net of transactions time) positive $\hat{q}^*_1>0$. Since cash balances held at the beginning of next period reduce transactions time, they increase next period's total product, $\hat{q}^*_2>0$. But, as the sector raises the wage rate it announces for next period it reduces, ceteris paribus, the productivity of money balances and thereby reduces next period's total product, $\hat{q}^*_3<0$.

All own second-order partials ($\hat{q}^*_{11}$, $\hat{q}^*_{22}$, and $\hat{q}^*_{33}$) are negative. As in the case of the current-period production function, cross-partial $\hat{q}^*_{12}$ is assumed to be positive (so that an increase in CU^{nd}_{t+1} raises the marginal product of labor) while $\hat{q}^*_{13}$ is assumed to be negative (an increase in w_{t+1} reduces the marginal product of next period's labor). In addition, $\hat{q}^*_{23}$ is positive.

Substituting the right hand side of (4.26) for q*(.) in (4.24) yields the following expression for next period's anticipated revenue:

$$R^{*e} = R^{*e}\{\hat{q}^*(N1^d_{t+1}, Cu^{nd}_{t+1}, w_{t+1}), v^{*c}\} \tag{4.27}$$

The Business Sector's Optimizing Problem at Time t

Substituting the right hand sides of (4.21) and (4.27) for $R^e\{.\}$ and $R^{e}*\{.\}$ respectively in (4.11) produces the following unconstrained objective function for the business sector at time t:

$$p^n_o = \pi^n_t + \pi^n_{t+1} = \frac{1}{S_n} [R^e\{\hat{q}(h_tN_t, Cu^n_t, w_t, w_{t+1}, N^d_{t+1}) + Q_t, v^c\}$$

$$- w_th_tN_t - (Cu^{nd}_{t+1} - Cu^n_t) + p^n_t(Sn^{de}_{t+1} - Sn_t)]$$

$$+ \frac{1}{Sb^{de}_{t+1}} [R^{*e}\{q^*(N^d_{t+1}, Cu^{nd}_{t+1}, w_{t+1}), v^*_c)\}$$

$$- w_{t+1}hN^d_{t+1} + Cu^{nd}_{t+1}] \tag{4.28}$$

The business sector's objective at time t is to maximize p^n_0 with respect to the choice variables h_t, N^d_{t+1}, w_{t+1}, Cu^{nd}_{t+1} and p^n_t.

Before this problem can be solved, however, we must specify the sector's estimate at time t of the household sector's end-of-period demand for equity shares, Sn^{de}_{t+1}. Based upon equation (3.27), see Chapter 3, suppose that the business sector's estimate of the household sector's demand for equity shares is given by (4.29):

$$Sn^{de}_{t+1} = Sn^{de}_{t+1}(\underset{-}{p^n_t}, \underset{+}{v_s}) \tag{4.29}$$

where v_s denotes a vector of shift parameters and where the signs of the first-order partials are presented below the respective variables. All second-order partials are ignored. Substitution of the right hand side of (4.29) for $Sn^{de}_{t+1}(.)$ in (4.28) completes the specification of the business sector's objective function at time t.

First-order Necessary Conditions

The first-order necessary conditions corresponding to the business sector's choice variables are presented below. Since each choice variable is constrained to be non-negative, two first-order conditions apply to each choice variable. The first stipulates that if the optimal value of the choice variable equals zero, the partial derivative of (4.29) with respect to the choice variable must be non-positive; the second condition specifies that if the optimal value of the choice variable is positive, the partial derivative must in fact equal zero. The strict-concavity of $\hat{q}(.)$ and $\hat{q}^*(.)$, coupled with the strict-concavity of $R^e\{.\}$ and $R^{*e}\{.\}$, insures that p^n_o is a strictly concave function of h_t, N^d_{t+1}, w_{t+1} and Cu^{nd}_{t+1}. Assume p^n_o is also strictly concave with respect to p^n_t. Consequently the first-order conditions are associated with a maximum rather than a minimum for an inflection point in case of positive values of the choice variables).

$$\text{If } h^*_t = 0, \ \frac{R^e_1\hat{q}_1N_t - w_tN_t}{Sn_t} \leq 0;$$

$$\text{If } h^*_t = 0, \ \frac{R^e_1\hat{q}_1N_t - w_tN_t}{Sn_t} = 0. \tag{4.30}$$

The term $R^e_1\hat{q}_1N_1$ in condition (4.30) represents the current period marginal revenue product of raising the average working time of the existing workers one hour. The term w_tN_t represents the current-period marginal cost of doing so. If the sector produces nothing during the current period, i.e., if $h_t = 0$, then the marginal cost of h_t is at least as large as is marginal revenue product. Assume that N_t, w_t and the marginal product of labor, $\hat{q}_1$, are all positive. If $h_t > 0$, then R^e_1 must also be positive. This is the well-known result that a price-setter, faced with positive marginal costs, will set product price, p^c_t, in the elastic range of is estimate of the demand function for its product.

Differentiating (4.28) partially with respect to N^d_{t+1} yields the following conditions for a non-negative solution for N^d_{t+1}:

$$\text{If } N^d_{t+1} \equiv 0, \ \frac{R^e_1\hat{q}_4}{Sn} + \frac{R^{*e}_1\hat{q}^*_1h - w_{t+1}h}{Sn^{de}_{t+1}} \leq 0$$

$$\text{If } N^d_{t+1} > 0, \quad \frac{R^e{}_1\hat{q}_4}{Sn_t} + \frac{R^{*e}{}_1\hat{q}^*{}_1h - w_{t+1}h}{Sn^{de}_{t+1}} = 0 \tag{4.31}$$

The term $R^e{}_1\hat{q}_4$ represents the loss in current revenue associated with diverting current labor from commodity production to search and recruitment of an additional employee for next period. Therefore, $R^e{}_1\hat{q}_4/Sn_t$ depicts the marginal cost per share to existing owners associated with searching for an additional worker. The term $R^{*e}{}_1\hat{q}_1{}^*h$ represents the anticipated marginal revenue product next period from an additional worker and $w_{t+1}h$ represents the marginal cost next period of using this worker the standard "h" hours. Consequently $R^{*e}{}_1\hat{q}^*h - w_{t+1}h)/Sn^{de}{}_{t+1}$ denotes the (present value of) next period's anticipated net income per share to existing shareholders from hiring one more worker for next period. If $N^d{}_{t+1} = 0$, the marginal current-period search cost is at least as great as the present value of the new income per share from a unit of labor. Otherwise, the sector will continue to add workers until the two dollar amounts are equal.

The first-order conditions under which the business sector will announce (at time t) a non-negative hourly money wage, w_{t+1}, that it will pay everyone who works next period are presented in (4.32):

$$\text{If } w_{t+1} = 0, \quad \frac{R^e{}_1\hat{q}_5}{Sn_t} + \frac{R^{*e}{}_1\hat{q}^*{}_3 - hN^d{}_{t+1}}{Sn^{de}_{t+1}} \leq 0 \tag{4.32}$$

$$\text{If } w_{t+1} > 0, \quad \frac{R^e{}_1\hat{q}_5}{Sn_t} + \frac{R^{*e}{}_1\hat{q}^*{}_3 - hN^d{}_{t+1}}{Sn^{de}_{t+1}} = 0$$

The term $-hN^d{}_{t+1}$ represents the anticipated reduction in the present value of the firm resulting from the increase in next period's anticipated wage bill caused by a unit increase in w_{t+1}. The term $R^{*e}{}_1\hat{q}^*{}_3$ is also negative. It denotes the anticipated reduction in future revenue resulting from diverting labor time next period from commodity production to transactions time. The anticipated increase in future transactions time arises because an increase in w_{t+1}, ceteris paribus, reduces the purchasing power of the currency which the busienss sector plans to hold at the beginning of next period (i.e., at the end of the current period). Consequently $(R^{*e}{}_1\hat{q}^*{}_3 - hN^d{}_{t+1})$

$/Sn^{de}_{t+1}$ represents the present value of the marginal reduction in next period's dividends per share resulting from a unit increase in w_{t+1}.

The term $R^e_1\hat{q}_4$ in conditions (4.32) depicts the effect upon current-period revenues associated with an adjustment in current commodity production stemming from a concomitant change in current-period search costs arising from a unit in increase in w_{t+1}. As noted above, if the business sector decides to produce at all in the current period, it will announce a product price, p^c_t, such that R^e_1 is positive. Therefore, if the firms announce a positive value for w_{t+1}, expression (4.32) stipulates that $\hat{q}_5$ must also be positive (so that the sum in parentheses in that expression may equal zero). But, from (4.20), $q_5=q'\gamma_2 N^{se}_1$. Assuminng that the marginal physical product of labor devoted to current commodity production, q', is positive and assuming that marginal search time in the current period is a decreasing function of the supply of labor (i.e. $\gamma_2<0$) then a necessary and sufficient condition for $\hat{q}_5$ to be positive is that the slope of the estimated labor supply function with respect to w_{t+1} be positive. In other words, the present-value maximizing business sector, if it decides to announce a positive money wage, w_{t+1}, will set that money wage in the positively sloped portion of the estimated supply function for labor. (Presumably, if w_{t+1} is set equal to zero, N^{se}_{t+1} also equals zero. Since we have assumed that $N^{se}_{t+1} \geq N^d_{t+1}$ this implies that if w_{t+1} is set equal to zero, then both N^d_{t+1} and $q^*(.)$ are zero.)

The first-order necessary conditions for the business sector's decision at time t to hold non-negative cash balances at the end of the current period are presented in (4.33):

$$\text{If } Cu^{nd}_{t+1} = 0, \; -\frac{1}{Sn_t} + \frac{R^{*e}_1\hat{q}^*_1 + 1}{Sn^{de}_{t+1}} \leq 0 \tag{4.33}$$

$$\text{If } Cu^{nd}_{t+1} > 0, \; -\frac{1}{Sn_t} + \frac{R^{*e}_1\hat{q}^* + 1}{Sn^{de}_{t+1}} = 0$$

term $-1/Sn_t$ represents the reduction in current income per share to existing owners if the business sector decides to increase its end-of-period cash balances by one dollar. The term $R^{*e}_1\hat{q}^*_2$ represents the anticipated marginal revenue product from the extra labor that will be released from transactions and applied to commodity production next period as a result of the extra dollar the sector decides (at time t) to hold at time t+1. Since the sector plans at time t to distribute next period its end-of-current-period cash balances plus next period's net income to the owners, the sum $R^{*e}_{1}\hat{q}^{*}_{2} + 1$ denotes the anticipated extra payment to the oweners next period resulting from an extra dollar of currency held by the business sector at the end of the current period. Division of this sum by Sn^{de}_{t+1} represents (the present value of) the anticipated increase in income per share to existing owners.

According to (4.33), if, when $Cu^{nd}_{t+1} = 0$, the reduction in current income per share from increasing Cu^{nd}_{t+1} one dollar is at least as great as the present value of the anticipated inrcease in future income per share. But, if $Cu^{nd}_{t+1} > 0$, the sector will continue to raise its demand for currency until the marginal reduction in current income just equals the present value of the anticipated increase in future income (per share). An implication of (4.33) is that the business sector will plan to set the current market price of equity shares, p^{n}_{t}, at a level at which the number of shares it plans to have outstanding at the end of the current period exceeds the initial number outstanding if and only if the anticipated marginal revenue product from currency next period, $R^{*e}_{1}\hat{q}^{*}_{2}$, is positive. This can be shown simply by setting the sum in (4.33) equal to zero and re-writing as:

$$\frac{Sn^{de}_{t+1}}{Sn_{t}} = R^{*e}{}_{1}\hat{q}^{*}_{2} + 1. \tag{4.34}$$

The first-order necessary conditions for the business sector to announce a non-negative current market price, p^{n}_{t}, for equity shares are given by (4.35)

$$\text{If } p^{n}_{t} = 0, \frac{(Sn^{de}_{t+1} - Sn_{t}) + p^{n}Sn^{de}_{1}}{Sn_{t}} + \frac{\pi^{n}_{t+1}}{Sn^{de}_{t+1}} Sn^{de}_{1} \geq 0 \tag{4.35}$$

$$\text{If } p^{n}_{t} > 0, \frac{(Sn^{de}_{t+1} - Sn_{t}) + p^{n}Sn^{de}_{1}}{S^{n}_{t}} \quad \frac{\pi^{n}_{t+1}}{Sn^{de}_{t+1}} Sn^{de}_{1} = 0$$

where Sn^{de}_1 represents the partial derivative of Sn^{de}_{t+1} with respect to p^n_t in (4.29) and where π^n_{t+1} was defined in (4.10). According to these conditions, the issuance of new shares during the current period by the business sector potentially affects both current dividends per share and future dividends per share. Current dividends per share are affected in that any revenue received from current sales of new shares, to the extent that it is not used to meet current expenses or to add to currency holdings, can be distributed to the current owners. Future dividends per share are also affected, ceteris paribus, because by issuing more shares this period the sector will have to distribute a given total amount of dividends next period among a greater number of shares, thereby reducing next period's dividends per share.

The second term, $-(\pi^n_{t+1}/Sn^{de}_{t+1})Sn^{de}_1$, in condition (4.35) is positive. It represents the addition to the present value of an equity share at time t, p^n_o, that results from raising the market price of an equity share for the current period, p^n_t, one dollar. In particular as p^n_t is raised, the estimated number of shares which the sector will have issued by time t+1 falls because $Sn^{de}_1 < 0$. Therefore, the present value of the future dividends per share increases as p^n_t is raised because the given total dividend will be divided among fewer shares.

Given that the second term in brackets on the left hand side of (4.35) is positive, condition (4.35) stipulates that the first term must be negative if the sector sets a positive market price for its shares. Since the numerator of the first term represents the current marginal revenue from raising p^n_t one dollar, and since this extra revenue must be negative if the firm is maximizing p^n_o, condition (4.35) therefore implies that for a positive p^n_t the sector will set the current market price of equity shares within the elastic portion of its estimate of the household sector's "flow" demand function for equity shares. The estimated "flow" demand is simply the estimated end-of-period demand, Sn^{de}_{t+1}, minus the number of shares outstanding at time t, Sn_t.

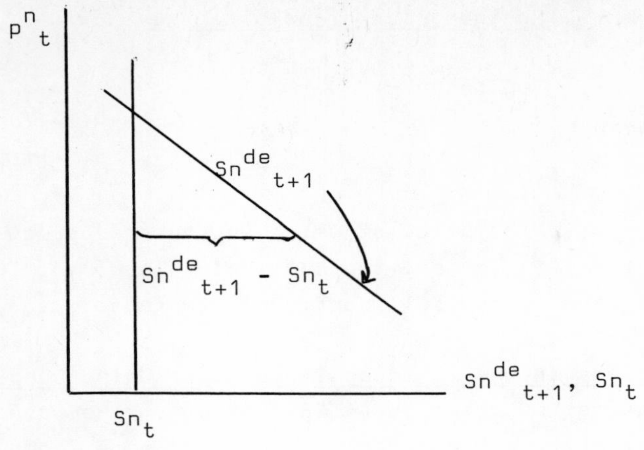

Figure 4.6 - The Estimated "Flow"Demand for Equity Shares, $Sn^{de}{}_{t+1} - Sn_t$.

<u>Conditions for Liquidation</u>

If the sector selects zero values for all of its choice variables, then it decides at time t to produce nothing during either the current or next periods. It will also decide not to hold any currency at the end of the current period and not to trade in equity shares during the period. Given these conditions, the objective of the business sector becomes, from expression (4.28), the maximization of:

$$p^n{}_o = \frac{R\{Q_t, v_c\} + Cu^n{}_t}{Sn_t} \qquad (4.36)$$

In other words, the sector will set the current period price of commodities, $p^c{}_t$, at the level that maximizes current revenue, $p^c{}_t Q_t$, from the sale of its initial inventory. Valuing the initial inventory at this price, the existing balance sheet at time t for the liquidating firm becomes, from expression (4.36):

Business Sector Balance Sheet

$p^c{}_t Q_t$	
$Cu^n{}_t$	$p^n{}_o Sn_t$

where $p^n{}_o$ represents the price at which equity shares would trade among households at time t, provided the households knew the plans of the business sector and placed full confidence in those plans.

Response Functions of the Business Sector as a Going Concern

If an interior solution to (4.28) exists, the behavior of the business sector at time t becomes considerably more complicated. The planned optimal levels of current and future production, employment and dividends as well as the optimal level of the end-of-period cash balances and the optimal prices which the sector announces at time t for commodities, labor and equity shares now all depend upon a variety of factors. These factors include not only the technical aspects of commodity production, the payments mechanism, and employee recruitment, but also the business sector's estimates of (a) the household sector's supply of labor function and (b) its demand functions for commodities (in both the current and next periods) and equity shares. The remainder of this section details these influences upon each of the business sector's choice variables at time t.

Assuming an interior solution exists to (4.28), expressions (4.30) - (4.33) and (4.35), all hold as equalities. Totally differentiating these first-order conditions yields a system of five linear equations in the differentials associated with the choice variables. Assuming the strict concavity of the objective function with respect to these variables, the coeffieient matrix of the endogenous variables in the system of five equations is negative definite.

The solution to (4.28) yields the following functions for: current labor hours, the business sector's demand for employees for next period, the optimal money wage rate for next period, the sector's desired currency holdings for the end of the period and the optimal equity-share price:

$$h_t = h_t(N_t, w_t, Cu^n{}_t, Q_t, Sn_t, v_c, v^*{}_c, v_n, v_s) \tag{4.37}$$

$$N^d_{t+1} = N^d_{t+1}(w_t, Cu^n_t, Q_t, Sn_t, v_c, v^*_c, v_n, v_s) \quad (4.38)$$

$$w_{t+1} = w_{t+1}(w_t, Cu^n_t, Q_t, Sn_t, v_c, v^*_c, v_n, v_s) \quad (4.39)$$

$$Cu^{nd}_{t+1} = Cu^{nd}_{t+1}(w_t, Cu^n_t, Q_t, Sn_t, v_c, v^*_c, v_n, v_s) \quad (4.40)$$

$$p^n_t = p^n_t(w_t, Cu^n_t, Q_t, Sn_t, v_c, v^*_c, v_n, v_s) \quad (4.41)$$

Substituting (4.37), (4.38) and (4.39) into (4.20) yields the following expression for current production by the business sector:

$$q = q(w_t, Cu^n_t, Q_t, Sn_t, v_c, v^*_c, v_n, v_s) \quad (4.42)$$

Adding existing inventories, Q_t, to this amount yields the business sector's estimated (real) sales of commodities for the current period, c^{de}_t:

$$c^{de}_t = c^{de}_t\ (w_t, Cu^n_t, Q_t, Sn_t, v_c, v^*_c, v_n, v_s) \quad (4.43)$$

Substitution of (4.43) into (4.49) yields the following function for the optimal current period price of commodities as viewed by the business sector at time t:

$$p^c_t = p^c_t(w_t, Cu^n_t, Q_t, Sn_t, v_c, v^*_c, v_n, v_s) \quad (4.44)$$

The optimal current period dividends per share, π^n_t, which the business sector also announces at time t is found by substituting the solutions for h_t, Cu^{nd}_{t+1} and p^n_t into (4.6). The optimal level of current dividends per share therefore is given by the following function:

$$\pi^n_t = \pi^n_t(w_t, Cu^n_t, Q_t, Sn_t, v_c, v^*_c, v_n, v_s) \quad (4.45)$$

Consequently, the solution to (4.28) ultimately yields mutually consistent optimal values for <u>all</u> the business sector's choices on the income and capital accounts, whether real or financial, for both the current and next periods with respect to quantities as well as prices. This fully-integrated, internally-consistent model of the business sector constitutes an integral part of the complete model of collective economic choice presented later in this study.

The discussion of functions (4.37) - (4.45) proceeds with an analysis of the effects of a change in each of the various parameters upon each choice variable. The effects of a change in N_t will be considered first.

Effects of a change in N_t

Only the total number of labor hours matters in the present specification of the business sector's production function. Consequently the greater the number of employees, N_t, with which the sector begins the current period, ceteris paribus, the smaller will be the average number of hours, h_t, that the business sector asks these people to work during the current period. The fall in h_t will be in proportion to the rise in N_t so that the optimal total number of hours remain unchanged.

The optimal levels of all of the business sector's other decision variables also remain unchanged. Therefore the parital derivative of h_t with respect to N_t in (4.37) equals $-h_t/N_t$ and the partial derivatives of all other choice variables with respect to N_t equal zero. That is why N_t does not appear in (4.38) - (4.45).

Effects of a change in w_t

The higher w_t happens to be at the beginning of the current period, the greater will be the marginal cost to the business sector of raising the average number of labor hours in the current period. Consequently, a higher w_t causes the business sector, ceteris paribus, to reduce h_t. The sector will produce less output during the current period and, given its estimate of the market demand for its product, will announce a higher market price for consumption goods. Marginal revenue will rise, but total revenue fall. The drop in total current revenue combined with the increase in current expenses caused by the higher wage bill reduces current net income and also reduces the dividends that the business sector pays its owners this period. The rise in marginal revenue increases the opportunity cost of devoting a portion of current labor time to search for employees for next period rather than to current production. Ceteris paribus, this encourages the sector to reduce its demand for workers for next period and to announce a higher money wage for next period in order to conserve current search effort. However,there are indirect effects operating as well. For instance, by reducing N^d_{t+1} the sector reduces current search effort thereby lowering the marginal revenue from raising w_{t+1}. Consequently, the sector may decide to adjust next period's money wage downward rather than upward.

Besides raising the marginal cost of h_t, a higher w_t also reduces the purchasing power of the business sector's initial cash balances over labor services. The drop in its initial 'real' balances causes current transactions time to rise thereby reducing current production and setting in motion forces comparable to those associated with the drop in h_t discussed in the last paragraph.

The effect of a higher w_t upon the business sector's demand for currency for the end of the current period depends upon whether the sector raises or lowers its estimate of next period's marginal revenue product of currency. Given the sector's estimate of next period's product demand curve, if the sector decides to reduce its labor force, N^d_{t+1}, for that period, it necessarily plans to reduce output next period. By itself, this tends to raise marginal revenue and hence the marginal revenue product of currency. However, the marginal revenue product of currency will depend as well upon the money wage, w_{t+1} that the sector plans to announce for next period. If the sector decides to adjust w_{t+1} above what it would have annonced if w_t had been lower, then even though next period's real cash balances fall, ceteris paribus, the <u>marginal</u> product of those balances increase. This would reinforce the tendency to raise Cu^{nd}_{t+1} in response to a fall in N^d_{t+1}. But, as mentioned above, the sector may decide to reduce w_{t+1} below what it would have announced otherwise. In either case, if the sector does decide to increase its end-of-period cash balances, it will tend to distribute less to its owners during the current period as dividends, ceteris paribus.

The effect of a higher w_t upon the current market price which the business sector announces for its equity shares at time t depends upon the sector's revised estimate of next period's dividends (i.e. net income). If the sector revises downward its estimate of next period's net income due to smaller anticipated production that period, this reduces the marginal cost to existing shareholders of issuing additional shares. The <u>fall</u> in future dividends <u>per share</u> (i.e. the marginal cost to existing shareholders) of issuing one more share this period is smaller the smaller the amount of dividends involved. This encourages the business sector to reduce the price of its shares, given its estimate of the end-of-period demand curve for its shares.

A simple example may be useful for illustrating this point. Suppose that at time t the business sector were to set p^n_t at the level at which it anticipates households will want to hold 100 shares at the beginning of next period. If anticipated dividends next period equal \$1,000, the marginal cost to existing shareholders would be 10¢ per share if the sector were to adjust p^n_t so that 101 shares were outstanding at time t+1. (Increasng the number of shares from 100 to 101 reduces next period's dividends per share from \$10 to \$9.90.) But if next period's anticipated dividends were only \$500, then if the number of outstanding shares were to be 101 rather than 100, the fall in dividends per share would be only 5¢ (from \$5 per share to \$4.95 per share). This example illustrates the role of the second term (i.e., the one involving π^n_{t+1}) in condition (4.35).

Effects of a change in Cu^n_t

The more money held by the nonfinancial business sector at time t, the greater the purchasing power of its initial balances over current labor services. To the extent that this reduces current transactions time, the sector will be able to apply a greater portion of its labor services to the production of commodities. The effect is just the opposite of the real balance effect associated with a rise in w_t, discussed above. In particular, as the sector decides to produce more commodities during the current period with the resources released by the added real balances it announces a lower price for current consumption goods than it would have otherwise. Total current revenue increases as marginal revenue falls. The increase in total revenue accompanied by the reduced labor expenses raises current net income and, therefore, current dividends. The fall in marginal revenue reduces the opportunity cost of devoting more resources to current search, thereby encouraging the sector to increase N^d_{t+1}(and reduce w_{t+1}). If current search costs do increase due to the rise in N^d_{t+1}, the sector may announce a higher (rather than a lower) money wage for next period. If, as a result of its decision to hire more labor in order to produce more consumption goods next period, the sector raises its estimate of next period's net income (and dividends), it will tend to raise the current market price of its equity shares. Also, as the sector's estimate of next period's marginal revenue falls in response to its plans to produce more next period, the marginal revenue product of currency it plans to hold at the beginning of next period falls. By itself, this tends to reduce the sector's end-of-period demand for currency for next period and to distribute more dividends to existing owners during the current period. But if the sector announces a higher money wage for next period, this raises the marginal physical product of the currency it plans to hold by the end of the period, which tends to increase the sector's demand for that asset. The net effect is indeterminate without the aid of further assumptions.

Effects of a change in Q_t

The following analysis is based upon the assumption that the business sector does not alter its estimate of either the current period's or next period's demand curve for its product in the face of an unanticipated change in its inventory of consumption goods at time t. Suppose that at time t, the sector finds that these inventories are larger than earlier planned. If the sector were to keep current production constant, it will have to lower the current price of consumption goods (below what it would have set if the higher Q_t had not occurred). Since the estimated demand curve is elastic, the sector anticipates that total current revenue is higher, but that marginal revenue is lower. This reduces the marginal revenue product of current labor services and induces the sector to reduce h_t and therefore to reduce current production. The reduction in current production raises the marginal physical product of labor, thereby raising the opportunity cost of current search. But the fall in marginal revenue (as the sector lowers commodity price in the current period) reduces the opportunity cost of current search. The net effect upon current search and therefore upon the sector's demand for labor for next period is indeterminate. The effects upon w_{t+1}, $p^n{}_t$ and $Cu^{nd}{}_{t+1}$ are also unclear a priori.

Effects of a change in Sn_t

An increase in Sn_t produces a number of effects upon the first-order conditions facing the business sector. The increase in Sn_t directly reduces (a) the cost per share of engaging in employee search in the current period, (b) the amount per share that an increase in w_{t+1} conserves employee search and (c) the cost per share of retaining an extra dollar of currency during the current period. These direct effects tend to cause the sector to lower w_{t+1} and to raise $N^d{}_{t+1}$ and $Cu^{nd}{}_{t+1}$. To the extent that the sector increases its end-of-period demand for currency, it reduces current dividends per share.

Next consider the effect of an increase in Sn_t upon the current price of equity shares. Given the sector's estimate of the end-of-period demand for these shares, the first term in (4.35) may be expressed as: $[(Sn^{de}{}_{t+1} + p^n{}_t\ Sn^{de}{}_1)/Sn_t] - 1$. If the sum in the numerator of the bracketed expression is negative, an increase in Sn_t makes the ratio larger (i.e., closer to zero) and encourages the sector to raise $p^n{}_t$. Consequently, if the "stock" demand for equity is elastic at the equity price set by the sector, an increase in the existing number of shares outstanding reduces the marginal revenue to the sector from issuing an additioinal share, thereby encouraging the sector to raise $p^n{}_t$. To the extent that $Sn^{de}{}_{t+1}$ falls in response to the rise in $p^n{}_t$, the marginal revenue product of labor next period rises, the marginal cost per share of raising w_{t+1} increases, and the marginal revenue per share from currency held next period rises. This will cause the sector to lower w_{t+1} and to raise $N^d{}_{t+1}$ and $Cu^{nd}{}_{t+1}$. As it reduces w_{t+1} and raises $N^d{}_{t+1}$, the sector will raise current search costs and reduce current output, thereby reducing h_t but raising $p^c{}_t$. Current net income will fall as will current dividends per share. The reduction in current dividends due to the drop in current net income is reinforced by the tendency by the sector to increase the amount of currency it plans to hold by the end of the period. These effects reinforce the more direct ones on w_{t+1}, $N^d{}_{t+1}$ and $Cu^{nd}{}_{t+1}$ discussed in the preceding paragraph.

To this point we have been concerned with changes in the initial conditions N_t, w_t, $Cu^n{}_t$, Q_t and Sn_t. Now we turn to shifts in the sector's estimates of: the demand curves for its product in the current and next periods, the supply curve of labor and the demand curve for its equity shares. The effects of each estimated shift will be considered in turn, starting with a change in v_c.

Effects of a shift in c^{de} (change in v_c)

As the business sector revises upward its estimate of the demand for its product, its estimate of the price it can receive for a given quantity of goods rises. This induces the sector to raise $p^c{}_t$. But estimated marginal revenue also rises. This encourages the sector to increase current labor services and to produce more output. The rise in the marginal revenue also raises the opportunity cost of engaging in current search. But to the extent that the rise in current output reduces the marginal physical product of labor it reduces the marginal cost of search. The term $R^e{}_1\hat{q}_4$ in (4.31) may rise or fall. The term $R^e{}_1\hat{q}_5$ in (4.32) may also rise or fall, since even though $R^e{}_1$ rises, $\hat{q}_5$ falls as the marginal product of labor, q', falls. Therefore the net effects upon both the sector's demand for labor for next period and upon the wage rate it announces for next period are unclear a priori.

Consequently, the effects upon next period's output, marginal revenue and net income are also unclear. Also, we cannot determine the effect upon the sector's end-of-period demand for currency or the current market price of equity shares without making further assumptions.

Effects of a shift in c^{de*} (a change in v_c)

As the business sector's estimate of next period's product demand curve shifts outward, the sector raises is estimate of $R^{e*}{}_{1}$ This causes it to increase its end-of-period demand for workers, N^d_{t+1}, as well as its end-of-period demand for currency. The sector will decide to increase current search which may also cause it to raise w_{t+1}. In either case, the sector will decide to increase retained earnings during the current period in order to accumulate the additional currency. Consequently, ceteris paribus, it will tend to reduce current dividends. However, the outward shift in its estimate of next period's demand for its output raises its estimates of next period's revenue and net income (provided next period's costs rise by a smaller amount). This induces the sector to raise the current market price of its equity shares.

Effects of a shift in N^{se} (change in v_n)

As N^{se}_{t+1} shifts outward, the marginal cost of engaging in current search falls, so that firms will tend to increase the number of people they want to employ next period. Furthrmore, the marginal return, in terms of conserving search costs, from raising the money wage also diminishes. Consequently, firms will tend to reduce w_{t+1} as N^{se}_{t+1} shifts outward.

The reduced search costs release resources for commodity production in the current period. Current production will increase even though total current labor time falls. To sell the extra product, firms will reduce current commodity prices. (The price they plan to charge for commodities next period also falls.) Current net income increases. Current dividends increase to the extent that current ex ante business saving does not rise by more than the increase in current income.

Since firms intend to hire more workers next period, future transactions time rises, causing the business sector's demand for currency to rise. But because firms also intend to announce a lower w_{t+1} than they originally planned, the purchasing power of a given amount of currency rises, thereby tending to reduce the sector's nominal demand for these balances.

Because firms now can hire more workers at a lower wage, next period's wage bill may not rise significantly. In fact it may even fall. This consideration coupled with the anticipated extra revenue from the extra commodities the added labor will be able to produce, implies that next period's net income may rise. If next peiod's anticipated net income does rise, the cost per share to existing owners from increasing the number of shares outstanding by next period also rises. This induces the business sector to raise the current market price of equity shares.

Shift in Sn^{de}_{t+1} (change in v_s)

An outward shift in the business sector's estimate of the household sector's demand for its equity shares produces two opposite effects upon the market price it announces for those shares. On the one hand, the increased demand, Sn^{de}_{t+1}, reduces the (flow) elasticity of demand at the equity price it originally planned to announce. In terms of condition (4.35), reproduced here for convenience,

$$\frac{(Sn^{de}_{t+1}-Sn_t) + p^n_t Sn^{de}_1}{Sn_t} - \frac{\pi^n_{t+1}}{Sn^{de}_{t+1}} \cdot Sn^{de}_1 = 0 \qquad (4.35)$$

the sum in the numerator of the first term becomes less negative. This reduces the current marginal revenue per share to existing shareholders from issuing an additional share. In other words, it reduces the marginal cost per share (to existing shareholders) of raising the current market price of equity shares. Therefore, the business sector will tend to raise p^n_t in response to the incraase in Sn^{de}_{t+1}.

On the other hand, at the original equity share price, an increase in the estimated demand for shares means that, ceteris paribus, next period's dividends per share will fall. This in turn implies that the cost per share (to the existing owners) of increasing the number of outstanding shares by the beginning of next period falls. In other words, it reduces the marginal revenue (to existing owners) from raising the current market price of an equity share, thereby inducing the business sector to lower the price of equity shares.

Assuming that the first of these two effects dominates, the sector will raise the market price of shares that it annnounces at time t. If that new price is set at a level consistent with a greater planned number of outstanding shares, say S^{de}_B, (see Figure 4.7), then as the estimated demand shifts from Sn^{de} to Sn^{de*} in Figure 4.7, the business sector plans to raise the market price from p^n_A to p^n_B and still have more shares outstanding by the end of the period than it previously planned.

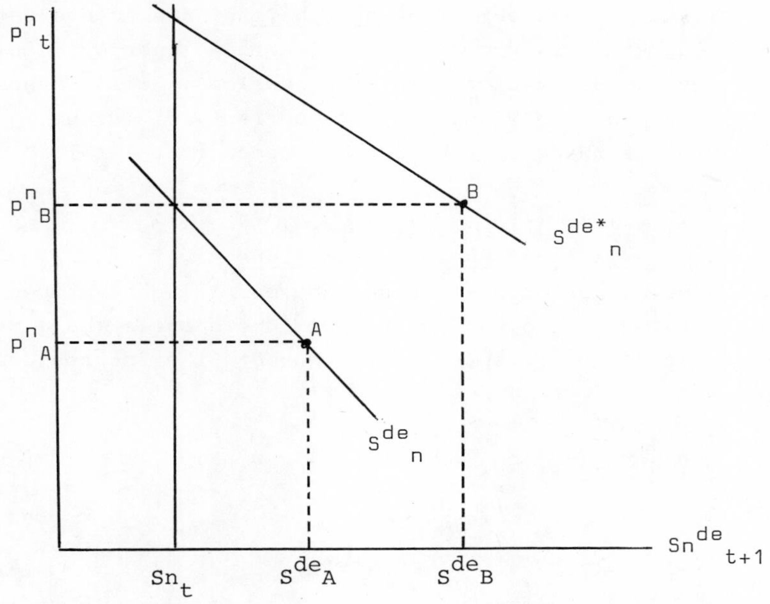

Figure 4. 7 - Potential Effects upon Market Price and Estimated Number of Outstanding Shares in Respone to an Increase in the Estimated Demand for Equity Shares

Assuming Sn^{de} rises in spite of the business sector's planned adjustment in p^n_t (so that $S^{de}_B > S^{de}_A$), the present value <u>per share</u> of next period's net marginal revenue from labor falls (see equation (4.33)) causing the business sector to reduce both its demand for labor for next period and its planned future production. As Sn^{de}_{t+1} rises, the present value <u>per share</u> of next period's marginal cost of raising w_{t+1} falls. As a result, the business sector will tend to raise w_{t+1} (see equation (4.31)).

Both of these effects tend to reduce the business sector's current search effort, allowing more commodity production using fewer total hours of current labor time. To sell the greater output, the sector will reduce the price of commodities. The extra revenue coupled with the lower expenses cause estimated current business income to rise. Ceteris paribus, the rise in current income induces the sector to raise current dividends. This is reinforced by the tendency to increase the number of shares it issues during the current period.

As Sn^{de}_{t+1} rises, the present value <u>per share</u> of the future return from currency held at the end of the current period falls. Consequently, the business sector, ceteris paribus, will tend to decrease its demand for currency and to raise current dividends. The fall in N^d_{t+1} reinforces these effects but the tendency to raise w_{t+1} undermines them.

<u>Summary of the Business Sector's Response Functions</u>

According to the preceding discussion, the partial derivatives of functions (4.37) - (4.45) are given as follows (where the symbol below the variable in question represents the sign of the corresponding partial derivative):

$$h_t = h_t(\underset{-}{N_t}, \underset{-}{w_t}, \underset{+}{Cu^n_t}, \underset{-}{Q_t}, \underset{?}{Sn_t}, \underset{+}{v_c}, \underset{?}{v^*_c}, \underset{+}{v_n}, \underset{+(?)}{v_s}) \tag{4.37}$$

$$N^d_{t+1} = N^d_{t+1}(\underset{-}{w_t}, \underset{+}{Cu^n_t}, \underset{+(?)}{Q_t}, \underset{+(?)}{Sn_t}, \underset{?}{v_c}, \underset{+}{v^*_c}, \underset{+}{v_n}, \underset{-(?)}{v_s}) \tag{4.38}$$

$$w_{t+1} = w_{t+1}(\underset{-(?)}{w_t}, \underset{+(?)}{Cu^n_t}, \underset{?}{Q_t}, \underset{-(?)}{Sn_t}, \underset{?}{v_c}, \underset{+(?)}{v^*_c}, \underset{-}{v_n}, \underset{+(?)}{v_s}) \tag{4.39}$$

$$Cu^{nd}_{t+1} = Cu^{nd}_{t+1}(\underset{?}{w_t}, \underset{?}{Cu^n_t}, \underset{?}{Q_t}, \underset{+(?)}{Sn_t}, \underset{?}{v_c}, \underset{+}{v^*_c}, \underset{?}{v_n}, \underset{-(?)}{v_s}) \tag{4.40}$$

$$p^n_t = p^n_t(\underset{?}{w_t}, \underset{?}{Cu^n_t}, \underset{?}{Q_t}, Sn_t, \underset{?}{v_c}, \underset{+}{v^*_c}, \underset{+(?)}{v_n}, \underset{+}{v_s}) \tag{4.41}$$

$$q = q(\underset{-}{w_t}, \underset{+}{Cu^n_t}, \underset{-}{Q^n_t}, \underset{?}{Sn_t}, \underset{+}{v_c}, \underset{?}{v^*_c}, \underset{?}{v_n}, \underset{+(?)}{v_s}) \tag{4.42}$$

$$c^{de}_t = c^{de}_t(\underset{-}{w_t}, \underset{+}{Cu^n_t}, \underset{+}{Q_t}, \underset{?}{Sn_t}, \underset{+}{v_c}, \underset{?}{v^*_c}, \underset{+}{v_n}, \underset{+(?)}{v_s}) \tag{4.43}$$

$$p^c_t = p^c_t(\underset{+}{w_t}, \underset{-}{Cu^n_t}, \underset{-}{Q_t}, \underset{?}{Sn_t}, \underset{+}{v_c}, \underset{?}{v^*_c}, \underset{-}{v_n}, \underset{-(?)}{v_s}) \tag{4.44}$$

$$\pi^n_t = \pi^n_t(\underset{-}{w_t},\ \underset{+}{Cu^n_t},\ \underset{+}{Q_t},\ \underset{-(?)}{Sn_t},\ \underset{+(?)}{v_c},\ \underset{-}{v^*_c},\ \underset{+(?)}{v_n},\ \underset{+(?)}{v_s}) \qquad (4.45)$$

In Chapter 5 the household and business sectors (the topics of Chapter 3 and Chapter 4 respectively) are combined to form a dynamic disequilibrium macro-model exhibiting persistent involuntary unemployment despite variable wages and prices. Furthermore, these wages and prices are set by economic agents rather than by the conventional fictitious auctioneer.

References

Anderson, W. H. Locke, 1979, "National Income Theory and its Price Theoretic Foundations" (New York, McGraw-Hill)

Jorgenson, Dale, 1976, The Theory of Investment Behavior in R. Ferber (ed.), "Determinants of Investment Behavior" (New York: Columbia University Press)

Modiglioni, F. and M. Miller, 1958, The Cost of Capital, Corporation Finance, and the Theory of Investment, American Economic Review, 48: 261-97, June.

Sandmo, Agnar, 1971, Investment and the Rate of Interest, Journal of Political Economy, 1335-1345, Nov./Dec.

Saving, T. R, 1972, Transactions Costs and the Firm's Demand for Money, Journal of Money, Credit, and Banking, 245-59, May.

Whitmore, H. W., 1975, A Temporal General Equilibrium Approach to the Firm's Demand for Money, Southern Economic Journal, 42: 201-211, October.

5 - National Product and the Dynamic Properties of the Simple Model

Equations (3.26) - (3.28) above depict the household sector's demand functions for commodities, currency and equity shares. Equation (3.29) portrays its supply of labor function. The business sector's price-setting functions for labor (w_{t+1}), equity shares (p^n_t) and commodities (p^c_t) are provided by expressions (4.39), (4.41) and (4.44) respectively. The remaining equations in the set numbered (4.37) - (4.45) represent the business sector's desired levels of labor (current hours and future employees), currency, current production, (real) sales and current dividends. These equations are combined in the present chapter to form a simple model of national income and product. To complete this model, the actual end-of-period stocks and the actual quantities traded also must be specified. These issues will be addressed before presenting the entire model.

In a manner consistent with earlier assumptions, the actual values of the levels of current-period labor time (h_t) current period production (q_t) and current-period dividends (π^n_t) are assumed to correspond to the values that the business sector decides are optimal at time t. Furthermore, the actual prices that prevail during the current period (namely, p^c_t, w_{t+1} and p^n_t) are assumed to correspond to the levels that the business sector deems optimal at time t. The business sector announces these prices based upon the amount of commodities it expects to sell, the number of people it plans to employ and the number of equity shares it plans to have outstanding by the end of the current period. Therefore in the present model the business sector has no incentive to re-evaluate its announced prices until time t+1. Consequently equations (4.37), (4.39), (4.41), (4.42), (4.44) and (4.45) presumably establish the actual values of h_t, w_{t+1}, p^n_t, q_t, p^c_t and π^n_t respectively.

In the commodity market, the actual quantity sold during the current period, c_t, presumably equals household demand, c^h_t:

$$c_t = c^h_t. \tag{5.1}$$

This means that the actual end-of-period inventory, Q_{t+1}, equals the difference between the business sector's planned sales (since those plans in this model are consistent with zero end-of-period inventories), c^{de}_t, and actual sales, c^h_t:

$$Q_{t+1} = c^{de}{}_{t} - c^{h}{}_{t} \tag{5.2}$$

Although measured real national product, q_t, is established by equation (4.42), actual total real national product, y_a, also includes household production, $\mu(.)$:

$$y_a = q + \mu(h^*N - h_t N_t). \tag{5.3}$$

In the labor market, the number of people, N_{t+1}, employed by time t+1 to work next period, is defined to be the minimum of the household sector's supply of labor, $N^{s}{}_{t+1}$, and the number of people the business sector planned to hire, $N^{d}{}_{t+1}$.

$$N_{t+1} = \min(N^{s}{}_{t+1}, N^{d}{}_{t+1}) \tag{5.4}$$

At time t the business sector announces a money wage, w_{t+1}, consistent with an estimated labor supply, $N^{se}{}_{t+1}$, at least as great as its own demand, $N^{d}{}_{t+1}$. But, by the time t+1 arrives, the business sector may find that the actual labor supply is smaller than the number it planned to hire. Labor shortages therefore may exist.

As for the financial markets, assume that the actual number of equity shares outstanding at the end of the current period, Sn_{t+1}, corresponds to the household sector's demand for that stock. (If security dealers, whose behavior remains implicit in this model, are viewed as part of the business sector and if they are viewed as the ones setting the market price for equity shares, then their portfolios could be what adjust to accommodate the household sector's demand.)

$$Sn_{t+1} = Sn^{d}{}_{t+1} \tag{5.5}$$

The household sector presumably knows h_t, Sn_t, $\pi^{n}{}_{t}$, $p^{c}{}_{t}$ and $p^{n}{}_{t}$ when it formulates its own plans at time t. From (5.5), the actual amount of equity shares it holds at time t+1 equals the amount it planned at time t for t+1. From (5.1), the sector buys the number of goods during the period that it planned at time t to buy. Therefore, from the household sector's budget constraint for the current period, the actual amount of currency, $Cu^{h}{}_{t+1}$, the household sector actually holds at the end of the current period equals the amount, $Cu^{hd}{}_{t+1}$, it planned at time t to hold by the end of the period. Therefore, the actual amount of currency held by the households at the end of the period is given by (5.6):

$$Cu^{h}_{t+1} = Cu^{hd}_{t+1} \tag{5.6}$$

Lacking any mechanism that alters the total stock of currency, the actual amount of currency held by the business sector, Cu^{n}_{t+1}, at the end of the peiod equals the exogenously given total stock, Cu^*, minus the quantity, Cu^{h}_{t+1}, which the households hold at the end of the current period:

$$Cu^{n}_{t+1} = Cu^* - Cu^{h}_{t+1}. \tag{5.7}$$

Derivation of Walras' Law in a Setting without Market-Clearing

From the assumptions made to this point, the household sector takes its current labor and dividend incomes as given. Since these amounts are presumably announced before the household sector formultes its plans for the current period, no discrepancies exist among the business sector's plans, the household sector's plans and the actual amounts of either the number of hours that people work during the current period or the amount of current dividends. Therefore, the household sector's and the business sector's ex ante budget constraints at time t are given respectively by (5.8) and (5.9):

$$Cu^{hd}_{t+1} = w_t h_t N_t + \pi^{n}_{t} Sn_t - p^{c}_{t} c^{h}_{t} - p^{n}_{t}(Sn^{d}_{t+1} - Sn_t) + Cu^{h}_{t} \tag{5.8}$$

$$Cu^{nd}_{t+1} = p^{c}_{t} c^{de}_{t} - w_t h_t N_t - \pi^{n}_{t} Sn_t + p^{n}_{t}(Sn^{de}_{t+1} - Sn_t) + Cu^{n}_{t} \tag{5.9}$$

Adding (5.8) and 85.9) yields:

$$(Cu^{hd}_{t+1} + Cu^{nd}_{t+1} - Cu^*) + p^{c}_{t}(c^{h}_{t} - c^{de}_{t}) + p^{n}_{t}(Sn^{d}_{t+1} - Sn^{de}_{t+1}) = 0 \tag{5.10}$$

Since c^{de}_{t} represents the number of commodities the business sector planned at time t to sell during the current period, it also represents the business sector's supply of commodities. Similarly, Sn^{de}_{t+1} represents the ex ante supply of equity shares in the sense that it denotes the number of shares which the business sector planned at time t to have outstanding by the end of the period. In the same manner, the exogenously given stock of currency may be viewed as the "supply" of currency. Consequently, expression (5.10) stipulates that the sum of the values of the "excess demands" for currency, commodities and equity shares must equal zero.

The Discrepancy between the Business Sector's Desired and Actual Cash Balances

Substituting the actual values Cu^h_{t+1}, c_t and Sn_{t+1} into the household sector's budget constraint, (5.8), and then adding the result to (5.9) produces (5.11):

$$Cu^{nd}_{t+1} - Cu^n_{t+1} = p^c_t(c^{de}_t - c_t) + p^n_t(Sn^{de}_{t+1} - Sn_{t+1}) \qquad (5.11)$$

According to (5.11) the amount of currency which the business sector actually holds at the end of the current period falls short of the amount it planned at time t to hold at the end of the period by an amount equal to the sum of the values of (a) its over-estimation of commodity sales and (b) its over-estimation of the number of shares the households would hold at the end of the current period.

National Income and Product

According to the expenditures approach, measured national product in current dollars, Y_m, is the sum of the value of household expenditures on commodities, $p^c_t c^h_t$, and the value of the business sector's addition to inventories, $p^c_t(Q_{t+1} - Q_t)$. But, since $Q_{t+1} = c^{de}_{t+1} - c^h_t$, national product (in current dollars) may be represented as:

$$Y_m = p^c_t c^h_t + p^c_t(Q_{t+1} - Q_t) = p^c_t(c^{de}_t - Q_t) = p^c_t q. \qquad (5.12)$$

Measured national income, on the other hand, consists of the sum of labor income ($w_t h_t N_t$), dividends ($\pi^n_t Sn_t$) and net business saving (s^n_t) where net business saving is defined as the net income of the business sector minus dividends. The net income of the business sector in this simple model consists of the value of sales plus the value of inventory accumulation minus the wage bill. Consequently according to the income approach the value of national product (in current dollars) is represented by:

$$\begin{aligned} Y_m &= w_t h_t N_t + \pi^n_t Sn_t + s^n_t \\ &= w_t h_t N_t + \pi_t Sn^n_t + (p^c_t c^h_t + p^c_t(Q_{t+1} - Q_t) - w_t h_t N_t - \pi^n_t Sn_t) \\ &= p^c_t[c^h_t + (Q_{t+1} - Q_t)] = p^c_t q. \end{aligned} \qquad (5.13)$$

Therefore both the "expenditure" and "income" approaches yield the same measure of national product.

Specification of the Complete Model

Equations (3.26) - (3.29),(4.37) - (4.45), (5.1) - (5.7) and equation (5.12) constitute a model in the unknowns: c^h_t, Cu^{hd}_{t+1}, Sn^d_{t+1}, N^s_{t+1}, h_t, N^d_{t+1}, w_{t+1}, Cu^{nd}_{t+1}, p^n_t, q_t, c^{de}_t, p^c_t, π^n_t, c_t, Q_{t+1}, y_a, N_{t+1}, Sn_{t+1}, Cu^h_{t+1}, Cu^n_{t+1} and Y_m. Reduction of the model to one expressed in terms of "measured" or "observed" variables requires only a few simple adjustments. First, substiitute the right hand side of (3.26) for c^h_t in (5.1) and (5.2). Equation (5.1) then becomes an expression for c_t. Second, substiitute the right hand side of (4.43) for c^{de}_t in (5.2), making (5.2) an expression for Q_{t+1}. Third, substitute (3.29) and (4.38) into (5.4) to obtain an expression for N_{t+1}. Forth, substitute the right hand side of (3.28) into (5.5) to find an expression for Sn_{t+1}. Fifth, substitute the right hand side of (3.27) into (5.6) to find an expression for Cu^h_{t+1}. The actual values may then be represented as follows:

$$h_t = h(N_t, w_t, Cu^n_t, Q_t, Sn_t, v_c, v^*_c, v_n, v_s) \quad (5.14)$$

$$p^c_t = p^c(w_t, Cu^n_t, Q_t, Sn_t, v_c, v^*_c, v_n, v_s) \quad (5.15)$$

$$w_{t+1} = w(w_t, Cu^n_t, Q_t, Sn_t, v_c, v^*_c, v_n, v_s) \quad (5.16)$$

$$p^n_t = p^n(w_t, Cu^n_t, Q_t, Sn_t, v_c, v^*_c, v_n, v_s) \quad (5.17)$$

$$\pi^n_t = \pi^n(w_t, Cu^n_t, Q_t, Sn_t, v_c, v^*_c, v_n, v_s) \quad (5.18)$$

$$q_t = q(w_t, Cu^n_t, Q_t, Sn_t, v_c, v^*_c, v_n, v_s) \quad (5.19)$$

$$c_t = c^h(h_t, p^c_t, w_{t+1}, p^n_t, \pi^n_t, w_t, Cu^h_t, Sn_t, N_t) \quad (5.20)$$

$$Cu^h_{t+1} = Cu^{hd}(h_t, p^c_t, w_{t+1}, p^n_t, \pi^n_t, w_t, Cu^h_t, Sn_t, N_t) \quad (5.21)$$

$$Sn_{t+1} = Sn^d(h_t, p^c_t, w_{t+1}, p^n_t, \pi^n_t, w_t, Cu^h_t, Sn_t, N_t \quad (5.22)$$

$$N_{t+1} = \min[N^s(h_t, p^c_t, w_{t+1}, p^n_t, \pi^n_t, w_t, Cu^h_t, Sn_t, N_t),$$

$$N^d(w_t,\ Cu^n_t,\ Q_t,\ Sn_t,\ v_c,\ v^*_c,\ v_n,\ v_s)] \qquad (5.23^*)$$

$$Cu^n_{t+1} = Cu^* - Cu^h_{t+1} \qquad (5.24)$$

$$Q_{t+1} = c^{de}(w_t,\ Cu^n_t,\ Q_t,\ Sn_t,\ v_c,\ v^*_c,\ v_n,\ v_s) - \quad t \qquad (5.25)$$

Real national income and product are given by q_t in (5.19), while national product in current dollars is found by multiplying p^c_t in (5.15) by q_t. Assuming unemployment exists, (5.23*) may be re-written as (5.23):

$$N_{t+1} = N^d(w_t,\ Cu^n_t,\ Q_t,\ Sn_t,\ v_c,\ v^*_c,\ v_n,\ v_s) \qquad (5.23)$$

This assumption will be retained throughout the rest of this chapter.

System (5.14) - (5.25) may be linearized and written in the following condensed form:

$$\left[\begin{array}{c|c} I_6 & 0 \\ \hline A_{21} & A_{22} \end{array}\right] y_t = \left[\begin{array}{c|c} C & D \\ \hline E & F \end{array}\right] y_{t-1} + \left[\begin{array}{c} B \\ \hline B^* \end{array}\right] z_t \qquad (5.26)$$

where

$$\underset{6\times 6}{A_{21}} = \begin{bmatrix} a_{11} & \cdots & a_{15} & 0 \\ a_{21} & \cdots & a_{25} & 0 \\ a_{31} & \cdots & a_{35} & 0 \\ 0 & \cdots & 0 & 0 \\ 0 & \cdots & 0 & 0 \\ 0 & \cdots & 0 & 0 \end{bmatrix};\quad \underset{6\times 6}{A_{22}} = \begin{bmatrix} 1 & 0 & 0 & 0 & 0 & 0 \\ 0 & 1 & 0 & 0 & 0 & 0 \\ 0 & 0 & 1 & 0 & 0 & 0 \\ 0 & 0 & 0 & 1 & 0 & 0 \\ 0 & 1 & 0 & 0 & 1 & 0 \\ 1 & 0 & 0 & 0 & 0 & 1 \end{bmatrix};\quad \underset{6\times 6}{C} = \begin{bmatrix} 0 & 0 & c_{13} & 0 \cdots 0 \\ \cdot & \cdot & \cdot & \cdot & \cdot \\ \cdot & \cdot & \cdot & \cdot & \cdot \\ \cdot & \cdot & \cdot & \cdot & \cdot \\ \cdot & \cdot & \cdot & \cdot & \cdot \\ 0 & 0 & c_{63} & 0 & 0 \end{bmatrix}$$

$$\underset{6\times 6}{D} = \begin{bmatrix} 0 & 0 & d_{13} & d_{14} & d_{15} & d_{16} \\ \cdot & \cdot & \cdot & 0 & \cdot & \cdot \\ \cdot & \cdot & \cdot & 0 & \cdot & \cdot \\ \cdot & \cdot & \cdot & 0 & \cdot & \cdot \\ \cdot & \cdot & \cdot & 0 & \cdot & \cdot \\ 0 & 0 & d_{63} & 0 & d_{65} & d_{66} \end{bmatrix};\quad \underset{6\times 6}{E} = \begin{bmatrix} 0 & 0 & e_{13} & 0 & 0 & 0 \\ \cdot & \cdot & \cdot & \cdot & \cdot & \cdot \\ \cdot & \cdot & \cdot & \cdot & \cdot & \cdot \\ \cdot & \cdot & \cdot & \cdot & \cdot & \cdot \\ \cdot & \cdot & \cdot & \cdot & \cdot & \cdot \\ 0 & 0 & e_{63} & 0 & 0 & 0 \end{bmatrix}$$

$$\underset{6\times6}{F} = \begin{bmatrix} 0 & f_{12} & f_{13} & f_{14} & 0 & 0 \\ 0 & f_{22} & f_{23} & f_{24} & 0 & 0 \\ 0 & f_{32} & f_{33} & f_{34} & 0 & 0 \\ 0 & 0 & f_{43} & 0 & f_{45} & f_{46} \\ 0 & 0 & 0 & 0 & 0 & 0 \\ 0 & 0 & f_{63} & 0 & f_{65} & f_{66} \end{bmatrix} ; \underset{6\times5}{B} = \begin{bmatrix} b_{11} & b_{12} & b_{13} & b_{14} & 0 \\ . & . & . & . & . \\ . & . & . & . & . \\ . & . & . & . & . \\ . & . & . & . & . \\ b_{61} & b_{62} & b_{63} & b_{65} & 0 \end{bmatrix}$$

$$\underset{6\times5}{B^*} = \begin{bmatrix} 0 & 0 & 0 & 0 & 0 \\ 0 & 0 & 0 & 0 & 0 \\ 0 & 0 & 0 & 0 & 0 \\ b_{41} & b_{42} & b_{43} & b_{44} & 0 \\ 0 & 0 & 0 & 0 & b_{55} \\ b_{61} & b_{62} & b_{63} & b_{64} & 0 \end{bmatrix}$$

$$y'_t = (h_t, p^c_t, w_{t+1}, p^n_t, \pi^n_t, q_t, c_t, Cu^h_{t+1}, Sn_{t+1}, N_{t+1}, Cu^n_{t+1}, Q_{t+1})$$

and

$$z'_t = (v_c, v^*_c\ v_n, v_s, Cu^*)$$

Premultiplying all terms in (5.26) by the inverse of the coefficient matrix of y_t yields the following reduced form equations for the endogenous variables:

$$\underset{12\times1}{y_t} = \underset{12\times12}{\left[\begin{array}{c|c} I_6 & 0 \\ \hline A_{21} & A_{22} \end{array}\right]^{-1}} \underset{12\times12}{\left[\begin{array}{c|c} C & D \\ \hline E & F \end{array}\right]} \underset{12\times1}{y_{t-1}} + \underset{12\times12}{\left[\begin{array}{c|c} I_6 & 0 \\ \hline A_{21} & A_{22} \end{array}\right]^{-1}} \underset{12\times4}{\left[\begin{array}{c} B \\ \hline B^* \end{array}\right]} \underset{4\times1}{z_t}$$

or

$$y_t = Py_{t-1} + Vz_t \qquad (5.27)$$

Dynamic Properties of the Model

This section draws heavily upon Chow [1983, pp. 145-151] and Sydsaeter [1981, pp. 404-415]. Assume that the coefficients comprising matrices P and V are constants. Starting at t = 1 and letting the t subscript advance by units yields:

$$y_1 = Py_o + Vz_1 \tag{5.28}$$

$$y_2 = P^2y_o + PVz_1 + Vz_2$$

$$\vdots$$

so that in general the "final form" may be written as:

$$y_t = P^ty_o + P^{t-1}Vz_1 + \ldots + PVz_{t-1} + Vz_t \tag{5.29}$$

The matrix V comprises "impact multipliers" of changes in the current exogenous variables. The PV, P^2V, etc. matrices depict the "delayed multipliers" of one period, two periods, etc. The "short-run or intermediate-run" multipliers of k+1 periods, showing the effects on y_t of a unit change in z_t lasting from period t-k to the current period, are represented by:

$$\sum_{i=0}^{k} P^iV.$$

System (5.29) is said to be inherently stable (globally asymptotically stable) if P^ty_o approaches the zero vector. A necessary and sufficient condition for the system (5.29) to be stable is that all the characteristic roots of the matrix P have moduli strictly less than one. If, for each row (column) of P, the sum of the absolute values of all coefficients in that row (column) is less than one, all characteristic roots of P will have moduli less than one and the system will be stable.

Assuming the system is stable, the solution to (5.29) then approaches (5.30) as $t\to\infty$, assuming z_t is constant over time:

$$y_t = (P^{t-1} + \ldots + P + I)Vz \tag{5.30}$$

But

$$(P^{t-1} + \ldots. + P + I) . (I - P) = I - P^t. \tag{5.31}$$

Therefore, if (5.29) is stable, so that P has all characteristic roots less than one, then $|I - P| \neq 0$. This implies that $(I - P)$ has an inverse. Post-multiplying both sides of (5.31) by $(I - P)^{-1}$ yields:

$$P^{t-1} + \ldots + P + I = (I - P^t)(I - P)^{-1} \qquad (5.32)$$

Therefore, if the system is stable y_t approaches

$$y_t = (I - P)^{-1} Vz \qquad (5.33)$$

as $t \to \infty$, where $(I - P)^{-1}Vz$ represents a constant vector. The "long-run multipliers" are given by $(I - P)^{-1}V$.

In general the time path of y_t and even its "equilibrium" solution (as shown by (5.33)) depend upon the household sector's tastes; the technical aspects of commodity production; employee search and transactions involving commodities and labor; the exogenously determined stock of currency; and the business sector's estimates of the household sector's demands for commodities and equity shares as well as its supply of labor.

Some Implications of the Model

The only event even remotely related to a policy action by an autonomous authority in the present model pertains to an exogenous change in the amount of currency, Cu*, in existence. As will be shown below, the impact (i.e. the "first-period") effects of an autonomous change in Cu* depend not only upon which one of the business or household sectors experiences the change in cash balances, but also upon the extent to which the business sector anticipates the household sector's response to any alteration of its balances.

Besides an autonomous change in Cu*, the present section also addresses the effects resulting from an autonomous change in household preferences. Three cases will be considered: an increase in the household sector's demand for current consumption goods accompanied by a reduction in its planned saving in the form of money accumulation, an increase in current consumption accompanied by a reduction in planned household saving via acquisitions of equity shares, and an increase in the household sector's end-of-period demand for money accompanied by a reduction in its end-of-period demand for equity shares. The last case amounts to a change in preferences regarding the compositon of a given amount of current saving.

As a means of transisting from the two-sector model developed above to the three-sector model presented in Chapter 6, we then consider the conventional method of inserting exogenous government activity into the two-sector model. The short-term implications of (a) a balanced budget increase in government spending, (b) a money-financed increase in government spending and (c) a money-financed reduction in lump-sum taxes are considered seriatim. As one might expect, the results will depend in part upon the expectations of the business sector.

To facilitate the analysis, calendar time will be represented by t*, t*+1, t*+2, etc. Each of the events considered below presumably begins at time t*.

An Exogenous Increase in the Household Sector's Initial Cash Balances

Suppose some additional currency, dCu*, falls into the lap of the household sector at time t*, i.e. assume $dCu^h_t = dCu^* > 0$. According to the analysis provided in Chapter 3, the households will respond by increasing current consumption (and reducing current saving) as well as by increasing their end-of-period demands for currency and equity shares according to the following constraint:

$$1 = \frac{\partial c^h_t}{\partial Cu^h_t} + \frac{\partial Cu^{hd}_{t+1}}{\partial Cu^h_t} + \frac{\partial Sn^{hd}_{t+1}}{\partial Cu^h_t}$$

The effects of the increase in Cu^h_t upon current period prices, production, employment and dividends will depend upon whether the business sector anticipated not only the rise in Cu^h_t but also its effects upon c^h_t and Sn^{hd}_{t+1} when it formulted its plans and announced current market prices at time t*.

If the business sector does not learn of the rise in Cu^h_t until after it has set its production level and prices for the current period and if the sector either did not anticipate the increase in Cu_t or did not anticipate the impact upon c^h_t and Sn^{hd}_{t+1}, then the rise in the households' cash balances will not affect current commodity prices, current equity prices, the wage rate, employment or production. Assuming that the business sector would have correctly estimated the current period demand functions for both c^h_t and Sn^{hd}_{t+1} if the rise in Cu^h_t had _not_ occurred, the business sector in this case discovers by time t*+1 that its current period sales of commodities and equity shares both exceed what it anticipated at time t*. Consequently, at time t*+1 the business sector's inventory of consumption goods is lower than it previously planned and the number of its equity shares outstanding greater than it previously planned. As a result, the amount of currency actually held by the business sector at t*+1 exceeds the amount it previously planned to hold at time t*+1.

How the business sector reacts at time t*+1 to the unanticipated sales of commodities and equity shares during the period just ended depends heavily upon whether it views these unanticipated sales as anomolies or as indicative of shifts in the respective demand functions for these items which will be maintained for the foreseeable future. If it views the unanticipated increases in its sales of commodities and equity shares as anomolies, these unanticipated results will not cause it to revise its estimate of the demand functions for these items for the upcoming "current" period. (Of course, the sector may alter its previous estimate of the upcoming period's demand functions for some other reason.) But even if its estimates of the new current period's flow demands for commodities and equity shares were to remain unchanged and equal to what the sector expected they would be last period, the business sector's behavior at time t*+1 will nevertheless differ from what it would have been at time t*+1 if the unantiticpated sales had not occured.

In particular, as the discussion in Chapter 4 indicates, the drop in commodity inventories at the beginning of the period at time t*+1 causes the sector to increase current production by increasing the number of hours it has its current employees work during the current period. The corresponding rise in the current wage bill, ceteris paribus, reduces the level of dividends the sector announces at time t*+1. The rise in current labor payments also tends to increase current transactions time, which causes the sector to decide to sell fewer goods and to charge a higher price for them than it would have if the transactions time remained unchanged. The larger beginning-of-period cash balances held by the sector at time t*+1 (due to last period's unanticipated sales) has the opposite effect upon current transactions time. These larger balances tend, ceteris paribus, to reduce transactions time thereby freeing more labor for commodity production, allowing the sector to plan to sell more consumption goods than otherwise, but at a lower price. The effects of the larger number of equity shares outstanding at time t*+1 have no clear impact upon any of the sector's decisions.

If at time t*+1 the business sector decides that the unanticipated drop in Q and the unanticipated rise in Sn indicat that the demand curves for commodities and equity shares have shifted and will remain in their new positions, then, the sector essentially revises upward its value for v_c and v_s at time t*+1. The upward revision in the new estimate of the demand for commodities, ceteris paribus, causes the sector to increase current production, current planned sales and current commodity prices. If at time t*+1 the sector anticipates that the shift in demand will persist into the new "next period", it will also plan to hire more people by time t*+2, to announce a higher wage rate in order to attract these workers and to produce more output next period than it would have otherwise. These effects would then have to be added to the ones discussed in the paragraph above in order to obtain the sector's total response at time t*+1.

On the other hand, if the business sector knew at time t* about the rise in Cu* and correctly anticipated the effects of this increase upon the household sector's behavior (perfect foresight), then the effects discussed in the paragraph immediately above this one would occur at time t* rather than at time t*+1. That is, the sector would not wait until time t*+1 or later to raise prices, production and employment. And the sector would not experience any unexpected changes in initial inventories, equity shares outstanding, or initial cash balances.

To summarize, although it is not true that "anything can happen" in this model in response to a change in the household sector's initial cash balances, it is true that several responses are possible depending upon the significance of transactions costs and search costs and upon the expectations formed by the business sector. The speed at which prices change will be due, in part, to the speed at which the business sector recognizes the shifts in demand.

An Exogenous Increase in the Business Sector's Initial Cash Balances

If the business sector's, rather than the household sector's, cash balances at time t* should grow due to an external artifical manipulation by a "policy authority", the immediate effect will be to reduce the current period's transactions time. On the margin, this will free labor for the production of additional commodities and induce the sector to lower the price it charges for those goods. The net effect initially will be deflationary rather than inflationary (as in the previous case of a "drop" of additional money into the lap of the household sector).

An Increase in c^h_t Accompanied by a Decrease in Cu^{hd}_{t+1}

If the households shift outward their demand for consumption goods in the current period by deciding to save less in the form of currency accumulation and if the business sector does not recognize that this shift has occurred, then by time t*+1 the business sector will find its inventory of consumption goods lower and its holdings of cash balances greater than otherwise. This case is very similar to the one associated with an exogenous increase in the household sector's cash balances except that the business sector will not experience an unexpected change in its equity share sales (unless it had otherwise incorrectly estimated the demand for those shares).

An Increase in c_t Accompanied by a Decrease in Sn^{hd}_{t+1}

In this case, the business sector will find by time t*+1 that its inventory of consumption goods is lower than expected and that the number of equity shares outstanding is also lower than expected. But it will not experience an unanticipated change in its cash balances in this case. The drop in its inventory induces the sector to increase current employment (via longer hours) and to increase current production. If the sector feels that the drop in inventories signals a sustained shift in the demand for commodities, it will also (a) raise the price of those goods, (b) attempt to hire more workers for the next period and (c) raise the wage rate it is willng to pay those workers next period.

An Increase in Cu^d_{t+1} Accompanied by a Decrease in Sn^{hd}_{t+1}

If the business sector does not anticipate this shift in household preferences, it will find that it has fewer shares outstanding at time t*+1 than otherwise. As a result it will also hold less currency at time t*+1 than otherwise. To the extent that the reduction in its currency holdings raises transactions costs and to the extent the rise in transactions costs reduces the production of consumption goods during the period commencing at time t*+1, the business sector will reduce output of consumption goods at time t*+1 and raise their price.

The Conventional Approach to Introducing Government Activity

Within the confines of the model developed to this point, the conventional approach to introducing government activity treats government spending, taxes and (fiat) currency in circulation, $\hat{Cu}$, as policy variables manipulated by an outside authority. Suppose real government spending, c^g_t, and nominal taxes, Tx_t, are treated as exogenous. Then, the volume of fiat money outstanding at the end of the period, $\hat{Cu}_{t+1}$, must exceed the volume outstanding at the beginning of the period, $\hat{Cu}_t$, by the nominal amount of the government's deficit during the current period, as shown by the following budget restriction:

$$\hat{Cu}_{t+1} - \hat{Cu}_t = p^c_t \, c^g_t - Tx_t. \tag{5.34}$$

To account for the effects of government activity upon the decisions facing the household and nonfinancial business sectors, several adjustments are necessary. First, the household sector's budget constraints for both the current and next periods must reflect, respectively, the current and anticipated future levels of taxes:

$$w_t h_t N_t + \pi^n_t \, Sn_t - Tx_t = p^c_t c^h_t + p^n_t (Sn^d_{t+1} - Sn_t) + (Cu^{hd}_{t+1} - Cu^h_t) \tag{5.35}$$

$$w_{t+1} h N^s_{t+1} + \pi^{ne}_{t+1} Sn^{hd}_{t+1} - Tx^*_{t+1} = p^c_{t+1} c^h_{t+1} - Cu^{hd}_{t+1} \tag{5.36}$$

As a result, both current and anticipated future taxes now enter as arguments in the household sector's demand curve for current consumption goods, its end-of-period demands for currency and equity shares, an its supply of labor:

$$c^h_t = c^h_t(h_t, p^c_t, w_{t+1}, p^n_t, \pi^n_t, w_t, N_t, Tx_t, Cu^h_t, Sn_t, Tx^*_{t+1}) \tag{5.37}$$

$$Cu^{hd}_{t+1} = Cu^{hd}_{t+1}(h_t, p^c_t, w_{t+1}, p^n_t, \pi^n_t, w_t, N_t, Tx_t, Cu^h_t, Sn_t, Tx^*_{t+1}) \tag{5.38}$$

$$Sn^{hd}_{t+1} = Sn^{hd}_{t+1}(h_t, p^c_t, w_{t+1}, p^n_t, \pi^n_t, w_t, N_t, Tx_t, Cu^h_t, Sn_t, Tx^*_{t+1}) \tag{5.39}$$

$$N^s_{t+1} = N^s_{t+1}(h_t, p^c_t, w_{t+1}, p^n_t, \pi^n_t, w_t, N_t, Tx_t, Cu^h_t, Sn_t, Tx^*_{t+1}) \tag{5.40}$$

Since an increase in current taxes (or current tax rates) reduces current disposable income, the households will plan to consume less and save less both in the form of currency and in equity shares during the current period. But the sector will decide to send more people into the labor force next period to replace at least some of the loss in future income due to the reduction in current saving. (Next period's anticipated taxes represent an unobserved variable at time t.)

The second adjustment to the above model is based upon the fact that now both the government and the household sectors are purchasing commodities from the businesses. Consequently, total actual nominal spending on consumption goods now is represented by $p^c_t(c^h_t + c^g_t)$. In addition, the business sector must include (its estmate of) government spending in its estimate of the market demand for commodities: $c^{de} = c^g + c^h_t$. If the government announces c^g_t before the business sector formulates its own plans at time t, the business sector views c^g_t as a known parameter. Essentially c^g_t then denotes a parameter affecting the position (but not the slope) of the business sector's estimate of the current period demand for commodities. Therefore, the sign of c^g_t in the functions denoting the business sector's decisions at time t corresponds to the sign of the shift parameter v_c in the respective functions:

$$h_t = h_t(N_t, w_t, Cu^n_t, Q_t, Sn_t, c^g_t, v_c, v^*_c, v_n, v_s) \quad (5.41)$$

$$p^c_t = p^c_t(w_t, Cu^n_t, Q_t, Sn_t, c^g_t, v_c, v^*_c, v_n, v_s) \quad (5.42)$$

$$w_{t+1} = w_{t+1}(w_t, Cu^n_t, Q_t, Sn_t, c^g_t, v_c, v^*_c, v_n, v_s) \quad (5.43)$$

$$p^n_t = p^n_{t+1}(w_t, Cu^n_t, Q_t, Sn_t, c^g_t, v_c, v^*_c, v_n, v_s) \quad (5.44)$$

$$\pi^n_t = \pi^n_t(w_t, Cu^n_t, Q_t, Sn_t, c^g_t, v_c, v^*_c, v_n, v_s) \quad (5.45)$$

$$q_t = q_t(w_t, Cu^n_t, Q_t, Sn_t, c^g_t, v_c, v^*_c, v_n, v_s) \quad (5.46)$$

$$N^d_{t+1} = N^d_{t+1}(w_t, Cu^n_t, Q_t, Sn_t, c^g_t, v_c, v^*_c, v_n, v_s) \quad (5.47)$$

The third adjustment amounts to revising the stock of currency to include fiat money, $\hat{C}u$, as well as private money, Cu*. Assuming that the household sector holds the amount of currency at time t+1 that it planned to hold, then

$$Cu^h_{t+1} = Cu^{hd}_{t+1}. \quad (5.48)$$

The quantity of fiat currency outstanding at time t+1 is given by the governrment sector's budget constraint, presented above as (5.34). Consequently the total amount of currency in the hands of the private sector at time t+1 is given by (5.49):

$$Cu_{t+1} = Cu^{*} + \hat{C}u_{t} + p^{c}_{t}\, c^{g}_{t} - Tx_{t}. \qquad (5.49)$$

Therefore, the amount of currency held by the private business sector at time t+1, Cu^{n}_{t+1}, equals total currency, Cu_{t+1}, minus the amount held by the households:

$$Cu^{n}_{t+1} = Cu_{t+1} - Cu^{h}_{t+1} \qquad (5.50)$$

In addition assume the following

$$c_{t} = c^{g}_{t} + c^{h}_{t} \qquad (5.51)$$

$$Sn_{t+1} = Sn^{nd}_{t+1} \qquad (5.52)$$

$$N_{t+1} = N^{d}_{t+1} \qquad (5.53)$$

denote, respectively, actual current consumption, the actual number of equity shares outstanding at time t+1, and the actual number of people employed at time t+1.

As before, actual real national product, y, is given by:

$$y_{a} = q(.) + \mu(.) \qquad (5.54)$$

while measured real national product is expressed by y_{m}:

$$y_{m} = q(.). \qquad (5.55)$$

According to the "expenditures approach", measured national product (in current dollars) is given by:

$$\begin{aligned}(Ym)_{t} &= p^{c}_{t}(c^{h}_{t} + c^{g}_{t}) + p^{c}_{t}(Q_{t+1} - Q_{t}) \\ &= p^{c}_{t}(c^{h}_{t} + c^{g}_{t}) + p^{c}_{t}(c^{de} - c^{h}_{t} - c^{g}_{t}) - p^{c}_{t}\, Q_{t} \qquad (5.56) \\ &= p^{c}_{t}\, q(.)\end{aligned}$$

where Q_{t+1} equals expected (real) sales of commodities, c^{de}, minus actual sales, $c^h_t + c^g_t$. The income approach to national product yields:

$$(Ym)_t = w_t h_t N_t + \pi^n_t\, Sn_t + s^n_t$$

$$= w_t h_t N_t + \pi^n_t\, Sn_t + p^c_t(c^h_t + c^g_t) + p^c_t(Q_{t+1} - Q_t) \qquad (5.57)$$

$$- w_t h_t N_t - \pi^n_t\, Sn_t$$

$$= p^c_t(c^h_t + c^g_t + (Q_{t+1} - Q_t)) = p^c_t\, q(.)$$

As expected, the 'expenditures' and 'income' approaches yield idenitcal measures of national product.

To this point we have shown that introducing government activity in the conventional manner creates the following model of aggregate economic choice:

$$h_t = h_t(N_t, w_t, Cu^n_t, Q_t, Sn_t, c^g_t, v_c, v^*_c, v_n, v_s) \qquad (5.58)$$

$$p^c_t = p^c_t(w_t, Cu^n_t, Q_t, Sn_t, c^g_t, v_c, v^*_c, v_n, v_s) \qquad (5.59)$$

$$w_{t+1} = w_{t+1}(w_t, Cu^n_t, Q_t, Sn_t, c^g_t, v_c, v^*_c, v_n, v_s) \qquad (5.60)$$

$$p^n_t = p^n_t(w_t, Cu^n_t, Q_t, Sn_t, c^g_t, v_c, v^*_n, v_s) \qquad (5.61)$$

$$\pi^n_t = \pi^n_t(w_t, Cu^n_t, Q_t, Sn_t, c^g_t, v_c, v^*_c, v_n, v_s) \qquad (5.62)$$

$$q_t = q_t(w_t, Cu^n_t, Q_t, Sn_t, c^g_t, v_c, v^*_c, v_n, v_s) \qquad (5.63)$$

$$c_t = c_t(h_t, p^c_t, w_{t+1}, p^n_t, \pi^n_t, w_t, Cu^h_t, Sn_t, N_t) + c^g_t \qquad (5.64)$$

$$Cu^h_t = Cu^h_{t+1}(h_t, p^c_t, w_{t+1}, p^n_t, \pi^n_t, w_t, Cu^h_t, Sn_t, N_t) \qquad (5.65)$$

$$Sn_{t+1} = Sn_{t+1}(h_t, p^c_t, w_{t+1}, p^n_t, \pi^n_t, w_t, Cu^h_t, Sn_t, N_t) \qquad (5.66)$$

$$N_{t+1} = N^d(w_t, Cu^n_t, Q_t, Sn_t, c^g_t, v_c, v^*_c, v_n, v_s) \qquad (5.67)$$

$$Cu^n_{t+1} = Cu_{t+1} - Cu^h_{t+1} \qquad (5.68)$$

$$Cu_{t+1} = Cu^* + \hat{Cu} + p^c_t\, c^g_t - Tx_t \tag{5.69}$$

$$Q_{t+1} = c^{de}(w_t, Cu^n_t, Q_t, Sn_t, c^g_t, v_c, v^*_c, v_n, v_s) - c_t \tag{5.70}$$

As in the simpler model without a government sector, equations (5.58) - (5.70) constitute a disequilibrium model of aggregate behavior in which involuntary unemployment may persist even though wages, prices and output are free to vary. Rather than adjusting instantaneously to "clear" their respective markets, however, the wages and prices are decided by a real economic agent, the business sector, at the beginning of each period. Because it is too costly to change prices instantaneously, the business sector presumably sets prices at the beginning of each period in light of its estimates of the relevant market demand and supply functions. Because it is constrained by imperfect information, its estimates may turn out to be incorrect. But in the labor market, the sector deliberately sets the wage rate above the level it estimates is necessary to attract the desired number of employees in order to reduce its own search costs. Consequently, involuntary unemployment may exist even though the business sector correctly estimates the household sector's supply of labor. Furthermore, the system (5.58) - (5.70) is derived from a mutually consistent set of optimizing decisions for the household and business sectors.

In the following sections we examine briefly the (short-run) impacts of several events involving exogenous changes in government activity. In particular, we consider a balanced-budget increase in government spending, a money-financed tax cut and a money-financed increase in government spending.

Balanced-Budget Increase in c^g_t

Suppose government spending rises in the current period by the real amount Δc^g_t in the above model. By itself, this rise in government spending shifts outward the market demand for commodities by the same amount. However, because the increase in c^g_t is tax-financed in this example, a change in real taxes, $\Delta(Tx_t/p^c_t)$, also occurs equal to Δc^g_t. Consequently, the household sector's current-period real disposable income falls by Δc^g_t, causing the household sector to reduce current-period real consumption by the marginal propensity to consume, MPC, times Δc^g_t. Therefore, in real terms, the balanced-budget increase in c_t causes total current-period demand for commodities, c^h_t, to shift outward by (1-MPC) Δc^g_t. This will also represent the rise in real expenditures for commodities _if_ the business sector does not change current period prices.

The effects upon current-period prices, output and employment depend upon whether the business sector knows about or anticipates the rise in government spending and the concomitant reduction in household demand and the extent to which the business sector expects these shifts to presist when it makes its own plans at time t*.

For the case in which the government announces the rise in c^g_t (and Tx_t) before the business sector announces current-period prices and decides current output, the business sector, ceteris paribus, will revise upward its estimate of the current-period demand for commodities. If the business sector also anticipates correctly the effect of the increase in taxes upon the household sector's demand for commodities, its upward revision in the current-period demand for commodities will not be as large as otherwise. In either case, the business sector will decide to raise p^c_t, to work its current-period employees longer hours (h_t), and to produce more goods in the current period (q). If the business sector anticipates that the shift in the demand for commodities will persist for the foreseeable future, it will increase its demand for workers (N^d_{t+1}) for next period. It may also raise the money wage (w_{t+1}) it announces at time t* that it is willing to pay next period in order to attract the extra workers. But, in any case, if the business sector increases current output, it will raise its current wage bill and thereby increase current labor income to the household sector, thereby offsetting, at least partially, the negative impact on household spending due to the rise in taxes. The fact that the business sector is also raising current-period commodity prices works against this positive impact on household labor income.

If, on the other hand, the business sector does not know about the currrent-period rise in c^g_t and Tx_t and does not anticipate these increases as it formultes its plans and announces current-period prices at time t*, then it will not raise current period prices, production or employment. Instead, by time t*+1, ceteris paribus, it will find its end-of-period inventory of consumption goods are lower by the amount of the unanticipated real sales, (1-MPC) Δc^g_t.

The business sector's cash balances at time t*+1 will be greater, by the amount p^c_t(1-MPC) Δc_t, than the sector anticipated at time t* due to the unanticipated sales of commodities. However, the increase in Tx_t also reduces the household sector's end-of-period demand for equity-shares, which, if unanticipated by the business sector, <u>reduces</u> its end-of-period cash balances by the amount $p^n_t \Delta Sn^{hd}_{t+1}$ where ΔSn^{hd}_{t+1} denotes the unanticipated change in the demand for equity due to the rise in Tx_t. Therefore, the <u>net</u> (unanticipated) change in the business sector's cash balances by time t*+1 will equal $p^c_t(1\text{-}MPC)\ \Delta c^g_t + p^n_t\ \Delta Sn^{hd}_{t+1}$, where $\Delta Sn^{hd}_{t+1} < 0$.

In this case, the unanticipated increase in the cash balances of the business sector by time t*+1 just matches the reduction in the household sector's demand for currency due to the increase in taxes. For, ceteris paribus, a given change in taxes affects household sector behavior in such a fashion that the following restriction holds:

$$- \Delta Tx_t = \Delta Cu^{hd}_{t+1} + p^n_t\ \Delta Sn^{hd}_{t+1} - MPC.\Delta Tx_t \tag{5.71}$$

where $p^c_t \Delta c^h_t = - MPC.\Delta Tx_t$. Solving for ΔCu^{hd}_{t+1} yields

$$\Delta Cu^{hd}_{t+1} = - (1\text{-}MPC).\Delta Tx_t - p^n_t\ \Delta Sn^{hd}_{t+1}.$$

Therefore, since total currency in circulation remains constant, $\Delta Cu^n_{t+1} = \Delta Cu^{hd}_{t+1}$. In other words, a balanced-budget increase in government spending on commodities leaves total currency in circulation unchanged. But at least in the present case it also causes unanticipated movements in money between the household and business sectors.

In the case in which the increase in commodity demand was unanticipated by the business sector at time t*, that sector must decide at time t*+1 whether (what is now) last period's unanticipated increase in sales was only an anomoly or whether it will persist during the new current period and, if so, whether it will also continue into next period. Suppose, for instance, that the business sector anticipates at time t*+1 that last period's unanticipated sales will not persist and that the demand for commodities in the upcoming period will be what the business sector estimated at time t* that demand would be last period. In other words, in spite of last period's unanticipatred sales, the business sector has not altered its estimate of the demand function for commodities. Under these conditions, the primary tendency of the business sector at time t*+1 with respect to its activity in the commodity market will be to announce the same price for commodities that it announced last period, but to increase production above what it was last period in order to replenish the unanticipated depletion of last period's inventories. In other words, it will respond to the drop in the "Q" parameter in its behavioral functions (5.58) - (5.63), but it will not perceive any change in the parameter "v_c". But, as we have seen above, the nonfinancial business sector's cash balances at time t*+1 also influence its decisions at that time and these cash balances, Cu^n, will be larger than they would have been if the balanced-budget increase in government spending had not occurred.

Money-Financed Increase in c^g_t

In the case of an increase in c^g_t which the government finances by issuing more currency rather than by raising taxes, the net shift in the market demand for comodities in the current period equals the change in real government spending, Δc^g_t. Since the effect of an increase in taxes upon the household sector's demand for commodities is absent in this case, the net effect upon commodity demand is larger than for the balanced-budget rise in c_t. If the business sector estimates correctly the effect upon the demand for commoditis, it will raise current output and prices by a greater amount than in the balanced-budget case. If the sector does not foresee the shift in demand, it will find a larger reduction in its inventory of consumption goods by time t*+1 than if the increase in government spending were tax-financed, but as in the tax-financed case no immediate change in production will occur.

If the business sector does not foresee the change in demand and does not alter current production, household income also will not change the household sector's end-of-period demands for currency and equity shares will also remain unchanged. But the business sector's end-of-period cash balances will rise by a greater amount than they would under a balanced-budget increase in government spending. In particular, the unanticipated increase in its cash balances will equal the dollar value of its unanticipated sales of consumption goods to the government. By the end of the current period, the extra currency issued by the government to pay for the increase in its commodity purchases will be in the hands of the business sector. And if this increase in the government's demand remains at this higher level over time, the cash balanes held by the business sector, ceteris paribus, will continue to grow.

Money-Financed Decrease in Taxes

If the cut in taxes equals the dollar value of the rise in government spending (and taxes) considered in the previous two cases, the household sector will increase current consumption in the current period by: - MPC. $\Delta(Tx_t/p^c{}_t)$. This shift will be smaller than that for a money-financed change in government spending of the same "real" amount. But, if the MPC > 0.5, this shift will be larger than that associated with a balanced-budget increase in government spending of the same "real" amount.

If the business sector does not foresee the shift in commodity demand, its inventories will fall by the amount: MPC.ΔTx_t (in nominal terms) and its end-of-period cash balances will rise by - MPC.ΔTx_t due to this unanticipated change in inventories. But the lower taxes imposed upon the household sector will increase its demand for equity shares by $p^n{}_t \Delta Sn^{hd}{}_{t+1}$ which raises the business sector's cash balances by the same amount. Therefore, the total increase in the business sector's cash balances by t*+1 will be - MPC.ΔTx_t + $p^n{}_t \Delta Sn^{hd}{}_{t+1}$ dollars. This is greater than that associated with the tax-financed increase in government spending (provided MPC > 0.5), but smaller than that associated with the money-financed increase in government spending. In the present case, the household sector's cash balances by the end of the period increase by - $(1-MPC)\Delta Tx_t$ + $p^n{}_t \Delta Sn^{hd}{}_{t+1}$. Together, the business sector's and household sector's end-of-period cash balances increase by $-\Delta Tx_t$. As in the other two cases, the time path of production, employment and prices that resut from the tax cut depends upon the speed with which the private business sector recognizes that a shift in demand has occurred as well as upon the sector's anticipations as to the degree to which the shift will extend into the future.

To this point government activity has been treated as exogenously determined by an outside policy authority. Although this assumption may be relevant to dictatorships, it hardly describes democracies in which the government is "of the people, by the people and for the people". In the next chapter, the household sector is viewed as ultimately deciding the level of government-produced goods it deems optimal in light of (a) the taxes it must pay to receive those goods and (b) its opportunities in the private markets. The role of government will not be to control the private economy but instead to provide the household sector with government-produced goods at minimum cost.

References

Chow, G. C., 1983, Econometrics (McGraw-Hill, New York).

Sydsaeter, K., 1981, Topics in Mathematical Analysis for Economists (Academic Press, New York).

6. Government Activity and Aggregate Economic Choice

Introduction

The traditional approach to incorporating government activity into macroeconomic models views the government as an autonomous agent who manipulates government spending and taxes in order to achieve desired changes in national income, prices or economic growth. In the conventional model, government spending (to the extent it does not "crowd out" private spending) serves only to generate earned income (and national product) to the factors which are used to produce the goods or services purchased by the government. The standard model ignores the usefulness to the private sector of any goods or services which the government provides as a result of these purchases. Consequently it cannot address the factors that affect the private sector's willingness for the government to engage in spending.

As indicated in Chapter 5, the standard approach to introducing government activity merely involves: adding a government demand for goods to the household sector's demand for commodities, subtracting taxes from personal income (and possibly from business income), and treating government spending, taxes (or income tax rates) and the stock of money as "policy" variables. The government's budget constraint dictates that at most two of these three policy parameters may be manipulated exogenously. The conventional analysis then proceeds by examining various combinations of changes in the policy variables to discover if they achieve some stated objective of the policy authority.

In the present model, I ignore the "stabilization" potential of government "policy" variables and instead investigate the manner in which a democratic society chooses for itself the optimal levels of government production and taxes. In the following simple framework, the government combines labor and privately produced consumption goods to produce "government goods." Its total expenditure on labor and private goods constitutes "government spending on goods and services." The community incorporates government-produced goods directly into its utility function. Based upon a "menu" prepared for it by the government showing the (maximum) amount of goods and services the government can provide at each level of taxes, the household sector selects the optimal combination of government-produced goods and taxes. This selection is made in light of not only the level of taxes and household sector must agree to pay for the goods the government produces but also the household sector's preferences and opportunities in the labor, commodity and financial markets. Once the private sector selects the level of government-produced goods it wants, the government attempts to produce those goods at minimum cost.

A few authors have incorporated the usefulness of government production directly into an aggregate economic framework. Grossman and Lucas (1974), for instance, construct a macroeconomic model in which public goods improve the productivity of those factors used in producing private goods. Drawing upon earlier works by Samuelson (1954, 1955, 1958, 1969), Atkinson and Stiglitz (1980), for instance, instead insert public goods directly into the community's utility function. However, neither model permits unbalanced government budgets or accommodates endogenously determined real wages under conditions of involuntary unemployment.

The model developed below is specified in discrete time with each sector formulating its plans at time t (representing the beginning of the "current" period) so as to optimize an objective function within a two-period time horizon. The number of employees and the stocks of all financial assets held at time t are viewed as effective constraints by everyone. Therefore no sector contemplates restructuring its beginning-of-period balance sheet at time t. Assets held at time t will yield returns during the current period. Assets acquired anytime during the current period, i.e. before time t+1 (which represents the beginning of "next" period), will not begin to yield returns until next period. Because of the two-period time horizon, each sector plans at time t to sell all assets and retire all liabilities by time t+2, marking the close of next period. Of course when t+1 actually arrives, each sector will face a new two-period time horizon extending beyond t+2. Therefore, at time t+1 each sector will be free to alter the plans it made at time t with respect to its desired balance sheet for time t+2.

The Government Sector

As the current period opens the government presumably knows not only the level of goods and services, g_t, which the household sector wants it to produce this period but also its current-period tax revenue, Tx_t. Transfer payments from one household to another, either directly or through the government, are ignored in this study. At the beginning of the period, the current-period's government workers, N^g_t, have already been hired at an hourly money wage, w_t, which was announced earlier by the business sector. The current hourly wage paid by the government corresponds to the rate which the private business sector, as the principal employer, announced last period that it guaranteed to pay its employees this period. Even though both the government and the private business sectors fully anticipated last period that they would use their current employees the standard "h" hours this period, no guarantees were made last period as to the average number of hours an employee would be asked to work this period. Therefore, each employer is free at the beginning of the current period to set the average hours per worker at a level different from h.

In its first phase of decision-making at time t the government selects the optimal combination of average hours per worker, h^g_t, and privately-produced goods, c^g_t, with which to produce g_t. The government's current production of "national defense", for instance, involves its strategic and tactical deployment of people with their weapons, ammunition and other supplies purchased from the private business sector. In this first phase the government also prepares a menu of alternative levels of government-produced goods, g_{t+1}, for next period and the corresponding levels of next period taxes, Tx_{t+1}, necessary to finance them. It presents this menu to the household sector. The household sector then selects the optimal level of g_{t+1} from this menu in light of its preferences and opportunities in the private sector.

As it calculates next period's minimum tax for each alternative level of g_{t+1}, the government must plan that it will sell all assets and retire all outstanding liabilities by the end of next period. For if the government were permitted to plan at time t to carry outstanding debt beyond time t+2, it could artificially reduce next period's tax burden for a given g_{t+2} without forcing the community to reckon with the private goods it eventually must sacrifice in order to retire the debt which the government plans to carry forward beyond t+2. (The means by which taxes are collected is not addressed in this study.)

After the household sector selects what it feels is the optimal level of g_{t+1} from this menu, the government then enters the second phase of its current-period decision-making. In particular, the government now decides the number of people, N^g_{t+1}, it will seek to employ by the end of the current period to produce g_{t+1} next period. (The question, addressed by the public choice literature, as to how households resolve differences of opinion as to the optimal level of g_{t+1} is ignored here.)

Let the government's production function for g_t be represented by the following strictly concave function (6.1):

$$g_t = \hat{g}(h^g_t N^g_t, c^g_t) \tag{6.1}$$

where $\hat{g}_1$, $\hat{g}_2$, > 0; $\hat{g}_{11}$, $\hat{g}_{22}$ < 0 and $\hat{g}_{12} = \hat{g}_{21} > 0$. As noted above, N^g_t is given at time t.

In light of the above discussion, the government's current wage bill is given by $w_t h^g_t N^g_t$ where w_t represents the money wage rate announced by the private business sector last period and which the government also agreed to pay its own employees in the current period. If the government anticipates a commodity price p^{cg}_t in the current period, its anticipated current period expenses are then represented by $w_t h^g_t N^g_t + p^{cg}_t c^g_t$. The relative inability of the government to react quickly to market signals is shown here by assuming that the government formultes its plans for current spending before the business sector actually announces current period prices, p^c_t. Given that its current tax revenue is known to be Tx_t, the amount the sector plans at time t to save during the current period is represented by $Tx_t - w_t h^g_t N^g_t - p^{cg}_t c^g_t$. At time t the amount the sector plans to save on the income account must be consistent with its plans on the capital account.

In the simple model presented here, the government's balance sheet at time t contains no tradeable assets. Its only liability presumably consists of fiat currency outstanding, $\hat{Cu}_t$. The government's balance sheet at time t is taken as a constraint by the government sector; at time t the government cannot plan a new balance sheet for that moment. However the government is free at time t to plan a new balance sheet for time t+1, marking the end of the current period. Let Cu^s_{t+1} represent the amount of currency which the government plans at time t to have outstanding by time t+1. Then, at time t the government faces the following budget constraint:

$$w_t h^g_t N^g_t + p^{cg}_t c^g_t = Tx_t + (\hat{Cu}^s_{t+1} - \hat{Cu}_t) \tag{6.2}$$

According to expression (6.2) the government must plan at time t to finance current expenses, $w_t h^g_t N^g_t + p^{cg}_t c^g_t$, from either current tax revenue, Tx_t, or a new currency issue, $Cu^s_{t+1} - Cu_t$. The choice variables entering expression (6.2) at time t include the average number of hours government employees work during the current period, h^g_t, the number of commodities the government plans to purchase from the business sector this period, c^g_t, and the amount of currency which the government plans to have outstanding by the end of the current period, $\hat{C}u^s_{t+1}$. The significance of (6.2) is that the government cannot arbitrarily decide the levels of all three of these variables at time t. Once it has selected any two of them, it also has automatically selected the third.

As the current period opens, the government devises a "menu" showing the level of taxes, Tx_{t+1}, which the household sector will have to pay next period for each alternative level of goods and services, g_{t+1}, it decides it wants the government produce next period. The government's objective as it develops this menu is to minimize the level of Tx_{t+1} necessary to finance the production of each given level of g_{t+1}.

In order to produce a given level of g_{t+1} next period, the government will require the servies of labor as well as commodities it purchases from the private business sector. For simplicity assume that the government plans at time t that everyone it employs for next period, N^{gd}_{t+1}, will work the standard number of hours, h. Then its total anticipated labor time next period is represented by $h.N^{gd}_{t+1}$. Let c^g_{t+1} represent the number of commodities which the government sector plans at time t to purchase next period. Then, as viewed at time t, next period's production function may be represented by the following strictly concave function

$$g_{t+1} = g*(hN^{gd}_{t+1}, c^g_{t+1}) \tag{6.3}$$

where $g*_1, g*_2 > 0$, $g*_{11}, g*_{22} < 0$ and $g*_{12}, g*_{21} > 0$.

If w^g_{t+1} represents the money wage which the government anticipates at time t that the business sector will announce, then the government's anticipated wage bill for next period will be $w^g_{t+1}hN^{gd}_{t+1}$. If p^{cg}_{t+1} denotes the price which the government expects at time t to pay for commodities next period, then its planned expenditures on commodities next period is shown by $p^{cg}_{t+1}c^g_{t+1}$ and its planned total expenses equal $w^g_{t+1}hN^{gd}_{t+1} + p^{cg}_{t+1}c^g_{t+1}$. With next period's planned tax revenue represented by Tx_{t+1}, the amount the government plans at time t to save next period is shown by $Tx_{t+1} - w^g_{t+1}hN^{gd}_{t+1} - p^{cg}_{t+1}c^g_{t+1}$. As the government formulates its plans at time t, this planned saving on the income account next period must coincide with its capital account plans for that period.

As noted above, the government at time t presumably plans to have $\hat{Cu}^s_{t+1}$ dollars of fiat currency outstanding by the end of the current period. As also noted above, the household sector's time horizon presumably extends only to the end of next period. As a result, the government is precluded in this model from planning at time t to have any fiat currency outstanding at time t+2. For to permit it to do so would enable the government to misrepresent to the household sector at time t the future cost of next period's production by the government of goods and services. In particular, each dollar of currency which the government might plan at time t to have outstanding at time t+2 represents one less dollar it would have to collect in taxes next period. Since the household sector does not see beyond the end of next period at time t, it would not reckon with the future tax liabilitiy that would have to be incurred eventually in order to redeem fiat money with private money (which in previous chapters was the only type of money in the economy). Consequently the reduced tax burden the household sector would face for next period would distort its view of the true opportunity cost of selecting government-produced goods over privately-produced goods.

Since the government sector plans to have $\hat{Cu}^s_{t+1}$ dollars outstanding at the beginning of next period but zero dollars outstanding by the end of that period, the sector must plan to save $\hat{Cu}^s_{t+1}$ dollars on the income account next period in order to redeem that amount of fiat currency. As a result, the government sector's budget constraint for next period, as viewed at time t, is given by (6.4):

$$Tx_{t+1} - w^g_{t+1} hN^{gd}_{t+1} - p^{cg}_{t+1} c^g_{t+1} = \hat{Cu}^s_{t+1} \tag{6.4}$$

The objective of the government sector at time t is to determine for each possible value of future government production, g_{t+1}, the minimum level of taxes, Tx_{t+1}, the government must collect next period in order to finance that production. As it calculates the minimum tax, the government is constrained by conditions (6.1)-(6.4). From condition (6.4), for instance, the government can reduce next period's tax burden dollar-for-dollar as it reduces the amount of currency it plans to have outstanding at the end of the current period. Therefore, to minimize next period's tax bill the government necessarily minimizes current period expenses in order to keep $\hat{Cu}^{s}_{t+1}$ as small as possible (see condition (6.2)).

Solving (6.2) for $\hat{Cu}^{s}_{t+1}$ and substituting into (6.4) yields:

$$Tx_{t+1} = w^{g}_{t+1}hN^{dg}_{t+1}+p^{cg}_{t+1}c^{g}_{t+1}+\hat{Cu}_{t}+w_{t}h^{g}_{t}N^{g}_{t}+p^{cg}_{t}c^{g}_{t}-Tx_{t} \qquad (6.5)$$

The government's objective, then, may be viewed as attempting to minimize (6.5) subject to the production functions (6.1) and (6.3). Or, in terms of the Lagrangian function (6.6), the government attempts to minimize:

$$Tx_{t+1} = w^{g}_{t+1}hN^{gd}_{t+1}+p^{cg}_{t+1}c^{g}_{t+1}+\hat{Cu}_{t}+w_{t}h^{g}_{t}N^{g}_{t}+p^{cg}_{t}c^{g}_{t}-Tx_{t} \qquad (6.6)$$

$$+ \lambda_1(g_t - \hat{g}(h^{g}_{t}N^{g}_{t},\ c^{g}_{t})) + \lambda_2(g_{t+1} - g^*(hN^{gd}_{t+1} - c^{g}_{t+1})$$

For an interior solution with the government constrained by its production functions (i.e. for the case in which h^{g}_{t}, c^{g}_{t}, N^{dg}_{t+1}, c^{g}_{t+1}, λ_1 and λ_2 are all positive), the following first-order conditions must hold:

$$\frac{\partial TX_{t+1}}{\partial h^{g}_{t}} = w_{t}N^{g}_{t} - \lambda_1\hat{g}_1N^{g}_{t} = 0 \qquad (6.7)$$

$$\frac{\partial TX_{t+1}}{\partial c^{g}_{t}} = p^{cg}_{t} - \lambda_1\hat{g}_2 = 0 \qquad (6.8)$$

$$g_t - \hat{g}(h^{g}_{t}N^{g}_{t},\ c^{g}_{t}) = 0 \qquad (6.9)$$

$$\frac{\partial TX_{t+1}}{\partial N^{gd}_{t+1}} = w^{g}_{t+1}h - \lambda_2 g^*_1 h = 0 \qquad (6.10)$$

$$\frac{\partial TX_{t+1}}{\partial h^{g}t} = p^{cg}_{t+1} - \lambda_2 g^*_2 = 0 \qquad (6.11)$$

$$g_{t+1} - g^*(hN^{dg}_{t+1},\ c^{g}_{t+1}) = 0 \qquad (6.12)$$

Together equations (6.7) and (6.8) stipulate that the government combine its factors of production, privately -produced commodities in current period and current labor time, so that the rate of technical substitution between them, $\hat{g}_1N^{g}_{t}/\hat{g}_2$ (as shown by the slope of the isoquant in Figure 6.1), equals their market rate of substitution, $w_t N^g_t / p^{cg}_t$.

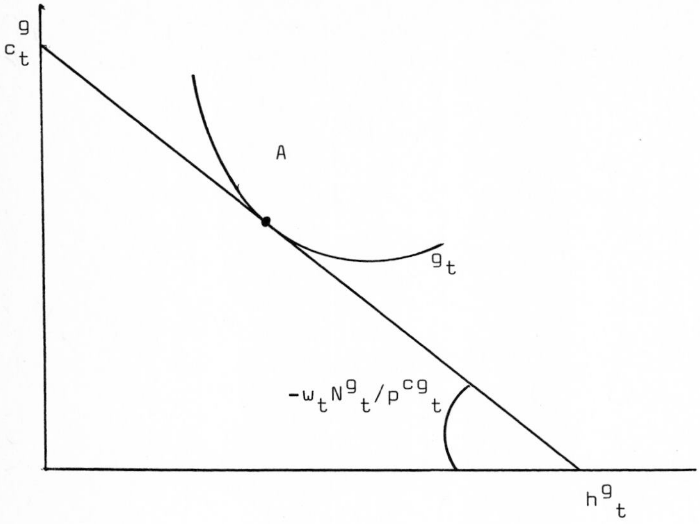

Figure 6.1 - The Given g_t is Produced by the Combination of Inputs Satisfying Conditions (6.7) and (6.8).

Equations (6.10) and (6.11) together constitute an analogous condition as to the government's use of N^{gd}_{t+1} and c^g_{t+1} next period in producing a given amount of g_{t+1}. In this case the rate of technical substitution is shown by $g^*_1 h/g^*_2$, while the market rate of substitution is estimated to be $w^g_{t+1} h/p^{cg}_{t+1}$. Equations (6.9) and (6.12), on the other hand, merely re-state the condition that the government must formulte its plans at time t in a manner consistent with its current and next-period production functions.

Since variables h^g_t, c^g_t and λ_1 appear only in conditions (6.7)-(6.9) while variables N^{gd}_{t+1}, c^g_{t+1} and λ_2 appear only in conditions (6.10)-(6.12), the system (6.7)-(6.12) may be treated as two separate sub-systems, both of which are necessary for the minimization of Tx_{t+1}.

Government Demand Functions for Current Labor Services and Current Consumption Goods

In this simple framework, the government's current demand for labor services, h^g_t, depends upon four parameters while its demand for commodities currently produced by the private sector c^g_t, depends on only three:

$$h^g_t = h^g_t(\underset{-}{N^g_t}, \underset{-}{w_t}, \underset{+}{p^{cg}_t}, \underset{+}{g_t}) \quad (6.13)$$

$$c^g_t = c^g_t(\underset{+}{w_t}, \underset{-}{p^{cg}_t}, \underset{+}{g_t}). \quad (6.14)$$

The greater the level of government-produced goods, g_t, that the household sector has instructed the government to produce this period, the greater is the government's current-period demand for both factors. An increase in the anticipated current-period price of privately produced commodities, p^{cg}_t, causes the government to plan to work its current employees longer and to use fewer commodities. (The government will instruct workers, for instance, to take greater care in planning work and in performing tasks so as to use materials more efficiently.) An increase in w_t causes the government to conserve labor by adding to its purchases of commodities. (As labor becomes more expensive relative to materials, workers will be instructed to make sure their material inventories are always adequate in order to reduce labor idleness.) Finally, an increase in N^g_t causes the government to cut back proportionately on the average number of hours, h^g_t, in order to keep total labor hours unchanged; it will not alter its demand for c^g_t in response to a change in N^g_t. These results imply the signs of the partial derivatives that are presented below their respective parameters in (6.13) and (6.14).

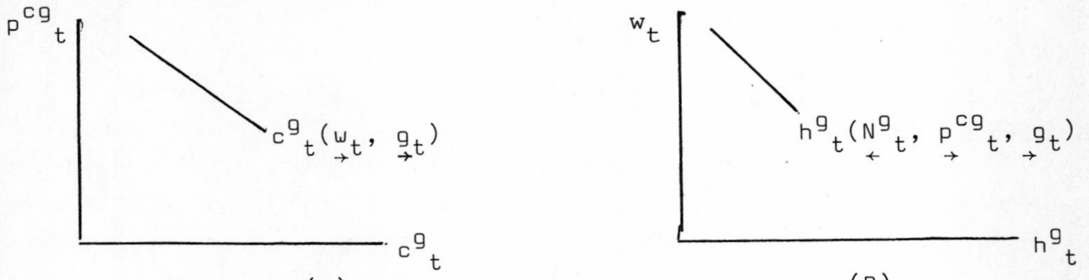

(A) (B)

Figure 6.2 - (A) The Government's Demand for Commodities and (B) Its Demand for Current Labor Time.

One of the unique features of this model is that endogenous "government spending on goods and services" includes government activity in the labor market as well as in the commodity market. As a result, an increase in "government spending" may directly affect not only the aggregate demand for commodities, as it does in conventional macro models, but also the market demand for labor. One of the major weaknesses of conventional models is that they fail to recognize the direct impact of government purchases of goods and services upon the labor market. (Foley and Sidrauski (1971) and Fair (1974) explicitly recognize government activity in the labor market, but only as an exogenous variable.)

Government's Demands for Workers and for Next Period's Privately-Produced Commodities

Solving system (6.10)-(6.12) simultaneously yields the optimal levels of N^{gd}_{t+1}, c^{g}_{t+1} and λ_2. The economic significance of λ_2 will be discussed shortly. But first, in a manner directly analogous to the discussion of the last section, note that an increase in g_{t+1} raises the government's demands for both factors. On the other hand, an increase in the anticipated price of one factor reduces the government's demand for that factor and increases the government's demand for the other factor. Consequently, the government's demand functions for N^{gd}_{t+1} and c^{g}_{t+1} may be presented as functions (6.15) and (6.16) with the signs of the partial derivatives shown below the corresponding parameters:

$$N^{gd}_{t+1} = N^{gd}_{t+1}(\underset{-}{w^{g}_{t+1}}, \underset{+}{p^{g}_{t+1}}, \underset{+}{g_{t+1}}) \qquad (6.15)$$

$$c^{g}_{t+1} = c^{g}_{t+1}(\underset{+}{w^{g}_{t+1}}, \underset{-}{p^{g}_{t+1}}, \underset{+}{g_{t+1}}) \qquad (6.16)$$

The Menu of Choices for Next Period's Government Production and Taxes

As mentioned several times above, at time t the government prepares and presents to the households a menu of alternative levels of government production of goods and services for next period, g_{t+1}, and their corresponding tax levels, Tx_{t+1}. The household sector then selects the optimal combination of g_{t+1} and Tx_{t+1} from that menu in concert with its other choices in the commodity, labor and equity markets.

From equation (6.59) it is clear that an increase in the government sector's initial currency outstanding, its anticipated current expenses or its anticipated future expenses, ceteris paribus, raises the amount of Tx_{t+1} the government must collect next period in order to produce a given amount of g_{t+1} that period. On the other hand, the greater Tx_t happens to be, ceteris paribus, the smaller Tx_{t+1} needs to be. Substituting (6.13) -(6.16) into (6.5) allows Tx_{t+1} to be written as follows:

$$
\begin{aligned}
Tx_{t+1} &= w^g_{t+1}h \cdot N^{gd}_{t+1}(w^g_{t+1},\ p^{cg}_{t+1},\ g_{t+1}) \\
&\quad + p^{cg}_{t+1}c^g_{t+1}(w^g_{t+1}, p^{cg}_{t+1}, g_{t+1}) \\
&\quad + \hat{C}u_t + w_t N^g_t h^g_t(N^g_t,\ w_t,\ p^{cg}_t,\ g_t) \\
&\quad + p^c_g c^g_t(w_t,\ p^{cg}_t,\ g_t) - Tx_t
\end{aligned} \tag{6.17}
$$

Assuming that all inputs are "normal", an increase in the price of any input will increase the anticipated expense of undertaking a given amount of government production that period. Consequently the signs of the first-order partials of (6.17) with respect to the various parameters are immediately evident; they are presented in (6.18):

$$
\begin{aligned}
Tx_{t+1} &= Tx_{t+1}(\underset{+}{\hat{C}u_t},\ \underset{-}{Tx_t},\ \underset{+}{w_t},\ \underset{+}{p^{cg}_t},\ \underset{+}{g_t},\ \underset{+}{w^g_{t+1}},\ \underset{+}{p^{cg}_{t+1}},\ \underset{+}{g_{t+1}}) \\
&= Tx_{t+1}(\underset{+}{g_{t+1}},\ k)
\end{aligned} \tag{6.18}
$$

where k represents the vector of shift parameters. Based upon (6.18), the government sector presumably prepares a menu of alternative combinations of g_{t+1} and Tx_{t+1} given the values of $C\hat{u}_t$, Tx_t, w_t, p^{cg}_t, g_t, w^g_{t+1} and p^{cg}_{t+1}.

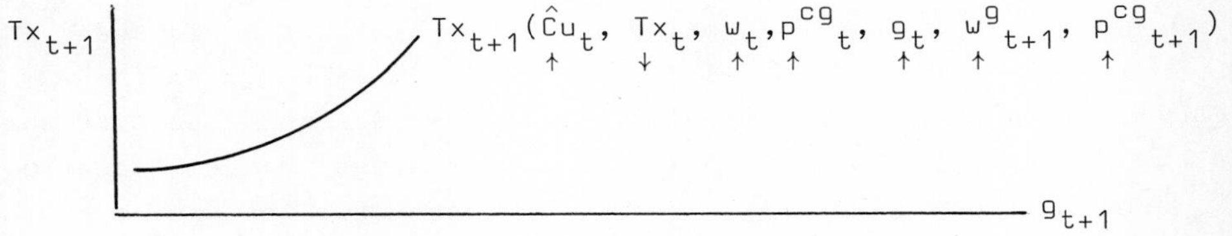

Figure 6.3 - The Menu of Next Period's Government Production and Tax Levels

The reason Tx_{t+1} rises at an increasing rate as g_{t+1} rises is evident from the solution for λ_2 in the sub-system (6.10)-(6.12) given above. From equation (6.6), the Lagrange multiplier $\lambda_2 (> 0)$ represents the slope of the government-production-tax menu in Figure 6.3. Specifically, λ_2 represents the minimum change in Tx_{t+1} for a unit change in g_{t+1}. But the solution for λ_2 in system (6.10)-(6.12) indicates that λ_2 is an increasing function of g_{t+1}, i.e. that the slope of the function in Figure 6.3 is increasing. This increasing slope results from the strict concavity of next period's production function. The amount of additional labor and privately-produced goods which the government requires to produce one more unit of g_{t+1} increases as g_{t+1} becomes larger. Therefore the marginal cost of g_{t+1} rises as g_{t+1} becomes larger, meaning that the marginal increase in next period's taxes to finance this higher marginal cost must also rise. Since λ_2 is also an increasing function of p^{cg}_{t+1} and w^g_{t+1}, an increase in either parameter not only shifts Tx_{t+1} upward but also increases the slope of the government-production tax menu. But subsequent analysis will ignore these effects.

Summary of Government Activity

The government sector's decisions at time t may be summarized as a two-stage process. In the first phase, the government decides the optimal levels of c^g_t and h^g_t in order to produce the amount of g_t in the current period that the household sector selected last period. In this first stage, the governmental so prepares a menu of combinations of g_{t+1} and Tx_{t+1} from which the households will choose during the current period. The government is able to decide c^g_t and h^g_t in the first stage even though it does not yet know what combination of g_{t+1} and Tx_{t+1} the households will select for next period. The reason is that no matter what level of g_{t+2} the households selcet, the government must minimize current expenses as well in order to minimize Tx_{t+1} and the combination of c^g_t and h^g_t which minimizes current expenses is independent of g_{t+1} in this model.

The government's ex ante supply of currency for the end of the current period is also determined in the first stage. From equation (6.2), the government's ex ante supply of currency for the end of the period is given by:

$$\begin{aligned} \hat{Cu}^s_{t+1} &= \hat{Cu}_t - Tx_t - w_t N^g_t h^g_t(N^g_t, p^{cg}_t, g_t) \\ &\quad - p^{cg}_t\, c^g_t(w_t, p^{cg}_t, g_t) \qquad (6.19) \\ &= \hat{Cu}^s_{t+1}(\hat{Cu}_t, Tx_t, w_t, p^{cg}_t, g_t) \end{aligned}$$

The signs of the partials in (6.19) are known once the assumption is made that both h^g_t and c^g_t are "normal" factors.

After the household sector has selected what it considers to be the optimal combination of Tx_{t+2} and g_{t+2} (i.e. a point on the curve in Figure 6.3), the government sector is then ready to decide, using functions (6.15) and (6.16), the number of people it wants to hire for next period, N^{gd}_{t+1}, and the number of privately-produced goods it (tentatively) wants to buy next period. These choices constitute the second stage of the government sector's decision-making process at time t.

By the time the government is ready to enter into the second stage of decision-making at the beginning of the current period, the business sector has presumably announced w_{t+1}. Therefore, in the second stage, w_{t+1} replaces the anticipated money wage, w^g_{t+1}. But, since the next-period commodity price will not be announced until next period, its anticipated value, p^{cg}_{t+1}, remains the relevant variable in (6.15) and (6.16) even in the second stage.

In light of the above model of government activity it becomes necessary to modify the household sector model presented in Chapter 3 in order to accommodate the household sector's selection of the optimal combination of government production and taxes for next period. These modifications are presented in the next section.

Modifications of Household Sector Behavior

The incorporation of government activity into the simple framework entails certain adjustments in the household sector's objective function as well as in the constraints facing that sector.

The first adjustment involves inserting current government-produced goods and service, g_t, and next period's government produced goods and services, g_{t+1}, into the household sector's utility function. Therefore, equation (3.14) in Chapter 3 becomes:

$$\begin{aligned} U = {} & U_1(c^h_t) + U_2(h^*N - h_tN_t) + U_3(Cu^h_t/p^c_t) + U_4(c^h_{t+1}) \\ & + U_5(h^*N - hN^s_{t+1}) + U_6(Cu^{hd}_{t+1}/p^{ch}_{t+1}) + U_7(g_t) \\ & + U_8(g_{t+1}) \end{aligned} \qquad (6.20)$$

where $U_7(.)$, $U_8(.)$, U'_7, $U'_8 > 0$; U''_7, $U''_8 < 0$. Now h_tN_t denotes the sum $h^n{}_t N^n{}_t + h^g{}_t N^g{}_t$ where $h^n{}_t N^n{}_t$ and $h^g{}_t N^g{}_t$ represent, respectively, the number of hours the households work for the nonfinancial business and government sectors this period.

At time t, the household sector's objective is to maximize U with respect to $c^h{}_t$, $c^h{}_{t+1}$, $N^s{}_{t+1}$, $Cu^{hd}{}_{t+1}$, $Sn^d{}_{t+1}$ and g_{t+1}. The household sector's current period budget constraint becomes:

$$w_t h_t N_t + \pi^n{}_t Sn_t - Tx_t = p^c{}_t c^h{}_t + (Cu^{hd}{}_{t+1} - Cu^h{}_t) + p^n{}_t(Sn^{hd}{}_{t+1} - Sn_t) \qquad (6.21)$$

while its budget constraint for next period becomes:

$$w_{t+1} hN^s{}_{t+1} + \pi^{nh}{}_{t+1} Sn^{hd}{}_{t+1} + Cu^{hd}{}_{t+1} - Tx_{t+1} = p^{ch}{}_{t+1} c^h{}_{t+1} \qquad (6.22)$$

with the added restriction imposed by the menu prepared by the government at time t that

$$Tx_{t+1} = Tx_{t+1}(g_{t+1}, k) \qquad (6.23)$$

where Tx'_{t+1}, $Tx''_{t+1} > 0$.

Solve (6.21) for $Sn^{hd}{}_{t+1}$, substitute the result into (6.22), then substitute (6.23) into (6.22) for Tx_{t+1}. Finally, solve the new (6.22) for $c^h{}_{t+1}$ and substitute into (6.20). This yields (6.24):

$$\begin{aligned} \text{Max } U = {} & U_1(c^h{}_t) + U_2(h^*N - h_t N_t) + U_3(Cu^h{}_t / p^c{}_t) \qquad (6.24) \\ & + U_4\left(\frac{w_{t+1} hN^s{}_{t+1}}{p^{ch}{}_{t+1}} + \frac{\pi^{nh}{}_{t+1}}{p^n{}_t p^{ch}{}_{t+1}} [w_t h_t N_t + (\pi^n{}_t + p^n{}_t) Sn_t - Tx_t \right. \\ & \left. - p^c{}_t c_{ht} + Cu^h{}_t] + \left(1 - \frac{\pi^{nh}{}_{t+1}}{p^n{}_t}\right) \frac{Cu^{hd}{}_{t+1}}{p^{ch}{}_{t+1}} - \frac{Tx_{t+1}(g_{t+1}, k)}{p^{ch}{}_{t+1}} \right) \\ & + U_5(h^*N - hN^s{}_{t+1}) + U_6(Cu^{hd}{}_{t+1} / p^h{}_{t+1}) + U_7(g_t) + U_8(g_{t+1}) \end{aligned}$$

The household sector in this model attempts at time t to maximize

(6.24) with respect to c^h_t, N^s_{t+1}, Cu^{hd}_{t+1} and g_{t+1}. Its optimal behavior with respect to c^h_{t+1}, Sn^{hd}_{t+1} and Tx_{t+1} may be found by substituting the solution for c^h_t, N^s_{t+1}, Cu^{hd}_{t+1} and g_{t+1} into equations (6.22), (6.21) and (6.23) respectively.

The Fist-Order Necessary Conditions

Partially differentiating (6.24) with respect to each of the four choice variables just mentioned yields the following four necessary conditions:

$$\frac{\partial U}{\partial c^h_t} \equiv U'_1 - \frac{\pi^{nh}_{t+1} \, p^c_t}{\pi^n_t \, p^{ch}_{t+1}} U'_4 = 0 \qquad (6.25)$$

$$\frac{\partial U}{\partial N^s_{t+1}} \equiv U'_4\left(\frac{w_{t+1}h}{p^{ch}_{t+1}}\right) - U'_5 h = 0 \qquad (6.26)$$

$$\frac{\partial U}{\partial Cu^{hd}_{t+1}} \equiv U'_4\left(1 - \frac{\pi^{nd}_{t+1}}{p^n_t}\right)\frac{1}{p^{ch}_{t+1}} + U'_6 \frac{1}{p^{ch}_{t+1}} = 0 \qquad (6.27)$$

$$\frac{\partial U}{\partial g_{t+1}} \equiv U'_4\left(-\frac{Tx'_{t+1}}{p^{ch}_{t+1}}\right) + U'_8 = 0 \qquad (6.28)$$

The first three of these conditions are identical to the ones derived in Chapter 3 and will not be discussed in detail here. The fourth condition stipulates that the household sector will increase the amount of goods it wants the government to produce next period until the marginal utility, U'_8, of the consumption of an extra unit of these goods just equals the marginal loss in utility from the extra sacrifice of privately-produced goods next period. A unit increase in g_{t+1} increases next period's taxes by Tx'_{t+1}, causing the household sector to reduce its anticipated (real) purchases of privately-produced goods next period by Tx'_{t+1}/p^{ch}_{t+1}. Consequently $U'_4(- \; Tx'_{t+1}/p^{ch}_{t+1})$ represents the loss in utility next period due to the reduction in the consumption of privately-produced goods.

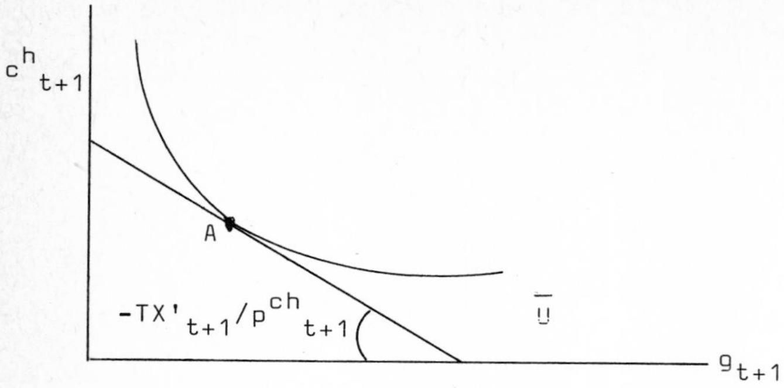

Figure 6.4 - Equality between the Subjective Rate of Substitution of g_t for c_{t+1} and the "Market" Rate (at Point A).

The Household Sector's Demand and Supply Functions

In Chapter 3 we discussed the effects of changes in each of the following parameters

$$p^c_t,\ w_{t+1},\ p^n_t,\ w_t,\ h_tN_t,\ \pi^n_t\ Sn_t,\ Cu^h_t,\ p^{ch}_{t+1} \text{ and } \pi^{nh}_{t+1}$$

upon the household sector's labor supply function as well as upon its demands for currency, equity shares and privately-produced goods. However that discussion concerned a household sector that did not have the option of obtaining publicly-produced goods. The introduction of this option complicates our earlier discussion in several respects. First, the addition of another first-order condition provides another channel through which the above parametric changes may affect the labor supply function and the three demand functions already mentioned. Our earlier discussion of these effects is incomplete within the present context. Second, the household sector now must decide as well the volume of goods and services it wants the government to produce next period. This demand for publicly-produced goods also will be influenced by the ten parameters mentioned above. Third, the existence of current taxes as well as next period's menu of alternative levels of government-produced goods and their corresponding tax burdens introduces a new set of parameters that potentially affect not only the household sector's demand for publicly-produced goods but also its other demand and supply functions.

Current price, p^c_t, of privately-produced goods

The following analysis is based upon the assumption that the "government-produced goods-tax menu" is announced prior to the business sector's announcement of p^c_t so that the function in Figure 6.3 does not shift in response to a change in p^c_t. The analysis also abstracts from any changes in expectations of future prices as p^c_t changes.

As discussed earlier, an increase in p^c_t produces both a substitution effect, which causes the households to tend to increase c^h_{t+1} and decrease c^h_t, and an income effect, which causes them to decrease both c^h_{t+1} and c^h_t. If the business sector sets p^c_t so that the household sector's current consumption is price elastic, then $p^c_t c^h_t$ falls as p^c_t rises. Since current nominal income is unchanged, this means that current saving rises as p^c_t rises, allowing households to purchase more goods produced by the private business sector next period. To the extent that this is so, Cu^{hd}_{t+1} rises along with Sn^{hd}_{t+1}; that is, households will decide to accumulate more of both financial assets during the current period. Sn^{hd}_{t+1} increases because the real return from equity increases, ceteris paribus, as p^c_t rises. Cu^{hd}_{t+1} rises because the increase in c^h_{t+1} reduces the opportunity cost (in terms of forgone utility) of saving in the form of currency rather than equity shares. In addition, as households decide to save more during the current period in order to purchase more c^h_{t+1}, the falling marginal utility of c^h_{t+1} causes the households to reduce N^s_{t+1}. The falling marginal utilty of c^h_{t+1} also makes households more willing to forgo some c^h_{t+1} in order to obtain an additional unit of government-produced goods next period. Consequently, ceteris paribus, if c^h_t is indeed own-price elastic, an increase in p^c_t will produce the following results:

$$\frac{\partial c^h_t}{\partial p^c_t} < 0,\ \frac{\partial c^h_{t+1}}{\partial p^c_t} > 0,\ \frac{\partial g_{t+1}}{\partial p^c_t} > 0,\ \frac{\partial Cu^{hd}_{t+1}}{\partial p^c_t} > 0,\ \frac{\partial Sn^{hd}_{t+1}}{\partial p^c_t} > 0 \text{ and}$$

$$\frac{\partial N^s_{t+1}}{\partial p^c_t} < 0. \tag{6.29}$$

<u>Next period's money wage, w_{t+1}.</u>

The business sector's announcement of w_{t+1} presumably takes place after the government has announced next period's menu, but before the household sector solves (6.24). These assumptions are outlined in greater detail in the discussion of the complete model that begins in Chapter 7.

An increase in w_{t+1} also produces an income effect and a substitution effect. The former enables households to enjoy more c^h_{t+1} without working longer hours, causing c^h_{t+1} to rise and N^s_{t+1} to fall. The latter makes the opportunity cost of home production greater, causing the households to increase N^s_{t+1} and c^h_{t+1}. Although the net effect on N^s_{t+1} is not clear, total anticipated future labor income, $w_{t+1}hN^s_{t+1}$, does increase with w_{t+1}, enabling c^h_{t+1} to rise. The rise in c^h_{t+1} reduces its marginal utility relative to both c^h_t and g_{t+1}. Consequently c^h_t tends to increase, as does g_{t+1}. In order to obtain the extra g_{t+1}, households agree to pay more taxes next period. The fallng marginal utility of c^h_{t+1} reduces the opportunity cost of saving in the form of currency during the current period so that Cu^{hd}_{t+1} increases with c^h_{t+1}. But since c^h_t increases while current income remains unchanged, total current saving must fall. Therefore, the household sector's demand for equity for the end of the current period must fall. This is the only way, in this simple model, that the currency component of current saving can increase as total current saving falls. To summarize:

$$\frac{\partial c^h_t}{\partial w_{t+1}} > 0, \frac{\partial c^h_{t+1}}{\partial w_{t+1}} > 0, \frac{\partial g_{t+1}}{\partial w_{t+1}} > 0, \frac{\partial Cu^{hd}_{t+1}}{\partial w_{t+1}} > 0, \frac{\partial Sn^{hd}_{t+1}}{\partial w_{t+1}} < 0 \text{ and}$$

$$\frac{\partial N^s_{t+1}}{\partial w_{t+1}} \lessgtr 0. \tag{6.30}$$

<u>Current equity price, p^n_t.</u>

An increase in p^n_t produces two substitution effects and an income effect. A negative income effect arises to the extent that households plan to save during the current period by accumulting equity shares, i.e. to the extent that $(Sn^{hd}_{t+1} - Sn_t) > 0$. As p^n_t rises, it costs households more to purchase a given number of shares. Therefore in spite of the often-discussed "wealth effect" associated with the greater value associated with its initial shares, the net effect of the increase in p^n_t is to <u>reduce</u> current household income in proportion to the excess of Sn^{hd}_{t+1} over Sn_t. Wealth effects, which are highly touted by monetarists and others, realize their full impact only if the end-of-period demands equal zero for those assets whose prices have appreciated in value. The tendency for economists to overlook this fact may be linked to their tendency to focus upon beginning-of-period demands rather than the end-of-period asset demands found in the present model.

The negative income effect tends to cause households to reduce c^h_t and current saving. To the extent that current saving falls, c^h_{t+1} also falls, increasing its marginal utility. As the marginal utility of c^h_{t+1} rises, households will plan to increase their supply of labor and to reduce their demand for government-produced goods next period. The increased marginal utililty of c_{t+1} also raises the opportunity cost of saving in the form of currency accumulation during the current period.

Ceteris paribus, an increase in p^n_t also reduces the anticipated real rate of return on equity, thereby causing the household sector to (a) substitute present consumption for future consumption on the margin and (b) substitute currency for equity shares on the margin in the portfolio it plans for the end of the current period. Both substitution effects are away from c^h_{t+1}. Therefore, the income and substitution effects upon c^h_{t+1} are all in the same direction. Since c^h_{t+1} falls, its marginal utility increases causing N^s_{t+1} to rise and g_{t+1} to fall. The net effects upon c^h_t and Cu^{hd}_{t+1} are unclear. To summarize:

$$\frac{\partial c^h_t}{\partial p^n_t} \gtrless 0, \quad \frac{\partial c^h_{t+1}}{\partial p^n_t} < 0, \quad \frac{\partial g_{t+1}}{\partial p^n_t} < 0, \quad \frac{\partial Sn^{hd}_{t+1}}{\partial p^n_t} < 0, \quad \frac{\partial Cu^{hd}_{t+1}}{\partial p^n_t} > 0, \text{ and}$$

$$\frac{\partial N^s_{t+1}}{\partial p^n_t} > 0 \tag{6.31}$$

Current wage income, $w_t h_t N_t$, current dividends per share, π^n_t, initial equity shares, Sn_t, and initial currency balances, Cu^h_t.

An increase in $w_t h_t N_t$ or π^n_t increases current income of the household sector, allowing it to increase c^h_t. As c^h_t rises, the subjective rate of substitution of c^h_t for c^h_{t+1} falls and households also increase their demand for c^h_{t+1}. Consequently, the household sector will tend to increase the amount it saves in the current period (in the form of equity shares). The diminishing marginal utility of c^h_{t+1} causes N^s_{t+1} to decrease, Cu^{hd}_{t+1} to rise and g_{t+1} to rise. Consequently as $w_t h_t N_t$ or π^n_t rises:

$$\frac{\partial c^t_t}{\partial x_t} > 0, \quad \frac{\partial c^h_{t+1}}{\partial x_t} > 0, \quad \frac{\partial g_{t+1}}{\partial x_t} > 0, \quad \frac{\partial Sn^{hd}_{t+1}}{\partial x_t} > 0, \quad \frac{\partial Cu^{hd}_{t+1}}{\partial x_t} > 0,$$

$$\frac{\partial N^s_{t+1}}{\partial x_t} < 0. \tag{6.32}$$

where x_t repesents either $\hat{w}_t h_t N_t$ or $\pi^n{}_t$.

Even though an increase in $Cu^h{}_t$ does not affect current market income, it does increase the amount of $c^h{}_t$ that the households can enjoy in the current period without jeopardizing their end-of-period portfolio. In other words, as $Cu^h{}_t$ rises the household sector needs to save less currency, $Cu^{hd}{}_{t+1} - Cu^h$, in order to have the same amount of currency by the end of the period. Consequently the households can spend part of an increase in $Cu^h{}_t$ on current consumption, use part of the increase to purchase equity shares, $Sn^{hd}{}_{t+1}$, and still add to its end-of-period balances of currency (even though the rise in $Cu^{hd}{}_{t+1}$ will be smaller than the rise in $Cu^h{}_t$). In fact, this is how we would expect the household sector to react. For as it adds to current consumption, the marginal utility of $c^h{}_t$ falls relative to future private-goods consumption, thereby inducing the household to buy more equity shares during the current period. As it does so, the marginal utility of future private-goods consumption also falls, thereby reducing the opportunity cost of raising $Cu^{hd}{}_{t+1}$. In addition the fall in the marginal utility of $c^h{}_{t+1}$ also induces the household sector (a) to increase the amount it instructs the government to produce next period and (b) to reduce its supply of labor for next period.

An increase in Sn_t raises both current dividend income, $\pi^n{}_t Sn_t$, and initial equity wealth, $p^n{}_t Sn_t$. In light of the above discussion, the "income" and "wealth" effects generated by an increase in Sn_t will be reinforcing and will show the same signs as presented in (6.32) above.

<u>Anticipated price of commodities, $p^{ch}{}_{t+1}$, and next period's anticipated equity income, $\pi^{nh}{}_{t+1}$.</u>

An increase in the anticipated level of the price of privately-produced commodities next period produces three substitution effects, a wealth effect and an income effect.

An increase in $p^{ch}{}_{t+1}$, by reducing the anticipated real rate of return on equity shares, causes the households to tend to substitute current consumption for future consumption. Second, the increse in $p^{ch}{}_{t+1}$ reduces the anticipated real wage from labor, inducing the sector to substitute home-produced goods for goods produced by the private business sector. This substitution effect, therefore, directly causes N^s_{t+1} and c^h_{t+1} to fall, just as the first one directly causes c^h_t to rise and c^h_{t+1} to fall. Third, an increase in p^{ch}_{t+1} reduces the real value of the privately-produced goods which the households anticipate they will sacrifice next period by selecting an additional unit of government-produced goods. This drop in the real marginal tax burden associated with a unit increase in g_{t+1} entices the household sector to substitute g_{t+1} for c^h_{t+1} on the margin.

The wealth effect produced by an increase in the anticipated level of next period's commodity prices concerns the portfolio which the household sector is planning for the end of the current period. In particular, as p^{ch}_{t+1} rises, the anticipated purchasing power next period of the currency which the sector plans to hold at the end of the current period falls. The drop in these real balances presumably increases their marginal utiliy, causing the sector to increase its nominal demand for currency for the end of the current period by saving more in the form of currency during the current period and less in the form of equity shares. As it diverts some saving from equity share accumulation to currency accumulation, the sector plans to sacrifice some future consumption of privately-produced commodities, c^h_{t+1}.

Finally, the increase in p^{ch}_{t+1} by making future consumption more expensive, is tantamount to a reductioin in next period's income. This effect will also tend to cause the household sector to plan to reduce c^h_{t+1} in the face of an increase in p^{ch}_{t+1}.

If the "own" substitution effects between c^h_t and c^h_{t+1}, between N^s_{t+1} and c^h_{t+1}, and between g_{t+1} and c^h_{t+1} dominate in terms of the net effect upon c^h_t, N^s_{t+1} and g_{t+1} respectively, then as p^{ch}_{t+1} rises, c^h_t and g_{t+1} tend to increase while N^s_{t+1} falls. If the wealth effect dominates in terms of dictating the net effect upon Cu^{hd}_{t+1}, then Cu^{hd}_{t+1} increases with p^{ch}_{t+1}. (The real demand for currency will fall, however, since the household sector plans to buy fewer c^h_{t+1}.) However the income effect of an increase in p^{ch}_{t+1} tends to reverse the signs in every case, so that any assertions as to the effect of an increase in p^{ch}_{t+1} upon any variable other than c^h_{t+1} must involve further assumptions as to the relative strength of the various effects mentioned above.

An increase in the anticipated income per share from equity next period, π^{nh}_{t+1}, produces two substitution effects and an income effect. First, by increasing the anticipated real rate of return on equity, the rise in π^{nh}_{t+1} causes the households to substitute future consumption for current consumption. Second, as π^{nh}_{t+1} rises the opportunity cost of saving an extra dollar in the current period as currency also rises. This causes Cu^{hd}_{t+1} to fall and c^{h}_{t+1} to rise; a dollar shifted from Cu^{hd}_{t+1} to Sn^{hd}_{t+1} yields more income next period with which to buy c^{h}_{t+1}. Furthermore, the increase in π^{nh}_{t+1} represents an increase in future income. This also encourages c^{h}_{t+1} and raises Sn^{hd}_{t+1}.

Since all three effects cause c^{h}_{t+1} to increase, its marginal utility will fall inducing the households to increase g_{t+1} and reduce N^{s}_{t+1}. If the first substitution effect dominates in terms of providing the net effect on c^{h}_{t}, current consumption falls as π^{nh}_{t+1} rises; if the second substitution effect dominates in terms of providing the net effect upon Cu^{hd}_{t+1}, Cu^{hd}_{t+1} also falls. However, the income effect tends to oppose both of these influences. Therefore, without additional assumptions, the signs of the partials of c^{h}_{t} and Cu^{hd}_{t+1} with respect to π^{nh}_{t+1} remain indeterminate.

<u>Current taxes, Tx_t</u>

Ignoring the effects on the menu offered by the government for next period, an increase in Tx_t reduces current disposable income. Therefore the signs of the partials with respect to a change in Tx_t are opposite those presented in (6.32).

<u>Shift in the government-produced goods-tax menu (k)</u>

As shown earlier in this chapter, an increase in the initial stock of fiat currency outstanding, $\hat{Cu}_t$, the current money wage, w_t, the current level of government production, g_t, the money wage which the government expects at time t to pay next period, w^{g}_{t+1}, or the price that the government expects to pay next period for privately-produced goods, p^{cg}_{t}, raises the level of taxes which the government must collect next period to finance a given amount of g_{t+1}. In other words, an increase in any one of these parameters shifts the tax menu upward in Figure 6.3. On the other hand, the higher Tx_t in this period, ceteris paribus, the lower Tx_{t+1} needs to be next period to produce a given level of g_{t+1}.

An upward shift in the tax level, Tx_{t+1}, for a given g_{t+1}, causes the household sector to revise downward is estimate of next period's disposable income for a given level of g_{t+1}. This means the sector will have to reduce its consumption of privately-produced goods next period. As c^h_{t+1} falls, its marginal utility rises causing the households to reduce c^h_t, Cu^{hd}_{t+1} and g_{t+1} and to increase N^s_{t+1} in order to restore the first-order necessary conditions. Since current disposable income is unaffected, the fall in c^h_t causes current household saving to increase. But the fall in Cu^{hd}_{t+1} means that the households plan to reduce the currency component of current saving. Therefore, the household sector's end-of-period demand for equity shares increases as the menu in Figure 6.3 shifts upward. It does so in order to partially offset the drop in next period's drop in disposable income due to the rise in Tx_{t+1}. Therefore:

$$\frac{\partial c^h_t}{\partial k} < 0, \quad \frac{\partial c^h_{t+1}}{\partial k} < 0, \quad \frac{\partial g_{t+1}}{\partial k} < 0, \quad \frac{\partial Sn^{hd}_{t+1}}{\partial k} > 0, \quad \frac{\partial Cu^{hd}_{t+1}}{\partial k} < 0,$$

$$\frac{\partial N^s_{t+1}}{\partial k} > 0. \tag{6.33}$$

With a government sector present, then, the household sector's demand and supply functions may be written:

$$c^h_t = c^h_t(\underset{-}{p^c_t}, \underset{+}{w_{t+1}}, \underset{?}{p^n_t}, \underset{+}{w_t} h_t N_t, \underset{+}{\pi^n_t}, \underset{+}{Sn_t}, \underset{+}{Cu^h_t}, \underset{?}{p^{ch}_{t+1}}, \underset{?}{\pi^{nh}_{t+1}}, \underset{-}{Tx_t}, \underset{-}{k}) \tag{6.34}$$

$$Cu^{hd}_{t+1} = Cu^{hd}_{t+1}(\underset{+}{p^c_t}, \underset{+}{w_{t+1}}, \underset{?}{p^n_t}, \underset{+}{w_t} h_t N_t, \underset{+}{\pi^n_t}, \underset{+}{Sn_t}, \underset{+}{Cu^h_t}, \underset{?}{p^{ch}_{t+1}}, \underset{?}{\pi^{nh}_{t+1}}, \underset{-}{Tx_t}, \underset{-}{k}) \tag{6.35}$$

$$Sn^{hd}_{t+1} = Sn^{hd}_{t+1}(\underset{+}{p^c_t}, \underset{-}{w_{t+1}}, \underset{-}{p^n_t}, \underset{+}{w_t} h_t N_t, \underset{+}{\pi^n_t}, \underset{+}{Sn_t}, \underset{+}{Cu^h_t}, \underset{?}{p^{ch}_{t+1}}, \underset{+}{\pi^{nh}_{t+1}}, \underset{-}{Tx_t}, \underset{-}{k}) \tag{6.36}$$

$$N^s_{t+1} = N^s_{t+1}(\underset{-}{p^c_t}, \underset{?}{w_{t+1}}, \underset{+}{p^n_t}, \underset{-}{w_t} h_t N_t, \underset{-}{\pi^n_t}, \underset{-}{Sn_t}, \underset{-}{Cu^h_t}, \underset{?}{p^{ch}_{t+1}}, \underset{-}{\pi^{nh}_{t+1}}, \underset{+}{Tx_t}, \underset{+}{k}) \tag{6.37}$$

$$g_{t+1} = g_{t+1}(\underset{+}{p^c_t}, \underset{+}{w_{t+1}}, \underset{-}{p^n_t}, \underset{+}{w_t} h_t N_t, \underset{+}{\pi^n_t}, \underset{+}{Sn_t}, \underset{+}{Cu^h_t}, \underset{?}{p^{ch}_{t+1}}, \underset{+}{\pi^{nh}_{t+1}}, \underset{-}{Tx_t}, \underset{-}{k}) \tag{6.38}$$

The derivation of (6.38) represents one of the unique aspects of the present model. For this equation reveals the economic variables that will tend to influence public opinion as to the approprite level of government-produced goods for next period. One of the factors which the public confronts in this model is the tax bill that will be necessary to finance these goods. Consequently rather than passively accepting the levels of government-produced goods and taxes which some outside policy authority arbitrarily decides is best for the community, as is done in conventional models, the community itself decides in the present case the optimum combination of these items in the context of its other choices in the private commodity, labor and financial markets. Although the government sector prepares the menu of alternatives, the community makes the actual selection. According to (6.38), the household sector will tend to demand more government-produced goods as its disposable income grows, as its own wealth grows, and as privately-produced goods become more expensive (provided the rise in p^c_t does not shift the tax menu upward). On the other hand, as the government asks for more taxes to provide a given level of g_{t+1}, the households will tend to reduce their demand for those goods and demand more privately-produced goods.

Modification of Business Sector Behavior

The introduction of government activity into the simple model produces few modifications in business sector behavior. To some extent this is due to the fact that all taxes are levied upon the household sector in this model and that government-produced goods and services provide utility directly to the households but do not make businesses more efficient. These simplifications are made so that business sector behavior may be complicated in other ways in later chapters. Specifically, later chapters allow the nonfinancial business sector to produce capital goods as well as consumption goods and to hold checkable deposits. Incorporating business taxes and government-produced goods as a factor of production would encumber an already complicated model.

There are two noteworthy adjustments which the business sector must make in the presence of a government sector in this model, however. It must revise its estimates of the market demand for its commodities, c^{de}, to include the government's demand for these goods and it must subtract its estimate, N^{ge}_{t+1}, of the government's demand for labor from its estimate, N^{se}_{t+1}, of the household sector's supply of labor.

Figures 6.5 and 6.6 show, respectively, the business sector's estimate of the total real market demand, c^{de}_t, for its commodities in the current period and its estimate of the net supply of labor, $N^{se}_{t+1} - N^{ge}_{t+1}$. From the analysis of the government sector presented

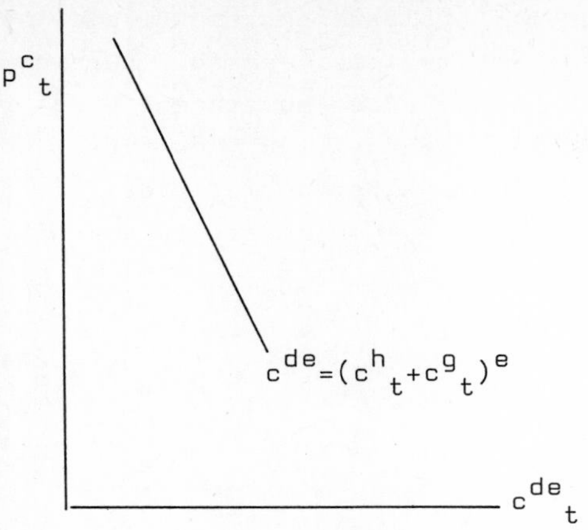

Figure 6.5 - The Estimated Market Demand for Commodities

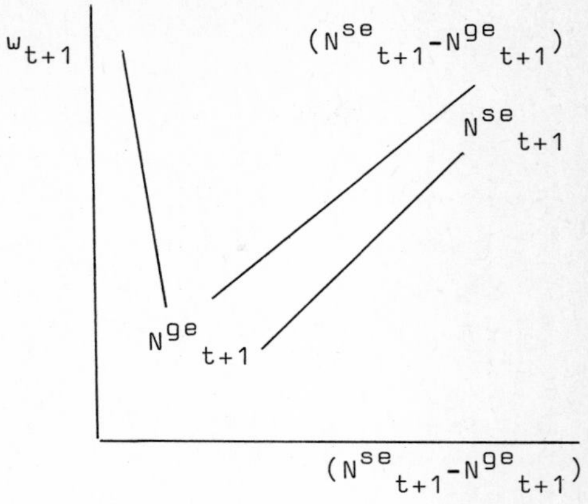

Figure 6.6 - The Estimated Net Supply of Labor as the Difference between N^{se}_{t+1} and N^{ge}_{t+1}.

earlier, the government's current demand for commodities c^g_t, increases with w_t and g_t while its demand for employees for next period increases with g_{t+1} but falls with w_{t+1}. Since the government sector presumably decides c^g_t before p^c_t is actually announced, the business sector knows c^g_t when it estimates c^{de}_t.

The outward shift in its estimate of current commodity demand due to an increase in c^g_t, ceteris paribus, causes the business sector to announce a higher current price, p^c_t, to produce more in the current period, q, and to use its current employees longer hours, h_t. These

$$\frac{\partial h_t}{\partial c^g_t} > 0, \frac{\partial q}{\partial c^g_t} > 0, \frac{\partial c^{de}_t}{\partial c^g_t} > 0, \frac{\partial p^c_t}{\partial c^g_t} > 0 \qquad (6.39)$$

results are based upon the discussion in Chapter 4 as to the effects of an outward shift in the business sector's estimate of the current demand function for commodities.

As shown in Figure 6.6, the reduction in the quantity of labor the government demands in response to an increase in w_{t+1} merely makes the business sector's estimate of the net supply of labor more elastic than its estimate of N^s_{t+1}.

The revised response functions for the business sector (i.e. its price and wage setting functions as well as its labor demand, currency demand and dividend functions) in the presence of a government sector are shown below as (6.40) - (6.48) where the parameter v_c now refers to a shift in the current period's estimated demand for commodities for a reason other than a change in c^g_t. Parameter v_n now refers to a shift in $(N^{se}_{t+1} - N^{ge}_{t-1})$ for any reason.

$$h^n_t = h^n_t(N^n_t, w_t, Cu^n_t, Q_t, Sn_t, c^g_t, v_c, v^*_c, v_n, v_s) \qquad (6.40)$$

$$p^c_t = p^c_t(w_t, Cu^n_t, Q_t, Sn_t, c^g_t, v_c, v^*_c, v_n, v_s) \qquad (6.41)$$

$$w_{t+1} = w_{t+1}(w_t, Cu^n_t, Q_t, Sn_t, c^g_t, v_c, v^*_c, v_n, v_s) \qquad (6.42)$$

$$p^n_t = p^n_t(w_t, Cu^n_t, Q_t. Sn_t, c^g_t, v_c, v^{*c}, v_n, v_s) \qquad (6.43)$$

$$N^{nd}_{t+1} = N^{nd}_{t+1}(w_t, Cu^n_t, Q_t, Sn_t, c^g_t, v_c, v^*_c, v_n, v_s) \qquad (6.44)$$

$$Cu^{nd}_{t+1} = Cu^{nd}_{t+1}(w_t, Cu_t, Q_t, Sn_t, c^g_t, v_c, v^*_c, v_n, v_s) \qquad (6.45)$$

$$q_t = q_t(w_t, Cu^n_t, Q_t, Sn_t, c^g_t, v_c, v^*_c, v_n, v_s) \qquad (6.46)$$

$$\pi^n_t = \pi^n_t(w_t, Cu^n_t, Q_t, Sn_t, c^g_t, v_c, v^*_c, v_n, v_s) \qquad (6.47)$$

$$c^{de}_t = c^{de}_t(w_t, Cu^n_t, Q_t, Sn_t, c^g_t, v_c, v^*_c, v_n, v_s) \qquad (6.48)$$

National Product and Economic Fluctuations

At time t the government must make several choices. On the one hand, it must decide the most efficient way to produce the given amount of government-produced goods, g_t, which the households have already selected for the current period. This involves choosing the optimal combination of privately-produced commodities, c^g_t, and labor time, h^g_t. The relevant equations here are (6.13) and (6.14). On the other hand the government must decide, see (6.18), the number of dollars it must collect as taxes next period to finance the production of each alternative level of government-produced goods next period. Once the households have selected the optimal g_{t+1} from this menu, the government then determines the number of people, N^{gd}_{t+1}, it wants to employ next period, using (6.15).

In order to portray a relative inability of the government sector to respond quickly to market pressures, I assume that the government decides c^g_t and announces h^g_t as well as the menu $Tx_{t+1}(.)$ at time t just prior to the business sector's announcement at that time as to the market prices for commodities, p^c_t, labor, w_{t+1}, and equity shares, p^n_t. In this way none of c^g_t, h^g_t, or $Tx_{t+1}(.)$, shown respectively by (6.13), (6.14) and (6.18)), is responsive to the levels of p^c_t, w_{t+1} and p^n_t actually announced at time t.

At the same time that it announces these market prices (see equations (6.41) - (6.43)) the private business sector presumably also decides the level of current production, q_t, and announces both the average number of hours, h^n_t, its current employees will work during the period and the dividends per share, π^n_t, it will pay its current shareholders. Therefore equations (6.46), (6.40) and (6.47) depict the actual values of these three variables in the current-period. Concomitantly, the business sector also plans N^{nd}_{t+1}, Cu^{nd}_{t+1} and c^{de}_t in accordance with (6.44), (6.45) and (6.48) respectively. However, these may not turn out to be actual values by time t+1.

Once the household sector has received (and processed) the information contained in the announcements made by the government and business sectors, it then selects (at time t) its desired levels of c^h_t, Cu^{hd}_{t+1}, Sn^{hd}_{t+1}, N^s_{t+1} and g_{t+1} in accordance with equations (6.34) - (6.38). It is not until the households have chosen g_{t+1} that the government becomes ready to decide N^{gd}_{t+1} in a manner consistent with (6.15).

From the discussion to this point, the actual values of h^g_t and c^g_t are determined from (6.13) and (6.14). Next, the actual values of h^n_t, w_{t+1}, p^n_t, q_t, p^c_t and π^n_t are determined from (6.40), (6.42), (6.43), (6.46), (6.41) and (6.47) respectively. Then the actual value of g_{t+1} is determined, in light of (6.18), by (6.38).

To establish the actual amounts traded during the current period in the commodity, equity and labor markets, assume the following:

$$c_t = c^h_t + c^g_t \tag{6.49}$$

$$Sn_{t+1} = Sn^{hd}_{t+1} \tag{6.50}$$

$$N_{t+1} = \min(N^s_{t+1}, N^{gd}_{t+1} + N^{nd}_{t+1}) \tag{6.51}$$

Equatiion (6.49) stipultes that the number of privately-produced commodities sold during the current period equals the sum of the ex ante demands by the household and government sectors. This implies that the end-of-period inventory of commodities is given by:

$$Q_{t+1} = c^{de}_{t} - c_{t} \qquad (6.52)$$

Equation (6.50) states that the number of equity shares outstanding at the end of the period equals the household sector's demand for those shares. According to (6.51), the number of people actually employed by the end of the current period to work next period is the minimum of the household sector's supply and the sum of the demands by the government and private business sector.

Since Tx_t and N_t are known at time t and since the government presumably announces h^g_t and the private business sector presumably announces h^g_t and π^n_t at time t before the household sector formulates its plans for the current period, it follows that current disposable income, $w_t h^g_t N^g_t + w_t h^n_t N^n + \pi^n_t Sn_t - Tx_t$, is also known to the household sector as it formulates its demands for current consumption, currency and equity shares. In light of (6.49) and (6.50) and in light of the fact that p^c_t and p^n_t have already been announced when the household sector formultes its plans with respect to c^h_t, Sn^{hd}_{t+1} and Cu^{hd}_{t+1}, it follows from the household sector's ex-post budget constraint:

$$w_t h^g_t N^g_t + w_t h^n_t N^n_t + \pi^n_t Sn_t - Tx_t = p^c_t c^h_t + p^n_t (Sn_{t+1} - Sn_t) + (Cu^h_{t+1} - Cu^h_t) \qquad (6.53)$$

that the amount of currency, Cu^h_{t+1}, which the household sector actually holds at the end of the period corresponds to the amount of currency, Cu^{hd}_{t+1}, which it planned at time t to hold by the end of the period. The reason is that the household sector's current period budget constraint in ex ante terms is represented by (6.54):

$$w_t h^g_t N^g_t + w_t h^n_t N^n_t + \pi^n_t Sn_t - Tx_t = p^c_t c^h_t + p^n_t (Sn^{nd}_{t+1} - Sn_t) + (Cu^{hd}_{t+1} - Cu^h_t) \qquad (6.54)$$

Equations (6.49) and (6.50) insure that the households in fact buy the commodities they planned to buy and that they also accumulate the number of equity shares they planned to accumulate. Consequently,

(6.53) and (6.54) together imply that:

$$Cu^{h}_{t+1} = Cu^{hd}_{t+1} \tag{6.55}$$

Recall the government sector's ex ante current-period budget constraint:

$$Tx_t - w_t h^g_t N^g_t - p^{cg}_t c^g_t = -\hat{C}u^s_{t+1} + \hat{C}u_t. \tag{6.2}$$

Since Tx_t, w_t, N^g_t and $\hat{C}u_t$ were determined prior to time t, they are taken as given by the government sector at time t. The government sector's ex post current-period budget constraint:

$$Tx_t = w_t h^g_t N^g_t - p^c_t c^g_t = -\hat{C}u_{t+1} + \hat{C}u_t. \tag{6.56}$$

may be re-written to reveal the actual amount of fiat currency outstanding at the end of the current period:

$$\hat{C}u_{t+1} = \hat{C}u_t + w_t h^g_t N^g_t + p^c_t c^g_t - Tx_t \tag{6.57}$$

In expression (6.2), p^{cg}_t is the price of commodities the government expects to prevail. In (6.56) and (6.57), p^c_t is the actual price of commodities announced by the business sector at the beginning of the period. Since the government presumably announces h^g_t and c^g_t before the business sector announces p^c_t, the government may find that by the end of the current period its actual spending on privately-produced goods, $p^c_t c^g_t$, is greater or less than the amount it planned to spend, $p^{cg}_t c^g_t$, on those goods. The actual stock of fiat currency at the end-of-the period will differ from the government's ex ante supply by the amount of its unanticipated expenditures on privately produced goods in the current period:

$$\hat{C}u_{t+1} - \hat{C}u^s_{t+1} = (p^c_t - p^{cg}_t)c^g_t \tag{6.58}$$

The ex ante supply of money on the other hand is the amount of fiat currency outstanding which the government feels at time t is consistent with minimizing current expenses in producing a predetermined level of g_t.

The amount of currency which the nonfinancial business sector holds at the end of the current period, namely Cu^n_{t+1}, is found by rearranging the ex post version of that sector's current period budget constraint:

$$Cu^n_{t+1} = p^c_t(c^h_t+c^g_t)-w_th^n_tN^n_t-\pi^n_tSn_t+p^n_t(Sn_{t+1}-Sn_t))+ Cu^n_t \qquad (6.59)$$

To show that the amounts Cu^h_{t+1} in (6.53), $\hat{Cu}_{t+1}$ in (6.57) and Cu^n_{t+1} in (6.59) are consistent, note that

$$\begin{aligned} Cu_{t+1} - Cu^h_{t+1} - Cu^n_{t+1} &= (\hat{Cu}_t+w_th^g_tN^g_t+p^c_tc^g_t-Tx_t) + Cu^* \qquad (6.60)\\ &- [-Tx_t+\pi^n_tSn_t+w_th^n_tN^n_t+w_th^g_tN^g_t-p^c_tc^h_t \\ &- p^c_t(Sn_{t+1}-Sn_t) + Cu^h_t] \\ &- [p^c_t(c^h_t+c^g_t) - w_th^n_tN^n_t - \pi^n_tSn_t \\ &+ p^n_t(Sn_{t+1}-Sn_t)+Cu^n_t] = \hat{Cu}_t+Cu^*-Cu^h_t-Cu^n_t \\ &= Cu_t - Cu^h_t - Cu^n_t. \end{aligned}$$

where <u>total</u> currency in circulation at any moment, Cu_t, equals fiat money, $\hat{Cu}_t$, plus (a constant level of) private money, Cu^*.

$$Cu_t = Cu_t + Cu^* = Cu^h_t + Cu^n_t \qquad (6.61)$$

Therefore, the right hand side of (6.60) equals zero, so that:

$$Cu_{t+1} + Cu^* = Cu^h_{t+1} + Cu^n_{t+1} \qquad (6.62)$$

The actual amount of private money plus fiat money outstanding at the end of the period equals the actual amont of money held by the households plus the amount held by the private business sector, jusst as was the case at the beginning of the period.

As the current period opens, the government's current tax revenues, Tx_t, are predetermined, since they were decided by the private sector last period in conjunction with the current volume of government production, g_t. At the beginning of the current period the government must select the combination of factors it estimates will minimize its current expenditures, $p^c_tc^g_t + w_th^g_tN^g_t$, in producing g_t before it knows all factor prices. Consequently, in general, the government's tax revenues in any period will not match its expenditures on goods and services. Whenever an unbalanced budget occurs during a period, the stock of money held by the private sector changes between the beginning and the end of that period. Therefore movements in the stock of money occur over time neither as random shocks nor as events manipulated by an interventionist authority. Instead they arise because the government has incomplete information not only when it presents its menu to the household sector, but also when it formulates its budget for next period in light of the household sector's choices. If the government were required to balance the budget each period, then the household sector's choice of g_t could only be tentative. For, given Tx_t, the government would attempt to maximize g_t subject to Tx_t. However, even under these circumstances the budget may not balance initially if the government must commit itself to purchasing certain factors before their prices are announced. In the expanded model that begins in Chapter 7, the private stock of money is also endogenously determined through the interactions of nor only the three sectors discussed in this chapter but also a central bank and a private finanical sector.

Walras' Law (in a Non-Walrasian Model)

The ex ante versions of the current-period budget constraints facing the households, the nonfinancial businesses and the government are repeated below for the reader's convenience:

$$w_t h^g{}_t N^g{}_t + w_t h^n{}_t N^n{}_t + \pi^n{}_t Sn_t - Tx_t = p^c{}_t c^h{}_t + p^n{}_t (Sn^{hd}{}_{t+1} - Sn_t) + (Cu^{hd}{}_{t+1} - Cu^h{}_t) \qquad (6.63)$$

$$p^c{}_t c^{de}{}_t - w_t h^n{}_t N^n{}_t - \pi^n{}_t Sn_t = (Cu^{nd}{}_{t+1} - Cu^n{}_t) - p^n{}_t (Sn^{de}{}_{t+1} - Sn_t) \qquad (6.64)$$

$$Tx_t - w_t h^g{}_t N^g{}_t - p^{cg}{}_t c^g{}_t = -\hat{C}u^s{}_{t+1} + \hat{C}u_t. \qquad (6.65)$$

where $\hat{C}u_t + Cu^* = Cu^h{}_t + Cu^n{}_t$ with Cu^* representing a nonnegative amount of private money (that exchanges dollar-for-dollar with fiat money). Summing equations (6.63) - (6.65) produces:

$$(p^c{}_t c^{de}{}_t - p^{cg}{}_t c^g{}_t - p^c{}_t c^h{}_t) = p^n{}_t (Sn^{hd}{}_{t+1} - Sn^{de}{}_{t+1}) + (Cu^{hd}{}_{t+1} + Cu^{nd'}{}_{t+1} - Cu^s{}_{t+1} - Cu^*) \qquad (6.66)$$

Since c^{de}_t represents the number of commodities which the private business sector anticipates selling, the difference on the left-hand side of (6.66) denotes the value of the excess supply of privately produced goods. Let $\hat{C}u^s_{t+1} + Cu^*$ represent the market "supply" of currency for time t+1 and interpret the business sector's anticipated stock of equity shares outstanding at time t+1 as its "supply" of equity shares. Then, according to (6.66), the sum of the values of the excess demands for equities and money must equal the value of the excess supply of privately produced goods. In other words, (6.66) states that the sum of the values of the excess demands across all three markets must equal zero, even when prices are announced by economic agents rather than by an auctioneer.

National Income and Product

According to the expenditure approach, measured national product (in current dollars), Ym_t, is the sum of household spending on privately-produced goods, $p^c_t c^h_t$, government spending on goods and services, $p^c_t c^g_t + w_t h^g_t N^g_t$, and the value of the business sector's net addition to inventories, $p^c_t(Q_{t+1} - Q_t)$:

$$Ym_t = p^c_t c^h_t + p^c_t c^g_t + w_t h^g_t N^g_t + p^c_t(Q_{t+1} - Q_t) \tag{6.67}$$

But $Q_{t+1} = c^{de}_t - c^h_t - c^g_t$. Therefore Ym_t becomes

$$\begin{aligned} Ym_t &= p^c_t c^h_t + p^c_t c^g_t + w_t h^g_t N^g_t + p^c_t(c^{de}_t - c^h_t - c^g_t - Q_t) \qquad (6.68)\\ &= p^c_t(c^{de}_t - Q_t) + w_t h^g_t N^g_t = p^c_t q_t + w_t h^g_t N^g_t \end{aligned}$$

since q_t, the real production of the business sector, is the difference between its planned sales and its initial inventory. If household production is ignored and if the value added by the government is defined as equal to its wage payments, then (6.68) in fact reveals the value of national product in current dollars.

Measured national income (also in current dollars) consists of the sum of a labor income, $w_t h^g_t N^g_t + w_t h^n_t N^n_t$, dividends, $\pi^n_t Sn_t$, and net business saving, where net business saving is defined as the business sector's net income minus dividends. The business sector's net income is defined as the value of sales plus the value of its net addition to inventories minus its wage bill:

$$Yi_t = w_t h^g{}_t N^g{}_t + w_t h^n{}_t N^n{}_t + \pi^n{}_t Sn_t \tag{6.69}$$

$$+ (p^c{}_t[c^h{}_t + c^g{}_t + (Q_{t+1} - Q_t)] - w_t h^n{}_t N^n{}_t - \pi^n{}_t Sn_t)$$

$$= w_t h^g{}_t N^g{}_t + p^c{}_t q_t$$

Therefore national product measured according to the expenditure approach in (6.68)equals national income as shown by (6.69).

Specification of the Reduced- and Final- Forms

In light of our earlier discussion,the actual values of $h^g{}_t$, $h^n{}_t$, w_{t+1}, $p^n{}_t$, Q_t, $p^c{}_t$, $\pi^n{}_t$, and g_{t+1} are given respectively by (6.13), (6.40), (6.42), (6.43), (6.46), (6.41), (6.47) and (6.38). These equatiions are repeated immediately below as (6.70) - (6.77):

$$h^g{}_t = h^g{}_t(N^g{}_t, w_t, p^{cg}{}_t, g_t) \tag{6.70}$$

$$h^n{}_t = h^n{}_t(N_t, w_t, Cu^n{}_t, Q_t, Sn_t, c^g{}_t, v_c, v^*{}_c, v_n, v_s) \tag{6.71}$$

$$w_{t+1} = w_{t+1}(w_t, Cu^n{}_t, Q_t, Sn_t, c^g{}_t, v_c, {}^*v_c, v_n, v_s) \tag{6.72}$$

$$p^n{}_t = p^n{}_t(w_t, Cu^m{}_t, Q_t, Sn_t, c^g{}_t, v_c, v^*{}_c, v_n, v_s) \tag{6.73}$$

$$q_t = q_t(w_t, Cu^n{}_t, Q_t, Sn_t, c^g{}_t, v_c, v^*{}_c, v_n, v_s) \tag{6.74}$$

$$p^c{}_t = p^c{}_t(w_t, Cu^n{}_t, Q_t, Sn_t, c^g{}_t, v_c, v^*{}_c, v_n, v_s) \tag{6.75}$$

$$\pi^n{}_t = \pi^n{}_t(w_t, Cu^n{}_t, Q_t, Sn_t, c^g{}_t, v_c, v^*{}_c, v_n, v_s) \tag{6.76}$$

$$g_{t+1} = g_{t+1}(p^c{}_t, w_{t+1}, p^n{}_t, w_t h_t N_t, \pi^n{}_t, Sn_t, Cu^h{}_t, p^{ch}{}_{t+1},$$

$$\pi^{nh}{}_{t+1}, Tx_t, k) \tag{6.77}$$

Given g_{t+1}, Tx_{t+1} is found from (6.18) and repeated here as (6.78):

$$Tx_{t+1} = Tx_{t+1}(Cu_t, Tx_t, w_t, p^c{}_t, g_t, w_{t+1}, p^{cg}{}_{t+1}, g_{t+1}) \tag{6.78}$$

Substituting (6.34) and (6.14) into (6.49) yields an expression for the actual number of privately produced goods, c_t, actually sold during the current period:

$$c_t = c_t(w_t,\ p^{cg}_t,\ g_t,\ p^c_t,\ w_{t+1},\ p^n_t,\ h^g{}_tN^g{}_t + h_tN^n{}_t,\ \pi^n{}_t,\ Sn_t,\ Cu^h{}_t,$$
$$p^{ch}{}_{t+1},\ \pi^{nh}{}_{t+1},\ Tx_t,\ k) \qquad (6.79)$$

while Sn_{t+1} is found by substituting (6.36) into (6.50) yielding:

$$Sn_{t+1} = Sn_{t+1}(p^c{}_t,\ w_{t+1},\ p^n{}_t,\ w_t\ (h_tN^g{}_t + h_tN^g{}_t),\ \pi^n{}_t,\ Sn_t,$$
$$Cu^h{}_t,\ p^{ch}{}_{t+1},\ \pi^{nh}{}_{t+1},\ Tx_t,\ k) \qquad (6.80)$$

Assuming $N^s{}_{t+1} \geq N^{gd}{}_{t+1} + N^{nd}{}_{t+1}$, then $N^{gd}{}_{t+1}$ and $N^{nd}{}_{t+1}$ are given respectively by (6.15) and (6.44), repeated here as (6.83) and (6.84):

$$N^g{}_{t+1} = N^{gd}{}_{t+1}(w_{t+1},\ p^{cg}{}_{t+1},\ g_{t+1}) \qquad (6.81)$$

$$N^n{}_{t+1} = N^{nd}{}_{t+1}(w_t,\ Q_t,\ Cu^n{}_t,\ Sn_t,\ c^g{}_t,\ v_c,\ v^*{}_c,\ v_n,\ v_s) \qquad (6.82)$$

The end-of-period level of inventories, Q_{t+1}, is given by:

$$Q_{t+1} = Q_t + q_t - c_t \qquad (6.83)$$

The household sector's end-of-period holdings of currency is found by substituting (6.35) into (6.55):

$$Cu^h{}_{t+1} = Cu^{hd}{}_{t+1}(p^c{}_t,\ w_{t+1},\ p^n{}_t,\ w_t(h^n{}_tN^n{}_t + h^g{}_tN^g{}_t),\ \pi^n{}_t,\ Sn_t,$$
$$Cu^h{}_t,\ p^{ch}{}_{t+1},\ \pi^{nh}{}_{t+1},\ Tx_t,\ k) \qquad (6.84)$$

The amount of fiat currency outstanding at the end of the period, $\hat{C}u_{t+1}$ is given by (6.57), which is repeated here as (6.85):

$$\hat{C}u_{t+1} = \hat{C}u_t + w_th^g{}_tN^g{}_t + p^c{}_tc_t - Tx_t \qquad (6.85)$$

From (6.62), the amount of currency held by the nonfinancial business sector at the end of the period is denoted by

$$Cu^n{}_{t+1} = Cu^* + \hat{C}u_{t+1} - Cu^h{}_{t+1} \qquad (6.86)$$

Finally, measured national income and product, Y_t, is:

$$Y_t = w_t h^g_t N^g_t + p^c_t q_t \tag{6.87}$$

What emerges is a system of eighteen equations, namely (6.70) - (6.87), in the variables h^g_t, h^n_t, w_{t+1}, $p^n_{\hat{t}}$, q_t, p^c_t, π^n_t, g_{t+1}, Tx_{t+1}, c_t, Sn_{t+1}, N^g_{t+1}, N^n_{t+1}, Q_{t+1}, Cu^h_{t+1}, $\hat{C}u_{t+1}$, Cu^n_{t+1} and Y_t. The unique features of this system include viewing the government's use of labor, the level of government production, and the stock of fiat currency as endogenous variables. Typically, these variables are left unexplained in macroecononomic analysis. In addition, wages and prices are announced by real economic agents in the above model.

In terms of current-period variables, the above system is recursive. In particulr although the current values of h^g_t, h^n_t, w_{t+1}, p^n_t, q_t, p^c_t and π^n_t depend upon the past values of a number of varibales as well as upon anticipated current or future values of a number of others, none of these seven variables depends upon observed values of any other current endogenous variable. This corresponds with our earlier assumption that the government sector first annonces h^g_t, c^g_t and the menu $Tx_{t+1}(.)$. Then based, among other things, upon its initial inventories and its estimatess of household activity in the commodity, labor and equity markets, the business sector announces the current period values of h^n_t, w_{t+1}, p^n_t, p^c_t and π^n_t (and decides q_t and N^{nd}_{t+1}). Armed with the information as to h^g_t, h^n_t w_{t+1}, p^n_t, p^c_t and π^n_t, the household sector then decides c^h_t, Cu^{hd}_{t+1}, Sn^{hd}_{t+1}, N^s_{t+1} and the optimal combination of g_{t+1} and Tx_{t+1} from the menu prepared for it by the government. Once p^c_t is announced, the government's current expenses are determined along with the amount of fiat currency that will be outstanding at the end of the period. Once g_{t+1} has been selected by the households, the government is ready to decide the number of people it will employ next period. The remaining items determined are the amount of currency which the business sector holds at the end of the period, the business sector's end of period inventory of commodities and national producct (and income).

The eighteen structural equations (6.70) - (6.87) may be linearized and written in compact form as:

$$Ay_t = By_{t-1} + Cz_t \tag{6.88}$$

where y_t represents the vector of endogenous variables and where z_t

represents a vector consisting of various expectations as well as the level of the exogneously determined stock of private money. The elements in A, B and C depend upon (a) various technical factors associated with the production of private and government produced goods, transactions costs and employer search (b) the coefficients of various estimated functions and (c) household sector's tastes and preferences. Assuming the coefficient matrices are constant over time, and premultiplying every term in (6.88) by the inverse of A yields the reduced form (6.89) which, upon successive iterations, leads to the final form, (6.90):

$$y_t = Py_{t-1} + Vz_t \tag{6.89}$$

$$y_t = P^t y_o + Vz_t + PVz_{t-1} + P^2Vz_{t-2} + \ldots + P^{t+1}Vz_1. \tag{6.90}$$

If the system is stable, P^t approaches the zero matrix as time progresses. Under these circumstances the time paths of the economic variables embodied in y_t are influenced by current and past values of the exogenously determined expectations as well as by the technical factors, the forecasting coefficients and the tastes and preferences underlying matrices A, B and C.

Some Implications of the Model

In contrast to the conventional approach to government-sector behavior summarized in Chapter 5, the households ultimately determine the volume of goods produced by the government in the present model. The government refrains from arbitrarily manipulating either expenditures or taxes. Instead, it attempts to produce at minimum cost the level of government-goods chosen by the households. As the analysis presented earlier in this chapter indicates, the household sector will tend to instruct the government to produce more government-goods as (a) household income and wealth increase, (b) privately-produced goods become relatively more expensive and (c) the government becomes more efficient by being able to lower taxes and still provide the same volume of government-produced goods.

Suppose, for instance, that the government discovers at time t a means of providing a given amount of government services next period using fewer factors of production. In other words, in the menu it prepares at time t for the household sector for next period, it requires lower taxes, Tx_{t+1}, than otherwise for each possible level of g_{t+1}. This improvement in government-sector efficiency, ceteris paribus, increases the household sector's anticipated disposable income for next period. The household sector will therefore plan to increase next period's consumption above what it would otherwise. This increase raises the marginal product of currency households plan to hold by the end of the period, which induces the household sector to raise its end-of-period demand for currency. In addition, as planned future consumption of private goods increases their marginal utility presumably falls relative to next-period's government-produced goods and current consumption of privately-produced goods. Consequently the household sector will tend to increase is demands for g_{t+1} and c_t.

But even though the selection of a higher level of g_{t+1}, ceteris paribus, causes the household sector to opt for a higher level of taxes next period, this new level of taxes will nevertheless still be lower than what they would have been if the improvement in government efficiency had not occured. Point A in Figure 6.7 presumably denotes the optimal level of g_{t+1} (and corresponding Tx_{t+1}) chosen by the household sector if the improved efficiency had not materialized. Point B denotes the higher g_{t+1} (but lower Tx_{t+1} than at A) chosen by the household sector in response to the improved efficiency.

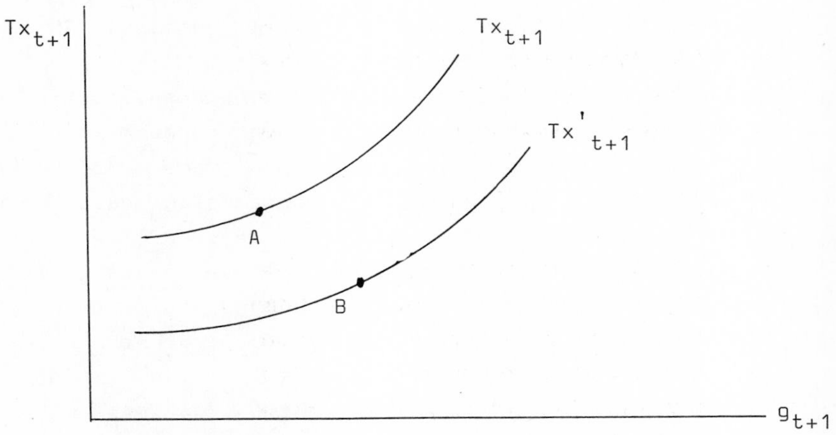

Figure 6.7 Effects of an Increase in Government Efficiency upon The Household Sector's Choice of Goverment-Produced Goods.

As mentioned, the reduced level of taxes in moving from A to B will be used by the household sector not only to buy more privately produced goods next period but also to buy more privately-produced goods in the current period. But since current-period disposable income remains unaffected, ceteris paribus, the household sector must plan to save less during the current period in order to finance the increase in its current consumption. Since the household sector plans to save more via currency accumulation this period to build its end-of-period balances and thereby reduce next period's transactions costs associated with next period's added consumption, it must plan to save less this period via equity-share accumulation.

The effects of the above adjustments upon (a) current-period production, (b) current-period product price, (c) the average number of hours worked by employees this period, (d) the business sector's demand for workers for next period and (e) the wage rate announced for next period all depend upon the business sector's expectations at time t. For instance, if the business sector at time t does not foresee the effect of an improvement in government efficiency upon the current-period demand for privately-produced goods,it will not alter any of the items listed in the preceding sentence. Therefore, if the business sector had otherwise correctly estimated the current-period demand for its product, it will find by time t+1 that its inventory of goods is lower than it anticipated it would be. At time t+1 in this case the business sector will have to decide whether the unanticipated increase in sales was an anomoly or whether it will continue into the future.

On the other hand, suppose at time t the business sector does correctly anticipate the effect of the gain in government efficiency upon the demand for its product. In this case, the business sector's estimate of the current-period demand for consumption goods rises, causing the sector to raise not only the current price of its product, but also current production and current average labor hours. If the sector also foresees at time t the increased demand for its product next period, it will also increase its demand for workers for next period.

But, in spite of the increase in its demand for workers for next period, the business sector may lower or at least leave unchanged the wage rate it announces for next peiod. For the increased government efficiency may be labor-saving. If the business sector estimates that the government's demand for labor will be less than otherwise after the gain in efficiency, the business sector may feel it will be able to hire the additional workers it wants for next period without adjusting (or, possibly, even though it reduces) the money wage it announces for next period.

If the business sector does raise the current-period price of its product,the government will have to pay more during the current period to buy the same number of consumption goods. As its ex post budget constraint indicates, the government will therefore have to issue more currency by the end of the current period than it would have otherwise. Consequently, it is possible that current government spending, current-period prices, the stock of money, private production and employment all grow together endogenously. This stands in sharp contrast to conventional models that attribute movements in production and/or prices to exogenous movements in government spending or the stock of money.

Parenthetically this example also highlights a difficulty in measuring the contribution of the government sector to national product in terms of factor cost. For in this example, the improvement in government efficiency may result in the government needing less labor even though it provides the households with more government-produced goods. The fall in the government's wage bill translates into a reduction in the value of goverment production under the standard measure of national product even though more goods are being produced by both the government and private sectors.

In the simple model presented in this chapter, endogenous changes in the stock of money arise only through unbalanced government budgets. In the extended model, to be developed in Chapters 7-12, the stock of money is ultimately determined by the interactions of the households, the nonfinancial businesses, the government, the central bank and the private depository institutions. Each of the household, government and nonfinancial business sectors select their respective holdings of checkable deposits at private depository institutions in light of the interest rates announced by these institutions. Households may also decide to hold currency rather than checkable deposits. Therefore, both the composition and the quantity of money are influenced by private-sector choices.

The function of the central bank in the extended model is to provide a flexible monetary base which is responsive to the needs of the rest of the economy. The central bank does not arbitrarly manipulate the quantity of high-powered money through open-market operations. Nor does it manipulate the required reserve ratio to influence the level of excess reserves. Instead, it stands ready to lend freely at the discount rate it announces. Therefore the private sector also utlitmately determines both the level and composition of high-powered money in the extended model.

What emerges from Chapter 7-12, then, is a model of aggregate economic choice for a closed economy in which wages, prices, interest rates, all government activity and all monetary aggregates are determined endogenously within a single unified framework.

References

Anderson, W.H.L., 1979, National Income Theory and Its Price Theoretic Foundations (McGraw-Hill, New York).

Atkinson, A. and J. Stiglitz, 1980, Lectures on Public Economics (McGraw-Hill, New York).

Blatt, J. M., 1983, Dynamic Economic Systems (M.E. Sharpe, Inc., New York).

Brunner, K., A. Cukierman and A. Meltzer, 1983, Money and Economic Activity, Inventories and Business Cycles, Journal of Monetary Economics, May, 281-319.

Chow, G.C., 1983, Econometrics (McGraw-Hill, New York).

Fair, R., 1974, A Model of Macroeconomic Activity, Vol. 1: The Theoretical Model (Ballinger, Cambridge).

Foley, D. and M. Sidruski, 1971, Monetary and Fiscal Policy in a Growing Economy (Macmillan, New York).

Grandmont, J., 1977, Temporary General Equilibrium Theory, Econometrica 45, 535-573.

Grossman, H. and R . Lucas, 1974, The Macro-Economic Effects of Productive Public Expenditures, The Manchester School 42, 162-170.

Hahn,F., 1978, On Non-Walrasian Equilibria, Review of Economic Studies 45, 1-17.

Iwai,K., 1981, Disequilibrium Dynamics, Cowles Foundation Monograph 27 (Yale University Press, New Haven).

Nagatani, K., 1981, Macroeconomic Dynamics (Cambridge University Press, Cambridge).

Negishi, T., 1979, Microeconomic Foundations of Keynesian Macroeconomics (North Holland, New York).

Samuelson, P., 1954, The Pure Theory of Public Expenditures, Review of Economics and Statistics, 387-89

________, 1955, Diagrammatic Expositioion of a Theory of Public Expenditure, Review of Economics and Statistics, 350-356.

________, 1958, Aspects of Public Expenditure Theories, Review of Economiics and Statistics, 332-338.

________, 1969, Pure Theory of Public Expenditures and Taxation in J. Margolis and H. Guitton (eds.) Public Economics (Macmillan, New York).

Sargent, T., 1979, Macroeconomic Theory (Academic Press, New York).

Saving, T. R., 1971, Transactions Costs and the Demand for Money, American Economic Review, June, 4077-420.

Siven, C., 1979, A Study in the Theory of Inflation and Unemployment (North Holland, New York).

Sweeney, R. J., 1974, A Macro Theory with Micro Fondations (South-Western Publishing, Cincinnati).

Tobin, J., 1969, A General Equilibrium Approach to Monetary Theory, Journal of Money Credit and Banking, Feb., 15-29.

________, 1982, Money and Finance in the Macroeconomic Process, Nobel Lecture printed in: Journal of Money, Credit and Banking 14, May, 171-204.

Turnovsky, S., 1977, Macroeconomic Analysis and Stabilization Policy (Cambridge University Press, Cambridge).

Weintraub, E.R., 1979, Microfoundations: The Compatibility of Micro-economics and Macroeconomics (Cambridge University Press, Cambridge).

7. - The Government Sector in the Expanded Model

Introduction

As discussed in Chapter 2, the expanded model, which we begin to develop in the present chapter, contains two new sectors (depository institutions and a central bank) in addition to the three sectors contained in Chapter 6. Before specifying the behavior of these new sectors in Chapters 10 and 11, the present chapter and the next two are devoted to reformulating respectively the behavior of the government, household and nonfinancial business sectors within the context of the expanded framework. The model present in Chapter 6 contained only three markets (labor, consumption goods and equity shares issued by the nonfinancial business sector) which together simultaneously constitutes a market for currency. The model developed in this and the next four chapters contains markets for labor, consumption goods, capital goods, bonds, personal loans, checkable deposits, advances from the central bank, equity shares issued by the nonfinancial business sector and equity shares issued by the private depository insitutions. Together these nine markets simultaneously constitute a market for high-powered money (consisting of currency held outside the central bank and the private depository institutions plus the reserves of the private depository institutions).

In the expanded model the government participates in markets for privately-produced consumption goods, privately-produced capital goods, labor, bonds and checkable deposits. The government presumably makes all its expeditures from and places all its receipts in checkable deposits at private depository institutions. (In the United States, the federal government transfers funds from its accounts at private depository institutions to the central bank prior to making payments to the private sector. These temporary transfers are ignored in the present study.) It holds no currency at the beginning of the current period nor does it plan to hold any currency by the end of either the current or next periods. Unlike the simple model, the central bank is responsible for issuing currency to the private sector in the expanded model. How it does so will be discussed in Chapters 10 and 11.

The number of people who have been hired by the government to work during the current period, N^g_t is known at time t. But the number of hours they will work this period, h^g_t, must be decided by the government at time t. The government will combine labor with the services of privately-produced consumption goods, which it purchases this period, to produce and distribute "free of charge" goods and services, g_t, to the household sector during the period.

In the expanded model, the government requires the services of labor not only to provide government-produced goods and services for the household sector but also to purchase labor and privately-produced consumption goods. Its beginning-of-period balances of checkable deposits at depository institutions presumably help to conserve the amount of labor time associated with these transactions. Consequently, because of their ability to conserve transactions time, governmental checkable deposits represent a productive resource similar to privately-held money balances.

Since current tax revenues were selected by the household sector last period, current government expenses incurred in producing this period's previously determined level of government-produced goods and services may exceed or fall short of these taxes. In this expanded model, the government is free to borrow (or retire outstanding debt) in the bond market during the current period to finance its deficits (or surpluses). However, just as in the simple framework, it must formulate its plans at time t as if it were going to sell all its assets and retire all its liabilities by the end of next period.

Formal Model of Government Activity

The government's balance sheet at the beginnig of the current period is taken as given; the sector is constrained at time t to plan a balance sheet for that moment which corresponds exactly to the existing one. Its existing balance sheet contains two assets and one liability. Let $D^g{}_t$ represent the government's volume of checkable deposits at private institutions, $K^g{}_t$ the number of units of physical capital held by the government and $B^g{}_t$ the number of government bonds outstanding at time t. All bonds issued by the government presumably mature one period later. Therefore no market will exist during the current period for $B^g{}_t$. Assume each bond pays a total of $1 in principal and interest during the maturity period. Assume also that the bonds issued by the government last period sold at price $p^b{}_{t-1}$. Then, at time t the government faces an outstanding liability, in dollars, equal to $p^b{}_{t-1}B^g{}_t$. During the current period the government will also incur ($1 - p^b_{t-1})B^g_t dollars as interest expense. Assuming that p^{kg}_t represents the current-period price of capital anticipated by the government at time t, the government's balance sheet at time t may be represented as:

Government's Balance Sheet at Time t

Assets	Liabilities
D^g_t	$p^b_{t-1}B^g_t$
$p^{kg}_t K^g_t$	
	Net Wealth
	NW^g_t

Although its existing balance sheet represents an effective constraint, the government is free at time t to plan a new balance sheet for the end of the current period. Let D^{gd}_{t+1}, K^{gd}_{t+1} and B^{gs}_{t+1} respectively represent the planned volume of government-held checkable deposits, the planned level of government-owned physical capital and the planned number of government bonds outstanding for the end of the current period. Let p_t^{bg} represent the current-period price of bonds anticipated by the government at time t. Then in terms of anticipated current period prices the balance sheet the government plans at time t for time t+1 appears as follows:

Government's Planned Balance Sheet at Time t+1

Assets	Liabilities
D^{gd}_{t+1}	$p^{bg}_t B^{gs}_{t+1}$
$p^{kg}_t K^{gd}_{t+1}$	
	Net Wealth
	NW^g_{t+1}

When tradeable assets and liabilities in both the beginning of-period and planned end-of-period balance sheets are valued in terms of the prices at which they can be traded (or in terms of the prices at which the sector anticipates they can be traded) during the current period, then the planned increment to net wealth, $NW^g_{t+1}-NW^g_t$, between the beginning and the end of the period must agree with the government's planned saving on the income account in the current period. In other words, government saving on the income account is both necessary and sufficient for adding to governmental wealth during the period. The reason is two-fold. First, when measured in terms of the prices at which the government anticipates they can be traded during the period, any planned net additions to assets minus liabilities during the period must be finanaced by an equal amount of saving on the income account. Second, every dollar saved on the current account will take some tangible form, i.e. it will amount to the net accumulation of some asset or to the net retirement of some liability of equal value during the period.

At time t the government anticipates receiving revenue from three separate sources during the current period. Let Tx_t denote the level of taxes which the households collectively agreed last period to pay during the current period. Let π^{cg}_t represent the income which the government anticipates the central bank will earn during the current period and distribute to the government. And let $r^d_{t-1}D^g_t$ represent the interest income which the government will earn during the current period on checkable deposits it holds at time t. Assume that checkable deposits accumulated between time t and time t+1 will not begin to pay interest until next period. The symbol r^d_{t-1} represents the interest rate which depository institutions announced last period that they will pay this period on all deposits held at time t. Then the government's anticipated current revenue is denoted by $Tx_t + \pi^{cg}_t + r^d_{t-1}D^g_t$.

As mentioned above, the government's current interest expense is denoted by $(\$1 - p^b_{t-1})B^g_t$. Its other expenses on the income account consist of its current wage bill, $w_t h^g_t N^g_t$, and its anticipated purchases of consumption goods (in dollars), $p^{cg}_t c^g_t$, from the private nonfinancial business sector. Symbol w_t denotes the money wage which the nonfinancial sector announced last period it will pay this period, h^g_t depicts the average number of hours the government plans to use the people whom it has employed, N^g_t, by time t to work this period. Symbol p^{cg}_t represents the price of consumption goods which the government anticipates that the nonfinancial business sector will announce this period and c^g_t

represents the physical number of consumption goods the government plans to buy this period. Anticipated current government saving, s^g_t, defined as anticipated current revenue less current expenses, is therefore shown by (7.1)

$$s^g_t = Tx_t + \pi^{cg}_t + r^d_{t-1} D^g_t - (\$1 - p^b_{t-1}) B^g_t - p^{cg}_t c^g_t - w_t h^g_t N^g_t \qquad (7.1)$$

The dollar value of current government saving displayed by (7.1) must agree with the planned accumulation of net wealth between time t and t+1. In particular, as it formulates its plans at time t, the government is constrained by the following:

$$Tx_t + \pi^{cg}_t + r^d_{t-1} D^g_t - (\$1 - p^b_{t-1}) B^g_t - p^{cg}_t c^g_t - w_t h^g_t N^g_t$$

$$= (D^g_{t+1} - D^g_t) + p^{kg}_t (K^g_{t+1} - K^g_t) \qquad (7.2)$$

$$- p^{bg}_t B^g_{t+1} p^b_{t-1} B^g_t$$

or

$$Tx_t + \pi^{cg}_t + r^d_{t-1} D^g_t - \$1.B^g_t - p^{cg}_t c^g_t - w_t h^g_t N^g_t$$

$$= (D^g_{t+1} - D^g_t) + p^{kg}_t (K^g_t - K^g_t) - p^{bg}_t B^g_{t+1} \qquad (7.3)$$

The significance of (7.3) is that the government can independently select only four of the variables c^g_t, h^g_t, D^{gd}_{t+1}, K^{gd}_{t+1} and B^{gs}_{t+1}.

Let Tx_{t+1} represent next period's tax revenue, let π^{cg}_{t+1} denote next period's anticipated income from the central bank's operations and let r^{dg}_t represent the interest rate which the government anticipates at time t that the private depository institutions will announce this period (that they will pay next period on checkable deposits held at time t+1). Then the government's anticipated revenue for next period is denoted by $Tx_{t+1} + \pi^{cg}_{t+1} + r^{dg}_t D^{gd}_{t+1}$.

Let N^{gd}_{t+1} represent the number of people that the government plans to employ next period for the standard h hours. Let w^g_{t+1} denote the hourly money wage which the government anticipates that the private nonfinancial business sector will announce this period that it will pay next period. Then at time t, the government's anticipated wage bill for next period is denoted by $w^g_{t+1} h N^{gd}_{t+1}$. Let p^{cg}_{t+1} represent the price of consumption goods which the government anticipates will be announced next period. Then its anticipated expenditures on consumption goods may be denoted by $p^{cg}_{t+1}c^{g}_{t+1}$ where c^{g}_{t+1} depicts the number of those goods the government anticipates it will buy next period. Since p_t^{bg} represents the current anticipated market price of bonds, $(\$1 - p^{bg}_{t})B^{g}_{t+1}$ denotes the interest expense that the government plans at time t to incur next period. Therefore, the amount, s^{g}_{t+1}, which the government plans at time t to save next period is given by (7.4):

$$s^{g}_{t+1}=Tx_{t+1}+ \pi^{cg}_{t+1}+r^{dg}_{t}D^{gd}_{t+1}-w^{g}_{t+1}hN^{gd}_{t+1}$$

$$-p^{cg}_{t+1}c^{g}_{t+1}-(\$1-p^{bg}_{t})B^{gs}_{t+1} \qquad (7.4)$$

The amount that the government plans to save on the income account next period must agree with its plans to accumulate net wealth on the capital account next period. At time t, the anticipated values of the government's checkable deposits and physical capital for time t+1 are denoted respectively by D^{gd}_{t+1} and $p^{kg}_{t+1}K^{gd}_{t+1}$, where p^{kg}_{t+1} represents the price of physical capital which the government anticipates will be announced next period. At time t the govenment also anticipates its outstanding bond indebtedness at time t+1 will equal $p^{bg}_{t}{}^{gs}_{t+1}$. Therefore, at time t, the government anticipates a net wealth at time t+1 equal to $D^{gd}_{t+1} + p^{kg}_{t+1}K^{gd}_{t+1} - p_t^{bg}B^{gs}_{t+1}$. Because the government is precluded from planning beyond the community's time horizon, we stipulate that it plans to hold no assets and to have no liabilities outstanding by time t+2). Therefore at time t its anticipated accumulation of net wealth during next period is shown by $0 - (D^{gd}_{t+1}+p^{kg}_{t+1}K^{gd}_{t+1}-p_t^{bg}B^{gs}_{t+1})$. Therefore, as it formulates its plans at time t, the government's next-period budget constraint appears as:

$$s^{g}_{t+1} = p^{bg}_{t+1}B^{gs}_{t+1} - D^{gd}_{t+1} - p^{kd}_{t+1}K^{gd}_{t+1} \qquad (7.5)$$

or

$$Tx_{t+1}+ \pi^{cg}_{t+1}+r^{dg}_{t} D^{gd}_{t+1}-w^{g}_{t+1}hN^{gd}_{t+1}-p^{cg}_{t+1}c^{g}_{t+1}-\$1.B^{gs}_{t+1} \qquad (7.6)$$

$$= -D^{gd}_{t+1} - p^{kg}_{t+1}K^{gd}_{t+1}$$

At time t the government prepares a menu of government-produced goods, g_{t+1}, and corresponding taxes, Tx_{t+1}, for next period. As it prepares this menu, the government attempts to minimize the level of Tx_{t+1} associated with any given g_{t+1}. Among other things, this involves producing the previously determined level of current goods and services, g_t, as efficiently as possible. Once the household sector selects its optimal combination of g_{t+1} and Tx_{t+1}, the government then decides the number of people it wants to hire for next period and the quantity of physical capital it wants to hold by the beginning of that period in order to produce g_{t+1}.

As mentioned above, the government employs labor during the current period for two purposes. First, it combines labor and privately-produced consumption goods with physical capital to produce government-produced goods and services which it distributes "free of charge" to the households. Second, it uses some labor to engage in transactions with the other sectors of the economy. In particular, assume that the government needs additional labor to purchase the labor and privately-produced consumption goods that it uses in the production of the government-produced goods. Suppose $\alpha(.)$ represents the amount of labor time which the government sector must devote to transactions during the current period. Then $h^g_t N^g_t - \alpha(.)$ denotes the portion of the government's current-period labor time which is available for producting the government-produced goods and services, g_t, for the households.

In a manner consistent with our earlier treatment of private transactions time, assume that $\alpha(.)$ is a positive strictly-convex function that increases with the government's purchases of labor, $h^g_t N^g_t$, and privately-produced goods, c^g_t, but decreases with the government's beginning-of-period "real" holdings of checkable deposits. In particular, suppose $\alpha(.)$ takes the following specification:

$$\alpha(.) = \alpha(h^g_t N^g_t,\ c^g_t,\ D^g_t,\ w_t,\ p^{cg}_t) \qquad (7.7)$$

with $\alpha(.)$, α_1, α_2, α_4, $\alpha_5 > 0$; $\alpha_3 < 0$; $\alpha ii > 0$ for $i=1,...,5$; $\alpha_{ij} > 0$ for all i, j = 3; $\alpha_{i3} = \alpha_{3i} < 0$ for all $i \neq 3$.

According to (7.7), a ceteris paribus increase in $h^g_t N^g_t$ or c^g_t increases current transactions time at an increasing rate while a ceteris paribus increase in D_t^d reduces current transactions time at a decreasing (absolute) rate. In addition for given current-period levels of labor hours, privately-produced consumption goods, and beginning-of-period checkable deposits, an increase in w_t or p^{cg}_t increases current-period transactons time because it reduces the purchasing power of the government's checkable deposits held at time t.

Assume that the current production function, $\hat{g}(.)$, for government-produced goods and services, g_t, is a positive, increasing, strictly concave function of current labor time devoted to that production, $h^g{}_tN^g{}_t - \alpha(.)$, the quantity of privately-produced consumption goods purchased from the private nonfinancial business sector, $c^g{}_t$, and the quantity of physical capital, $K^g{}_t$, with which the government begins the current period:

$$g_t = \hat{g}(h^g{}_tN^g{}_t - \alpha(h^g{}_tN^g{}_t,\ c^g{}_t,\ D^g{}_t,\ w_t,\ p^{cg}{}_t),\ c^g{}_t,\ K^g{}_t) \qquad (7.8)$$

or:

$$g_t = g(h^g{}_tN^g{}_t,\ c^g{}_t,\ D^g{}_t,\ K^g{}_t,\ w_t,\ p^{cg}{}_t) \qquad (7.9)$$

where g(.) is assumed to be a strictly-concave, positive function with $g_i > 0$ for i=1, ..., 4 but $g_i < 0$ for i=5, 6. Since all other variables are taken as given by the government at time t, the only choice variables appearing in (7.9) are $h^g{}_t$ and $c^g{}_t$.

Analogously, let $\beta(.)$ depict the amount of time the government anticipates at time t that it will spend undertaking transactions next period. Presumably this transactions time (a) increases at an increasing rate as next period's total labor time, $hN^g{}_{t+1}$, rises; (b) increases at an increasing rate as next period's purchases of privately-produced consumption goods, $c^g{}_{t+1}$, rises; and (c) decreases at a decreasing rate as (the purchasing power of) next period's beginning-of-period checkable deposits, $D^g{}_{t+1}$, rises. In particular, assume that next period's transactions time is given according to the following function:

$$\beta(.) = \beta(hN^g{}_{t+1}, c^g{}_{t+1},\ D^g{}_{t+1},\ w^g{}_{t+1},\ p^{cg}{}_{t+1}) \qquad (7.10)$$

where $w^g{}_{t+1}$ represents the money wage which the government anticipates will prevail next period and where $p^{cg}{}_{t+1}$ denotes the price of privately-produced consumption goods which the government anticipates for next period. Also, let $\beta(.)$, $\beta_i > 0$, $i \neq 3$; $\beta_3 < 0$; $\beta_{ii} > 0$ for all i, $\beta_{ij} > 0$ for all i, $j \neq 3$; and $\beta_{3i} = \beta_{i3} < 0$ for $i \neq 3$. The amount of labor time available for the production of government produced goods next period is given by $hN^g{}_{t+1} - \beta(.)$.

Let next period's production function, $g^+(.)$, for government produced goods, g_{t+1}, be a positive, increasing strictly concave function of next period's available labor, $hN^g{}_{t+1} - \beta(.)$, the quantity of privately-produced consumption goods, c^g_{t+1}, which the government plans to purchase next period, and the stock of physical capital, K^g_{t+1}, which the government plans to hold at the beginning of next period:

$$g_{t+1}=g^+(hN^g_{t+1}-\ \beta(hN^g_{t+1},c^g_{t+1},D^g_{t+1},w^g_{t+1},p^{cg}_{t+1}),c^g_{t+1},K^g_{t+1}) \quad (7.11)$$

$$\text{or:}\quad g_{t+1} = g^*\ (hN^g_{t+1},c^g_{t+1},\ K^g_{t+1},\ D^g_{t+1},\ w^g_{t+1},\ p^{cg}_{t+1}), \quad (7.12)$$

where $g^*_1 = g^+_1(1-\beta_1)$ $\qquad g^*_4 = -g^+_1\ \beta_3 > 0$

$g^*_2 = g^+_2-g^+_1\beta_2$ $\qquad g^*_5 = -g^+_1\ \beta_4 < 0$

$g^*_3 = g^+_3 > 0$ $\qquad g^*_6 = -g^+_1\ \beta_5 < 0$

Assume that the marginal products of labor and consumption goods net of the transactions costs associated with their purchase are positive so that g^*_1 and g^*_2 are both positive. Given that $g^+(.)$ is strictly concave, so is $g^*(.)$.

At time t the government's objective is to find for each possible value of future government production, g_{t+1}, the minimum level of taxes, Tx_{t+1}, it must collect next period in order to finance that production. As it calculates the minimum tax, the government is constrained by expressions (7.3), (7.6), (7.9) and (7.12). From condition (7.6), we see that the government is able at time t to reduce next period's tax burden by one dollar for each dollar reduction in the number of bonds it plans to have outstanding at the end of the current period. Therefore, from condition (7.3), a necessary condition for minimizing next period's taxes is that the government minimize the cost of producing the predetermined level of current government-produced goods, g_t.

Solving equation (7.3) for B^g_{t+1} and substituting the result into (7.6) yields the following expression for Tx_{t+1}:

$$\begin{aligned} Tx_{t+1} = {} & p^{cg}_{t+1}\cdot c^g_{t+1}+w^g_{t+1}hN^g_{t+1}-(1+r^{dg}_t)D^g_{t+1} \\ & - \pi^{cb}_{t+1} - p^{kg}_{t+1}K^g_{t+1} \\ & + (\$1/p^{bg}_t)(D^g_{t+1} - D^g_t)+(p^{kg}_t/p^{bg}_t)(K^g_{t+1} - K^g_t) \\ & + (\$1/p^{bg}_t)(\$1.B^g_t+p^{cg}_t c^g_t+w_t h^g_t N^g_t-Tx_t-\pi^{cg}_t-r^d_{t-1}D^g_t) \end{aligned} \quad (7.13)$$

Let the next period's interest payment, $\$1+p^{bg}_{t}$, expressed as a percentage of the current anticipated bond price, p^{bg}_{t}, be denoted by r^{b}_{t}. Then $\$1/p^{bg}_{t}$ in equation (7.13) represents the "capitalization" factor, $1+r^{b}_{t}$.

The objective of the government at time t is to generate a menu for the household sector showing for each level of g_{t+1} the corresponding minimum level of Tx_{t+1}. In other words, the government's objective is to find for each possible g_{t+1}, the corresponding minimum Tx_{t+1} subject to the production functions (7.9) and (7.12). In terms of a Lagrangian function, the objective is to minimize (7.14) with respect to the choice variables c^{g}_{t}, h^{g}_{t}, c^{g}_{t+1}, N^{g}_{t+1}, K^{g}_{t+1}, and D^{g}_{t+1} with g_{t+1} serving as a parameter:

$$\begin{aligned}
Tx_{t+1} = {} & p^{cg}_{t+1}c^{b}_{t+1}+w^{g}_{t+1}hN^{g}_{t+1}-(1 + r^{dg}_{t})D^{g}_{t+1} \\
& - \pi^{cg}_{t+1}-p^{kg}_{t+1}K^{g}_{t+1} \qquad (7.14) \\
& + (\$1/p^{bg}_{t}) \cdot (D^{g}_{t+1} - D^{g}_{t})+(p^{kg}_{t}/p^{bg}_{t})(K^{g}_{t+1} - K^{g}_{t}) \\
& + (\$1/p^{bg}_{t})(\$1.B^{g}_{t}+p^{cg}_{t}c^{g}_{t}+w_{t}h^{g}_{t}N^{g}_{t}-Tx_{t}-\pi^{cg}_{t}-r^{d}_{t-1}D^{g}_{t}) \\
& + \lambda_{1}[g_{t} - g(h^{g}_{t}N^{g}_{t}, c^{g}_{t}, D^{g}_{t}, K^{g}_{t}, w_{t}, p^{cg}_{t})] \\
& + \lambda_{2}[g_{t+1}- g^{*}(h^{g}_{t}N^{g}_{t+1}, c^{g}_{t+1}, K^{g}_{t+1}, D^{g}_{t+1}, w^{g}_{t+1}, \\
& \quad p^{cg}_{t+1})]
\end{aligned}$$

For an interior solution with the government constrained by its production functions, it is necessary that the following "first-order" conditions hold:

$$\frac{\partial Tx_{t+1}}{\partial h^{g}_{t}} \equiv (\$1/p^{bg}_{t})w_{t}N^{g}_{t} - \lambda_{1}g_{1}N^{g}_{t} = 0 \qquad (7.15)$$

$$\frac{\partial Tx_{t+1}}{\partial c^{g}_{t}} \equiv (\$1/p^{bg}_{t})p^{cg}_{t} - \lambda_{1}g_{2} = 0 \qquad (7.16)$$

$$g_{t} - g(h^{g}_{t}N^{g}_{t}, c^{g}_{t}, D^{g}_{t}, K^{g}_{t}, w_{t}, p^{cg}_{t}) = 0 \qquad (7.17)$$

$$\frac{\partial Tx_{t+1}}{\partial N^{g}_{t+1}} \equiv w^{g}_{t+1}h_{t} - \lambda_{2}g^{*}_{1}h = 0 \qquad (7.18)$$

$$\frac{\partial Tx_{t+1}}{\partial c^g_{t+1}} \equiv p^{cg}_{t+1} - \lambda_2 g^*_2 = 0 \qquad (7.19)$$

$$\frac{\partial Tx_{t+1}}{\partial K^g_{t+1}} \equiv (p^{kg}_t/p^{bg}_t) - p^{kg}_{t+1} - \lambda_2 g^*_3 = 0 \qquad (7.20)$$

$$\frac{\partial Tx_{t+1}}{\partial D^g_{t+1}} \equiv (\$1/p^{bg}_t) - (1+r^{dg}_t) - \lambda_2 g^*_4 = 0 \qquad (7.21)$$

$$g_{t+1} - g^*(hN^g_{t+1},\ c^g_{t+1},\ K^g_{t+1},\ D^g_{t+1},\ w^g_{t+1},\ p^{cg}_{t+1}) = 0 \qquad (7.22)$$

The term $g_1N^g_t$ in equation (7.15) represents the marginal physical product of an hour of labor time net of the marginal product sacrificed due to the transactions time involved in purchasing that unit of labor time. Since the price of an hour of labor is postive and since the Lagrange multiplier, λ_1, is also positive, condition (7.15) stipulates that the government will use labor in the current period only if its net marginal physical product is positive.

The term g_2 in equation (7.16) represents the marginal physical product of a unit of privately produced consumption goods net of the marginal product of labor that is sacrificed due to the transactions time involved in purchasing that unit of consumption goods from the private business sector. Since λ_1 is positive and since the current price of privately produced consumption goods is also anticipated to be positive, condition (7.16) requires that the government continue to purchase consumption goods only if its net marginal product is positive.

Dividing (7.15) by (7.16) yields the condition that the government combine labor hours and privately produced commodities in the current period so that the rate of technical substitution between these two factors, $g_1N^g_t/g_2$, equals the market rate of substitution, $w_tN^g_t/p^{cg}_t$.

In equation (7.18) g^*_1 represents the anticipated net marginal product of an additional worker (who is expected to work the standard h hours) next period while the term g^*_2 in (7.19) denotes the net marginal physical product of privately-produced commodities next period. Just as in the current period, both of these net marginal products must be positive.

The term g^*_3 in (7.20) depicts the extra output the government can produce next period by adding one unit to its stock of physical capital by the beginning of that period. The difference $(p_t^{kg}/p_t^{bg}) - p^{kg}_{t+1}$

in that expression represents what is commonly referred to as the user cost of capital. As mentioned above, in terms of the anticipated interest rate in the bond market, r^{bg}_t, the term $(\$1/p^{bg}_t$ may be represented as $1 + r^{gb}$. Consequently the above difference may be written as $r^{bg}_t p^{kg}_t - (p^{kg}_{t+1} - p^{kg}_t)$. This last expression represents the user cost of capital in discrete time if physical depreciation is ignored. The following analysis is based upon the assumption of a positive user cost of capital.

In (7.21) the term g^*_4 represents the anticipated marginal physical product of a dollar of governmental deposits held at depository insitutions by the end of the current period. In particular a one dollar increase in those deposits will reduce next period's transactions time and will thereby release labor time for the production of goods to be distributed to the household sector. Therefore by raising D^g_{t+1} one dollar, the government expects to be able to increase its output of government produced goods next period by g^*_4. The difference $(\$1/p^{bg}_t)-(1+r^{dg}_t)$ in (7.21) represents the opportunity cost to the government of holding a dollar of deposits at time t+1 rather than using that dollar to reduce the government's outstanding bonds. In particular, this difference amounts to $r^{bg}_t - r^{dg}_t$, the anticipated difference in interest rates between bonds and checkable deposits. As long as this difference is positive, equation (7.21) stipulates that the marginal product of governmental deposits must also be positive.

Together equations (7.18)-(7.21) may be viewed as producing six conditions equating the rates of technical substitution between any two of the factors N^g_{t+1}, c^g_{t+1}, K^g_{t+1} and D^g_{t+1} to their respective market rates of substitution.

Finally, conditions (7.17) and (7.22) merely restate the fact that the government must formulate its plans in a manner consistent with the production functions for g_t and g_{t+1}.

Just as in the simple model discussed above, the system of first-order conditions may be separated into two sub-systems, both of which are necessary for the minimization of Tx_{t+1}. In particular, equations (7.15)-(7.17) constitute a system in the unknown h^g_t, c^g_t and λ_1 while equations (7.18)-(7.22) form a separate system in the unknowns N^g_{t+1}, c^g_{t+1}, K^g_{t+1}, D^g_{t+1} and λ_2.

<u>The Government's Demand Functions for Current Labor Services and Current Consumption Goods.</u>

In this expanded model the government's demand for h^g_t depends upon six parameters while its demand for c^g_t depends upon five:

$$h^g_t = h^g_t(\underset{-}{N^g_t}, \underset{-}{w_t}, \underset{+}{p^{cg}_t}, \underset{+}{g_t}, \underset{-}{K^g_t}, \underset{-}{D^g_t}) \tag{7.23}$$

$$c^g_t = c^g_t(\underset{+}{w_t}, \underset{-}{p^{cg}_t}, \underset{+}{g_t}, \underset{-}{K^g_t}, \underset{-}{D^g_t}) \tag{7.24}$$

Just as in the simple model, the greater the number of workers at the beginning of the current period, ceteris paribus, the smaller the average number of hours they will be used to produce the predetermined level of g_t. The proportionate reduction in h^g_t arises from the simplifying assumption that current production depends on total labor hours but not the composition of those hours in terms of number of people and the average number of hours they work. Since the total number of hours remains unchanged in this model as N^g_t rises, the quantity of c^g_t the government uses to produce g_t also remains unchanged.

Just as in the simple model, the greater g_t happens to be, ceteris paribus, the greater the amounts of h^g_t and c^g_t the government will demand in order to produce g_t.

The effects of changes in p^{cg}_t and w_t are more complicated than in the simple model due to the presence of transactions time. Consider, first, and increase in p^{cg}_t. Just as in the simple model, this increase makes privately produced goods more expensive relative to labor, causing the government to tend to substitute the latter for the former in producing a given level of g_t. But there are other effects as well. In particular as p^{cg}_t rises, the purchasing power of nominal money balances falls causing the government to have to devote more labor time in order to complete a given volume of transactions (and therefore less time to producing goods and services) than it did before the increase in p^{cg}_t. In effect, the rise in p^{cg}_t reduces the amount of labor available to produce the given g_t, causing the government to increase its demands for both h^g_t and c^g_t. But this is not all. For as the purchasing power of government deposits falls in response to the rise in p^{cg}_t, the net marginal products of both h^g_t and c^g_t are also affected. In particular as $h^g_t N^g_t - \alpha(.)$ falls in response to the rise in p^{cg}_t, the marginal product of labor, $\hat{g}_1$, used in the production of

g_t rises. But as $\hat{g}_1$ rises, the net marginal product of c^g_t, $g_2 = \hat{g}_2 - \hat{g}_1 \alpha_2$, falls. Both of these last two effects cause the government to increase h^g_t but to reduce the amount of c^g_t it uses to produce the given amount of g_t. The net effect of an increase in p^{cg}_t upon c^g_t is negative provided the substitution effect mentioned at the beginning of this paragraph and these last two effects more than offset the second effect. In any case, the net effect of an increase in p_t^{cg} upon h^g_t is positive.

An increase in w_t produces effects similar to those associated with a change in p^{cg}_t. In particular, by making h^g_t more expensive relative to c^g_t, it induces the government to increase its use of the latter and to reduce its use of the former. But the rise in w_t also reduces the purchasing power of nominal money, causing $h^g_t N^g_t - \alpha(.)$ to fall thereby effectively reducing the amount of labor time available for producing the given level of g_t. This causes the government to increase its demands for both h^g_t and c^g_t. But the drop in $h^g_t N^g_t - \alpha(.)$ due to the rise in w_t also increases the marginal product of h^g_t and reduces the net marginal product of c^g_t, causing the government's demand for h^g_t to rise and its demand for c^g_t to fall in spite of the increase in w_t. Assuming that the substitution effect mentioned first is the strongest, then as w_t rises, the government's demand for h^g_t will fall and its demand for c^g_t will rise.

Next, consider a ceteris paribus increase in D^g_t. This rise in D^g_t reduces $\alpha(.)$ thereby effectively increasing the amount of labor time the government has available for producing goods to be distributed to the households. This "direct effect" means that the government will need less of both c^g_t and h^g_t in order to produce the unchanged level of g_t, thereby causing its demands for both factors to fall. But as $h^g_t N^g_t - \alpha(.)$ rises, the net marginal product of h^g_t falls and the <u>net</u> marginal product of c^g_t increases because $\hat{g}_1$ falls. These "indirect effects" operating through the net marginal products induce the government to decrease its demand for h^g_t but to increase its use of c^g_t. If the "direct effect" dominiates, then c^g_t will fall. But both the direct and indirect effects induce the government to hire less labor in the current period.

Finally, a ceteris paribus increase in K^g_{t+1} means that the government is able to produce the unchanged amount of g_t using less of each of the factors h^g_t and c^g_t. Therefore, the government's demands for h^g_t and c^g_t will both tend to fall as K^g_t rises.

The above discussion explains the signs of the partial derivatives shown underneath the corresponding parameters in equations (7.23) and (7.24). Next the discussion turns to the derivation of the government-produced goods-tax menu and to derivation of the sector's demands for capital, workers, and deposits for the beginning of next period.

The Menu of Choices for Next Period's Government Production and Taxes and the Government's Demand Functions for Next Period

Solving the simultaneous system (7.18)-(7.22) yields the government sector's demand functions for N^g_{t+1}, c^g_{t+1}, K^g_{t+1} and D^g_{t+1} as well as an expression for λ_2. The expression for λ_2 reveals the responsiveness of the slope of the government-goods-tax menu to various parametric changes. Not suprisingly, the government's demands for workers, physical capital, and checkable deposits for the beginning of next period as well as its anticipated next period demand for privately-produced goods all depend upon the level of g_{t+1} which the household sector selects from this menu. The government's demand functions for N^g_{t+1}, c^g_{t+1}, K^g_{t+1}, and D^g_{t+1} are presented below as equations (7.25)+(7.28):

$$N^{gd}_{t+1} = \mathbf{N}^g_{t+1}(\underset{-}{w^g_{t+1}}, \underset{+}{p^{cg}_{t+1}}, \underset{+}{p^{kg}_t}, \underset{-}{p^{kg}_{t+1}}, \underset{-}{p^{bg}_t}, \underset{-}{r^{dg}_t}, \underset{+}{g_{t+1}}) \quad (7.25)$$

$$c^{gd}_{t+1} = c^g_{t+1}(\underset{+}{w^g_{t+1}}, \underset{-}{p^{cg}_{t+1}}, \underset{+}{p^{kg}_t}, \underset{-}{p^{kg}_{t+1}}, \underset{-}{p^{bg}_t}, \underset{-}{r^{dg}_t}, \underset{+}{g_{t+1}}) \quad (7.26)$$

$$K^{gd}_{t+1} = K^g_{t+1}(\underset{+}{w^g_{t+1}}, \underset{+}{p^{cg}_{t+1}}, \underset{-}{p^{kg}_t}, \underset{+}{p^{kg}_{t+1}}, \underset{+}{p^{bg}_t}, \underset{-}{r^{dg}_t}, \underset{+}{g_{t+1}}) \quad (7.27)$$

$$D^{gd}_{t+1} = D^g_{t+1}(\underset{+}{w^g_{t+1}}, \underset{+}{p^{cg}_{t+1}}, \underset{+}{p^{kg}_t}, \underset{-}{p^{kg}_{t+1}}, \underset{+}{p^{bg}_t}, \underset{+}{r^{dg}_t}, \underset{+}{g_{t+1}}) \quad (7.28)$$

Effects of a change in w^g_{t+1}

A revision in the government's anticipated value of next period's wage rate, w^g_{t+1}, or next period's price of privately-produced consumption goods, p^{cg}_{t+1}, produces several effects. Consider first the effects of change in w^g_{t+1}. As w^g_{t+1} rises, for instance, labor services become more expensive relative to privately-produced consumption goods, c_{t+1}, and privately-produced capital goods, K_{t+1}. Consequently the government will tend to a substitute both of these privately-produced goods for labor in the production of a given amount of g_{t+1} next period. Furthermore, as w^g_{t+1} grows the government will tend to increase D^g_{t+1} in order to conserve transactons time and therefore to conserve total labor time.

However there are some additional effects arising from the change in w^g_{t+1} which are less direct. In particular, as w^g_{t+1} rises the purchasing power of checkable deposits falls causing the sector, ceteris paribus, to have to divert more labor to transactions time than it would otherwise. As a result, in order to maintain production of a given level of g_{t+1} the sector will tend to increase its demands for c^g_{t+1}, N^g_{t+1} and K^g_{t+1}; it will also tend to increase its demand for D^g_{t+1} in order to further conserve transactons time. These tend to reinforce the "substitution" effects upon c^g_{t+1}, K^g_{t+1} and D^g_{t+1} discussed above, but to work against the substitution effect upon N^g_{t+1}.

In addition, by reducing the purchasing power of D^g_{t+1} and causing the government to divert some labor from production of g_{t+1} to the undertaking of transactions, the increase in w^g_{t+1} causes the marginal product of labor in producing g_{t+1} to rise. This causes (a) the marginal product of N^g_{t+1} to increase, (b) the net marginal product of c^g_{t+1} to fall and (c) the marginal product of D^g_{t+1} to increase. The reason the net marginal product of c^g_{t+1} falls is that the marginal amount of transactions time associated with a unit increase in c^g_{t+1} now represents a greater sacrifice of government produced goods.

But if we assume the "substitution" effects dominate, the government's responses to an increase in w^g_{t+1} will correspond to the signs associated with that parameter in expression (7.25)-(7.28).

Effects of a change in p^{cg}_{t+1}

Next, consider an increase in p^{cg}_{t+1}. As p^{cg}_{t+1} rises the government will plan to use less c^g_{t+1} but more K^g_{t+1} and N^g_{t+1} in the production of g_{t+1} because the factor c_{t+1} has become relatively more expensive. Unlike the case for an increase in w^g_{t+1}, however, the substitution effect upon D^g_{t+1} due to an increase in p^{cg}_{t+1} is unclear.

To see why, notice that as the government reduces N^g_{t+1} (but keeps the other factors c^g_{t+1} and K^g_{t+1} constant) in response to an increase in w^g_{t+1}, it must increase D^g_{t+1} in order to release enough labor from transactions to apply to the production of government produced goods so that the unchanged g_{t+1} may be maintained. On the other hand, as the government reduces c^g_{t+1} (keeping the other factors, N^g_{t+1} and K^g_{t+1} constant) in response to an increase in p^{cg}_{t+1}, it may not have to increase D^g_{t+1} in order to maintain the production of a given amount of g_{t+1}. The reason is that as c^g_{t+1} is reduced, the amount of transactions time also falls and the labor time which is released in the process may be applied to the production of g_{t+1}. Consequently, the substitution effect of an increase in p^{cg}_{t+1} upon D^g_{t+1} is unclear. However, if the amount of labor time released from transactions is small as c^g_{t+1} is reduced, then the government will increase its demand for D^g_{t+1}, ceteris paribus. This assumption will be followed in the remainder of the analysis.

Besides producing the above substitution effects, the increase in p^{cg}_{t+1}, also reduces the purchasing power of D^g_{t+1}. This causes the government to divert more labor time to transactions. In order to maintain production of g_{t+1} at a given level, therefore, the government will tend to increase its demands for all four factors c^g_{t+1}, N^g_{t+1}, D^g_{t+1} and N^g_{t+1}. These "scale" effects tend to reinforce the above substitution effects in every case except upon the demand for c^g_{t+1}.

In addition to the substitution and scale effects, by reducing the purchasing power of D^g_{t+1} and therefore causing some labor time to be diverted from the production of g_{t+1} to undertaking transactions, the increase in p^{cg}_{t+1}causes the marginal product of labor in production of g_{t+1} to rise. Just as in the case of an increase in w^g_{t+1}, this in turn causes (a) the marginal product of N^g_{t+1} to rise, (b) the net marginal product of c^g_{t+1} to fall and (c) the marginal product of D^g_{t+1} to increase.

Assuming the first-mentioned substituion effects dominate, the government's reaction to an upward revision of its estimate of p^{cg}_{t+1} are summarized by the signs corresponding to that parameter in expressions (7.25)-(7.28) above.

Effects of a change in p^{kg}_t or p^{kg}_{t+1}

If p^{kg}_t increases, the government will tend to reduce its demand for K^g_{t+1} and to increase its demands for N^g_{t+1}, c^g_{t+1} and D^g_{t+1}. In this case the substitution effect upon D^g_{t+1} is determinate because I have abstracted from any transactions time involved in purchasing additional units of physical capital. Consequently, if the government were to reduce K^g_{t+1} (holding c^g_{t+1} and N^g_{t+1} constant) it would have to increase D^g_{t+1} in order to release enough labor from transactions in order to maintain a given level of g_{t+1} production. Assuming that the government anticipates that the capital goods it holds at time t+1 will be tradeable at the price p^{kg}_{t+1} next period, an increase in that expected price reduces the user cost of capital and produces effects opposite to those associated with an increase in p^{kg}_t.

Effects of a change in p^{bg}_t

An increase in the price at which the government anticipates bonds will be traded during the current period reduces not only the user cost of physical capital but also the opportunity cost of holding checkable deposits at depository insitutions at time t+1. The reduction in the user cost of capital induces the government to increase its demand for K^g_{t+1} but to reduce its demands for c^g_{t+1}, N^g_{t+1} and D^g_{t+1}. The reduction in the opportunity cost of holding D^g_{t+1}, on the other hand, causes the government to increase D^g_{t+1} but to reduce c^g_{t+1} and N^g_{t+1}. Clearly, as p^{bg}_{t+1} rises both c^g_{t+1} and N^g_{t+1} tend to fall. If we assume that the own price effects upon K^g_{t+1} and D^g_{t+1} more than offset the cross effects, then both K^g_{t+1} and D^g_{t+1} increase.

Effects of a change in r^{dg}_t or g_{t+1}

An increase in r^{dg}_t increases the return to holding checkable deposits at depository institutions. As a result, the government will tend to increase its demand for D^g_{t+1}. To the extent that this frees labor time from undertaking transactions and permits the government to apply the labor to the production of a given level of g_{t+1}, the government will reduce its demands for N^g_{t+1}, c^g_{t+1} and K^g_{t+1}.

An increase in g_{t+1} increases the government's scale of production of goods and services and causes it to demand more of all factors of production. Consequently, its demands for N^g_{t+1}, c^g_{t+1}, K^g_{t+1} and D^g_{t+1} will increase as the households select higher values of g_{t+1}.

The Menu of Alternative g_{t+1} - Tx_{t+1} Combinations

Substituting (7.23)-(7.28) into (7.13) produces the following expression for Tx_{t+1} in terms of parameters facing the government sector at time t:

$$Tx_{t+1}=p^{cg}_{t+1}\cdot c^{g}_{t+1}(\underset{+}{w^{g}_{t+1}},\ \underset{-}{p^{cg}_{t+1}},\ \underset{+}{p^{kg}_{t}},\ \underset{-}{p^{kg}_{t+1}},\ \underset{-}{p^{bg}_{t}},\ \underset{-}{r^{dg}_{t}},\ \underset{+}{g_{t+1}})$$

$$+\ w^{g}_{t+1}h\ \cdot\ N^{g}_{t+1}(\underset{-}{w^{g}_{t+1}},\ \underset{+}{p^{cg}_{t+1}}\cdot\ \underset{+}{p^{kg}_{t}},\ \underset{-}{p^{kg}_{t+1}},\ \underset{-}{p^{bg}_{t}},\ \underset{-}{r^{dg}_{t}},\ \underset{+}{g_{t+1}})$$

$$+[(\frac{\$1}{p^{bg}_{t}})-(1+r^{dg}_{t})]D^{g}_{t+1}(\underset{+}{w^{g}_{t+1}},\underset{+}{p^{cg}_{t+1}},\ \underset{+}{p^{kg}_{t+1}},\ \underset{-}{p^{kg}_{t}},\ \underset{+}{p^{bg}_{t+1}},\ \underset{+}{r^{dg}_{t}},\ \underset{+}{g_{t+1}})$$

$$+\ \ (p^{kg}_{t}/p^{bg}_{t})-p^{bg}_{t+1}]\ k^{g}_{t+1}(\underset{+}{w^{g}_{t+1}},\underset{+}{p^{cg}_{t+1}},\underset{-}{p^{kg}_{t}},\underset{+}{p^{kg}_{t+1}},\underset{+}{p^{bg}_{t}},\underset{-}{r^{dg}_{t}},\underset{-}{g_{t+1}})$$

$$-\ \pi^{cg}_{t+1}-(\$1/p^{bg}_{t})D^{g}_{t}-(p^{kg}_{t}/p^{bg}_{t})K^{g}_{t}$$

$$+(1/p^{bg}_{t})\ .\ [\$1B^{g}_{t}\ +\ p^{cg}_{t}\ \cdot\ c^{g}_{t}(\underset{+}{w_{t}},\ \underset{-}{p^{cg}_{t}},\ \underset{+}{g_{t}},\ \underset{-}{K^{g}_{t}},\ \underset{-}{D^{g}_{t}})$$

$$+w_{t}N^{g}_{t}\ \cdot\ h^{g}_{t}(\underset{-}{N^{g}_{t}},\ \underset{-}{w_{t}},\ \underset{+}{p^{cg}_{t}},\ \underset{+}{g_{t}},\ \underset{-}{K^{g}_{t}},\ \underset{-}{D^{g}_{t}})$$

$$-Tx_{t}\ -\ \pi^{cg}_{t}\ -\ r^{d}_{t+1}D^{g}_{t}] \tag{7.29}$$

or:

$$Tx_{t+1}=Tx_{t+1}(g_{t+1};\ w_{t},\ \ p^{cg}_{t},\ g_{t},\ K^{g}_{t},\ D^{g}_{t},\ B^{g}_{t},\ Tx_{t},\ \pi^{cg}_{t},\ r^{d}_{t-1},$$

$$\pi^{cg}_{t+1},\ w^{g}_{t+1},\ p^{cg}_{t+1},\ p^{kg}_{t},\ p^{kg}_{t+1},\ p^{bg}_{t},\ r^{dg}_{t}) \tag{7.30}$$

or:

$$Tx_{t+1}\ =\ Tx_{t+1}(\underset{+}{g_{t}+1};\ k) \tag{7.31}$$

where k represents a vector of sixteen shift parameters. Given the actual and anticipated values of the parameters contained in k, the government at time t presents the menu depicted in (7.30) to the households. The households then select the optimal combination of g_{t+1} and Tx_{t+1} for next period. After the households have made their selection, the government substitutes the chosen value of g_{t+1} into expressions (7.25)-(7.28) in order to obtain its optimal demands for N^{g}_{t+1}, c^{g}_{t+1}, K^{g}_{t+1} and $D^{g}_{t}+1$.

It its clear from (7.29) that, ceteris paribus, an increase in g_{t+1} induces the government to announce it must collect more taxes next period. In fact, ceteris paribus, Tx_{t+1} must increase at an increasing rate as g_{t+1} grows larger. This result is obtained, just as in the simple model presented earlier, by examining the solution for λ_2 in system (7.18)-(7.22) as a function of g_{t+1}. In particular, λ_2 represents the minimum amount by which taxes must increase next period as g_{t+1} increases one until that is, λ_2 represents the slope of the menu presented in Figure 7.2.

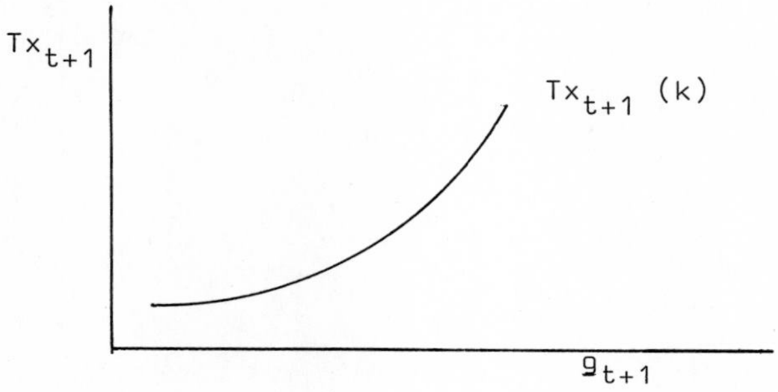

Figure 7.2 - Next Period's Menu of Alternative Levels of g_{t+1} and Corresponding Tx_{t+1}.

Totally defferentiating system (7.18)-(7.22) produces the following system, where g_{t+1} is the only parameter which is allowed to change:

$$\begin{bmatrix} \\ A \\ \\ \end{bmatrix} \begin{bmatrix} dN^g_{t+1} \\ dc^g_{t+1} \\ dK^g_{t+1} \\ dD^g_{t+1} \\ d\lambda_2 \end{bmatrix} = \begin{bmatrix} 0 \\ 0 \\ 0 \\ 0 \\ -dg_{t+1} \end{bmatrix} \tag{7.32}$$

Let $|A_{55}|$ represent the cofactor of element a_{55}. Then $\partial\lambda_2/\partial g_{t+1} = -|A_{55}|/|A|$. It can be shown that $A_{55} > 0$ while $|A| < 0$. Consequently, $\partial\lambda_2/\partial g_{t+1} > 0$; the slope of the menu in Figure 7.2 increases as g_{t+1} rises.

The Government's Bond Supply Function

The government's supply of bonds, $p^{bg}{}_t B^g{}_{t+1}$ (in dollars), for the end of the current period is found by substituting (7.23)-(7.28) into (7.3) and solving for $p^{bg}{}_t B^g{}_{t+1}$:

$$p^{bg}_t B^g_{t+1} = \$1.B^g_t + p^{cg}_t \cdot c^g_t(\underset{+}{w_t},\ \underset{-}{p^{cg}_t},\ \underset{+}{g_t},\ \underset{-}{K^g_t},\ \underset{-}{D^g_t}) \qquad (7.33)$$

$$+w_t N^g_t \cdot h^g_t(\underset{-}{N^g_t},\ \underset{-}{w_t},\ \underset{+}{p^{cg}_t},\ \underset{+}{g_t},\ \underset{-}{K^g_t},\ \underset{-}{D^g_t})$$

$$-Tx_t - \pi^{cg}_t - (1+r^d_{t+1})D^g_t - p^{kg}_t K^g_t$$

$$+D^g_{t+1}(\underset{+}{w^g_{t+1}},\ \underset{+}{p^{cg}_{t+1}},\ \underset{+}{p^{kg}_t},\ \underset{-}{p^{kg}_{t+1}},\ \underset{+}{p^{bg}_t},\ \underset{+}{r^{dg}_t},\ \underset{+}{g_{t+1}})$$

$$+\ p^{kg}_{t+1} \cdot K^g_{t+1}(\underset{+}{w^g_{t+1}}, \underset{+}{p^{cg}_{t+1}}, \underset{+}{p^{kg}_t}, \underset{-}{p^{kg}_{t+1}}, \underset{+}{p^{bg}_t}, \underset{+}{r^{dg}_t}, \underset{+}{g_{t+1}})$$

or:

$$p^{bg}_t B^g_{t+1} = B^{gs}_{t+1}(\underset{+}{p^{bg}_t};\ \underset{+}{B^g_t},\ \underset{+}{w_t},\ \underset{+}{p^{cg}_t},\ \underset{+}{g_t},\ \underset{+}{K^g_t},\ \underset{-}{D^g_t},\ \underset{-}{Tx_{t+1}},\ \underset{-}{\pi^{cg}_t},$$

$$\underset{-}{r^d_{t+1}},\ \underset{?}{p^{kg}_t},\ \underset{?}{p^{kg}_{t+1}},\ \underset{+}{w^g_{t+1}},\ \underset{+}{p^{cg}_{t+1}},\ \underset{?}{r^{dg}_{t+1}},\ \underset{+}{g_{t+1}}) \qquad (7.34)$$

or:

$$p^{bg}_t B^g_{t+1} = B^{gs}_{t+1}(p^{bg}_t,\ v)$$

where v represents a vector of fifteen shift parameters. The signs of the partial derivatives in (7.34) with respect to w_t and p^{cg}_t are based upon the assumption that an increase in either factor price raises current expenses, causing the government to borrow more. Also, note that $h^g_t N^g_t$ is independent of N^g_t.

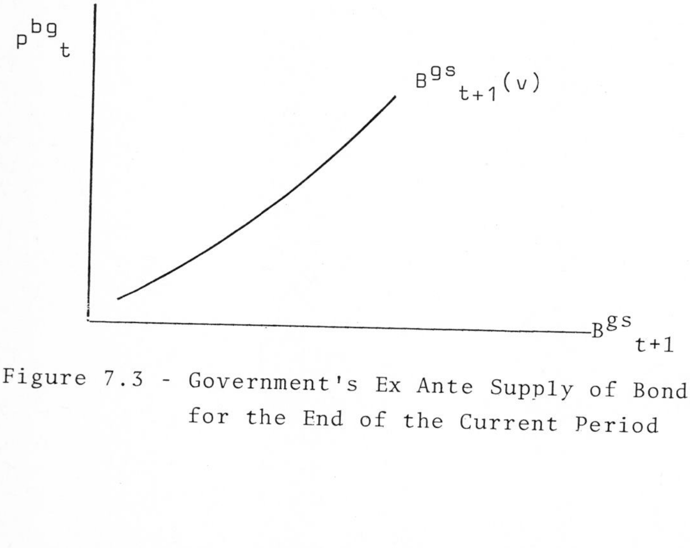

Figure 7.3 - Government's Ex Ante Supply of Bonds at Time t for the End of the Current Period

In the chapters that follow, the households at time t will use the menu prepared by the government to select the optimal combination of g_{t+1} and Tx_{t+1} for next period; the non-financial business sector at time t will estimate c_t^{gd}, N^{gd}_{t+1} and K^{gd}_{t+1} in an attempt to select the optimal levels of p^c_t, w_{t+1} and p^k_t; and the private depository institutions at time t will be interested in estimating D^{gd}_{t+1} and B^{gs}_{t+1} in their attempt to select the optimal levels of r^d_t and p^b_t. Therefore, government activity, or anticipated government activity, will play an important role in the decision-making of each of the private sectors. Furthermore, government activity will directly influence private sector behavior in the markets for labor, privately-produced goods, checkable deposits and bonds. The next chapter focuses upon the behavior of the household sector in this expanded model.

8. - Household Sector Behavior in the Expanded Model

In the expanded model currently under construction, the household sector faces a variety of decisions at time t with respect to its activities in the labor, commodity and financial markets. It must decide the number of people who will attempt this period to find jobs for next period, the volume of consumption goods it will buy, the amount of physical capital it will accumulate, the amount it will borrow from depository institutions, as well as the amounts of currency, checkable deposits, and equity shares it will hold at the end of the current period. In the simple model, presented earlier, the household sector purchased equity shares only from private nonfinancial businesses. However in this expanded version it also buys shares from private depository institutions. Because household expenditures on capital goods are assumed to be too large to be financed out of current household saving (defined as current disposable income less current expenditures on consumption goods), the sector presumably finances its capital goods expenditures by borrowing from the private depository institutions.

In addition to making the above market decisions, the household sector also selects next period's combination of government-produced goods and taxes from the menu prepared for it by the government sector. The household sector makes this selection in a manner which is mutually consistent with every one of its decisions in the private markets. This mutual consistency represents one of the fundamental factors that distinguishes the current treatment from the standard macro model.

Formal Model of Household Behavior

At time t, the household sector holds certain amounts of physical capital, K^h_t, checkable deposits, D^h_t, currency, Cu^h_t, equity shares issued by private nonfinancial businesses, Sn_t, and equity shares issued by private depository institutions, Sf_t. The household sector also has a certain amount of debt, L_t, outstanding at time t in the form of notes payable to depository institutions (i.e. "personal loans"). All these balance sheet items are viewed as constraints by the household sector at time t. That is, at time t the household sector's planned amounts of these balance sheet items for time t correspond exactly to their respective actual amounts. Let p^{kh}_t denote the price at which the household sector anticipates at time t that physical capital will trade during the current period. Also, let p^{nh}_t and p^{fh}_t represent the prices which the household sector anticipates at time t will prevail during the current period for equity shares issued by the nonfinancial businesses and the private financial institutions respectively. Then the household sector's existing balance sheet at time t, expressed in terms of anticipated current period prices, appears as follows.

Household Sector's Balance Sheet at Time t

Assets	Liabilities
$p^n_t\ Sn_t$	L_t
$p^f_t\ Sf_t$	
D^h_t	Net Wealth
Cu^h_t	
$p^k_t\ K^h_t$	NW_t

Household net wealth at time t, NW^h_t, is defind as the residual: $p^n{}_tSn_t + p^f{}_tSf_t + D^h_t + Cu^h_t + p^k{}_tK^h_t - L_t$.

Although its existing balance sheet represents an effective constraint,the household sector is free at time t to plan a new balance sheet for the end of the current period. Let Sn^{hd}_{t+1}, Sf^{hd}_{t+1}, D^{hd}_{t+1}, Cu^{hd}_{t+1} and K^{hd}_{t+1} respectively represent the amounts of equity shares issued by nonfinancial businesses, equity shares issued by private financial (depository) institutions, checkable deposits, currency and physical capital which the household sector plans to hold at the end of the current period. Then $D^{hd}_{t+1} + Cu^{hd}_{t+1}$ denotes the household sector's demand for money for time t+1, $p^{nh}{}_tSn^{hd}_{t+1} + p^{fh}{}_tSf^{hd}_{t+1}$ represents the dollar value of its demand for nonmonetary financial assets for time t+1, and $p^{kh}{}_tK^{hd}_{t+1}$ depicts the dollar value of its demand for capital goods for time t+1. Also, let L^{hd}_{t+1} represent the number of dollars of personal IOU's which the household sector plans to have outstanding at time t+1. Then the balance sheet it plans at time t for the end of the current period may be shown as:

Household Sector's Planned Balance Sheet for Time t+1
(in anticipated current-period prices)

Assets	Liabilities
Cu^{hd}_{t+1}	L^{hd}_{t+1}
D^{hd}_{t+1}	
$p^{hd}_{t}\ K^{hd}_{t+1}$	Net Wealth
$p^{fh}_{t}\ Sf^{hd}_{t+1}$	
$p^{nh}_{t}\ Sn^{hd}_{t+1}$	NW_{t+1}

where $NW_{ht+1} = Cu^{hd}_{t+1} + D^{hd}_{t+1} + p^{kh}{}_{t}K^{hd}_{t+1} + p^{fh}{}_{t}Sf^{hd}_{t+1} + p^{nh}Sn^{hd}_{t+1} - L^{hd}_{t+1}$. The household sector's planned increment to net wealth, $NW^{h}_{t+1} - NW^{h}_{t}$, during the current period must agree with the amount it plans to save on the income account during the current period. The reason is simple. Not only is current saving the only way to accumulate net wealth at the prices which prevail during the current period but current saving also necessarily involves accumulating net wealth at those prices. Therefore, for a given set of actual or anticipated prices, current saving on the income account is both necessary and sufficient for net wealth accumulation on the capital account. The household sector's current period plans must reflect that condition.

During the current period, the household sector will receive wage income from three employers (nonfinancial businesses, depository institutions and the government), dividend income from two business sectors (nonfinancial businesses and depository institutions) and interest income from checkable deposits held at depository institutions.

As the current period opens, N_t people already have been hired to work during the current period (at the money wage w_t) for either the government (N^{g}_{t}), the nonfinancial businesses (N^{n}_{t}) or the private financial institutions (N^{f}_{t}). Therefore $N_t = N^{g}_{t} + N^{n}_{t} + N^{f}_{t}$. At time t each employer decides the average number of hours its employees will work during the current period. Then $h^{g}{}_{t}N^{g}{}_{t}$, $h^{n}{}_{t}N^{n}{}_{t}$ and $h^{f}{}_{t}N^{f}{}_{t}$ respectively represent the total number of labor hours used by the government, the nonfinancial businesses and the depository institutions during the current period. Since each employer presumably pays the same money wage in the current period, the household sector's total labor income is represented by $w_t(h^g{}_tN^g{}_t + h^n{}_tN^n{}_t + h^f{}_tN^f{}_t)$ or $w_th_tN_t$ where h_t denotes the (weighted) average, $(h^g{}_tN^g{}_t + h^n{}_tN^n{}_t + h^f{}_tN^f{}_t)/(N^g{}_t + N^n{}_t + N^f{}_t)$, of the hours worked in the current period.

The household sector holds Sn_t shares of ownership in the nonfinancial businesses at time t and Sf_t shares of ownership in the private depository institutions. Let $\pi^n{}_t$ and $\pi^f{}_t$ represent the current dividend income which the households receives on each of the nonfinancial and financial equity shares respectively. Then the household sector's total current dividend income amounts to $\pi^n{}_tSn_t + \pi^f{}_tSf_t$.

Last period the private depository institutions announced that every dollar held as checkable deposits by the end of that period (i.e. by time t) would earn $r^d{}_{t-1}$ in interest during the current period. Therefore $r^d{}_{t-1}$ represents the interest rate on checkable deposits announced by the depository institutions last period. Since $D^h{}_t$ represents the number of dollars which the household sector holds as deposits at time t, its current period interest from checkable deposits is denoted by $r^d{}_{t-1}D^h{}_t$. Also, current period personal income equals $w_th_tN_t + \pi^n{}_tSn_t + \pi^f{}_tSf_t + r^d{}_{t-1}D^h{}_t$.

As discussed above, the household sector last period presumably selected the current level of personal taxes from a menu of government-produced goods and taxes prepared for it by the government. Therefore at time t both current-period taxes, Tx_{t+1}, and the current-period level of government produced goods, g_t, are known. Consequently, current period disposable income is also known at time t and is depicted by $w_th_tN_t + r^d{}_{t-1}D^h{}_t + \pi^n{}_tSn_t + \pi^f{}_tSf_t - Tx_t$.

Let $p^{ch}{}_t$ represent the price of consumption goods which the household sector anticipates at time t will prevail during the current period. Let $c^h{}_t$ denote the household sector's real demand for consumption goods during the current period. Then at time t ex ante personal consumption (in dollars) becomes $p^{ch}{}_tc^h{}_t$. Also, let $r^1{}_{t-1}$ denote the interest rate which depository institutions announced last period that households would have to pay during the current period on each dollar of personal loans, L_t, outstanding at time t. Then the household sector's current outlay as interest payments to business equals $r^1{}_{t-1}L_t$. Since personal saving is defined as disposable income minus personal consumption minus personal interest payments to business, ex ante current personal savings, s^h_t, at time t may be defined as:

$$s^h_t = w_t h_t N_t + r^d_{t-1} D^h_t + \pi^n_t Sn^h_t + \pi^f_t Sf^h_t - Tx_t - p^c_t c^h_t - r^1_{t-1} L_t. \qquad (8.1)$$

But s^h_t must be consistent with the household sector's planned increment to net wealth during the period, $NW^h_{t+1} - NW^h_t$. Therefore at time t the following budget constraint faces the household sector for the current period:

$$w_t h_t N_t + r^d_{t-1} D^h_t + \pi^n_t Sn_t + \pi^f_t Sf_t - Tx_t - p^c_t c^h_t - r^1_{t-1} L_t.$$

$$= p^{kh}_t (K^{hd}_{t+1} - K^h_t) + p^{nh}_t (Sn^{hd}_{t+1} - Sn_t) + p^{fh}_t (Sf^{hd}_{t+1} - Sf_t)$$

$$+ (D^{hd}_{t+1} - D^h_t) + (Cu^{hd}_{t+1} - Cu^h_t) - (L^{hd}_{t+1} - L_t) \qquad (8.2)$$

In words, expression (8.2) stipultes that the amount which the household sector plans at time t to save on the income account during the current period must equal the sum of the values of the physical capital, equity shares and money it plans to accumulate during the period minus any additional amount it plans to borrow during the current period.

In order to simplify the following analysis, assume that expenditures by the household sector on physical capital are large relatiive to personal saving so that they must be financed through additional borrowing. In other words, we impose the added restriction:

$$p^{kh}_t (K^{hd}_{t+1} - k^h_t) = (L^{hd}_{t+1} - L_t). \qquad (8.3)$$

At time t the household sector also formulates plans for next period. As discussed earlier, at the beginning of the current period the nonfinancial business sector (as the principal employer) calls out the hourly money wage, w_{t+1}, which it guarantees to pay next period's employees. Although it does not guarantee that everyone will work the standard h hours next period, the nonfinancial business sector nevertheless formualtes its plans for next period based upon the assumption that eveyone will indeed work that number of hours next period. Furthermore, it announces its bona fide intention that everyone will work h hours next period. The other employers, namely the government and the private depository institutions, presumably follow suit. They guarantee the same hourly money wage, w_{t+1}, that the private nonfinancial business sector announes and also plan to employ all their workers next period for the standard h hours. In order to confine the analysis to a single labor market, I assume that despite current or past experience to the contrary, the household sector places full confidence in the ability of each of its potential employers to correctly access its labor requirements for next period. Furthermore, I assume away any non-pencuniary factors which may cause the households to prefer working for a particular employer. Therefore, the households are equally willing to be employed by any one of the three potential employers and they anticipate at time t that no matter for whom they work next period, they will earn $w_{t+1}\bar{h}$ dollars per person. On the basis of this information, the household sector must decide at time t how many people, N^s_{t+1}, it wants to have working next period. The number N^s_{t+1} refers to its "supply of labor" for next period and must be no larger than the sum of the number of people which the household sector anticipates that each potential employer will want to employ by the end of the current period to work next period. On this basis, the term $w_{t+1}hN^s_{t+1}$ represents the total wage income which the households anticipate at time t that they will earn next period.

Let π^{fh}_{t+1} represent the total income per share which the household sector anticipates at time t receiving next period on each equity share of the private financial business sector that it plans to hold by the end of the current period. Let π^{nh}_{t+1} represent the corresponding income associated with each share of the private nonfinancial business sector that it plans to hold by the end of the current period. Also, let r^{dh}_t represent the interest rate which the household sector anticipates at time t that the private financial institutions will announce this period that they will pay next period on each dollar their customers hold as checkable deposits at time t+1. Then at time t the level of personal income which the household sector anticipates receiving next period is represented by $w_{t+1}hN^s_{t+1}$ + $\pi^{fh}_{t+1}Sf^{hd}_{t+1}$ + $\pi^{nh}_{t+1}Sn^{hd}_{t+1}$ + $r^{dh}_tD^{hd}_{t+1}$. Consequently, the disposable income it anticipates receiving next period is $w_{t+1}hN^s_{t+1}$ + $\pi^{fh}_{t+1}Sf^{hd}_{t+1}$ + $\pi^{nh}_{t+1}Sn^{hd}_{t+1}$ + $r^{dh}_tD^{hd}_{t+1}$ - Tx_{t+1} where Tx_{t+1} is yet to be decided by the household sector at time t.

Let p^{ch}_{t+1} depict the price of consumption goods which the households at time t anticipate incurring next period. Also, let c^h_{t+1} represent the real number of consumption goods which the households at time t anticipate buying next period. In addition suppose r^{lh}_t represents the interest rate on loans which the households at time t anticipate that the private financial institutions will announce this period. This rate depicts what households anticipate they will have to pay next period on each dollar of personal loans outstanding at time t+1. Then the level of personal saving, s^h_{t+1}, which the household sector at time t anticipates for next period is defined by (8.4):

$$s^h_{t+1} \equiv w_{t+1}hN^s_{t+1} + \pi^{fh}_{t+1}Sf^{hd}_{t+1} + \pi^{nh}_{t+1}Sn^{hd}_{t+1} + r^{dh}_t D^{hd}_{t+1} - Tx_{t+1}$$
$$- p^{ch}_{t+1}c^h_{t+1} - r^1_t L^{hd}_{t+1} \qquad (8.4)$$

The amount it plans to save next period must be consistent with its plans on the capital account for that period.

In particular, suppose that the households anticipate at time t that no markets will exist next period for the equity shares they hold at the beginning of that period. Furthermore, let p^{kh}_{t+1} denote the market price of physical capital which the households anticipate will prevail next peirod. Then, when valued in terms of next period's anticipated prices, the household sector's planned balance sheet for time t+1 becomes:

Household Sector's Planned Balance Sheet for Time t+1
(in terms of next period's anticipated prices)

Assets	Liabilities
Cu^{hd}_{t+1}	L^{hd}_{t+1}
D^{hd}_{t+1}	Net Welath
$p^{kh}_{t+1}K^{hd}_{t+1}$	NW^{h*}_{t+1}

Since the household sector at time t presumably cannot see beyond time t+2, assume that the households plan at time t to hold no assets and to have no liabilities outstanding at time t+2. Therefore, as the current period opens the sector's plans to save on the income account next period, s^h_{t+1}, must equal its planned decumulation of net wealth on the capital account next period, $0 - NW^{h*}_{t+1}$. Consequently, the household sector at time t faces the following budget constraint with respect to next period:

$$w_{t+1}hN^{s}_{t+1} + \pi^{fh}_{t+1}Sf^{hd}_{t+1} + \pi^{nh}_{t+1}Sn^{hd}_{t+1} + r^{dh}_{t}D^{hd}_{t+1} - Tx_{t+1}$$

$$-p^{ch}_{t+1}c^{h}_{t+1} - r^{1}_{t}L^{hd}_{t+1} = - Cu^{hd}_{t+1} - D^{hd}_{t+1} - p^{kh}_{t+1}K^{hd}_{t+1} + L^{hd}_{t+1} \quad (8.5)$$

In words, the household sector must plan at time t to save out of next period's disposable income exactly the amount it will still need in order to retire its outstanding personal loans after it has sold its physical capital and applied the proceeds from that sale as well as the money with which plans to start next period to the retiement of its debt.

In addition to conditions (8.2), (8.3) and (8.5),the household sector also is confronted by the government goods - tax menu prepared for it by the government sector. This menu, derived in Chapter 7 as expression (7.31) and presented here as (8.6):

$$Tx_{t+1} = Tx_{t+1}(g_{t+1}, k) \quad (8.6)$$

provides households with alternative combinations of Tx_{t+1} and g_{t+1} for next period. The objctive of the household sector at time t is to choose the optimal combination in a manner consistent with its choices in the private markets. That is, the household sector at time t attempts to maximize present utility by choosing the optimal levels of c^{h}_{t}, Cu^{hd}_{t+1}, D^{hd}_{t+1}, N^{s}_{t+1}, Sf^{hd}_{t+1}, Sn^{hd}_{t+1}, K^{hd}_{t+1} and g_{t+1} in light of restrictions (8.2), (8.3), (8.5) and (8.6).

In accordance with the analysis presented in Chapter 3, the household sector presumably attempts at time t to maximize its present utility (i.e. its feeling of well-being at that time). Present utility in turn presumably depends upon the volume of consumption goods, c^{h}_{t}, that the sector plans to purchase from the nonfinancial business sector this period; the consumption goods, c^{h}_{t+1}, it plans to buy next period; the volume of goods and services, μ^*, the sector plans to produce itself this period using "leisure" time and the services of physical capital; the volume of household-produced goods and services, μ, it plans for next period; the transactions time τ^*, the household sector anticpates it will incur during the current period; the transactions time, τ, it anticipates next period; the volume of goods and services, g_t, that the government will produce and distribute "free of charge" during the current period; the goods and services, g_{t+1}, which the households direct the government to produce next period; and the "security" or "safety" it associates with the portfolio it plans for the end of the current period in terms of its purchasing power over consumption goods next period. In particular assume that present utility is an additively separable concave function of each of these nine items. Furthermore, assume that present utility increases as the volume of consumption goods the households plan to consume in either period increases, as the volume of household-produced goods and services in either period increases, as the volume of government-produced goods and services in either period increases, or as the degree of "safety" it attaches to its anticipated end-of-period portfolio increases. In addition, assume that present utility diminishes, ceteris paribus, as anticipated transactions time in either period rises. Then the household sector's objective function may be written as:

$$U = \tilde{U}_1 (c^h_t) + \tilde{U}_2(\mu^*) + \tilde{U}_3(\tau^*) + \tilde{U}_4(g_t) + \tilde{U}_5(c^h_{t+1}) + \tilde{U}_6(\mu) \qquad (8.7)$$

$$+ \tilde{U}_7(\tau) + \tilde{U}_8(g_{t+1}) + \tilde{U}_9(.)$$

where $\tilde{U}_1(.)$, $\tilde{U}_2(.)$, $\tilde{U}_4(.)$, $\tilde{U}_5(.)$, $\tilde{U}_6(.)$, $\tilde{U}_8(.)$ and $\tilde{U}_9(.) > 0$; $\tilde{U}_3(.)$ and $\tilde{U}_7(.) < 0$; $\tilde{U}'_1, \tilde{U}'_2, \tilde{U}'_4, \tilde{U}'_5, \tilde{U}'_6, \tilde{U}'_8$ and $\tilde{U}'_9 < 0$; $\tilde{U}'_3$ and $\tilde{U}'_7 < 0$; $\tilde{U}''_1, \tilde{U}''_2, \tilde{U}''_4, \tilde{U}''_5, \tilde{U}''_6, \tilde{U}''_8$ and $\tilde{U}''_9 < 0$. For simplicity, assume $\tilde{U}''_3$ and $\tilde{U}''_7 = 0$. The term $\tilde{U}_9(.)$ denotes the present utility derived from the degree of security the sector attaches to its anticipated end-of-current-period portfolio.

The household production functions in this chapter are slightly more complicated than the ones presented earlier because the household sector now uses not only leisure time (i.e. time not spent working for another sector) but also the services of physical capital with which it begins a given period to produce other goods and services that period. Specifically assume the household production functions for the current and next periods are given by (8.8) and (8.9) respectively:

$$\mu^* = \mu^*(h^*N - h_t N_t, K^h_t) \qquad (8.8)$$

$$\mu = \mu(h^*N - hN^s_{t+1}, K^{hd}_{t+1}) \qquad (8.9)$$

where $\mu^*_1, \mu^*_2, \mu_1, \mu_2 > 0$; $\mu^*_{11}, \mu^*_{22}, \mu_{11}, \mu_{22} < 0$.

The transactions-time functions facing the household sector are also more complicated than the ones used earlier because at the beginning of any period, the sector now may hold two types of money--namely, currency and checkable deposits--rather than just one. In particular, the amount of transactions time the household sector anticipates at time t that it will incur during a particular period now presumably increases as the number of consumption goods it plans to purchase that period increases, but decreases as either the quantity of (real) currency or (real) checkable deposits with which the sector begins that period increases. More formally, suppose the transactions time functions for the current and next periods are given respectively by (8.10) and (8.11):

$$\tau^* = \tau^*(c^h_t,\ Cu^h_t/p^{ch}_t,\ D^h_t/p^{ch}_t) \tag{8.10}$$

$$\tau = \tau(c^h_{t+1}, Cu^{hd}_{t+1}/p^{ch}_{t+1}, D^{hd}_{t+1}/p^{ch}_{t+1}) \tag{8.11}$$

where $\tau^*(.)$, $\tau(.) > 0$; τ^*_1, $\tau_1 > 0$; τ^*_2, τ^*_3, τ_2, $\tau_3 < 0$; and all own second-order partials are negative.

To address the question of the degree of safety which the household sector attaches to the portfolio it plans for the end of the current period, re-write equation (8.5) as:

$$c^h_{t+1} = \frac{w_{t+1}hN^s_{t+1}}{p^{ch}_{t+1}} + \frac{p^{kh}_{t+1}K^{hd}_{t+1}}{p^{ch}_{t+1}} - \frac{Tx_{t+1}}{p^{ch}_{t+1}} - \frac{(1 + r^1_t)\ L^{hd}_{t+1}}{p^{ch}_{t+1}} \tag{8.5}$$
$$+ \frac{\pi^{nh}_{t+1}Sn^{hd}_{t+1}}{p^{ch}_{t+1}} + \frac{\pi^{fh}_{t+1}Sf^{hd}_{t+1}}{p^{ch}_{t+1}} + \frac{(1 + r^{dh}_t)D^{hd}_{t+1}}{p^{ch}_{t+1}} + \frac{Cu^{hd}_{t+1}}{p^{ch}_{t+1}}$$

To reveal a ceteris paribus change in the degree of safety of purchasing power over a given amount of future consumption, suppose we hold constant the amount of future consumption, c^h_{t+1}, the amount of government-produced goods, g_{t+1}, and next period's production by the households, μ. Also, suppose that we ignore any effects on transations time due to any changes in currency or checkable deposits. From (8.6), a constant level of g_{t+1} is associated with a constant amount of Tx_{t+1}. Therefore, Tx_{t+1} is constant as well. Also, suppose that in order to hold constant, we hold constant both N^s_{t+1} and K^{hd}_{t+1}. Then from (8.3), L^{hd}_{t+1} is held constant as well (given the initial values K^h_t and L_t). According to condition (8.5), a given level of c^h_{t+1} may be financed in alternative ways even though Tx_{t+1}, N^s_{t+1}, K^{hd}_{t+1}

and L^{hd}_{t+1} are held constant. The particular assertion offered here is that for a given total value of real financial assets, depicted by the sum of the last four terms in (8.5), the household sector will attach different degrees of safety or security to different mixes of Sn^{hd}_{t+1}, Sf^{hd}_{t+1}, D^{hd}_{t+1} and Cu^{hd}_{t+1} within that total. In other words, aside from the fact that currency and checkable deposits are useful in conserving transactions time, the household sector will view a given total value of real financial assets planned for the end of the current period as qualitatively different if it contains, say, more purchasing power in the form of money but less in the form of equity shares. More specifically, assume, arbitrarily, that the equity shares issued by the nonfinancial business sector are viewed as less safe than those issued by depository institutions. Then, for a given total value $(\pi^{nh}_{t+1}Sn^{hd}_{t+1} + \pi^{fh}_{t+1}Sf^{hd}_{t+1} + (1 + r^{dh}_{t})D^{hd}_{t+1} + Cu^{hd}_{t+1})/p^{ch}_{t+1}$, the degree of safety associated with this sum presumably increases as $(\pi^{fh}_{t+1}Sf^{hd}_{t+1} + (1 + r^{dh}_{t})D^{hd}_{t+1} + Cu^{hd}_{t+1})/p^{c}_{t+1}$ increases (and, therefore, as $\pi^{nh}_{t+1}Sn^{hd}_{t+1}$ falls). Therefore, ceteris paribus, assume present utility rises as $(\pi^{fh}_{t+1}Sf^{hd}_{t+1} + (1 + r^{dh}_{t})D^{hd}_{t+1} + Cu^{hd}_{t+1})/p^{c}_{t}$ grows, given the total referred to above.

But, the household sector may also view any purchasing power it anticipates holding as money as being qualitatively different ("safer") from an equal amount held as equity shares in financial institutions. Therefore, holding constant not only the total $(\pi^{nh}_{t+1}Sn^{hd}_{t+1} + \pi^{fh}_{t+1}Sf^{hd}_{t+1} + (1 + r^{dh}_{t})D^{hd}_{t+1} + Cu^{hd}_{t+1})/p^{ch}_{t+1}$ but also the subtotal $(\pi^{fh}_{t+1}Sf^{hd}_{t+1} + (1 + r^{dh}_{t})D^{hd}_{t+1} + Cu^{hd}_{t+1})/p^{ch}_{t+1}$ present utility presumably rises as the component $((1 + r^{dh}_{t})D^{hd}_{t+1} + Cu^{hd}_{t+1})/p^{c}_{t+1}$ rises. Therefore the term, $U_9(.)$ in (8.7) that depicts the present utiliy of the degree of safety associated with the purchasing power of the portfolio of financial assets planned for the end of the current period is hereby replaced by the two-term expression:

$$\hat{U}_9([\pi^{fh}_{t+1}Sf^{hd}_{t+1} + (1+r^{dh}_{t})D^{hd}_{t+1} + Cu^{hd}_{t+1}]/p^{c}_{t+1})$$

$$+ U_{10}([(1 + r^{dh}_{t})D^{hd}_{t+1} + Cu^{hd}_{t+1}]/p^{c}_{t+1})$$

with $\hat{U}_9(.), \hat{U}_{10}(.) > 0$; $\hat{U}'_9, \hat{U}'_{10} > 0$; and $\hat{U}''_9, \hat{U}''_{10} < 0$.

When these two terms are inserted into (8.7) they indicate that, for given values of c^{h}_{t+1}, g_{t+1}, Tx_{t+1}, K^{hd}_{t+1}, N^{s}_{t+1} and L^{h}_{t+1}, present utility will increase if the household sector decides to transfer a dollar (in real terms) from financial assets held as equity in the nonfinancial sector at the end of the period to a dollar held as equity in the depository institutions. Furthermore, they indicate that present utility will rise even more if the household sector should decide instead to transfer a (real) dollar from nonfinancial equity shares to money balances in the portfolio it plans for the end of the current period.

Substituting (8.8) - (8.11) for μ^*, μ, τ^* and τ respectively in (8.7) now yields the following expression for present utility:

$$
\begin{aligned}
U = {} & \tilde{U}_1(c^h{}_t) + \tilde{U}_2(\mu^*(h^*N - h_tN_t, K^h{}_t)) \\
& + \tilde{\tilde{U}}_3(\tau^*(c^h{}_t, Cu^h{}_t/p^{ch}{}_{t+1}, D^h{}_t/p^{ch}{}_{t+1})) \\
& + \tilde{U}_4(g_t) + \tilde{U}_5(c^h{}_{t+1}) + \tilde{U}_6(\mu(h^*N - hN^s{}_{t+1}, K^{hd}{}_{t+1})) \\
& + \tilde{U}_7(\tau(c^h{}_{t+1}, Cu^{hd}{}_{t+1}/p^{ch}{}_{t+1}, D^{hd}{}_{t+1}/p^{ch}{}_{t+1})) + \tilde{U}_8(g_{t+1}) \\
& + \hat{U}_9([\pi^{hf}{}_{t+1}Sf^{hd}{}_{t+1} + (1 + r^{dh}{}_t)D^{hd}{}_{t+1} + Cu^{hd}{}_{t+1}]/p^{ch}{}_{t+1}) \\
& + \hat{U}_{10}([(1 + r^{dh}{}_t)D^{hd}{}_{t+1} + Cu^{hd}{}_{t+1}]/p^{ch}{}_{t+1})
\end{aligned}
\tag{8.12}
$$

Assuming zero values for the cross-partials in $\tau^*(.)$ and $\tau(.)$, given that the second-order partials of $\tilde{U}_3(.)$ and $\tilde{U}_7(.)$ are assumed to be zero and given that a strictly concave function (either $\tilde{U}_2(.)$ or $\tilde{U}_6(.)$) of a strictly concave function ($\mu^*(.)$ or $\mu(.)$, respectively) is also strictly concave, then (8.12) may be written more simply as:

$$
\begin{aligned}
U = {} & U_1(c^h_t) + U_2(h^*N - h_tN_t, K^h_t) + U_3(Cu^h_t/p^{ch}_t) \\
& + U_4(D^h_t/p^{ch}_t) + U_5(c^h_{t+1}) + U_6(h^*N - hN^s_{t+1}, K^h_{t+1}) \\
& + U_7(Cu^h_{t+1}/p^{ch}_{t+1}) + U_8(D^h_{t+1}/p^{ch}_{t+1}) \\
& + U_9\left(\frac{\pi^{fh}_{t+1}Sf^h_{t+1} + (1 + r^{dh}_t)D^h_{t+1} + Cu^h_{t+1}}{p^{ch}{}_{t+1}}\right)
\end{aligned}
\tag{8.13}
$$

$$+ U_{10}\left(\frac{Cu^h_{t+1} + (1 + r^{dh}_t) D^h_{t+1}}{p^{ch}_{t+1}}\right) + U_{11}(\sigma_t) + U_{12}(\sigma_{t+1})$$

where

$$U'_1(.) = \tilde{U}'_1(.) + \tilde{U}'_3\tau^*_1 > 0; \; U''_1 = \tilde{U}''_1 + U'_3\tau^*_{11} < 0$$

$$U_2(.) = \tilde{U}_2(\mu^*(.)); \; (\tilde{U}_2)_1 = \tilde{U}'_2\mu^*_1 > 0; \; (U_2)_2 = \tilde{U}'_2\mu^*_2 > 0$$

$$U'_3 = \tilde{U}'_3\tau^*_2 > 0; \; \tilde{U}''_3 = \tilde{U}'_3\tau^*_{22} < 0$$

$$U'_4 = U'_3\tau^*_3 > 0; \; \tilde{U}''_4 = U'_3\tau^*_{33} < 0;$$

$$U'_5(.) = \tilde{U}'_5(.) + \tilde{U}'_7\tau^*_1 > 0$$

$$U''_5 = \tilde{U}''_5 + \tilde{U}'_7\tau^*_{11} < 0$$

$$U_6 = \tilde{U}_6(\mu(.)); \; (U_6)_1 = \tilde{U}'_6\mu_1 > 0; \; (U_6)_2 = \tilde{U}'_6\mu_2 > 0;$$

$$(U_6)_{11} = \tilde{U}'_6\mu_{11} + \tilde{U}''_6(\mu_1)^2 < 0; \; (U_6)_{22} = U'_6\mu_{22} + (U''_6)(\mu_2)^2 < 0$$

$$U'_7 = \tilde{U}'_7\tau_2 > 0; \; U''_7 = \tilde{U}'_7\tau_{22} < 0; \; U'_8 = \tilde{U}'_7\tau_3 > 0; \; U''_8 = \tilde{U}''_7\tau_{33} < 0;$$

$$U_9(.) = \hat{U}_9(.); \; U_{10}(.); \; U_{11}(.) = \tilde{U}_4(.) \text{ and } U_{12}(.) = \tilde{U}_8(.).$$

Again for simplicity, assume $(U_6)_{12} = 0$. Essentially, expression (8.13) depicts present utility at time t as a strictly-concave function of c^h_t, c^h_{t+1}, N^s_{t+1}, Cu^h_{t+1}, D^h_{t+1}, Sf^h_{t+1}, g_{t+1} and K^h_{t+1}.

To summarize, the objective of the household sector at time t is to maximize (8.13) subject to restrictions (8.2), (8.3), (8.5) and (8.6). Substitute (8.3) and (8.6) into (8.2) and (8.5). Then, solve (8.5) to obtain the following expression for c^h_{t+1}:

$$c^h_{t+1} = \left(\frac{1}{p^{ch}_{t+1}}\right) [w_{t+1}hN^s_{t+1} + \frac{\pi^{nh}_{t+1}}{p^n_t}\{w_t h_t N_t + \pi^n_t Sn_t + \pi^f_t Sf_t + r^d_{t-1}D^h_t$$

$$- r^{d}_{t-1}L_t - Tx_t - p^{ch}_t c^h_t - (Cu^h_{t+1} - Cu^h_t) - (D^h_{t+1} - D^h_t)$$

$$- p^{fh}_t(Sf^h_{t+1} - Sf_t) + p^{nh}_t Sn_t\}$$

$$+ \pi^{fh}_{t+1}Sf^h_{t+1} + (1 + r^{dh}_t)D^h_{t+1} - Tx_{t+1}(g_{t+1},k) + Cu^h_{t+1}$$

$$+ p^{kh}_{t+1}K^h_{t+1} - (1+r^{lh}_t)p^k_t(K^h_{t+1}-K^h_t) - (1+r^{lh}_t)L_t] \quad (8.14)$$

Substituting the right hand side of (8.1) for c^h_{t+1} in (8.13) then yields the following unconstrained objective function for the household sector:

$$U = U_1(c^h_t) + U_2(h^*N - h_tN_t,\ K^h_t) + U_3(Cu^h_t/p^{ch}_t) + U_4(D^h_t/p^{ch}_t)$$

$$+ U_5\{\frac{1}{p^{ch}_{t+1}}[w_{t+1}hN^s_{t+1} + \frac{\pi^{nh}_{t+1}}{p^n_t}\{w_th_tN_t + \pi^n_t Sn_t + \pi^f_t Sf_t + r^d_{t-1}D^h_t \quad (8.15)$$

$$- r^{\ell}_{t-1}L_t - Tx_t - p^{ch}_t c^h_t - (Cu^h_{t+1} - Cu^h_t) - (D^h_{t+1} - D^h_t) -$$

$$- p^{fh}_t(Sf^h_{t+1} - Sf_t) + p^{nh}_t Sn_t\} + \pi^{fh}_{t+1}Sf_{ht+1} + (1 + r^d_t)D^h_{t+1}$$

$$- Tx_{t+1}(g_{t+1},k) + Cu^h_{t+1} + p^{kh}_{t+1}K^h_{t+1} - (1 + r^{lh}_t)p^{kh}_t(K^h_{t+1} - K^h_t)$$

$$- (1 + r^{lh}_t)L_t]\}$$

$$+ U_6(h^*N - hN^s_{t+1},\ K^h_{t+1}) + U_7(Cu^h_{t+1}/p^{ch}_{t+1}) + U_8(D^h_{t+1}/p^{ch}_{t+1})$$

$$+ U_9(\frac{\pi^{fh}_{t+1}Sf^h_{t+1} + Cu^h_{t+1} + (1 + r^{dh}_t)D^h_{t+1}}{p^{ch}_{t+1}}) + U_{10}(\frac{Cu^h_{t+1} + (1 + r^{dh}_t)D^h_{t+1}}{p^{ch}_{t+1}})$$

$$+ U_{11}(g_t) + U_{12}(g_{t+1}).$$

First-Order Conditions

Differentiating (8.15) partially with respect to current purchases of consumption goods, c^h_t, yields the necessary condition (8.16):

$$U_1' - \frac{\pi^{nh}_{t+1}p^{ch}_t}{p^{nh}_t p^{ch}_{t+1}} U_5' = 0 \tag{8.16}$$

This condition, derived holding N^s_{t+1}, Sf^{hd}_{t+1}, Cu^{hd}_{t+1}, K^{hd}_{t+1} and g_{t+1} constant, allows only c^h_t, c^h_t and Sn^{hd}_{t+1} to vary. As a result the partial derivative of (8.15) with respcet to c^h_t which produced condition (8.16) refers to an increase in current consumption financed by reducing current saving by purchasing during the current period fewer equity shares issued by the nonfinancial business sector. This reduction in current saving effectively reduces the number of consumption goods which the household sector may purchase next period. The ratio π^{nh}_{t+1}/p^{nh}_t represents the anticipated total return (including principal) next period per share of nonfinancial equity as a percent of the current market price anticipated by the household sector. Therefore this ratio equals $1 + r^{nh}_t$ where r^{nh}_t equals the anticipated nominal rate of return on nonfinancial equity. Since p^{ch}_{t+1}/p^{ch}_t represents the ratio of the price of consumption goods which households expect next period to the current price of consumption goods, it may be written as $1 + p^{ch}$ where p^{ch} denotes the rate of change in the price of consumption goods anticipated by the household sector. Therefore the ratio $(\pi^{nh}_{t+1}p^{ch}_t)/(p^n_t p^{ch}_{t+1})$ may be represented as $(1 + r^{nh})/(1 + p^{ch})$, or $(1 + R^{nh})$, where R^{nh} is the "real" rate of return which the household sector expects to earn on an equity share issued by the nonfinancial business sector. The term $(1 + R^{nh})$ in the present context represents the number of consumption goods which the households anticipate they will sacrifice next period to obtain an additional unit of consumption goods in the current period. Therefore, transferring the second term in (8.16) to the right hand side and dividing both sides by U'_5 yields the standard intertemporal result that the household sector will continue to add to current consumption up to the point at which the rate at which it can substitute future goods for present goods in the market, $1 + R^{nh}$, just equals the rate at which it is willing to do so, U'_1/U'_5.

Differentiating (8.15) partially with respect to the number of people who would like to work next period, N^s_{t+1}, produces the necessary condition (8.17):

$$U_5'\left(\frac{w_{t+1}h}{p^{ch}_{t+1}}\right) - (U_6)_1 h = 0 \tag{8.17}$$

According to this condition, the household sector will continue to increase the number of people it sends into the labor force this period (to seek jobs for next period) until the marginal utility of the extra consumption next peiod which an extra employee will provide the household sector just equals the marginal loss in utility due to the reduction in goods and services produced within the household sector. The gain in marginal utility via the extra consumption goods provided by the last worker is shown in the first term on the left hand side of (8.17). The marginal loss in utility resulting from reduced home production is shown by the second term in that equation.

Differentiating (8.15) partially with respect to the number of equity shares issued by the financial sector which the household sector demands for the end of the current period, Sf^{h}_{t+1}, yields expression (8.18):

$$U_5'\left(-\frac{\pi^{nh}_{t+1}p^{fh}_{t}}{p^{nh}_{t}\,p^{ch}_{t+1}} + \frac{\pi^{fh}_{t+1}}{p^{ch}_{t+1}}\right) + U_9'\,\frac{\pi^{fh}_{t+1}}{p^{ch}_{t+1}} = 0. \tag{8.18}$$

This particular necessary condition for utility maximization is derived holding constant all choice variables <u>except</u> Sf^{hd}_{t+1}, c^{h}_{t+1} and Sn^{hd}_{t+1}. The latter two are free to vary implicitly due to the substitutions performed in producing expression (8.15). If the household sector decides at time t to add one share of financial sector stock to its portfolio by time t, it can expect to receive total receipts of π^{fh}_{t+1} next period from that share. The anticipated purchasing power of that amount is then represented by $(\pi^{fh}_{t+1}/p^{ch}_{t+1})$. On the other hand, if the household sector buys a share of financial sector equity this period, which the household sector anticipates at time t will cost p^{fh}_{t}, it must sacrifice purchasing (p^{fh}_{t}/p^{nh}_{t}) shares (or a fraction thereof) of nonfinancial equity this period, since p^{nh}_{t} denotes the current period price of that equity which the household sector anticipates at time t. Therefore, since π^{nh}_{t+1} depicts the anticipated total yield next period from a share of nonfinancial sector stock, the household sector expects to sacrifice $(\pi^{nh}_{t+1}p^{fh}_{t}/p^{nh}_{t}p^{ch}_{t+1})$ units of consumption goods next period by purchasing (p^{fh}_{t}/p^{nh}_{t}) fewer shares of that stock this period. The amount, $-(\pi^{nh}_{t+1}p^{nh}_{t}/p^{nh}_{t}p^{ch}_{t+1}) + (\pi^{fh}_{t+1}/p^{ch}_{t+1})$, if negative, represents the net reduction in the number of consumption goods which the household sector anticipates it will be able to buy next period if it decides to purchase one more share of financial sector equity this period rather than using that money to buy a share of nonfinancial sector stock. Under these conditions, then, the first term in (8.18) represents the marginal loss in present utility due to the forgone future consumption associated with purchasing an extra share of financial sector equity (rather than nonfinancial equity of equal value) in the current period.

The second term in (8.18) represents the marginal utility of the increment in anticipated purchasing power over future consumption which is in a form deemed "safer" than that provided by nonfinancial equity. Consequently, according to (8.18) the household sector will continue to add to its demand for financial sector stock (at the expense of nonfinancial sector equity) up to the point at which the marginal utility of the extra security of the puchasing power over future consumption provided by the marginal financial-sector share just equals the marginal disutility associated with forgoing the opportunity to <u>possibly</u> earn a higher yield and therefore enjoy greater consumption by instead purchasing extra equity in the nonfinancial sector. The difference in parentheses in the first term in (8.18) must be negative, since the second term in that expression is positive. As long as the extra security associated with financial equity yields positive marginal utility, the household sector will be willing to anticipate earning a rate of return on that equity, $(\pi^{fh}_{t+1}/p^{fh}_{t}) - 1$, which is lower than that anticipated on nonfinancial equity, $(\pi^{nh}_{t+1}/p^{nh}_{t}) - 1$.

The partial derivative of (8.15) with respect to the amount of currency which the household sector plans at time t to hold by the end of the current period, Cu^{hd}_{t+1}, produces the following necessary condition:

$$U_5'\left(-\frac{\pi^{nh}_{t+1}}{p^n_t p^{ch}_{t+1}} + \frac{1}{p^{ch}_{t+1}}\right) + U_7'\left(\frac{1}{p^{ch}_{t+1}}\right) + U_9'\left(\frac{1}{p^{ch}_{t+1}}\right) + U_{10}'\left(\frac{1}{p^{ch}_{t+1}}\right) = 0 \qquad (8.19)$$

Together the last two terms on the left hand side of (8.19) represent the marginal utility of adding to the safer financial asset in the portfolio planned for the end of the period. The second term, $U'_7(1/p^{ch}_{t+1})$, represents the marginal utility derived from the anticipated reduction in transactions time next period resulting from the marginal increase in currency holdings planned for the beginning of that period. According to condition (8.19), as long as the household sector continues to assign positive utility to either or both of the safety and resource conserving properties of currency, it will be willing to hold currency even though the anticipated yield on nonfinancial equity, $(\pi^{nh}_{t+1}/p^{nh}_{t}) - 1$, is greater than zero. In other words, as long as the sum of the last three terms on the left hand side of (8.19) is positive, the first term will be negative. The household sector under these conditions will continue to add to its demand for currency up to the point at which the marginal utility of the extra safety and time conserving properties of the last unit of currency is just offset by the marginal loss in utility due to the future consumption it anticipates it will forgo because it is placing the last dollar in currency holdings rather than into the income generating nonfinancial equity.

One of the advantages of the approach followed here is that it provides an explicit theoretical basis upon which to establish the optimal mix of currency, checkable deposits, and equity demanded by the households. Consequently, it provides an explicit microfoundation for the "desired ratios" commonly employed on an ad hoc basis in studies of the money supply process. In addition, in the present study these microfoundations are mutually consistent and fully integrated with the remainder of the model. Another example of this is provided by the following necessary condition for the maximization of present utility.

Partial differentiating (8.15) with respect to the volume of checkable deposits which the household sector demands for time t+1, D^{h}_{t+1}, yields the following condition:

$$U'_5\left(-\frac{\pi^{nh}_{t+1}}{p^{nh}_{t}\,p^{ch}_{t+1}} + \frac{1 + r^{dh}_{t}}{p^{ch}_{t+1}}\right) + U'_8\left(\frac{1}{p^{ch}_{t+1}}\right) + U'_9\left(\frac{1 + r^{dh}_{t}}{p^{ch}_{t+1}}\right) + U'_{10}\left(\frac{1 + r^{dh}_{t}}{p^{ch}_{t+1}}\right) = 0 \qquad (8.20)$$

Just as in (8.19), the sum of the last two terms on the left hand side represents the marginal utility of adding a dollar to the relatively safer financial asset, D^{h}_{t+1}. Because a dollar of D^{h}_{t+1} added to the portfolio by time t+1 represents $(1 + r^{dh}_{t})$ dollars of nominal purchasing power over commodities next period, ceteris paribus, a dollar increase in checkable deposits contributes more to present utility derived from safety of purchasing power than does a dollar of currency. The second term in (8.20) denotes the marginal utility derived from the ability of an extra dollar of checkable deposits to conserve transactions time. As long as the sum of this term and the last two terms on the left hand side of (8.20) remains positive, condition (8.20) stipulates that the difference in parentheses in the first term must be negative, i.e. that the anticipated return on nonfinancial equity, $(\pi^{nh}_{t+1}/p^{nh}_{t}) - 1$, must exceed the rate of interest, r^{dh}_{t}, which the household sector anticipates receiving on its checkable deposits next period. The entire first term then represents the marginal disutility of adding a dollar to checkable deposits rather than nonfinancial equity by the end of the current period because of the sacrifice of future consumption which this choice implies. According to (8.20) the sector will continue to plan to add to its holdings of checkable deposits until the marginal disutility of this forgone consumption is exactly offset by the marginal utility provided by the safety and transactions-time conserving properties of the last dollar of checkable deposits.

Subtracting (8.19) from (8.20) yields the following:

$$U_5'\left(\frac{r^{dh}_t}{p^{ch}_{t+1}}\right) + (U_8' - U_7')\left(\frac{1}{p^{ch}_{t+1}}\right) + (U_9' + U_{10}')\frac{r^{dh}_t}{p^{ch}_{t+1}} = 0 \qquad (8.21)$$

According to (8.21), if the household sector were to add one dollar to D^{h}_{t+1} by reducing its demand for Cu^{h}_{t+1} one dollar, then (a) present utility will rise because of the extra consumption goods the sector could purchase next period, $U'_5(r^{dh}_{t}/p^{ch}_{t+1})$, and (b) present utility will increase because each dollar placed in checkable deposits rather than currency adds r^{dh}_{t} dollar's worth of relatively safe purchasing power over commodities next period. However, (8.21) also stipulates that on the margin, the <u>net</u> increase in present utility resulting from a transfer of a dollar of currency to checkable deposits must equal zero. Therefore, the marginal utility of the extra transactions time which a dollar of currency conserves must exceed the marginal utility of the extra transactions time that a dollar of checkable deposits conserves when utility is maximized.

Partially differentiating (8.25) with respect to the amount of physical capital which the household sector plans to hold by the end of the current period, K^{h}_{t+1}, produces condition (8.22);

$$U_5'\left(\frac{\acute{p}^{kh}_{t+1} - (1 + r^{lh}_t)p^{kh}_t}{p^{ch}_{t+1}}\right) + (U_6)_2 = 0 \qquad (8.22)$$

The second term in (8.22) denotes the marginal utility of the extra household production of goods and services which the marginal unit of physical capital provides next period. The first term, which must be negative for (8.22) to hold, represents the marginal disutility associated with the reduction in the purchase of consumption goods next period caused by the expenditure in the current period on the extra unit of physical capital. For by purchasing an extra unit of physical capital costing p^{kh}_t in the current period, the household sector will have to repay $(1 + r^{lh}_t)p^{kh}_t$ in principal and interest to depository institutions next period. This amount less the anticipated "resale" value, p^{kh}_{t+1}, of the capital good next period represents the nominal amount that the sector will have to forgo spending on consumption goods next period. This net amount, $p^{kh}_t r^{lh}_t - (p^{kh}_{t+1} - p^{k}_t)$, is nothing more than the discrete version of the familiar "user cost of capital" for the case in which physical depreciation is ignored.

The last first-order condition is obtained by partially differentiating (8.15) with respect to the volume of government-produced goods, g_{t+1}, which the household sector decides the government should provide next period.

$$U_5'(-\frac{Tx'_{t+1}}{p^{ch}_{t+1}}) + U'_{12} = 0 \qquad (8.23)$$

The term U'_{12} represents merely the marginal utility of government-produced goods. The first term, however, represents the marginal disutility caused by the household sector's sacrifice of future private consumption in order to finance the increase in government-produced goods. Just as in every other case, expression (8.23) stipultes that the household sector will continue to increase the amont of government-produced goods it desires up to the point at which the marginal utility of those goods is just offset by the marginal disutility associated with the curtailed private expenditure on privately produced consumption goods.

Household Sector's Decision Variables

Totally differentiating (8.16) - (8.20), (8.22) and (8.23) and solving for the vector $dc^h_t, dN^s_{t+1}, dSf^{hd}_{t+1}, dD^{hd}_{t+1}$ and dg_{t+1} yields qualiative solutions for the responses in the corresponding decision variables to various parametric changes. The optimizing responses in Sn^{hd}_{t+1} and c^h_{t+1} may then be obtained using (8.2) (after substitutiting (8.3) and (8.6) into it) and (8.14) respectively. The changes in the optimal levels of L^{hd}_{t+1} and Tx_{t+1} may be found directly from (8.3) and (8.6) respectively. The effects of various parametric changes upon the household sector's decision variables are discussed immediately below.

Current disposable income

An increase in the household sector's current disposable income, $w_t h_t N_t + \pi^n_t Sn_t + \pi^f_t Sf_t + r^d_{t-1} D_t - Tx_t$, holding constant its current outlays for interest payments on personal loans, $r^\ell_{t-1} L_t$, causes the household sector to increase is desired level of current consumpton, $p^c_t c^h_t$, but by less than the increase in disposable income. A drop in current interest payments to depository institutions, $r^\ell_{t-1} L_t$, holding disposable income constant, produces a similar effect.

The household sector may direct the increase in current saving resulting from either greater disposable income or smaller interest payments on personal loans to acquisitions of currency, checkable deposits, equity issued by financial institutions and/or equity issued by nonfinancial businesses. Ceteris paribus, since current saving rises, the household sector is able to purchase more consumption goods next period. In terms of condition (8.19), this means that if Cu^h_{t+1} were to remain unchanged, the first term would become larger in algebraic value (smaller in absolute value), causing an inequaltiiy to result. In other words, if Cu^h_{t+1} were to remain unchanged, the marginal disutility of the forgone future consumption associated with accumulating a unit of currency (rather than nonfinancial equity) would become smaller than the marginal utility associated with the reduced transactions time and the relatively greater safety of nominal value provided by a unit of currency. Consequently, the houseuhold sector is encouraged to devote at least a portion of its greater current saving to acquiring additional currency with which to start next period; the household sector's demand for currency, Cu^h_{t+1}, rises.

The effect of an increase in disposable income upon the household sector's demand for checkable deposits, D^h_{t+1}, is not clear when the sector has available to it not only another monetary asset but also nonmonetary financial assets whose yields are higher than that on checkable deposits. It may be that the household sector increases its demands for both Cu^h_{t+1} and D^h_{t+1} or that it increases its demand for Cu^h_{t+1} but reduces its demand for D^h_{t+1}. But it will not increase its demand for D^h_{t+1} in response to an increase in disposable income and at the same time lower its demand for Cu^h_{t+1}.

To see why, consider expression (8.21) derived above for the case of an increase in current disposable income. Since current saving rises, future consumption rises, causing the first term in (8.21) to become smaller; the marginal utility of the extra future consumption provided by saving an additional dollar via checkable deposits rather than via currency falls. Also, if the sector were to increase D^h_{t+1} by one dollar but reduce Cu^h_{t+1} by that amount or less, the third term in (8.21) would also become less positive. Therefore, if the household sector decides as a result of an increase in disposable income to save more by increasng D^h_{t+1} but by reducing Cu^h_{t+1} (by a smaller absolute amount), then the middle term in (8.21) must become less negative in order to restore the equality exhibited by that necessary condition. However, this is not possible. For, if D^h_{t+1} were to rise, U'_8 would become smaller and if Cu^h_{t+1} were to fall, U'_7 would become larger. This means that the middle term in (8.21) would become <u>more</u> negative rather than less negative as the sector increased D^h_{t+1} and reduced Cu^h_{t+1}. Therefore, this response by the household sector is ruled out.

Although it is possible that the household sector will elect to increase its demand for Cu^{hd}_{t+1} but reduce its demand for D^h_{t+1} as disposable income rises, its total demand for money, $Cu^{hd}_{t+1} + D^{hd}_{t+1}$, definitely will increase. The household sector's total demand for money is "normal". Of course, it is possible that both components of this demand are normal as well.

The effect of an increase in current disposable income upon the household sector's demand for the "safer" of the two types of equity shares available to it is also uncertain. The sector may increase its demand for this asset or reduce it. However, the sector's total demand for money <u>plus</u> this financial asset, $Cu^{hd}_{t+1} + D^{hd}_{t+1} + p^{fh}_t Sf^{hd}_{t+1}$, is normal.

Furthermore, the analysis of the system generated by totally differentiating (8.16) - (8.20), (8.22) and (8.23) reveals that a unit increase in current disposable income, ceteris paribus, causes the sum $p^{ch}_t c^h_t + Cu^{hd}_{t+1} + D^{hd}_{t+1} + p^{fh}_t Sf^{hd}_{t+1}$ to increase by less than one unit. This implies that the equitiy which the household sector regards as the least safe haven of puchasing power over future consumption (namely, the equity issued by the nonfinancial sector in this particualr study) is also a normal good. This result conforms to empirical evidence. In fact, this evidence has discredited the competing mean-variance approach to portfolio analysis because the latter implies the "risky" asset is an inferior asset.

Turning to the household sector's demands for nonfinancial assets (physical capital) and government-produced goods for next period, the model developed above implies that both goods are normal. An increase in current disposable income increases both the household sector's demand for physical capital, K^{hd}_{t+1}, and the amount of government-produced goods it wants produced next period, g_{t+1}. Reference to expressions (8.22) and (8.23) yields the reason for these responses. In both cases, as the household sector increases its demand for next period's consumption goods, the marginal utility of those goods diminishes thereby reducing the opportunity cost (in terms of forgone utility) of acquiring an added unit of physical capital or of selecting an added unit of government-produced goods.

Since its purchases of physical capital are financed by obtaining a personal loan from depository institutions in this model, the household sector's desired indebtedness for the end of the current period, L^{hd}_{t+1}, will increase with the value of its demand for physical capital. In addition, because it selects the greater level of government-produced goods, g_{t+1}, from the menu prepared for it by the government and because that menu indicates that the greater volume of government-produced goods cannot be forthcoming unless the household sector agrees to pay higher taxes next period, the household sector simultaneously approves a greater tax liability for next period as it raises is desired level of g_{t+1}. Consequently, ceteris paribus, both L^{hd}_{t+1} and Tx_{t+1} will tend to rise as current disposable income rises.

Finally, for a given hourly money wage, w^{h}_{t+1}, which the households anticipate they will receive next period, the number of people who plan to work next period, N^{s}_{t+1}, will tend to diminish as current disposable income rises. From (8.17), as ex ante future consumption rises in response to the larger current saving generated by the rise in current income, the marginal utility of that consumption falls causing the marginal benefit from next period's labor to fall.

To summarize, an increase in current disposable income Y^{d}_{t}, produces the following responses in household sector behavior:

$$\frac{\partial c^{h}_{t}}{\partial Y^{d}_{t}} > 0, \quad \frac{\partial Cu^{hd}_{t+1}}{\partial Y^{d}_{t}} > 0, \quad \frac{\partial (Cu^{hd}_{t+1} + D^{hd}_{t+1})}{\partial Y^{d}_{t}} > 0, \quad \frac{\partial (Cu^{hd}_{t+1} + D^{hd}_{t+1} + pf^{h}_{t}\ Sf^{hd}_{t+1})}{\partial Y^{d}_{t}} > 0$$

$$\frac{\partial N^{s}_{t+1}}{\partial Y^{d}_{t}} < 0, \quad \frac{\partial(p^{nh}_{t} Sn^{hd}_{t+1})}{\partial Y^{d}_{t}} > 0, \quad \frac{\partial g_{t+1}}{\partial Y^{d}_{t}} > 0, \quad \frac{\partial K^{hd}_{t+1}}{\partial Y^{d}_{t}} > 0, \quad \frac{\partial Tx_{t+1}}{\partial Y^{d}_{t}} > 0 \qquad (8.24)$$

and $\frac{\partial L^{hd}_{t+1}}{\partial Y^{d}_{t}} > 0$

If we assume that checkable deposits and equity issued by the financial institutions (which we have arbitrarily selected as the "safer" of the two types of equity) are both normal goods, then, in addition, $D^{hd}_{t+1}/\partial Y^{d}_{t} > 0$ and $\partial(p^{fh}{}_{t} Sf^{hd}{}_{t+1})/\partial Y^{d}{}_{t} > 0$.

Initial net wealth

An increase in any one of (a) the number of shares equity held in nonfinancial businesses, Sn_{t}, (b) the number of depository-institution equity shares, Sf_{t}, (c) the initial stock of currency, $Cu^{h}{}_{t}$, (d) the initial stock of checkable deposits, $D^{h}{}_{t}$, or (e) the initial stock of physical capital, $K^{h}{}_{t}$, causes effects similar to the ones discussed above for an increase in current disposable income (or to a reduction in current interest on personal loans). A reduction in the volume of household debt outstanding, $L^{h}{}_{t}$, at the beginning of the current period also produces similar results. No matter which one of the above additions to initial net wealth occurs, the household sector will be able, because of the increase in net wealth, to increase current consumption and reduce future work even though current disposable income (less current interest on personal loans) remains unchanged. Also, a dollar increase in anyone of the initial assets (or dollar decrease in initial liabilities) would enable the sector to sell a portion of that increase and use the proceeds of that sale to buy consumption goods as well as to accumulate other assets. The portion of the increase in the initial asset which remains unsold constitutes an increase in the housheold sector's end-of-period demand for that asset. Therefore the signs of the partial derivatives in (8.24) associated with an increae in current disposable income correspond term by term with the signs of the partials associated with an increase in initial net wealth (for a reason other than a change in an asset's price).

Current price of consumption goods

An increase in the current price of consumption goods produces the familiar income and substitution effects. Current disposable income is effectively reduced as p^{ch}_t rises since it now takes more of the unchanged income to purchase a given amount of consumption goods. These income effects associated with a rise in p^{ch}_t are therefore opposite in sign to the partials displayed in (8.24) for an increase in disposable income.

The increase in p^{ch}_t also causes the household sector to substitute future consumption, future household-produced goods, and future government-produced goods for current consumption. As a result, the sector will decide (a) to consume less in the current period, (b) to save more in the current period by accumulating not only more money, $Cu^h_{t+1} + D^h_{t+1}$, but also more of the relatively safe assets, $Cu^h_{t+1} + D^h_{t+1} + p^{fh}_t Sf^h_{t+1}$, and more of the less safe asset, $p^{nh}_t Sn^h_{t+1}$, (c) to work less for other sectors next period; (d) to demand more physical capital for next period; and (e) to demand more government-produced goods.

Since the substitution and income effects work in opposite directions in every case except for current consumption, the only qualitative result that is known a priori is that current consumption will fall as its price increases.

Current period equity prices

An increase in the price of an equity share also produces income and substitution effects. The income effect associated with a change in the price of a financial asset is no different than that associated with a change in the price of consumption goods. In particular, if an agent plans to purchase additional units of an asset during the period, an increase in the price of that asset is tantamount to a reduction in that agent's disposable income with the reduction varying in proportion to the number of units of the asset which the agent originally planned to purchase. The only difference between the two cases in the present example is that the household sector's initial inventory of consumption goods is assumed to be zero at time t so that its planned purchases of goods during the current period also represents its total demand for consumption goods. But the household sector is permitted to hold an initial inventory of financial assets at time t. The number of units of an asset that it plans to buy during the period is simply the difference between the number of units it plans at time t to hold at the end of the period and the number of units with which it begins the period. If the market price of an asset which the household sector plans to purchase during the period rises, the household sector will be worse off in spite of the fact that the dollar value of that asset in its initial portfolio increases. Therefore the often recognized wealth effect attached to the initial portfolio actually constitutes only a part of the broader income effect.

Since the households are net savers in the present model, potentially they could decide to save by accumulating both types of equity during the current period. In this case an increase in the price of either p^{fh}_t or p^{nh}_t will effectively reduce the current disposable income of the household sector, causing it to demand less of all assets, to consume less in the current period, to demand fewer government-produced goods and to increase its supply of labor to the employing sectors. On the other hand if the household sector is planning at time t to be a net seller during the current period of the particular equity whose price rises, then the household sector experiences, in effect an increase in income. In this case the signs of the partials associated with the income effect will be the same as those shown in (8.24). The following discussion of the substitutition effects resulting from an increase in the current market price of an equity share will be based upon the assumption that checkable deposits and equity issued by the depository institutions are both normal goods.

Consider, first, the case of an increase in p^{fh}_t (holding constant the anticipated future income from financial-sector equity). As p^{fh}_t rises, the anticipated rate of return on this type of equity falls causing the household sector's demand for it to fall as well. The drop in this return also increases the opportunity cost of future consumption relative to current consumption; ceteris paribus, a unit increase in future consumption requires a larger sacrifice of current consumption than it did previously. Therefore the household sector will tend to increase current consumption and reduce future consumption demand at time t.

An increase in p^{fh}_t also produces a direct impact upon the household sector's demands for each of the other assets it plans to hold at the end of the current period. In particular, the household sector will tend to replace its reduced demand for equity in the private financial sector with all other assets, since their net returns remain unchanged when p^{fh}_t rises. Some indirect effects also exist, however, which work against these more direct ones. For instance, the direct effect tending to raise the sector's demand for checkable deposits also has an impact upon the marginal utility of holding currency. In particular, as the household sector plans to add to checkable deposits, these deposits provide added "security" or "safety" to the portfolio planned for the end of the period. This in turn reduces the marginal utility of holding currency. In particular, as the household sector plans to add to checkable deposits, these deposits provide added "security" or "safety" to the portfolio planned for the end of the period. This in turn reduces the marginal utility associated with the ability of a unit of currency to provide that service, which tends to cause the household sector to reduce its demand for currency, on the margin. Assuming that the "direct" effects dominate, the substitution effects upon current consumption, currency demand, the demand for durables, the demand for checkable deposits and the demand for nonfinancial-sector equity shares will all be positive. The substitution effects upon the demand for financial-sector equity and the household sector's supply of labor for next priod will be negative, however.

To understand the negative substition effect upon N^s_{t+1} as p^{fh}_t rises, form the following equality between two ratios using conditions (8.17) and (8.18):

$$\frac{w_{t+1}h}{\left(\frac{\pi^{nh}_{t+1}p^{fh}_t}{p^{nh}_t} - \pi^{fh}_{t+1}\right)} = \frac{(U_6)_1h}{U_9'\pi^{fh}_{t+1}} \tag{8.25}$$

The numerator on the left hand side of (8.25), $w_{t+1}h$, denotes the cost to the household sector next period (in terms of forgone income) of increasing by one the number of people that remain home next period and produce goods and servies within the household sector. The denominator on the left hand side denotes the cost to the household sector next period (in terms of forgone interest income) of forming a "safer" portfolio with which to begin next period by adding one share of equity in the private financial sector to that portfolio and simultaneously reducing the equity held in the private nonfinancial business sector by p^{fh}_t/p^{nh}_t shares. The forgone interest of this purchase of additional safety is then the denominator on the left hand side of (8.25). And the ratio on the left hand side therefore depicts the rate at which the household sector can substitute one more person to produce goods in the household sector for equity shares issued by the financial sector. For if the household sector were to retain one more person, it would potentially sacrifice $w_{t+1}h$ dollars of labor income. In order to offset that reduction in labor income, the sector would need to <u>reduce</u> the number of shares it holds in the financial institutions (i.e. sacrifice some safety of the portfolio it plans for the end of the period) in order to buy enough shares in the higher yielding shares issued by the nonfinancial business sector. The ratio on the right hand side of (8.25) shows the subjective rate at which the household sector is willing to substitute people to produce goods at home for equity issued by the private financial sector. According to (8.25) a necessary condition for utility maximization is that the market and subjective rates of substitution be equal.

Now consider the substitution effect upon N^s_{t+1} due to an increase in p^{fh}_t. The households must sacrifice shares of financial sector equity to acquire the nonfinancial sector shares they require to generate sufficient extra interest income so that one more person may stay home without jeopardizing next period's total income. Clearly, as p^{fh}_t rises the number of financial sector equity shares it must forgo is reduced, since a fewer number of these shares need to be sold to acquire the same number of shares of nonfinancial business sector equity. Therefore the market rate of substitution of people in home production for financial-sector equity falls. This encourages households on the margin to retain more people within the sector to provide household-produced goods. In other words, according to the substitution effect operating upon N^s_{t+1}, an increase in p^{fh}_t causes the households this period too send fewer people into the labor force to seek work for next period.

Dividing condition (8.23) by (8.18) produces an analogous equality between the market rate of substitution of government-produced goods for financial sector equity and the subjective rate of substitution between these items:

$$\frac{Tx'_{t+1}}{\left(\frac{\pi^{nh}_{t+1}p^{fh}_t}{p^{nh}_t} - \pi^{fh}_{t+1}\right)} = \frac{U'_{12}}{U'_9\pi^{fh}_{t+1}} \tag{8.26}$$

Ceteris paribus, as p^{fh}_t rises, the household sector needs to sacrifice fewer shares of financial sector equity in order to buy enough shares in the nonfinancial sector so that next period's disposable income is not reduced even though the household sector elects to pay Tx'_{t+1} more dollars in taxes next period in order to gain an additional unit of government-produced goods. Consequently as p^{fh}_t rises, the market rate of substitution of government-produced goods for financial sector equity falls, thereby encouraging the household sector to order more government-produced goods for next period.

Assuming that the household sector plans at time t to acquire financial sector shares during the current period, then in every case except one, the aforementioned substitution and income effects work in opposite directions. Therefore, a priori, the only definite net effect of an increase in p^{fh}_t is that the household sector's end-of-period demand for financial-sector equity will fall. That is the only case for which the (negative) income and substitution effects operate in the same direction.

As illustrated in conditions (8.16), (8.18), (8.19) and (8.20) respectively, an increase in p^n_t ceteris paribus (a) reduces the real rate of return on nonfinancial equity (thereby reducing the opportunity cost of current consumption), (b) reduces the opportunity cost of purchasing a share of equity in the financial institutions, (c) reduces the opportunity cost of adding a dollar to currency holdings during the current period and (d) reduces the opportunity cost of adding a dollar to checkable deposits during the period. These "direct" effects generate additional "indirect" substitution effects through their influence upon the marginal utility of the extra "safety" which these assets provide in the portfolio planned for the end of the period.

Should the "direct" substitution effects upon c^h_t, Sf^{hd}_{t+1}, Cu^{hd}_{t+1} and D^{hd}_{t+1} dominate not only the "indirect" effects just mentioned but also the contrary income effects (assuming the household sector begins the current period planning to accumulate nonfinancial-sector equity), then the quantity of nonfinancial equity demanded by the households will diminish as the anticipated current period price of that equity, p^{nh}_t, rises.

The substitution effects of an increase in p^{nh}_t upon the household sector's demand for physical capital, K^{hd}_{t+1}, and for government produced goods, g_{t+1}, are indirect and indeterminate within the analytical framework provided here.

Current price of capital goods and the current interest rate on personal loans

As either the current price of capital goods (consumer durables), p^{kh}_t, or the current interest rate on personal loans, r^1_t, rises, the households effectively experience a reduction in next period's anticipated disposable income. Ceteris paribus, the higher either one of these variables happens to be, the greater the number of dollars which the household sector must repay next period either as principal or interest on funds it borrows during the current period to finance the purchase of a given number of capital goods. The negative income effect causes the household sector to reduce its demands for all assets as well as current consumption, future government-produced goods and goods produced in the household sector itself next period. This implies that as a result of the fall in its effective income, the household sector will supply more labor to other sectors for next period.

On the other hand, an increase in p^{kh}_t or r^1_t also causes the household sector to substitute goods and assets which have now become relatively cheaper to acquire for physical capital. The substitution effect at least partially offsets the income effect in every case except the demand for physical capital. (In this last instance, the (negative) income and substitution effects reinforce each other.) The substitution effect upon the sector's supply of labor is negative since the households will tend to substitute human effort for physical capital in household production as p^{kh}_t or r^1_t rises thereby making less labor available to other sectors.

Next period's hourly money wage

The greater the money wage, w_{t+1}, which the employers guarantee to pay their workers next period, the greater will be the household sector's disposable income next period. Consequently the sector will increase its demands for current consumption, the level of government-produced goods for next period and the level of next period's home production. This last effect increases the sector's derived demand for durable goods and reduces its supply of labor to other sectors. Since the sector's demand for consumption next period also rises, so does its demand for nonfinancial-sector equity. However as the anticipated level of next period's consumption rises, its marginal utility falls, thereby causing the opportunity costs of acquiring currency, checkable deposits and financial sector equity to fall. Consequently the income effect of an increase in w_{t+1} upon each financial asset is positive.

Unlike the price changes considered to this point, the substitution effects upon every asset, upon current and future consumption, upon household production and upon government-produced goods reinforce rather than contradict the income effects presented above. Only in the case of the household's supply of labor does the positive substitution effect oppose the income effect (a familiar result). Therefore an increase in w_{t+1} produces the same net effects upon c^h_t, Sf^{hd}_{t+1}, Cu^{hd}_{t+1}, D^{hd}_{t+1}, K^{hd}_{t+1}, L^{hd}_{t+1}, Tx_{t+1}, and g_{t+1} as those presented in (8.24) above. We assume that in the case of N^s_{t+1} that the substitution effect dominates the income effect.

Interest rate on checkable deposits

An increase in the current interest rate, r^{dh}_t, on checkable deposits anticipated by the household sector produces several effects. The first is the income effect generated by the greater interest income next period from a given level of deposits held at the end of the current period. This income effect produces the familiar signs in (8.24) above.

However the greater return on checkable deposits also reduces the opportuniity cost of holding these deposits rather than higher yielding assets and increases the opportunity cost of holding currency rather than checkable deposits. Furthermore, since the safety of next period's anticipated purchasing power over consumption goods is derived not only from the checkable deposits themselves but also from the income they generate, an increase in r^{dh}_t also increases the safety associated with a given volume of checkable deposits planned for the end of the current period. In other words, the marginal cost of purchasing a dollar's worth of "safe" disposable income next period falls as r^{dh}_t rises. This reinforces the substitution effects just mentioned.

But this is not all. For as the safety of next period's future income rises with r^{dh}_t, the marginal utility of that safety presumably diminishes thereby reducing the marginal utilities of currency and financial-sector equity as well as the marginal utility of checkable deposits themselves.

Ignoring these last complicating influences, the net effect of an increase in r^{dh}_t will cause the household sector to increase its demand for checkable deposits. But without further assumptions as to the relative strengths of the income and substitution effects upon the other decision variables, the net effects upon these variables remain indeterminate.

Vertical shift in the government goods - tax menu

As discussed previously, a number of factors may shift the position as well as the slope of the tax menu prepared by the government sector. The present section briefly considers the effect of an increase in the shift parameter k in function (8.6) upon the economic behavior of the household sector. An increase in k merely reflects an increased cost to the government of providing a given amount of government-produced goods to the household sector next period.

An upward shift in the tax level Tx_{t+1}, for a given level of g_{t+1} causes the household sector to revise downward its estimate of next period's disposable income. This in turn induces the household sector to reduce its demand for privately produced consumption goods next period (and therefore its demand for nonfinancial sector equity as well) thereby raising the marginal utility of future consumption. This in turn raises (a) the disutility of saving during the current period in a form that yields less income than nonfinancial sector equity, (b) the disutility of the forgone future consumption associated with current purchases of capital goods and (c) the disutility of forgone future consumption associated with the taxes necessary to finance government-produced goods. As a result the household sector will reduce as well its demands for currency, checkable deposits, equity in the private financial sector, durable goods and next period's government-produced goods. The increased marginal utility of future consumption also induces the household sector to increase the number of people who enter (or remain in) the labor force in the current period seeking work for next period.

Should the increase in the shift parameter also increase the slope of the tax function, then further influences upon household sector behavior will be forthcoming. In particular, as Tx'_{t+1} rises, the sector will tend to substitute current consumption, future consumption and goods and services produced within the household sector itself for government-produced goods. These "substitution" effects tend to counteract the aforementioned "income" effects upon current consumption, and the demands for currency, checkable deposits, and equity in depository institutions and nonfinancial businesses. The positive substitution effect upon the household sector's supply of labor as well as the negative substitution effect upon the demand for government produced goods reinforce their respective income effects, however.

<u>Summary of the household sector's econmic behavior in the extended model</u>

The household sector's demand and supply functions may be summarized as follows:

$$c^h_t = c^h_t(\underset{+}{Yd_t},\ \underset{+}{Sn^h_t},\ \underset{+}{Sf^h_t},\ \underset{+}{Cu^h_t},\ \underset{+}{D^h_t},\ \underset{+}{K^h_t},\ \underset{+}{L_t},\ \underset{-}{p^{ch}_t},\ \underset{-}{p^{fh}_t},\ p^{nh}_t,\ p^{kh}_t,\ r^{lh}_t,\ r1^{dh}_t,\ \underset{+}{w_{t+1}},\ k). \qquad (8.27)$$

$$Sf^{hd}_{t+1} = Sf^h_{t+1}(\underset{+}{Yd_t},\ \underset{+}{Sn^h_t},\ \underset{+}{Sf^h_t},\ \underset{+}{Cu^h_t},\ \underset{+}{D^h_t},\ \underset{+}{K^h_t},\ \underset{-}{L_t},\ p^{ch}_t,\ \underset{-}{p^{fh}_t},\ p^{nh}_t,\ p^{kh}_t,\ r^{lh}_t,\ r^{dh}_t,\ \underset{+}{w_{t+1}},\ k). \qquad (8.28)$$

$$Sn^{hd}_{t+1} = Sn^h_{t+1}(\underset{+}{Yd_t},\ \underset{+}{Sn^h_t},\ \underset{+}{Sf^h_t},\ \underset{+}{Cu^h_t},\ \underset{+}{D^h_t},\ \underset{+}{K^h_t},\ \underset{-}{L_t},\ p^{ch}_t,\ p^{fh}_t,\ \underset{-}{p^{nh}_t},\ p^{kh}_t,\ r^{lh}_t,\ r^{dh}_t,\ \underset{+}{w_{t+1}},\ k). \qquad (8.29)$$

$$Cu^{hd}_{t+1} = Cu^h_{t+1}(\underset{+}{Yd_t},\ \underset{+}{Sn^h_t},\ \underset{+}{Sf^h_t},\ \underset{+}{Cu^h_t},\ \underset{+}{D^h_t},\ \underset{+}{K^h_t},\ \underset{-}{L_t},\ p^{ch}_t,\ p^{fh}_t,\ p^{nh}_t,\ p^{kh}_t,\ r^{lh}_t,\ r^{dh}_t,\ \underset{+}{w_{t+1}},\ k). \qquad (8.30)$$

$$D^{hd}_{t+1} = D^h_{t+1}(\underset{+}{Yd_t},\ \underset{+}{Sn^h_t},\ \underset{+}{Sf^h_t},\ \underset{+}{Cu^h_t},\ \underset{+}{D^h_t},\ \underset{+}{K^h_t},\ \underset{-}{L_t},\ p^{ch}_t,\ p^{fh}_t,\ p^{nh}_t,\ p^{nh}_t,\ p^{kh}_t,\ r^{lh}_t,\ r^{dh}_t,\ \underset{+}{w_{t+1}},\ k). \qquad (8.31)$$

$$K^{hd}_{t+1} = K^h_{t+1}(\underset{+}{Yd_t},\ \underset{+}{Sn^h_t},\ \underset{+}{Sf^h_t},\ \underset{+}{Cu^h_t},\ \underset{+}{D^h_t},\ \underset{+}{K^h_t},\ \underset{-}{L_t},\ p^{ch}_t,\ p^{fh}_t,\ p^{nh}_t,\ p^{kh}_t,\ r^{lh}_t,\ r^{dh}_t,\ \underset{+}{w_{t+1}},\ k). \qquad (8.32)$$

$$L^{hd}_{t+1} = L^h_{t+1}(\underset{+}{Yd_t},\ \underset{+}{Sn^h_t},\ \underset{+}{Sf^h_t},\ \underset{+}{Cu^h_t},\ \underset{+}{D^h_t},\ \underset{+}{K^h_t},\ \underset{-}{L_t},\ p^{ch}_t,\ p^{fh}_t,\ p^{nh}_t,\ p^{kh}_t,\ r^{lh}_t,\ r^{dh}_t,\ \underset{+}{w_{t+1}},\ k). \qquad (8.33)$$

$$N^{hd}_{t+1} = N^h_{t+1}(\underset{+}{Yd_t},\ \underset{+}{Sn^h_t},\ \underset{+}{Sf^h_t},\ \underset{+}{Cu^h_t},\ \underset{+}{D^h_t},\ \underset{+}{K^h_t},\ \underset{-}{L_t},\ p^{ch}_t,\ p^{fh}_t,\ p^{nh}_t,\ p^{kh}_t,\ r^{lh}_t,\ r^{dh}_t,\ \underset{+}{w_{t+1}},\ k). \qquad (8.34)$$

$$g^{hd}_{t+1} = g^{h}_{t+1}(\underset{+}{Yd_t},\ \underset{+}{Sn^h_t},\ \underset{+}{Sf^h_t},\ \underset{+}{Cu^h_t},\ \underset{+}{D^h_t},\ \underset{+}{K^h_t},\ \underset{-}{L_t},\ p^{ch}_t,\ p^{fh}_t,$$

$$p^{nh}_t,\ p^{kh}_t,\ r^{lh}_t,\ r^{dh}_t,\ \underset{+}{w_{t+1}},\ \underset{-}{k}). \qquad (8.35)$$

The next two chapters illustrate how the present-value maximizing business sectors will decide the optimal (ex ante) wages, prices and interest rates based upon their estimates of functions (8.27) - (8.35), the government sector's demands (7.24) - (7.28), and the government's supply of bonds, (7.35).

9. - The Nonfinancial Business Sector in the Expanded Model

The model of the nonfinancial business sector presented in this chapter extends the one developed in Chapter 4 by allowing the sector to produce capital goods as well as consumption goods. Consequently in addition to the decisions confronting it in Chapter 4, the sector now must determine (at least tentatively) how many capital goods it will produce in both the current and next periods as well as how many of the capital goods it produces this period it will sell to the household or government sectors and how many it will acquire itself in order to facilitate next period's production.

The only other modification of the model presented earlier concerns the type of money used by the nonfinancial business sector. In Chapter 4 currency constituted the only type of money available. But in the expanded model, depository institutions issue checkable deposits, which also serve as money. To simplify the following analysis, assume now that the nonfinancial business sector holds no currency at the beginning of any period and plans to hold none at the end of any period. Checkable deposits at depository institutions constitute the only type of money which the nonfinancial sector currently holds and/or plans to hold. This assumption does not preclude the nonfinancial business sector from receiving currency as payment during a particular period and then making payments with that currency during the same period.

The nonfinancial business sector appears in this chapter as a centralized decision-maker that begins the current period with given amounts of checkable deposits and physical capital. It also holds a beginning inventory of unsold consumption goods and has a given number of equity shares outstanding. At time t the nonfinancial business sector decides: (a) the number of hours during the current period it will employ the people it has hired by time t, (b) the hourly wage it will announce during the current period, which it will guarantee to everyone it employs by t+1 to work for it next period, (c) the number of people it plans to hire by the end of the current period to work next period, (d) the current period price it will announce for consumption goods, (e) the current period price it will announce for capital goods, (f) the price of consumption goods it anticipates it will announce next period, (g) the price of capital goods it anticipates it will announce next period, (h) the stock of physical capital it wants to hold at t+1, (i) the volume of checkable deposits it wants to hold at t+1, and (j) the price at which it will stand ready during the current period to trade its own equity shares. The sector decides these optimal values simultaneously in a mutually consistent manner that conforms to its overriding objective: the maximization of is present value.

In making these decisions the sector relies on its estimates at time t of the (net) supply function of labor facing it, the market demand functions for consumption and capital goods, and the household sector's demand function for is equity shares. The actual supply of labor to the nonfinancial business sector consists of the household sector's supply of labor (presented in Chapter 8) minus the government's demand for labor (obtained in Chapter 7) and minus the private financial sector's demand for labor (to be derived in Chapter 10). The actual market demand functions for consumption and capital goods consist of the sums of the corresponding demand functions (derived in Chapters 7 and 8) for the household and government sectors. The household sector's demand for shares of ownership in the nonfinancial business sector was derived in Chapter 8.

In the simple models presented in Chapters 3-6, currency represented the household sector's only financial-asset alternative to holding equity issued by the nonfinancial business sector. Since currency yields no market income, from the nonfinancial business sector's point of view the opportunity cost to its shareholders of holding its equity shares was also zero in the simple model. Consequently the nonfinancial business sector maximized its present value by maximizing the simple sum of its anticipated dividends per share over the current and next periods.

In the extended model, however, the households may hold the equity shares of private depository institutions as well as of nonfinancial businesses. Let π^{n}_{t+1} represent the amount which the nonfinancial businesses anticipate they will pay per share to their owners next period. Let π^{fn}_{t+1} denote the total return per share which the nonfinancial business sector anticipates that the private depository institutions will pay their owners next period. And let p^{fn}_{t} depict the price at which the nonfinancial business sector anticipates at time t that equity shares of financial institutions will trade during the current period. Then $\pi^{fn}_{t+1}/p^{fn}_{t}$ represents the anticipated total return next period per dollar spent on financial sector equity this period. It is identical to $1 + r^{fn}_{t}$, defined as the rate of return on financial sector equity anticipated by the nonfinancial business sector.

Given that the nonfinancial business sector anticipates that r^{fn}_t is positive, the sector's owners would need to place only $\pi^n_{t+1}/(1 + r^{fn}_t)$ dollars in their next best alternative (i.e. in financial-sector equity) this period to generate the same total return next period that the nonfinancial sector anticipates it will generate next period. Therefore, the present value of the nonfinancial sector at time t -- the amount which its owners would need to place in their next best alternative at time t in order to duplciate period-by-period the "dividend" stream which the nonfinancial sector anticipates it will generate -- is represented by the weighted sum $\pi^n_t + \pi^n_{t+1}/(1 + r^{fn}_t)$.

The income which the business sector plans at time t to earn during the current period equals the value of its planned current production plus its current interest income minus its current expenses. Its planned level of current (net) business saving, by definition, is the portion of this net income which it plans to retain rather than distribute to existing shareholders. The sector will plan at time t to retain net income during the current period as long as the sector will be able to increase the present value of the future dividends per share by at least as much as the retention of current income reduces its present value.

Formal Model of the Nonfinancial Business Sector

At the beginning of the current period the nonfinancial business sector holds two real assets: an initial inventory of consumption goods, Q_t, and an initial stock of physical capital, K^n_t. Its only financial asset presumably consists of an initial volume of checkable deposits, D^n_t, held at private financial institutions. For simplicity, borrowing by the nonfinancial business sector is ignored in this study. Therefore the nonfinancial businss sector is assumed to have no debt outstanding at time t. Let p^c_t and p^k_t represent the respective prices at which the nonfinancial business sector announces at time t that it stands ready to trade consumption goods and capital goods during the current period. Then in terms of these current-period prices the nonfinancial businss sector's initial balance sheet may be expressed as follows:

Nonfinancial Business Sector's Balance Sheet at Time t

Assets	Liabilities
$p^c_t Q_t$	
$p^k_t K^n_t$	
	Net Wealth
D^n_t	NW^n_t

where NW^n_t is simply the sum of the values of the assets on the left hand side. Let Sn_t denote the number of shares of nonfinancial sector equity outstanding at time t. If the sector decides to liquidate at time t, then its present value per share at time t equals NW^n_t/Sn_t. Otherwise, the sector's present value reflects its anticipated dividend stream over the next two periods.

Let $R^e\{.\}$ represent the current-period revenue which the sector anticipates at time t from its sales of consumption and capital goods. Also, let $r^d_{t-1}D^n_t$ denote the interest income which the nonfinancial sector will receive during the current period. The interest rate r^d_{t-1} was announced last period by the private depository institutions and is paid during the current period on each dollar of checkable deposits held by time t. Then the sector's current-period receipts are depicted by $R^e\{.\} + r^d_{t-1}D^n_t$.

Since all the goods which the nonfinancial business sector requires as factors of production are produced within the sector itself, its only current expense (in the form of outlays to other sectors) consists of wage payments to the households. As before, physical depreciation is ignored. The number of people, N^n_t, who will work for the nonfinancial sector during the current period has already been established by time t. Also each of these workers has already been guaranteed an hourly wage, w_t, for the current period. However at time t the nonfinancial business sector is still free to set the average number of hours, h^n_t, it will use these workers during the current period. Therefore its current-period wage bill, $w_t h^n_t N^n_t$, remains open to choice at time t.

Let K^{nd}_{t+1} represent the amount of physical capital which the nonfinancial business sector plans at time t to hold by time t+1. Then $p^n_t(K^{nd}_{t+1} - K^n_t)$ represents the value of its planned net (and gross) investment in capital goods during the current period. Assuming that the sector plans a zero inventory of consumption goods for the end of the current period, the value of its planned inventory investment for the current period is shown by $-p^c_tQ_t$. Since the anticipated value of the sector's current production equals the anticipated value of current sales plus its ex ante net investment, the anticipated value of its current production may be depicted as $R^e\{.\} + p^k_t(K^{nd}_{t+1}-K^n_t) - p^c_tQ_t$. The net income which the sector anticipates at time t that it will earn during the current period equals the anticipated value of its current production plus its current interest income minus its current wage bill: $R^e\{.\} + p^k_t(K^{nd}_{t+1}-K^n_t) - p^c_tQ_t + r^d_{t-1}D^n_t - w_th^n_tN^n_t$. Since corporate taxes are ignored, this amount also represents current income after taxes.

Ex ante net saving for the current period by the nonfinancial business sector, s^n_t, is defined as anticipated current net income (after taxes) minus current dividends. Let π^n_t denote the level of current-period dividends per share which the nonfinancial sector decides (and announces) at time t. Then ex ante current-period net saving by the sector at time t is represented by:

$$s^n_t = R^e\{.\} + p^k_t(K^{nd}_{t+1} - K^n_t) - p^c_tQ_t + r^d_{t-1}D^n_t - w_th^n_tN^n_t - \pi^n_tSn_t. \tag{9.1}$$

Let D^{nd}_{t+1} denote the volume of checkable deposits which the nonfinancial business sector plans at time t to hold at time t+1. The amount of money which the business sector plans at time t to accumulate during the current period, $D^{nd}_{t+1} - D^n_t$, necessarily equals the amount it plans to save on the income account during the current period, plus the value of its planned sales of equity shares during the period minus the value of is planned net physical investment during the period. Let Sn^e_{t+1} represent the number of its equity shares which the nonfinancial business sector anticipates at time t that the household sector will want to hold at time t+1. Let p^n_t denote the price at which the nonfinancial business sector decides (and announces) at time t that it stands ready to trade its own equity shares during the current period. Then the value of its planned sales of equity shares during the current period is denoted by $p^n_t(Sn^e_{t+1} - Sn_t)$. Since ex ante current saving is denoted by (9.1) and since ex ante net physical investment has been defined as $p^k_t(K^{nd}_{t+1} - K^n_t) - p^c_tQ_t$, it follows that the nonfinancial business sector's planned accumulation of money balances for the current period must obey constraint (9.2):

$$D^{nd} - D^{n}_{t} = [R^{e}\{.\} + p^{k}_{t}(K^{nd}_{t+1} - K^{n}_{t}) - p^{c}_{t}Q_{t} + r^{d}_{t-1}D^{n}_{t} \tag{9.2}$$
$$- w_{t}h^{n}_{t}N^{n}_{t} - \pi^{n}_{t}Sn_{t}] + p^{n}_{t}(Sn^{e}_{t+1} - Sn_{t})$$
$$- [p^{k}_{t}(K^{nd}_{t+1} - K^{n}_{t}) - p^{c}_{t}Q_{t}].$$

After canceling and rearranging terms, (9.2) becomes the following expression for current-period dividends per share:

$$\pi^{n}_{t} = \frac{[R^{e}\{.\} + r_{t-1}D^{n}_{t} - w_{t}h^{n}_{t}N^{n}_{t} + p^{n}_{t}(Sn^{e}_{t+1} - Sn_{t}) - (D^{nd}_{t+1} - D^{n}_{t})]}{Sn_{t}} \tag{9.3}$$

An analogous set of restrictions face the nonfinancial business sector at time t in terms of its plans for next period. Let $R^{e*}\{.\}$ represent the sector's anticipated sales revenue for next period. Since at time t the sector's time horizon extends only to the end of next period, the sector presumably plans to hold no assets and to have no liabilities outstanding at time t+2. Among other things, this implies that its planned inventory of consumption goods for time t+2 and its planned stock of physical capital for time t+2 both equal zero.

Let p^{kn}_{t+1} depict the price at which the nonfinancial business sector anticipates that it will announce (at time t+1) that it will stand ready to trade capital goods next period. Then at time t, the sector's ex ante net investment in capital goods <u>next</u> period is negative and represented by $- p^{kn}_{t+1}K^{nd}_{t+1}$. Since the sector plans at time t to hold no consumption-goods inventory either at the beginning or at the end of next period, the amount $- p^{kn}_{t+1}K^{nd}_{t+1}$ also represents the sector's ex ante total net physical investment for next period. In light of this, the anticipated value of the nonfinancial business sector's production next period is represented by $R^{e*}\{.\} - p^{kn}_{t+1}K^{nd}_{t+1}$.

Let r^{dn}_{t} represent the interest rate which the nonfinancial business sector anticipates at time t that the depository institutions will announce this period that they will pay next period on all checkable deposits held at time t+1. Then the nonfinancial business sector's anticipated interest income for next period from checkable deposits is represented by $r^{dn}_{t}D^{nd}_{t+1}$.

Let w_{t+1} represent the hourly money wage which the nonfinancial business sector announces at time t that it guarantees for next period.

Let N^{nd}_{t+1} represent the number of people which the nonfinancial business sector plans to employ next period for the standard number of hours, h. Then at time t, the sector's anticipated wage bill for next period is given by $w_{t+1}hN^{nd}_{t+1}$

From the discussion to this point, at time t the nonfinancial business sector's anticipated net after-tax income next period is given by: $R^{e*}\{.\} - p^{kn}_{t+1}K^{nd}_{t+1} + r^{dn}_{t}D^{nd}_{t+1} - w_{t+1}hN^{nd}_{t+1}$. Its ex ante net saving for next period is described at time t by (9.4):

$$s^{n}_{t+1} = R^{e*}\{.\} - p^{kn}_{t+1}K^{nd}_{t+1} + r^{dn}_{t}D^{nd}_{t+1} - w_{t+1}hN^{nd}_{t+1} - \pi^{n}_{t+1}Sn^{e}_{t+1} \qquad (9.4)$$

where π^{n}_{t+1} denotes the level of dividends per share which the nonfinancial sector anticipates at time t that it will distribute next period.

At time t the sector anticipates that no market will exist for its equity shares next period. For one thing, the sector will be unwilling to plan to buy back next period any shares it may have outstanding at time t+1. For even if it were to do so it would not be able to alter the amount it will pay out in dividends next period. That amount, $\pi^{n}_{t+1}Sn^{e}_{t+1}$, must be paid to those holding shares at time t+1 regardless of whether they decide to hold or sell their shares after that time. Furthermore, since any additional income to be generated from shares acquired by time t+2 must be received after that date and since the nonfinancial business sector anticipates that additional income will equal zero because it falls outside its time horizon, the sector therefore anticipates that no one will be willing to purchase equity shares from the nonfinancial sector next period. Therefore at time t the sector's anticipated sales of its own equity to the household sector next period equals zero.

Since the nonfinancial business sector plans at time t to hold no checkable deposits at the end of next period (i.e. at time t+2), the amount of money which the sector plans to accumulate during next period is represented by $-D^{nd}_{t+1}$. Since the sector anticipates no sales of its own equity next period, this planned amount of money accumulation necessarily equals the amount it plans to save on the income account next period minus the value of its planned physical investment for next period. In light of the above discussion, then, the following relationship must hold:

$$- D^{nd}_{t+1} = [R^{e*}\{.\} - p^{kn}_{t+1}K^{nd}_{t+1} + r^{dn}_{t}D^{nd}_{t+1} - w_{t+1}hN^{nd}_{t+1} - \pi^{n}_{t+1}Sn^{e}_{t+1}] - [- p^{kn}_{t+1}K^{nd}_{t+1}] \qquad (9.5)$$

Canceling and rearranging terms produces the following expression for the anticipated level of next period's dividends per share:

$$\pi^{n}_{t+1} = \frac{R^{e*}\{\cdot\} + (1 + r_{t})D^{nd}_{t+1} - w_{t+1}hN_{t+1}}{Sn^{e}_{t+1}} \qquad (9.6)$$

As stated in this chapter's introduction, the nonfinancial business sector's objective at time t is to maximize its present value defined as the sum $\pi^{n}_{t} + \pi^{n}_{t+1}/(1 + r^{fn}_{t})$. From expressions (9.3) and (9.6), this objective may be rewritten as:

$$\text{Maximize:} \frac{[R^{e}\{.\} + r^{d}_{t-1}D^{n}_{t} - w_{t}h_{t}N_{t} + p^{n}_{t}(Sn^{e}_{t+1} - Sn_{t}) - (D^{nd}_{t+1} - D^{n}_{t})]}{Sn_{t}}$$

$$+ \frac{R^{e*}\{.\} + (1 + r^{dn}_{t})D^{nd}_{t+1} - w_{t+1}hN^{nd}_{t+1}}{Sn^{e}_{t+1}(1 + r^{fn}_{t})} \qquad (9.7)$$

From the discussion in Chapter 4, this sum also may be viewed as the shadow price, p^{n}_{o}, of a share of nonfinancial sector equity at time t. Before (9.7) can be maximized, the anticipated sales revenue functions, $R^{e}\{.\}$ and $R^{e*}\{.\}$, and the sector's anticipated demand for its equity at the end of the current period, Sn^{e}_{t+1}, must be specified. These are matters to which we now turn.

Anticipated Current Sales Revenue

The nonfinancial business sector's anticipated sales revenue function for the current period is based upon its estimates at time t of the current-period demand functions for consumption goods of the household and government sectors as well as upon its estimates of their demand functions for physical capital for the end of the current period. By subtracting the existing stocks of physical capital held by the household and government sectors at time t from these respective estimated demand functions for capital, the nonfinancial sector then obtains corresponding estimated functions for the number of units of physical capital which these other two sectors plan to purchase during the current period.

According to the analysis of Chapter 7, the government sector knows by time t the volume of government-produced goods, g_t, it must provide in the current period. At time t the average number of hours it employs its workers during the current period, $h^g{}_t$, and the quantity of consumption goods it purchases the period, $c^g{}_t$, are the only two variable factors in the production of g_t. In order to infuse a degree of inflexibility on the part of the government in responding to market forces, assume arbitrarily that the government sector decides $h^g{}_t$ and $c^g{}_t$ at time t <u>before</u> any other sector makes its plans at time t. However, the government presumably does wait until the price setters have announced current-period prices and next-period's wage rate before it decides the number of people it wants to hire for next period or the amount of capital it wants to hold at the beginning of next period.

The importance of these assumptions for the nonfinancial business sector is that it may therefore view the government's current period demand for consumption goods as known and unresponsive to the price the nonfinancial business sector announces for those goods at time t. But the household sector's current period demands for consumption and capital goods and the government's current-period demand for capital goods are not known at time t; the nonfinancial business sector must estimate them.

For even though the nonfinancial business sector may know what variabls enter functions (7.27), (8.27) and (8.32), many of these variables are unobservable to the nonfinancial business sector at time t. For instance, unless that sector waits until after the private financial sector has announced current interest rates to make its own price announcements, it can only guess what interest rates the government and household sectors are assuming as they formulate their plans at time t. These demand functions are also partially based upon assumptions which the government and households make at time t as to the prices of consumption goods and capital goods which the nonfinancial business sector will not announce until time t+1. As it formulates its own plans at time t, the nonfinancial business sector itself does not know what these prices will be.

Because of the unobservable nature of the actual current market demand functions for its products, the nonfinancial business sector may turn to proxy variables or other information to gain knowledge about these functions. The possibilities are almost limitless. Rather than pursue these possibilities in any detail, I arbitrarily specify very simple forms for the sector's estimates of functions (7.27), (8.27) and (8.32).

The estimated current period household sector demand for consumption goods available to the nonfinancial business sector at time t is presumably negatively related to the price which the nonfinancial sector announces at time t for those goods. In particular, the nonfinancial business sector's estimated current market demand for consumption goods may be expressed as:

$$c^{de}_t = c^{de}(\underset{-}{p^c_t};\ \underset{+}{c^g_t},\ v_c) \tag{9.8}$$

where c^g_t represents the (known) government demand for those goods and v_c again denotes a vector of shift parameters other than c^g_t.

Since the household and the government sectors' actual demands for capital for time t+1 are both negatively related to the current price of those goods, p^k_t, assume that the nonfinancial business sector's estimate of the current demand function for its capital goods is also negatively related to p^k_t. This yields the following estimated market demand function (in physical units) for capital for t+1:

$$K^{de}_{t+1} = K^{de}_{t+1}(\underset{-}{p^k_t};\ v_k) \tag{9.9}$$

where v_k denotes a vector of shift parameters which the nonfinancial business sector feels affects the demand for its capital goods. At time t, the nonfinancial business sector's anticipated sales (in physical units) of capital goods during the current period is then represented by

$$\begin{aligned} i^{de}_t &= K^{de}_{t+1} - (K^h_t + K^g_t). \\ &= i^{de}_t(\underset{-}{p^k_t};\ v^k) \end{aligned} \tag{9.10}$$

where v_k now includes K^h_t and K^g_t as shift parameters.

The nonfinancial business sector's estimate of its current sales revenue, R^e, is simply its estimated current revenue from sales of consumption goods, $p^c_t c^{de}_t$, plus its estimated current sales of capital goods, $p^k_t i^{de}_t$. Since the partial derivative of (9.8) with respect to p^c_t is nonzero, expression (9.8) may be solved for p^c_t as a function of the remaining variables in that expression:

$$p^c_t = p^c_t(\underset{-}{c^{de}_t}, \underset{+}{c^g_t}, v_c) \tag{9.11}$$

In a similar fashion expression (9.10) may be solved for p^k_t as a function of the remaining variables in that expression:

$$p^k_t = p^k_t(\underset{-}{i^{de}_t}, v_k) \tag{9.12}$$

These expressions in turn lead to the following specification of the nonfinancial business sector's estimate of its current-period revenue function:

$$R^e = p^c_t(.)c^{de}_t + p^k_t(.)i^{de}_t$$

$$= R^e(c^{de}_t, i^{de}_t, \underset{+}{c^g_t}, v_c, v_k) \tag{9.13}$$

The next step involves respecifying (9.13) so that it incorporates the technical constraints facing the nonfinancial business sector during its current-period production of consumption and investment goods.

The nonfinancial business sector requires the services of labor during the current period not only to produce commodities, but also to undertake transactions and engage in search activities. In conformance with the specification in chapter 4, let the nonfinancial business sector's current transactions time, τ, be represented by the following function:

$$\tau = \tau(h^n_t N^n_t, D^n_t, w_t) \tag{9.14}$$

where $\tau(.) > 0$; $\tau_1, \tau_3, > 0$; $\tau_2 < 0$; $\tau_{ii} > 0$ for $i = 1, 2, 3$; $\tau_{12}, \tau_{23} < 0$; $\tau_{13} > 0$. According to (9.14), current transactions time for the nonfinancial business sector increases with the number of hours, h^n_t, its current-period employees, N^n_t, work during the current period. Ceteris paribus, by holding more money at the beginning of the period (this time in checkable deposits), D^n_t, the sector is able to reduce current transactions time. However the higher the hourly money wage, w_t, which the sector guaranteed last period to pay this period, the smaller is the ability of a given volume of D^n_t to conserve current transactions time.

Again in conformance with Chapter 4, the nonfinancial business sector also anticipates at time t that it will have to devote some time, γ, during the current period either searching for new employees for next period or providing "working conditions" or "perks" during the current period so that its current employees will wish to remain employed in the sector next period. Let (9.15) denote the anticipated current search effort:

$$\gamma = \gamma(N^{nd}_{t+1}, N^{se}_{t+1}(w_{t+1}, v_n)) \tag{9.15}$$

with $\gamma(.) > 0$; $\gamma_1 > 0$; $\gamma_2 < 0$; $\gamma_{11}, \gamma_{22}, > 0$; $\gamma_{12} < 0$ and $N^{nd}_{t+1} \leq N^{se}_{t+1}(.)$. Again as in Chapter 4, assume that the estimated labor supply curve is positively related to w_{t+1}, with v_n denoting a vector of shift parameters in $N^{se}_{t+1}(.)$. However N^{se}_{t+1} now represents the nonfinancial sector's estimate at time t of the number of people who will be available to work in the nonfinancial sector next period. This function is deduced by subtracting the sum of (a) the sector's estimates of the government's current demand for workers for next period, N^{ge}_{t+1}, and (b) the financial business sector's current demand for workers for next period, N^{fe}_{t+1}, from its estimate of the household sector's current ex ante supply of workers for next period, N^{he}_{t+1}, in symbols, $N^{se}_{t+1} = N^{he}_{t+1} - N^{ge}_{t+1} - N^{fe}_{t+1}$. The nonfinancial business sector presumably anticipates at time t that N^{se}_{t+1} is an increasing function of w_{t+1}, the hourly money wage it announces at time t (and which it guarantees to pay its employees next period). The reason is two-fold. First, as soon as w_{t+1} is announced by the nonfinancial business sector at time t, it is presumably adopted as well by both of the other employers. It becomes next period's universal hourly money wage. Second, since the household sector's actual ex ante supply of labor, N^{s}_{t+1}, is positively related to w_{t+1} (see equation (8.34)) and since the government and the financial business sector's actual demands for labor, N^{gd}_{t+1} and N^{fd}_{t+1} respectively, are both negatively related to w_{t+1} (see equations (7.25) and (10.34) respectively), the nonfinancial business sector's estimates of these functions presumably reflect these signs, making N^{se}_{t+1} positively related to w_{t+1}. Assume as well that the nonfinancial business sector never sets its ex ante demand for labor, N^{nd}_{t+1}, above the level, N^{se}_{t+1}, it anticipates will be available at the wage rate it selects.

In light of the above, the amount of labor time which the

nonfinancial business sector anticipates at time t will be available during the current period to produce commodities may be represented by $h^n{}_t N^n{}_t - \tau(.) - \gamma(.)$. Let the current-period production functions for consumption goods and capital goods be denoted by (9.16) and (9.17) respectively:

$$c_t = c^+(v^c{}_1, v^c{}_k) \tag{9.16}$$

$$i_t = i^+(v^i{}_1, v^i{}_k) \tag{9.17}$$

with (9.16) and (9.17) representing positive strictly-concave functions with positive (but diminishing) marginal products and with:

$$v^c{}_1 + v^i{}_1 = h^n{}_t N^n{}_t - \tau(.) - \gamma(.) \tag{9.18}$$

$$v^c{}_k + v^i{}_k = K^n{}_t. \tag{9.19}$$

To obtain the nonfinancial business sector's production possibilities frontier for the current period, simply solve (9.18) and (9.19) for $v^i{}_1$ and $v^i{}_k$ respectively and substitute these values into (9.17). Then, maximize (9.16) with respect to $v^c{}_1$ and $v^c{}_k$, subject to (9.17). The choice variables $v^c{}_1$ and $v^c{}_k$ will emerge as functions of i_t, $h^n{}_t N^n{}_t$, $K^n{}_t$, $D^n{}_t$, w_t, $N^{nd}{}_{t+1}$ and w_{t+1}. Substitution of the solution values for $v^c{}_1$ and $v^c{}_k$ (expressed in terms of these seven parameters) back into (9.16) then yields the maximum number of consumption goods that can be produced during the current period, given the values of each of the seven parameters:

$$c_t = q(\underset{-}{i_t}, \underset{+}{h^n{}_t N^n{}_t}, \underset{+}{K^n{}_t}, \underset{+}{D^n{}_t}, \underset{-}{w_t}, \underset{-}{N^{nd}{}_{t+1}}, \underset{+}{w_{t+1}}, v_n) \tag{9.20}$$

Since current production of investment goods diverts resources from the production of consumption goods, q(.) is diminishing function of i_t. An increase in w_t increases current transactions time and thereby reduces, ceteris paribus, the amount of labor devoted to the production of consumption goods. Therefore, the partial derivative of q(.) with respect to w_t is negative. An increase in the number of people, $N^{nd}{}_{t+1}$, which the nonfinancial sector plans to hire next period, ceteris paribus, increases the sector's current search effort thereby reducing the amount of time available for producing consumption goods this period. Therefore the partial derivative of q( ) with respect to N^{nd}_{t+1} is also negative.

The remaining four partial derivatives are positive however. In particular, an increase in either total current labor hours, $h^n_t N^n_t$, or the nonfinancial business sector's initial stock of physical capital, K^n_t, increases directly the sector's capacity to produce consumption goods this period. An increase in D^n_t, ceteris paribus, reduces current-period transactions time thereby releasing additional real resources to the production of consumption goods. Finally, the higher the nonfinancial sector sets w_{t+1} at the beginning of the current period the less time it anticipates, ceteris paribus, that it will have to spend on search activities during the current period. This too releases resources to the production of consumption goods.

Since q(.) is a positive strictly-concave function, all of the own second-order partials are negative. In order to simplify the ensuing analysis, all the cross-partials in q(.) are set equal to zero.

The number of consumption goods, c^{de}_t, which the nonfinancial business sector plans to sell during the current period necessarily equals the amont of those goods it plans to produce, q(.), during the current period minus its planned accumulation of consumption goods inventory, $0 - Q_t$, over the period. In symbols, the following ex ante relationship must hold.

$$c^{de}_t = q(.) + Q_t. \tag{9.21}$$

Analogously, the sector's anticipated current-period sales of investment goods (in physical units), i^{de}_t, necessarily equals its planned current production of those goods, i_t, minus its planned investment in physical capital, $K^{nd}_{t+1} - K^n_t$, during the period:

$$i^{de}_t = i_t - (K^{nd}_{t+1} - K^n_t). \tag{9.22}$$

Substituting the right hand sides of (9.21) and (9.22) for c^{de}_t and i^{de}_t respectively in (9.13) yields the following expression for the nonfinancial business sector's anticipated current revenue at time t:

$$R^e = R^e\{q(.) + Q_t, i_t - (K^{nd}_{t+1} - K^n_t); c^g_t, v_c, v_k\} \tag{9.23}$$

This new function is expressed in terms of the following four decision variables facing the nonfinancial business sector at time t: i_t,

K^{nd}_{t+1}, N^{nd}_{t+1}, and w_{t+1}. The right hand side of (9.23) will be substituted for $R^e\{.\}$ in (9.7) when it becomes time to maximize that function. However, the nonfinancial business sector's next-period revenue function must also be specified. That function is considered next.

Anticipated Future Sales Revenue

Suppose the nonfinancial business sector's estimates at time t of next period's market demand functions for consumption goods and capital goods take the following simple forms:

$$c^{de}_{t+1} = c^{de}_{t+1}(p^c_{t+1},\ v^*_c) \tag{9.24}$$

$$i^{de}_{t+1} = i^{de}_{t+1}(p^k_{t+1},\ v^*_k) \tag{9.25}$$

where v^*_c and v^*_k represent unspecified shift parameters and where the partials of (9.24) and (9.25) with respect to the relevant next period product prices are negative. In principle, these functions may be solved respectively for p^c_{t+1} and p^k_{t+1} in terms of next period's anticipated sales of consumption and capital goods:

$$p^c_{t+1} = p^c_{t+1}(c^{de}_{t+1},\ v^*_c) \tag{9.26}$$

$$p^k_{t+1} = p^k_{t+1}(i^{de}_{t+1},\ v^*_k) \tag{9.27}$$

where the first-order partials with respect to c^{de}_{t+1} and i^{de}_{t+1} in (9.26) and (9.27) respectively are both negative. Assume for simplicity that the second-order partials in (9.26) and (9.27) equal zero. At time t next period's anticipated sales revenue, R^{e*}, is then defined as:

$$\begin{aligned} R^{e*} &= p^c_{t+1} \cdot c^{de}_{t+1} + p^k_{t+1} i^{de}_{t+1} \\ &= p^c_{t+1}(c^{de}_{t+1},\ v^*_c) \cdot c^{de}_{t+1} + p^k_{t+1}(i^{de}_{t+1},\ v^*_k) \cdot i^{de}_{t+1} \\ &= R^{e*}\{c^{de}_{t+1},\ i^{de}_{t+1},\ v^*_c,\ v^*_k\} \end{aligned} \tag{9.28}$$

The own second-order partials with respect to c^{de}_{t+1} and i^{de}_{t+1} in (9.28) are negative. Their cross-partials equal zero. The signs of the first-order partials with respect to these two variables depend upon whether the sector plans to set next period's product prices in the elastic or inelastic regions of next period's estimated demand functions.

The nonfinancial business sector in this model presumably does not plan at time t to search next period for people willing to work after time t+2. However, it does anticipate it will engage in transactions that involve payments to labor next period. The amount of labor effort, $\hat{\tau}$, which the sector anticipates it will have to expend on transactions next period is presumably an increasing strictly convex function of next period's anticipated total labor time, hN^{nd}_{t+1}, but a decreasing strictly convex function of the purchasing power over labor of the checkable deposits, D^{nd}_{t+1}, it plans to hold at the end of the current period. In particular let:

$$\hat{\tau} = \hat{\tau}(hN^{nd}_{t+1}, \; D^{nd}_{t+1}, \; w_{t+1}) \tag{9.29}$$

with $0 < \hat{\tau}_1 < 1$, $\hat{\tau}_2 < 0$; $\hat{\tau}_3 > 0$, $\hat{\tau}_{ii} > 0$ for all $i = 1,2,3$; and $\hat{\tau}_{12}$, $\hat{\tau}_{23} < 0$; $\hat{\tau}_{13} > 0$. Since both w_{t+1} and D^{nd}_{t+1} represent choice variables of the nonfinancial business sector at time t, the ratio D^{nd}_{t+1}/w_{t+1} is neither convex nor concave in these choice variables. To circumvent the difficulty of attempting to maximize (9.17) when it is not concave with respect to choice variables, I simply assign a positive partial derivative to w_{t+1} in (9.29) to denote the adverse effect of an increase in w_{t+1} upon the purchasing power of checkable deposits and therefore upon transactions time.

In light of (9.29), the amount of labor time that the nonfinancial business sector anticipates at time t that it will be able to apply to the production of commodities next period is given by $hN^{nd}_{t+1} - \hat{\tau}(.)$. Let the next-period production function for consumption goods and capital goods be denoted by (9.30) and (9.31) respectively:

$$c_{t+1} = \hat{c}(\hat{v}^c_1, \; \hat{v}^c_k) \tag{9.30}$$

$$i_{t+1} = \hat{i}(\hat{v}^i_1, \; \hat{v}^i_k) \tag{9.31}$$

where both functions are strictly concave with positive (but diminishing) marginal products. The variables entering $\hat{c}(.)$ and $\hat{i}(\;.)$ are subject to the following restrictions:

$$\hat{v}^c_1 + \hat{v}^i_1 = hN^{nd}_{t+1} - \hat{\tau}(.) \tag{9.32}$$

$$\hat{v}^c_k + \hat{v}^i_k = K^{nd}_{t+1} \tag{9.33}$$

To obtain next period's production possibilities frontier, solve (9.32) and (9.33) respectively for $\hat{v}^i_1$ and $\hat{v}^i_k$ and substitute their values into (9.31). Next, maximize (9.30) with respect to $\hat{v}^c_1$ and $\hat{v}^c_k$ subject to the new (9.31). The solutions for $\hat{v}^c$ and $\hat{v}^c_k$ will emerge as functions of i_{t+1}, N^{nd}_{t+1}, K^{nd}_{t+1}, D^{nd}_{t+1} and w_{t+1}. Substitution of their solutions into (9.30) yields the following function depicting the maximum production of consumption goods next period for given values of each of the five variables just listed:

$$c_{t+1} = \hat{q}(\underset{-}{i}_{t+1}, \underset{+}{N}^{nd}_{t+1}, \underset{+}{K}^{nd}_{t+1}, \underset{+}{D}^{nd}_{t+1}, \underset{-}{w}_{t+1}) \tag{9.34}$$

The first-order partial derivative with respect to i_{t+1} is negative since the more capital goods the sector plans to produce next period, ceteris paribus, the fewer consumption goods it can produce. The partial derivative with respect to w_{t+1} is negative in (9.34) since the higher the wage rate the sector announces at time t for next period, the smaller the purchasing power of a given level of checkable deposits. This means more real resources must be diverted from the production of consumption goods, ceteris paaribus, to the provision of transactions services.

The first order partial derivatives of N^{nd}_{t+1}, K^{nd}_{t+1} and D^{nd}_{t+1} are all positive in (9.34). An increase in either of the first two variables means that the sector has more real resources with which to produce consumption goods next period. An increase in D^{nd}_{t+1}, however, reduces the portion of a given volume of real resources that needs to be devoted to undertaking transactions next period. Therefore an increase in D^{nd}_{t+1} releases real resources to next period's commodity production.

The function $\hat{q}(.)$ in (9.34) is a positive strictly concave function; all of the own second-order partials are negative. All of the cross-partials are assumed to equal zero.

Because the nonfinancial business sector plans at time t to hold no inventory of consumption goods either at the beginning or at the end of next period, the number of consumption goods it plans to produce next period, $\hat{q}(.)$, necessarily equals the number of these goods it plans to sell next period, c^{de}_{t+1}. On the other hand the sector's planned accumulation of physical capital next period is given by 0 - K^{nd}_{t+1}. The number of capital goods the sector plans at time t to produce next period, i_{t+1}, equals its planned sales next period, i^{de}_{t+1}, plus its planned accumulation of inventories, - K^{nd}_{t+1}. Therefore, we have

$$c^{de}_{t+1} = \hat{q}(.) \tag{9.35}$$

$$i^{de}_{t+1} = i_{t+1} + K^{nd}_{t+1}. \tag{9.36}$$

Substituting the right hand sides of (9.35) and (9.36) into (9.28) yields the following expression for the nonfinancial business sector's anticipated sales revenue next period:

$$R^{e*} = R^{e*}\{\hat{q}(.),\ i_{t+1} + K^{nd}_{t+1},\ v^*_c,\ v^*_k\} \tag{9.37}$$

The right hand side of (9.37) expresses next period's anticipated sales revenue in terms of the choice variables i_{t+1}, N^{nd}_{t+1}, K^{nd}_{t+1}, D^{nd}_{t+1} and w_{t+1}.

Estimated Demand for Nonfinancial Business Sector Equity

Besides estimating the sales revenue functions for the current period and the next, the nonfinancial business sector must also estimate at time t the household sector's demand for its equity shares for the end of the current period. According to the analysis presented in Chapter 8, the household sector's actual demand for nonfinancial-sector equity is negatively related to the current market price for that equity. In the ensuing analysis, the nonfinancial business sector's estimate of that demand function exhibits partial derivatives whose signs correspond to those found in the actual function. (Their estimated numerical values may not correspond to their actual values however.) Therefore let (9.38) represent the nonfinancial business sector's estimate at time t of the household sector's end-of-period demand for its equity shares:

$$Sn^e_{t+1} = Sn^e_{t+1}(\underset{-}{p^n_t},\ v_{sn}) \tag{9.38}$$

where v_{sn} denotes a vector of shift parameters.

Maximizing the Nonfinancial Business Sector's Present Value

Substituting the right hand sides of (9.23), (9.37) and (9.38) for $R^e\{.\}$, $R^{e*}\{.\}$ and Sn^e_{t+1} respectively in (9.7) yields the following objective function:

$$
\begin{aligned}
\text{Minimize } p^n_o &= \pi^n_t + \pi^n_{t+1}/(1 + r^{fn}_t) \\
&= \frac{1}{Sn_t} [R^e\{q(i_t, h^n_t N^n_t, K^n_t, D^n_t, w_t, N^{nd}_{t+1}, w_{t+1}, v_n) + Q_t \\
&\quad i_t - (K^{nd}_{t+1} - K^n_t),\ c^g_t,\ v_c,\ v_k\} \\
&\quad + r^d_{t-1} D^n_t - w_t h^n_t N^n_t + p^n_t (Sn^e_{t+1}(p^n_t,\ v_{sn}) - Sn_t) \\
&\quad - (D^{nd}_{t+1} - D^n_t)] \\
&\quad + \frac{1}{(1+r^{fn}_t) Sn^e_{t+1}(p^n_t,\ v_{sn})} \\
&\quad [R^{e*}\{q(i_{t+1},\ N^{nd}_{t+1},\ K^{nd}_{t+1},\ D^{nd}_{t+1},\ w_{t+1}), i_{t+1} \\
&\quad + K^{nd}_{t+1},\ v^*_c,\ v^*_k\} \\
&\quad + (1 + r^{dn}_t) D^{nd}_{t+1} - w_{t+1}\, h N^{nd}_{t+1}]
\end{aligned}
\qquad (9.38)
$$

The objective of the nonfinancial business sector at time t is to maximize its present value by maximizing the right hand side of (9.38) with respect to h^n_t, i_t, w_{t+1}, N^{nd}_{t+1}, i_{t+1}, K^{nd}_{t+1}, D^{nd}_{t+1} and p^n_t. The optimal level of current production of consumption goods is found by substituting the solution to (9.38) into (9.20). Optimal current sales of consumption and capital goods are then found from (9.21) and (9.22) respectively. The solutions to these last two variables, when substituted into (9.11) and (9.12), yield the optimal current-period prices for consumption and capital goods respectively. The optimal (ex ante) level of current dividends, π^n_t, is found by substituting the solution to (9.38) into (9.3).

First-Order Necessary Conditions for a Maximum

In the following discussion, an interior solution is assumed to exist. The first-order conditions presented below reflect that assumption.

Setting the partial derivative of (9.38) with respect to h^n_t equal to zero produces condition (9.39):

$$\frac{R^e{}_1 q_2 N^n{}_t - w_t N^n{}_t}{Sn_t} = 0 \qquad (9.39)$$

This condition is directly analogous to condition (4.30) derived in Chapter 4. The first term, $R^e{}_1 q_2 N^n{}_t$, represents the current period marginal revenue product resulting from increasing by one hour the average working time of its current employees. The second term, $w_t N^n{}_t$, is the current marginal cost of doing so. In conformance with the standard analysis, then, the present-value optimizing sector sets the current average number of employee hours at the level at which the marginal revenue product of $h^n{}_t$ just equals its marginal cost.

Differentiating (9.38) partially with respect to current production of capital goods, i_t, and setting the result equal to zero yields the necessary condition (9.40):

$$\frac{R^e{}_1 q_1 + R^e{}_2}{Sn_t} = 0 \qquad (9.40)$$

According to this condition the nonfinancial business sector should continue to increase current capital goods production until the marginal revenue per share from the sale of the last unit of these goods, $R^e{}_2/Sn_t$, just equals the marginal opportunity cost per share, -$R^e{}_1 q_1/Sn_t$. The opportunity cost takes the form of forgone current sales revenue, $R^e{}_1 q_1$, from the production of those consumption goods which the sector sacrifices by producing instead the last unit of capital goods.

The first-order condition associated with the hourly money wage, w_{t+1}, which the sector announces at time t that it will pay next period is found by setting equal to zero the partial derivative of (9.38) with respect to w_{t+1}:

$$\frac{R^e{}_1 q_7}{Sn_t} + \frac{R^{e*}{}_1 \hat{q}_5 - hN^{nd}{}_{t+1}}{Sn^e{}_{t+1}(1 + r^{fn}{}_t)} = 0 \qquad (9.41)$$

This condition, which is analogous to (4.32). states that the present-value maximizing sector will continue to raise w_{t+1} until the anticipated present value of the marginal wage expense per share next period, $hN^{dn}{}_{t+1}/Sn^{e}{}_{t+1}(1 + r^{fn}{}_{t})$, from raising w_{t+1} just equals the anticipated present value of the adjustment to the stream of sales revenue per share. The latter consists, first, of the anticipated current marginal revenue per share, Re_1q_7/Sn_t, from the added labor released from current search due to the higher money wage and, second, of the anticipated reduction in the present value of next period's sales revenue per share, $R^{e*}{}_1\hat{q}_5/Sn^{e}{}_{t+1}(1 + r^{fn}{}_{t})$, due to an increase in next period's transactions time. The anticipated increase in transactions time arises from the reduced purchasing power of a given amount of checkable deposits as w_{t+1} is raised. As labor effort is diverted next period from commodity production to transactions services, sales revenue will be sacrificed.

The partial derivative of (9.38) with respect to $N^{nd}{}_{t+1}$ when set equal to zero yields first-order condition (9.42):

$$\frac{R^{e}{}_1q_6}{Sn_t} + \frac{R^{e*}{}_1\hat{q}_2 - w_{t+1}h}{Sn^{e}{}_{t+1}(1 + r^{fn}{}_{t})} = 0 \qquad (9.42)$$

This condition is analogous to (4.31). It stipulates that the present-value maximizing sector will continue to increase the number of employees it decides to use next period until the present value of the marginal future wage expense per share, $w_{t+1}h/Sn^{e}{}_{t+1}(1 + r^{fn}{}_{t})$, just equals the present value of the adjustments in the stream of current and future revenue per share, $(R^{e}{}_1q_6/Sn_t) + R^{e*}{}_1\hat{q}_2/Sn^{e}{}_{t+1}(1 + r^{fn}{}_{t})$, associated with searching for and then using that extra worker. The term $R^{e}{}_1q_6/Sn_t$ denotes the reduction in current sales revenue per share from diverting current labor from commodity production to the recruitment of an additional worker for next period. The term $R^{e*}{}_1\hat{q}_2/Sn^{e}{}_{t+1}(1 + r^{fn}{}_{t})$ represents the anticipated present value per share of the marginal revenue product next period from an additional worker.

Partially differentiating (9.38) with respect to the production of capital goods next period, i_{t+1}, leads to the necessary condition (9.43):

$$\frac{R^{e*}{}_1q_1 + R^{e*}{}_2}{Sn^{e}{}_{t+1}(1 + r^{fn}{}_{t})} = 0 \qquad (9.43)$$

The interpretation of (9.43) is directly analogous to the one associated with (9.49). In particular the nonfinancial business sector will plan to increase next period's production of capital goods up to the point at which the anticipated present value per share of the marginal sales revenue of that production, $R^{e*}{}_{2}/Sn^{e}{}_{t+1}(1 + r^{fn}{}_{t})$, equals the anticipated present value per share of its opportunity cost: the forgone sales revenue on consumption goods, $-R^{e}*\hat{q}_{1}/Sn^{e}{}_{t+1}(1+r^{fn}{}_{t})$.

The first-order necessary condition for the optimal stock of physical capital, $K^{nd}{}_{t+1}$, to be held at the end of the current period appears as equation (9.44):

$$\frac{-R^{e}{}_{2}}{Sn_{t}} + \frac{R^{e*}{}_{1}\hat{q}_{3} + R^{e*}{}_{2}}{(1 + r^{fn}{}_{t})Sn^{e}{}_{t+1}} = 0 \qquad (9.44)$$

The sector will plan to continue adding to its end-of period stock of physical capital until the present value of next period's marginal revenue per share, $(R^{e*}{}_{1}\hat{q}_{3} + R^{e*}{}_{2})/Sn^{e}{}_{t+1}(1 + r^{fn}{}_{t})$, just equals the current marginal opportunity cost per share, $R^{e}{}_{2}/Sn_{t}$, from adding one more unit to the end-of-period stock. Next period's marginal revenue consists of the sum of the marginal revenue product next period, $R^{e*}{}_{1}\hat{q}_{3}$, of a unit of physical capital held at the beginning of that period plus the marginal revenue that period, $R^{e*}{}_{2}$, from next period's sale of the unit of capital it instead accumulates within the sector.

The first-order condition associated with the sector's optimal holding of checkable deposits at the end of the current period, $D^{n}{}_{t+1}$, is obtained by partially differentiating (9.38) with respect to that variable and setting the result equal to zero:

$$-\frac{1}{Sn_{t}} + \frac{R^{e*}{}_{1}\hat{q}_{4} + (1 + r^{dn}{}_{t})}{(1 + r^{fn}{}_{t})Sn_{t+1}} = 0 \qquad (9.45)$$

According to this condition, the nonfinancial business sector should continue to add to the amount of checkable deposits it plans to hold at the end of the current period until the marginal cost per share from doing so (in terms of reduced dividends to current shareholders), $\$1/Sn_{t}$, just equals the anticipated present value per share of the extra payment to shareholders next period from (a) the principal and interest, $1 + r^{dn}{}_{t}$, on the last dollar of checkable deposits and (b) the marginal sales revenue generated by that dollar of deposits. The extra sales revenue, $R^{e*}{}_{1}\hat{q}_{4}$, arises from the extra commodity production made possible by the real resources released from transactions services due to the increase in checkable deposits.

Finally, the first-order condition for the ex ante optimal price, p^n_t, of the nonfinancial sector's equity shares in the current period is presented as equation (9.46):

$$\frac{(Sn^e_{t+1}-Sn_t) + p^n_t(Sn^e_{t+1})_1}{Sn_t} - \frac{[R^e*\{.\} + (1+r^{dn}_t)D^{nd}_{t+1} - w_{t+1}hN^{nd}_{t+1}]}{(1 + r^{fn}_t)(Sn^e_{t+1})^2} \cdot (Sn^e_{t+1})_1 = 0 \qquad (9.46)$$

where $(Sn^e_{t+1})_1$ denotes the estimated slope of the household sector's end-of-period demand for equity shares. This condition is directly analogous to condition (4.35). It stipulates that the current-period optimal market price of nonfinancial sector equity is that value for which the potential marginal reduction in current payments per share to current shareholders, $[(Sn^e_{t+1} - Sn_t) + p^n_t(Sn^e_{t+1})_1]/Sn_t$, due to a unit increase in p^n_t just offsets the present value of the marginal increase in the payment per share to owners next period resulting from the increase in p^n_t. An increase in p^n_t reduces current payments to the owners because it discourages current sales of equity and therefore reduces the revenue from those sales (provided the household sector's demand is elastic with respect to p^n_t). But because an increase in p^n_t, ceteris paribus, reduces the number of shares the nonfinancial business sector plans to have outstanding at the end of the period, it thereby increases the anticipated payment <u>per share</u> to the owners next period. According to this condition, the nonfinancial sector will set the price of its equity in the elastic range of the estimated demand function for that equity.

Response Functions of the Nonfinancial Business Sector

Within the unified framework specified immediately above, the nonfinancial business sector simultaneously decides its mutually consistent combination of optimal levels of commodity production, investment, commodity prices, employment, wages, dividends, checkable deposits and the market price of its own equity. In general, these optimal values all depend upon the technical aspects of its commodity production, its transactions mechanism, and its employee recruitment as well as upon the sector's estimates of the market demand for its commodities, the market demand for its equity and the [net] market supply of labor. The present section details the factors influencing the nonfinancial business sector's choices at time t.

Totally differentiating first-order conditions (9.39) - (9.46) yields a simultaneous system of eight linear equations in the differentials of h^n_t, i_t, w_{t+1}, N^{nd}_{t+1}, i_{t+1}, K^{nd}_{t+1}, D^{nd}_{t+1} and p^n_t. Assuming the strict concavity of (9.38) with respect to each of these variables, the coefficient matrix of the new system is negative definite. Solving this system yields the following general functions:

$$h^n_t = h^n_t(N^n_t, K^n_t, D^n_t, w_t, Q_t, c^g_t, v_c, v_k, r^{dn}_t, r^{fn}_t, Sn_t, v^*_c, v^*_k, v_n, v_{sn}) \tag{9.47}$$

$$i_t = i_t(K^n_t, D^n_t, w_t, Q_t, c^g_t, v_c, v_k, r^{dn}_t, r^{fn}_t, Sn_t, v^*_c, v^*_k, v_n, v_{sn}) \tag{9.48}$$

$$w_{t+1} = w_{t+1}(K^n_t, D^n_t, w_t, Q_t, c^g_t, v_c, v_k, r^{dn}_t, r^{fn}_t, Sn_t, v^*_c, v^*_k, v_n, v_{sn}) \tag{9.49}$$

$$N^{nd}_{t+1} = N^{nd}_{t+1}(K^n_t, D^n_t, w_t, Q_t, c^g_t, v_c, v_k, r^{dn}_t, r^{fn}_t, Sn_t, v^*_c, v^*_k, v_n, v_{sn}) \tag{9.50}$$

$$i_{t+1} = i_{t+1}(K^n_t, D^n_t, w_t, Q_t, c^g_t, v_c, v_k, r^{dn}_t, r^{fn}_t, Sn_t, v^*_c, v^*_k, v_n, v_{sn}) \tag{9.51}$$

$$K^{nd}_{t+1} = K^{nd}_{t+1}(K^n_t, D^n_t, w_t, Q_t, c^g_t, v_c, v_k, r^{dn}_t, r^{fn}_t, Sn_t, v^*_c, v^*_k, v_n, v_{sn}) \tag{9.52}$$

$$D^n_{t+1} = D^n_{t+1}(K^n_t, D^n_t, w_t, Q_t, c^g_t, v_c, v_k, r^{dn}_t, r^{fn}_t, Sn_t, v^*_c, v^*_k, v_n, v_{sn}) \tag{9.53}$$

$$p^n_t = p^n_t(K^n_t, D^n_t, w_t, Q_t, c^g_t, v_c, v_k, r^{dn}_t, r^{fn}_t, Sn_t, v^*_c, v^*_k, v_n, v_{sn}) \tag{9.54}$$

The solutions for c_t, i^{de}_t, c^{de}_t, p^c_t and p^k_t are then found from (9.20), (9.22), (9.21), (9.11), and (9.12) respectively, repeated here for convenience:

$$c_t = q(i_t, h^n_t N^n_t, K^n_t, D^n_t, w_t, N^{nd}_{t+1}, w_{t+1}, v_n) \tag{9.20}$$

$$i^{de}_t = i_t - (K^{nd}_{t+1} - K^n_t) \tag{9.22}$$

$$c^{de}_t = c_t + Q_t \tag{9.21}$$

$$p^c_t = p^c_t(c^{de}_t, c^g_t, v_c) \qquad (9.11)$$

$$p^k_t = p^k_t(i^{de}_t, v_k) \qquad (9.12)$$

Finally, the optimal level of current dividends per share, π^n_t, is found by substituting the solutions for c^{de}_t and i^{de}_t into (9.23) and then substitutiing the resulting solution for $R^e\{.\}$ into (9.3):

$$\pi^n_t = \pi^n_t(K^n_t, D^n_t, w_t, Q_t, c^g_t, v_c, v_k, r^{dn}_t, r^{fn}_t, Sn_t, v^*_c, v^*_k, v_n, v_{sn}) \qquad (9.55)$$

Change in K^n_t

For given amounts of the other variables appearing in production functon q(.), the nonfinancial business sector will tend to produce more consumption goods during the current period the larger the amount of physical capital with which it begins the period. In order to sell these extra consumption goods, the sector will tend to reduce the current-period price, p^c_t, thereby lowering as well the estimated marginal revenue of consumption goods, R^e_1.

Ceteris paribus, the fall in R^e_1 reduces the marginal revenue product of current labor, causing the sector to reduce the average number of hours its current employees work this period. But the increase in K^n_t may raise the marginal physical product of labor, q_2, so that its marginal revenue product, $R^e_1 q_2$, rises despite the fall in R^e_1. If the increase in q_2 more than offsets the fall in R^e_1, the sector will rasie the average number of hours it uses its current employees.

Both terms in condition (9.40) are affected by the rise in K^n_t. First, holding constant the sector's end-of-period demand for physical capital, K^{nd}_{t+1}, the increase in K^n_{t+1} represents an equivalent increase in the number of capital goods that the business sector plans to sell during the current period. Assuming no shift in the sector's estimate of the current market demand function for its capital goods, the sector must reduce p^k_t in order to sell the extra goods. Therefore R^e_2 falls. Ceteris paribus the fall in R^e_2 induces the business sector to curtail its current output of capital goods.

Second, since the rise in K^n_t also reduces R^e_1, it reduces as well the marginal opportunity cost of producing capital goods (rather than consumption goods), R^e_1. This encourages the business sector to increase its current production of capital goods. Therefore, the net effect of a rise in K^n_t upon current production of capital goods is unclear.

The aforementioned drop in R^e_2 in response to an increase in K^n_t also reduces the opportunity cost to the nonfinancial business sector of accumulating physical capital within that sector (see condition (9.44)). Therefore, the sector will tend to increase its own end-of-period demand for physical capital, K^{nd}_{t+1}, as K^n_t rises. But the rise in K^{nd}_{t+1} is necessarily smaller than the rise in K^n_t. For K^{nd}_{t+1} will not rise unless R^e_2 falls and R^e_2 will not fall if the rise in K^{nd}_{t+1} exceeds the increase in K^n_t.

Summarizing the discussion to this point pertaining to a rise in K^n_t, the nonfinancial business sector will tend to reduce the prices for both consumption and capital goods, to increase its own end-of-period demand for capital goods, and to increase current production of consumption goods. The net effects upon (a) its current production of capital goods and (b) the average number of hours it uses its current employees are unclear.

If labor and physical capital are technical complements in next period's production function, the sector's increased end-of-period demand for physical capital tends to raise the marginal physical product of next period's labor, q_2, thereby raising the sector's end-of-period demand for labor, N^{nd}_{t+1}. Ceteris paribus, this raises current-period search time and induces the sector to rasie w_{t+1}.

But, a rise in K^n_t also lowers R^e_1, which by itself tends to reduce the opportunity cost of devoting labor effort to current search (see condition (9.41)), which induces the sector to lower w_{t+1}. Consequently, the net effect upon w_{t+1} due to a rise in K^n_t is unclear.

If the nonfinancial business sector's end-of-period demand for labor rises and if it raises w_{t+1} to conserve search effort in obtaining these employees, then next period's transactions time will increase, raising the marginal product of end-of-period checkable deposits and therefore raising the nonfinancial business sector's demand for those deposits, D^{nd}_{t+1}.

As noted above, an increase in K^n_t tends to cause the business sector to raise is end-of-period demand for physical capital, K^{nd}_{t+1}. From production function q( ), see (9.34), this tends to increase the number of consumption goods the business sector plans to produce and sell next period. (This tendency is reinforced if N^{nd}_{t+1} and D^{nd}_{t+1}

both rise.) The anticipated increase in c_{t+1} lowers the marginal revenue of those goods, R^{e*}_{1}, relative to the marginal revenue of capital goods. Consequently, the sector will tend, ceteris paribus, to raise its anticipated level of sales of capital goods next period as well.

Suppose that as a result of the increase in K^n_t, the nonfinancial business sector estimates that next period's net income will increase, i.e. that next period's revenues will increase more than next period's expenses. This increase in next period's anticipated net income increases the marginal cost to the business sector's current owners of issuing an additional share of equity during the current period. This encourages the business sector to raise the market price of its equity shares, p^n_t, in the current period in order to discourage sales. (If the business sector estimates that the household sector will correctly anticipate that the business sector will generate more net income next period, the business sector may simultaneously shift outward its estimate of the end-of-period demand curve for its shares. This will reinforce the tendency for the nonfinancial business sector to raise p^n_t.)

Change in D^n_t

The greater the nonfinancial business sector's holding of checkable deposits at time t, the fewer real resources the sector requires to complete a given volume of labor transactions during the current period. Ceteris paribus, these released resources may be applied to the production of consumption goods. As a result, an increase in D^n_t ceteris paribus enables the sector to expand its production of consumption goods. As this production rises, the marginal revenue of consumption goods falls causing the sector to divert some of the released resources to the production of capital goods as well. In the process the marginal revenue of capital goods sales this period, R^e_2, also falls. (In both cases marginal revenue falls as the sector lowers the product price.)

The drop in R^e_2 reduces the opportunity cost of accumulating physical capital within the nonfinancial business sector this period. Consequently, the end-of-period demand for capital by the sector, K^{nd}_{t+1}, may rise. If labor and physical capital are technical complements in next period's production function, the rise in K^{nd}_{t+1} raises next period's marginal product of labor and therefore the sector's demand for labor. The sector may raise w_{t+1} in order to be able to acquire the additional workers. But the fall in R^e_1 due to the extra production of current consumption goods reduces the opportunity cost of devoting current labor to current search. So the sector may decide instead to attempt to find the additional workers for next period without raising w_{t+1}.

If the sector does decide to increase its production of goods next period, the anticipated marginal revenues from those goods will also fall since the sector will plan to reduce the prices of those goods as well. By itself, this reduces the marginal revenue product of a unit of checkable deposits held by the sector at the end of the current period. But if the sector decides to use more labor next period, the extra transactions time associated with this increase may cause the marginal physical product and hence the demand for these checkable deposits to rise. Therefore, the net effect upon D^{nd}_{t+1} is indeterminate.

The fact that (as opposed to a rise in D^h_t) an increase in D^n_t may cause the business sector to <u>reduce</u> current period prices indicates that the response in current prices to a given rise in initial money balances may depend as much upon the distribution of those deposits across sectors as it does upon the size of the increase. Of course, in the present model a given increase in D^n_t may be accompanied by a drop in Q_t. This double change could arise, for instance, if there had been an unforeseen increase in the market demand for consumption goods last period. The present section considered only those effects directly related to the rise in D^n_t. The effects associated with a given change in Q_t will be discussed later.

<u>Change in w_t</u>

The higher w_t is at the beginning of the current period, the greater the current-period transactions time associated with a given labor input and therefore the smaller the current output of consumption and capital goods. More importantly, a higher w_t also raises the marginal cost of a unit of labor services during the current period and reduces the sector's demand for that labor. Current production goods falls, causing the sector to raise the price of consumption goods. The rising marginal revenue associated with these goods causes the sector to divert some resources from the production of capital goods. This in turn induces the firm to raise the current market price of capital goods.

The rising R^e_1 and R^e_2 induce the sector to reduce its demand for capital for the end of the current period since the opportunity cost of accumulating that capital has risen. The demand for K^{nd}_{t+1} falls. As K^{nd}_{t+1} falls, next period's anticipated sales of consumption goods and capital goods both fall. As a result, both R^{e*}_1 and R^{e*}_2 tend to increase as the sector plans to raise next period's commodity prices. The effect upon N^{nd}_{t+1} as a result of the drop in K^{nd}_{t+1} depends upon whether these factors are technical complements. If they are, the sector's demand for labor for next period will fall.

As R^{e*}_1 rises, the value of the marginal product of the sector's end-of-period holdings of checkable deposits tends to increase. However, if the sector's demand for labor for next period falls, the marginal product of these checkable deposits will also fall. The net effect upon D^{nd}_{t+1} is unclear. Furthermore, as the sector's demand for labor for next period falls, it will tend to announce a lower w_{t+1}; but the rising R^e_1 associated with the curtailment of current-period sales raises the opportunity cost of current search, inducing the sector to raise w_{t+1}. The net effect upon w_{t+1} is also indeterminate.

Finally, as w_t rises, the anticipated reduction in next period's total sales and net income reduces the marginal cost to the existing shareholders of issuing an additional share of equity this period. Consequently, the sector will tend to lower the current market price of its equity as w_t rises.

Change in Q_t

An increase in the nonfinancial business sector's initial inventory of consumption goods allows that sector to sell more goods in the current period without increasing current production. The extra units can be sold however only if the sector reduces the market price of consumption goods, thereby reducing as well the marginal revenue, R^e_1. This causes the marginal revenue product of current labor time, h^n_t, to fall inducing the sector to produce less during the current period by reducing the average number of hours it employs its current workers.

As R^e_1 falls, the opportunity cost of producing and sellng capital goods during the current period also falls. Hence the nonfinancial business sector will be encouraged to shift some current production from consumption goods to capital goods. The extra capital goods, if they are to be sold, must carry a lower price tag; the sector therefore will reduce p^k_t. As a result R^e_2 also falls. The fall in R^e_2 means that the opportunity cost of accumulating capital within the sector also falls; the sector's demand for K^{nd}_{t+1} increases as a result. Therefore, the nonfinancial business sector's ex ante physical investment for the current period increases along with its current production and anticipated sales of capital goods.

Because the nonfinancial business sector revises upward the amount of physical capital it plans to begin next period, its anticipated capacity to produce next period is also revised upward; the sector will plan to produce and sell more consumption goods next period (provided the unexpected increase in Q_t does not cause it to revise downward its estimate of next period's demand for consumption goods). Because of our assumption that the physical capital which the sector holds at the beginning of next period will be saleable to other sectors next period, the sector, by virtue of the rise in K^{nd}_{t+1}, also plans greater sales of capital goods next period. Consequently the marginal revenues anticipated next period for consumption and capital goods, R^{e*}_1 and R^{e*}_2, both fall.

Because R^{e*}_1 and R^{e*}_2 both fall, the net effect upon next period's production, i_{t+1}, of capital goods is unclear. The reason is that since R^{e*}_1 falls, the opportunity cost of producing capital goods next period falls; but since R^{e*}_2 also falls, so does next period's marginal revenue product of those goods.

With the drop in R^e_1, the opportunity cost of current search effort falls so that the marginal revenue product of a unit increase in w_{t+1} (in terms of the current search effort it tends to conserve) falls. By itself, this causes the nonfinancial sector to reduce the money wage it announces at time t. But the anticipated fall in R^{e*}_1 reduces the opportunity cost of devoting resources to transactions next period. This latter effect encourages the sector to raise w_{t+1}. In addition, because of the fall in R^{e*}_1 caused by the rise in K^{nd}_{t+1}, the anticipated marginal revenue product of labor falls causing the sector to reduce its demand for workers, N^{nd}_{t+1}. This in turn reduces the sector's anticipated out-of-pocket expenditures for labor services and reduces the marginal cost of raising w_{t+1}.

Since R^{e*}_1 falls, next period's anticipated marginal revenue product of checkable deposits falls causing, ceteris paribus, the sector's demand for checkable deposits for the end of the current period to fall.

Assuming that the increase in Q_t does not affect the nonfinancial business sector's estimates of the market demand functions for its products, the sector will anticipate greater total sales revenue during the current period and a lower current wage bill. Bouyed by the sector's reduced demand for checkable deposits for the end of the period, current dividends will tend to rise along with current income earned by the sector.

The current period market price which the sector sets at time t for its equity shares depends upon the sector's prospects for payments to its owners next period. Assuming once again that the increase in Q_t is not taken by the nonfinancial business sector as reflecting an adverse shift in the market demand for its product, the greater capital which the sector plans to hold at the beginning of next period represents the prospect of greater sales revenue in the future and, ceteris paribus, larger payments to its owners next period. This increase in anticipated future payments raises the cost to existing shareholders of the nonfinancial sector increasing the number of shares outstanding. Therefore, the sector will tend to increase p^n_t.

Changes in shift parameters affecting R^e_1 (namely c^g_t and v_c)

An increase in the nonfinancial business sector's estimate of the household sector's or the government's demand for consumption goods in the current period causes it to revise upward its estimate of the total and marginal revenues in the current period associated with a given current level of production and sales (in physical units) of consumption goods. The sector will raise the current-period market price, p^c_t, it announces at time t for consumption goods.

The increase in the sector's estimate of the current marginal revenue from consumption goods, R^e_1, causes the sector to increase its production of those goods in the current period by increasing the average length of time it uses its current employees.

The rise in R^e_1 also increases the opportunity cost of engaging in search during the current period. Therefore, even if the nonfinancial sector does not plan to alter the number of people it will hire next period (i.e. even if its estimate of next period's demands for consumption and capital goods remain unchanged) the sector will still tend to announce a higher money wage, w_{t+1}, today in order to facilitate its current-period search for those employees. As will be shown when a perceived outward shift in one of next period's commodity demand functions is considered, this effect upon w_{t+1} will be reinforced if the sector anticipates that the current outward shift in the demand for consumption goods is permanent.

Ceteris paribus, the increase in R^e_1 raises the opportunity cost of producing and selling capital goods during the current period. As a result, if the sector's estimate of R^e_2 remains unaffected when the perceived shift in the demand for consumption goods occurs, then the nonfinancial business sector will tend to shift current production away from capital goods as well as to reduce the amonut of physical capital it wants to hold itself by the end of the current period.

Change in v_k

An increase in the nonfinancial business sector's estimate of the current demand for capital goods causes R^e_2 to rise. The sector will shift production to capital goods at the expense of consumption goods, on the margin, and will announce higher current-period prices of both goods. Whether the sector decides to use its current workers more or less intensively will depend upon their relative marginal products in the production of consumption versus capital goods.

Change in r^{dn}_t

If the nonfinancial business sector revises upward is estimate of the interest rate on checkable deposits that it expects the private depository institutions to announce this period (and pay next period), this raises next period's income from checkable deposits and hence next period's dividends to current owners. In addition, the rise in r^{dn}_t also raises the return to D^{dn}_{t+1} causing the sector, ceteris paribus, to reduce current dividends in order to increase its holdings of checkable deposits by the end of the current period. To the extent that next period's transactions costs fall as a result of the rise in D^{nd}_{t+1}, next period's net income and dividends will rise. This reinforces the direct income effect from checkable deposits mentioned at the beginning of this paragraph. The rise in next period's dividends as a result of the rise in r^{dn}_t raises the marginal cost to the current owners of the nonfinancial business sector issuing additional shares this period. Therefore the sector will tend to raise the current period price of its shares in order to depress the demand for them.

Change in r^{fn}_t

If the nonfinancial business sector revises upward is estimate of the rate of return its shareholders could earn next period if they were to purchase a share of financial-sector equity, the present valus of the nonfinancial business sector's anticipated future revenues and costs will fall. Ceteris paribus, the present value of the nonfinancial business sector's dividends falls causing the sector to reduce the current market price of its own equity. In addition, the present values of the marginal revenue products of next period's labor and capital will fall. The sector will tend to demand fewer workers for next period and to demand less physical capital with which to begin next period. The reduction in its own demand for physical capital induces the sector to attempt to sell more capital goods this period (as well as to curtail current period production of those goods) by lowering the price of capital goods. The sector will shift production, on the margin, into consumption goods and reduce the price of those goods as well.

The fact that the nonfinancial sector reduces its demand for labor for next period lowers the marginal product of checkable deposits held by that sector at the end of the period. It also means the sector will tend to reduce w_{t+1} because the marginal product of raising w_{t+1} in order to avoid labor search falls as N^{nd}_{t+1} falls. The sector's end-of-period demand for checkable deposits falls not only because of its reduced marginal product but also because the present value of the corresponding marginal revenue product falls.

<u>Change in v^*_c</u>

Ceteris paribus, an increase in the nonfinancial business sector's estimate at time t of next period's demand for consumption goods, v^*_c, means that its estimate of the marginal revenue from those goods also increases. The sector raises the price it expects to charge for consumption goods next period. The increase in R^{e*}_1 raises the anticipated marginal revenue product of next period's labor causing N^{nd}_{t+1} to rise. As a result, the sector may estimate that it must raise the hourly money wage, w_{t+1}, it announces at time t to attract the desired number of employees for next period.

The increase in R^{e*}_1 raises next period's opportunity cost of using labor time to complete transactions. Furthermore, the increase in w_{t+1} means that, ceteris paribus, more labor time will be required next period to complete a given volume of transactions because the puchasing power of checkable deposits will be smaller. Both of these effects encourage the sector to increase the volume of checkable deposits, D^n_{t+1}, it plans to hold by the end of the current period in order to conserve labor time devoted to transactions next period.

As R^{e*}_1 rises, the opportunity cost of producing capital goods next period rises causing the sector to reduce its planned production, i_{t+1}, of those goods next period. However the rise in R^e_1 raises the anticipated value of the marginal product of capital held by the nonfinancial sector at the beginning of next period, K^{nd}_{t+1}, since this stock of capital will be used to produce consumption goods next period. The nonfinancial business sector will therefore plan to increase its holdings of physical capital by the end of the current period. If it reduces the number of capital goods it sells during the current period in order to accumulate more capital by the end of the period, it will be able to charge a higher current price, p^k_t, for the units of capital it does sell. As a result the marginal revenue of capital goods sold during the current period rises, thereby encouraging the sector to shift some resources in the current period from the production of consumption goods to the production of capital goods. The sector therefore raises the current price of consumption goods, p^c_t, as it anticipates an increase in next period's demand for those goods. It also raises the current period price of capital goods, p^k_t, and increases its current period production of those goods, i_t, in order to build the stock of physical capital it desires by the end of the period to produce more consumption goods next period.

But the reduction in next period's anticipated production of capital goods complicates the adjustments just described. For as the sector reduces its planned production of capital goods it may release more than sufficient labor and/or capital to satisfy the additional need for those factors in producing the extra consumption goods next period. In the final analysis the adjustment will depend upon the elasticities of demand for both products as well as the technical rates of substitution among the factors N^{nd}_{t+1}, K^{nd}_{t+1} (and D^n_{t+1}).

Even though the marginal revenues of consumption and capital goods increase in the current period, total revenue from the sales of these goods fall; the sector sacrifices some current revenue for the prospect of even greater revenue (and income) next period. Current dividends fall not only because the sector earns less in the current period but also because it saves more (in the form of checkable deposits) in order to prepare for next period's increased activity. But in spite of the reduction in current dividends, the sector will nevertheless announce a higher current-period market price for its equity shares. The greater anticipated level of payments to owners next period increases the cost to the current owners of the nonfinancial business sector issuing additional shares during the current period. The sector therefore raises p^n_t to discourage sales.

Change in v^*_k

An increase in the nonfinancial business sector's estimate at time t of next period's market demand of capital goods, v^*_k, ceteris paribus, raises its estimate of the marginal revenue, R^{e*}_2, from those goods. The sector revises upward the price, p^k_{t+1}, it anticipates it will announce next period for those goods. The rise in R^e*_2 represents an increase in the opportunity cost of producing consumption goods next period. As it reduces planned production of these goods, the sector raises the price, p^c_{t+1}, it plans to charge for these goods next period. As discussed under the case of a change in v^*_c, whether the sector will require more or less labor and/or more or less capital by the beginning of next period will depend upon the extent to which it reduces its planned production of consumption goods next period and the relative intensities with which labor and capital are to be used in the production of consumption and capital goods next period.

In any case, however, the rise in R^e*_1 and R^e*_2 raises the value of the marginal product of D^n_{t+1}, causing the sector's end-of-period demand for checkable deposits to rise. In addition, because of the rise in the anticipated level of net income next period, the sector will announce a higher current-period price for its equity shares, p^n_t, than it would have if the estimate of next period's demand for capital goods had not risen.

Change in the estimated demand for nonfinancial-sector equity (v_{sn})

Just as in Chapter 4, an outward shift in the nonfinancial business sector's estimate of the household sector's end-of-period demand for its equity shares produces two opposite effects upon the market price, p^n_t, it announces for those shares at time t. First, the increase in estimated demand, Sn^e_{t+1}, reduces the (flow) elasticity of demand at the price it was originally planning to announce. This reduces the current marginal revenue per share to existing shareholders of that sector issuing additional shares of equity, thereby inducing the sector to raise p^n_t.

Second, at the original market price, an increase in Sn^e_{t+1}, ceteris paribus, reduces the estimated return <u>per share</u> next period (since next period's total payment to shareholders is being held constant) to shareholders. This reduces the future marginal cost to current owners of issuing an additional share (via a manipulation of the price p^n_t) and induces the sector to reduce p^n_t.

As discussed in Chapter 4, assuming that the first of these two effects dominates, the sector may decide to raise p^n_t even though it plans to have more shares outstanding at the end of the period.

The analysis in Chapter 8 indicates that current disposable income and the household sector's current level of net wealth are the variables which are observable to the nonfinancial business sector at time t that shift the actual demand for nonfinancial sector equity. We might expect, therefore, that an increase in either of these variables will increase the nonfinancial business sector's estimate at time t of the position of the household sector's demand for its equity. Since these are the same variables that influence the household sector's demands for consumption goods and capital goods as well as its supply of labor, it follows that at the same time that the nonfinancial sector revises its estimate of the market demand for its own equity, it is also revising its estimates of its current revenue function $R^e\{.\}$ and of the household sector's labor supply function.

Ignoring any feedback effects, then, the responses of the nonfinancial business sector discussed to this point indicate that as its estimate of current disposable income or of the household sector's initial wealth increases, the nonfinancial sector will tend to increase current production of both consumption and capital goods, raise the market prices associated with both goods, and raise the current price of its equity shares.

Change in the estimated (net) labor supply function (v_n)

As N^{se}_{t+1} shifts outward, the marginal cost of engaging in current search falls, so that the nonfinancial business sector will tend to increase the number of people it wants to employ next period. Furthermore, the marginal return, in terms of conserving search costs, from raising the money wage also diminishes. Consequently, the sector will tend to reduce w_{t+1} as N^{se}_{t+1} shifts outward.

The reduced search costs release resources for commodity production in the current period. Current production will increase even though total current labor time falls. To sell the extra product, firms will reduce current commodity prices. (The price they plan to charge for comodities next period also falls.) Current net income increases. Current dividends increase to the extent that current ex ante business saving does not rise by more than the increase in current income. Since firms tend to hire more workers next period, future transactions time rises, causing the nonfinancial business sector's demand for currency to rise.

Because the sector now can hire more workrs at a lower wage, next period's wage bill may not rise significantly. In fact it may even fall. This consideration, coupled with the anticipated extra revenue from the extra commodities the added labor will be able to produce, implies that next period's net income may rise. If it does rise, the cost per share to existing owners from inreasing the number of shares outstanding by next period also rises. This induces the business sector to raise the current market price of equity shares.

Since the household sector's supply of labor constitutes a significant portion of the net supply of labor facing the nonfinancial business sector, estimated increases in either current disposable income or initial household net wealth will likely produce, ceteris paribus, a reduction in the estimated net supply of labor. Consequently the analysis contained in the section immediately preceding this one must be amended to include the effects (discussed in this section for the case of an increase in N^{se}_{t+1}) of a decrease in N^{se}_{t+1}.

Furthermore, since the nonfinancial business sector is only one of three potential employers, its estimated net supply, N^{se}_{t+1}, of employees depends as well upon its estimates of the government's and the financial business sector's demands for labor. The govenment's actual demand for labor was discussed in Chapter 7. The financial business sector's demand for labor is discussed in the next chapter. In conformance with our treatment of the govenment, household and nonfinancial business sectors, the financial business sector's demand for labor will not be presented in isolation. Instead it will be derived from the same present-value optimizing framework that yields the optimal values for all of its other decision variables at time t.

10. - The Private Financial Sector

The private financial sector in this study consists of depository institutions behaving as though they were a centralized unit. The objective of this sector at time t is to maximize its present value. It formulates its plans for the "current" and "next" periods in a manner that maximizes the amount which its shareholders would have to place in their next best alternative (presumably in equity shares issued by the nonfinancial business sector) at time t in order to duplicate (period by period) the income which the private financial sector contemplates distributing to its owners over each of the next two periods.

Because the private financial sector is free to sell or buy back its own equity shares during the current period, the number of shares it plans at time t to have outstanding at time t+1 may differ from the number outstanding at time t. In a manner consistent with our earlier treatment of the nonfinancial business sector, any new shares which the financial sector sells during the current period will not entitle the purchaser to receive income from those shares until next period. Also, any shares outstanding at time t will continue to pay dividends during the current period to the owners at time t whether or not the owners decide to sell the shares back to the financial sector during the current period.

The income per share which the private financial sector plans to distribute next period must be the same for both "old" and "new" shares. Therefore if the financial sector were to issue additional shares during the current period, those agents holding shares at time t would gain only if the proceeds of that sale increased the current income from an existing share by at least as much as the larger volume of shares outstanding next period would reduce the present value of next period's income per share. Consequently the objective of the private financial sector at time t must be to maximize the present value of the income <u>per share</u> to its owners over the next two periods.

But maximizing the present value of this income per share is tantamount to maximizing the shadow price of private financial sector equity at time t. The shadow price represents the maximum amount that someone would be willing to pay at time t for the right to receive one share's worth of income from the financial sector during each of the current and next periods, providing that person possessed the information held by the financial sector. The shadow price also represents the minimum amount that an existing owner at time t would ask for a share if that person also held the same information. Therefore the shadow price is also the present value of the income stream from that share. This value remains a shadow price in this study simply because we abstract from trading in existing shares among economic agents at time t.

To the extent that they purchase bonds directly from the government (a specialty function which no one else performs) and issue their own liabilities in the form of interest bearing checkable deposits, the private depository institutions truly serve as financial intermediaries in this study. They also grant personal loans to the household sector and trade their own equity shares.

Since the private financial sector is viewed here as a centralized depository institution and since the government, household and nonfinancial business sectors all hold their deposits at this institution, a transfer of deposits among its customers will not affect the institution's reserves. The financial institutions will lose reserves to other sectors only through a cash drain.

Because its lending activities and the activities of its depositors involve transactions between the private financial sector and its customers, the sector presumably requires the services of labor. To simplify the analysis, suppose the private financial sector requires neither the services of capital goods nor consumption goods. Excess reserves held by the depository institutions at the beginning of the period provide a service similar to that yielded by the currency and checkable deposits held by the household, government and nonfinancial business sectors. In particular the excess reserves it holds at the beginning of the period facilitate some transactions during the period and therefore help to conserve real resources (i.e. labor time). More specifically, the financial sector may experience an outflow of currency because a customer cashes a check or asks for currency as payment for interest earned on a checkable deposit. A currency drain also results if a borrower takes out a loan in the form of currency, if an employee asks for currency as payment for labor services it provides the financial sector, or if an owner asks for currency in exchange for equity shares it sells back to the financial sector. If the financial business sector were to hold no excess reserves at the time one of these transactions occurs, it would have to engage in at least one additional transaction in order to obtain sufficient currency to meet the currency drain. It would need to convert some other asset into currency before it could make the required currency payment. Ceteris paribus, then, the larger its excess reserves at the beginning of the period, the fewer of these extra transactions will be required during the period to meet even temporary cash drains. Since transactions require the services of labor, excess reserves serve, ceteris paribus, to reduce the quantity of labor the financial sector must hire to undertake transactions.

At time t the private financial sector must decide the interest rate on checkable deposits, the interest rate on personal loans, the price of (government) bonds, the price of its own equity shares, the average number of hours it will use its current employees, the number of people it will employ next period, and its desired end-of-period levels of total and excess reserves. In the next section the mutually consistent optimal levels of all these variables are derived simultaneously within a comprehensive model of a present-value maximizing financial sector.

Formal Model of the Private Financial Sector

As the current period opens the private financial sector holds three financial assets consisting of reserves, Rs_t (held either as vault cash or as deposits at the central bank), government bonds, B^f_t, and personal loans, L_t. As mentioned earlier, government bonds issued in one period presumably mature in the next period, paying one dollar total in principal and interest. The bonds held by the financial sector at time t were issued last period. (For the time being, government bonds may also be held by the central bank. The number of bonds in the central bank's portfolio equals the total number of government bonds outstanding at time t, defind earlier as B^g_t, minus B^f_t.) Since the government bonds were purchased by the private financial sector last period at price p^b_{t-1} per bond, the dollar value of the bond principal held by the private financial sector at time t equals $p^b_{t-1}B^f_t$. Therefore the total dollar value of its assets at time t may be denoted by $Rs_t + L_t + p^b_{t-1}B^f_t$.

On the liability side, the private financial sector has outstanding checkable deposits payable to the government, D^g_t, to the households, D^h_t, and to the nonfinancial business sector, D^n_t, at time t. In addition, it has a given volume of advances, A_t, outstanding at time t, which are simply notes payable to the central bank. Therefore, at time t, the total dollar value of the private financial sector's outstanding liabilities equals $D^g_t + D^h_t + D^n_t + A_t$.

The current revenue received by the depository institutions during the current period consists of the interest income it receives on personal loans outstanding at time t plus the interest income it receives during the current period on the government bonds it holds at time t. Let r^{ℓ}_{t-1} represent the rate of interest on personal loans that was announced last period and which is received during the current period. Based upon earlier statements, $\$1 - p^{b}_{t-1}$ represents the current interest income per bond held at time t. Therefore, the private financial sector's current revenue equals $r^{\ell}_{t-1}L_t + (\$1 - p^{b}_{t-1})B^{f}_{t}$.

Let D_t represent the total number of dollars held by the government, the household and the nonfinancial business sectors as checkable deposits at the beginning of the current period at depository institutions: $D_t = D^{g}_{t} + D^{h}_{t} + D^{n}_{t}$. Let r^{d}_{t-1} denote the interest rate which the depository institutions announced last period that they would pay this period on each dollar of checkable deposits outstanding at time t. Then the private financial sector's current interest expense on checkable deposits equals $r^{d}_{t-1}D_t$. Let ρ_{t-1} denote the "discount rate" which the central bank announced last period and which the private financial sector must pay during the current period on each dollar of advances outstanding at time t. Then the private financial sector's current interest expense on advances equals $\rho_{t-1}A_t$.

The private financial sector presumably uses current labor time only for the purpose of undertaking financial transactions. Let N^{f}_{t} represent the number of people whom the private financial sector has hired by time t to work during the current period. Let h^{f}_{t} denote the average number of hours that the private financial sector decides at time t that these N^{f}_{t} people will work this period. Then current labor time used by the private financial sector becomes $h^{f}_{t}\ N^{f}_{t}$.

Let $\tilde{\alpha}(.)$ represent the amount of transactions time the sector anticipates incurring during the current period. Suppose $\tilde{\alpha}(.)$ is a strictly convex function of the volume of personal loans, L_t, granted by the beginning of the period, the volume of checkable deposits, D_t, outstanding at the beginning of the period, and the amount of excess reserves, X_t, the private financial sector holds at the beginning of the period. Presumably current transactions time increases at an increasing rate with respect to both L_t and D_t and decreases at a decreasing rate with respct to S_t:

$$h^{f}_{t}N^{f}_{t} = \tilde{\alpha}(L_t, D_t, X_t) \qquad (10.1)$$

where $\tilde{\alpha}_1$, $\tilde{\alpha}_2$, $\tilde{\alpha}_{11}$, $\tilde{\alpha}_{22} > 0$; $\tilde{\alpha}_3 < 0$; $\tilde{\alpha}_{33} > 0$.

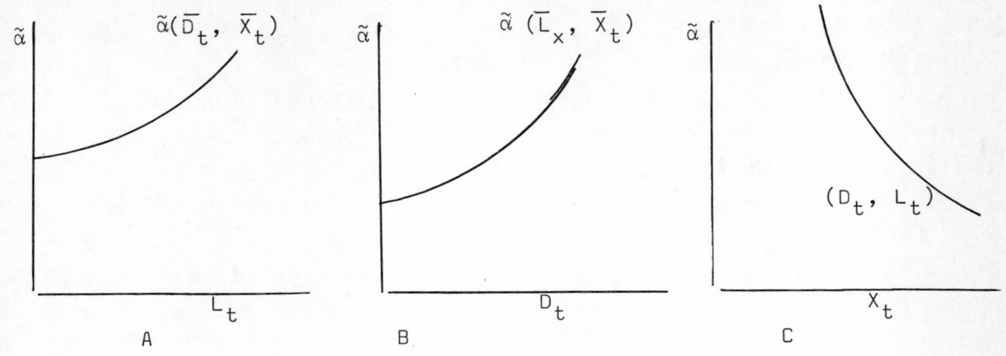

Figure 10.1 - Current Transactions Time (as an Increasing Function of L_t (Panel A), an Increasing Function of D_t (Panel B) and a Decreasing Function of X_t (Panel C))

The private financial sector's current wage bill constitutes the third component of is current expenses. The current hourly money wage, w_t, was announced last period by the nonfinancial business sector and was adopted by all employers, including the private financial sector. Therefore its current wage bill equals $w_t h^f{}_t N^f{}_t$. Hence, based upon the above discussion, its total current expenses equal $r^d{}_{t-1}D_t + \rho_{t-1}A_t + w_t h^f{}_t N^f{}_t$.

At time t the financial sector must decide, <u>inter alia</u>, the level of dividends it will announce at the beginning of the current period and distribute to its shareholders during the period. Let $\pi^f{}_t Sf_t$ denote the level of those dividends, where $\pi^f{}_t$ represents the current dividends per share announced at time t and where Sf_t, as previously, depicts the number of financial sector shares held by the households at time t. Then in terms of current income, current expenses and net business saving of the financial sector, current dividends may be represented by expression (10.2):

$$\pi^f{}_t Sf_t = r^\ell{}_{t-1}L_t + (\$1 - p^b{}_{t-1})B^f{}_t - r^d{}_{t-1}D_t - \rho_{t-1}A_t - w_t h^f{}_t N^f{}_t - s^f{}_t \quad (10.2)$$

where $s^f{}_t$ represents current net business saving of the private financial sector.

Let Rs^e_{t+1} denote the volume of reserves which the private financial business sector plans at time t to hold time t+1. Then the volume of reserves which the sector plans at time t to accumulate during the current period is represented by $Rs^e_{t+1} - Rs_t$. This difference necessarily equals the amount the sector plans to save, s^f_t, on the income account during the current period plus the value of the sector's planned addition to its checkable deposit liabilities plus the value of its planned addition to its notes payable to the central bank plus the value of its planned sales of its equity shares during the period minus the value of its planned addition to government bonds and minus the value of its planned increase in personal loans during the period.

Let D^e_{t+1} denote the volume of checkable deposits which the private financial sector plans at time t to have outstanding at time t+1, let A^e_{t+1} depict the dollar value of advances payable to the central bank which the sector plans at time t to have outstanding at time t+1, let p^f_t represent the current market price which the sector announces for its own equity shares, let Sf^e_{t+1} denote the number of its own shares which the sector plans at time t to have outstanding by time t+1, let B^{fe}_{t+1} equal the number of government bonds the sector plans at time t to hold at time t+1, let p^b_t denote the current market price of government bonds, and let L^e_{t+1} represent the dollar value of personal IOU's which the private financial sector plans to hold by time t+1. Then the last statement in the paragraph immediately above may be written as expression (10.3).

$$\begin{aligned}(Rs^e_{t+1} - Rs_t) = {} & [r^\ell_{t-1}L_t + (\$1 - p^b_{t-1})B^f_t - r^d_{t-1}D_t - \rho_{t-1}A_t \\ & - w_t h^f_t N^f_t - \pi^f_t Sf^h_t] \\ & + (D^e_{t+1} - D_t) + (A^e_{t+1} - A_t) + p^f_t(Sf^e_{t+1} - Sf_t) \\ & - (p^b_t B^{fe}_{t+1} - p^b_{t-1}B^f_t) - (L^e_{t+1} - L_t) \qquad (10.3)\end{aligned}$$

The terms involving $p^b_{t-1}B^f_t$ on the right hand side of (10.3) cancel. This reflects the fact that since B^f_t matures during the current period, no market exists for these bonds during the period. The number of bonds held at the end of the period, B^f_{t+1}, therefore also represents the number of bonds the private financial sector buys during the period.

As the above discussion suggests, the balance sheet of the private financial sector is closely tied to the central bank's balance sheet. In particular the volume of reserves, Rs_t, which the private financial sector actually holds at the beginning of a particular period necessarily equals the dollar value of "central bank credit" outstanding at that time, $p^b_{t-1}B^{cb}_t + A_t$, minus the volume of currency in circulation outside the central bank and the depository institutions (i.e. held by the household sector), Cu^h_t, at that time. This relationship is implied by the following balance sheet for the central bank:

Central Bank's Beginning-of-Period Balance Sheet

$p^b_{t-1}B^{cb}_t$	Rs_t
A_t	Cu^h_t

where B^{cb}_t equals the number of government bonds held by the central bank at the beginning of the current period. The exchange rates among D, Rs, Cu and A respectively are fixed at unity. Also, once the current - period price, p^b_t, of the one-period government bonds is announced, it presumably remains unchanged for the duration of the current period. Consequently, the central bank in this study earns neither capital gains nor losses on the items in its balance sheet. In addition the central bank presumably distributes its entire current income from operations to the "general fund" of the government sector. Therefore, since the "net worth" accont of the central bank cannot change (we abstract from equity issues by that bank), we ignore the net worth account altogether.

The close association between the balance sheets of the private financial sector and the central bank indicates that the anticipations which the private financial sector forms at time t with respect to its own end-of-period balance sheet will be influenced by its anticipations concerning the central bank's end-of-period balance sheet:

The Private Financial Sector's Anticipations
at Time t as to the Central Bank's End-of-Period Balance Sheet

$p^b_t B^{cbe}_{t+1}$	Rs^e_{t+1}
A_t	Cu^h_t

Clearly, the level of reserves, Rs^e_{t+1}, that the private financial sector anticipates at time t that it will hold at time t+1 equals the value of monetary base it anticipates for time t+1 (which, from the "sources" side, equals $p^b_t B^{cbe}_{t+1} + A^e_{t+1}$) minus the amount of currency, Cu^e_{t+1}, it anticipates the private nonfinancial sectors will hold at time t+1. These anticipated values reflect, in turn, the private financial sector's perception of the central bank's objective.

An "interventionist" view of central bank behavior currently prevails not only in the professional literature, but also in practice. According to this view, the central bank exists in order to control certain economic variables (e.g. the monetary base, the money stock or interest rates) for the purpose of producing favorable effects (or preventing unfavorable effects) upon certain other economic variables (e.g. commodity prices, employment and/or GNP). Since open-market operations and, to a lesser extent, discount policies provide the primary instruments of monetary control, the private financial sector must anticipate the central bank's activities in both the bond and discount markets under this regime. In terms of the balance sheet displayed in the paragraph immediately above, the private financial sector must estimate not only Cu^e_{t+1} but also $p^b_t B^{cbe}_{t+1}$ and A^e_{t+1} in order to arrive at an estimate of Rs_{t+1}.

Under this regime, the central bank may attempt to control bond prices, in which case the private financial institutions must guess what the other participants in the bond market will do before it can estimate at time t the size of the government securities component of central bank credit at time t+1. On the other hand, the central bank may decide (but not announce) B^{cb}_{t+1}, allowing p^b_t to be established in the marketplace. In this case, in order to estimate at time t the level of Rs_{t+1}, the private financial sector must estimate B^{cb}_{t+1}. With respect to the discount window, the central bank currently has the right not only to set the discount rate but also to limit the availability of borrowed reserves. As a result, the private financial sector must decide not only the amount of funds it would like to borrow by time t+1 at the interest rate it anticipates the central bank will announce but also whether the central bank will limit directly the availability of borrowed reserves.

In the next chapter a noninterventionist alternative is developed for the central bank. The bank is precluded from manipulating reserve requirements, from limiting directly the availability of borrowed reserves and from engaging in open-market operations. Instead, it sets the discount rate at what it estimates at the beginning of the period is the optimal level and then lends at that rate to private financial institutions on an unrestricted basis. The advantages of this alternative as well as the basis upon which the central bank decides the optimal level of the discount rate will be discussed in the next chapter. At this point we pursue only the implications of this alternative for the private financial sector's plans at time t with respect to Rs_{t+1}.

Under the scheme proposed in the next chapter, the central bank holds no government bonds. Therefore,

$$Rs_t = A_t - Cu_t \tag{10.4}$$

Also, from the private financial sector's point of view:

$$Rs^e_{t+1} = A^e_{t+1} - Cu^e_{t+1} \tag{10.5}$$

The private financial sector is able, under this alternative regime, to decide for itself the volume of advances it will have outstanding at time t+1. Therefore, the only source of uncertainty insofar as the private financial sector's planned end-of-period reserves, Rs^e_{t+1}, is concerned is the amount of currency it anticipates the private nonfinancial sectors (i.e. the households) will want to hold. The alternative role for the central bank advocated below reduces the degree of uncertainty surrounding the level of reserves the private financial sector anticipates it will hold at time t. The reason is simple. Under this alternative,the central bank is precluded from altering unilaterally the level of high-powered money. Only deliberate action by the private sector may bring about a change in the monetary base.

Returning to condition (10.3), it is evident that the private financial sector must also formulate its plans at time t with respect to the dollar values of checkable deposits, D^e_{t+1}, personal loans,

L^e_{t+1}, equity shares, $p^f_t Sf^e_{t+1}$, and government bonds, $p^b_t B^{fe}_{t+1}$, in its end-of-period balance sheet. Its anticipated levels of these items are derived from its estimates of the respective end-of-period market demand and supply functions for these items. These anticipated levels therefore depend upon the current-period interest rates on checkable deposits and personal loans as well as upon the current-period prices for government bonds and its own equity shares that the private financial sector announces at time t.

Suppose the private financial sector estimates the following simple end-of-period demand function for checkable deposits:

$$D^e_{t+1} = D^e_{t+1}(r^d_t, \xi_d) \tag{10.6}$$

where the partial derivative of $D^e_{t+1}(.)$, with respect to r^d_t, $(D^e_{t+1})_1$, is positive in conformance with functions (7.28), (8.31) and (9.53), depicting respectively the government, household and nonfinancial business sector's demands for checkable deposits. The symbol ξ_d denotes a vector of parameters which the depository institutions estimate determines the position of the market demand function for checkable deposits in the (r^d_t, D^e_{t+1}) plane.

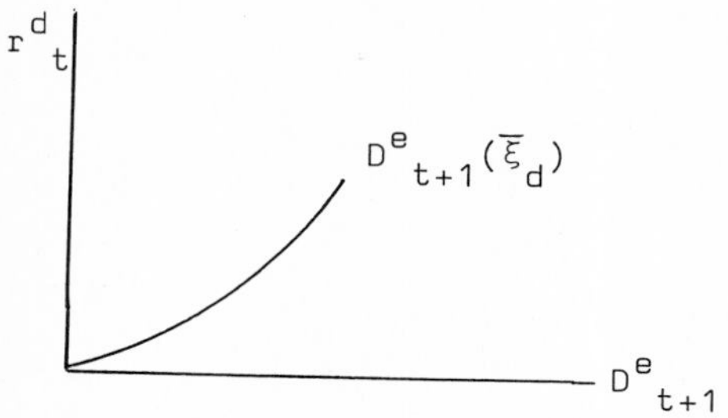

Figure 10.2 - The Private Financial Sector's Estimate of the End-of-Period Demand Function for Checkable Deposits

Let expression (10.7) represent the private financial sector's estimate of the end-of-period demand for personal loans L^{hd}_{t+1} (i.e. ex ante supply of IOU's).

$$L^e_{t+1} = L^e_{t+1}(r^\ell_t, \xi_\ell) \tag{10.7}$$

In conformance with the household sector's actual end-of-period demand, equation (8.33), suppose the partial derivative of L^e_{t+1}, with respect to r^{ℓ}_{t} is negative, i.e. $(L^{e}_{t+1})_{1} < 0$. The symbol ξ_{ℓ} denotes a vector of parameters which the private financial sector estimates determines the position of the household sector's end-of-period demand for loans.

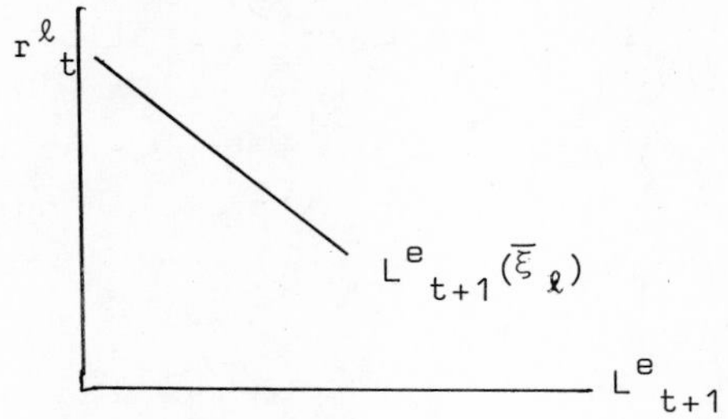

Figure 10.3 - The Financial Sector's Estimate of the End-of-Period Demand Function for Personal Loans

Assume the private financial sector's estimate of the household sector's end-of-period demand function for its own equity shares is represented by the following function:

$$Sf^{e}_{t+1} = Sf^{e}_{t+1}(p^{f}_{t}, \xi_{f}) \qquad (10.8)$$

where the partial derivative with respect to p^{f}_{t} is negative in conformance wiith the household sector's actual demand function, (8.28), and where ξ_{f} represents a vector of parameters which the financial sector estimates determines the position of this demand function in $(p^{f}_{t}, Sf^{e}_{t+1})$ space.

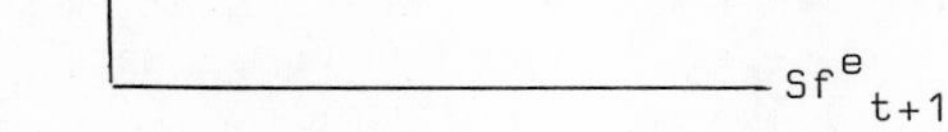

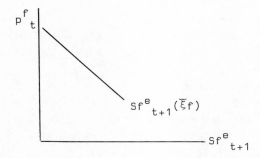

Figure 10.4 - The Financial Business Sector's Estimate of the End-of-Period Demand for Its Equity Shares

Given the noninterventionist role assigned to the central bank in this study, the government and the private financial sector constitute the only two partiicipants in the bond market. Consequently, at time t, $B^f_t = B^g_t$. The number of bonds held by the private financial sector at time t equals the number of government bonds outstanding at that moment. Furthermore, in deciding the optimal market price, p^b_t, to announce at time t, at which it will stand ready to purchase bonds during the current period, the private financial sector must rely upon its estimate of the government's end-of-period supply of bonds:

$$B^e_{t+1} = B^e_{t+1}(\underset{+}{p^b_t}, \xi_b) \tag{10.9}$$

where, in accordance with (7.35), the partial derivative with respect to p^b_t, $(B^e_{t+1})_1$, is positive. (More accurately, equation (7.35) stipulates that the dollar value of the government's supply of bonds is positively related to p^b_t whereas (10.9) portrays the estimated number of government bonds issued as increasing with p^b_t.) The symbol ξ_b denotes a vector of shift parameters..

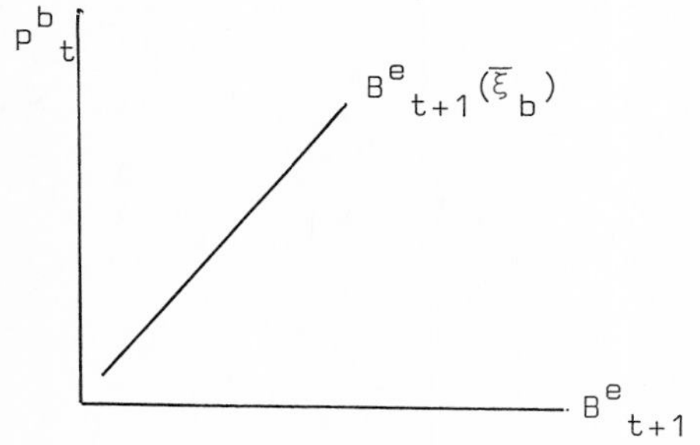

Figure 10.5 - The Private Financial Sector's Estimate of the End-of-Period Supply of Government Bonds.

Since the household sector's demand for currency for the end of the period directly affects the private financial sector's end-of-period reserves, the private financial sector must estimate at time t what that demand will be. In accordance with the actual demand derived in (8.30), suppose the private financial sector estimates the following end-of-period demand for currency by the household sector:

$$Cu^e_{t+1} = Cu^e_{t+1}(r^d_t, \xi_c) \tag{10.10}$$

where the partial derivative of that demand with respect to the interest rate on checkable deposits, $(Cu^e_{t+1})_1$, is negative. The symbol ξ_c denotes a vector of shift parameters which the private financial sector estimates also affects the household sector's end-of-period demand for currency:

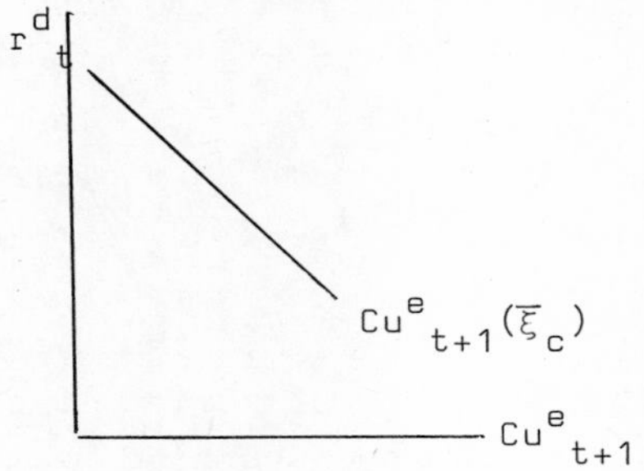

Figure 10.6 - The Private Financial Sector's Estimate of the Household Sector's End-of-Period Demand for Currency.

Substitute the right hand side of (10.10) for Cu^e_{t+1} in (10.5). Then substitute the right hand sides of (10.1) and (10.4)-(10.9) for $h^f_t N^f_t$, Rs_t, Rs^e_{t+1}, D^e_{t+1}, L^e_{t+1}, Sf^e_{t+1} and B^e_{t+1}, respectively, into (10.3). Rearranging terms in the new (10.3) yields the following expression for the private financial sector's current dividends per share:

$$\pi^f_t = \frac{1}{Sf_t}[r^\ell_{t-1}L_t + (\$1-p^b_{t-1})B^g_t - r^d_{t-1}D_t - \rho_{t-1}A_t - w_t\tilde{\alpha}(L_t, D_t, X_t)$$
$$+ Cu^e_{t+1}(r^d_t, \xi_c) - Cu_t + D^e_{t+1}(r^d_t, \xi_d) - D_t$$
$$- (L^e_{t+1}(r^\ell_t, \xi_\ell) - L_t)$$
$$- (p^b_t B^e_{t+1}(p^b_t, \xi_b) - p^b_{t-1}B^g_t) + p^f_t(Sf^e_{t+1}(p^f_t, \xi_f) - Sf_t)] \quad (10.11)$$

Next Period's Anticipated Dividends

Based upon the discussion to this point, the private financial sector's anticipated interest income next period will consist of interest from loans and bonds it holds at time t+1: $r^\ell_t \cdot L^e_{t+1}(r^\ell_t, \xi_\ell) + (\$1 - p^b_t)B^e_{t+1}(p^b_t, \xi_b)$. Its anticipated interest expense next period amounts to the interest it must pay on checkable deposits and advances outstanding at time t+1: $r^d_t D^e_{t+1}(r^d_t, \xi_d) + \rho_t A_{t+1}$. Next period's wage bill, $w_{t+1} hN^f_{t+1}$, constitutes the second component of the private financial sector's anticipated expenses next period, where w_{t+1} denotes next period's hourly money wage (announced at time t by the nonfinancial business sector), h depicts the standard number of hours each employer anticipates at time t that each of its employees will work next period and N^f_{t+1} represents the number of people which the financial sector plans at time t to employ next period. Therefore, the financial sector's anticipated level of net income next period may be denoted by $r^\ell_t L^e_{t+1}(r^\ell_t, \xi_\ell) + (\$1 - p^b_t)B^e_{t+1}(p^b_t, \xi_b) - r^d_t D^e_{t+1}(r^d_t, \xi_d) - \rho_t A_{t+1} - w_{t+1} hN^f_{t+1}$.

Suppose that the total labor time, hN^f_{t+1}, that the private financial sector anticipates it will require next period is related to the amount of transactions time it anticipates incurring next period. Specifically, assume that the amount of time the sector plans to spend undertaking transactions (and therefore the amount of labor time it will need) next period is an increasing function, $\alpha(.)$, of the levels of deposit liabilities, D^e_{t+1}, and loans, $L^e_{t+1}(.)$, it plans to have outstanding at time t+1. In addition, let the amount of excess reserves, X^d_{t+1}, it plans to hold at time t+1 serve to reduce, ceteris paribus, the amount of time required to "service" a given volume of D_{t+1} and L_{t+1}. To simplify the analysis, assume that $\alpha(.)$ is strictly convex in its arguments

$$hN^f_{t+1} = \alpha(D^e_{t+1}(r^d_t, \xi_d), L^e_{t+1}(r^\ell_t, \xi_\ell), X^d_{t+1}) \tag{10.12}$$

so that $\alpha_1, \alpha_2 > 0$, $\alpha_3 < 0$; $\alpha_{ii} > 0$ for all i. Ceteris paribus, then, an increase in either D^e_{t+1} or L^e_{t+1} will increase at an increasing rate the amount of labor the sector requires next period. This may be due either to a more than proportionate increase in the volume of transactions as D^e_{t+1} or L^e_{t+1} grows, or to a reduction in the marginal product of labor. Also, an increase in X^d_{t+1} presumably reduces next period's labor requirement but at a decreasing rate; the marginal product of excess reserves is diminishing.

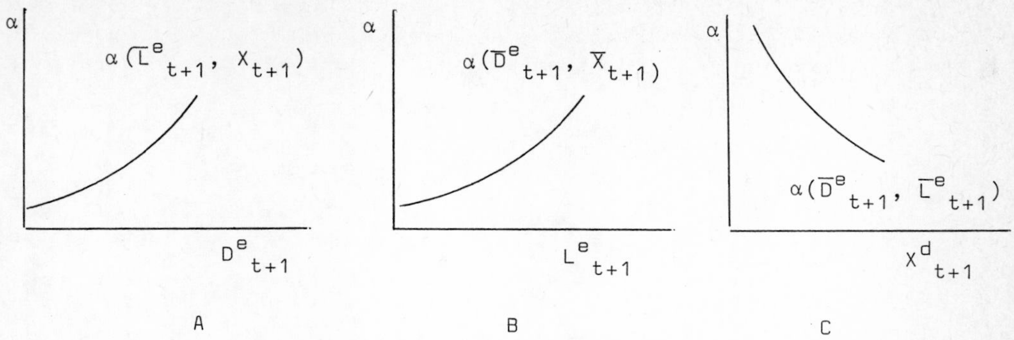

Figure 10.7 - Next Period's Transactions Time as an Increasing Function of D^e_{t+1} (Panel A), an Increasing Function of L^e_{t+1} (Panel B) and a Decreasing Function of X_{t+1} (Panel C).

The dividends which the private financial sector plans to distribute to its shareholders next period is represented by the product $\pi^f_{t+1}Sf^e_{t+1}(.)$, where π^f_{t+1} denotes dividends per share and $Sf^e_{t+1}(.)$ denotes the number of shares the sector anticpates will be outstanding at time t+1. In terms of next period's revenues and expenses, then, these dividends may be expressed according to (10.13):

$$\pi^f_{t+1}Sf^e_{t+1}(.) = r^\ell_t L^e_{t+1}(.) + (\$1 - p^b_t)B^e_{t+1}(.) - r^d_t D^e_{t+1}(.)$$

$$- \rho_t A_{t+1} - w_{t+1}\alpha(.) - s^f_{t+1} \qquad (10.13)$$

where s^f_{t+1} denotes the private financial sector's anticipated level of net saving next period.

The stipulation, repeated throughout this study, that every sector must plan at time t to hold no assets and to retire all liabilities by time t+2 is also imposed upon the private financial sector. In addition, the volume of reserves which the sector plans to accumulate next period, $0 - Rs^e_{t+1}$, necessarily equals the amount it plans to save next period, s^f_{t+1}, plus the planned increase in its deposit liabilities, $0 - D^e_{t+1}(.)$, plus the planned increase in its advances from the central bank, $0 - A_{t+1}$, minus the planned increase in government bonds, $0 - p^b_t B^e_{t+1}(.)$, minus the planned increase in loans to households, $0 - L^e_{t+1}(.)$:

$$- Rs^e_{t+1} = s^f_{t+1} - D^e_{t+1}(.) - A_{t-1} + p^b_t B^e_{t+1}(.) + L^e_{t+1}(.) \qquad (10.14)$$

Substituting the right hand side of (10.5) for Rs^e_{t+1} yields the following expression for the ex ante level of next period's net saving:

$$s^f_{t+1} = Cu^e_{t+1}(.) + D^e_{t+1}(.) - p^b_t B^e_{t+1}(.) - L^e_{t+1}(.). \quad (10.15)$$

Substituting the right hand side of (10.15) for s^f_{t+1} in (10.13) then produces the following expression for next period's anticipated dividends per share:

$$\pi^f_{t+1} = \frac{1}{Sf^e_{t+1}(.)}[(1 + r^{\ell}_t)L^e_{t+1}(.) + B^e_{t+1}(.) - (1 + r^d_t)D^e_{t+1}(.) - Cu^e_{t+1}(.) - \rho_t A_{t+1} - w_{t+1}\alpha(.)] \quad (10.16)$$

Before the present value of the private financial sector can be maximized, the relationship between total reserves and excess reserves must be recognized. In particular,

$$X_t = Rs_t - r^* D_t \quad (10.17)$$

$$X^d_{t+1} = Rs^e_{t+1} - r^* D^e_{t+1}(.) \quad (10.18)$$

where r* represents the required reserve ratio. In this study r* no longer denotes a "policy" parameter. It is a positive fraction only if the nonbanking public's confidence as to the safety of its checkable deposits is enhanced by the existence of required reserves, a questionable result in the presence of more visible deposit insurance. In light of (10.4) and (10.5), the above expressions for X_t and X^d_{t+1} become:

$$X_t = A_t - Cu_t - r^* D_t \quad (10.19)$$

$$X^d_{t+1} = A_{t+1} - Cu^e_{t+1}(.) - r^* D^e_{t+1}(.) \quad (10.20)$$

The Private Financial Sector's Objective Function

Substitute the right hand side of (10.19) for X_t in the $\tilde{\alpha}(.)$ term in expression (10.11). Next substitute the right hand side of (10.20) for X^d_{t+1} in the $\alpha(.)$ term appearing in expression (10.16). Dividing the new (10.16) by (π^n_{t+1}/p^n_t), to convert it to present value terms, and adding the result to the new (10.11) yields the following expression for the present value of the private financial sector:

$$p^f_o = \pi^f_t + \frac{\pi^f_{t+1}}{(\pi^{ne}_{t+1}/p^n_t)}$$

$$= \frac{1}{Sf_t}[r^\ell_{t-1}L_t + B^g_t - (1+r^d_{t-1})D_t - \rho_{t-1}A_t - w_t\tilde{\alpha}(D_t, L_t, A_t - Cu_t - r^*D_t)$$

$$+ Cu^e_{t+1}(r^d_t, \xi_c) - Cu_t + D^e_{t+1}(r^d_t, \xi_d) - D_t - L^e_{t+1}(r^\ell_t, \xi_\ell) + L_t$$

$$- p^b_t B^e_{t+1}(p^b_t, \xi_b) + p^f_t(Sf^e_{t+1}(p^f_t, \xi_f) - Sf_t)]$$

$$+ \frac{1}{(\pi^{ne}_{t+1}/p^n_t)Sf^e_{t+1}(p^f_t, \xi_f)}[(1+r^\ell_t)L^e_{t+1}(r^\ell_t, \xi_\ell)$$

$$+ B^e_{t+1}(p^b_t, \xi_b) - (1+r^d_t)D^e_{t+1}(r^d_t, \xi_d)$$

$$- Cu^e_{t+1}(r^d_t, \xi_c) - \rho_t A_{t+1}$$

$$- w_t\alpha(D^e_{t+1}(r^d_t, \xi_d), L^e_{t+1}(r^\ell_t, \xi_\ell), A_{t+1}$$

$$- Cu^e_{t+1}(r^d_t, \xi_c) - r^*D^e_{t+1}(r^d_t, \xi_d))] \qquad (10.21)$$

The objective of the private financial sector at time t is to maximize (10.21) with respect to the choice variables r^d_t, r^1_t, p^b_t, p^f_t and A_{t+1}. Substituting the optimal solution for r^d_t and A_{t+1} into (10.20) yields the optimal (ex ante) level of excess reserves for the end of the period, X^d_{t+1}. Substituting the optimal values for r^d_t and X^d_{t+1} into (10.18) then provides the amount of reserves, Rs^e_{t+1}, which the private financial business sector anticipates holding by the end of the period.

Implications for Private Financial Sector Behavior

The first-order necessary conditions for the (unconstrained) maximization of (10.21) are given below as conditions (10.22) - (10.26).

Consider, first, the necessary condition associated with the interest rate on checkable deposits, r^d_t:

$$\frac{\partial p^f_o}{\partial r^d_t} = \frac{(Cu^e_{t+1})_1 + (D^e_{t+1})_1}{Sf_t} - \frac{D^e_{t+1} + (1 + r^d_t)(D^e_{t+1})_1 + (Cu^e_{t+1})_1}{Sf^e_{t+1}(\pi^{ne}_{t+1}/p^n_t)}$$

$$- \frac{w_{t+1}[\alpha_1(D^e_{t+1})_1 + \alpha_3(-(Cu^e_{t+1})_1 - r^*(D^e_{t+1})_1)]}{Sf^e_{t+1}(\pi^{ne}_{t+1}/p^n_t)} = 0 \qquad (10.22)$$

This condition refers to a situation in which the financial sector holds constant (a) the amount it lends (either as personal loans or as bond purchases), (b) the number of equity shares it issues, and (c) the amount it borrows from the central bank. Ceteris paribus, as the private financial sector raises r^d_t, it reduces its estimate of the amount of currency which the households will want to hold by the end of the period and increases its estimate of the volume of checkable deposits that its customers will want to hold at the end of the period. Holding D^e_{t+1} constant temporarily, the decrease in Cu^e_{t+1} is tantamount to an increase in the level of reserves the private financial sector plans to hold at the end of the current period. Given that current revenues and expenses are unchanged, the increase in Rs^e_{t+1} is, in effect, financed via an increase in current saving by the private financial sector. In other words, the rise in Rs^e_{t+1} is financed by a reduction in current dividends to the current shareholders.

However, as r^d_t is raised, the estimated end-of-period demand for checkable deposits will rise. Ceteris paribus, this reduces the amount the private financial sector must save during the current period in order to obtain the unchanged optimal level of Rs^e_{t+1}. (If we temporarily hold Cu^e_{t+1} constant, then with A_{t+1} also held constant, the desired level of Rs^e_{t+1} remains unchanged as D^e_{t+1} rises.) Since the sector's ex ante net saving falls and since its current net income remains unchanged, the private financial sector tends to raise current dividends as D^e_{t+1} rises in response to the increase in r^d_t.

The net effect of the two opposing influences mentioned in the last two paragraphs above is readily apparent. First, according to the analysis in Chapter 8, as r^d_t rises the households will substitute checkable deposits for currency <u>and</u> other assets on the margin. In other words, for the household sector, the absolute value of the partial derivative of its end-of-period demand for checkable deposits with respect to r^d_t exceeds the absolute value of the corresponding partial of its demand for currency. Second, since neither the government nor the nonfinancial business sector demands currency for the end of the period, the absolute values of the partial derivatives of their end-of-period demands for checkable deposits with respect to r^d_t also exceed the zero values of the partials of their demands for currency. Hence $(D^e_{t+1})_1 + (Cu^e_{t+1})_1 > 0$. As the private financial sector raises r^d_t, its current period dividends per share will tend, ceteris paribus, to increase. According to condition (10.22), the private financial sector will continue to raise r^d_t until the fall in the present value of future dividends per share just offsets the above rise in current dividends per share, on the margin.

The anticipated net effect on the margin of an increase in r^d_t upon next period's dividends per share consists of the sum of the two fractions in (10.22) having the common denominator $Sf^e_{t+1}(\pi^{ne}_{t+1}/p^n_t)$. The first of these contains several terms pertaining to the effect upon the private financial sector's net income next period due to anticipated changes in the quantities demanded of currency and checkable deposits. The term $-D^e_{t+1}$ denotes the reduction in next period's net income due to the extra interest expense from raising r^d_t one point even if this increase does not attract additional deposits. The term $-(1 + r^d_t)(D^d_{t+1})_1$ represents the anticipated extra expenses next period for interest and deposit retirement resulting from the extra deposits attracted by the increase in r^d_t. The last term in this first fraction, $-(Cu^e_{t+1})_1$, represents the increase in next period's dividends because of the reduction in the quantity of currency demanded in response to a rise in r^d_t. The reduction in the quantity of currency demanded ceteris paribus increases the volume of reserves that the private financial sector holds at the end of the current period; this increases the amount that the sector can potentially pay its owners next period. Since the absolute value of this third term is less than the absolute value of the second, the first and second terms in this first fraction dominate the third. The net impact of an increase in r^d_t upon next period's anticipated dividends per share operating through the demands for currency and checkable deposits is negative.

The second fraction, depicting an impact upon the present value of next period's dividends due to a rise in r^d_t, concerns changes in next period's labor cost due to changes in the volume of transactions. The term $-w_{t+1}\alpha_1(D^e_{t+1})_1$ denotes the reduction in future dividends because of the higher wage expense next period associated with the greater demand for checkable deposits spurred by the unit increase in r^d_t. The larger the end-of-period volume of checkable deposits, the greater the transactions costs (in the form of labor time) that the private financial sector expects to incur.

The term $w_{t+1}\alpha_3(Cu^e_{t+1})_1$ represents the positive effect upon next period's dividends due to the anticipated reduction in next period's labor cost resulting from the estimated response in the demand for currency to a rise in r^d_t. As r^d_t rises, the demand for currency falls thereby raising, ceteris paribus, the level of excess reserves the financial sector will hold by the end of the period. Since excess reserves conserve real resources, the sector will be able to reduce next period's labor cost.

However another effect upon the financial sector's end-of-peiod excess reserves also exists if the required reserve ratio is positive. In particular as r^d_t rises, the corresponding rise in the anticipated level of checkable deposits at the end of the period raises the anticipated level of required reserves by the amount $r^*(D^e_{t+1})_1$. This reduces, ceteris paribus, the level of excess reserves by an equivalent amount, causing the financial sector to add labor services at a cost equal to $-\ w_{t+1}\alpha_3 r^*(D^e_{t+1})$. Minus one times this amount, $w_{t+1}\alpha_3 r^*(D^e_{t+1})_1$, denotes the anticipated corresponding reduction in next period's dividends; it appears as the last term in the second fraction pertaining to next period's dividends per share in expression (10.22). Assuming this entire second fraction is negative implies that an increase in r^d_t raises the private financial sector's estimate of next period's labor expense.

To summarize, condition (10.22) stipulates that the private depository institutions will continue to raise r^d_t until the marginal increase in current dividends per share is exactly offset by the marginal reduction in the present value of next period's dividends per share resulting from next period's greater interest and labor expenses.

Partially differentiating (10.21) with respect to r^1_t and setting the result equal to zero produces the following first-order condition for the optimal interest rate on personal loans:

$$\frac{\partial p^f_o}{\partial r^\ell_t} = \frac{-(L^e_{t+1})_1}{Sf_t} + \frac{L^e_{t+1} + (1 + r^\ell_t)(L^e_{t+1})_1 - w_{t+1}\alpha_2(L^e_{t+1})_1}{(\pi^{ne}_{t+1}/p^n_t)Sf^e_{t+1}} = 0 \qquad (10.23)$$

According to this condition, the financial sector, ceteris paribus, should continue to raise the interest rate it announces for personal loans until the increase in current dividends per share is offset by the reduction in the present value of next period's dividends per share. The former effect is illustrated by the first fraction in

(10.23); the latter is shown by the second.

As the sector raises r^{ℓ}_t, it discourages borrowing by its customers. Holding constant the anticipated levels of its deposit liabilities etc., the less the sector lends in the current period, the more it can potentially distribute to its shareholders in the current period. Consequently, on the margin, the unit increase in r^{ℓ}_t raises current dividends by $-(L^e_{t+1})_1$.

According to the numerator of the second fraction in (10.23), an increase in r^{ℓ}_t influences next period's dividends per share in three different ways. First, as r^{ℓ}_t rises by one point, next period's loan revenue will rise by L^e_{t+1} dollars, ignoring the effect of the change in r^{ℓ}_t will, in fact, discourage household borrowing, causing next period's principal plus interest (and therefore next period's dividends) to fall by $(1 + r^{\ell}_t)(L^e_{t+1})_1$. Third, the reduction in the anticipated loan volume at time t+1 in response to the increase in r^{ℓ}_t reduces next period's transaction time and labor cost. As a result of this saving, the financial sector anticipates it will be able to raise next period's dividends by $- w_{t+1}\alpha_2(L^e_{t+1})_1$.

Since the first fraction in (10.23) is positive, the second fraction must be negative. Since the denominator and the third term in the numerator of that second fraction are positive, the sum of the first two terms in the numerator of the second fraction must be negative. The sector will set the rate of interest on personal loans such that:

$$\frac{(1+r^{\ell}_t)(L^e_{t+1})_1}{L^e_{t+1}} < -1$$

Clearly, the price of a dollar borrowed in the current period is $(1 + r^{\ell}_t)$. Furthermore $(L^e_{t+1})_1$ denotes the partial derivative with respect to both $(1 + r^{\ell}_t)$ and r^{ℓ}_t. Therefore, according to the above expression the private financial sector will set the interest rate on personal loans in the elastic range of the estimated demand for those loans (in the $(L^e_{t+1}, 1 + r^{\ell}_t)$ plane).

Setting the partial derivative of (10.21) with respect to p^b_t equal to zero yields the following necessary condition for the optimal price of bonds announced by the private financial sector:

$$\frac{\partial p^f_o}{\partial p^b_t} = - \frac{B^e_{t+1} - p^b_t(B^e_{t+1})_1}{Sf_t} + \frac{(B^e_{t+1})_1}{(\pi^{ne}_{t+1}/p^n_t)Sf^e_{t+1}} = 0 \qquad (10.24)$$

The first ratio represents the effect upon the sector's current dividends per share from a ceteris paribus one-dollar increase in p^b_t. Since the increase in p^b_t raises not only the amount that the sector is willing to pay for a given number of bonds, but also the number of bonds the sector anticipates the government will offer, the financial sector reduces current dividends by raising the current market price of bonds. The second ratio in (10.24) shows the marginal increase in interest income from government bonds and hence the increase in next period's dividends per share from raising p^b_t one dollar.

Partially differentiating (10.21) with respect to p^f_t and setting the result equal to zero produces necessary condition (10.25):

$$\frac{\partial p^f_o}{\partial p^f_t} = \frac{p^f_t(Sf^e_{t+1})_1 + (Sf^e_{t+1} - Sf_t)}{Sf_t} + \frac{-(Sf^e_{t+1})_1\pi^f_{t+1}}{(Sf^e_{t+1})(\pi^{ne}_{t+1}/p^n_t)} = 0 \qquad (10.25)$$

The numerator of the first fraction in (10.25) denotes the effect upon current receipts from the sale of equity shares and therefore, ceteris paribus, upon potential current dividends to existing shareholders from a one-dollar increase in the current market price of private financial equity shares. As the private financial sector raises the current market price of its equity shares one dollar, it increases anticipated current receipts by an amount equal its anticipated sales, $Sf^e_{t+1} - Sf_t$, during the current period, provided the household sector's demand for those shares does not respond to the higher price. However, as p^f_t rises, the financial sector estimates that the number of shares demanded by the household sector will diminsh causing, ceteris paribus, a loss of $p^f_t(Sf^e_{t+1})_1$ in receipts from equity sales. Consequently, $(Sf^e_{t+1} - Sf_t) + p^f_t(Sf^e_{t+1})_1$ denotes the net marginal sales receipts from equity share sales in the current period from a one-dollar increase in p^f_t.

The numerator of the second fraction in (10.25), $-(Sf^e_{t+1})_1\pi^f_{t+1}$, portrays the effect of a one-dollar increase in p^f_t upon the anticipated dividends per share to owners next period. As p^f_t rises by one dollar the anticipated number of shares outstanding by the end of the current period falls. For a given previously anticipated level of dividends per share, π^f_{t+1}, the drop in the anticipated number of oustanding shares raises next period's anticipated total dividends by $-(Sf^e_{t+1})_1\pi^f_{t+1}$.

Since the second fraction in (10.25) is positive, the numerator of the first fraction must be negative. This implies that the private financial sector will set the current market price of financial sector equity in the elastic portion of the "flow" demand, $(Sf^e_{t+1} - Sf_t)$, for that equity:

$$\frac{p^f_t (Sf^e_{t+1})_1}{(Sf^e_{t+1} - Sf_t)} < -1.$$

This statement follows from the fact that since Sf_t is given at time t, the partial derivative of $(Sf^e_{t+1} - Sf_t)$ with respect to p^f_t equals the parital derivative of Sf^e_{t+1} with respect to p^f_t.

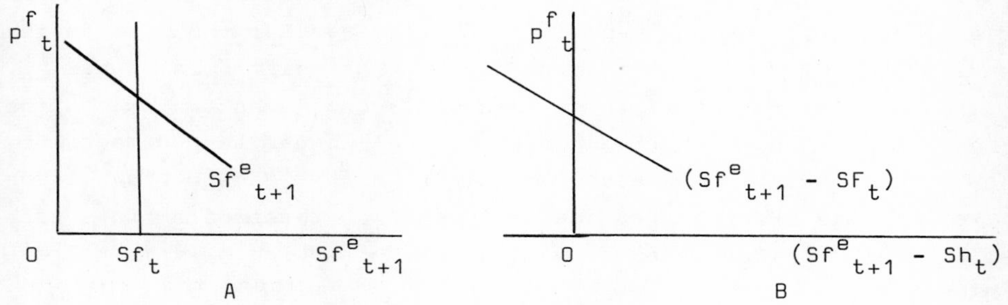

Figure 10.8 - The Anticipated End-of-Period "Stock" Demand (Panel A) and Current-Period "Flow" Demand (Panel B) for Private Financial-Sector Equity.

When set equal to zero, the partial derivative of (10.21) with respect to A_{t+1} yields the following necessary condition for maximizing the present value of the financial sector:

$$\frac{\partial p^f_o}{\partial A_{t+1}} = \frac{-\rho_t - w_{t+1}\alpha_3}{(\pi^{ne}_{t+1}/p^n_t)Sf^e_{t+1}} = 0 \qquad (10.26)$$

The private financial sector, according to this condition, will continue to increase the amount it borrows from the central bank until the marginal cost (i.e. the discount rate), ρ_t, just equals the value of the marginal product of the last dollar of advances. The latter refers to the fact that, ceteris paribus an additional dollar of advances amounts to an additional dollar of excess reserves. An additional dollar of excess reserves reduces the amount of labor the sector requires in order to undertake transactions during the current period. The resulting fall in next period's anticipated wage bill, $-w_{t+1}\alpha_3$, then represents the value of the marginal product of advances.

Total differentiation of (10.22) - (10.26) produces a simultaneous system in the unknowns r^d_t, r^ℓ_t, p^b_t, p^f_t and A_{t+1}. (The second-order sufficient conditions for the maximization of (10.21) stipulate that the principal minors of the coefficient matrix attached to the endogenous variables in the simultaneous system alternate in sign, beginning with a negative sign for principal minors of order one. I assume these conditions hold.) These endogenous variables may be viewed as functions of eight parameters consisting of the discount rate, ρ_t, the money wage, w_{t+1}, the market price of non-financial sector equity, p^n_t, the number of financial sector equity shares outstanding, Sf_t, and four shift parameters. The shift parameters ξ_b, ξ_c, ξ_d and ξ_ℓ refer to the private financial sector's estimates of the positions of the supply function for government bonds, the demand for currency, the demand for checkable deposits and the demand for loans respectively. The effects of a change in each of these parameters upon optimal financial sector behavior will be discussed in the remainder of this chapter.

Change in ρ_t

The higher the discount rate set by the central bank at time t, the greater is the marginal cost to the private financial sector of having a dollar of advances outstanding at the end of the current period. Therefore the private depository institutions will tend to reduce their end-of-period demand for advances, A_{t+1}, as ρ_t rises. This relationship is indicated in Figure 10.9.

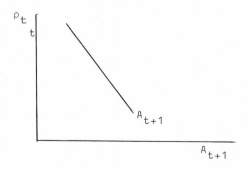

Figure 10.9 - The Private Financial Sector's Demand for Advances is Negatively Related to the Discount Rate

Ceteris paribus, as the depository institutions reduce the quantity of advanes they demand, they simultaneously reduce dollar-for-dollar the amount of excess reserves they plan to hold by the end of the period. As a result, the value of the marginal product of excess reserves increases. Every dollar of currency that the private depository institutions can entice into their vaults via new deposits represents an increase in their excess reserves equal to $(1 - r^*) \cdot \$1$. Therefore as ρ_t rises, the depository institutions will raise r^d_t, the interest rate on checkable deposits, in order to encourage the private nonfinancial sectors to hold less currency by the end of the period.

In addition, every dollar that depository institutions lend in the financial markets (either as personal loans or as bond-purchases from the government) could be used instead to reduce their own indebtedness at the central bank. Therefore as the discount rate rises the opportunity cost to the depository institutions of lending in the financial markets rises. The depository institutions will tend to raise the interest rates they charge for personal loans and to reduce the price they are willing to pay for government bonds. An increase in the discount rate induces higher interest rates throughout the financial markets. In addition as ρ_t rises, the depository institutions' anticipated costs next period increase; next period's anticipated dividends fall. This lowers the marginal cost of issuing additional equity shares and induces these firms to reduce the market price of their equity shares.

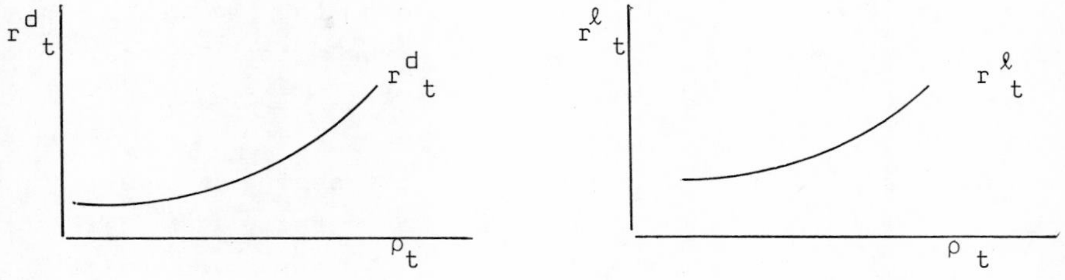

Figure 10.10 - The Optimal Interest Rates on Checkable Deposits, r^d_t, and Personal Loans, r^ℓ_t, Vary Directly with ρ_t.

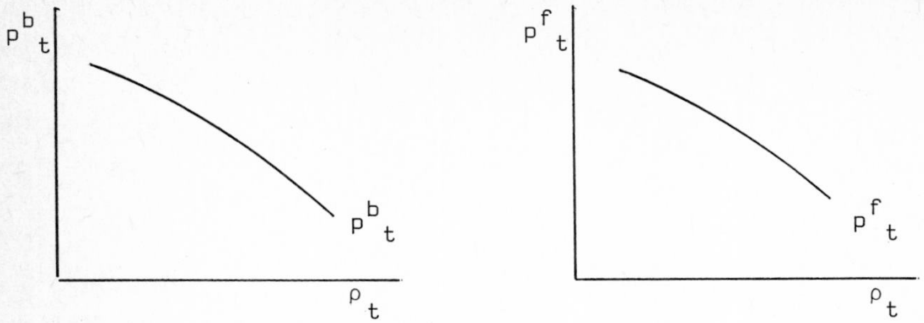

Figure 10.11 - The Optimal Prices of Government Bonds, p^b_t, and Financial-Sector Equity, p^f_t, Vary Inversely with the Discount Rate.

<u>Change in w_{t+1}</u>

An increase in w_{t+1} increases the marginal cost of raising the interest rate on checkable deposits. The reason is that as r^d_t is raised, more deposits are attracted, causing transactions time to grow. As w_{t+1} rises, the wage bill associated with this transactions time also rises, thereby increasing the marginal cost of raising r^d_t. As a result, the private financial sector tends to lower r^d_t as w_{t+1} rises.

This tendency to lower r^d_t is reinforced by the fact that as w_{t+1} rises, the <u>value</u> of the marginal product of excess reserves held at the end of the period also rises, since a dollar of excess reserves, by conserving the same amount of real resources, conserves a greater amount of money wages. This encourages the sector to borrow additional reserves from the central bank since the value of the marginal product of excess reserves rises above the discount rate. As the private financial sector obtains more reserves in this manner, the return from attracting an extra dollar of currency into the private financial institutions falls. This encourages the sector to lower r^d_t.

The more indirect effects work against the direct and indirect effects just mentioned. In particular, as w_{t+1} rises next period's income tends to fall, ceteris paribus. As a result the cost <u>per share</u> of issuing an additional share of financial sector equity falls. This causes the sector to lower p^f_t in order to raise Sf^e_{t+1}. The anticipated increase in Sf^e_{t+1} reduces the present value <u>per share</u> of the marginal interest and labor expense next period due to raising r^d_t one point. This encourages the financial sector to raise r^d_t. Secondly, as w_{t+1} rises, the marginal cost of administering the transactions associated with personal loans goes up causing the private financial sector to raise the interest rate on loans in order to discourage personal borrowing. In the process of reducing its lending, the financial institutions will release some real resources which can be applied to servicing checkable deposits, therby encouraging the sector to raise the interest rate it is willing to pay on those deposits. Assuming that the two indirect effects mentioned in this paragraph are small relative to the direct effect mentioned in the first paragraph of this section, the net effect of an increase in w_{t+1}, ceteris paribus, will be for the financial sector to reduce r^d_t.

The direct effects of an increase in w_{t+1} upon the financial sector's demand for advances, its optimal price of equity and its optimal interest rate on personal loans have already been discussed in the above paragraphs. Assuming that these effects dominate, an increase in w_{t+1} will cause A_{t+1} and r^d_t to rise but will induce the sector to lower p^f_t. The net effect upon p^b_t is indeterminate since a change in w_{t+1} produces no direct influence upon condition (10.24), relating the marginal revenue of raising p^b_t to its marginal cost. A change in w_{t+1} only produces indirect effects upon p^b_t.

The average number of hours, h^f_t, that the private financial sector uses its employees during the current period is determined by the amounts of checkable deposits and personal loans outstanding at the beginning of the period as well as the volume of excess reserves the sector holds at the beginning of the period. These amounts are known at the beginning of the current period and completely determine h^f_t, given that the current number of employees have already been hired by time t. The sector's demand for h^f_t therefore is unrelated to w_{t+1}.

However, the financial sector's demand for workers for next period, N^f_{t+1}, is related to w_{t+1}. The total number of hours of labor that the financial sector plans at time t that it will need next period is given by $\alpha(.)$. Division of α (.) by the standard number of hours, h, that the sector plans to use each person next period then determines the number of people it plans to employ next period. But we have just seen that the arguments included in $\alpha(.)$ are dependent upon w_{t+1}, thereby making N^f_{t+1} dependent upon w_{t+1} as well.

As w_{t+1} rises, the financial sector's optimal value for r^d_t falls while its optimal value for r^ℓ_t rises. Therefore, as w_{t+1} rises the sector will plan a balance sheet for the end of the period that contains fewer deposit liabilities and fewer personal loans. Both of these adjustments tend to conserve transactions time, α, and cause the sector to reduce the quantity of labor it demands. Furthermore, the analysis above suggests that as w_{t+1} rises the financial sector will increase its demand for advances, A_{t+1}. This, coupled with the anticipated reduction in required reserves, causes anticipated excess reserves at the beginning of next period to rise, which also causes the sector's demand for N^f_{t+1} to become smaller. Assuming that the anticipated reduction in reserves due to the greater demand for currency following the reduction in r^d_t does not offset this anticipated increase in excess reserves, the changes in all three arguments of $\alpha(.)$ induce the private financial sector to demand less labor as w_{t+1} rises.

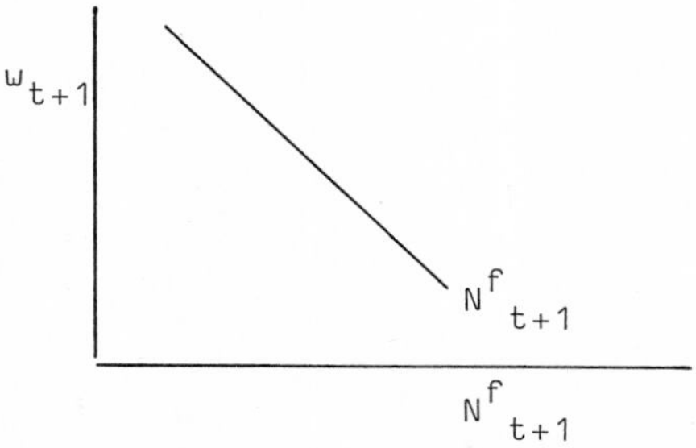

Figure 10.12 - The Private Financial Sector's Demand for Workers for Next Period is Inversely Related to w_{t+1}.

Change in p^n_t

An increase in p^n_t reduces the anticipated rate of return in the nonfinancial business sector, making the present value of the financial sector's anticipated future dividends larger. This increases the cost per share to existing owners (in terms of the reduction in dividends per share) from an increase in the number of financial-sector shares outstanding. This induces the sector to raise the price of its own shares in order to reduce Sf^e_{t+1}. The resulting anticipated drop in Sf^e_{t+1} means that the marginal interest cost per share next period from raising the interest rate on loans one point rises, causing the sector to lower r^ℓ_t. Also, the marginal return per share next period from raising the current price of government bonds rises as Sf^e_{t+1} falls. Therefore, the financial sector will tend to announce a higher market price for bonds in the current period. Finally, as Sf^e_{t+1} falls, the marginal cost per share next period in terms of interest and labor expenses associated with a one point increase in the interest rate on checkable deposits tends to rise. This induces the financial sector to reduce r^d_t. As a result, a drop in the rate of return on nonfinancial sector equity due to an increase in p^n_t causes the financial sector not only to raise the price of its own equity shares but also to reduce the interest rates on checkable deposits, loans and bonds.

Change in Sf_t

The greater the number of shares of financial sector equity outstanding at the beginning of the current period, the smaller the current revenue per share from an additional dollar of checkable deposits issued. This reduces the marginal revenue from raising r^d_t and thereby induces the firm to lower r^d_t. Analogously, the rise in Sf_t reduces the current marginal dividends per share from raising r^ℓ_t; the sector tends to lower r^ℓ_t as Sf_t grows. Also, as the number of these oustanding shares becomes larger, the marginal cost (in terms of foregone dividends) per share of purchasing government bonds falls. The financial sector will therefore tend to raise the market price of bonds. In addition, the reduction in current revenue per share from raising the price of financial sector equity falls, encouraging the sector to raise that price. The tendency for the financial sector to buy more bonds, to lend more to households, to issue fewer checkable deposits (attract less currency) and to issue fewer equity shares also causes it to borrow more funds from the central bank at a given discount rate.

Change in ξ_c

An outward shift in the private financial sector's estimate of the end-of-period demand for currency, see Figure 10.13, means, ceteris

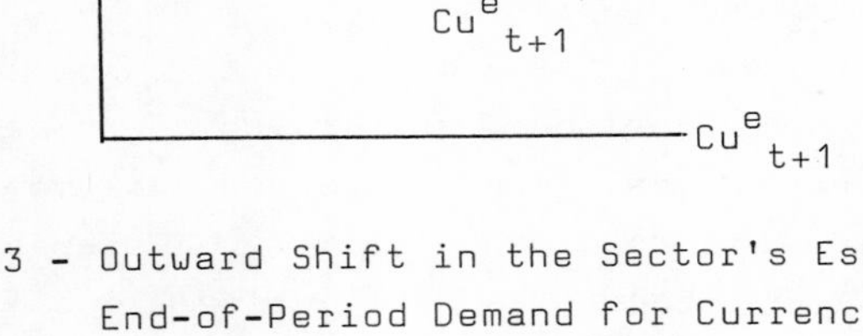

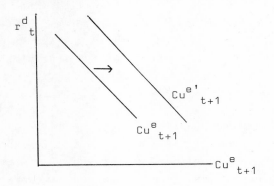

Figure 10.13 - Outward Shift in the Sector's Estimate of the End-of-Period Demand for Currency

paribus, that the sector must revise downward dollar for dollar its estimate of the volume of excess reserves it plans to hold at the end of the period. This raises the marginal product of those reserves and encourages the sector to increase the amount it plans to borrow from the central bank. The sector's end-of-period demand for advances shifts outward.

The anticipated fall in excess reserves due to the estimated rise in the demand for currency causes the sector's estimate of next period's dividends to fall. This encourages the sector to reduce the current market price of its equity shares in order to stimulate sales of those shares. As Sf^e_{t+1} rises, the fall in the present value of future dividends <u>per share</u> that results from an increase in r^ℓ_t becomes smaller; the sector will tend to raise r^ℓ_t, thereby discouraging borrowing by the household sector.

As condition (10.24) illustrates, the rise in Sf^e_{t+1} due to the lower p^f_t announced by the sector in response to the shift in Cu^e_{t+1} causes the present value of the increase in next period's dividends <u>per share</u> due to a rise in p^b_t to become smaller. This induces the private financial sector to lower the market price of government bonds.

<u>Change in ξ_d</u>

An outward shift in the private financial sector's estimate of the end-of-period demand for checkable deposits, see Figure 10.14, means

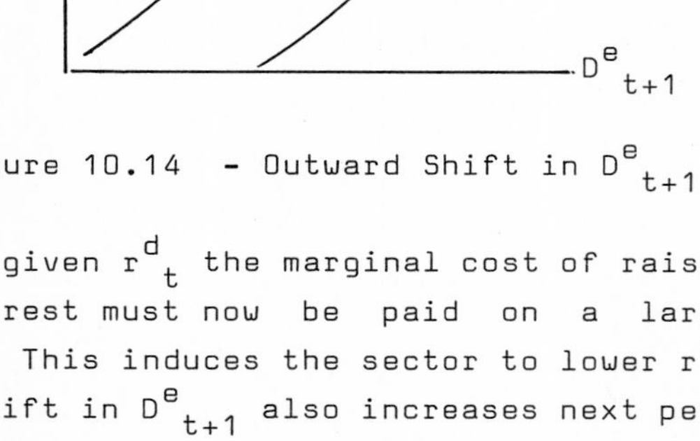

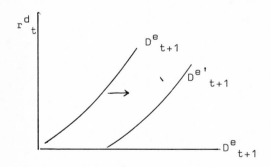

Figure 10.14 - Outward Shift in D^e_{t+1}

that at a given r^d_t the marginal cost of raising r^d_t rises, since the extra interest must now be paid on a larger volume of checkable deposits. This induces the sector to lower r^d_t. Ceteris paribus, the outward shift in D^e_{t+1} also increases next period's costs reducing next period's dividends thereby inducing the sector to lower the price of its shares and thereby increasing Sf^e_{t+1}. The sector will tend to raise the interest rate it announces for personal loans and to reduce the market price of bonds. By itself, the outward shift in D^e_{t+1} also increases next period's anticipated required reserves and so reduces the amount of excess reserves the sector plans to hold by the beginning of next period. This raises the marginal product of those reserves, inducing the sector to increase its demand for advances from the central bank.

Change in ξ_ℓ

An outward shift in the private depository institutions' estimate of the end-of-period demand for personal loans, see Figure 10.15,

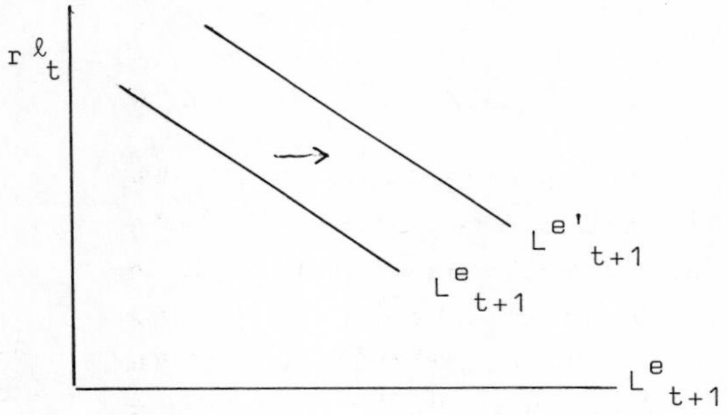

Figure 10.15 - Shift in L^e_{t+1}

lowers the marginal cost of raising r^ℓ_t. Given that the estimated slope of L^e_{t+1} remains unchanged, the outward shift in this curve means that the estimated demand for loans is less elastic at the original interest rate. The sector will tend to raise r^ℓ_t. With the shift in L^e_{t+1}, the marginal revenue product of excess reserves held at the beginning of next period grows. This induces the sector to increase its demand for excess reserves by increasing its demand for advances from the central bank.

Also, with the estimated increase in L^e_{t+1}, the sector revises upward is estimate of next period's revenue and, therefore, next period's dividends per share. This in turn induces the sector to raise p^f_t in order to discourage sales of additional shares.

Change in ξ_b

An outward shift in the sector's estimate of the government's supply of bonds, see Figure 10.16, means that at a given price of bonds

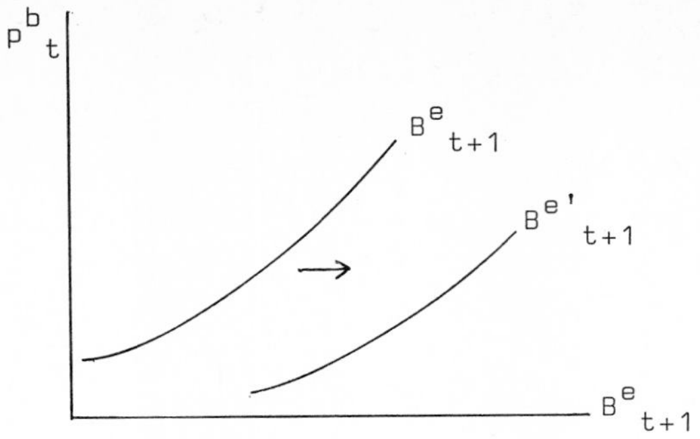

Figure 10.16 - Shift in B^e_{t+1}

B^e_{t+1} is larger than before. This increases the current-period marginal cost of raising p^b_t (since the sector estimates it will have to buy more bonds than before at each price) thereby inducing the private financial sector to lower p^b_t. The increase in B^e_{t+1} raises next period's estimated dividends per share, thereby inducing the sector to raise p^f_t.

Change in ξ_f

An outward shift in the private financial sector's estimate of the market demand for its own shares induces the sector to raise p^f_t because it raises Sf^e_{t+1}. The rise in Sf^e_{t+1} also encourages the sector to raise r^d_t and r^ℓ_t but to lower p^b_t. The sector's demand for advances for the end of the period will depend upon the net effect on next period's transactions costs. As the sector raises r^d_t, these anticipated costs grow, but as it raises r^ℓ_t, they tend to fall. If transactions costs rise, the marginal product of excess reserves will grow, inducing the sector to increase its demand for advances.

Summary

The analysis contained in the present chapter produces the following functions for the private financial sector:

$$r^d_t = r^d_t(\underset{+}{\rho_t}, \underset{-}{w_{t+1}}, \underset{-}{p^n_t}, \underset{-}{Sf_t}, \xi_b, \underset{+}{\xi_c}, \underset{-}{\xi_d}, \underset{+}{\xi_f}, \xi_\ell) \tag{10.27}$$

$$r^\ell_t = r^\ell_t(\underset{+}{\rho_t}, \underset{+}{w_{t+1}}, \underset{-}{p^n_t}, \underset{-}{Sf_t}, \xi_b, \underset{+}{\xi_c}, \underset{+}{\xi_d}, \underset{+}{\xi_f}, \underset{+}{\xi_\ell}) \tag{10.28}$$

$$p^b_t = p^b_t(\underset{-}{\rho_t}, w_{t+1}, \underset{+}{p^n_t}, \underset{+}{Sf_t}, \underset{-}{\xi_b}, \underset{-}{\xi_c}, \underset{-}{\xi_d}, \underset{-}{\xi_f}, \xi_\ell) \tag{10.29}$$

$$p^f_t = p^f_t(\underset{-}{\rho_t},\ \underset{-}{w_{t+1}},\ \underset{+}{p^n_t},\ \underset{+}{Sf_t},\ \xi_b,\ \underset{-}{\xi_c},\ \xi_d,\ \underset{+}{\xi_f},\ \underset{+}{\xi_\ell}) \tag{10.30}$$

$$A_{t+1} = A_{t+1}(\underset{-}{\rho_t},\ \underset{+}{w_{t+1}},\ \underset{-}{p^n_t},\ \underset{+}{Sf_t},\ \xi_b,\ \xi_c,\ \underset{+}{\xi_d},\ \xi_f,\ \underset{+}{\xi_\ell}) \tag{10.31}$$

$$\pi^f_t = \pi^f_t(\rho_t,\ w_{t+1},\ p^n_t,\ \underset{-}{Sf_t},\ \xi_b,\ \xi_c\ \xi_d\ \xi_f,\ \xi_\ell) \tag{10.32}$$

$$h^f_t = h^f_t(N^f_t,\ D_t,\ L_t,\ A_t - Cu_t - r^*D_t) \tag{10.33}$$

$$N^f_{t+1} = N^f_{t+1}(\rho_t,\ \underset{-}{w_{t+1}},\ p^n_t,\ Sf_t,\ \xi_b,\ \xi_c,\ \xi_d,\ \xi_f,\ \xi_\ell) \tag{10.34}$$

The model of the private financial sector presented in this chapter differs from the conventional models of commercial bank behavior and the money supply process in at least one important respect. In particular, all of the existing models view the banking sector as selecting its beginning-of-period balance sheet (or certain components of that balance sheet or certain interest rates that influence it) so as to maximize (expected) current-period net income. In the present case, the amounts in the private financial sector's beginning-of-period balance sheet are given data. The sector's objective is to divide the current net income associated with that balance sheet between dividends and net business saving and to plan an end-of-period balance sheet consistent with its decisions on the income account in such a way as to maximize its present value. This approach to financial sector behavior, though unconventional, is nevertheless consistent, for instance, with the conventional microfoundations underlying the household sector's intertemporal consumption decision. For the balance sheet decisions associated with the household sector's decision to save during the current period are necessarily end-of-period decisions; current saving occurs only by accumulating assets or by retiring liabilities during the period. In addition, the "end-of-period" approach followed here for the private financial sector is also consistent with our development of both the nonfinancial business and government sectors.

According to the view adopted in this study, a central bank should not attempt to control the economy. Instead it should provide the private sector with the high-powered money it needs. The next chapter explores the implications of this view in terms of central bank operations.

11. The Central Bank

The world's central banks currently operate under a philosophy of control rather than accommodation. According to the implicit assumption underlying this philosophy, a central bank somehow possesses superior information, knowledge, or ability to determine the appropriate level of whatever economic variable(s) it seeks to control. Consequently it is justified in attempting to prevent or offset business conditions it considers adverse and to promote conditions it deems desirable. In the U.S., for example, the Federal Reserve is allowed to select from an array of potentially conflicting goals the rate of inflation, level of unemployment, rate of economic growth, or the exchange rate it considers best for the economy. It neither consults a constituency in making its selection nor offers any specific information to the private sector either as to its long-run objectives or as to precisely how it expects to attain those objectives. It does announce broad ranges for twelve-month target rates of growth for several monetary arrgregates. But it is not uncommon to find one or more of these aggregates lying outside is targeted range. Becasue the Fed does not reveal the extent to which it is committed to keeping these measures within their targeted bounds, the financial markets must continually guess what the Fed will or will not do next.

Since 1971, when the U.S. suspended covertibility of the dollar into gold, the Fed has been unencumbered in its monetary actions. Despite this freedom to pursue whatever monetary policy it deemed appropriate to stabilize the economy, the U.S. has continued to experience wide fluctuations in interest rates, prices, employment, and real income. Recent historical experience fails to support the claim that interventionist monetary policy is effective, whether that policy be discretionary or guided by some arbitrary rule.

For instance, just since 1980 the annual rate of change in real GNP (1972 dollars) has fluctuated dramatically from quarter to quarter. Between the first and second quarters of 1980 (1-80 to 2-80), for example, the rate of change was -9.0 percent. But between 4-80 and 1-81 it jumped +10.0 percent. Between 3-81 and 4-81 the rate of change became negative again, -5.4 percent. But from 1-83 to 2-83 it skyrocketed +10.1 percent. Even the year-to-year changes in real GNP have been irregular. Real GNP changed -2.0 percent from 1-81 to 1-82, for example, but registered an 8.0 percent gain from 1-83 to 1-84. The interest rates on 3-month Treasury Bills rose above 15% early in 1980, dropped to 7% at mid-year and finished the year again above 15%. By the end of 1981, the rate on these bills had fallen below 11%, but was soon above 13% in 1982. By the end of 1982, this interest rate was below 8% again. (Sources: "National Economic Trends" (February 1985) Federal Reserve Bank of St. Louis. Table: Gross National Product in 1972 Dollars, Compounded Annual Rates of Change, p. 12. Also, "Monetary Trends" (February 1985) Federal Reserve Bank of St. Louis. Chart: Money Market Rates, p. 12.)

Even if a central bank were able to stablize an economy, it is questionable whether it should be allowed to do so. A decision to stabilize presumes that the targeted values are somehow the correct ones. The application of countercyclical measures simply because they are countercyclical presumes that movement away from current levels is undesirable. But if price and quantity movements are viewed at the mirco level as necessary for transmitting information to buyers and sellers as to the costs and availability of various products and factors of production, why are the same movements undesirable at the aggregate level? Of course unemployed labor implies that some goods are not being produced that could be produced, and that some people are not earning incomes who could be doing so. But an interventionist policy will not necessarily cause the unemployed to become employed or cause them to become employed in those industries that the private sector would have chosen for them if the central bank had not distorted its choices.

For whenever a central bank intervenes in the bond market through open market operations it adversely affects those private participants who happen to be on the same side of the market. If the central bank enters as a buyer, it makes it more expensive for others who are planning to purchase bonds to do so; this distorts their decision to save, i.e., their choices between present and future goods. If the central bank enters the bond market as a seller, it reduces the price that private sellers can receive. This distorts their decision to invest, i.e., their choices as to producing comsumption goods or expanding production capacity. In short, unilateral intervention by a central bank distorts private choices and makes some participants worse off. It violates the fundamental tenet of free markets--namely, that economic welfare is enhanced by free trade in markets that contain a minimum number of distortions. (Society is still free to transfer income from those with jobs to those who do not have them and to devote resources to improving the employability of the unemployed.)

Modern economies require an institutional arrangement whereby both the volume and the composition of the monetary base respond to the needs of the private sector. In the U.S., the Fed does permit the private sector to determine the composition of the monetary base by allowing depository institutions to exchange their deposits at the Fed for currency (and vice versa). The private depository institutions in turn allow their customers to exchange their deposits for currency (and vice versa). But, primarily through open market operations, the Fed attempts to maintain control over the size of the monetary base.

Assume that the cost of producing high-powered money is zero. Microeconomic theory stipulates that economic welfare is maximized with respect to a standard good if the price of that good is set equal to its marginal cost. Therefore, if money were similar to other goods, it should be made available free of charge since it costs nothing to produce. However, high-powered money is a special asset in that one of its components, currency, serves as the medium of exchange while its other component, bank reserves, limits the amount of checkable deposits, the other component of the medium of exchange, that depository institutions can issue. (Since depository institutions must stand ready to exchange currency for the checkable deposits they issue, the volume of their reserves places an upper limit upon the volume of checkable deposits they can issue.) If the central bank were to charge a zero price for high-powered money, the private sector would continue to demand more of it until the marginal product of the medium of exchange were equal to zero, at which time the mrginal product of high-powered money would also equal zero. But the productivity of money is inextricibly tied to its value in terms of other goods and services. For by definition its marginal product pertains to its ability to facilitate exchange. As long as money has a positive value, people are willing to accept it in exchange for other goods. As its value falls (i.e., as the money prices of other goods rise), its ability to do work also falls. Both the marginal and total products of money fall to zero if and only if money's value in terms of other goods falls to zero. Therefore, if high-powered money were to be given away, the private sector would continue to demand more of it until the medium of exchange became worthless in terms of other goods, i.e., until whatever was serving as the medium of exchange (in our case, currency and checkable deposits) would no longer do so. The disappearance of an asset that previously conserved real resources by facilitating transactions would reduce economic welfare. Therefore, even if high-powered money were costless to produce, it must be issued at a positive price.

The present proposal provides a simple, yet automatic, mechanism that limits the quantity of high-powered money to levels consistent with a positive price for that asset and simultaneously permits the private sector to ultimtely determine both the size and composition of the stock of money and the monetary base. Under this proposal, the central bank would be prevented from unilaterally altering either the quantity of high-powered money or the level of excess reserves held by the private depository institutions because it would be prohibited from engaging in open market opeations or from altering the required reserve ratio on checkable deposits. It would be limited to lending high-powered money to depository institutions and it would set the discount rate at the level that maximizes its own anticipated income from advances to these institutions.

As the monopolistic lender of high-powered money, the central bank faces the downward sloping market demand for advances. Even though the marginal cost of producing and lending high-powered money may be zero, the revenue-maximizing central bank will set a positive interest rate on these advances. Also, under this system additional high-powered money will be made available to the private sector, but only if it demands it and only if it is willing to pay a higher discount rate to obtain it. For an outward shift in the demand for advances will automatically induce the central bank to raise the discount rate, but not to raise it so high so that no additional funds enter the hands of the private sector. By the same token, if the private sector were to reduce its demand for high-powered money, the central bank would automatically absorb the unwanted funds, but it would simultaneously lower the discount rate to encourage the private sector to hold at least part of them.

Formal Model of Central Bank Behavior

In the extremely simple model of central bank behavior presented here, the central bank presumably administers the discount window without incurring any costs. The revenue it receives during the current period, π^{cb}_t, is derived exclusively from the advances it has granted to private depository institutions by the beginning of the period, A_t. Presumably the discount rate which these institutions must pay this period, ρ_{t-1}, was announced by the central bank sometime last period. Therefore the central bank's current period income, $\pi^{cb}_t = \rho_{t-1}A_t$, is already known at the beginning of the period.

At the beginning of the current period, then, the only decision facing the central bank is the discount rate, ρ_t, to announce that will apply to all advances outstanding by the end of the current period. As derived in Chapter 10, the depository institutions' end-of-period demand for advances, A^d_{t+1}, is negatively related to the interest rate that they must pay next period on those advances. Suppose that the central bank's beginning-of-period estimate, A^e_{t+1}, of this end-of-period demand is also negatively related to ρ_t. The central bank's objective at the beginning of the current period is to set ρ_t at the level it anticipates will maximize next period's revenues. Let π^{cb}_{t+1} denote the central bank's anticipated income next period. Then the central bank may be viewed as attempting to maximize (11.1):

$$\pi^{cb}_{t+1} = \rho_t A^e_{t+1}(\rho_t, v) \tag{11.1}$$

where v denotes a vector of shift parameters. As noted, the partial derivative of A^e_{t+1} with respect to ρ_t, namely $(A^e_{t+1})_1$, is assumed to be negative. Maximizing (11.1) with respect to ρ_t yields condition (11.2):

$$\rho_t \frac{(A^e_{t+1})_1}{A^e_{t+1}} = -1. \tag{11.2}$$

Condition (11.2) stipulates that the revenue maximizing central bank will set the discount rate at the level at which its estimated demand curve for advances is unitary elastic. The second order condition, $2(A^e_{t+1})_1 + \rho_t(A^e_{t+1})_{11} < 0$, is assumed to be satisfied.

Given values of the shift parameters, v, suppose the optimal discount rate is estimated to be ρ^* and that the central bank estimates that at this interest rate the depository institutions will demand A^* dollars of advances by the end-of-period. These conditions correspond to point x in Figure 11.1.

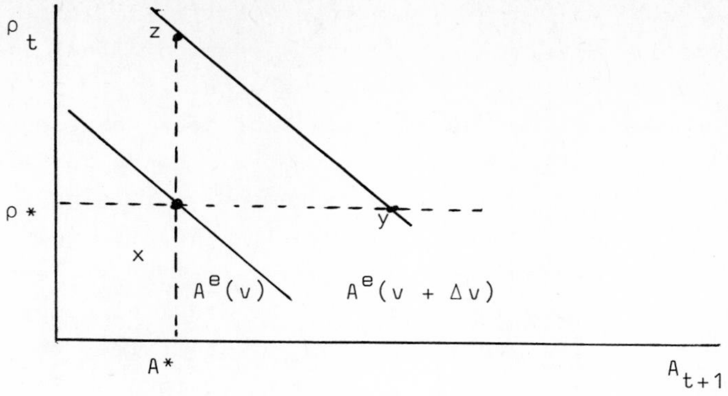

Figure 11.1 Outward Shift in A^e

Next, consider a change in the shift parameters, Δv, such that the central bank's estimate of the demand for advances at each possible discount rate increases. Assuming that the central bank's estimate of the slope of this function has not changed, the shift in its position causes the central bank to announce a higher rate than ρ^*. Assuming both estimated demand curves are linear with common slope, the central bank will not raise the discount rate so high as to completely offset the increase in the demand for advances.

At point x in Figure 11.1 the following condition holds:

$$\frac{\rho^*(A^*)_1}{A^*} = -1. \tag{11.3}$$

For all points directly to the right of point x, the numerator in the expression on the left hand side of (11.3) remains unchanged, but the denominator increases. Therefore, if the estimated demand curve should shift to the right, point y in Figure 11.1 will represent a point at which demand is inelastic (i.e., the expression on the left hand side of (11.3) becomes greater than -1 at point y). In addition all points directly above point x in Figure 11.1 correspond to positions at which the denominator is the same as at x, but the numerator is larger in absolute value (smaller in algebraic value) than at x. Therefore point z on the new estimated demand curve represents a position at which demand is elastic. Since the central bank will set the discount rate at the point at which demand is unitary elastic, it will set the new discount rate somewhere between the levels corresponding to points y and z in Figure 11.1. Therefore, if the central bank were to set the discount rate at the level at which it estimates will maximize its own income, it will automatically accommodate the needs of the private sector while simultaneously "leaning against the wind."

Suppose the demand for high-powered money increases in response to an expansion in national product. As the central bank raises the discount rate in response to the increased demand for high-powered money, it affects other interest rates as well. For example, the currency held by the "nonbank" public constitutes an alternative source of base money for the depository institutions. As the discount rate rises, these institutions will raise the interest rates they are willing to pay on checkable deposits held by their customers in order to encourage them to exchange some of their currency for checkable deposits. In addition, every dollar that depository institutions lend in the financial markets could be used instead to reduce their indebtedness at the central bank. Therefore as the discount rate rises, the opportunity cost to the depository institutions of lending in the financial markets rises. As a result they will raise the interest rates they charge in the loan market and will reduce the prices they are willing to pay for bonds in order to discourage potential borrowers. Therefore, the rise in the discount rate set by the central bank induces higher interest rates throughout the financial markets, which in turn work against those factors that caused the initial increase in the demand for base money.

Answers to Criticisms of Profit-Maximization and a Reliance Upon Discounting

The above proposal to allow the central bank to behave as a profit maximizer and to restrict its operations to discounting appears on the surface to ignore the lessons taught by earlier central bank experiences. Both concepts presumably have been tried before, although not simultaneously, in the U.S. and have been rejected as inadequate. This section offers a brief summary of the objections that have been raised against these concepts as well as an attempt to dispel those objections.

During the early 1800s both the First and Second Banks of the United States attempted to maximize profits and at the same time perform certain central banking functions. In both cases, it became evident that the optimal strategy for a central bank may contradict the objective of a profit maximizing commercial bank. At the onset of a potential banking panic, for example, with the private nonfinancial sector clamoring for additional currency, the prudent reaction for commercial banks would be to contract their lending to customers. In fact the concomitant drain in reserves caused by the shift to currency may force this reaction. In contrast, as the depository institutions attempt to obtain more funds to meet their currency drain, the optimal strategy for a central bank would be to expand, rather than contract, its lending in order to stem the tide. In Bagehot's (1873) words, "In times of panic it must advance freely and vigorously ... at a very high rate of interest." This contradiction in the roles of profit-maximizing depository institutions and the central bank has been used to discredit the notion that the central bank might operate as a profit maximizer.

It should be noted however that the First and Second Banks were first and foremost commercial banks, not central banks. They competed openly and directly with other commercial banks for deposits and loan applications. It was this direct competition--not the fact that the Banks were attempting to maximize profits--which conflicted with their effectively serving as central banks. The fact that two institutions have conflicting goals and that one of them is pursuing maximum profits does not imply that the other should not also attempt to maximize its own profits. A simple example will suffice to illustrate this point.

Consider the case of a firm that earns its income by selling its product to another firm. The firms have conflicting goals in the sense that, ceteris paribus, the first raises its income to the extent it is able to sell its product at a higher price to the second, but the second firm raises its net income by buying this product at a lower price. Yet each best serves its owners by attempting to maximize its own income. The conflict between private depository institutions and the central bank may imply that they should be separate institutions, but it does not imply that only the former should be allowed to maximize profits. The experience of the First and Second Banks of the United States may have illustrated the inappropriateness of allowing the central bank to compete directly with private depository institutions for deposits and loan applications. But it certainly did not illustrate the inappropriateness of allowing the central bank to maximize its income.

Under the present proposal, the central bank is not permitted to engage in open market operations: it may not enter the bond market to earn its income. Advances to depository institutions represent its only source of revenue. By setting the discount rate at the level that maximizes its income, the central bank will automatically behave as Bagehot suggests it should behave at the onset of a potential banking panic. In particular, as depository institutions scramble for additional high-powered money to meet their currency drains, they shift the demand for advances outward. As we have seen, this induces the central bank to lend additional reserves to the depository institutions, but at a higher discount rate.

The proposal to limit central banking activity to discount operations also is not new. In fact discounting constituted the primary instrument of monetary policy when the Federal Reserve opened in 1914. Reliance upon the discount mechanism continued until the 1930s, when it was abondoned. With the Treasury Accord of 1951, discounting again emerged as a tool of monetary policy, but a relatively minor one.

When discounting was first established in the U.S., several conditions prevailed which diminished its usefulness. Until the early 1930s the gold standard "ruled supreme". The Fed's overriding objective during this period was to maintain the gold standard, which sometimes conflicted with appropriate discount policy for the domestic economy. The autumn of 1931 serves as an excellent case in point. When Great Britain left the gold standard in September of that year, concern grew that the U.S. may be the next to do so. In order to restrain the resulting outflow of gold from the U.S., the Fed decided to raise the discount rate even though the domestic economy was languishing in a deep recession. Although this response by the Fed has been viewed by some as an indictment against discounting, it actually represents merely the dilemma confronting a monetary authority attempting to pursue conflicting goals.

The Fed again set conflicting goals between World War I and the Treasury Accord. During this period the Fed felt its primary responsibility was to keep bond prices high in order to minimize the Treasury's cost of servicing its debt. In this case the Fed's role as fiscal agent or a public bank superceded any discounting operations for the purpose of "stabilizing" the economy. The fact that the Fed set interest rates either too high or too low during these periods does not blemish the efficiency of discounting; it only shows the futility of attempting to pursue multiple goals.

In addition to its conflicting goals prior to the Accord, the Fed also imposed two important nonprice impediments to an effective countercyclical discount mechanism during this period. For one thing, the Fed initially stipulted that only short-term self-liquidating paper was eligible for discount at its discount window. For another, it openly discouraged commercial banks from using the discount window, claiming that use of the window was a privilege and not a right. Consequently, during the Great Depression, for instance, not only was self-liquidating paper extremely scarce in the face of large amounts of unsold inventories, but to the extent such paper was available commercial banks were reluctant to take it to the Fed for discounting. Once again these represent difficulties associated with the imposition of certain nonprice restrictions, not an intrinsic defect in the discount mechanism.

In A Program for Monetary Stability, Friedman (1960) offers several objections to the current discount mechanism. His objections center primarily upon the defects of the discount mechanism as a device for controlling the economy. In particular, he discusses the fact that discounting occurs at the initiative of the private depository institutions rather than the central bank, that the appropriate discount rate is difficult to establish because the same rate can represent "easy" policy under certain conditions but "tight" policy under other conditions, that the discount window allows private institutions to short-circuit open-market operations of the central bank, and that changes in the discount rate often produce announcement effects that cause market participants to guess (incorrectly) the direction in which the Fed is attempting to steer the economy.

None of Friedman's objections referred to above is applicable to the present proposal. Under the present proposal, the fact that discounting occurs at the initiative of the private institutions is a desirable feature of that mechanism because the premise underlying this proposal asserts that the market knows better than the central bank the appropriate level of high-powered money. Throughout its history the discount mechanism has been incomplete because it has failed to provide an objective basis for setting the discount rate. But the present proposal includes a discount rate setting mechanism that is simple and automatic. Furthermore, the discount rate would always move in the direction that opposes a change in the demand for high-powered money under this proposal. It would never be too "tight" or too "easy". Friedman's third criticism of the current discount mechanism is not relevant either since the present proposal would preclude the central bank from engaging in open market operations. Furthermore, any announcement effects associated with changes in the discount rate under this proposal would be minimal. Because the central bank would not be pursuing any particular policy, a change in the discount rate would not signal a change in policy. A change in the discount rate certainly would not signal that the Fed intends either to "ease" or "tighten" monetary conditions in the near future.

The notion that discounting is by its very nature "procyclical" and therefore "destabilizing" is potentially the most damaging charge that can be leveled against it. But the procyclical argument does not allow for the discount rate -- or other interest rates, for that matter -- to rise or fall in response to a change in the demand for money. It is true that extra high-powered money would become available during expansions and that some high-powered money would become absorbed by the central bank during contractions under the present proposal. But these changes in high-powered money would be accompanied automatically by a change in the discount rate that would tend to discourage this "procyclical" movement in high-powered money. The private sector would obtain additional high-powered money only if it were willing to pay a higher interest rate to obtain it; and as it attempts to reduce its holdings of high-powered money, the discount rate would automatically fall to induce the private sector to hold some of the unwanted balances. This adjustment mechanism is no different than that found in any other market. In the commodity markets, for instance, if market demand should increase, producers will be willing to produce and sell the additional goods albeit at a higher price; if market demand should fall, they will produce and sell fewer goods, but will also charge a lower price to stimulate sales. To the extent that producers adjust their production in the same direction as the change in the demand for their product, they are behaving "procyclically". Yet few would suggest that their actions were intrinsically destabilizing.

Conclusion

In a recent article, Barro and Gordon (1983) develop a natural-rate model for which "the economist has no useful day-to-day advice to offer to the monetary authority". They conclude that "the most likely general rule for policy advice consists of identifying and designing improvements in present policy institutions. In the monetary area the major issue concerns arrangements that are preferable replacements for the present discretionary setup. We would like to know which mechanisms ... would effectively (and cheaply) restrict the course of future money and prices". The institutional arrangement proposed in the present chapter may provide the mechanism they are seeking.

References

Bagehot, Walter. The Money Market New York: Scribner, Armstrong 1873 (reprinted by R.D. Irwin, Inc., Homewood, IL 1962).

Barro, Robert J., and Gordon, David B., "A Positive Theory of Monetary Policy in a Natural Rate Model." JPE 91 (August 1983): 589-609.

Federal Reserve Bank of St. Louis. "National Economic Trends," February 1985.

_______________. "Monetary Trends," February 1985.

Friedman, Milton. A Program for Monetary Stability. New York: Fordham University Press, 1960.

_______________ and Schwartz, Anna J., A Monetary History of the United States 1867-1960. Princeton: Princeton University Press, 1963.

Hardy, Charles O. Credit Policies of the Federal Reserve System. Washington, D.C.: The Brookings Institution, 1932.

Hawtrey, R.G., The Art of Central Banking. New York: Longmans, Green and Co., 1932.

McKinney, George W., Jr. The Federal Reserve Discount Window. New Brunswick: Rutgers University Press, 1960.

Timberlake, Richard H., Jr. The Origins of Central Banking in the United States. Cambridge: Harvard University Press, 1978.

12. The Complete Model of a Closed Economy

The models of the five individual optimizing sectors presented in Chapters 7-11 provide the basis for the unified model of collective economic choice developed in the present chapter. This combined model contains markets for consumption goods, capital goods, labor, equity shares of the private financial sector, equity shares of the nonfinancial business sector, personal loans, checkable deposits, government bonds and advances. Together these markets also constitute a market for high-powered money.

The complete dynamic model developed here permits economic agents themselves to set all wages, prices and interest rates in accordance with their attempts to optimize their respective objective functions. The nonfinancial business sector announces the hourly wage rate and the market prices of consumption goods, capital goods and its own equity shares. The private financial sector announces the interest rates on checkable deposits and personal loans as well as the market prices of government bonds and its own equity shares. The central bank announces the discount rate.

The prices which these price-setters announce at the beginning of the period are the ones they anticipate will generate optimal "sales" (or "purchases") for them by the end of the period. However the price-setters base their decisions on estimates of market demand and supply functions which are derived using incomplete information. Consequently their forecasts may prove to be incorrect. As a result, at least some markets may fail to clear by the end of the period, possibly causing credit rationing, unwanted inventories, unanticipated accumulations of cash balances and/or involuntary unemployment. According to the analysis contained in Chapter 9, in order to conserve its own search cost for employees, the nonfinancial business sector may announce an hourly wage rate which it anticipates will correspond to some involuntary unemployment. In this case some people become involunarily unemployed even though the nonfinancial business sector forecasts correctly the households' supply of labor as well as the demands for labor by the government and private financial sectors.

In the present model, neither the government nor the central bank intervenes into the market process for the purpose of stabilizing national income, employment or prices. The government sector presents to the household sector a menu of alternative levels of government-goods production and corresponding level of taxes it calculates would be necessary to finance each separate alternative. The household sector then selects the optimal level of government goods (and its accompanying tax burden) in a manner consistent with the sector's objective function, its budget constraints and its choices in private markets. The goverment then attempts to produce at minimum cost the level of goods selected by the households. (Programs designed to redistribute income among households are viewed as separate from the provision of government-produced goods and are not addressed here.) The central bank also operates in its own self-interest rather than attempting to manipulate the aggregate economy. It sets the discount rate on advances at the level it anticipates will maximize its own income. (But the central bank also passes on to the government the income it earns from its loans to the private financial sector.) The private depository institutions then decide the optimal amount to borrow. In light of these non-interventionist roles assigned to the government and the central bank, the private sector itself ultimately decides not only the optimal combination of government-produced goods and taxes but also the optimal levels of the money stock and the monetary base.

In summary, no ad hoc adjustment mechanism or interventionist monetary or fiscal policy is used in the present study to explain production, employment, wages, prices, interest rates, public expenditures on goods and services, taxes, the stock of money or the monetary base. Each of these variables is determined instead through the interactions of the various optimizing economic agents. It is this feature which distinguishes the present model from existing ones.

Fair's (1984) theoretical disequilibrium macro model is the closest existing model to the one presented here. Both his model and this one stress the relationships between a sector's ex ante saving or cash flow and its ex ante changes over the period in various balance sheet items. Both models also view economic agents as forming "certainty equivalent" forecasts on the basis of limited information. And both models treat the nonfinancial business sector as setting commodity prices and wages. However, our models differ in several important respects.

First, Fair relies on simulation techniques rather than analysis to examine the properties of his theoretical model. As revealed by the preceding chapters, on the other hand, the present study specifies the first-order necessary conditions explicitly and then analyzes the qualitative effects of various parametric changes upon each sector's behavioral functions. These functions are then combined (in the present chapter) with certain market-trading conditions to form the complete model.

Second, Fair's financial markets are severely underdeveloped. Bank reserves consist entirely of deposits at the central bank in Fair's model because currency does not exist. As a result the nonfinancial private sector cannot induce any cash flows which might affect bank reserves. Fair also specifies an ad hoc proportion between bank borrowing and bank reserves which depends upon the difference between the discount rate and the interest rate on bonds. But to the extent that the interest rate on bonds is explicitly determined in his model, it is manipulated by the government through an ad hoc "reaction function" based upon the rates of unemployment and inflation. Since the government also controls the discount rate, the government therefore can control the ratio of bank borrowing to bank reserves in his model. The government controls bank reserves (and therefore, indirectly, bank borrowing) by deciding what portion of its deficit will be financed by issuing government bonds. Since Fair assumes the stock of money is a given multiple of the level of bank reserves, his government sector can effectively control the money stock as well. In this case he requires the interest rate on bonds to be the rate that satisfies the government's budget constraint. Fair's banking firms do not behave as profit maximizers. Instead they passively grant loans and accept deposits at the exogenously determined interest rates on these items.

The inadequacies of his financial markets are also attested to by the lack of a market for the fixed number of equity shares held by the household sector. For the purpose of determining the value of household wealth at the beginning of the period and the "capital gains" component of its disposable income over the period, Fair arbitrarily values these equity shares at whatever is consistent with making its expected rate of return equal to the government-controlled interest rate. This procedure is rationalized by the assumption that the households view equity shares and bonds as perfect substitutes. But equality of the expected rates of return on these perfect substitutes is only a necessary, not a sufficient condition for the households to hold both assets.

Third, Fair treats his government/central banking sector as an autonomous policy authority that arbitrarily manipulates public expenditures, income tax rates, the discount rate and the rate of interest (or the stock of money).

In the following sections, the behavioral functions developed in the previous chapters are brought forward to form the basis of a combined model of national income determination. In order to complete the specification of the model, certain equations must be added that specify the amounts actually traded in the various markets if the actions of the price-takers happen to differ from the forecasts of the price-setters. The exact sequence in which prices are announced by the price-setters must also be specified.

In the standard Walrasian general-equilibrium models, the actual quantity traded in a given market is determined by the intersection of the ex ante market demand and supply functions for that item. In the present study, the actual amount traded is determined differently in different markets.

In the markets for personal loans and labor, the actual amount traded corresponds to the minimum of the price-takers' ex ante demands (or supplies) of that item and the price-setter's ex ante supply (or demand) for that item based upon its beginning-of-period forecast of the market demand (or supply) for that item at the price it announced. Consequently, the depository institutuions are not obligated to grant more personal loans during the period than they plannned to extend when they announced the interest rate on those loans at the beginning of the period. They may decide to ration credit. In the labor market, if the number of people who decide at the beginning of the period that they would like to work next period exceeds the demand for that labor by the government and the private business sectors, then involuntory unemployment will prevail at the end of the period.

A different situation presumably exists in the markets for bonds, consumption goods, capital goods, equities, advances, and checkable deposits. In each of these markets, the amount actually traded or held by the end of the period presumably always corresponds to the price taker's ex ante supply or demand. The degree to which the amount traded also corresponds to the price-setter's desired amount is determined by the accuracy of the price-setter's beginning-of-period estimate of the relevant supply or demand function. For instance, the private financial sector sets the interest rate on checkable deposits at the level which it estimates at the beginning of the period will attract the desired volume of deposits by the end of the period. However, it must stand ready during the period to accept <u>all</u> deposits at the interest rate it announces. The same is true in the other markets mentioned above.

As will be shown, when the household and government budget constraints are combined are combined with the cash-flow identities facing the business sectors and the central bank to form a single constraint for the entire community, they imply that the net dollar value of the nonfinancial business sector's unanticipated inventory accumulation (or, if negative, the net dollar value of unfilled orders for commodities) exactly equals the net dollar value of the discrepancies accross the various financial markets between the price-taker's demand or ex ante supply of an item and the price-setter's beginning-of-period estimate of that demand or supply.

As discussed earlier, every market price and interest rate is set by some economic agent at the beginning of every period. Because no price or interest rate is observable until it is actually announced, the sequence in which the price-setters announce their prices at the beginning of each period determines which variables are observable to the price-setters who have yet to announce their own prices. The sequence of the pricing announcements influences the specification of the price-setter's behavioral functions. For instance, if the nonfinancial business sector is viewed as announcing its prices before the private financial sector announces its prices and interest rates, then the latter knows the wage rate it must pay its workers next period when it makes its announcements. That wage rate would then represent a potential observable variable influencing the financial sector's decisions. On the other hand, if the nonfinancial business and the private financial sectors are seen as announcing their prices and interest rates simultaneously at the beginning of the period, then the financial sector must do so without knowing the wage rate it must pay its workers next period. In this case, its expectation of that wage rate would be included in the functions influencing the financial sector's announcements.

Among the decisions facing the government sector at the beginning of the current period are (a) the quantities of consumption goods and labor hours it willneed in order to produce the predetermined level of government-produced goods this period and (b) the level of taxes it anticipates will be necessary to produce a particular level of government-produced goods next period (without having any government bonds outstanding by the end of that period). In order to depict, however crudely, the notion that the government possesses the least flexibility of all the decision-makers, suppose that it must make these decisions at the beginning of the period before any price-setter announces its current-period wages, prices and/or interest rates. Therefore, the government decides its current-period combination of consumption goods and labor hours without actually knowing the current-period price of consumption goods. It also prepares the menu of government-produced goods (and taxes) for the household sector for next period before it knows how much it will have to pay its employees next period, the interest rate at which it will be able to borrow in the bond market, the price of capital goods this period, the price of next period's consumption goods or the income which the central bank anticipates it will generate for the government next period through its discount operations. As a result, even though the government plans at time t to have no debt outstanding by time t+2, when t+1 actually arrives it will be unlikely that the government will still plan to have no outstanding debt by time t+2 (even though it will plan at time t+1 to retire all outstanding debt by t+3).

After the government makes these decisions, I assume it is the nonfinancial business sector's turn to set the current-period prices of consumption goods, capital goods, and its own equity shares as well as the wage that it promises to pay workers next period. The central bank presumably waits for the nonfinancial business sector to make its price announcements before announcing the discount rate. But it announces this rate before the private financial sector makes its interest rates and prices known. The private financial sector then announces curent period interest rates on checkable deposits and personal loans as well as the price of its equity shares and of government bonds.

Once the private price-setters have announced these wages, prices and interest rates, the household sector then decides its demands for consumption goods, capital goods, personal loans equity shares, checkable deposits and currency as well as its supply of workers for next period. The household sector simultaneously decides the optimal level of government production for next period (and, therefore, next period's taxes as well). Having learned the amount that the households want it to produce next period, the government then decides the number of workers it wants to hire for next period as well as the number of capital goods it wants to hold by the beginning of that period.

In light of these assumptions, the government's demands for consumption goods and labor hours will not be a function of actual current prices or interest rates, since they are not announced by the time the government formulates these demands in the present model. By the same token, the nonfinancial business sector's demand, supply and price-setting functions will be dependent upon their unobservable anticipations of current-period interest rates rather that their actual values. The private financial sector's interest rate and price-setting functions however will include the current discount rate as an argument since it is announced before the financial sector announces its own interest rates rather than their actual values. The private financial sector's interest rate and price-setting functions however will include the current discount rate as an argument since it is announced before the financial sector announces its own interest rates and prices. Therefore, the specification of the complete model presented below depends heavily upon the sequence of announcements assumed above. If prices were announced either simultaneously or in a different sequence, the behavioral functions given below would have to be specified differently.

The remainder of the present chapter contains, first, a specification of the behavioral functions and the "quantity-traded" equations under the respective pricing arrangements. The "quantity-traded" equations replace the customary equilibrium conditions of the standard model and reveal the end-of-period stocks for the following period. This is one way the model generates time paths for the various endogenous variables.

Typically, theoretical macroeconomic models are constructed in order to assess the ability of an exogenous policy authority to control or stabilize the private economy by manipulating various fiscal or monetary instruments. A primary purpose in constructing the present model, however, is to examine how the private sector itself will select the optimal combination of government-produced goods, taxes, bank reserves, and the money supply when assisted by an accommodating government and central bank. Consequently, instead of focusing upon the effects of various autonomous monetary or fiscal policy actions, the present chapter explores some of the factors influencing our collective economic choices between public and private goods, between production of market and nonmarket goods, and between present and future goods.

The complete model will be linearized to form a recursive system of equations containing as explanatory variables various exogenous variables and the endogenous variables lagged one period. The reduced form then will be derived and the stability conditions briefly examined. The wild gyrations in prices, interest rates and employment during the 1970's and early 1980's suggest, however, that an analysis of the short-run impacts of various changes in certain "initial conditions" may prove to be at least as interesting as stability analysis. Therefore, the analysis of the present model will conclude with an examination of some short-run responses to various "shocks" in the initial conditions.

Formal Specification of the Complete Model

The first phase of the government's decision-making at the beginning of the period consists of (a) deciding the optimal combination of labor hours, h^g_t, and consumption goods, c^g_t, to combine with the predetermined level of capital, K^g_t, in order to produce the predetermined level of government produced goods, g_t, and (b) preparing next period's government goods-tax menu (i.e. combinations of Tx_{t+1} and g_{t+1}) for the household sector. These decision functions were derived earlier as equations (7.23), (7.24) and (7.31) and are repeated here as equations (12.1) - (12.3):

$$h^g_t = h^g_t(N^g_t, w_t, g_t, K^g_t, D^g_t) \tag{12.1}$$

$$c^g_t = c^g_t(w_t, g_t, K^g_t, D^g_t) \tag{12.2}$$

$$Tx_{t+1} = Tx_{t+1}(g_{t+1}, k_g) \tag{12.3}$$

Note that since the government presumably makes these decisions prior to the private sector's announcements of current commodity prices, these prices do not enter functions (12.1) - (12.3). These functions instead depend upon the government sector's unobservable anticipations of these prices, which are left unspecified in (12.1) - (12.3).

Once the government has announced next period's menu of government-produced goods, the nonfinancial business sector presumably decides the average number of hours, h^n_t, it will use its current employees; the current-period volume of capital goods production, i_t; next period's hourly money wage, w_{t+1}; the number of people, N^{nd}_{t+1}, it wants to hold by the end of the period, the volume of checkable deposits, D^n_{t+1}, it wants to hold by the end of the period; the current period price, p^n_t, of its equity shares; the current-period volume of consumption goods production, c_t; the current-period price of consumption goods, p^c_t; the current-period price of capital goods, p^k_t;

and current-period dividends per share, π^n_t. The optimizing values for these variables were derived earlier according to functions (9.47) - (9.50), (9.52) - (9.54), (9.20), (9.11), (9.12) and (9.3) respectively. These eleven functions are reproduced here as equations (12.4) - (12.14):

$$h^n_t = h^n_t(N^n_t, K^n_t, D^n_t, w_t, Q_t, c^g_t, v_{ct}, v_{kt}, r^{dn}_t, r^{fn}_t, Sn_t, v_c^*, v_k^*, v_n, v_{sn}) \quad (12.4)$$

$$i_t = i_t(K^n_t, D^n_t, w_t, Q_t, c^g_t, v_c, v_k, r^{dn}_t, r^{fn}_t, Sn_t, v_c^*, v_k^*, v_n, v_{sn}) \quad (12.5)$$

$$w_{t+1} = w_{t+1}(K^n_t, D^n_t, w_t, Q_t, c^g_t, v_c, v_k, r^{dn}_t, r^{fn}_t, Sn_t, v_c^*, v_k^*, v_n, v_{sn}) \quad (12.6)$$

$$N^{nd}_{t+1} = N^{nd}_{t+1}(K^n_t, D^n_t, w_t, Q_t, c^g_t, v_c, v_k, r^{dn}_t, r^{fn}_t, Sn_t, v_c^*, v_k^*, v_n, v_{sn}) \quad (12.7)$$

$$K^{nd}_{t+1} = K^{nd}_{t+1}(K^n_t, D^n_t, w_t, Q_t, c^g_t, v_c, v_k, r^{dn}_t, r^{fn}_t, Sn_t, v_c^*, v_k^*, v_n, v_{sn}) \quad (12.8)$$

$$D^{nd}_{t+1} = D^n_{t+1}(K^n_t, D^n_t, w_t, Q_t, c^g_t, v_c, v_k, r^{dn}_t, r^{fn}_t, Sn_t, v_c^*, v_k^*, v_n, v_{sn}) \quad (12.9)$$

$$p^n_t = p^n_t(K^n_t, D^n_t, w_t, Q_t, c^g_t, v_c, v_k, r^{dn}_t, r^{fn}_t, Sn_t, v_c^*, v_k^*, v_n, v_{sn}) \quad (12.10)$$

$$c_t = c_t(K^n_t, D^n_t, w_t, Q_t, c^g_t, v_c, v_k, r^{dn}_t, r^{fn}_t, Sn_t, v_c^*, v_k^*, v_n, v_{sn}) \quad (12.11)$$

$$p^c_t = p^c_t(K^n_t, D^n_t, w_t, Q_t, c^g_t, v_c, v_k, r^{dn}_t, r^{fn}_t, Sn_t, v_c^*, v_k^*, v_n, v_{sn}) \quad (12.12)$$

$$p^k_t = p^k_t(K^n_t,\ D^n_t,\ w_t,\ Q_t,\ c^g_t,\ v_c,\ v_k,\ r^{dn}_t,$$

$$r^{fn},\ Sn_t,\ v_c{}^*,\ v_k{}^*,\ v_n,\ v_{sn}) \qquad (12.13)$$

$$\pi^n_t = \pi^n_t(K^n_t,\ D^n_t,\ w_t,\ Q_t,\ c^g_t,\ v_c,\ v_k,\ r^{dn}_t,$$

$$r^{fn}_t,\ Sn_t,\ v_c{}^*,\ v_k{}^*,\ v_n,\ v_{sn}) \qquad (12.14)$$

where $N^h_t = N^g_t + N^f_t + N^n_t$ and where the actual current interest rates are not included because they have yet to be announced when the nonfinancial business sector formulates its plans at the beginning of the period.

Immediately after the nonfinancial business sector announces its prices, the central bank presumably announces the current discount rate in accordance with its own objective function. It also announces the income it will be generating for the government in the current period from the advances outstanding at the end of last period. The central bank's discount rate function is derived directly from the condition (11.3) in Chapter 11, while its current income from operations is denoted by (11.1). These functions are written here as (12.15) and

$$\rho_t = \rho_t(\xi_a) \qquad (12.15)$$

$$\pi^{cb}_t = \rho_{t-1}A_t \qquad (12.16)$$

(12.16) respectively where ξ_a denotes a vector of shift parameters that places the central bank's estimate of the demand function for advances in the $(\rho_t,\ A_{t+1})$ plane (see Figure 11.1).

Following the central bank's discount rate announcement, the private financial sector is presumably the next to formulate its plans for the current period. In particular it decides the interest rate on checkable deposits. r^d_t, the interest rate on loans, r^ℓ_t, the market price of government bonds, p^b_t, the amount it plans to borrow by the end of the current period, A_{t+1}, current dividends per share, π^f_t, the average number of hours, h^f_t, it will use its current employees, and the number of people, N^f_{t+1}, it plans to employ by the beginning of next period. The present-value maximizing values for these variables were derived in Chapter 10 as functions (10.27) - (10.34). They are reproduced here as functions (12.17) - (12.24).

$$r^d_t = r^d_t(\rho_t,\ w_{t+1},\ p^n_t,\ Sf_t,\ \xi_b,\ \xi_c,\ \xi_d,\ \xi_f,\ \xi_\ell) \qquad (12.17)$$

$$r^{\ell}_{t} = r^{\ell}_{t}(\rho_t, w_{t+1}, p^n_t, Sf_t, \xi_b, \xi_c, \xi_d, \xi_f, \xi_{\ell}) \tag{12.18}$$

$$p^{b}_{t} = p^{b}_{t}(\rho_t, w_{t+1}, p^n_t, Sf_t, \xi_b, \xi_c, \xi_d, \xi_f, \xi_{\ell}) \tag{12.19}$$

$$p^{f}_{t} = p^{f}_{t}(\rho_t, w_{t+1}, p^n_t, Sf_t, \xi_b, \xi_c, \xi_d, \xi_f, \xi_{\ell}) \tag{12.20}$$

$$A^{d}_{t+1} = A^{d}_{t+1}(\rho_t, w_{t+1}, p^n_t, Sf_t, \xi_b, \xi_c, \xi_d, \xi_f, \xi_{\ell}) \tag{12.21}$$

$$\pi^{f}_{t} = \pi^{f}_{t}(\rho_t, w_{t+1}, p^n_t, Sf_t, \xi_b, \xi_c, \xi_d, \xi_f, \xi_{\ell}) \tag{12.22}$$

$$h^{f}_{t} = h^{f}_{t}(\rho_t, w_{t+1}, p^n_t, Sf_t, \xi_b, \xi_c, \xi_d, \xi_f, \xi_{\ell}) \tag{12.23}$$

$$N^{f}_{t+1} = N^{f}_{t+1}(\rho_t, w_{t+1}, p^n_t, Sf_t, \xi_b, \xi_c, \xi_d, \xi_f, \xi_{\ell}) \tag{12.24}$$

Next, in light of: menu (12.3); the current disposable income implied by (12.1), (12.4), (12.14), (12.22) and (12.24); the current commodity and asset prices implied by (12.10), (12.12), (12.13) and (12.20); and the current interest rates on checkable desposits and personal loans implied by (12.17) and (12.18), the household sector decides the optimal levels of current household consumption, c^h_t, equity shares in the private financial sector, Sf^d_{t+1}, equity shares in the nonfinancial business sector, Sn^d_{t+1}, currency balances, Cu^{hd}_{t+1}, checkable deposit balances, $D^{hd'}_{t+1}$, physical capital, K^{hd}_{t+1}, and personal loans, L^d_{t+1}, for the end of the current period. It also decides, using the same framework, the number of people, N^s_{t+1}, it would like to have working by the beginning of next period and the volume of government-produced goods, g_{t+1}, it would like to enjoy next period. (Given menu (12.3), the household sector automatically selects next period's taxes, Tx_{t+1}, as it decides g_{t+1}). These behavioral functions for the household sector were derived in Chapter 8 as functions (8.27) - (8.35). They are repeated here as functions (12.25) -(12.33).

$$c^{h}_{t} = c^{h}_{t}(Y_{dt}, Sn^h_t, Sf^h_t, Cu^h_t, D^h_t, K^h_t, L_t, p^c_t, p^f_t,$$
$$p^n_t, p^k_t, r^{\ell}_t, r^d_t, w_{t+1}, k_h) \tag{12.25}$$

$$Sf^{hd}_{t+1} = Sf^{hd}_{t+1}(Y_{dt}, Sn^h_t, Sf^h_t, Cu^h_t, D^h_t, K^h_t, L_t, p^c_t, p^f_t,$$

$$p^n_t,\ p^k_t,\ r^\ell_t,\ r^d_t,\ w_{t+1},\ k_h) \qquad (12.26)$$

$$Sn^{hd}_{t+1}=Sn^{hd}_{t+1}(Y_{dt},\ Sn^h_t,\ Sf^h_t,\ Cu^h_t,\ D^h_t,\ K^h_t,\ L_t,\ p^c_t,\ p^f_t,$$

$$p^n_t,\ p^k_t,\ r^\ell_t,\ r^d_t,\ w_{t+1},\ k_h) \qquad (12.27)$$

$$Cu^{hd}_{t+1}=Cu^{hd}_{t+1}(Y_{dt},\ Sn^h_t,\ Sf^h_t,\ Cu^h_t,\ D^h_t,\ K^h_t,\ L_t,\ p^c_t,\ p^f_t,$$

$$p^n_t,\ p^k_t,\ r^\ell_t,\ r^d_t,\ w_{t+1},\ k_h) \qquad (12.28)$$

$$D^{hd}_{t+1}=D^{hd}_{t+1}(Y_{dt},\ Sn^h_t,\ Sf^h_t,\ Cu^h_t,\ D^h_t,\ K^h_t,\ L_t,\ p^c_t,\ p^f_t,$$

$$p^n_t,\ p^k_t,\ r^\ell_t,\ r^d_t,\ w_{t+1},\ k_h) \qquad (12.29)$$

$$K^{hd}_{t+1}=K^{hd}_{t+1}(Y_{dt},\ Sn^h_t,\ Sf^h_t,\ Cu^h_t,\ D^h_t,\ K^h_t,\ L_t,\ p^c_t,\ p^f_t,$$

$$p^n_t,\ p^k_t,\ r^\ell_t,\ r^d_t,\ w_{t+1},\ k_h) \qquad (12.30)$$

$$L^d_{t+1}=L^d_{t+1}(Y_{dt},\ Sn^h_t,\ Sf^h_t,\ Cu^h_t,\ D^h_t,\ K^h_t,\ L_t,\ p^c_t,\ p^f_t,$$

$$p^n_t,\ p^k_t,\ r^\ell_t,\ r^d_t,\ w_{t+1},\ k_h) \qquad (12.31)$$

$$N^s_{t+1}=N^s_{t+1}(Y_{dt},\ Sn^h_t,\ Sf^h_t,\ Cu^h_t,\ D^h_t,\ K^h_t,\ L_t,\ p^c_t,\ p^f_t,$$

$$p^n_t,\ p^k_t,\ r^\ell_t,\ r^d_t,\ w_{t+1},\ k_h) \qquad (12.32)$$

$$g_{t+1}=g_{t+1}(Y_{dt},\ Sn^h_t,\ Sf^h_t,\ Cu^h_t,\ D^h_t,\ K^h_t,\ L_t,\ p^c_t,\ p^f_t,$$
$$p^n_t,\ p^k_t,\ r^\ell_t,\ r^d_t,\ w_{t+1},\ k_h) \qquad (12.33)$$

After the household sector has selected what it feels is the optimal level of next period's government-produced goods, the government sector is able to decide the number of people, N^{gd}_{t+1}, it wants to employ next period, the amount of physical capital, K^{gd}_{t+1}, it wants to hold by the beginning of next period, its demand for checkable deposits, D^g_{t+1}, and its ex ante supply of bonds, $p^b_t B^{gs}_{t+1}$ (in dollars), for the end of the current period. These functions were derived in Chapter 7 (as (7.25), (7.27), (7.28) and (7.34)) in accordance with the government's objective of minimizing next period's tax burden for each given level of g_{t+1}. They are repeated here as equations (12.34) - (12.37).

$$N^{gd}_{t+1} = N^{gd}_{t+1}(w_{t+1}, p^k_t, p^b_t, r^d_t, g_{t+1}) \tag{12.34}$$

$$K^{gd}_{t+1} = K^{gd}_{t+1}(w_{t+1}, p^k_t, p^b_t, r^d_t, g_{t+1}) \tag{12.35}$$

$$D^{gd}_{t+1} = D^{gd}_{t+1}(w_{t+1}, p^k_t, p^b_t, r^d_t, g_{t+1}) \tag{12.36}$$

$$p^b_t B^{gs}_{t+1} = p^b_t B^{gs}_{t+1}(p^b_t, B^g_t, w_t, p^c_t, p^b_t, g_t, K^g_t, D^g_t, Tx_t, \pi^{cb}_t, r^d_{t-1}, Tx_{t+1}, r^d_t, w_{t+1}, g_{t+1}) \tag{12.37}$$

The Non-Walrasian Counterpart to Walras' Law

When aggregated into a single community budget constraint, the respective current-period ex ante budget or cash-flow restrictions on the various decision-makers imply a relationship among the differences between the ex ante demands (or supplies) in the commodity and financial markets and the price-setters' corresponding estimates of those demands (or supplies). To derive this relationship consider, first, the government sector's budget constraint presented above as equation (7.3) and repeated here as equation (12.38):

$$Tx_t + \pi^{cb}_t + r^d_{t-1}D^g_t - \$1 \,.\, B^g_t - p^c_t c^g_t - w_t h^g_t N^g_t = (D^{gd}_{t+1} - D^g_t) + p^k_t(K^{gd}_{t+1} - K^g_t) - p^b_t B^{gs}_{t+1} \tag{12.38}$$

Next, consider the household sector's budget constraint derived as equation (8.2) and repeated here as (12.39):

$$w_t\,(h^g_t N^g_t + h^f_t N^f + h^n_t N^n_t)\; r^d_{t-1}D^h_t + \pi^n_t Sn_t + \pi^f_t Sf_t - Tx_t - p^c_t c^h_t - r^\ell_{t-1} L^h_t = p^k_t(K^{hd}_{t+1} - K^h_t) + p^n_t(Sn^{hd}_{t+1} - Sn_t) + p^f_t(Sf^{hd}_{t+1} - Sf_t) + (D^{hd}_{t+1} - D^h_t) + (Cu^{hd}_{t+1} - Cu^h_t) - (L^{hd}_{t+1} - L^h_t) \tag{12.39}$$

Equation (12.40) below depicts the nonfinancial business sector's cash-flow constraint developed as equation (9.2) in Chapter 9. Equation (12.40) is found by substituting the right hand sides of (9.21) and (9.22) for c_t^{de} and i_t^{de} respectively into the first expression in (9.13) and substituting that result for $R^e(.)$ in (9.2):

$$p^c_t c^{de}_t + p^k_t i^{de}_t + r^d_{t-1} D^n_t - w_t h^n_t N^n_t - \pi^n Sn_t = (D^n_{t+1} - D^n_t)$$

$$- p^n_t (Sn^e_{t+1} - Sn_t) \qquad (12.40)$$

The private financial sector's cash-flow constraint, presented earlier as expression (10.3) is reproduced here as equation (12.41). Expression (12.41) incorporates the assumptions (developed later in Chapter 10) that only the government issues bonds and that only the private financial sector purchases these bonds.

$$r^{\ell}_{t+1} L^h_t + \$1.B^g_t - r^d_{t-1} D_t - \rho_{t-1} A_t - w_t h^f_t N^f_t - \pi^f_t Sf_t$$

$$= (Rs^e_{t+1} - Rs_t) + p^b_t B^{ge}_{t+1} + (L^{de}_{t+1} - L^h_t) \qquad (12.41)$$

$$- (D^e_{t+1} - D_t) - (A^d_{t+1} - A_t) - p^f_t (Sf^e_{t+1} - Sf_t)$$

Finally, consider the cash-flow constraint facing the central bank. The revenue which the central bank receives during the current period, $\rho_{t-1} A_t$, minus the amount, π^{cb}_t, it transfers to the government's "general fund" necessarily equals the value of its planned additions to assets, $A^e_{t+1} - A_t$, minus the value of its planned additions to liabilities. The latter constitutes the monetary base, MB, and consists of reserves of the private depository instituitons, Rs, plus currency in the hands of the household and nonfinancial business sector, Cu. Therefore, the central bank's cash-flow constraint may be written as (12.42):

$$\rho_{t-1} A_t - \pi^{cb}_t = (A^e_{t+1} - A_t) - (MB^e_{t+1} - MB_t) \qquad (12.42)$$

where A^e_{t+1} denotes the dollar value of advances which the central bank anticipates it will hold by time t+1 and MB^e_{t+1} denotes the volume of the monetary base it anticipates for time t+1.

Assuming all beginning-of-period announcements as to current market interest rates, prices, dividends and labor-hours have been made, then summing across expressions (12.48)-(12.52) yields the following condition:

$$p^c_t (c^{de}_t - c^h_t - c^g_t) + p^k_t (i^{de}_t - (K^{hd}_{t+1} - K^h_t) - (K^{gd}_{t+1} - K^g_t))$$

$$+ p^n_t(Sn^e_{t+1} - Sn^{hd}_{t+1}) + p^f_t(Sf^e_{t+1} - Sf^{hd}_{t+1}) + p^b_t(B^{gs}_{t+1} - B^e_{t+1})$$

$$+ (A^d_{t+1} - A^e_{t+1}) + (L^{hd}_{t+1} - L^e_{t+1})$$

$$+ (D^e_{t+1} - D^g_{t+1} - D^h_{t+1} - D^n_{t+1}) + (MB^e_{t+1} - Rs^d_{t+1} - Cu^{hd}_{t+1}) = 0 \quad (12.43)$$

According to this condition, the sum across all markets of the discrepancy between the price-setter's estimate of the market demand or supply and the actual market demand or supply must equal zero. Alternatively, since the nonfinancial business sector sets the prices of consumption goods, capital goods and its equity shares at the levels which it feels will induce the household sector to purchase the optimal amounts of those items (from the nonfinancial business sector's point of view), the quantities c^{de}, i^{de} and Sn^e may be viewed as ex ante supplies. In a like manner, the private financial sector's estimate of the government's supply of bonds at the price it announces, B^{ge}, may be viewed as its own ex ante demand for those bonds; its estimate of the household sector's demand for loans (supply of IOU's), L^{de}, may be viewed as the financial sector's demand for those IOU's; its estimate of the market demand for checkable deposits, D^e, may be viewed as its own ex ante supply of checkable deposits; and its estimate of the market demand for its equity shares, Sf^e, may be regarded as its ex ante supply of those shares. By the same token, the central bank's estimate of the private financial sector's demand for advances, or supply of IOU's, A^e, may be viewed as the central bank's ex ante demand for those IOU's. Finally, the level of the monetary base which the central bank anticipates at the discount rate it sets may be viewed as its ex ante supply of base money. Under this interpretation, equation (12.43) stipulates that the values of the excess supplies across the markets for consumption goods, capital goods, equity shares, government bonds, the IOU's issued by households in exchange for personal loans, the IOU's issued by private depository institutions in exchange for advances from the central bank, checkable deposits and base money must sum to zero. The labor market cancels out in deriving (12.43) because all participants in the market presumably know at the beginning of the current period the number of hours each employee will work in each sector during the period. No potential discrepancy in the plans of the various sectors with respect to current labor hours exists at time t.

Within this interpretation, then, expression (12.43) is directly analogous to Walras' Law associated with general-equilibrium models.

The analogy between Walras' Law as commonly stated and expression (12.53) may be drawn more closely if we are willing to consider the amount $MB^e - Rs^d$ in the latter expression as representing the amount of currency in the hands of the "nonbank public" consistent with the plans of the central bank and the private depository institutions. Amount $MB^e - Rs^d$ may then be regarded as the (combined) "banking sector's" ex ante "supply" of currency to the nonbank public. And the sum of the terms in the last two sets of parentheses in (12.43), namely $(D^e_{t+1}-D^{gd}_{t+1}-D^{hd}_{t+1}-D^{nd}_{t+1}) + (MB^e_{t+1}-Rs^d_{t+1}-Cu^{hd}_{t+1})$, then may be interpreted as the "excess supply of money."

Actual Quantities Traded and End-of-Period Stocks

Since the unit time interval between the beginning and the end of a particular period is irreducible into shorter planning periods in this model, no price-setter has occasion until the end of the period to reevaluate the prices it announced at the beginning of that period. Each price that a price-setter announces at the beginning of the period is the one which that sector anticipates will yield the desired level of sales or purchases of the item in question by the end of the period. The analysis of the price-setters' behavior presented in Chapters 9, 10 and 11 assumed that it was costless to change at the beginning of a particular period a price that prevailed during the immediately preceding period. If we were to relax this assumption, then besides solving the optimizing problems presented in these chapters, each price-setter would also need to compute the anticipated loss in present value if it were to keep its prices unchanged from last period and compare this potential loss with the cost of announcing a new set of prices. But, the analysis that follows continues the assumption that new price announcements at the beginning of the period are costless to make (or at least are less costly than the anticipated short-fall in present value if the old prices are maintained).

Because all prices are announced at the beginning of the period and are not altered until the beginning of next period, a particular market will "clear" by the end of the period only if the price-setter's beginning of period forecast of the price-takers' current demand or supply for that item happens to coincide with the actual amount demanded or supplied by the price takers. Depending upon the market in question, the actual amount traded in a particular market may differ from the price-setter's beginning-of-period estimate of the price takers' demand (or supply), or it may differ from the price-takers' beginning-of-period demand for (or ex ante supply of) that item, or it may differ from both magnitudes.

In the consumption goods market, the amount actually traded during the period presumably equals the household and government sectors' combined beginning-of-period demand, $c^h_t + c^g_t$. Assuming the nonfinancial business sector plans at the beginning of the period to hold a zero inventory of consumption goods by the end of the period, its estimate of combined demand for these goods coincides with the sum of its current production of consumption goods, c_t, and its initial inventory, Q_t, of these goods. Therefore, the quantity of consumption goods in the nonfinancial business sector's end-of-period inventory, Q_{t+1}, is given by (12.44):

$$Q_{t+1} = c_t + Q_t - c^h_t - c^g_t \tag{12.44}$$

To appreciate the actual transactons in the capital goods market, it may be best to begin with the market for personal loans. In this market, the volume of loans outstanding, L^h_{t+1}, at the end of the current period is the minimum of the household sector's demand for loans, L^{hd}_{t+1}, and the private financial sector's beginning-of-period estimate, L^{de}_{t+1}, of that demand.

$$L^h_{t+1} = \min (L^{hd}_{t+1}, L^{de}_{t+1}) \tag{12.45}$$

Clearly, if $L^{hd}_{t+1} > L^{de}_{t+1}$, "credit rationing" exists during the current period.

To find the impact of "credit rationing" in the loan market upon the capital goods market, consider restriction (8.3), which we imposed upon the household sector in Chapter 8 and which is repeated here as condition (12.46):

$$p^k_t(K^{hd}_{t+1} - K^h_t) = (L^{hd}_{t+1} - L^h_t) \tag{12.46}$$

Condition (12.46) is a restriction upon ex ante magnitudes. It stipulates that given the household sector's utility maximizing demand for physical capital, K^{hd}_{t+1}, the amount of loans which the households plan to have outstanding by the end of the period must exceed the amount of personal debt outstanding at the beginning of the period by the value of that sector's planned purchase of capital goods. But suppose that before the household sector can actually purchase capital goods during the period, it must first obtain approval for its personal loans. And suppose as well that the possibility exists that it will not be able to borrow all that it wants to borrow during the period. In this case, we can consider an ex post version of (12.46) which reveals the value of the household sector's "effective" (flow) demand for physical capital given the maximum amount it is permitted to borrow in the loan market. In other words,

$$p^k_t(K^h_{t+1} - K^h_t) = (L^h_{t+1} - L^h_t) \tag{12.47}$$

where L^h_{t+1} is defined in (12.45).

In physical units, the actual market (flow) demand for capital goods (i.e. desired purchases) is presumed to equal the sum of the household sector's effective demand, $K^h_{t+1} - K^h_t$, and the government's ex ante (and effective) demand, $K^{gd}_{t+1} - K^g_t$. Assuming that the nonfinancial business sector does not ration physical capital, the amount actually traded during the period will equal $(K^h_{t+1} - K^h_t) + (K^{gd}_{t+1} - K^g_t)$. The nonfinancial business sector's beginning-of-period ex ante supply of capital goods (i.e. its beginning-of-period anticipated sales of capital goods) necessarily coincides with its current production of capital goods. i_t, minus its own beginning-of-period ex ante investment, $K^{nd}_{t+1} - K^n_t$. But the actual stock of physical capital held by the nonfinancial business sector by the end of the period is given by (12.48):

$$K^n_{t+1} = K^n_t + i_t - (K^h_{t+1} - K^h_t) - (K^{dg}_{t+1} - K^g_t) \tag{12.48}$$

The level of unintended investment by the nonfinancial business sector in physical capital is then given by the difference $K^n_{t+1} - K^{nd}_{t+1}$. Consequently, the actual amount of physical capital traded during the current period, $(K^h_{t+1} - K^h_t) + (K^{dg}_{t+1} - K^g_t)$, may differ from both the nonfinancial business sector's beginning-of-period estimate of that demand, $i_t - (K^{nd}_{t+1} - K^n_t)$, and the combined "notional" demand of the price-takers, $(K^{dh}_{t+1} - K^h_t) + (K^{dg}_{t+1} - K^g_t)$.

In the labor market, the total number of people hired during the current peiod to work next period, N_{t+1}, is represented by the minimum of the household sector's ex ante supply of labor, N^s_{t+1}, and the sum of the demands for labor by the government, N^{gd}_{t+1}, the private financial sector, N^{fg}_{t+1}, and the nonfinancial business sector, N^{nd}_{t+1}.

$$N_{t+1} = \min(N^{s}_{t+1}, N^{gd}_{t+1} + N^{fd}_{t+1} + N^{nd}_{t+1}) \tag{12.49}$$

Unemployment, U_{t+1}, exists (in the sense that some people who wish to work next period at the wage rate, w_{t+1}, will not be hired during the current period) to the extent that N^{s}_{t+1} exceeds $N^{gd}_{t+1} + N^{fd}_{t+1} + N^{nd}_{t+1}$. As mentioned above, the nonfinancial sector typically sets w_{t+1} at a level at which it anticipates U_{t+1} will be positive:

$$U_{t+1} = N^{s}_{t+1} - N^{gd}_{t+1} - N^{fd}_{t+1} - N^{nd}_{t+1} \tag{12.50}$$

Underemployment and/or overtime may also exist in the present framework. In particular, by time t, N^{g}_{t} people have been hired by the government to work during the current period, N^{f}_{t} have been hired by the private financial sector and N^{n}_{t} have been hired by the nonfinancial sector. All employers and potential employees presumably planned last period that everyone would work the standard number of hours, h, during the current period. However, at time t each employer is free to alter the average number of hours its employees work during the current period even though the current number of employees and the current period wage rate, w_t, cannot be changed. Consequently, at the beginning of the current period the nonfinancial business sector, for instance, could decide to "layoff" its workers for a portion of the period by deciding to use them less than h hours, on the average. But, at the same time, the private financial sector, for instance, could decide that its employees will work "overtime" during the current period, i.e. work longer than the standard h hours, on the average. In this model some people can be working overtime during the current period even though (a) others are being "laid off" (or reduced to "part-time") and (b) not everyone who wants to work next period is able to find a job. This situation may exist even though labor is homogeneous.

In the remaining financial markets, the price setters are obligated to buy, sell or issue all the bonds, equity shares, checkable deposits, and advances that the price-takers want to trade, acquire or borrow. Consequently, the volume of government bonds, B^{g}_{t+1}, outstanding at the end of the period corresponds to the government's ex ante supply, B^{gs}_{t+1}; the volume of shares of financial sector equity held by the households at the end of the period, Sf^{h}_{t+1}, corresponds to the household sector's demand for those shares, Sf^{hd}_{t+1}; the volume of shares of nonfinancial business sector equity held by the households at the end of the period, Sn^{h}_{t+1}, corresponds to the household sector's demand, Sn^{hd}_{t+1}; and the volume of advances outstanding at time t+1, A_{t+1}, equals the private financial sector's demand, A^{d}_{t+1}.

$$B^{g}_{t+1} = B^{gs}_{t+1} \tag{12.51}$$

$$Sf^{h}_{t+1} = Sf^{hd}_{t+1} \tag{12.52}$$

$$Sn^{h}_{t+1} = Sn^{hd}_{t+1} \tag{12.53}$$

$$A_{t+1} = A^{d}_{t+1} \tag{12.54}$$

The end-of-period stocks of the various components of the medium of exchange--"checkable deposits" and "currency" for those outside the private financial sector and "bank reserves" for the private financial sector itself--are the only values that remain unspecified. These will be considerd next.

Consider, for instance, the nonfinancial business sector's end-of-period holdings of checkable deposits, D^{n}_{t+1}. The value of these deposits may be obtained from the ex post version of its cash-flow constraint!

$$D^{n}_{t+1} = D^{n}_{t} + p^{n}_{t}(Sn^{h}_{t+1} - Sn^{h}_{t}) + p^{c}_{t}c_{t} + p^{k}_{t}i_{t} + r^{d}_{t} D^{n}_{t} - w_{t}h^{n}_{t}N^{n}_{t} - \pi^{n}s_{t}n^{h}_{t} \tag{12.55}$$

The degree to which these actual end-of-period deposits differ from the sector's beginning-of-period ex ante demand, D^{nd}_{t+1}, may be found by solving (12.40) for that ex ante demand and then subtracting that expression from (12.55):

$$D^{n}_{n+1} = D^{nd}_{t+1} - p^{c}_{t}(c^{de}_{t} - c_{t}) - p^{k}_{t}(i^{de}_{t} - i_{t}) - p^{n}_{t}(Sn^{e}_{t+1} - Sn^{h}_{t}) \tag{12.56}$$

In words, the nonfinancial business sector's checkable deposits at the end of the period will fall short of the amount it planned to hold by that time to the extent that the sector overestimated at the beginning of the period its current period sales of consumption goods, capital goods and equity shares.

The households sector's end-of-period holdings of currency, Cu^{h}_{t+1} presumably equals the ex ante demand, Cu^{hd}_{t+1}:

$$Cu^{h}_{t+1} = Cu^{hd}_{t+1} \tag{12.57}$$

Then, substituting (12.47), (12.52) and (12.53) into (12.39) yields the following expression for the household sector's holdings of checkable deposits, D^{h}_{t+1}, at the end of the period:

$$\begin{aligned} D^{h}_{t+1} = {} & D^{h}_{t} + w_t h_t N_t + r^{d}_{t+1} D^{h}_{t} + \pi^{n}_{t} Sn^{h}_{t} \\ & + \pi^{f}_{t} Sf^{h}_{t} - Tx_t - p^{c}_{t} c^{h}_{t} - r_{t-1} L^{h}_{t} \\ & + p^{n}(Sn^{h}_{t+1} - Sn^{h}_{t}) + p^{f}(Sf^{h}_{t+1} - Sf^{h}_{t}) \\ & + (Cu^{h}_{t+1} - Cu^{h}_{t}) \end{aligned} \tag{12.58}$$

Since the household sector is unconstrained with respect to Sf, Sn, and Cu, this end-of-period stock also equals the ex ante demand, D^{hd}_{t+1}, presented in (12.29). Therefore,

$$D^{h}_{t+1} = D^{hd}_{t+1}. \tag{12.59}$$

The government's end-of-period stock of checkable deposits, D^{g}_{t+1}, may be found from the ex post version of (12.38):

$$\begin{aligned} D^{g}_{t+1} = {} & Tx_t + \pi^{cb}_{t} + r^{d}_{t+1} D^{g}_{t} - B^{g}_{t} - p^{c}_{t} c^{g}_{t} - w_t h^{g}_{t} N^{g}_{t} \\ & + D^{g}_{t} - p^{k}(K^{g}_{t+1} - K^{g}_{t}) + p^{b}_{t} B^{g}_{t+1} \end{aligned} \tag{12.60}$$

However, since K^{g}_{t+1}, B^{g}_{t+1} and c^{g}_{t} all equal their ex ante values, it follows from a comparison of (12.38) and (12.60) that

$$D^{g}_{t+1} = D^{gd}_{t+1}. \tag{12.61}$$

In other words, the volume of checkable deposits which the government holds at the end of the period corresponds to the amount it planned at the beginning of the period to hold by time t+1.

Total checkable deposits at time t+1 is denoted by

$$D_{t+1} = D^n{}_{t+1} + D^h{}_{t+1} + D^g{}_{t+1} \tag{12.62}$$

while the stock of money held by the private nonfinancial sectors at time t+1 corresponds to :

$$M_{t+1} = Cu^h{}_{t+1} + D_{t+1}. \tag{12.63}$$

The actual volume of reserves, Rs_{t+1}, held by the private depository institutions at the end of the period may be obtained from the ex post version of (12.41):

$$\begin{aligned} Rs_{t+1} = {} & r^{\ell}{}_{t+1}L^h{}_t + B^g{}_t - r^d{}_tD_t - \rho_{t-1}A_t \\ & - w_th^f{}_tN^f{}_t - \pi^f{}_tSf^h{}_t \\ & + Rs_t - p^b{}_tB^g{}_{t+1} - (L^h{}_{t+1} - L^h{}_t) \\ & + (D_{t+1} - D_t) + A_{t+1} - A_t) \\ & + p^f{}_t(Sf^h{}_{t+1} - Sf^h{}_t). \end{aligned} \tag{12.64}$$

The actual volume of excess reserves, X_{t+1}, at the end of the period is given by (12.65)

$$X_{t+1} = Rs_{t+1} - r^*D_{t+1}. \tag{12.65}$$

Subtracting (12.41) from (12.64) with $A^d{}_{t+1} = A_{t+1}$, yields

$$\begin{aligned} Rs_{t+1} = {} & Rs^d{}_{t+1} + p^b{}_t(B^{ge}{}_{t+1} - B^{gs}{}_{t+1}) \\ & + (L^{de} - L^{hd}) - (D^e - D_{t+1}) \\ & + p^f{}_t\,(Sf^e{}_{t+1} - Sf^h{}_t). \end{aligned} \tag{12.66}$$

According to (12.66), actual reserves at time t+1 will exceed the volume of reserves the depository institutions planned at the beginning of the period to hold at time t+1 by the sum of: the dollar amount by which the sector over-estimated the government's supply of bonds plus the amount by which it over-estimated the household sector's demand for loans minus the amount by which it over-estimated the demand for checkable deposits minus the amount to which it overestimated the demand for its own equity shares.

Finally, from the central bank's end-of-period balance sheet, the actual volume of the monetary base outstanding at time t+1, MB_{t+1}, equals the volume of advance at that time.

$$MB_{t+1} = A_{t+1}. \qquad (12.67)$$

National Income and Product

The value of national income and product depends upon the assumptions one is willing to make not only as to what constitutes productive activity but also as to what productive activity can be measured at reasonable cost. In the U.S., for example, household and government production are measured by the compensation of the sectors' employees. This view presumes that (a) interest payments by households and the government are not associated with productive activity and (b) any production originating in these sectors that is uncompensated by an explicit market payment is too costly to measure. Therefore according to the official U.S. measure, no income or product originates in the household sector in the present model. Furthermore the income and product originating in the government sector consists only of its wage payments, $w^g{}_t h^g{}_t N^g{}_t$. This amount appears under national income as a component of wage income and under the "expenditures" approach to national product as part of "government spending on goods and services."

Ignoring imputed interest, the official measures of income and product originating in the nonfinancial business sector may be derived directly from that sector's (ex post) income statement:

$$p^c{}_t q_t + p^k{}_t i_t = w^n{}_t h^n{}_t N^n{}_t + Pr^n{}_t - r^d{}_t D^n{}_t \qquad (12.68)$$

where q_t represents current production of consumption goods, i_t represents current production of capital goods, and $Pr^n{}_t$ represents current "profits" (i.e. dividends plus additions to retained earnings) of the nonfinancial business sector. The value of output currently produced by that sector is shown on the left side of (12.68) with the income charges against that product depicted on the right.

Still ignoring inputed interest, the official measures of income and product originating in the private financial sector may be derived directly from that sector's income statement:

$$0 = w^f{}_t h^f{}_t N^f{}_t + Pr^f{}_t - B^g{}_t - r^\ell{}_t L_t + r^d{}_t D_t \tag{12.69}$$

where $Pr^f{}_t$ denotes current "profits" of the private financial sector. In the absence of imputed interest, then, the value of product originating in the private financial sector equals zero, as shown by the left hand side of (12.69). The net income originating in this sector also equals zero; the income accruing to labor and the owners is simply paid for by the net interest received by the depository institutions.

Adding (12.68) and (12.69) and then adding wages paid by the government sector to both sides of the result produces the following expression:

$$\begin{aligned} &p^c{}_t[c^h{}_t + c^g{}_t + (Q_{t+1} - Q_t)] + p^k{}_t[(K^g{}_{t+1} - K^g{}_t) \\ &+ (K^h{}_{t+1} - K^h{}_t) + (K^n{}_{t+1} - K^n{}_t)] + w^g{}_t h^g{}_t N^g{}_t \\ &= w_t h_t N_t + Pr^n{}_t + Pr^f{}_t + (r^d{}_t(D^h{}_t + D^g{}_t) - B^g{}_t - r^d{}_t L_t) \end{aligned} \tag{12.70}$$

But $p^c{}_t c^h{}_t + p^k{}_t(K^h{}_{t+1} - K^h{}_t)$ = personal consumption, C_t

$p^c{}_t c^g{}_t + p^k{}_t(K^g{}_t - K^g{}_t) + w^g{}_t h^g{}_t N^g{}_t =$ government expenditures on goods and services, G_t

and $p^c{}_t(Q_{t+1} - Q_t) + p^k{}_t(K^n{}_{t+1} - K^n{}_t)$ = gross (and net) private domestic investment, I_t.

Therefore, ignoring imputed interest, the sum on the left-hand side of (12.70) measures national product as the sum of expenditures $C_t + I_t + G_t$. The sum on the right hand side of (12.70) measures national income (the charges against national product) as the sum of wages, profits and net interest (paid by the business sector to households and government).

One of the disadvantages of the above approach is that the product originating is the financial sector equals zero. Therefore the national income accountants have devised a measure of "imputed interest" paid by depository institutions which simultaneously denotes "services furnished without payment by financial intermediaries." Currently, this imputed interest is measured as "the property income earned on the investment of deposits less monetary interest paid on deposits." In the present context, let the imputed interest paid by the private financial sector be represented as $r^1{}_tL_t - r^d{}_tD_t$. This amount would then be added to both the left and right hand sides of (12.69), making the product originating in that sector equal to:

$$r^{\ell}{}_tL_t - r^d{}_tD_t = w^f{}_th^f{}_tN^f{}_t + Pr^f{}_t - B^g{}_t \tag{12.71}$$

Suppose that the imputed interest total is allocated among the nonfinancial business, household and government sectors on the basis of the relative sizes of the accounts held by each. Then the respective amounts will equal

$r^{\ell}{}_tL_t\left(\frac{D^n{}_t}{D_t}\right) - r^d{}_tD^n{}_t$ = imputed interest paid to the nonfinancial business sector

$r^{\ell}{}_tL_t\left(\frac{D^h{}_t}{D_t}\right) - r^d{}_tD^h{}_t$ = imputed interest paid to the household sector

$r^{\ell}{}_tL_t\left(\frac{D^g{}_t}{D_t}\right) - r^d{}_tD^g$ = imputed interest paid to the government sector

where $D^n{}_t + D^h{}_t + D^g{}_t = D_t$. (Note that the sum of these three imputed interest payments equals $r^d{}_tL_t - r^d{}_tD_t$.)

Since the nonfinancial business sector holds some of the checkable deposits issued by the private financial institutions, it receives a portion of both the "imputed interest" and the "services furnished without payment by financial intermediaries." Subtracting the corresponding portion from both sides of (12.68) yields

$$\begin{aligned} p^c{}_tq_t + p^k{}_ti_t - \left(r^{\ell}{}_tL_t\left(\frac{D^n{}_t}{D_t}\right) - r^d{}_tD^n{}_t\right) \\ = w^n{}_th^n{}_tN^n{}_t + Pr^n{}_t - r^d{}_tD^n{}_t \\ -\left(r^{\ell}{}_tL_t\left(\frac{D^n{}_t}{D_t}\right) - r^d{}_tD^n{}_t\right) \end{aligned} \tag{12.72}$$

Net monetary interest paid by the nonfinancial sector is then $-\ r^d{}_tD^n{}_t$

and net imputed interest paid by that sector equals $-(r^{\ell}_t(D^n_t/D_t) - r^d_tD^n_t)$. The value of the production of consumption and capital goods overstates the value of product originating in the nonfinancial sector because it includes as part of the value added by that sector the value of the intermediate good "financial services in kind." Therefore the value of these services must be subtraced from the value of the consumption and capital goods produced to obtain the value added by the nonfinancial business sector, as we have done in (12.72).

Adding equations (12.71) and (12.72) and then adding government wage payments to both sides of the new equation provides an alternative to (12.70) as the definition for national income and product:

$$Y^m_t = p^c_tc_t+p^k_ti_t+w^g_th^g_tN^g_t + r^{\ell}_tL_t\left(\frac{D^h_t + D^g_t}{D_t}\right) - r^1_t(D^h_t+D^g_t)$$

$$= w_th_tN_t + Pr^n_t + Pr^f_t - B^g_t - r_tL_t\left(\frac{D^n_t}{D_t}\right) \tag{12.73}$$

where Y^m_t = measured national income and product

$p^c_tc^h_t + p^k_t(K^h_{t+1} - K^h_t) + r^{\ell}_tL_t\left(\frac{D^n_t}{D_t}\right) - r^d_tD^h_t$
= personal consumption, C_t

$p^c_tc^h_t + p^k_t(K^h_{t+1} - K^h_t)+r^{\ell}_tL_t\left(\frac{D^g_t}{D_t}\right) - r^d_tD^h_t + w^g_th^g_tN^g_t$
= government spending on goods and services, G_t

$p^c_t(Q_{t+1} - Q_t) + p^k_t(K^n_{t+1} - K^n_t)$ =private domestic investment, I_t

with $p^c(c_t = \cdot p^c(c^h + c^g+(Q_{t+1} - Q_t))$

and $p^k_ti_t = p^k_t(K^h_{t+1}+ K^g_{t+1}+ K^n_{t+1} - K^h_t - K^g_t - K^n_t)$.

The term $-(B^g_t + r^1_tL_t(D^n_t/D_t))$ represents net monetary interest plus net imputed interest paid by the business sector.

In light of the discussion to this point, then, the functions (12.1), (12.2), (12.4) - (12.6), (12.10) - (12.23), (12.25) - (12.29), (12.33), (12.35), (12.36) and (12.37) depict the actual values for h^g_t, c^g_t, h^n_t, i_t, w_{t+1}, p^n_t, c_t, p^c_t, p^k_t, π^n_t, ρ_t, π^{cb}_t, r^d_t, r^1_t, p^b_t, p^f_t, A_{t+1}, π^f_t, h^h_t, c^h_t, Sf^h_{t+1}, Sn^h_{t+1}, Cu^h_{t+1}, D^h_{t+1}, g_{t+1}, K^g_{t+1}, D^g_{t+1} and $p^b_tB^g_{t+1}$ respectively. Substitution of g_{t+1} from (12.33) into (12.2) then yields the actual value of Tx_{t+1} and (12.44) yields the actual value of Q_{t+1}.

The nonfinancial business sector's end-of-period stock of physical capital is not determined until the household sector decides how much capital to purchase in the current period. The household sector in turn cannot make this decision until it discovers whether the private financial sector "rations" personal loans. Substituting the actual value of r^1_t as revealed by (12.18) into the unobserved function $L^e_{t+1}(.)$ will produce the private financial sector's estimate of the household sector's demand for loans, and presumably, the maximum volume of loans that the financial sector is willing to extend by time t+1. Substitution of this value and the right hand side of (12.31), denoting the household sector's ex ante demand for personal loans, into (12.45) reveals the actual level of L^h_{t+1}:

$$L^h_{t+1} = L^h_{t+1}(\ldots) \tag{12.74}$$

Then the actual values of K^h_{t+1} and K^n_{t+1} may be found from (12.47) and (12.48) respectively.

If we assume that the government and private financial sectors always are able to hire by the end of the period the number of people they set out to hire (i.e. $N^g_{t+1} = N^{gd}_{t+1}$ and $N^f_{t+1} = N^{fd}_{t+1}$) then equations (12.24) and (12.34) reveal the actual amounts of N^f_{t+1} and N^g_{t+1} respectively. Then the number of people actually hired by the nonfinancial business sector will be found from

$$N^n_{t+1} = \min\,(N^{nd}_{t+1}, N^s_{t+1} - N^f_{t+1} - N^g_{t+1}) \tag{12.75}$$

<u>after</u> substituting the right hand sides of (12.7) and (12.32) for N^{nd}_{t+1} and N^s_{t+1} respectively into (12.75). Then the actual number of people hired by the end of the period will be given by:

$$N_{t+1} = N^f_{t+1} + N^g_{t+1} + N^n_{t+1} \tag{12.76}$$

Equation (12.55) reveals the nonfinancial sector's end-of-period checkable deposits, D^n_{t+1}. The end-of-period stocks of money, M_{t+1}, bank reserves, R_{t+1}, excess reserves, X_{t+1}, and the monetary base, MB_{t+1}, are denoted by equations (12.63) - (12.65) and (12.67) respectively. Equation (12.73) then completes the model by revealing the current level of measured national income and product, Y^m_t, (Other equations could be added to denote personal and disposable income, if the reader prefers.) What results, then, is a recursive system in 45 endogenous variables, which may be linearized and written in condensed form as:

$$A_t y_t = B_t y_{t-1} + C_t z_t \qquad (12.77)$$

where

y_t (45x1) $= [h^g_t, c^g_t, h^n_t, i_t, w_{t+1}, N^n_{t+1}, p^n_t, c_t, p^c_t, p^k_t, \pi^n_t, \rho_t, \pi^{cb}_t, r^d_t, r^l_t,$

$p^b_t, p^f_t, A_{t+1}, \pi^f_t, h^f_t, N^f_{t+1}, c^h_t, Sf_{t+1}, Sn_{t+1}, Cu_{t+1},$

$D^h_{t+1}, L^{dh}_{t+1}, N^s_{t+1}, g_{t+1}, N^g_{t+1}, K^g_{t+1}, D^g_{t+1}, Tx_{t+1},$

$B^g_{t+1}, Q_{t+1}, L_{t+1}, K^h_{t+1}, K^n_{t+1},$

$N_{t+1}, D^n_{t+1}, M_{t+1}, R_{t+1}, X_{t+1} MB_{t+1}, Y^m_t]'$

A_t = a lower triangular matrix with ones along the 45 X 45 main diagonal.

and z_t (px1) $= [\alpha^c, \alpha^k, \varepsilon_a \cdot \varepsilon_b, \varepsilon_c, \varepsilon_d, \varepsilon_f, \varepsilon_1, \ldots]'$, a vector of exogeneous shift parameters affecting the anticipated positions of the functions estimated by the price-setters and/or the actual positions of the true market demand and supply funtions.

Unlike standard macroeconomic systems, the one displayed in (12.77) includes no "policy parameters" in the vector of exogenous variables. The purpose of the present model is to show the basic functions served by each sector in a democratic society and the implications for the movement of the economy over time. In the present setting, economic agents themselves, not some autonomous policy authority, determine the course of economic activity.

In general, the coefficients in the A. B and C matrices in (12.77) are not constant over time. However, instead of shifting in response to anticipated maneuvers by a policy authority, these coefficients change for a variety of non-policy reasons. These include shifts in household sector tastes; the technical aspects of household, government or nonfinancial business sector production; technical factors associated with transactons undertaken by the government or private sectors; technical factors affecting employee search; institutional arrangements pertaining to the bond, loan and equity markets; and the price-setters' estimates of the price-takers' demand and supply functions.

Since A is triangular, with 1's along its main diagonal, its inverse exists. The reduced form of (12.77) therefore may be found by premultiplying all terms in (12.77) by the inverse of A_t. This yields

$$y_t = P_t y_{t-1} + V_t z_t \tag{12.78}$$

where $P_t = A_t^{-1} B_t$ and $V_t = A_t^{-1} C_t$. As is well known, depending upon the size and sign of P_t, the vector of endogenous variables may show either oscillatory or nonoscillatory movement and either explosive or damped growth or decay. If, in spite of the above warnings, one were to assert that coefficient matrices P and V are constant over time, successive substitution produces the following "final form" for the system.

$$y_t = P^t y_o + P^{t-1} V z_1 + \ldots + PVz_{t-1} + Vz_t \tag{12.79}$$

Matrix V contains the "impact multipliers" on the current endogenous variables associated with an increase in the current exogenous variables. The "delayed multipliers" are represented by PV, P^2V, etc., showing the effects on the current endogenous variables in response to exogenous changes one period earlier, two periods earlier, etc. The sum $\Sigma^k_{i=0} P^i V$ denotes the short-or intermediate-run multiplier of a unit change in z lasting from period t-k to the present.

<u>Long-run Properties</u>

System (12.79) is said to be inherently stable (globally asymptotically stable) if $P^t y_o$ approaches the zero vector. A necessary and sufficient condition for this system to be stable is that all the characteristic roots of the matrix P have moduli strictly less than one. If, for every row (column) of P, the sum of the absolute values of all coefficients in that row (column) is less than one, all characteristic roots of P will have moduli less than one and the system will be stable.

Assuming the system is stable, the solution to (12.79) then approaches (12.80) as t approaches infinity, assuming z_t is constant over time:

$$Y_t = (P^{t-1}+\ldots P + I)Vz \qquad (12.80)$$

But

$$(P^{t-1}+\ldots+P + I) \,.\, (I-P^t) = I - P^t \qquad (12.81)$$

Therefore, if (12.79) is stable, so that P has all characteristic roots less than one, then $|I - P| = 0$. This implies that $(I - P)$ has an inverse.
Post-multiplying both sides of (12.78) by $(I - P)^{-1}$ yields:

$$P^{t-1}+\ldots+P + I = (I - P^t)\,(I - P)^{-1} \qquad (12.82)$$

Therefore, if the system is stable, y_t approaches

$$Y_t = (I - P)^{-1}Vz \qquad (12.83)$$

as t approaches infinity, where $(I - P)^{-1}Vz$ represents a constant vector. The "long-run multipliers" are then given by $(I - P)^{-1}V$.

Because of the likelihood that the coefficient martices P_t and V_t as well as the exogenous variables, z_t, are not constant over time, these long-run properties are of limited interest. Of greater interest are the short-run responses to exogenous shocks.

Virtually every existing macroeconomic model has been developed for the purpose of discussing the consequences of stabilization policies involving exogenous changes in government spending, taxes (or tax rates) and/or the money stock (or monetary base). In the present model, however, changes in these so-called policy parameters are induced by market conditions, technological factors and household preferences rather than by an automonous policy authority. Consequently exogenous changes in government spending, taxes and/or the monetary base simply do not occur in this model. The economy essentially runs itself with real economic agents, rather than an outside interventionist, making the crucial economic choices. Therefore, the following analysis provides no monetary or fiscal policy prescriptions for bringing about "desirable" changes in any "target" variables.

Instead the following conceptual experiments are meant to shed some light upon how an economy supported by a government and central bank dedicated to serving the private sector rather than to controlling it might react in the very short run to exogenous changes in technology. In particular, the following discussion attempts to provide some insight as to how economic agents will alter production, employment, prices, interest rates, the monetary base and the level of government production in response to (a) a technological improvement in government-goods production, (b) an exogenous technological advance in the current-period production of private goods and (c) an exogenous technological advance in next-period's production function for consumption goods.

Effects of a Technological Advance in Government-Goods Production

As in Chapter 6, suppose the government discovers at time t a means of providing a given level government-produced goods next period using fewer units of labor and physical capital. As a result the memu it prepares at time t for the household sector for next period will require lower taxes, Tx_{t+1}, than otherwise for each alternative level of government-produced goods. The reduction in Tx_{t+1} raises the household sector's anticipated disposable income for next period, inducing it to raise next period's planned consumption.

The prospect of higher future consumption expenditures not only reduces the marginal utility of future consumption, but also raises the marginal product of currency and checkable deposits held by the households by the end of the current period. As a result, the household sector increases its demands for government-produced goods and household-produced goods for next period, its current-period demand for consumption goods and its end-of-period demands for currency and checkable deposits. Because the sector plans to produce more goods within the sector next period, its end-of-current-period demand for capital goods rises along with its demand for personal loans from private depository institutions. Since current-period disposable income remains unchanged, the household sector plans to save less during the current period in order to transfer some of next period's disposable income to the present. It therefore reduces its end-of-period demands for currency and checkable deposits. The anticipated increase in disposable income next period also induces the sector to reduce its supply of labor for next period.

As noted in Chapter 6, the new level of taxes selected by the households for next period will be lower than if the increased government efficiency had not occured even after allowing for the household sector's decision to have the government produce more goods next period. Therefore, ceteris paribus, the government's planned expenses for labor, consumption goods and/or capital goods services next period will be lower than if the increased government efficiency had not occurred.

As it formulates its own plans at time t, the nonfinancial business sector may or may not foresee the effects of the increased efficiency in government operations upon the market demands for its own products or upon the number of workers that will be available for next period. We have noted that because of the technical improvement the household sector tends to increase its current and future demands for privately-produced consumption goods, its end-of-period demand for physical capital and to reduce its supply of labor for next period. The government tends to reduce its future demand for consumption goods, its end-of-period demand for physical capital and its demand for labor for next period.

Suppose the nonfinancial business sector does not foresee any of the above effects at time t. Then, by time t+1 its inventory of consumption goods will be lower than it had anticipated (in the form of unfilled orders) because of the household sector's increased current-period demand for consumption goods. The nonfinancial business sector's holdings of physical capital by time t+1 will be greater or smaller than it anticipated, depending upon whether the government's reduction in demand for physical capital is greater or less than the household sector's increased demand during the period from time t to t+1. Also, the level of unemployment at time t+1 may be greater or less than the nonfinancial business sector anticipated at time t. In fact, if the household sector's reduced supply of labor is sufficiently larger than the government sector's reduced demand, the nonfinancial business sector could conceivably find at time t+1 that it has been unable to hire all the workers it planned to hire when it announced next period's wage rate at time t.

If the nonfinancial business sector does find an unanticipated change in its inventory of consumption goods, its stock of physical capital, or the number of its employees by time t+1, it must then decide whether the unanticipated events of the current perirod were anomolies or whether they signal a more permanent change in market conditions.

On the otehr hand, if the nonfinancial business sector correctly foresses at time t the increase in the household sector's current-period demand for consumption goods, it will raise not only the price at time t but also its current-period production of those goods. If it also estimates a change in the market demand for physical capital and/or the net available supply of labor, the nonfinancial sector may also adjust the price of physical capital and the money wage.

If the private depository institutions foresee the increase in the household sector's demand for loans to finance its increased demand for physical capital, they will, ceteris paribus, tend to raise the interest rate they announce at time t on personal loans. If they also foresee the reduction in the government's demand for bonds, due to its reduced demand for physical capital, then they will also tend to raise at time t the price they are willing to pay for bonds during the current period. As a result, the effective interest rates in the markets for personal loans and government bonds will tend to move in opposite directions.

The interest rate which the private financial sector announces at time t on checkable deposits will be affected by its estimate at time t of the end-of-period demands for checkable deposits by the government, the households and the nonfinancial business sector. From the discussion above, it is clear that the household sector's demand for checkable deposits rises because of the extra spending it anticipates for next period. The government's demand for deposits falls, however, even though it may produce more goods next period; the technological advance enables the government to produce more goods using fewer resources and hence making fewer expenditures next period. Therefore the government needs fewer checkable deposits by the beginning of next period. The nonfinancial business sector's demand for checkable deposits may rise or fall depending upon whether the shifts in the government and household sectors' next-period demands for its goods cause the nonfinancial businesses to plan to use more or less labor services next period. If they decide to use more labor, the marginal revenue product of checkable deposits will tend to grow and the nonfinancial business sector's demand for checkable deposits will grow. In any case, if the financial business sector foresees an increase in the demand for checkable deposits, it will tend to reduce the interest rate it announces on those deposits.

As noted above, the household sector's end-of-period demand for currency will tend to grow as it contemplates spending more on consumption goods next period. This causes the private financial sector to revise downward the volume of excess reserves it anticipates for time t+1. But the productivity of a given volume of excess reserves at time t+1 depends upon the volume of checkable deposits the sector plans to have outstanding and upon the volume of personal loans the sector plans to grant by time t+1. We have seen that the household sector's demand for personal loans tends to rise but that the shift in market demand for checkable deposits is indeterminate. Nevertheless, it is possible that the private financial sector will revise upward its estimate of next-period's marginal revenue product associated with a given level of excess reserves at time t+1. If this is so, the sector will increase its demand for advances from the central bank. If this is the response of the private financial sector and if the central bank correctly anticipates this response, it will announce a higher discount rate at time t than it would otherwise.

As discussed in Chapters 10 and 11, the higher discount rate will tend to induce the private depository institutions to raise the interest rate on loans, lower bond prices and lower the interest rate on checkable deposits. The higher interest rate on loans will discourage household expenditures on physical capital and the lower bond prices will tend to raise the cost of government operations next period, which further affects the household sector's choice of the optimal level of government product for next period.

A Technological Advance in the Nonfinancial Business Sector's Production Function

Consider, alternatively, an exogenous disembodied technological improvement in the production of consumption goods (see function (9.16)) and capital goods (see function (9.17)). In the former case, the nonfinancial business sector will not change either the level or the combination of resourses it devotes to the production of either type of good. Therefore, at least initially, its current-period production of capital goods remains unchanged while its current output of consumption goods grows because of the technical advance. The initial response of the sector will be to produce more consumption goods and to announce a lower price for these goods in the current period. But, the fall in the current market price will lower the opportunity cost of producing capital goods, so the sector will tend to produce more of both types of goods in the current period, switch some factors from consumption goods production to capital goods production, and to announce a lower market price for both goods.

In the latter case, i.e. for a technical advance in the production if capital goods, the sector will tend to produce more capital goods using less labor, thereby freeing labor to the production of more consumption goods. Once again the technical advance tends to raise current production of both consumption and capital goods and to induce the private sector to announce lower market prices for both goods at time t.

The reduction in the price of consumption and capital goods induces the household sector to buy more of both goods in the current period. To finance the latter, the household sector also increases its demand for personal loans. As the sector increases its planned spending on consumption goods, the marginal utility of these goods falls relative to next period's consumption and government-produced goods. Consequently, the household sector will tend to instruct the government sector to produce more goods next period than it would otherwise. And it will also tend to decrease its supply of labor for next period. Provided it does not alter its expectations as to next period's prices, the household sector will tend to save more during the current period in order to transfer purchasing power to the future. Part of its extra saving will take the form of increased end-of-period demands for currency and checkable deposits, since the sector anticipates larger real purchases of goods next period.

However, if the households revise downward their expectations of next period's prices in light of lower current-period prices, then a given amount of nominal money balances held by the end of the current period represents a greater real value in terms of next period's goods. Since the marginal products of the end-of-period balances of currency and checkable deposits are diminishing, the sector will tend in this case to reduce its nominal demand for currency and checkable deposits even though its real demand for each type of money rises.

Once the government is instructed to produce more next period, its demand for labor for next period as well as its end-of-period demands for physical capital and checkable deposits will increase. Since its outlays for capital goods grows in the current period, the government will also increase its end-of-period supply of bonds.

If the private financial sector foresees the increase in the household sector's demand for loans, it wlll announce a higher interest rate for loans in the current period. If it foresees the increase in the government sector's demand for bonds, it will lower bond prices this period. And if it revises downward its estimate of the end-of-period demand for nominal checkable deposits, the sector will tend to raise the interest rate on those deposits. If the household sector's nominal end-of-period demand for currency falls, the financial sector will tend to experience an increase in excess reserves. The larger demand for personal loans by the households tends to increase the marginal product of excess reserves held at the end of the period. But, more importantly, the fall in the nominal demand for checkable deposits tends to reduce the marginal product of excess reserves. With the fall in prices, then, the private sector simply needs less nominal high-powered money. Consequently the private financial sector's demand for advances diminishes. If the central bank foresees the reduction in the private financial sector's demand for advances, it will tend to lower the discount rate as it absorbs the unwanted high-powered money. The reduction in the discount rate will at least partially offset the tendency for the level of high-powered money to diminish.

A Technological Advance in Next-Period's Household Production Function

Suppose a technological improvement raises the marginal product of physical capital in the household sector's next-period production function. This causes the households to demand more physical capital for the end of the current period and to substitute home-produced goods for consumption goods produced by the nonfinancial business sector next period. As the anticipated level of future consumption falls, its marginal utility rises, causing the households to decide to supply more labor to the labor market next period and to instruct the government sector to produce fewer government-produced goods next period. Since the sector's anticipated expenditures on consumption goods next period diminishes, the household sector also reduces its end-of-period demands for currency and checkable deposits. Its current demand for consumption goods will also fall as the marginal utility of future consumption rises. In order to finance its increased demand for capital goods, the household sector will increase its end-of-period demand (and hence its current-period demand) for personal loans.

In response to the household sector's instructions to curtail its production next period, the government sector will reduce its end-of-period demands for labor and capital as well as its end-of-period demand for checkable deposits and its supply of bonds.

If the household sector's increased demand for capital exceeds the drop in the government's demand for those goods, the nonfinancial business sector will tend to raise the current price of physical capital, assuming it correctly foresees these relative shifts. The business sector will lower the price of consumptin goods this period in response to the drop in the household sector's demand for those goods. Depending upon the strengths of the estimated shifts in demand and depending upon the technical coefficients in the nonfinancial business sector's production function, the sector may employ its current workers longer or shorter hours this period. But since the sector plans to produce less next period, its demand for labor will fall for next period. Since the government's demand for labor also falls and since the household sector's supply of labor rises, the nonfinancial business sector will tend to reduce next period's money wage.

Assuming the private financial sector correctly anticipates the effects on the asset markets in which it particiaptes, it will tend to raise the interest rate on checkable deposits and raise the price of bonds. If the sector anticipates fewer checkable deposits outstanding by the end of the period, the marginal revenue product of excess reserves falls. If the sector also correctly anticipates a reduction in the household sector's end-of-period demand for currency, it anticipates that its actual excess reserves will be higher than otherwise. Therefore, the sector will tend to borrow fewer reserves from the central bank. If the central bank correctly foresees this shift, it will reduce the discount rate.

This third example contrasts with the second in that the private sector's need for nominal high-powered money fell in the second example because of an anticipated drop in future prices by the household sector. In the present example, the private sector's need for high-powered money diminishes because households are deciding to substitute household-produced goods for goods produced by the business sector next period.

All three of the above examples illustrate how the private sector ultimately determines all prices, wages and interest rates as well as the level of government activity and the stock of high-powered money. These examples also illustrate that all prices and/or all interest rates do not necessarily move in the same direction. Consequently, these results are more general than those found in conventional models of aggregate economic activity. Since every wage, price and interest rate is set by some optimizing economic agent in the present model, our results are also more realistic than relying upon a fictitious auctioneer to establish these values. The next chapter extends the analysis to a large open economy.

13. Model of a Large Open Economy

The theoretical construct presented in this chapter contains the five domestic decision-making units analyzed in Chapters 7-12 plus a foreign sector. Four of the five domestic sectors interact with the foreign sector through the product and financial markets. The domestic household and government sectors purchase not only domestically-produced consumption and capital goods but also foreign-produced commodities. The private nonfinancial business sector also imports commodities from the foreign sector. Domestic private depository institutions, domestic nonfinancial businesses and the domestic government sector carry out transactions involving foreign exchange. They also hold deposits denominated in foreign exchange at foreign depository institutions. The "rest-of-the-world" or foreign sector holds checkable deposits denominated in the domestic currency at domestic private depositiory institutions. The foreign sector also holds bonds issued by domestic borrowers and buys goods produced by domestic firms. Domestic private depository institutions hold both domestic and foreign bonds. The only domestic decision-making unit not engaging in transactions with the foreign sector is the central bank. It continues to deal only with domestic private depository institutions. Furthermore, no foreign firm or worker attempts to buy or sell labor in the domestic economy and no domestic firm or national enters the foreign labor market. Foreign commodity prices, foreign bond prices and interest rates on checkable deposits at foreign banks are treated as exogenous.

As the dominant dealer in the foreign exchange market, the domestic depository institutions presumably set not only the price of domestic bonds, the interest rate on domestic loans and the interest rate on domestic checkable deposits but also the exchange rate between the domestic and foreign currencies. The private domestic financial sector (i.e., domestic depository institutions) announces the exchange rate in conformance with its estimates of the market demand and supply for foreign currency and its objective of optimizing its present value. Consequently, just as every domestic price, wage and interest rate is announced by some real optimizing economic agent in this model, so is the exchange rate between currencies.

The model of the single large open economy is developed sector-by-sector below, beginning with governmental economic activity.

The Government Sector

The analysis of the present section extends the model of the government sector appearing in Chapter 7 to allow the government to procure foreign-produced goods and to hold deposits denominated in foreign exchange. The government combines the goods it imports from the foreign sector with domestic labor and domestically-produced goods to provide the domestic household sector with government-produced goods. In the same manner as its balances of domestic money, the government's balances of foreign money serve both as a store of value and as a means of conserving real resources -- those used in the process of purchasing goods from the foreign sector.

In light of these considerations, the initial and planned balance sheets of the government sector presented in Chapter 7 must be amended to include its actual and planned holdings of checkable deposits denominated in foreign exchange. Let e^g_t denote the exchange rate which the government anticipates at time t will prevail during the current period (i.e., the government's anticipated current-period value of foreign money in terms of the domestic unit of account). Let D^{*g}_t represent the government's actual holding of foreign money (in terms of foreign money) at time t. And, let D^{*gd}_{t+1} depict the volume of checkable deposits denominated in foreign exchange which the government plans at time t to hold at time t+1. Then, in terms of anticipated current-period values expressed in terms of the domestic unit of account, the government's actual balance sheet at time t and its planned balance sheet for time t+1 become:

Government's Actual Balance Sheet at Time t

Assets	Liabilities
D^g_t	$p^b_{t-1}B^g_t$
$p^{kg}_tK^g_t$	Net Wealth
$e^g_tD^{*g}_t$	NW^g_t

Government's Planned Balance Sheet for Time t+1

Assets	Liabilities
D^{gdt+1}	$p^{bg}_tB^{gs}_{t+1}$
$p^{kg}_tK^{gdt+1}$	Net Wealth
$e^g_tD^{*gd}_{t+1}$	NW^g_{t+1}

In the present framework the government at time t anticipates receiving revenue during the current period from taxes, Tx_t, income generated by the central bank, π^{cg}_t, interest income from checkable deposits at domestic depository institutions, $r^d_{t-1}D^g_t$, and interest income from checkable deposits at foreign depository institutions, $e^g_t r^{*d}_{t-1} D^{*g}_t$, where r^{*d}_{t-1} represents the interest rate which foreign depository institutions announced last period that they would pay this period on each unit of foreign deposits outstanding at time t. Therefore, its total anticipated current-period revenue is given by $Tx_t + \pi^{cg}_t + r^d_{t-1} D^r_t + e^g_t r^{*d}_{t-1} D^{*g}_t$.

The government's current expenses include its interest payments, $(\$1 - p^b_{t-1}) B^g_t$, on government-bonds outstanding at time t, its purchases of domestically-produced consumption goods, $p^{cg}_t c^{gd}_t$, its purchases of domestic labor time, $w^g_t h^g_t N^g_t$, and its purchases of foreign-produced goods, $e^g_t p^{*g}_t im^{*gd}_t$, where p^{*g}_t denotes the anticipated current-period price of imported goods (expressed in terms of the foreign curerency) and where im^{*gd}_t represents the physical number of units of foreign-produced goods that the government plans to import this period. Therefore, its total anticipated current expenses are denoted by $(\$1 - p^b_{t+1}) B^g_t + p^{cg}_t c^{gd}_t + w^g_t h^g_t N^g_t + e^g_t p^{*g}_t im^{gd}_t$.

Since the government's planned saving on the income account (its planned revenue minus its planned expenses) must be consistent with its planned accumulation of net wealth on the capital account (the planned level of net wealth in its end-of-period balance sheet minus its existing net wealth), the government's current-period decisions are constrianed by the following condition at time t:

$$\begin{aligned} & Tx_t + \pi^{cg}_t + r^d_{t-1} D^g_t + e^g_t r^{*d}_{t-1} D^{*g}_t - \$1.B^g_t \\ & - p^{cg}_t c^{gd}_t - w^g_t h^g_t N^g_t - e^g_t\ p^{*g}_t im^{*gd}_t \qquad (13.1) \\ & = (D^{gd}_{t+1} - D^g_t) + p^{kg}_t (K^{gd}_{t+1} - K^g_t) + e^g_t (D^{*gd}_{t+1} - D^{*g}_t) - p^{bg}_t B^{gs}_{t+1}. \end{aligned}$$

Expression (13.1) represents the open-economy counterpart of the government's budget constraint presented in (7.3).

Let e^g_{t+1} denote the exchange rate which the government anticipates at time t will prevail next period and let r^{*dg}_t represent the interest rate which the government anticipates at time t that foreign depository institutions will announce this period that they will pay next period on checkable deposits held at those institutions by time t+1. Since D^{*g}_{t+1} represents (in units of foreign currency) the amount the government plans at time t to hold as checkable deposits in foreign depository institutions at time t+1, its anticipated income (in terms of domestic currency) from those deposits next period is denoted by $e^g_{t+1}r^{*dg}_tD^{*dg}_{t+1}$. Tx_{t+1} represents the tax revenue the government anticipates receiving next period, π^{cg}_{t+1} represents the income it anticipates the central bank will earn (and return to the treasury) next period and $r^{dg}_tD^g_{t+1}$ denotes the interest income which the government anticipates at time t receiving as interest income from domestic deposits next period. Therefore at time t, the government's anticipated total revenue next period is given by: $Tx_t+1 + \pi^{cg}_{t+1}$ $r^{dg}_tD^{gd}_{t+1} + e^g_{t+1}r^{*dg}_tD^{*dg}_{t+1}$.

Let p^{*g}_{t+1} represent the price (in terms of foreign money) of imported goods which the goverment anticipates at time t will prevail next period. Then at time t the government anticipates spending (in terms of the domestic unit of account) $e^g_{t+1}p^{*g}_{t+1}im^{*gd}_{t+1}$ on foreign-produced goods next period. As in Chapter 7, let $w^g_{t+1}hN^{gd}_{t+1}$ denote the amount the government plans to spend next period for labor services, let $p^{cg}_{t+1}c^{gd}_{t+1}$ represent the amount it plans to spend next period on domestically-produced consumption goods, and let $(\$1 - p^{bg}_t)B^{gs}_{t+1}$ depict the amount it plans to pay out next period as interest on bonds. Then at time t the government's anticipated next-period expenses are given by:

$$w^g_{t+1}hN^{gd}_{t+1} + p^{cg}_{t+1}c^{gd}_{t+1} + (\$1 - p^{bg}_t)B^{gs}_{t+1} + e^g_{t+1}p^{*g}_{t+1}im^{*gd}_{t+1}.$$

Based upon the above discussion, the government plans at time t to save the amount $Tx_{t+1} + \pi^{cg}_{t+1} + r^{dg}_tD^{gd}_{t+1} + e^g_{t+1}r^{*dg}_tD^{*gd}_{t+1} - w^g_{t+1}hN^{gd}_{t+1} - p^{cg}_{t+1}c^{gd}_{t+1} - (\$1 - p^{bg}_t)B^{gs}_{t+1} - e^g_{t+1}p^{*g}_{t+1}im^{*gd}_{t+1}$ next period. This amount of planned saving on the income account must be consistent with the net wealth that the government plans to accumulate next period on the asset account. In particular, re-write the government's planned balance sheet for time t+1 in terms of next period's prices. Since those prices are the ones at which the items in that balance sheet can be traded next period either to finance government dissaving or to channel government saving, the difference in net wealth associated with the balance sheet planned for t+2 and the level of net wealth in the balance sheet planned for t+1 must equal the amount the government plans to save on the income account next period.

But the government is precluded from planning beyond the community's time horizon, which at time t extends only to time t+2. Therefore the government at time t must plan to hold no assets and to have no liabilities outstanding by time t+2. As a result, its planned change in net wealth between time t+1 and t+2, expressed in terms of next period's anticipated prices, is given by: $- D^{gd}_{t+1} - e^{g}_{t+1}D^{*gd}_{t+1} - p^{kg}_{t+1}K^{gd}_{t+1} + p^{bg}_{t}B^{gs}_{t+1}$. Consequently, at time t the government anticipates confronting the following budget constraint next period.

$$Tx_{t+1} + \pi^{cg}_{t+1} + r^{dg}_{t}D^{gd}_{t+1} + e^{g}_{t+1}r^{*d}_{t}D^{*gd}_{t+1} - w^{g}_{t+1}hN^{gd}_{t+1}$$

$$- p^{cg}_{t+1}c^{gd}_{t+1} - \$1 \, . \, B^{gs}_{t+1} - e^{g}_{t+1}p^{*g}_{t+1}im^{*gd}_{t+1} = - D^{gd}_{t+1}$$

$$- e^{g}_{t+1}D^{*gd}_{t+1} - p^{kg}_{t+1}K^{gd}_{t+1}. \qquad (13.2)$$

Expression (13.2) represents the open-economy counterpart of equation (7.6).

As in the closed-economy version, the government's objective at time t includes not only producing the predetermined current level of government-produced goods, g_t, at minimum cost, but also developing a menu of alternative combinations of government-produced goods, g_{t+1}, and corresponding tax burdens, Tx_{t+1}, from which the household sector may choose this period for next period. As the government attempts to meet these objectives it is constrained at time t by the above-specified budget restrictions as well as by various technical factors.

In the closed-economy version, government-produced goods required labor services, domestically-produced consumption goods and domestically-produced capital goods as inputs. In this open-economy version, foreign-produced goods also serve as a factor of production for government-produced goods. But the adjustments to the government's current-period production function involve more than merely inserting foreign-produced goods as a factor input. In particular, current labor effort now must be devoted not only to the productin of goods and services for the households as well as to transactions involving the purchases of labor and domestically-produced consumption goods, but also to transactions devoted to acquiring foreign-produced goods. Let $\alpha(.)$ represent anticipated current-period transactions time inclusive of time devoted to purchasing imported goods. In particular assume the transactions time function assumes the following form:

$$\alpha(.) = \hat{\alpha}(h^{g}{}_{t}N^{g}{}_{t}, c^{gd}{}_{t}, D^{g}{}_{t}, w^{g}{}_{t}, p^{cg}{}_{t}) + \tilde{\alpha}(im^{*gd}{}_{t}, D^{*g}{}_{t}, p^{*g}{}_{t}) \qquad (13.3)$$

with $\hat{\alpha}_1$, $\hat{\alpha}_2$, $\hat{\alpha}_4$, and $\hat{\alpha}_5 > 0$; $\hat{\alpha}_3 < 0$; $\hat{\alpha}_{ii} > 0$ for $i = 1...5$; $\hat{\alpha}_{13}$, $\hat{\alpha}_{23} < 0$; $\hat{\alpha}_{43}$, $\hat{\alpha}_{53} > 0$; and with $\tilde{\alpha}_1$, $\tilde{\alpha}_3 > 0$; $\tilde{\alpha}_2 < 0$; $\tilde{\alpha}_{ii} > 0$ for $i = 1...3$; $\tilde{\alpha}_{12} < 0$ and $\tilde{\alpha}_{32} > 0$.

According to this specification a ceteris paribus increase in either current labor hours or consumption goods purchased in the current period increases current transactions time at an increasing rate while a ceteris paribus increase in initial checkable deposits at domestic depository institutions decreases current transactions time, but at a decreasing rate. Furthermore an increase in D^g_t decreases the rate at which a unit increase in $h^g_t N^g_t$ or c^g_t raises current transactions time. A rise in w^g_t or p^{cg}_t presumably increases current transactions time at an increasing rate and reduces the marginal productivity of D^g_t. Similarly, a ceteris paribus increase in imports by the government increases its current transactions time at an increasing rate while an increase in its beginning-of-period balances of checkable deposits denominated in the foreign unit of account decreases current transactions time at a decreasing rate. In addition, an increase in the foreign currency price of these foreign-produced goods increases current transactions time at an increasing rate and reduces the marginal product of a unit of D^{*g}_t.

Assume the current-period production function for government-produced goods, $g(.)$, is a positive, increasing, strictly concave function of (a) labor time devoted to that production, $h^g_t N^g_t - \alpha(.)$; (b) the quantity of privately-produced consumption goods purchased from the domestic nonfinancial business sector, c^g_t; (c) the quantity of imported goods, im^{*g}_t; and (d) the quantity of physical capital with which the government begins the current period, K^g_t. Then the current-period production function for government-produced goods may be represented by:

$$g_t = g(h^g_t N^g_t - \hat{\alpha}(h^g_t N^g_t,\ c^{gd}_t,\ D^g_t,\ w^g_t,\ p^{cg}_t) - \tilde{\alpha}(im^{*gd}_t,\ D^{*g}_t,\ p^{*g}_t),\ c^{gd}_t,\ im^{*gd}_t,\ K^g_t) \qquad (13.4)$$

where $g_i > 0$, $g_{ii} < 0$ for $i = 1, \ldots, 4$. At time t variables N^g_t, D^g_t, D^{*g}_t and K^g_t are predetermined so that the only choice variables appearing in $g(.)$ at time t are h^g_t, c^g_t and im^{*g}_t.

In an analogous manner, let $\beta(.)$ denote the amount of time the government anticipates at time t that it will spend undertaking transactions next period. Suppose, in particular, that $\beta(.)$ assumes the following form:

$$\beta(.) = \hat{\beta}(hN^{gd}_{t+1}, c^{gd}_{t+1}, D^{gd}_{t+1}, w^{g}_{t+1}, p^{cg}_{t+1}) + \tilde{\beta}(im*^{gd}_{t+1},$$

$$D^{*gd}_{t+1}, p^{*g}_{t+1}) \qquad (13.5)$$

where $\hat{\beta}_1$, $\hat{\beta}_2$, $\hat{\beta}_4$, $\hat{\beta}_5 > 0$; $\hat{\beta}_3 < 0$; $\hat{\beta}_{ii} > 0$, $i = 1,..., 5$; $\hat{\beta}_{13}$, $\hat{\beta}_{23} < 0$; and $\tilde{\beta}_{34}$, $\beta_{35} > 0$; and where $\tilde{\beta}_1$, $\tilde{\beta}_3 > 0$; $\tilde{\beta}_{ii} > 0$, $i = 1,2,3$; $\beta_{12} < 0$ and $\tilde{\beta}_{23} > 0$. The interpretation of (13.5) is directly analogous to that associated with (13.3).

Assume the government anticipates at time t that the next-period production function for government-produced goods, $\hat{g}(.)$, is a positive, increasing, strictly concave function of (a) the amount of labor time devoted to producing goods and services for the households, $hN^{gd}_{t+1} - \beta(.)$; (b) the number of domestically-produced consumption goods it purchases next period, c^{gd}_{t+1}; (c) the number of goods it imports from the foreign sector next period, im^{*gd}_{t+1}; and (d) the stock of physical capital the government plans to hold by the beginning of next period, K^{gd}_{t+1}. In particular let the next-period production function for government-produced goods by represented by:

$$g_{t+1} = \hat{g}(hN^{gd}_{t+1} - \hat{\beta}(hN^{gd}_{t+1}, c^{gd}_{t+1}, D^{gd}_{t+1}, w^{g}_{t+1}, p^{cg}_{t+1})$$

$$- \tilde{\beta}(im^{*gd}+1, D^{*gd}_{t+1}, p^{*g}_{t+1}), c^{gd}_{t+1}, im^{*gd}_{t+1}, K^{gd}_{t+1}) \qquad (13.6)$$

with $g_i > 0$, $g_{ii} < 0$ $i = 1, ..., 4$.

The government's objective at time t is to find for each possible value of future government production, the minimum level of taxes it must collect next period to finance that production. As it calculates the minimum tax, Tx_{t+1}, the government is constrained by conditions (13.1), (13.2), (13.4) and (13.6). Solving (13.1) for B^{gs}_{t+1} and substituting the result into (13.2) produces the following expression for Tx_{t+1}:

$$Tx_{t+1} = p^{cg}_{t+1}c^{gd}_{t} + w^{g}_{t+1}hN^{gd}_{t+1} + e^{g}_{t+1}p^{*g}_{t+1}im*^{gd}_{t+1}$$

$$- (1 + r^{dg}_{t})D^{g}_{t} - (1 + r^{*g}_{t})e^{g}_{t+1}D^{*gd}_{t+1} - \pi^{cb}_{t+1} - p^{kg}_{t+1}K^{gd}_{t+1}$$

$$+ (\$1/p^{bg}_{t})(D^{gd}_{t+1} - D^{g}_{t}) + (\$1/p^{bg}_{t})e^{g}_{t}(D^{*gd}_{t+1} - D^{*g}_{t})$$

$$+ (\$1/p^{bg}_{t})p^{kg}_{t}(K^{gd}_{t+1} - K^{g}_{t}) + (\$1/p^{bg}_{t})(\$1 \cdot B^{g}_{t} + p^{cg}_{t}c^{gd}_{t}$$

$$+ w^g{}_t h^g{}_t N^g{}_t + e^g{}_t p^{*g}{}_t im^{*gd}{}_t - Tx_t - \pi^{cb}{}_t$$

$$- r^d{}_{t-1} D^g{}_t - r^{*d}{}_{t-1} e^g{}_t D^{*g}{}_t) \qquad (13.7)$$

The government's objective at time t becomes the minimization of (13.7), subject to (13.4) and (13.6). By varying g_{t+1} parametrically the government is able to generate a menu of alternative levels of g_{t+1} and corresponding minimum taxes, Tx_{t+1}, necessary to finance each level of government-produced goods. It is then up to the household sector to decide the level of g_{t+1} it wants the government to produce next period. Knowing g_{t+1} enables the government to select the optimal levels of $c^{gd}{}_{t+1}$, $N^{gd}{}_{t+1}$, $K^{gd}{}_{t+1}$, $D^{gd}{}_{t+1}$, $D^{*gd}{}_{t+1}$ and $im^{*gd}{}_{t+1}$. The optimal levels of $c^{gd}{}_t$, $h^g{}_t$ and $im^{*gd}{}_t$, on the other hand, are independent of g_{t+1}, as the following analysis shows.

To solve the above optimization problem, minimize the following Lagrangian function with respect to the choice variables $c^{gd}{}_t$, $h^g{}_t$, $im^{*gd}{}_t$, λ_1, $c^{gd}{}_{t+1}$, $N^{gd}{}_{t+1}$, $K^{gd}{}_{t+1}$, $D^{gd}{}_{t+1}$, $D^{*gd}{}_{t+1}$, $im^{*gd}{}_{t+1}$ and λ_2.

$$Tx_{t+1} = p^{cg}{}_{t+1} c^{gd}{}_{t+1} + w^g{}_{t+1} h N^{gd}{}_{t+1} + e^g{}_{t+1} p^{*g}{}_{t+1} im^{*gd}{}_{t+1}$$

$$- (1+r^{gd}{}_t) D^{gd}{}_{t+1} - (1+r^{*g}{}_t) e^g{}_{t+1} D^{*gd}{}_{t+1} - \pi^{cb}{}_{t+1} - p^{kg}{}_{t+1} K^{gd}{}_{t+1}$$

$$+ (\$1/p^{bg}{}_t)(D^{gd}{}_{t+1} - D^g{}_t) + (\$1/p^{bg}{}_t) e^g{}_t (D^{*gd}{}_{t+1} - D^{*g}{}_t)$$

$$+ (\$1/p^{bg}{}_t) p^{kg}{}_t (K^{gd}{}_{t+1} - K^g{}_t) + (\$1/p^{bg}{}_t)(\$1.B^g{}_t + p^{cg}{}_t c^{gd}{}_t$$

$$+ w^g{}_t h^g{}_t N^g{}_t + e^g{}_t p^{*g}{}_t im^{*gd}{}_t - Tx_t - \pi^{cb}{}_t - r^d{}_{t-1} D^g{}_t$$

$$- r^{*d}{}_{t-1} e^g{}_t D^{*g}{}_t) \qquad (13.8)$$

$$+ \lambda_1 (g_t - g(h^g{}_t N^g{}_t - \hat{\alpha}(h^g{}_t N^g{}_t, c^{gd}{}_t, D^g{}_t, w^g{}_t, p^{cg}{}_t)$$

$$- \tilde{\alpha}(im^{*gd}{}_t, D^{*g}{}_t, p^{*g}{}_t), c^{gd}{}_t, im^{*gd}{}_t, K^g{}_t))$$

$$+ \lambda_2 (g_{t+1} - \hat{g}(hN^{gd}{}_{t+1} - \hat{\beta}(hN^{gd}{}_{t+1}, c^{gd}{}_{t+1}, D^{gd}{}_{t+1}, w^g{}_{t+1}, p^{cg}{}_{t+1})$$

$$- \tilde{\beta}(im^{*gd}{}_{t+1}, D^{*gd}{}_{t+1}, p^{*g}{}_{t+1}), c^{gd}{}_{t+1}, im^{*gd}{}_{t+1}, K^{gd}{}_{t+1}))$$

Partially differentiating (13.8) with respect to each of the choice variables produces the following eleven first-order necessary conditions:

$$\frac{\partial Tx_{t+1}}{\partial h^{gt}} = (\$1/p^{bg}_{t})w^{g}_{t}N^{g}_{t} + \lambda_1[-g_1(1-\hat{\alpha}_1)N^{g}_{t}] = 0 \qquad (13.9)$$

$$\frac{\partial Tx_{t+1}}{\partial c^{gd}_{t}} = (\$1/p^{bg}_{t})p^{cg}_{t} + \lambda_1[-g_1(-\hat{\alpha}_2) - g_2] = 0 \qquad (13.10)$$

$$\frac{\partial Tx_{t+1}}{\partial im^{*gd}_{t}} = (\$1/p^{bg}_{t})e^{g}_{t}p^{*g}_{t} + \lambda_1[-g_1(-\tilde{\alpha}_1) - g_3] = 0 \qquad (13.11)$$

$$\frac{\partial Tx_{t+1}}{\partial \lambda_1} = g_t - g(h^{g}_{t}N^{g}_{t} - \hat{\alpha}(h^{g}_{t}N^{g}_{t}, c^{gd}_{t}, D^{g}_{t}, w^{g}_{t}, p^{cg}_{t})$$

$$- \tilde{\alpha}(im^{*gd}_{t}, D^{*g}_{t}, p^{*g}_{t}), c^{gd}_{t}, im^{*gd}_{t}, K^{g}_{t}) = 0 \qquad (13.12)$$

$$\frac{\partial Tx_{t+1}}{\partial N^{gd}_{t+1}} = w^{g}_{t+1}h + \lambda_2[-\hat{g}_1(1-\hat{\beta}_1)h] = 0 \qquad (13.13)$$

$$\frac{\partial Tx_{t+1}}{\partial c^{gd}_{t+1}} = p^{cg}_{t+1} + \lambda_2[-\hat{g}_1(-\hat{\beta}_2) - \hat{g}_2] = 0 \qquad (13.14)$$

$$\frac{\partial Tx_{t+1}}{\partial im^{*gd}_{t+1}} = e^{g}_{t+1}p^{*g}_{t+1} + \lambda_2[-\hat{g}_1(-\tilde{\beta}_1) - \hat{g}_3] = 0 \qquad (13.15)$$

$$\frac{\partial Tx_{t+1}}{\partial K^{gd}_{t+1}} = (\$1/p^{bg}_{t})p^{kg}_{t} - p^{kg}_{t+1} + \lambda_2[-\hat{g}_4] = 0 \qquad (13.16)$$

$$\frac{\partial Tx_{t+1}}{\partial D^{gd}_{t+1}} = (\$1/p^{bg}_{t}) - (1 + r^{dg}_{t}) + \lambda_2[-\hat{g}_1(-\hat{\beta}_3)] = 0 \qquad (13.17)$$

$$\frac{\partial Tx_{t+1}}{\partial D^{*gd}_{t+1}} = (\$1/p^{bg}_{t})e^{g}_{t} - (1+r^{*g}_{t})e^{g}_{t+1} + \lambda_2[-\hat{g}_1(-\tilde{\beta}_2)] = 0 \qquad (13.18)$$

$$\frac{\partial Tx_{t+1}}{\partial \lambda_2} = g_{t+1} - \hat{g}(hN^{gd}_{t+1} - \hat{\beta}(hN^{gd}_{t+1}, c^{gd}_{t+1}, D^{gd}_{t+1}, w^{g}_{t+1}, p^{cg}_{t+1}) \qquad (13.19)$$

$$- \tilde{\beta}(im^{*gd}_{t+1}, D^{*gd}_{t+1}, p^{*g}_{t+1}), c^{gd}_{t+1}, im^{*gd}_{t+1}, K^{gd}_{t+1}) = 0$$

Since conditions (13.9) - (13.12) depend only upon choice variables c^{gd}_t, h^g_t, im^{*gd}_t and λ_1 while conditions (13.13) - (13.19) depend only upon variables g^{gd}_{t+1}, N^{gd}_{t+1}, K^{gd}_{gd}, D^{dg}_{t+1}, D^{*gd}_{t+1}, im^{*gd}_{t+1} and λ_2, the system (13.9) - (13.19) consists of two separate subsystems. The first subsystem is necessary for the minimization of Tx_{t+1}, given g_t; the second set is necessary for the minimization of Tx_{t+1}, given g_{t+1}.

Transferring the second terms in (13.9) - (13.11) to their respective right-hand sides and then dividing each of (13.9) and (13.10) by (13.11) yields the following two conditions:

$$\frac{w^g_t N^g_t}{e^g_t p^{*g}_t} = \frac{g_1(1 - \hat{\alpha}_1)N^g_t}{g_3 - g_1\tilde{\alpha}_1} \tag{13.20}$$

$$\frac{p^{cg}_t}{e^g_t p^{*g}_t} = \frac{g_2 - g_1\hat{\alpha}_2}{g_3 - g_1\tilde{\alpha}_1} \tag{13.21}$$

These two conditions in turn imply the following relationship which was obtained earlier for a government sector operating in a clsosed economy:

$$\frac{w^g_t N^g_t}{p^{cg}_t} = \frac{g_1(1 - \hat{\alpha}_1)N^g_t}{g_2 - g_1\hat{\alpha}_2} \tag{13.22}$$

According to (13.20) - (13.22), the cost-minimizing government will combine resources in producing a given level of g_t so that the market rate of substitution between any two factors just equals the (marginal) rate of technical substitution between them. An increase in the price (denominated in the domestic currency) of any one of current labor hours, current domestic consumption goods, or current imported goods causes the government to substitute more of the other two variable factors for some of the factor whose price has risen. Ceteris paribus, the larger the quantity of g_t that the government is asked to produce in the current period, the more it must use of at least one of these three factors. If the government employs more of only one or two factors, their marginal products will fall relative to those whose use has remained unchanged, causing the government to increase the amount it uses of all factors. An increase in K^g_t enables the government to produce a given level of g_t using less of all three of the variable inputs, causing its demand for each of these factors to fall. An increase in $D^g{}_t$ releases some labor that was previously devoted to undertaking transactions associated with buying domestic labor or consumption goods, thereby enabling the government to produce a given level of g_t with less of all variable inputs. An increase in $D^{*g}{}_t$ leads to a similar response by the government since it releases some labor that was previously used in acquiring the imported factor. As in the discussions of the government sector in Chapters 6 and 7, an increase in $N^g{}_t$ simply affects $h^g{}_t$ proportionately in the opposite direction since total labor hours, but not the composition of those hours, matter in this model.

To summarize, the government sector's demands for current labor hours, current consumption goods and current imported goods may be expressed as follows, where the signs below the parameters reflect the signs of the corresponding partial derivatives:

$$h^g{}_t = h^g{}_t(\underset{-}{N^g{}_t},\ \underset{-}{w_t},\ \underset{+}{p^{cg}{}_t},\ \underset{+}{e^g{}_t p^{*g}{}_t},\ \underset{-}{D^g{}_t},\ \underset{-}{D^{*g}{}_t},\ \underset{+}{g_t}) \tag{13.23}$$

$$c^g{}_t = c^g{}_t(\underset{+}{w_t},\ \underset{-}{p^{cg}{}_t},\ \underset{+}{e^g{}_t p^{*g}{}_t},\ \underset{-}{D^g{}_t},\ \underset{-}{D^{*g}{}_t},\ \underset{+}{g_t}) \tag{13.24}$$

$$im^{*g}{}_t = im^{*g}{}_t(\underset{+}{w_t},\ \underset{+}{p^{cg}{}_t},\ \underset{-}{e^g{}_t p^{*g}{}_t},\ \underset{-}{D^g{}_t},\ \underset{-}{D^{*g}{}_t},\ \underset{+}{g_t}) \tag{13.25}$$

Transferring the second term in each of equations (13.13) - (13.18) to their respective right hand sides and then dividing (13.13), (13.14) and (13.16) - (13.18) by (13.15) produces the following set of conditions:

$$\frac{w^g{}_{t+1}h}{e^g{}_{t+1}p^{*g}{}_{t+1}} = \frac{\hat{g}_1(1 - \hat{\beta}_1)h}{\hat{g}_3 - \tilde{\beta}_1\hat{g}_1} \tag{13.26}$$

$$\frac{p^{cg}{}_{t+1}}{e^g{}_{t+1}p^{*g}{}_{t+1}} = \frac{\hat{g}_2 - \hat{\beta}_2\hat{g}_1}{\hat{g}_3 - \tilde{\beta}_1 g_1} \tag{13.27}$$

$$\frac{r^{bg}{}_t p^{kg}{}_t - (p^{kg}{}_{t+1} - p^{kg}{}_t)}{e^g{}_{t+1}p^{*g}{}_{t+1}} = \frac{\hat{g}_4}{\hat{g}_3 - \tilde{\beta}_1 g_1} \tag{13.28}$$

$$\frac{r^b g_t - r^{gd}{}_t}{e^g{}_{t+1}p^{*g}{}_{t+1}} = \frac{-\hat{\beta}_3\hat{g}_1}{\hat{g}_3 - \tilde{\beta}_1\hat{g}_1} \tag{13.29}$$

$$\frac{(1-r^{bg}_{t})e^{g}_{t} - (1+r^{*g}_{t})e^{g}_{t+1}}{e^{g}_{t+1}p^{*g}_{t+1}} = \frac{-\tilde{\beta}_2\hat{g}_1}{\hat{g}_3 - \tilde{\beta}_1\hat{g}_1} \qquad (13.30)$$

As shown by these relations, the government's end-of-period portfolio decisions at time t (i.e., its plans at time t for K^{gd}_{t+1}, D^{gd}_{t+1} and D^{*gd}_{t+1}), its decisions to hire labor for next period, and its tentative decisions to buy domestic consumption goods and to import goods from the foreign sector next period are all jointly determined. The amount of physical capital, or checkable deposits which the government decides to hold by the end of the period affects either directly or indirectly its demands for labor, domestic consumption goods, and imported goods and vice versa. As a first approximation, an increase in the anticipated future domestic price of labor, consumption goods, or imported goods or an increase in the anticipated user cost of physical capital will cause the government to reduce its demand for the factor whose anticipated price has risen and to increase its demands for all other real factors. If the government plans to increase its purchases of both labor and domestic consumption goods, its nominal demand for domestic checkable deposits will tend to grow as well, since the increased transactions tend to raise the marginal product of these deposits. (If its demands for labor and domestic consumption goods, move in opposite directions, the net effect on the government's demand for domestic checkable deposits is less clear.) If the government plans to increase its imports from the foreign sector next period in response to a change in relative factor prices, this increase in demand for imports raises the anticipated marginal product of checkable deposits denominated in the foreign currency, causing the government"s demand for those deposits to rise as well.

As a first approximation, the higher the interest rate in the domestic bond market, the higher the opportunity cost of holding checkable deposits denominated in either currency and the higher the user cost of physical capital. The government will tend to reduce the volume of physical capital it plans to use in producing a given amount of g_{t+1} and therefore will tend to increase the number of people it plans to employ next period as well as to increase its purchases of domestic consumption goods and its imports from the foreign sector next period.

In general the government sector's demands for labor, domestic consumption goods and imported goods for next period as well as its end-of-period demands for physical capital and both types of checkable deposits will be influenced by the same array of parameters, as indicated below:

$$N^{gd}_{t+1} = N^{g}_{t+1}(w^{g}_{t+1}, p^{cg}_{t+1}, p^{*g}_{t+1}, p^{bg}_{t}, p^{kg}_{t}, p^{kg}_{t+1}, r^{dg}_{t}, r^{*g}_{t}, e^{g}_{t}, e^{g}_{t+1}, g_{t+1}) \qquad (13.31)$$

$$c^{gd}_{t+1} = c^{g}_{t+1}(w^{g}_{t+1}, p^{cg}_{t+1}, p^{*g}_{t+1}, p^{bg}_{t}, p^{kg}_{t}, p^{kg}_{t+1}, r^{dg}_{t}, r^{*g}_{t}, e^{g}_{t}, e^{g}_{t+1}, g_{t+1}) \qquad (13.32)$$

$$im^{*gd}_{t+1} = im^{*g}_{t+1}(w^{g}_{t+1}, p^{cg}_{t+1}, p^{g}_{t+1}, p^{bg}_{t}, p^{kg}_{t}, p^{kg}_{t+1}, r^{dg}_{t}, r^{*g}_{t}, e^{g}_{t}, e^{g}_{t+1}, g_{t+1}) \qquad (13.33)$$

$$K^{gd}_{t+1} = K^{g}_{t+1}(w^{g}_{t+1}, p^{cg}_{t+1}, p^{*g}_{t+1}, p^{bg}_{t}, p^{kg}_{t}, p^{kg}_{t+1}, r^{dg}_{t}, r^{*g}_{t}, e^{g}_{t}, e^{g}_{t+1}, g_{t+1}) \qquad (13.34)$$

$$D^{gd}_{t+1} = D^{g}_{t+1}(w^{g}_{t+1}, p^{cg}_{t+1}, p^{*g}_{t+1}, p^{bg}_{t}, p^{kg}_{t}, p^{kg}_{t+1}, r^{dg}_{t}, r^{*g}_{t}, e^{g}_{t}, e^{g}_{t+1}, g_{t+1}) \qquad (13.35)$$

$$D^{*gd}_{t+1} = D^{*g}_{t+1}(w^{g}_{t+1}, p^{cg}_{t+1}, p^{*g}_{t+1}, p^{bg}_{t}, p^{kg}_{t}, p^{kg}_{t+1}, r^{dg}_{t}, r^{*g}_{t}, e^{g}_{t}, e^{g}_{t+1}, g_{t+1}) \qquad (13.36)$$

Substitution of (13.31) - (13.36) into (13.7) yields an expression for the minimum taxes, Tx_{t+1}, the government will need to collect from the households next preriod as a function of the parameters appearing not only in (13.31) - (13.36) but also in (13.7). Of particular importance in this study is the fact that, ceteris paribus, an increase in g_{t+1} increases next period's minimum taxes at an increasing rate. Therefore, the "menu" which the government presents to the households, although influenced by more factors, still assumes the same shape with respect to g_{t+1} as the menus specified in Chapters 6 and 7. Let this "tax function" be represented by (13.37)

$$Tx_{t+1} = Tx_{t+1}(\underset{+}{g_{t+1}};\ k^*) \tag{13.37}$$

where k* denotes the relevant vector of shift parameters. In addition, the government's supply of bonds is found by substituting (13.23) - (13.25) and (13.34) - (13.36) into (13.1):

$$p^{bg}{}_t B^{gs}{}_{t+1} = B^g{}_{t+1}(\underset{+}{p^{bg}{}_t};\ v) \tag{13.38}$$

where v also denotes a vector of parameters.

The Household Sector

Because of the wide range of choices confronting the household sector in the closed-economy version presented in Chapter 8, the open-economy extension of that sector's activities in the present section will be limited to allowing the household sector to import goods from the foreign sector. Domestic nationals are precluded from emigrating to the foreign sector and the domestic households are viewed as holding no financial assets denominated in foreign currency.

Let the household sector's actual balance sheet at time t and its planned balance sheet at time t for time t+1 be the same as those respective balance sheets presented in Chapter 8. Then the amount the household sector plans to save out of current income this period, namely, $s^h{}_t$, must correspond to the planned increment in net wealth, $NW^h{}_{t+1} - NW^h{}_t$, or:

Household Sector's Actual Balance Sheet at Time t	
Assets	**Liabilities**
$p^{nh}_t Sn_t$	L_t
$p^{fh}_t Sf_t$	**Net Wealth**
D^h_t	NW^h_t
Cu^h_t	
$p^{kh}_t K^h_t$	

Household Sector's Planned Balance Sheet for Time t+1	
Assets	**Liabilities**
$p^{nh}_t Sn^{hd}_{t+1}$	L^{hd}_{t+1}
$p^{fh}_t Sf^{hd}_{t+1}$	**Net Wealth**
D^{hd}_{t+1}	NW^h_{t+1}
Cu^{hd}_{t+1}	
$p^{kh}_t K^{hd}_{t+1}$	

$$s^h_t = p^{nh}_t(Sn^{hd}_{t+1} - Sn^h_t) + p^{fh}_t(Sf^{hd}_{t+1} - Sf^h_t) + p^{kh}_t(K^{hd}_{t+1} - K^h_t)$$
$$+ (D^{hd}_{t+1} - D^h_t) + (Cu^{hd}_{t+1} - Cu^h_t) - (L^{hd}_{t+1} - L^h_t). \qquad (13.39)$$

As in Chapter 8, let $w_t h_t N_t + r^d_{t-1} D^h_t + \pi^n_t Sn^h_t + \pi^f_t Sf^h_t - Tx_t$ denote the household sector's current disposable income. In addition, let $p^{ch}_t c^{hd}_t$ denote its ex ante spending on domestic consumption goods, let $e^h_t p^{*h}_t \, im^{*hd}_t$ represent its anticipated current spending on imported goods and let $r^\ell_{t-1} L_t$ depict the household sector's current outlay for interest on personal loans. Then ex ante current household saving, s^h_t, is defined as:

$$s^h_t = w_t h_t N_t + r^d_{t-1} D^h_t + \pi^n_t Sn^h_t + \pi^f_t Sf^h_t - Tx_t - p^{ch}_t c^{hd}_t$$
$$- e^h_t p^{*h}_t im^{*hd}_t - r^\ell_{t-1} L_t \qquad (13.40)$$

where e^h_t = the dollar value of foreign exchange during current period as anticipated by the domestic households at time t

p^{*h}_t = household sector's anticipated current-period price (in terms of foreign exchange) of foreign goods

im^{*h}_t = the physical units of foreign goods demanded by the households in the current period.

Assuming, for simplicity, as was done in Chapter 8, that household expenditures on capital goods are financed exclusively through personal borrowing:

$$p^{kh}_{t}(K^{hd}_{t+1} - k^{h}_{t}) = (L^{hd}_{t+1} - L^{h}_{t}) \qquad (13.41)$$

then the household sector's current-period budget constraint may be written as

$$w_t h_t N_t + r^{d}_{t-1} D^{h}_{t} + \pi^{n}_{t} Sn^{h}_{t} + \pi^{f}_{t} Sf^{h}_{t} - Tx_t - p^{c}_{t} c^{hd}_{t}$$
$$- e^{h}_{t} p^{*h}_{t} im^{*hd}_{t} - r^{\ell}_{t-1} L_t = p^{nh}_{t} (Sn^{hd}_{t+1} - Sn^{h}_{t})$$
$$+ p^{fh}_{t}(Sf^{hd}_{t+1} - Sf^{h}_{t}) + (D^{hd}_{t+1} - D^{h}_{t}) + (Cu^{hd}_{t+1} - Cu^{h}_{t}) \qquad (13.42)$$

Let e^{h}_{t+1} denote the exchange rate which the household sector anticipates at time t will prevail next period, let p^{*h}_{t+1} denote the price of foreign goods (expressed in terms of foreign currency) which the household sector anticipates at time t will prevail next period and let im^{*h}_{t+1} represent the number of imported goods the household anticipates at time t that it will purchase next period. Then the household setctor's ex ante saving for next period is defined as:

$$s^{h}_{t+1} = w_{t+1} h N^{s}_{t+1} + \pi^{fh}_{t+1} Sf^{hd}_{t+1} + \pi^{nh}_{t+1} Sn^{hd}_{t+1} + r^{dh}_{t} D^{hd}_{t+1}$$
$$- Tx_{t+1} - p^{ch}_{t+1} c^{hd}_{t+1} - e^{h}_{t+1} p^{*h}_{t+1} im^{*hd}_{t+1} - r^{\ell}_{t}(L^{h}_{t}$$
$$+ p^{hk}_{t}(K^{hd}_{t+1} - K^{h}_{t})) \qquad (13.43)$$

Except for incorporating expenditures on foreign-produced goods and the relationship between purchases of physical capital and personal loans, depicted by (13.41), expression (13.43) corresponds to the definition given in (8.4).

In terms of next period's anticipated prices, the household sector's planned balance sheet for time t+1 is given by:

Household Sector's Planned Balance Sheet for Time t+1 (in terms of next period's anticipated prices)

Assets	Liabilities
Cu^{hd}_{t+1}	L^{hd}_{t+1}
D^{hd}_{t+1}	Net Wealth
$p^{kh}_{t+1}K^{hd}_{t+1}$	NW^{h*}_{t+1}

Since at time t the household sector's time horizon extends only to t+2, the sector plans at time t to hold no assets and no liabilities by time t+2. Therefore, at time t, s^{h}_{t+1} must equal $-NW^{h*}_{t+1}$. Or, in light of (13.41) and (13.43), the following must hold:

$$w_{t+1}hN^{s}_{t+1} + \pi^{fh}_{t+1}Sf^{hd}_{t+1} + \pi^{nh}_{t+1}Sn^{hd}_{t+1} + r^{dh}_{t}D^{hd}_{t+1} - Tx_{t+1} - p^{ch}_{t+1}c^{hd}_{t+1} - e^{h}_{t+1}p^{*h}_{t+1}im^{*hd}_{t+1} - r^{\ell}_{t}(L^{h}_{t} + p^{kh}_{t}(K^{hd}_{t+1}-K^{h}_{t})) = -Cu^{hd}_{t+1} - D^{hd}_{t+1} - p^{kh}_{t+1}K^{hd}_{t+1} + L^{h}_{t} + p^{kh}_{t}(K^{hd}_{t+1} - K^{h}_{t}). \quad (13.44)$$

At time t, the household sector's objective presumably is to maximize present utility subject to budget restrictions (13.42) and (13.44) as well as to the "tax menu" (13.37). The household sector's objective function is assumed to be a modified verion of (8.13). In particular, that objective function is extended to allow anticipated purchases of foreign-produced goods this period and next to affect present utility. To accommodate this extension in the simplest fashion, two new arguments, $U_{13}(im^{*}_{t})$ and $U_{14}(im^{*}_{t+1})$, are added to the utiility function appearing as (8.13). Assume these components are positive, increasing, strictly concave functions of their respective arguments. Then U, defined in (13.45), is also strictly concave:

$$U = U_1(c^{hd}_{t}) + U_2(h^{*}N - h_tN_t, K^{h}_{t}) + U_3(Cu^{h}_{t}/p^{ch}_{t}) + U_4(D^{h}_{t}/p^{ch}_{t}) + U_5(c^{hd}_{t+1}) + U_6(h^{*}N - hN^{s}_{t+1}, K^{hd}_{t+1})$$

$$+ U_7(Cu^{hd}_{t+1}/p^{ch}_{t+1}) + U_8(D^{hd}_{t+1}/p^{ch}_{t+1}) \quad (13.45)$$

$$+ U_9((\pi^{fh}_{t+1}Sf^{hd}_{t+1} + (1+r^{dh}_t)D^{hd}_{t+1} + Cu^{hd}_{t+1})/p^{ch}_{t+1})$$

$$+ U_{10}((Cu^{hd}_{t+1} + (1+r^{dh}_t)D^{hd}_{t+1})/p^{ch}_{t+1})$$

$$+ U_{11}(g_t) + U_{12}(g_{t+1}) + U_{13}(im^{*hd}_t) + U_{14}(im^{*hd}_{t+1})$$

Solve (13.42) for Sn^{hd}_{t+1} then substitute the expression for this variable as well as the tax menu into budget constraint (13.44) and then solve it for c^{hd}_{t+1}. Substituting the resulting expression for c^{hd}_{t+1} into (13.45) produces the following unrestricted strictly concave objective function:

$$U = U_1(c^{hd}_t) + U_2(h^*N - h_tN_t,\ K^h_t) + U_3(Cu^h_t)$$

$$+ U_3(Cu^h_t/p^{ch}_t) + U_4(D^h_t/p^{ch}_t)$$

$$+ U_5((\frac{1}{p^{ch}_{t+1}})\ [w_{t+1}hN^s_{t+1} + \pi^{fh}_{t+1}Sf^{hd}_{t+1} + (1+r^{hd}_t)D^{hd}_{t+1}$$

$$+ Cu^{hd}_{t+1} + (p^{kh}_{t+1} - (1+r^1_t)p^{kh}_t)K^{hd}_{t+1} + (1+r^1_t)p^{kh}_tK^h_t$$

$$- (1+r^{\ell}_t)L_t - Tx_{t+1}(g_{t+1};\ k) + \frac{\pi^{nh}_{t+1}}{p^{nh}_{t+1}} w_th_tN_t + (1+r^{dh}_{t-1})D^h_t$$

$$+ \pi^{fh}_tSf^h_t + (\pi^{nh}_t+p^{nh}_t)Sn^h_t - D^{hd}_{t+1} - (Cu^{hd}_{t+1}-Cu^h_t)$$

$$- p^{fh}_t(Sf^{hd}_{t+1}-Sf^h_t) - Tx_t - r^{\ell}_{t-1}L_t - p^c_tc^{hd}_t \quad (13.46)$$

$$- e^h_tp^{*h}_tim^{*hd}_t - e^h_{t+1}p^{*h}_{t+1}im^{*hd}_{t+1}])$$

$$+ U_6(h^*N - hN^s_{t+1},\ K^{hd}_{t+1}) + U_7(Cu^{hd}_{t+1}/p^{ch}_{t+1})$$

$$+ U_8(D^{hd}_{t+1}/p^{ch}_{t+1})$$

$$+ U_9((\pi^{fh}_{t+1}Sf^{hd}_{t+1} + (1+r^{dh}_t)D^{hd}_{t+1} + Cu^{hd}_{t+1})/p^{ch}_{t+1})$$

$$+ U_{10}(Cu^{hd}_{t+1} + (1+r^{hd}_{t})D^{hd}_{t+1}/p^{ch}_{t+1}) + U_{11}(g_t) + U_{12}(g_{t+1})$$

$$+ U_{13}(im^{*hd}{}_t) + U_{14}(im^{*hd}_{t+1})$$

Expression (13.46) depicts present utility at time t as a strictly concave function of c^{hd}_t, N^s_{t+1}, Sf^{hd}_{t+1}, Cu^{hd}_{t+1}, D^{hd}_{t+1}, K^{hd}_{t+1}, g_{t+1}, im^{*hd}_t and im^{*hd}_{t+1}. The first-order necessary conditions associated with the first seven of these nine choice variables correspond exactly with conditions (8.16)-(8.20), (8.22) and (8.23) respectively. These first-order conditions were discussed in detail in Chapter 8; that discussion will not be repeated here. The first-order conditions associated with im^{*hd}_t and im^{*hd}_{t+1} are found by partially differentiating (13.46) with respect to each of those variables. The results are presented in (13.47) and (13.48) respectively.

$$\frac{U'_{13}}{U'_5} = \frac{\pi^{nh}_{t+1}}{p^{ch}_{t+1}p^{nh}_{t+1}}(e^h_t p^{*h}_t) \tag{13.47}$$

$$\frac{U'_{14}}{U'_5} = \frac{e^h_{t+1}p^{*h}_{t+1}}{p^{ch}_{t+1}} \tag{13.48}$$

According to condition (13.47), the household sector will continue to import goods during the current period up to the point at which the subjective rate of substitution between current imports and future domestic consumption goods just equals the market rate of substitution between them. The product $(\pi^{nh}_{t+1}/p^{ch}_{t+1}p^{nh}_{t+1})e^h_t p^{*h}_t$ denotes the number of domestic consumption goods that the household sector anticipates it could buy next period if it were to purchase one less unit of imported goods this period, place the funds so released into equity shares and use next period's total return form those shares to buy domestic consumption goods. Condition (13.48) stipulates that the household sector will plan at time to to continue to import goods next period up to the point at which the subjective rate of substitution between next period's imports and next period's domestic consumption goods equals the market rate of substitution between them. The term $e^h_{t+1}p^{*h}_{t+1}/p^{ch}_{t+1}$ represents the number of consumption goods the household sector anticipates it could purchase next period if it were to reduce its imports of foreign-produced goods by one unit that period.

Assuming that the goods it imports from the foreign sector are viewed as normal goods by the domestic household sector, its current demand for imports will vary directly with current disposalbe income as well as with its initial holdings of equity shares, currency, checkable deposits and physical capital. But its demand for current imports will vary inversely with initial household debt outstanding. Ceteris paribus, an increase in the current-period exchange rate, e^h_t, anticipated by the household sector or in the current (foreign currency) price of foreign goods, p^{*h}_t, reduces the household sector's demand for imports, but an increase in next period's domestic money wage raises that demand. In addition the exchange rate and the current (foreign currency) price of foreign goods also affects the household sector's demand for domestic consumption goods, its financial and real asset demands, its demand for loans, its supply of labor and its demand for government-produced goods. The general forms of these functions are presented below as equations (13.49) - (13.58):

$$c^{hd}_t = c^h_t(\underset{+}{Y^d_t}, \underset{+}{Sn^h_t}, \underset{+}{Sf^h_t}, \underset{+}{Cu^h_t}, \underset{+}{D^h_t}, \underset{+}{K^h_t}, \underset{-}{L_t}, \underset{-}{p^{ch}_t}, p^{fh}_t, p^{nh}_t,$$

$$p^{kh}_t, p^{*h}_t, e^h_t, r^{\ell h}_t, r^{dh}_t, w_{t+1}, k) \qquad (13.49)$$

$$Sf^{hd}_{t+1} = Sf^h_{t+1}(\underset{+}{Y^d_t}, \underset{+}{Sn^h_t}, \underset{+}{Sf^h_t}, \underset{+}{Cu^h_t}, \underset{+}{D^h_t}, \underset{+}{K^h_t}, \underset{-}{L_t}, p^{ch}_t, \underset{-}{p^{fh}_t},$$

$$p^{nh}_t, p^{kh}_t, e^h_t, r^{\ell h}_t, r^{dh}_t, w_{t+1}, k) \qquad (13.50)$$

$$Sn^{hd}_{t+1} = Sn^h_{t+1}(\underset{+}{Y^d_t}, \underset{+}{Sn^h_t}, \underset{+}{Sf^h_t}, \underset{+}{Cu^h_t}, \underset{+}{D^h_t}, \underset{+}{K^h_t}, \underset{-}{L_t}, p^{ch}_t, p^{fh}_t,$$

$$\underset{-}{p^{nh}_t}, p^{kh}_t, p^{*h}_t, e^h_t, r^{\ell h}_t, r^{dh}_t, w_{t+1}, k) \qquad (13.51)$$

$$Cu^{hd}_{t+1} = Cu^h_{t+1}(\underset{+}{Y^d_t}, \underset{+}{Sn^h_t}, \underset{+}{Sf^h_t}, \underset{+}{Cu^h_t}, \underset{+}{D^h_t}, \underset{+}{K^h_t}, \underset{-}{L_t}, p^{ch}_t, p^{fh}_t,$$

$$p^{nh}_t, p^{kh}_t, p^{*h}_t, e^h_t, \underset{-}{r^{\ell h}_t}, \underset{+}{w_{t+1}}, k) \qquad (13.52)$$

$$D^{hd}_{t+1} = D^{h}_{t+1}(\underset{+}{Y^{d}_{t}}, \underset{+}{Sn^{h}_{t}}, \underset{+}{Sf^{h}_{t}}, \underset{+}{Cu^{h}_{t}}, \underset{+}{D^{h}_{t}}, \underset{+}{K^{h}_{t}}, \underset{-}{L_{t}}, p^{ch}_{t}, p^{fh}_{t},$$

$$p^{nh}_{t}, p^{kh}_{t}, p^{*h}_{t}, e^{h}_{t}, r^{\ell h}_{t}, \underset{+}{r^{dh}_{t}}, \underset{+}{w_{t+1}}, k) \qquad (13.53)$$

$$K^{hd}_{t+1} = K^{h}_{t+1}(\underset{+}{Y^{d}_{t}}, \underset{+}{Sn^{h}_{t}}, \underset{+}{Sf^{h}_{t}}, \underset{+}{Cu^{h}_{t}}, \underset{+}{D^{h}_{t}}, \underset{+}{K^{h}_{t}}, \underset{-}{L_{t}}, p^{ch}_{t}, p^{fh}_{t},$$

$$p^{nh}_{t}, p^{kh}_{t}, \underset{-}{p^{*h}_{t}}, e^{h}_{t}, r^{\ell h}_{t}, r^{dh}_{t}, w_{t+1}, k) \qquad (13.54)$$

$$L^{hd}_{t+1} = L^{h}_{t+1}(\underset{+}{Y^{d}_{t}}, \underset{+}{Sn^{h}_{t}}, \underset{+}{Sf^{h}_{t}}, \underset{+}{Cu^{h}_{t}}, \underset{+}{D^{h}_{t}}, \underset{+}{K^{h}_{t}}, \underset{-}{L_{t}}, p^{ch}_{t}, p^{fh}_{t},$$

$$p^{nh}_{t}, p^{kh}_{t}, p^{*h}_{t}, \underset{-}{e^{h}_{t}}, r^{\ell h}_{t}, r^{dh}_{t}, \underset{+}{w_{t+1}}, k) \qquad (13.55)$$

$$N^{s}_{t+1} = N^{s}_{t+1}(\underset{-}{Y^{d}_{t}}, \underset{-}{Sn^{h}_{t}}, \underset{-}{Sf^{h}_{t}}, \underset{-}{Cu^{h}_{t}}, \underset{-}{D^{h}_{t}}, \underset{-}{K^{h}_{t}}, \underset{+}{L_{t}}, p^{ch}_{t}, p^{fh}_{t},$$

$$p^{nh}_{t}, p^{kh}_{t}, p^{*h}_{t}, e^{h}_{t}, r^{\ell}_{ht}, \underset{+}{r^{dh}_{t}}, w_{t+1}, k) \qquad (13.56)$$

$$g_{t+1} = g_{t+1}(\underset{+}{Y^{d}_{t}}, \underset{+}{Sn^{h}_{t}}, \underset{+}{Sf^{h}_{t}}, \underset{+}{Cu^{h}_{t}}, \underset{+}{D^{h}_{t}}, \underset{+}{K^{h}_{t}}, \underset{-}{L_{t}}, p^{ch}_{t}, p^{fh}_{t},$$

$$p^{nh}_{t}, p^{kh}_{t}, p^{*h}_{t}, e^{h}_{t}, r^{\ell h}_{t}, \underset{+}{r^{dh}_{t}}, w_{t+1}, k) \qquad (13.57)$$

$$im^{*hd}_{t} = im^{*h}_{t}(\underset{+}{Y^{d}_{t}}, \underset{+}{Sn^{h}_{t}}, \underset{+}{Sf^{h}_{t}}, \underset{+}{Cu^{h}_{t}}, \underset{+}{D^{h}_{t}}, \underset{+}{K^{h}_{t}}, \underset{-}{L_{t}}, p^{ch}_{t}, p^{fh}_{t},$$

$$p^{nh}_{t}, \underset{-}{p^{kh}_{t}}, p^{*h}_{t}, e^{h}_{t}, \underset{+}{r^{\ell h}_{t}}, r^{dh}_{t}, w_{t+1}, k) \qquad (13.58)$$

The Nonfinancial Business Sector

This section extends the analysis of Chapter 9 by allowing the private nonfinancial business sector to also sell physical capital to the foreign sector and purchase a foreign-produced good which it uses as an input in its own production. In order to conserve the real resources involved in purchasing the intermediate good from the foreign sector, the private nonfinancial business sector also holds some foreign money in the form of checkable deposits at foreign depository institutions.

In light of these adjustments, the domestic nonfinancial business sector's balance sheet at time t includes four assets, rather than the three discussed in Chapter 9. Let $p^c_t Q_t$ denote its inventory of consumption goods at time t, let $p^k_t K^n_t$ depict the value of its stock of physical capital, let D^n_t denote the value of its holdings of checkable deposits at domestic depository institutions and let $e^n_t D^{*n}_t$ show the value (in terms of the domestic unit of account) of its holdings of checkable deposits at foreign depository institutions, where e^n_t denotes the exchange rate that the domestic nonfinancial business sector anticipates will prevail during the current period and where D^{*n}_t represents the stock of foreign money it holds at time t.

Since the domestic nonfinancial business sector receives interest income in the current period from the foreign checkable deposits it holds at time t, its current-period receipts must reflect that income. Therefore, its current-period receipts are given by $R^e\{.\} + r^d_{t-1}D^n_t + r^{*d}_{t-1}e^n_t D^{*n}_t$, where, as in Chapter 9, $R^e\{.\}$ denotes anticipated current-period sales revenue, $r^d_{t-1}D^n_t$ depicts current period interest income from domestic checkable deposits, and $r^{*d}_{t-1}e^n_t D^{*n}_t$ denotes current-period interest income from foreign checkable deposits with r^{*d}_{t-1} representing the interest rate which the foreign depository institutions announced last period that they would pay during the current period on deposits held by their customers at time t.

The current-period expenses of the domestic nonfinancial business sector now include not only its current wage bill, $w_t h^n_t N^n_t$, but also its current purchases of foreign-produced intermediate goods, $e^n_t p^{*n}_t im^{*nd}_t$, where p^{*n}_t denotes the price of foreign-produced goods (expressed in terms of the foreign unit of account) which the domestic business sector anticipates at time t will prevail during the current period and where im^{*nd}_t represents the number of foreign-produced goods which the sector plans to buy during the period. Since the sector presumably holds no beginning-of-period inventory of foreign-produced goods and plans a zero inventory of those goods for the end of the period, its current ex ante inventment coreresponds to that shown in Chapter 9. Current net income equals the anticipated value of current production, $R^e\{.\} + p^k_t(K^{nd}_{t+1} - K^n_t) - p^c_tQ_t$, plus current period interest income, $r^d_{t-1}D^n_t + e^n_tr^{*d}_{t-1}D^*_{nt}$, minus current expenses, $w_th^n_tN^n_t + e^n_tp^{*n}_tim^{*nd}_t$. Since corporate taxes equal zero in this model, $R^e\{.\} + p^k_t(K^{nd}_{t+1} - K^n_t) - p^c_tQ_t + r^d_{t-1}D^n_t + e^n_tr^{*d}_{t-1}D^{*n}_t - w_th^n_tN^n_t - e^n_tp^{*n}_tim^{*nd}_t$ also represents current income after taxes.

Since current-period ex ante saving, s^n_t, equals anticipated current net income after taxes minus dividends, where the latter is denoted by $\pi^n_tS^n_t$, we have:

$$s^n_t = R^e\{.\} + p^k_t(K^{nd}_{t+1} - K^n_t) - p^c_tQ_t + r^d_{t-1}D^n_t + e^n_tr^{*d}_{t-1}D^{*n}_t - w_th^n_tN^n_t - e^n_tp^{*n}_tim^{*nd}_t - \pi^n_tS^n_t. \tag{13.59}$$

The amount of domestic money which the business sector plans to accumulate during the current period, $D^{nd}_{t+1} - D^n_t$, necessarily equals the amount it plans to save on the current account, s^n_t, plus the value of its planned sales of equity shares, $p^n_t(Sn^e_{t+1} - Sn_t)$, minus the value of its planned physical investment, $p^k_t(K^{nd}_{t+1} - K^n_t) - p^c_tQ_t$, and minus the (domestic-money) value of its planned accumulation of foreign money, $e^n_t(D^{*nd}_{t+1} - D^{*n}_t)$. Therefore:

$$\begin{aligned} D^{nd}_{t+1} - D^n_t = {} & R^e\{.\} + r^d_{t-1}D^n_t + e^n_tr^{*d}_{t-1}D^{*n}_t - w_th^n_tN^n_t \\ & - e^n_tp^{*n}_tim^{*nd}_t - \pi^n_tSn_t + p^n_t(Sn^e_{t+1} - Sn_t) \\ & - e^n_t(D^{*nd}_{t+1} - D^{*n}_t) \end{aligned} \tag{13.60}$$

Rearranging terms yields the following expression for current-period dividends:

$$\begin{aligned} \pi^n_t = {} & [R^e\{.\} + r^d_{t-1}D^n_t + e^n_tr^{*d}_{t-1}D^{*n}_t - w_th^n_tN^n_t - e^n_tp^{*n}_tim^{*nd}_t \\ & + p^n_t(Sn^e_{t+1} - Sn_t)]/Sn_t - e^n_t(D^{*nd}_{t+1} - D^{*n}_t) - (D^{nd}_{t+1} - D^n_t))/Sn_t \end{aligned} \tag{13.61}$$

In a manner consistent with the notation used in Chapter 9, let $R^{e*}\{.\} - p^{kn}_{t+1}K^{nd}_{t+1}$ represent the anticipated value of next period's production, let $r^{dn}{}_t D^{nd}{}_{t+1}$ represent anticipated interest income next period from domestic checkable deposits, let $e^n{}_{t+1} r^{*d}{}_t D^{*nd}{}_{t+1}$ represent next period's anticipated interest income (in domestic money) from foreign checkable deposits, let $w_{t+1} hN^{nd}{}_{t+1}$ denote the sector's anticipated wage bill next period, let $e^n{}_{t+1} p^{*n}{}_{t+1} im^{*nd}{}_{t+1}$ represent its planned purchases (in domestic currency) next period of foreign-produced goods, and let $\pi^n{}_{t+1} Sn^e{}_{t+1}$ denote next period's anticipated dividends. Then at time t, next period's ex ante saving, $s^n{}_{t+1}$, is denoted by

$$s^n{}_{t+1} = R^{e*}\{.\} - p^{kn}{}_{t+1} K^{nd}{}_{t+1} + r^{dn}{}_t D^{nd}{}_{t+1} + e^n{}_{t+1} r^{*dn}{}_t D^{*nd}{}_{t+1}$$

$$- w_{t+1} hN^{nd}{}_{t+1} - e^n{}_{t+1} p^{*n}{}_{t+1} im^{*nd}{}_{t+1} - \pi^n{}_{t+1} Sn^e{}_{t+1}. \quad (13.62)$$

Also, the amount of domestic money the domestic nonfinancial business sector plans to accumulate next period, $- D^{nd}{}_{t+1}$, must equal next period's ex ante saving, $s^n{}_{t+1}$, minus the value of its planned physical investment that period, $- p^{kn}{}_{t+1} K^{nd}{}_{t+1}$, and minus the (domestic money) value of its planned accumulation of foreign money, $- e^n{}_{t+1} D^{*nd}{}_{t+1}$:

$$- D^{nd}{}_{t+1} = R^{e*}\{.\} + r^{dn}{}_t D^{nd}{}_{t+1} + e^n{}_{t+1} r^{*dn}{}_t D^{*nd}{}_{t+1} - w_{t+1} hN^{nd}{}_{t+1}$$

$$- e^n{}_{t+1} p^{*n}{}_{t+1} im^{*nd}{}_{t+1} - \pi^n{}_{t+1} Sn^e{}_{t+1} + e^n{}_{t+1} D^{*nd}{}_{t+1} \quad (13.63)$$

Rearranging terms in (13.63) yields the following expression for next period's dividends per share:

$$\pi^n{}_{t+1} = \frac{R^{e*}\{.\} + (1+r^{dn}{}_t) D^{nd}{}_{t+1} + e^n{}_{t+1}(1+r^{*dn}{}_t) D^{*dn}{}_t - w_{t+1} hN^{nd}{}_{t+1}}{Sn^e{}_{t+1}}$$

$$+ \frac{-e^n{}_{t+1} p^{*n}{}_{t+1} im^{*nd}{}_{t+1}}{Sn^e{}_{t+1}} \quad (13.64)$$

The nonfinancial business sector's objective at time t is to maximize its present value, $\pi^n{}_t + \pi^n{}_{t+1}/(1 + r^{fn}{}_t)$. Before we can consider this problem in detail, we must first reformulate the sector's anticipated sales-revenue functions, $R^e\{.\}$ and $R^{e*}\{.\}$, in light of its dealings with the rest-of-the-world.

Let (13.65) represent the nonfinancial business sector's estimate at time t of the market demand (the sum of the household and government sectors' demands) for current consumption goods and let (13.66) denote the nonfinancial business sector sector's estimate at time t of the total (stock) demand for physical capital for time t+1 by the household, government and foreign sectors:

$$c^{de}_t = c^{de}_t(p^c_t, k^c) \tag{13.65}$$

$$K^{de}_t = K^{de}_t(p^k_t, k^k) \tag{13.66}$$

where k^c and k^k represent vectors of variables besides the own-price that are estimated to affect these market demands. Presumably in both (13.65) and (13.66) the estimated demand is inversely related to its own price. Subtracting the sum of the existing stocks of physical capital held by the households, K^h_t, the government, K^g_t, and the foreign sector, K^*_t, at the beginning of the current period from (13.66) yields the nonfinancial business sector's estimate of its current-period sales of physical capital:

$$i^{de}_t = i^{de}_t(p^k_t, k^i) = K^{de}_t(p^k_t, k^k) - (K^h_t + K^g_t + K^*_t) \tag{13.67}$$

Since the partial of (13.65) with respect to p^c_t is presumably nonzero, as is the partial of (13.67) with respect to p^k_t, these two expressions may be solved (jointly, if necessary) for p^c_t and p^k_t as functions of the other variables in those respective expressions:

$$p^c_t = p^c_t(c^{de}_t, \ldots) \text{ and } p^k_t = p^k_t(i^{de}_t, \ldots) \tag{13.68}$$

Then, since anticipated current revenue is defined as

$$R^e = p^c_t \cdot c^{de}_t + p^k_t \cdot i^{de}_t, \tag{13.69}$$

substitution of (13.68) for p^c_t and p^k_t in (13.69) yields an expression for current revenue in terms of anticipated current sales of consumption goods, anticipated current sales of capital goods and various shift parameters, k_r:

$$R^e = R^e(c^{de}_t, i^{de}_t, k_r) \tag{13.70}$$

Turn next to the production activity of the nonfinancial business sector. This sector essentially requires the services of the labor it has hired by the beginning of the period, the stock of capital it has in place by the beginning of that period and the goods it imports from the foreign sector in the current period in order to produce consumption and capital goods during the current period. However, as in Chapter 9, assume that the nonfinancial business sector requires labor services during the current period for producing commodities, for undertaking transactions involving purchases of labor and foreign-produced goods, and for engaging in search activities.

Let the nonfinancial business sector's current transactions time be represented as the sum of two strictly convex functions: the first pertaining to transations associated with purchasing the services of domestic labor and the second associated with importing goods from the foreign sector.

$$\tau = \hat{\tau}(h^n_t N^n_t,\ D^n_t,\ w_t) + \tau^*(im^{*nd}_t,\ D^{*n}_t,\ p^{*n}_t) \qquad (13.71)$$

where $\hat{\tau}_1, \hat{\tau}_3 > 0$; $\hat{\tau}_2 < 0$; $\hat{\tau}_{ii} > 0$, $i = 1,2,3$; $\hat{\tau}_{12} < 0$; $\hat{\tau}_{23} < 0$; $\hat{\tau}_{13} > 0$ and where $\tau^*_1, \tau^*_3 > 0$; $\tau^*_2 < 0$; $\tau^*_{ii} > 0$, $i = 1,2,3$; $\tau^*_{12} < 0$; $\tau^*_{23} < 0$; $\tau^*_{13} > 0$. Also, let the nonfinancial business sector's anticipated current-period search time, α, for employees for next period be a positive, decreasing, convex function of (a) the number of people it estimates will be available during the current period for work next period after deducting the sum of its estimates of the government and private financial sectors' demands for those workers and (b) the number of people it wants to employ in its own sector by the beginning of next period:

$$\alpha = \alpha(N^{se}_{t+1}(w_{t+1}),\ N^{nd}_{t+1}) \qquad (13.72)$$

with $\alpha(.)$, $N^{se}_{t+1}(.)$ and N^{nd}_{t+1} discussed in more detail in Chapter 9. Then the net number of labor hours available to the nonfinancial business sector during the current period is anticipated at time t as the amount $h^n_t N^n_t - \hat{\tau}(.) - \tau^*(.) - \alpha(.)$.

Let the current-period production functions for consumption goods and capital goods be denoted by (13.73) and (13.74) respectively:

$$c_t = c^+(v^c_1,\ v^c_k,\ v^c_m) \qquad (13.73)$$

$$i_t = i^+(v^i_1, v^i_k, v^i_m) \tag{13.74}$$

where $c^+(.)$ and $i^+(.)$ are both positive, increasing strictly concave functions and where

$$v^c_1 + v^i_1 = h^n_t N^n_t - \hat{\tau}(.) - \tau^*(.) - \alpha(.) \tag{13.75}$$

$$v^c_k + v^i_k = K^n_t \tag{13.75}$$

$$v^c_m + v^i_m = im^{*nd}_t . \tag{13.75}$$

Solve (13.75) - (13.77), respectively, for v^i_l, v^i_k and v^i_m and substitute these values into (13.74). Then maximize (13.73) with respect to v^c_l, v^c_k and v^c_m subject to the new (13.74). The choice variables v^c_1, v^c_k and v^c_m emerge as functions of i_t, $h^n_t N^n_t$, K^n_t, im^{*nd}_{t+1}, D^n_t, D^{*n}_t, w_t, p^{*n}_t, N^{nd}_{t+1} and w_{t+1}. Substitution of the solution values for v^c_1, v^c_k and v^c_m, expressed in terms of these ten parameters, back into (13.73) then yields the maximum number of consumption goods that can be produced during the current period for given values of each of these ten parameters:

$$c_t = q(\underset{-}{i_t}, \underset{+}{h^n_t N^n_t}, \underset{+}{K^n_t}, \underset{+}{im^{*nd}_t}, \underset{+}{D^n_t}, \underset{+}{D^{*n}_t}, \underset{-}{w_t}, \underset{-}{p^{*n}_t}, \underset{-}{N^{nd}_{t+1}}, \underset{+}{w_{t+1}}) \tag{13.78}$$

This function is similar to expression (9.20), except that now (a) foreign-goods, im^{*nd}_t, are added as an input, (b) beginning balances of foreign exchange, D^{*n}_t, conserve transactions time, allowing for greater production of c_t, and (c) the higher the foreign-exchange price of foreign goods, the smaller the productivity of foreign money balances. Assume q(.) is a positive strictly concave function. To simplify the analysis, suppose that all cross-partials in q(.) equal zero.

As in Chapter 9, it must be true that

$$c^{de}_t = q(.) + Q_t \tag{13.79}$$

$$i^{de}_t = i_t - (K^{nd}_{t+1} - K^n_t) \tag{13.80}$$

Substituting the right hand sides of (13.79) and (13.80) into (13.70) yields the following following expression for the nonfinancial business sector's anticipated current revenue at time t:

$$R^e = R^e\{q(.) + Q_t, i_t - (K^{nd}_{t+1} - K^n_t), k_r\} \tag{13.81}$$

In the analysis which follows, the right hand side of (13.81) is substituted for $R^e\{.\}$ in (13.61).

In a similar fashion, the private nonfinancial business sector must also estimate at time t the revenue it anticipates receiving next period, $R^{e*}\{.\}$. Let (13.82) denote the sector's estimate at time t of next period's market demand for consumption goods and let (13.83) depict its estimate of next period's sales of capital goods:

$$c^{de}_{t+1} = c^{de}_{t+1}(p^c_{t+1}, \alpha^c) \tag{13.82}$$

$$i^{de}_{t+1} = i^{de}_{t+1}(p^k_{t+1}, \alpha^k) \tag{13.83}$$

where the own-price partials are assumed to be negative. Solving these two expressions for p^c_{t+1} and p^k_{t+1} and substituting into the definition of next period's anticipated revenue, $R^{e*}\{.\} = p^c_{t+1}c^{de}_{t+1} + p^k_{t+1}i^{de}_{t+1}$, yields an expression for next period's anticipated revenue in terms of the prices that the nonfinancial business sector anticipates at time t that it will announce next period:

$$R^{e*} = R^{e*}\{c^{de}_{t+1}, i^{de}_{t+1}, \alpha^c, \alpha^k\}. \tag{13.84}$$

As in the current period, the nonfinancial business sector will require the services of labor, physical capital and imported goods next period in order to produce consumption and capital goods. However, unlike the current period, it will need labor services only for transactions. Since at time t it does not plan beyond time t+2, the sector does not plan to search for workers next period who would begin working a time t+2.

Let next period's anticipated transactions time consist of the sum of transactions time associated with purchasing labor hours next period and with transactions time associated with purchasing foreign-produced goods, im^{*nd}_{t+1}, next period:

$$\tau^+ = \tau^-(hN^{nd}_{t+1}, D^n_{t+1}, w_{t+1}) + \tilde{\tau}(im^{*nd}_{t+1}, D^{*nd}_{t+1}, p^{*n}_{t+1}) \tag{13.85}$$

where $\tau^{-}(.)$ has the same properties as $\hat{\tau}(.)$ and where $\tilde{\tau}(.)$ has the same properties as $\tau^{*}(.)$ in (13.71). Then the anticipated net number of labor hours available to the nonfinancial business sector next period is given by $hN^{nd}_{t+1} - \tau^{-}(.) - \tilde{\tau}(.)$.

Assume that next period's production functions for consumption goods and capital goods are given by (13.86) and (13.87) respectively:

$$c_{t+1} = c(\hat{v}^{c}_{1}, \hat{v}^{c}_{k}, \hat{v}^{c}_{m}) \tag{13.86}$$

$$i_{t+1} = i(\hat{v}^{i}_{1}, \hat{v}^{i}_{k}, \hat{v}^{i}_{m}) \tag{13.87}$$

where $\hat{c}(.)$ and $\hat{i}(.)$ are both positive, increasing, strictly-concave functions with:

$$\hat{v}^{c}_{1} + \hat{v}^{i}_{1} = hN^{nd}_{t+1} - \tau^{-}(.) - \hat{\tau}(.) \tag{13.88}$$

$$\hat{v}^{c}_{k} + \hat{v}^{i}_{k} = K^{nd}_{t+1} \tag{13.89}$$

$$\hat{v}^{c}_{m} + \hat{v}^{i}_{m} = im^{*nd}_{t+1} \tag{13.90}$$

Solve (13.88) - (13.90), respectively, for $\hat{v}^{i}_{1}$, $\hat{v}^{i}_{k}$, and $\hat{v}^{i}_{m}$ and substitute the resulting expressions into (13.87). Next, maximize (13.86) with respect to $\hat{v}^{c}_{1}$, $\hat{v}^{c}_{k}$ and $\hat{v}^{c}_{m}$ subject to the new (13.87). The choice variables emerge as functions of i_{t+1}, N^{nd}_{t+1}, K^{nd}_{t+1}, im^{*nd}_{t+1}, D^{nd}_{t+1}, D^{*nd}_{t+1}, w_{t+1} and p^{*n}_{t+1}. Substituting the solutions for $\hat{v}^{c}_{1}$, $\hat{v}^{c}_{k}$ and $\hat{v}^{c}_{m}$ into (13.86) yields an expression showing the maximum number of consumption goods that the nonfinancial business sector anticipates it will be able to produce next period for given values of the eight parameters just mentioned:

$$c_{t+1} = \hat{q}(\underset{-}{i_{t+1}}, \underset{+}{N^{nd}_{t+1}}, \underset{+}{K^{nd}_{t+1}}, \underset{+}{im^{*nd}_{t+1}}, \underset{+}{D^{nd}_{t+1}}, \underset{-}{D^{*nd}_{t+1}}, \underset{-}{w_{t+1}}, \underset{-}{p^{*n}_{t+1}}) \tag{13.91}$$

This function conforms to expression (9.34), except that it (a) also includes foreign goods as an input, (b) recognizes the productivity of foreign money balances in conserving real resources, and (c) recognizes the effect of a change in the foreign currency price of foreign-produced goods upon the productivity of its foreign money balances. Presumably $\hat{q}(.)$ is positive and strictly concave with all cross-partials set equal to zero, for convenience.

Since the sector plans at time t to hold no inventory of consumption goods at either time t+1 or time t+2, its planned sales of consumption goods next period must equal its planned production of those goods. Furthermore, the sector's planned sales of capital goods next period presumably exceeds its planned production of those goods by the amount of its planned beginning of period inventory of those goods next period. Consequently, we have:

$$c^{de}_{t+1} = \hat{q}(.) \tag{13.92}$$

$$i^{de}_{t+1} = i_{t+1} + K^{nd}_{t+1} \tag{13.93}$$

Substituting (13.92) and (13.93) for c^{de}_{t+1} and i^{de}_{t+1} respectively in (13.84) yields the following expression for next period's anticipated revenue at time t:

$$R^{e*}\{.\} = R^{e*}\{\hat{q}(.),\ i_{t+1} + K^{nd}_{t+1}, \alpha^{c}, \alpha^{k}\} \tag{13.94}$$

where $\hat{q}(.)$ is given by the right hand side of (13.91).

As already mentioned, the objective of the nonfinancial business sector at time t is to maximize its present value, $\pi^{n}_{t} + \pi^{n}_{t+1}/(1+r^{fn}_{t})$, where π^{n}_{t} and π^{n}_{t+1} are defined in (13.61) and (13.64) respectively. Substituting (13.81) for $R^{e}\{.\}$ in (13.61), substituting (13.94) for $R^{e*}\{.\}$ in (13.64), and substituting (9.38) for Sn^{e}_{t+1} (the sector's estimate of the household sector's demand for nonfinancial sector equity for time t+1) in (13.64) produces the following expression for the nonfinancial business sector's objective function at time t.

Maximize

$$\begin{aligned} p^{o}_{n} = [R^{e}\{ & q(i_{t}, h^{n}_{t}N^{n}_{t}, K^{n}_{t}, im*^{nd}_{t}, D^{n}_{t}, D*^{n}_{t}, w_{t}, p*^{n}_{t}, N^{nd}_{t+1}, w_{t+1}) \\ & + Q_{t}, i_{t} - (K^{nd}_{t+1} - K^{n}_{t}), k^{r}\} + r^{d}_{t-1}D^{n}_{t} + e^{n}_{t}r*^{d}_{t-1}D*^{n}_{t} \\ & - w_{t}h^{n}_{t}N^{n}_{t} - e^{n}_{t}p*^{n}_{t}im*^{nd}_{t} + p^{n}_{t}(Sn^{e}_{t+1} - Sn_{t}) \end{aligned}$$

$$- e^n_t(D^{*n}_{t+1} - D^{*n}_t) - (D^n_{t+1} - D^n_t)]/Sn_t \qquad (13.95)$$

$$+ [R^{e*}\{\hat{q}(i_{t+1}, N^{nd}_{t+1}, K^{nd}_{t+1}, D^{nd}_{t+1}, D^{*nd}_{t+1}, w_{t+1}, p^{*n}_{t+1}),$$

$$i_{t+1} + K^{nd}_{t+1}, \alpha^c, \alpha^k\} + (1+r^{dn}_t)D^{nd}_{t+1} + e^n_{t+1}(1+r^{*d}_t)D^{*nd}_{t+1}$$

$$- w_{t+1}hN^{nd}_{t+1} - e^n_{t+1}p^{*n}_{t+1}im^{*n}_{t+1}]/(1+r^{fn}_t)Sn^e_{t+1}(.).$$

with respect to h^n_t, i_t, im^{*nd}_t, w_{t+1}, N^{nd}_{t+1}, i_{t+1}, im^{*nd}_{t+1}", K^{nd}_{t+1}, D^{nd}_{t+1}, D^{*nd}_{t+1} and p^n_t. The optimal level of current production of c_t is then found by substituting the solution to (13.95) into (13.78). The optimal levels of desired sales c^{de}_t and i^{de}_t are then obtained from (13.79) and (13.80) respectively. These values, in turn, may then be substituted into (13.68) to obtain the commodity prices that the nonfinancial sector feels at time t are optimal for the current period. The nonfinancial business sector presumably announces these prices at the beginning of the current period. The optimal (ex ante) level of current-period dividends is found by substituting the solution to (13.95) into (13.61). The sector announces these dividend payments at the beginning of the period.

Partially differentiating (13.95) with respect to each of the eleven choice variables h^n_t, i_t, im^{*nd}_t, w_{t+1}, N^{nd}_{t+1}, i_{t+1}, im^{*nd}_{t+1}, K^{nd}_{t+1}, D^{nd}_{t+1}, D^{*nd}_{t+1} and p^n_t yields an equal number of first-order necessary conditions. The conditions associated with h^n_t, i_t, w_{t+1}, N^{nd}_{t+1}, i_{t+1}, K^{nd}_{t+1} and D^{nd}_{t+1} correspond exactly with conditions (9.39) - (9.45), repeated here for convenience as expressions (13.96) - (13.102):

$$\frac{R^e_1 q_2 N^n_t - w_t N^n_t}{Sn_t} = 0 \qquad (13.96)$$

$$\frac{R^e_1 q_1 + R^e_2}{Sn_t} = 0 \qquad (13.97)$$

$$\frac{R^e_1 q_{10}}{Sn_t} + \frac{R^{e*}_1 \hat{q}7 - hN^{nd}_{t+1}}{(1+r^{fn}_t)Sn^e_{t+1}} = 0 \qquad (13.98)$$

$$\frac{R^{e}{}_{1}q_{9}}{Sn_{t}} + \frac{R^{e*}{}_{1}\hat{q}_{2} - w_{t+1}h}{(1+r^{fn}{}_{t})Sn^{e}{}_{t+1}} = 0 \tag{13.99}$$

$$\frac{R^{e*}{}_{1}\hat{q}_{1} + R^{e*}{}_{2}}{(1+r^{fn}{}_{t})Sn^{e}{}_{t+1}} = 0 \tag{13.100}$$

$$\frac{-R^{e}{}_{2}}{Sn_{t}} + \frac{R^{e*}{}_{1}\hat{q}_{3} + R^{e*}{}_{2}}{(1+r^{fn}{}_{t})Sn^{e}{}_{t+1}} = 0 \tag{13.101}$$

$$\frac{-1}{Sn_{t}} + \frac{R^{e*}{}_{1}\hat{q}_{5} + (1+r^{dn}{}_{t})}{(1+r^{fn}{}_{t})Sn^{e}{}_{t+1}} = 0 \tag{13.102}$$

The first-order partial derivative of (13.95) with respect to $p^{n}{}_{t}$ is also very similar to condition (9.46). The only difference is that next period's anticipated dividends now also depend upon the sector's anticipated (explicit and implicit) income from foreign deposits and upon the productivity and expense associated with next period's imports of foreign-produced goods. Therefore the first-order condition associated with $p^{n}{}_{t}$ now appears as:

$$\frac{(Sn^{e}{}_{t+1} - Sn_{t}) + p^{n}{}_{t}(Sn^{e}{}_{t+1})_{1}}{Sn_{t}} - \frac{\left[\begin{array}{l} R^{e*}\{.\} + (1+r^{dn}{}_{t})D^{n}{}_{t+1} + e^{n}{}_{t+1}(1+r^{*dn}{}_{t})D^{*n}{}_{t} - w_{t+1}hN^{dn}{}_{t+1} \\ \qquad - e^{n}{}_{t+1}p^{*n}{}_{t+1}im^{*n}{}_{t+1} \cdot (Sn^{e}{}_{t+1})_{1} \end{array}\right](Sn^{e}{}_{t+1})_{1}}{(1+r^{fn}{}_{t})Sn^{e}{}_{t+1}} = 0 \tag{13.103}$$

The last three first-order conditions relate to the above three new decision variables $im^{*nd}{}_{t}$, $im^{*nd}{}_{t+1}$ and $D^{*nd}{}_{t+1}$ respectively. Partially differentiating (13.95) with respect to $im^{*nd}{}_{t}$ yields (13.104):

$$\frac{R^{e}{}_{1}q_{4} - e^{n}{}_{t}p^{*n}{}_{t}}{Sn_{t}} = 0 \tag{13.104}$$

According to this condition, the sector will purchase foreign-produced goods during the current period up to the point at which the value of the marginal product of those goods this period, $R^{e}{}_{1}q_{4}$, equals their marginal cost, in terms of domestic money. Similarly, setting the partial derivative of (13.95) with respect to $im^{*nd}{}_{t+1}$ equal to zero produces (13.105):

$$\frac{R^{e*}{}_{1}\hat{q}_{4} - e^{n}{}_{t+1}p^{*n}{}_{t+1}}{(1 + r^{fn}{}_{t})Sn^{e}{}_{t+1}} = 0 \tag{13.105}$$

The private nonfinancial business sector will plan at time t to purchase foreign-produced goods next period up to the point at which the anticipated value of their marginal product, $R^{e*}{}_{1}\hat{q}_{4}$, equals their anticipated marginal cost, $e^{n}{}_{t+1}p^{*n}{}_{t+1}$. Finally, setting the partial of (13.95) with respect to $D^{*nd}{}_{t+1}$ equal to zero yields (13.106):

$$\frac{-e^{n}{}_{t}}{Sn_{t}} + \frac{R^{e*}{}_{1}\hat{q}_{6} + e^{n}{}_{t+1}(1+r^{*dn}{}_{t})}{(1 + r^{fn}{}_{t})Sn^{e}{}_{t+1}} = 0 \tag{13.106}$$

The first term, $- e^{n}{}_{t}/Sn_{t}$, denotes the reduction in current dividends per share from the accumulation of one more unit of foreign deposits during the current period. The second terms, $[R^{e*}{}_{1}\hat{q}_{6} + e^{n}{}_{t+1}(1+r^{*dn}{}_{t})]/(1+r^{fn}{}_{t})Sn^{e}{}_{t+1}$, represents the present value per share of the anticipated return next period from foreign deposits held by the nonfinancial business sector at time t+1. This anticipated return consists of the value of the extra product the sector can produce next period with the resources released from the task of undertaking transactions because of the additional unit of foreign money balances held at the beginning of that period, $R^{e*}{}_{1}\hat{q}_{6}$, plus the explicit principal and interest, expressed in terms of the domestic unit of account, to be earned next period from that unit of foreign money. The optimizing nonfinancial business sector will accumulate foreign money up to the point at which the present value per share of next period's anticipated marginal return just equals the marginal current dividends per share which the sector sacrifices by accumulating the last unit of foreign deposits during the current period.

Totally differentiating conditions (13.96) - (13.106) yields a simultaneous system of eleven linear equations in the differentials of h^n_t, i_t, w_{t+1}, N^{nd}_{t+1}, i_{t+1}, K^{nd}_{t+1}, D^{nd}_{t+1}, p^n_t, im^{*nd}_t, im^{*nd}_{t+1}, and D^{*nd}_{t+1}. In general, the solution to this system indicates that the values of these variables selected by the optimizing nonfinancial business sector will depend upon the parameters listed in equations (9.47) - (9.54) plus the new parameters associated with the sector's purchases of foreign-produced goods and its acquisition of deposits at foreign depository institutions. In this case the additional parameters in the sector's choice functions at time t include D^{*n}_t, p^{*n}_t, p^{*n}_{t+1}, r^{*dn}_t, e^n_t and e^n_{t+1}. Consequently the general solution to (13.95) will include the following functions:

$$h^n_t = h^n_t(K^n_t, D^n_t, w_t, Q_t, \alpha^c, \alpha^k, r^{dn}_t, r^{fn}_t, Sn_t, Sf_t, c^g_t, N^h_t,$$
$$Tx_t, Cu^h_t, D^h_t, L_t, K^h_t, K^g_t, D^{*n}_t, p^{*n}_t, p^{*n}_{t+1}, r^{*dn}_t, e^n_t, e^n_{t+1}) \quad (13.107)$$

$$i_t = i_t(.) \quad (13.108) \qquad D^{nd}_{t+1} = D^{nd}_{t+1}(.) \quad (13.112)$$

$$w_{t+1} = w_{t+1}(.) \quad (13.109) \qquad D^{*nd}_{t+1} = D^{*nd}_{t+1}(.) \quad (13.113)$$

$$N^{nd}_{t+1} = N^{nd}_{t+1}(.) \quad (13.110) \qquad im^{*nd}_t = im^{*nd}_t(.) \quad (13.114)$$

$$K^{nd}_{t+1} = K^{nd}_{t+1}(.) \quad (13.111) \qquad p^n_t = p^n_t(.) \quad (13.115)$$

where the parameters appearing in functions (13.108) - (13.115) correspond to those appearing in (13.107), but not necessarily with the same signs. Substituting the solution to (13.95) into (13.78) - (13.80) and (13.68) yields (optimal) values of current production of consumption goods, c_t, current estimated real sales of consumption goods, c^{de}_t, current estimated real sales of capital goods, i^{de}_t, the current-period price of consumption goods, p^c_t, and the current period price of capital goods, p^k_t:

$$c_t = c_t(.) \quad (13.116) \qquad p^c_t = p^c_t(.) \quad (13.1119)$$

$$c^{de}_t = c^{de}_t(.) \quad (13.117) \qquad p^k_t = p^k_t(.) \quad (13.120)$$

$i^{de}_t = i^{de}_t(.)$ (13.118)

Assume that the effects of the domestic parameters upon the decision variables h^n_t, i_t, w_{t+1}, N^{nd}_{t+1}, i_{t+1}, K^{nd}_{t+1} and D^{nd}_{t+1} are essentially the same in this open-economy version as in the closed economy version of the nonfinancial business sector presented in Chapter 9. Consequently, only the effects of the foreign parameters on these variables are discussed here. In addition, the present discussion also includes the effects of all parameters - domestic and foreign - upon the sector's new decision variables: im^{*nd}_t, im^{*nd}_{t+1}, and D^{*nd}_{t+1}. Because of the relatively large number of decision variables only the "direct effects" (i.e., only those effects operating through the first-order condition of the variable in question) will be considered explicitly.

Effects of the Foreign Parameters (p^{*nt}, r^{*dn}_t, e^n_t)

An increase in p^{*n}_t or e^n_t raises the marginal cost of the imported factor of production, im^*_t. Ceteris paribus, the nonfinancial business sector will therefore tend to purchase fewer goods from abroad and, by implication, to use relatively more domestic factors in the production of consumption and capital goods. This rise in the price of one of the factors, ceteris paribus, tends to cause the sector to reduce the amount it plans to produce of both types of goods in the current period, which in turn implies that the sector will tend to produce less during the current period and to charge a higher price for its output than it would if p^*_t or e_t had not risen.

But this is not all. For to the extent that domestically produced goods are substitutes for foreign goods, the rise in p^*_t or e_t also causes the nonfinancial business sector to revise upward its estimate of the demand for its own products. In light of this, the sector will plan to produce more of both types of goods instead of less (at higher prices) and to use more of at least the domestic factors of production. The net effect of an increase in p^*_t or e_t may then be to increase current production of both goods, to raise their current market prices, to reduce the quantity of the imported factor and to increase the amount of current labor hours. If the rise in p^*_t or e_t is expected to persist through next period, then the sector will also raise w_{t+1} above the level it would otherwise announce at time t in order to attract additional employees for next period. Finally, from (13.106) it is clear that as e_t rises, it raises the current marginal cost of adding a unit to the sector's end-of-period holdings of foreign checkable deposits. Unless the sector's estimate of next period's exchange rate rises sufficiently, the sector will, ceteris paribus, reduce its demand for foreign checkable deposits as e_t rises. This drop in demand for D^{*n}_{t+1} will be reinforced if the sector plans at time t to import fewer foreign goods next period and if this drop in demand reduces next period's marginal product of foreign checkable deposits held at time t+1.

An increase in the interest rate, r^{*d}_t, that the foreign sector can earn this period (and receive next period) on foreign checkable deposits it holds by time t+1 raises the anticipated return form D^{*n}_{t+1}, thereby increasing the sector's demand for those deposits. In addition, to the extent that the sector plans to hold such deposits at time t+1, an increase in r^{*d}_t increases next preriod's anticipated dividends per share thereby raising the marginal cost of issuing an additional share of equity during the current period. This in turn causes the sector to raise the current market price of its own equity shares.

<u>Effects of Selected Domestic-Economy Parameters upon im^{*nd}_t and D^{*nd}_{t+1}</u>

The effects of K^n_t, w_t, Q_t and c^{gd}_t upon the nonfinancial business sector's current-period demand for imports, im^{*nd}_t, and its current end-of-period demand for foreign checkable deposits, D^{*nd}_{t+1}, are examined in the present section. An increase in K^n_t, ceteris paribus, implies that the nonfinancial business sector will require fewer variable factors in the current period in order to produce a given volume of consumption and capital goods that period. Ignoring any impacts of the larger beginning-of-period stock of physical capital upon the marginal physical product of imported goods, the larger stock of K^n_t will tend to enable the sector to conserve its use of the imported factor. The rise in K^n_t may also cause the marginal physical product of imported goods to rise (fall) thereby mitigating (reinforcing) this effect. Thus the sector may decide to produce more consumption goods in the current period and to use more imported goods in the production process; its demand for im^*_t may rise as K^n_t rises. Furthermore, if the change in K^n_t affects the amount of physical capital with which the sector plans to begin next period, the change in K^n_t may also affect the amount the sector plans to import, im^{*nd}_{t+1}, next period. To the extent that the sector alters its plans for

im^{*nd}_{t+1}, it affects the anticipated marginal product of foreign checkable deposits it plans to hold by time t+1. In particular, an increase in the planned level of imports next period raises the marginal product of these checkable deposits, causing its demand, D^{*nd}_{t+1}, to rise.

The higher w_t happens to be at the beginning of the current period, ceteris paribus, the smaller will be the sector's demand for current labor hours and the higher the marginal cost of current production of domestic consumption and capital goods. The nonfinancial business sector will tend to import more goods from abroad as a factor in the production process (assuming that the quantity of labor leaves the marginal product of the imported good unaffected) since as it reduces production, the marginal revenue product of the imported factor tends to rise. But the effect of a change in w_t upon the sector's end-of-period demand for foreign checkable deposits is unclear.

The higher Q_t happens to be at time t, ceteris paribus, the less the nonfinancial business sector plans to produce of consumption goods in the current period. To the extent that the sector decides to reduce that production (and ignoring any feedback effect upon the current production of capital goods) the sector will demand less of all factors in the current period, including im^{*nd}_t. If the rise in consumption goods inventories at time t is viewed as reflecting reduction in product demand which the sector now anticipates will persist through next period, the sector will revise downward its estimate of next period's demand for consumption goods as well. By itself this will induce the sector to plan to purchase fewer foreign factors next period thereby reducing its current end-of-period demand for foreign checkable deposits.

Ceteris paribus, an increase in the government sector's current demand for domestically produced goods will produce effects which are opposite to those just discussed for an increase in Q_t. The increased demand for foreign checkable deposits by the nonfinancial sector in this case would arise if the sector anticipates that the government's increased demand will persist through next period.

The next section represents the central contribution of the present chapter. It analyzes the factors affecting the optimal exchange rate set by the private financial institutions in a large open economy. In particular the domestic private financial sector sets the market exchange rate at a level which is consistent with its central objective of maximizing its own present value. As a result, the rate it deems optimal at time t is consistent with the other prices and interest rates it announces at the beginning of the current period.

The Private Depository Institutions

This section extends the analysis of the private depository institutions presented in Chapter 10 by permitting this sector to set the market exchange rate between the domestic and foreign currencies in addition to domestic interest rates on personal loans and checkable deposits and the market prices of domestic bonds and financial-sector equity shares. As the dominant participant in the foreign exchange market, the domestic private financial sector announces at the beginning of the period the exchange rate it estimates will maximize its own present value in accordance with its other business decisions. It then stands ready during the current period to trade foreign exchange at the announced rate. To meet demands for foreign exchange, the sector presumably holds an inventory of that money in the form of checkable deposits at foreign financial institutions. It also holds foreign bonds as an income earning asset, but it is assumed to be a price-taker in that market. As in the closed-economy model, the domestic private financial sector also borrows from its own central bank. But the domestic private financial sector may not exchange foreign currency for domestic high-powered money at the central bank; the central bank therefore refrains from intervening into the foreign exchange market in this model.

As the current period opens, the domestic private financial sector holds five assets, rather than only the three it held in the closed-economy version. These assets consist of reserves, Rs_t (held either as vault cash or as deposits at the central bank), domestic government bonds, $B^f{}_t$, foreign bonds, $B^{*f}{}_t$, checkable deposits (denominated in the foreign unit of account) held at foreign financial institutions, $D^{*f}{}_t$, and personal loans to domestic households, L_t. Expressed in terms of the domestic currency, the total value of the sector's assets at time t equals $Rs_t + L_t + p^b{}_{t-1}B^f{}_t + e_t p^{*b}{}_{t-1}B^{*f}{}_t + e_t D^{f*}{}_t$ where $p^{*b}{}_{t-1}$ denotes last period's market price of foreign bonds expressed in terms of the foreign unit of value and e_t represents the current-period exchange rate, which the domestic private financial sector has yet to announce at time t.

The domestic financial sector's outstanding liabilities at time t include advances payable to the central bank, A_t, and checkable deposits held by the domestic government, D^g_t, domestic household, D^h_t, the domestic nonfinancial business, D^n_t, and the foreign, D^r_t, sectors, where superscript "r" denotes the "rest-of-the-world". Therefore the domestic-money value of these liabilities at time t equals $A_t + D^g_t + D^h_t + D^n_t + D^n_t + D^r_t$, or $A_t + D_t$ where $D_t = D^g_t + D^h_t + D^n_t + D^r_t$.

The private depository institutions' current revenue consists of the current interest income on personal loans outstanding at time t, $r^{\ell}_{t-1}L_t$, plus the current interest income on domestic government bonds, $(\$1 - p^b_{t-1})B^f_t$, plus the current interest income (in domestic money) on foreign bonds, $e_t(1 - p^{*b}_{t-1})B^{*f}_t$, plus the current interest income on checkable deposits held at foreign financial institutions, $e_t r^{*d}_{t-1}D^{*f}_t$. The sector's current expenses include its interest payments on checkable deposits, $r^d_{t-1}D_t$, its interest payments on advances outstanding at time t, $\rho_{t-1}A_t$, and its current labor expenses $w_t h^f_t N^f_t$. Subtracting the private financial business sector's net saving in the current period, s^f_t, from its current income yields the following expression for the dividends, $\pi^f_t Sf_t$, it distributes to its owners during the current period.

$$\pi^f_t Sf_t = r^{\ell}_{t-1}L_t + (\$1-p^b_{t-1})B^f_t + e_t(1-p^{*b}_{t-1})B^{*f}_t + e_t r^{*d}_{t-1}D^{*f}_t - r^d_{t-1}D_t - \rho_{t-1}A_t - w_t h^f_t N^f_t - s^f_t. \tag{13.121}$$

The symbol r^{*d}_{t-1} denotes the interest rate on checkable deposits announced by foreign financial institutions last period.

The volume of reserves which the private financial sector plans to accumulate during the current period, $Rs^e_{t+1} - Rs_t$, necessarily equals the amount it plans to save on the income account, s^f_t, plus the amount of its planned increment to checkable deposit liabilities, $D^e_{t+1} - D_t$, plus its planned increment in advances from the central bank, $A^d_{t+1} - A_t$, plus the value of its planned sales of its own equity shares, $p^f_t(Sf^e_{t+1} - Sf_t)$, minus the value of its planned additions to domestic government bonds, $p^b_t B^{fe}_{t+1} - p^b_{t-1}B^f_t$, minus the value of its planned additions to foreign bonds, $e_t(p^{*b}_t B^{*fd}_{t+1} - p^{*b}_{t-1}B^{*f}_t)$, minus the value of its planned accumulation of checkable deposits at foreign financial institutions, $e_t(D^{*fe}_{t+1} - D^{*f}_t)$, and minus its planned acccumulation of IOU's issued by the domestic household sector, $L^e_{t+1} - L_t$, during the current period. Solving (13.121) for s^f_t and inserting the value for s^f_t into the relationship delineated in the last sentence yields the following relationship between the sector's "income" and "capital" accounts in the current period:

$$(Rs^e_{t+1} - Rs_t) = [r^{\ell}_{t-1}L_t + (\$1-p^b_{t-1})B^f_t + e_t(1-p^{*b}_{t-1})B^{*f}_t$$
$$+ er^{*d}_{t-1}D^{*f}_t - r^d_{t-1}D_t - \rho_{t-1}A_t - w_t h^f_t N^f_t - \pi^f_t Sf_t]$$
$$+ (D^e_{t+1} - D_t) + (A^d_{t+1} - A_t) + p^f_t(Sf^e_{t+1} - Sf_t)$$
$$- (p^b_t B^{fe}_{t+1} - p^b_{t-1}B^f_t) - e_t(p^{*b}_t B^{*fd}_{t+1} - p^{*b}_{t-1}B^{*f}_t)$$
$$- e_t(D^{*fe}_{t+1} - D^{*f}_t) - (L^e_{t+1} - L_t). \qquad (13.122)$$

From Chapter 10, since the central bank holds no assets other than the discounts of the domestic private financial institutions, the reserves of these institutions simply equal the value of discounts minus the amount of currency held by the domestic household sector:

$$Rs_t = A_t - Cu_t. \qquad (13.123)$$

Furthermore, the domestic private depository institutions at time t can estimate the amount of their reserves at time t+1 simply by substracting from their planned level of advances outstanding at t+1, A^d_{t+1}, the amount of currency they anticipate the domestic household sector will want to hold at time t+1:

$$Rs^e_{t+1} = A^d_{t+1} - Cu^e_{t+1} \qquad (13.124)$$

Substituting the right hand sides of (13.123) and (13.124) for Rs_t and Rs^e_{t+1} respectively in (13.122) yields the following expression for the current dividends per share announced by the private financial institutions at time t:

$$\pi^f_t = \frac{1}{Sf_t}[r^{\ell}_{t-1}L_t + B^f_t + e_t B^{*f}_t + er^{*d}_{t-1}D^{*f}_t - r^d_{t-1}D_t - \rho_{t-1}A_t$$
$$- w_t h^f_t N^f_t + (D^e_{t+1} - D_t) + (Cu^e_{t+1} - Cu_t) + p^f_t(Sf^e_{t+1} - Sf_t)$$
$$- p^b_t B^{fe}_{t+1} - e_t p^{*b}_t B^{*fd}_{t+1} - e_t(D^{*fe}_{t+1} - D^{*f}_t) - (L^e_{t+1} - L_t)] \qquad (13.125)$$

The private financial sector's anticipated interest income next period consists of the interest from: personal loans outstanding at time t+1, $r^{\ell}_{t}L^{e}_{t+1}$, domestic government bonds held at time t+1, $(\$1-p^{b}_{t})B^{fe}_{t+1}$, foreign bonds held at time t+1, $e_{t+1}(1-p^{*b}_{t})B^{*fd}_{t}$, and checkable deposits held at foreign financial institutions, $e_{t+1}r^{*de}_{t}D^{*fe}_{t+1}$. The sector's anticipated expenses next period equals the interest it must pay on checkable deposits, $r^{d}_{t}D^{e}_{t+1}$, and advances outstanding at time t+1, $\rho_{t}A^{d}_{t+1}$, plus its anticipated wage bill, $w^{e}_{t+1}hN^{fd}_{t+1}$. Therefore, at time t the sector's anticipated next-period net income is denoted by:

$$r^{\ell}_{t}L^{e}_{t+1} + (\$1-p^{b}_{t})B^{fe}_{t+1} + e_{t+1}(1-p^{*b}_{t})B^{*fd}_{t+1} + e_{t+1}r^{*de}_{t}D^{*fe}_{t+1}$$

$$- r^{d}_{t}D^{e}_{t+1} - \rho_{t}A^{d}_{t+1} - w^{e}_{t+1}hN^{fd}_{t+1}.$$

As in Chapter 10, let $\pi^{f}_{t+1}Sf^{e}_{t+1}$ represent the dividends that the sector anticipated distributing to its owners next period. Clearly, these dividends equal next period's anticipated net income less the sector's anticipated level of saving next period, s^{f}_{t+1}:

$$\pi^{f}_{t+1}Sf^{e}_{t+1} = r^{\ell}_{t}L^{e}_{t+1} + (\$1-p^{b}_{t})B^{fe}_{t+1}$$

$$+ e_{t+1}r^{*de}_{t}D^{*fe}_{t+1} - r^{d}_{t}D^{e}_{t+1} - \rho_{t}A^{d}_{t+1}$$

$$- w^{e}_{t+1}hN^{fd}_{t+1} - s^{f}_{t+1}. \qquad (13.126)$$

The volume of reserves which the sector plans at time t to accumulate next period, $0 - Rs^{e}_{t+1}$, necessarily equals the amount it plans to save next period, s^{f}_{t+1}, plus the planned increase in its checkable deposit liabilities, $0-D^{e}_{t+1}$, plus the planned increment in advances from the central bank, $0-A^{d}_{t+1}$, minus the planned increase in its holdings of domestic government bonds, $0-p^{b}_{t}B^{fe}_{t+1}$, minus the planned increment in its holdings of foreign bonds, $e_{t+1}(0-p^{*b}_{t}B^{*fd}_{t+1})$, minus the planned increment in its holdings of personal loans to households, $0-L^{e}_{t+1}$, and minus the planned increase in its holdings of checkable deposits at foreign depository institutions, $e_{t+1}(0 - D^{*fe}_{t+1})$. Substituting the right hand side of (13.124) for Rs^{e}_{t+1} and substituting the expression obtained in (13.126) for s^{f}_{t+1} into the relationship just discussed yields the following expression for next period's anticipated dividends per share:

$$\pi^{f}_{t+1} = \frac{1}{S^{fe}_{t+1}}[(1+r^{\ell}_{t})L^{e}_{t+1}+B^{fe}_{t+1}+e_{t+1}B^{*fd}_{t+1}+e_{t+1}(1+r^{*de}_{t})D^{*fe}_{t+1}$$
$$- (1+r^{d}_{t})D^{e}_{t+1} - Cu^{e}_{t+1} - \rho_{t}A^{d}_{t+1} - w_{t+1}hN^{df}_{t+1}]. \qquad (13.127)$$

The present value of the private financial sector, p^{o}_{f}, at time t is denoted by the sum $\pi^{f}_{t} + \pi^{f}_{t+1}/(1+r^{ne}_{t})$ where $(1+r^{ne}_{t})$ equals π^{ne}_{t+1}/p^{n}_{t}, the total return per share that the private financial sector anticipates at time t will be earned by the private nonfinancial business sector for its shareholders (i.e., for the household sector) next period. I assume the private financial sector at time t formulates its plans and announces the relevant interest rates and prices of financial instruments in a manner that maximizes its present value.

Just as it did in the closed-economy model, the private financial sector at time t sets the interest rates on domestic checkable deposits, r^{d}_{t}, and personal loans, r^{1}_{t}, as well as the prices of domestic government bonds, p^{b}_{t}, and its own equity shares, p^{f}_{t}. The optimal (ex ante) values for these variables depend, in part, upon the sector's estimates at time t of the end-of-eriod, demand for checkable deposits, D^{e}_{t+1}, the demand for personal loans, L^{e}_{t+1}, the supply of government bonds, B^{e}_{t+1}, the demand for its own equity shares, Sf^{e}_{t+1}, and the demand for currency, Cu^{e}_{t+1}. The open-economy model developed here adds a new dimension to two of thse estimated functions because of the foreign sector's participation in the domestic markets for checkable deposits and bonds. The domestic depository institutions' estimate of the end-of-period market demand for checkable deposits, D^{e}_{t+1}, now includes its estimate of the foreign sector's demand for those deposits. Its estimate of the market supply of government bonds, B^{e}_{t+1}, is a <u>net</u> supply equal to its estimate of the number of bonds the government will be willing to offer at each value of p^{b}_{t} minus its estimate of the number of bonds, B^{re}_{t+1}, that the foreign sector will be willing to purchase. The difference represents the net amount of domestic government bonds that the financial sector itself must stand ready to hold by time t+1. For simplicity, let functions $D^{e}_{t+1}(.)$, $B^{e}_{t+1}(.)$, $L^{e}_{t+1}(.)$, $Sf^{e}_{t+1}(.)$ and $Cu^{e}_{t+1}(.)$ all take fundamentally the same forms that they took previously:

$$D^{e}_{t+1} = D^{ge}_{t+1}(r^{d}_{t}, \xi_{dg}) + D^{he}_{t}(r^{d}_{t}, \xi_{dh}) + D^{ne}_{t+1}(r^{d}_{t}, \xi_{dn})$$

$$+ D^{ne}_{t+1}(r^d_t, \xi_{dr}) = D^e_{t+1}(r^d_t, \xi_d); (D^e_{t+1})^1 > 0 \tag{13.128}$$

where ξ_d and ξ_{dj}(j = g, h, n and r) represent vectors of shift parameters in the estimated demand functions for checkable deposits

$$L^e_{t+1} = L^e_{t+1}(r^1_t, \xi_1); (L^e_{t+1})_1 < 0 \tag{13.129}$$

$$B^e_{t+1} = B^{ge}_{t+1}(p^b_t, \xi_{bg}) - B^{re}_{t+1}(p^b_t, \xi_{br}) \tag{13.130}$$

$$= B^e_{t+1}(p^b_t, \xi_b); (B^e_{t+1})_1 > 0$$

where $B^{ge}_{t+1}(.)$ denotes the number of bonds the private depository institutions estimate the domestic government sector will have outstanding at time t+1; $B^{re}_{t+1}(.)$ denotes the number of domestic (government) bonds that the private depository institutions estimate the foreign sector will want to hold at time t+1, and $B^e_{t+1}(.)$ denotes the number of bonds the depository institutions estimate they will hold as a result at time t+1; ξ_b, ξ_{bg} and ξ_{br} denote vectors of shift

$$Sf^e_{t+1} = Sf^e_{t+1}(p^f_t, \xi_f); (Sf^e_{t+1})_1 < 0 \tag{13.131}$$

$$Cu^e_{t+1} = Cu^e_{t+1}(r^d_t, \xi_c); (Cu^e_{t+1})_1 < 0 \tag{13.132}$$

parameters where ξ_f and ξ_c denote vectors of shift parameters.

In this open-economy model, the domestic private financial sector sets the exchange rate between the domestic and foreign monies. In addition, it stands ready to buy or sell foreign checkable deposits (in exchange for domestic money) during the current period at the exchange rate it announces at the beginning of the period. Therefore the volume of foreign checkable deposits that the domestic private financial sector itself plans to hold by the end of the current period will be influenced by the net payments or receipts that the sector plans to make during the period. Consequently in deciding the optimal level of the exchange rate, the sector must estimate what will be the "balance of payments" at each alternate exchange rate that it might announce.

Many economists argue that since the foreign exchange market involves a large number of participants dealing in a homogeneous commodity that can be traded quickly and cheaply, this market is best characterized as being devoid of any price-setters. They assume exchange rates are determined instantaneously by market demand and supply. These arguments notwithstanding, foreign exchange dealers do in fact announce exchange rates and stand ready to deal at those rates for a real length of time, however short. When exchange dealers announce their prices they have no knowledge that a customer will indeed buy or sell at that price. At least momentarily, then, foreign-exchange dealers may experience unanticipated accumulations or reductions in their inventories of foreign exchange. More generally Franklin Fisher (1983) asserts that "If 'equilibrium' is to have any substantive meaning, one must be willing to countenance the possibility of encountering disequilibrium states." Furthermore "...[A] satisfactory underpinning for equilibrium analysis must be a theory in which the adjustments to disequilibrium made by agents are made optimally." This is the spirit in which the behavior of the private financial sector is developed in the present study.

Consider, first, the relationship between the domestic private financial sector's anticipated net accumulation of foreign checkable deposits and the international transactions involving foreign exchange that it anticipates will occur during the current period. The net value (in terms of the domestic unit of account) of the foreign money that the domestic private despository institutions anticipate accumulating during the current period, $e_t(D^{*fe}_{t+1} - D^{*f}_t)$, necessarily equals the value of the domestic economy's anticipated exports during the current period, $p^c_t ex^d_t$, plus the domestic government's anticipated current-period borrowing from abroad, $p^b_t B^{re}_{t+1} - p^b_{t-1} B^r_t$, plus the current interest income received by domestic depository institutions from foreign bonds, $e_t(1-p^{b*}_{t-1})B^{*f}_t$, plus the current interst income on foreign checkable deposits received by the domestic government, private financial and nonfinancial business sectors, $e_t r^{d*}_{t-1}(D^{*g}_t + D^{*n}_t + D^{*ft})$, plus the anticipated current hoarding of domestic money by foreigners, $(D^{re}_{t+1} - D^r_t)$, minus the value of domestic imports, $e_t p^{c*}_t im_t(e_t)$, minus current interest payments by the domestic government to the foreign sector, $(\$1 - p^b_{t-1})B^r_t$, minus current interest payments by domestic depository institutions to foreigners, $r^d_{t-1} D^r_t$, minus the current (net) purchases of foreign bonds by private domestic depository institutions, $e_t(p^{b*}_t B^{*f}_{t+1} - p^{b*}_{t-1} B^{*f}_t)$, minus the anticipated foreign money hoarded by the domestic government, $e_t(D^{*g}_{t+1} - D^{*g}_t)$ and by the domestic nonfinancial business sector, $e_t(D^{*n}_{t+1} - D^{*n}_t)$:

$$
\begin{aligned}
e_t(D^{*fe}_{t+1}-D^{*f}_t) = {} & p^c_t ex^{de}_t(.) - e_t p^{c*}_t im^e_t(.) \\
& + p^b_t B^{re}_{t+1}(.) - p^b_{t-1}B^r_t + e_t(1-p^{b*}_{t-1})B^{*f}_t \\
& + e_t r^{d*}_{t-1}(D^{*g}_t+D^{*n}_t+D^{*f}_t) + (D^{re}_{t+1}(.)-D^r_t) \\
& - (\$1-p^b_{t-1})B^r_t - r^d_{t-1}D^r_t \\
& - e_t(p^{b*}_t B^{*f}_{t+1} - p^{b*}_{t-1}B^{*f}_t) \qquad (13.134) \\
& - e_t(D^{*ge}_{t+1}(.) - D^{*g}_t) - e_t(D^{*ne}_{t+1}(.)-D^{*n}_t).
\end{aligned}
$$

Since the domestic central bank is precluded from exchanging foreign money for domestic high-powered money (or vice versa) in this model, the amount on the left hand side of (13.134) denotes the change in the level of the checkable deposits (denominated in foreign exchange) held by domestic depository institutions at foreign financial institutions between the beginning and the end of the current period. In order to forecast at time t what the change in these deposits will be, the private domestic financial sector must estimate the various components on the right-hand side of (13.134) and their responses to the choice variables facing that sector at time t.

The domestic demand for imports is the sum of the import demands of the domestic government, household and business sectors: $im^*_t(.) = im^{*g}_t(.) + im^{*h}_t(.) + im^{*n}_t(.)$. Rewrite functions (13.33), (13.58), and (13.114) so that only the choice variables of the depository institutions appear explicitly:

$$im^{*g}_t(.) = im^{*g}_t(p^b_t,\ r^d_t,\ e_t,\ k^i_g) \qquad (13.33)$$

$$im^{*h}_t(.) = im^{*h}_t(r^d_t,\ e_t,\ k^i_h) \qquad (13.58)$$

$$im^{*n}_t(.) = im^{*n}_t(r^d_t,\ e_t,\ k_n) \qquad (13.114)$$

where k^i_g, k^i_n and k^i_n represent shift parameters beyond the direct control of the depository institutions. Then the real level of domestic imports during the current period estimated by the depository institution at time t, $im^{*e}_t(.)$, may be depicted as (13.135):

$$im^{*e}_t = im^e_t(p^b_t, r^d_t, e_t, k^i_g, k^i_h, k^i_n) \qquad (13.135)$$

Presumably the financial business sector estimates that current domestic imports will fall if it raises the current exchange rate, raises the current interest rate on checkable deposits or reduces the current-period price at which it is willing to buy domestic bonds. These assumptions are consistent with the substitution effects operating upon the demands for imports by the government, household and nonfinancial business sectors.

An increase in p^b_t reduces the interest rate that foreigners can earn on domestic bonds. Consequently, it is reasonable to suppose that foreigners will demand fewer domestic bonds as p^b_t rises and that the domestic private financial sector correctly estimates at least the direction of this response. Thereforee, I assume $B^{re}_{t+1}(.)$ is negatively related to p^b_t. An increase in r^d_t, on the other hand, increases the demands for domestic checkable deposits by the domestic government, household and nonfinancial business sectors. I assume an increase in r^d_t also raises, ceteris paribus, the foreign sector's demand for domestic checkable deposits. Consequently, I assume that the domestic private financial sector's estimate of the demand for its checkable deposits by foreigners, $D^{re}_{t+1}(.)$, is positively related to r^d_t.

Since checkable deposits held in foreign exchange represent an alternative form of holding financial wealth for the domestic government and nonfinancial business sectors, an increase in r^d_t, ceteris paibus, reduces the demands by these sectors for foreign money. Assuming that the domestic private financial sector's estimate of these demands for foreign exchange reflect these responses, then both $D^{*ge}_{t+1}(.)$ and D^{*ne}_t are negatively related to r^d_t.

Finally, I assume that the domestic private financial sector estimates that the foreign sector's current-period demand for domestically-produced goods is directly related to one of the variables announced by the private financial sector at time t, namely e_t. Since an increase in e_t makes domestic goods relatively cheaper to foreigners, I suppose that the private financial sector's etimate of current period exports, $ex^e_t(.)$, is directly related to e_t.

Expressing the above-mentioned components of the private financial sector's estimate of the current period "balance-of-payments" (in terms of the household, government, foreign and nonfinancial business sectors' net (flow) demands for domestic currency, as shown by the right-hand side of (13.134)) as dependent upon some of the variables under the control of the private financial sector, yields the following restatement of (13.134):

$$e_t(D^{*fe}_{t+1}-D^{*f}_t) = p^c_t ex^{de}_t(e_t) - e_t p^{c*}_t im^{*e}_t(p^b_t, r^d_t, e_t)$$
$$+ p^b_t B^{re}_{t+1}(p^b_t) + p^b_{t-1}B^r_t + e_t(1-p^{b*}_{t-1})B^{*f}_t$$
$$+ e_t r^{d*}_{t-1}(D^{*g}_t+D^{*f}_t) + D^{re}_{t+1}(r^d_t) - D^r_t \qquad (13.136)$$
$$- (\$1-p^b_{t-1})B^r_t - r^d_{t-1}D^r_t - e_t(p^{b*}_{t-1}B^{*fd}_{t+1}-p^{b*}_{t-1}B^{*f}_t)$$
$$- e_t(D^{*ge}_{t+1}(r^d_t)-D^{*g}_t) - e_t(D^{*ne}_{t+1}(r^d_t) - D^{*n}_t).$$

Analogously (remembering that every sector presumabnly faces a two-period time horizon at which time it plans to hold no assets and have no outstanding liabilities), the private financial sector's planned accumulation of foreign checkable deposits next period (expressed in units of domestic money), $- e_{t+1}D^{*fe}_{t+1}$, necessarily equals the anticipated value of next period's net exports, $p^{ce}_{t+1}ex^{de}_{t+1}(e_{t+1}) - e_{t+1}p^{c*}_{t+1}im^{*e}_{t+1}(e_{t+1})$, <u>plus</u> the government sector's borrowing from abroad, $- p^b_t B^{re}_{t+1}(p^b_t)$, <u>plus</u> the interest income the domestic depository institutions will receive from foreign bonds held at time t+1, $e_{t+1}(1-p^{b*}_t)B^{*fd}_{t+1}$, <u>plus</u> the interest income on foreign checkable deposits that will be received by the domestic government, private financial and nonfinancial business sectors, $e_{t+1}r^{d*e}_t(D^{*ge}_{t+1} + D^{*ne}_{t+1} + D^{*fe}_{t+1})$, <u>plus</u> hoarding of domestic currency by the foreign sector, $- D^{re}_{t+1}$, <u>minus</u> interest payments by the domestic government to the foreign sector, $(\$1 - p^b_t)B^{re}_{t+1}(p^b_t)$, minus the interest payments by domestic depository institutions to foreigners, $r^e_t D^{re}_{t+1}$, <u>minus</u> the net purchases of foreign bonds by private depository institutions, $- e_{t+1}p^{b*}_t B^{*fd}_{t+1}$, <u>minus</u> the foreign money accumulated by the domestic government, $-e_{t+1}D^{*ge}_{t+1}$, and by the domestic nonfinancial business sector, $- e_{t+1}D^{*ne}_{t+1}$, next period.

$$- e_{t+1}D^{*fe}_{t+1} = p^{ce}_{t+1}ex^e_{t+1}(.) - e_{t+1}p^{c*e}_{t+1}im^{*e}_{t+1}(.)$$
$$- p^b_t B^{re}_{t+1}(.) + e_{t+1}(1-p^{b*}_t)B^{*fd}_{t+1} + e_{t+1}r^{d*}_t(D^{*ge}_{t+1}(.)$$
$$+ D^{*ne}_{t+1}(.) + D^{*fe}_{t+1}) - D^{re}_{t+1}(.) - (\$1-p^b_t)B^{re}_{t+1}(.)$$

$$- r^d_t D^{re}_{t+1}(.) + e_{t+1}p^{b*}_t B^{*fd}_{t+1} + e_{t+1}(D^{*ge}_{t+1}(.)$$

$$+ D^{*ne}_{t+1}(.)). \qquad (13.137)$$

To simplify the analysis, I assume that the domestic private financial sector at time t anticipates that next period's domestic exports, ex^e_{t+1}, will depend directly upon the exhange rate, e_{t+1}, that the sector announces at the beginning of that period. Furthermore, assume that it anticipates that next period's domestic imports, $im^{*e}_{t+1}(.)$, will vary inversely with respect to e_{t+1}. Then , expressing $ex^e_{t+1}(.)$, $im^{*e}_{t+1}(.)$, $B^{re}_{t+1}(.)$, $D^{*ge}_{t+1}(.)$, $D^{*ne}_{t+1}(.)$ and $D^{re}_{t+1}(.)$ as functions of variables which are announced by the private financial sector produces the following form for (13.137):

$$- e_{t+1}D^{*fe}_{t+1} = p^{ce}_{t+1}ex^e_{t+1}(e_{t+1}) - e_{t+1}p^{c*e}_{t+1}im^{*e}_{t+1}(e_{t+1})$$

$$-p^b_t B^{re}_{t+1}(p^b_t) + e_{t+1}(1-p^{b*}_t)B^{*fd}_{t+1}$$

$$+ e_{t+1}r^{d*}_t(D^{*ge}_{t+1}(r^d_t) + D^{*ne}_{t+1}(r^d_t) \qquad (13.138)$$

$$+ D^{*fe}_{t+1}) - D^{re}_{t+1}(r^d_t) - (\$1-p^b_t)B^{re}_{t+1}(p^b_t)$$

$$- r^d_t D^{re}_{t+1}(r^d_t) + e_{t+1}p^{b*}_t B^{*fd}_{t+1}$$

$$+ e_{t+1}(D^{*ge}_{t+1}(r^d_t) + D^{*ne}_{t+1}(r^d_t)).$$

Equations (13.136) and (13.138) each may be viewed as representing an implicit function with a continuous partial derivative in the dependent variable e_t or e_{t+1} respectively:

$$F(e_t, \ldots) = 0 \qquad (13.139)$$

$$G(e_{t+1}, \ldots) = 0 \qquad (13.140)$$

It is then possible, in principle, to find the partial derivatives of each of the variables e_t and e_{t+1} with respect to each of the variables which are "independent" (at least for the purpose of these equations) -- D^{*f}_t, D^{*g}_t, D^{*n}_t, D^{*fe}_{t+1}, p^{c*}_t, p^c_t, p^b_{t-1}, p^b_t, p^{b*}_{t-1}, p^{*b}_t, B^r_t, r^d_{t-1}, r^{d*}_{t-1}, r^{d*}_t, D^r_t, B^{*f}_t and B^{*fd}_{t+1} -- in the following "reduced form" equations:

$$e_t = e(.) \tag{13.141}$$

$$e_{t+1} = e(.) \tag{13.142}$$

Consequently, just as the downward sloping product demand curve facing an imperfect competitor may be converted into an expression showing the maximum price which the producer could charge for a given level of goods it plans to sell, the "balance of payments" equations (13.136) and (13.138) may be converted into expressions showing the exchange rate that the financial sector estimates it would have to announce at the beginning of the period in question in order to acquire or divest itself of a given amount of foreign exchange that period. In the optimizing problem presented below, the sector will decide the optimal level of its end-of-period balance of foreign exchange in conjunction with its optimal announcements for current interest rates and prices of various financial assets using expressions (13.141) and (13.142). Substituting the solution to the optimizing problem into these two equations will then provide the values of e_t and e_{t+1} which the private financial sector deems optimal at time t.

The partial derivatives of (13.141) and (13.142) are obtaianed by finding the total differentials of each of (13.139) and (13.140), then dividing every term in (13.139) by the (non-zero) coefficient of de_t and dividing every term in (13.140) by the (non-zero) coefficient of de_{t+1}. The new coefficients attached to the differentials of all variables except e_t in (13.139) depict the partial derivatives of e(.) in (13.141). Analogously, the new coefficients attached to the differentials of all variables except e_{t+1} in (13.140) represent the partial derivatives of e(.) in (13.142). From (13.136) and (13.137) it follows that $\partial F/\partial e$ and $\partial G/\partial e_{t+1}$ are given respectively by:

$$\frac{\partial F}{\partial e_t} = -(D^{*f}_{t+1} - D^{*f}_t) + p^c_t(ex^{de}_t)' - p^{c*}_t im^e_t - e_t p^{c*}_t (im^e_t)_3$$
$$+ B^{*f}_t - p^{b*}_t B^{*f}_{t+1} + r^{d*}_{t-1}(D^{*g}_t + D^{*n}_t + D^{*f}_t) - (D^{*ge}_{t+1} - D^{*g}_t)$$
$$- (D^{*ne}_{t+1} - D^{*n}_t)$$

$$\frac{\partial G}{\partial e_{t+1}} = D^{*fe}_{t+1} + p^{ce}_{t+1}(ex^{de}_{t+1})' - p^{c*e}_{t+1} im^e_t - e_{t+1} p^{c*e}_{t+1}(im^e_{t+1})'$$
$$+ B^{*fe}_{t+1} + r^{d*}_t (D^{*ge}_{t+1} + D^{*ne}_{t+1} + D^{*fe}_{t+1}) + (D^{*ge}_{t+1} + D^{*ne}_{t+1})$$

Let x_j represent any variable other than e_t in F( ) and let y_j represent any variable other than e_{t+1} in G( ). Then the partial derivatives of e_t with respect to each x_j in (13.141) are given by $\partial e_t/\partial x_j = -(\partial F/\partial x_j)/(\partial F/\partial e_t)$. Analogously, the partial derivatives of e_{t+1} with respecct to each y_j in (13.142) are given by $\partial e_{t+1}/\partial y_j = -(\partial G/\partial y_j)/(\partial G/\partial e_{t+1})$. Since the signs of $\partial G/\partial e_{t+1}$ and (especially) $\partial F/\partial x_j$ both depend upon the magnitudes of the anticipated capital flows relative to interest payments and the responsiveness of the balance of trade to changes in the exchange rate, neither sign is determinate a priori. Consequently the signs of the partials in (13.141) and (13.142) cannot be established without making further assumptions.

Suppose that $\partial F/\partial e_t > 0$. Then the signs of the partial derivatives in (13.41) will appear as:

$$e_t = e(\underset{+}{r^d_{t-1}},\ \underset{-}{r^d_t},\ \underset{-}{p^b_{t-1}},\ \underset{+}{p^b_t},\ \underset{+}{D^{*f}_{t+1}},\ \underset{+}{B^{*f}_{t+1}},\ \underset{-}{D^{*f}_t + D^{*g}_t + D^{*n}_t}$$

$$\underset{-}{r^{*d}_{t-1}},\ \underset{+}{r^{*d}_t},\ p^{b*}_t,\ \underset{+}{D^r_t},\ \underset{-}{B^{*f}_t},\ \underset{+}{B^r_t},\ \underset{+}{p^c_t},\ \underset{-}{p^{*c}_t})$$

if the Marshall-Lerner condition holds with respect to p^c_t and p^{*c}_t. Analogously, suppose $\partial G/\partial e_{t+1} > 0$. Then the signs of the partial derivatives in (13.142) become:

$$e_{t+1} = e(\underset{+}{r^d_t},\ \underset{-}{p^b_t},\ \underset{-}{D^{*f}_{t+1}},\ \underset{-}{B^{*f}_{t+1}},\ \underset{+}{p^{ce}_{t+1}},\ \underset{-}{p^{*ce}_{t+1}},\ \underset{-}{r^{*d}_t},\ \underset{+}{p^{*b}_t})$$

Just as in the closed-economy model presented in Chapter 10, suppose that the domestic private financial sector anticipates at time t that it will incur transactions costs during both the current and next periods associated with the volume of domestic loans the sector has, or plans to have, outstanding and with the volume of checkable deposit liabilities it has, or plans to have, outstanding at the beginning of the period in question. Furthermore, as in Chapter 10, assume that the domestiic private financial sector anticipates that the amount of excess reserves it holds, or anticipates holding, at the beginning of the period in question will serve to conserve transactions time during that period. To this point then, the amount of current labor effort, $h^f_tN^f_t$, that the private financial sector anticipates devoting to current transactions may be expressed as a strictly convex function, $\alpha(\ )$, which increases (at an increasing rate) with respect to each of L_t and $D_t = D^g{}_t + D^n{}_t + D^r{}_t + D^h{}_t$, but which decreases (at a decreasing absolute rate) with respect to X_t:

$$h^f{}_tN^f{}_t = \alpha(L_t, D_t, X_t) \qquad (13.143)$$

Also, the amount of labor time, $hN^{fd}{}_{t+1}$, that the private financial sector anticiptes directing toward financial transactions next period may be expressed as a strictly convex function, $\tilde{\alpha}(\ )$, which increaes (at an increasing rate) with respect to each of $L^e{}_{t+1}$ and $D^e{}_{t+1} = D^{ge}{}_{t+1} + D^{he}{}_{t+1} + D^{ne}{}_{t+1} + D^{re}{}_{t+1}$, but which decreases (at a decreasing absolute rate), as X_{t+1} rises:

$$hN^{fd}{}_{t+1} = \tilde{\alpha}(L^e{}_{t+1}, D^e{}_{t+1}, X_{t+1}) \qquad (13.144)$$

However, in the open-economy model developed here, the domestic private financial sector also stands ready during a given period to trade currencies at the exchange rate it announed at the beginning of that period. If a customer wishes to sell foreign currency to the domestic private financial sector, that customer will merely deposit a check denominated in the foreign unit of account at the private financial institutions in exchange for checkable deposits denominated in the domestic currency. The private financial sector transfers the check to the foreign financial sector and receives an addition to its deposits denominated in the foreign unit of account. On the other hand, if a customer wishes to buy foreign currency from the domestic private financial institutions, the customer will either write a check against its domestic-money account at these institutions or deposit domestic currency at these institutions in exchange for a check written by these institutions against their accounts at foreign financial institutions. The <u>gross</u> payments of foreign exchange (measured in the foreign unit of account) which the domestic private institutions anticipate at time t that they will make to customers during the current period is represented by:

$$z^e{}_t = p^{c*}{}_tim^e{}_t(e_t) + (1 - p^b{}_{t-1})B^r{}_t/e_t + r^{d*}{}_{t-1}D^r{}_t/e_t + (D^{*ge}{}_{t+1}(r^d{}_t)$$

$$- D^{*g}{}_t) + (D^{*ne}{}_{t+1}(r^d{}_t) - D^{*n}{}_t) = z^e{}_t(\ ). \qquad (13.145)$$

Ceteris paribus, the domestic private institutions presumably anticipate at time t that their current-period transactions time will increase at an increasing rate as their anticipated gross current-period payments rise but that their initial balances of foreign exchange, D^{*f}_t, will conserve transactions time, albeit at a decreasing (absolute) rate. Letting $\hat{\alpha}(.)$ represent anticipated current transactions time associated with payments of foreign exchange, then $\hat{\alpha}(.)$ is assumed to be positive and strictly convex with a positive first-order partial derivative with respct to anticipated current-period payments and a negative first-order partial with respect to D^{*f}_t. Then at time t, the sector's anticipated total current period transactions time is given by:

$$h^f_t N^f_t = \alpha(L_t, D_t, X_t) + \hat{\alpha}(z^e_t, D^{*f}_t) \qquad (13.146)$$

where z^e_t represents the anticipated current-period gross payments of foreign exchange, expressed in terms of the foreign unit of account. For simplicity, ignore the anticipated effects operating upon z^e_t through (13.141). That is, ignore effects on z^e_t due to changes in e_t.

Analogously, the gross payments of foreign exchange which the domestic private financial institutions anticipate at time t that they will make next period, z^e_{t+1}, presumably increases their anticipated transactions time for next period at an increasing rate. But the

$$\begin{aligned} z^e_{t+1} &= p^{c*e}_{t+1} im^{*e}_{t+1} + B^{re}_{t+1}/e_{t+1} + (1 + r^d_t) D^{re}_{t+1}(r^d_t)/e_{t+1} \\ &= z^e_{t+1}(.) \end{aligned} \qquad (13.147)$$

volume of checkable deposits, D^{*fe}_{t+1}, they plan to hold at foreign depository institutions by time t+1 presumably reduces next period's anticipated transactons time, albeit at a decreasing rate. In particular, letting $\alpha^+(.)$ denote anticipated transactions time associated with payments of foreign exchange next period, assume $\alpha^+(.)$ is a positive, strictly convex, increasing funtion of z^e_{t+1}, but a decreasing function of D^{*fe}_{t+1}. Then at time t, next period's anticipated total transactions time may be represented by:

$$hN^{fd}_{t+1} = \tilde{\alpha}(L^e_{t+1}, D^e_{t+1}, X_{t+1}) + \alpha^+(z^e_{t+1}, D^{*fe}_{t+1}). \qquad (13.148)$$

Again, for simplicity, ignore the effect of a change in e_t upon z^e_{t+1} in (13.148).

Once again, excess reserves at the beginning of the current period, X_t, and at the beginning of next period, X^e_{t+1}, are defined by (10.19) and (10.20), repeated here as (13.149) and (13.150) respectively:

$$X_t = A_t - Cu_t - \hat{r}D_t \tag{13.149}$$

$$X_{t+1} = A^d_{t+1} - Cu^e_{t+1} - \hat{r}D^e_{t+1} \tag{13.150}$$

where $\hat{r}$ now denotes the required reserve ratio on all checkable deposits and where D_t and D^e_{t+1} now also include checkable deposits issued by domestic depository institutions and held by the foreign sector.

The analysis to this point leads to the following expression for the objective funcion of the private financial sector at time t: Maximize

$$p^f_o = \pi^f_t + \frac{\pi^f_{t+1}}{(\pi^{ne}_{t+1}/p^n_t)}$$

$$= \frac{1}{Sf_t} = [r^{\ell}_{t-1}L_t + B^f_t + e(.)\{B^{*f}_t + r^{*d}_{t-1}D^{*f}_t - p^{*b}_t B^{*fd}_{t+1}$$

$$- (D^{*f}_{t+1} - D^{*f}_t)\}$$

$$- r^d_{t-1}D_t - \rho_{t-1}A_t + (D^e_{t+1}(.) - D_t) + (Cu^e_{t+1}(.) - Cu_t)$$

$$+ p^f_t(Sf^e_{t+1}(.) - Sf_t) - p^b_t(B^e_{t+1}(.) - B^{re}_{t+1}) - (L^e_{t+1}(.) - L_t)$$

$$- w_t\{\alpha(L_t, D_t, X_t) + \hat{\alpha}(z^e_t(.), D^{*f}_t)\}]$$

$$+ \frac{1}{(\pi^{ne}_{t+1}/p^n_t)Sf^e_{t+1}(.)} [(1 + r^{\ell}_t)L^e_{t+1}(.) + (B^e_{t+1}(.) - B^r_{t+1})$$

$$+ e(.)\{B^{*fd}_{t+1} + (1 + r^{*de}_t)D^{*fe}_{t+1}\}$$

$$- (1 + r^d_t)D^e_{t+1}(.) - Cu^e_{t+1}(.) - \rho_t A^d_{t+1}$$

$$- w_{t+1}\{\tilde{\alpha}(L^e_{t+1}(.), D^e_{t+1}(.), A^d_{t+1} - Cu^e_{t+1}(.) - \hat{r}(D^e_{t+1}(.))$$

$$+ \alpha^+(z^e_{t+1}(.), D^{fe}_{t+1})\}] \tag{13.151}$$

with respect to decision variables: r^d_t, r^ℓ_t, p^b_t, p^f_t, A_{t+1}, D^{*f}_{t+1} and B^{*f}_{t+1}.

The dependency of z^e_t upon e_t is ignored in $z^e_t(.)$; similarly, ignore the dependency of z^e_{t+1} upon e_{t+1} in $z^e_{t+1}(.)$. These simplifying assumptions allow abstraction from the indirect effects of certain variables upon z^e_t and z^e_{t+1} operating through (13.141) and (13.142). However the more direct effects of these variables upon z^e_t and z^e_{t+1} are not ignored since both z^e_t and z^e_{t+1} are viewed here as depending upon all the variables other than e_t and e_{t+1} which appear in the definitions of z^e_t and z^e_{t+1}.

Partially differentiating (13.151) with respect to each of the seven choice variables, taken separately, and then setting these derivatives equal to zero produces the following first-order necessary conditions:

$$\frac{\partial p^o_f}{\partial r^d_t} = \frac{[(D^e_{t+1})_1 + (Cu^e_{t+1})_1 + (\partial e/\partial r^d_t)\{.\} - w_2\hat{\alpha}_1(\partial z^e_t/\partial r^d_t)]}{Sf_t}$$

$$+ \frac{\begin{bmatrix} -(1+r^d_t)(D^e_{t+1})_1 + D^e_{t+1} + (Cu^e_{t+1})_1 + w_{t+1}\{\tilde{\alpha}_2(D^e_{t+1})_1 \\ -\tilde{\alpha}_3[(Cu^e_{t+1})_1 + \hat{r}(D^e_{t+1})_1] \end{bmatrix}}{(\pi^{ne}_{t+1}/p^n_t)Sf^e_{t+1}(.)}$$

$$+ \frac{[(\partial\hat{e}/\partial r^d_t)\{B^{*fd}_{t+1} + (1+r^{*de}_t)D^{*fe}_{t+1}\} - w_{t+1}\overset{+}{\alpha}_1(\partial z^e_{t+1}/\partial r^d_t)]}{(\pi^{ne}_{t+1}/p^n_t)Sf^e_{t+1}(.)} = 0 \qquad (13.152)$$

$$\frac{\partial p^o_f}{\partial r^\ell_t} = \frac{-(L^e_{t+1})_1}{Sf_t} + \frac{(1+r^\ell_t)(L^e_{t+1})_1 + L^e_{t+1} - w_{t+1}\tilde{\alpha}_1(L^e_{t+1})_1}{(\pi^{ne}_{t+1}/p^n_t)Sf^e_{t+1}(.)} = 0 \qquad (13.153)$$

$$\frac{\partial p^o_f}{\partial p^b_t} = \frac{[-(B^e_{t+1}(.) - B^{re}_{t+1}) - p^b_t(B^e_{t+1})_1]}{Sf_t} + \frac{(B^e_{t+1})_1}{(\pi^{ne}_{t+1}/p^n_t)Sf^e_{t+1}(.)} \qquad (13.154)$$

$$\frac{\partial p^o_f}{\partial p^f_t} = \frac{(Sf^e_{t+1} - Sf_t) + p^f_t(Sf^e_{t+1})_1}{Sf_t} - \frac{\pi^f_{t+1}}{(\pi^{ne}_{t+1}/p^n_t)(Sf^e_{t+1})}(Sf^e_{t+1})_1 = 0 \qquad (13.155)$$

$$\frac{\partial p^{o}{}_{f}}{\partial A^{d}{}_{t+1}} = \frac{-\rho_{t} - w_{t+1}\tilde{\alpha}_{3}}{(\pi^{ne}{}_{t+1}/p^{n}{}_{t})(Sf^{e}{}_{t+1})} = 0 \tag{13.156}$$

$$\frac{\partial p^{o}{}_{f}}{\partial p^{*fe}{}_{t+1}} = \frac{-e(.) + (\partial e/\partial D^{*fe}{}_{t+1})}{Sf_{t}}$$

$$+ \frac{[(\partial\hat{e}/\partial D^{*fe}{}_{t+1}\{.\} + \hat{e}(.)(1 + r^{*de}{}_{t}) - w_{t+1}\alpha^{+}{}_{2}]}{(\pi^{ne}{}_{t+1}/p^{n}{}_{t})Sf^{e}{}_{t+1}(.)} = 0 \tag{13.157}$$

$$\frac{\partial p^{f}{}_{o}}{\partial B^{*f}{}_{t+1}} = \frac{(\partial e/\partial B^{*fd}{}_{t+1})\{.\} - p^{*b}{}_{t}e(.)}{Sf_{t}} + \frac{\hat{e}(.) + (\partial\hat{e}/\partial B^{*fd}{}_{t+1})}{(\pi^{ne}{}_{t+1}/p^{n}{}_{t})Sf^{e}{}_{t+1}(.)} = 0 \tag{13.158}$$

First-order conditions (13.153) - (13.156) are exactly the same as their closed-economy counterparts, except that $\pi^{f}{}_{t+1}$ in the second term of (13.155) is defind differently than the corresponding term in (10.25). The reader is referred to Chapter 10 for a discussion of these variables. However several additional terms appear in the first-order condition associated with the optimal interest rate on checkable deposits, expression (13.152), which do not appear in the closed-economy version,equation (10.22). Also, the first-order conditions associated with the private financial sector's anticipated optimal holdings of foreign exchange (in the form of checkable deposits at foreign depository institutions) and foreign bonds, conditions (13.157) and (13.158), are new; they have no closed-economy counterparts.

Turning to the new features found in (13.152), notice that the condition now contains three complex terms which sum to zero. The first of these terms now includes the anticipated effects of an increase in $r^{d}{}_{t}$ upon current dividends arising from balance of payments considerations. For one thing, if the domestic private financial sector were to raise $r^{d}{}_{t}$, it would discourage the domestic government and domestic nonfinancial business sectors from accumulating foreign checkable deposits in the current period and encourage the foreign sector to accumulate domestic checkable deposits. Ceteris paribus, this will increase the "flow" demand for domestic money outside the domestic private financial sector. Holding constant the domestic private financial sector's end-of-period demand for foreign exchange, the sector will tend to lower the exchange rate, if it estimates that by doing so it will diminsh the flow demand for domestic money by the other sectors. Suppose we adopt the standard assumption that a redution in e_t does reduce the flow demand for the domestic money and suppose that the private financial sector correctly anticipates at least the direction of this response. Then as the sector reduces e_t, in order to offset the anticipated effect on the flow demand for domestic money by other sectors in response to the rise in r^d_t, it reduces the domestic-money value of its own anticipated current-period net receipts from abroad, $e_t[B^{*f}_t + r^{*d}_{t-1}D^{*f}_t - p^{*b}_t B^{*fd}_{t+1} - (D^{*fe}_{t+1} - D^{*f}_t)]$. Consequently, if the domestic private financial sector plans that its current-period acquisitions of foreign bonds and foreign checkable deposits will be smaller than its current-period receipts of principal and interest from foreign bonds and checkable deposits it holds at the beginning of the period, then the effects of an increase in r^d_t upon the dollar value of its current dividends arising from its own transactions with the foreign sector will be negative as shown by the term $(\partial e/\partial r^d_t)\{B^{*f}_t + r^{*d}_{t-1}D^{*f}_t - p^{*b}_t B^{*fd}_{t+1} - (D^{*fe}_{t+1} - D^{*f}_t)\}$ in the numerator of the first term in condition (13.152).

An increase in r^d_t also exerts another effect upon the current-period dividends of the private financial sector because of its transactions in foreign exchange. In particular, from (13.145) it is evident that a rise in r^d_t reduces the sector's anticipated gross payments of foreign exchange as it stands ready to trade in that market at the exchange rate it announces, i.e. $\partial z^e_t/\partial r^d_t < 0$. According to our earlier assumptions, the drop in the level of these transactions reduces current transactions time, permitting the private financial sector to conserve current labor expenses and thereby raise current dividends to its shareholders.

Besides the above two effects upon current-period dividends, a change in r^d_t also introduces two more effects upon the anticipated level of <u>next</u> period's dividends per share that were not present in the closed-economy model. These are shown by the third complex term on the left-hand side of (13.152) and are directly analogous to the two effects on current-period dividends just discussed. In particular, if the private financial sector raises r^d_t it will, as has been mentioned, encourage the foreign sector's end-of-period demand for domestic checkable deposits and dampen the domestic government and nonfinancial business sectors' demands for foreign deposits. Therefore, next period, ceteris paribus, the interest income and principal from domestic deposits paid to foreigners will be larger than otherwise while the interest income and principal from foreign deposits paid to the domestic nonfinancial sectors will be smaller. Therefore, an increase in r^d_t, ceteris paribus, reduces the anticipated net (flow) demand for the domestic currency next period by those sectors outside the domestic private financial sector. An increase in r^d_t, then, produces the opposite effect upon next period's anticipated (flow) demand for domestic currency than it does upon this period's anticipated demand. Assume that the private financial sector anticipates that next period's (flow) demand for domestic currency will be positively related to the exchange rate it announces at the beginning of next period. Then, holding constant the amount of foreign exchange that the private financial sector plans to hold at both the beginning and the end of next period, the private financial sector must at time t revise upward its planned value for e_{t+1} if it decides to raise r^d_t. This will raise next periods dividends per share to the financial sector's owners because it will increase the domestic-currency value of the income which the private financial sector itself plans to receive on foreign assets next period. This impact upon next period's anticipated dividends is shown by $(\partial\hat{e}/\partial r^d_t)\{B^{*fd}_{t+1} + (1 + r^{*de}_t)D^{*fe}_{t+1}\}$ in the numerator of the third term.

The second effect on next period's anticipated dividends per share results from the assumption that an increase in r^d_t increases the gross payments of foreign exchange that the financial sector anticipates making next period (see (13.147)). This presumably raises next period's anticipated transactions time and also next period's anticipated labor expense, thereby reducing next period's anticipated dividends per share. This effect upon next period's anticipated dividends per share is shown by $- w_{t+1}\alpha^+_1(\partial z^e_{t+1}/\partial r^d_t)$ in the numerator of the third term in (13.152).

The above discussion of the additional terms in the first-order condition for r^d_t is directly relevant to the two new first-order conditions, (13.157) and (13.158). Consider first the condition associated with the private financial sector's end-of-period demand for checkable deposits denominated in foreign exchange. If the sector increases by one unit the amount it plans to hold in checkable deposits at foreign institutions by the end of the current period, it reduces current revenues by e_t units of domestic currency. But the unit rise in D^{*fe}_{t+1} also means that the sector will need to adjust e_t, ceteris paribus, in order to generate the additional (flow) demand for domestic money outside that sector which will provide the extra unit of foreign exchange to the sector. If we assume that an increase in e_t generates an increase in the flow demand for domestic currency, then in order to acquire the extra unit of foreign exchange, the private financial sector will need to raise e_t. Assuming that its own current-period net receipts from abroad are positive, then as it raises e_t in order to gain the added unit of foreign exchange, the sector simultaneously raises the value (in terms of the domestic currency) of its own current-period net receipts from foreign assets it holds at time t. This second effect, then, raises current-period dividends to the sector's owners.

If the private financial sector decides to hold an additional unit of foreign exchange at the beginning of next period (but not by the end of that period) the decision will also affect next period's anticipated net income. For one thing, the additional unit of D^{*fe}_{t+1} will provide an additional $e_{t+1}(1 + r^{*de}_t)$ units of principal and interest next period, measured in domestic currency. In addition, the extra unit of foreign exchange held at the beginning of next period presumably conserves next period's transactions costs thereby increasing next period's dividends by $- w_{t+1}\alpha^+_2$, the value of the marginal product of D^{*fe}_{t+1}. These two effects on next period's net income are tempered by the fact that if the sector decides to hold one more unit of D^{*f}_{t+1} by the beginning of next period but still plans to hold zero balances of foreign exchange by the end of that period, it must adjust the level of e_{t+1} it plans to announce at the beginning of next period in order to divest itself of that extra unit of foreign exchange. Assuming that the anticipated flow demand for foreign exchange by the other sectors next period is negatively related to e_{t+1}, the private financial sector will plan to announce a lower value for e_{t+1} than it would otherwise. But as it lowers e_{t+1}, it reduces the domestic-currency value of its own anticipated income from foreign assets next period, $(\partial e/\partial D^{*fe}_{t+1})\{B^{*fd}_{t+1} + (1 + r^{*de}_t)D^{*fe}_{t+1}\}$. According to condition (13.157), the private financial sector will continue to add to the amount of foreign exchange it plans to hold by the end of the period up to the point at which the present value of the (net) marginal contribution to the dividend stream equals zero.

First-order condition (13.158) may be interpreted analogously. If the private financial sector plans to add one unit to the number of foreign bonds it holds by the end of the period, ceteris paribus, it will demand foreign exchange in order to purchase those bonds. In order to induce the other sectors to demand the extra dollars it is supplying, the sector will tend to raise e_t. As it raises e_t, the value of its current period income (measured in domestic currency) from foreign assets it holds at time t also rises, as shown by the sum $(\partial\hat{e}/\partial B^{*f}_{t+1})\ B^{*f}_t + r^{*d}_{t-1}D^{*f}_t - p^{*b}_t B^{*fd}_{t+1} - (D^{*fe}_{t+1} - D^{*f}_t)$. But the mere fact that it decides to add one more foreign bond to its end-of-period portfolio reduces current dividends by the amount $p^{b*}_t e_t$.

Each additional bond the private financial sector holds at time t+1 yields an anticipated total of one unit of foreign exchange in principal and interest next period, which translates into an additional e_{t+1} units of net income next period to shareholders in terms of domestic currency. But for each additional foreign bond it holds at the beginning of next period, the sector will demand e_{t+1} units of domestic currency in the foreign exchange market, ceteris paribus. Keeping its balances of foreign exchange constant, this means the sector must plan to lower e_{t+1} below the level it previously planned in order to induce the other sectors to provide it with the extra domestic currency it will demand next period. But, as the sector lowers the value of e_{t+1}, it plans to announce next period, it simultanously reduces the present value (measured in domestic currency) of the income it anticipates next period from foreign assets it holds at time t+1. This last effect is shown by $(\partial\hat{e}/\partial B^{*fd}_{t+1})\ \{B^{*fd}_{t+1} + (1 + r^{*de}_t)D^{*fe}_{t+1}\}$ in the numerator of the second term in (13.158).

Totally differentiating (13.152) - (13.158) and solving the resulting system for the differentials of the choice variables r^d_t, r^ℓ_t, p^b_t, p^f_t, A^d_{t+1}, D^{*fe}_{t+1}, and B^{*fd}_{t+1} yields the signs of the partial derivaties of these variables with respect to the parameters which the domestic private financial sector at time t takes as given:

$$r^d_t = r^d_t(\rho_t,\ w_{t+1},\ p^n_t,\ Sf_t,\ \xi_b,\ \xi_c,\ \xi_d,\ \xi_f,\ \xi_\ell,\ B^{*f}_t,\ D^{*f}_t$$

$$r^{*d}_{t-1},\ r^{*d}_t,\ p^{*b}_t,\ p^c_t,\ p^{*c}_t) \qquad (13.159)$$

$$r^{\ell}_t = r^{\ell}_t(\rho_t,\ w_{t+1},\ p^n_t,\ Sf_t,\ \xi_b,\ \xi_c,\ \xi_d,\ \xi_f,\ \xi_\ell,\ B^{*f}_t,\ D^{*f}_t$$
$$r^{*d}_{t-1},\ r^{*d}_t,\ p^{*b}_t,\ p^c_t,\ p^{*c}_t) \qquad (13.160)$$

$$p^b_t = p^b_t(\rho_t,\ w_{t+1},\ p^n_t,\ Sf_t,\ \xi_b,\ \xi_c,\ \xi_d,\ \xi_f,\ \xi_\ell,\ B^{*f}_t,\ D^{*f}_t$$
$$r^{*d}_{t-1},\ r^{*d}_t,\ p^{*b}_t,\ p^c_t,\ p^{*c}_t) \qquad (13.161)$$

$$p^f_t = p^f_t(\rho_t,\ w_{t+1},\ p^n_t,\ Sf_t,\ \xi_b,\ \xi_c,\ \xi_d,\ \xi_f,\ \xi_\ell,\ B^{*f}_t,\ D^{*f}_t$$
$$r^{*d}_{t-1},\ r^{*d}_t,\ p^{*b}_t,\ p^c_t,\ p^{*c}_t) \qquad (13.162)$$

$$A^d_{t+1} = A^d_{t+1}(\rho_t,\ w_{t+1},\ p^n_t,\ Sf_t,\ \xi_b,\ \xi_c,\ \xi_d,\ \xi_f,\ \xi_\ell,\ B^{*f}_t,\ D^{*f}_t$$
$$r^{*d}_{t-1},\ r^{*d}_t,\ p^{*b}_t,\ p^c_t,\ p^{*c}_t) \qquad (13.163)$$

$$D^{*fe}_{t+1} = D^{*f}_{t+1}(\rho_t,\ w_{t+1},\ p^n_t,\ Sf_t,\ \xi_b,\ \xi_c,\ \xi_d,\ \xi_f,\ \xi_\ell,\ B^{*f}_t,\ D^{*f}_t$$
$$r^{*d}_{t-1},\ r^{*d}_t,\ p^{*b}_t,\ p^c_t,\ p^{*c}_t) \qquad (13.164)$$

$$B^{*fd} = B^{*f}_{t+1}(\rho_t,\ w_{t+1},\ p^n_t,\ Sf_t,\ \xi_b,\ \xi_c,\ \xi_d,\ \xi_f,\ \xi_\ell,\ B^{*f}_t,\ D^{*f}_t$$
$$r^{*d}_{t-1},\ r^{*d}_t,\ p^{*b}_t,\ p^c_t,\ p^{*c}_t) \qquad (13.165)$$

The effects of each of the first nine parameters in each of the first five functions were discussed in detail in Chapter 10 in connection with a closed economy. For simplicity, assume that these effects do not change significantly as the economy is opened to a foreign sector. We concentrate instead upon (a) the effects of the foreign parameters (B^{*f}_t, D^{*f}_t, r^{*d}_{t-1}, r^{*d}_t, p^{*d}_t and p^{*c}_t) upon the domestic financial sector's end-of-period demand for advances and the prices and interest rates it announces at time t and (b) the effects of all sixteen parameters upon the domestic financial sector's end-of-period demands for checkable deposits and bonds issued by the foreign sector.

Effects of B^{*f}_t,, D^{*f}_t and r^{*d}_{t-1} upon r^d_t, r^1_t,p^b_t, p^f_t and A^d_{t+1}

Consider, first, the effects of an increase in the private financial sector's initial holdings of foreign bonds, B^{*f}_t, its initial holdings of foreign checkable deposits, D^{*f}_{t}, or the interest income, r^{*d}_{t-1}, it earns in the current period on checkable deposits denominated in foreign currency. An increase in any one of these three parameters, ceteris paribus, increases the private financial sector's current-period receipts from abroad and raises the current-period flow of dividends to its owners. This increase in income from the foreign sector raises the marginal cost (in terms of the resulting reduction in the value of that income denominated in the domestic currency) of a unit reduction in the current-period exchange rate. This increased marginal cost of raising e_t is relevant for determining the optimal interest rate on checkable deposits, r^{d}_{t}, to be set by the domestic private financial sector at time t. For given the amount of foreign currency which the private financial sector plans to hold by the end of the current period, the sector will need to lower e_t as it raises r^{d}_{t} in order to maintain a given "flow" demand for domstic currency by those sectors outside the domestic private financial sector. Consequently, the greater B^{*f}_{t}, D^{*f}_{t} or r^{*d}_{t-1} happen to be, the greater the marginal cost of increasing r^{d}_{t} one unit, thereby inducing the private financial sector to reduce r^{d}_{t}.

Of course, this effect upon r^{d}_{t} is merely the "direct effect" operating through first-order condition (13.152). Indirect effects upon r^{d}_{t} are also produced by a change in B^{*f}_{t}, D^{*f}_{t} or r^{*d}_{t-1} which operate through the other first-order conditions. For instance, an increase in one of these parameters will also effect, among other choice variables, the private financial sector's end-of-period demand for foreign exchange (in the form of deposits it holds in the foreign sector), D^{*fe}_{t-1}. As it adjusts this demand, it will also need to adjust e_t accordingly which in turn will affect the marginal cost of adjusting r^{d}_{t}. In the following discusson of the parametric effects upon r^{1}_{t}, p^{b}_{t}, p^{f}_{t}, A^{d}_{t+1}, D^{*fe}_{t+1}, and B^{*fd}_{t+1} we will limit the analysis to the "direct effects", i.e. the effects operating through the first-order condition associated with the choice variable under discussion.

In light of this, an increase in D^{*f}_{t}, B^{*f}_{t} or r^{*d}_{t-1} does not directly affect the marginal cost or marginal revenue of a unit change in r^{d}_{t}, p^{b}_{t}, p^{f}_{t} or A^{d}_{t+1}. Therefore an increase in one of these foreign parameters will not directly affect the optimal values of these particular choice variables. However, an increase in D^{*f}_{t}, B^{*f}_{t} or r^{*d}_{t-1} does affect directly the sector's end-of-period demands for foreign checkable deposits, D^{*fe}_{t+1}, and foreign bonds, B^{*fd}_{t+1}. These will be discussed in a later section along with the effects of the domestic parameters upon these end-of-period demands. Before investigating those effects, however, we will first consider the "direct" effects of a change in r^{*d}_t and p^{*b}_t, respectively, upon the seven decision variables r^d_t, r^ℓ_t, p^b_t, p^f_t, A^d_{t+1}, D^{*fe}_{t+1} and B^{*fd}_{t+1}.

Effects of a change in r^{*d}_t

Consider an increase in the interest rate, r^{*d}_t, which the foreign sector announces at time t that it will pay next period on each unit of checkable deposits (denominated in the foreign currency) held at foreign financial institutions at time t+1. Suppose that as a result the domestic financial institutions (a) reduce their estimate of the end-of-period demand for checkable deposits, D^e_{t+1}, (b) increase their estimates of the domestic government and nonfinancial business sectors' end-of-period demands for foreign checkable deposits, D^{*ge} and D^{*ne}, and (c) reduce their estimate of the foreign demand for domestic government bonds, B^{re}_{t+1}. The anticipated drop in D^e_{t+1} reduces next period's marginal cost of raising the interest rate on domestic checkable deposits. This induces the domestic private financial sector to raise r^d_t. The estimated fall in B^{re}_{t+1}, on the other hand, increases the current marginal cost of raising the current price of bonds (since the sector now expects more bonds will be sold to it at a given announced price), thereby causing the private financial sector to reduce the current-period price of those bonds.

The above revised estimates have implications for the domestic depository institutions' estimates of the nation's balance of payments in both the current and next periods. For as r^{*d}_t rises, the domestic sectors will tend to lend more abroad and the foreign sector will tend to lend less to the domestic sectors. This tends to reduce the domestic economy's balance of payments (defined as receipts less outlays in the current period), but to increase next period's balance of payments, at which time the interest payments and repayment of principal will occur on the international loans granted during the current period. As the current balance of payments falls, the customers of the domestic private financial sector will tend to exchange domestic money for foreign money. As a result, the domestic private financial sector will anticipate, ceteris paribus, a drop in its own end-of-period holdings of foreign checkable deposits. Assuming for the moment that the sector's end-of-period demand for these deposits remains unchanged, it will tend to raise the current exchange rate (i.e. devalue the domestic currency) in order to reduce the outside-pressure for it to transfer its own foreign deposits to others.

But the domestic private financial sector may not want just to maintain its anticipated end-of-period holdings of foreign deposits. For one thing, those deposits will now pay a higher return next period. This tends to raise the sector's demand for those deposits. For another, next period's anticipated gross payments to foreigners will fall as the sector anticipates foreigners receiving less interest income from domestic sectors. This reduces the marginal product of deposits held by the domestic financial sector in foreign institutions at the end-of-period. This tends to reduce the sector's end-of-period demand for foreign deposits.

In the present model the domestic household sector is the only one that holds domestic equity shares. But this sector does not have access to foreign checkable deposits in this model. Consequently an increase in r^{*d}_t does not directly affect the private financial sector's estimate of the end-of-period demand function for its shares. Therefore the price it announces at time t for these shares will be affected only by its estimate of the net effect upon its net income next period due to the rise in r^{*d}_t.

If the sector anticipates holding more domestic government bonds next period (due to the foreign sector's reduced demand for those bonds) it will anticipate a greater interest income next period, not only from government bonds but also from its own holdings of foreign deposits. In addition, if the sector anticipates paying out less next period as interest to its own depositors, next period's net income will be higher than otherwise. In this case, the cost to existing owners of issuing additional shares rises, thereby inducing the private financial sector to raise the current-period price of its equity. If the household sector is assumed to be unable to anticipate the effect on the financial sector's income next period and is expected to reduce the quantity it demands these shares in the face of their higher market price, the financial sector will lower its estimate of the number of shares it anticipates it will have outstanding by time t+1. This increases the marginal cost of raising r^{ℓ}_t for the demand for personal loans is assumed to be elastic with respect to this interest rate and the drop in future revenue from raising r^{ℓ}_t, translates into a greater drop in revenue per share as Sf^{e}_{t+1} falls. Under these conditions, the private depository institutions will tend to reduce r^{ℓ}_t.

As r^{*d}_t rises the opportuniy cost of holding foreign bonds at the end of the period rises. The domestic private financial sector's demand for those bonds will fall. In the present model the opportunity cost appears in a unique way, since a change in D^{*d}_{t+1} has implications for next period's exchange rates. According to (13.158) if the sector increases its end-of-period demand for foreign bonds, it must lower e_{t+1}. As it does so, any interest income from abroad next period represents fewer units of domestic currency and the drop in domestic-currency-equivalent income associated with a given drop in e_{t+1} will be higher the greater the interest income the sector anticipates in terms of foreign currency. Therefore, as r^{*d}_t rises, the marginal cost of adding a unit of foreign bonds to the private financial sector's portfolio grows. This induces it to reduce its demand for those bonds.

Finally, as r^{*d}_t rises and the domestic private financial sector revises downward its estimate of domestic checkable deposits outstanding at the end of the period, it revises downward its estimate of the marginal revenue product of excess reserves it plans to hold by the beginning of next period. This causes it to reduce its end-of-period demand for advances from the central bank. Less domestic high-powered money is needed when r^{*d}_t rises since the various sectors of the world will decide to hold more foreign money and less domestic money.

Effects of a change in p^{*b}_t

An increase in the current market price (denominated in foreign exchange) of foreign bonds makes foreign bonds more expensive for the domestic financial sector to purchase. Suppose that this increase also causes the domestic private financial sector to raise its estimate of the end-of-period demand for domestic checkable deposits, D^e_{t+1}, and raise its estimate of the foreign sector's demand, B^{re}_{t+1}, for domestic government bonds. As a result, the domestic private financial sector will tend to reduce its own demand for foreign bonds, to reduce the interest rate it announces for domestic checkable deposits and raise the current price of domestic bonds.

As p^{*b}_t rises, the domestic depository institutions will generally anticipate that the domestic sectors (including itself) will lend less abroad and that foreign sectors will lend more to domestic sectors during the current period. This tends to "improve" the domestic economy's balance of payments this period, causing the domestic financial sector's estimate of its own end-of-period balance of foreign exchange to rise, ceteris paribus. Assuming that its desired level of these balances remains unchanged, the sector would then lower the current exchange rate (revalue the domestic currency) in order to offset the initial tendency for the balance of payments to "improve".

However the domestic sector may anticipate that the rise in p^{*b}_t and the corresponding rise in foreign lending in the domestic markets in the current period will raise next period's gross payments to foreigners in the form of interest and the repayment of principal. In this case the marginal product of deposits held by the sector in foreign institutions by the beginning of next period rises. Consequently its demand for checkable deposits at foreign institutions will rise. This may at least partially offset the sector's tendency to reduce e_t.

Since the domestic financial sector anticipates holding fewer foreign bonds next period and since it anticipates having more checkable deposits outstanding next period, it anticipates lower receipts but higher expenses next period. This reduces the marginal cost to the sector of issuing additional shares, thereby inducing it to reduce the current price of its shares. The sector may, in light of an anticipated increase in the number of its shares outstanding by the end of the period, decide to raise the interest rate on personal loans.

Finally, since the domestic financial sector revises upward is estimate of the volume of its checkable deposit liabilities for the end of the current period, the anticipated marginal product of excess reserves held at that time rises. In addition, because the sector decides to reduce the interest rate on checkable deposits, it may expect the households will hold more domestic currency than otherwise, thereby reducing the financial sector's end-of-period reserves. Both of these effects tend to cause the sector to increase its end-of-period demand for advances from the central bank.

Direct effects upon D^{*fe}_{t+1}

In the present section we consider the factors affecting the desired level of D^{*fe}_{t+1} due to changes in other parameters. The next section analyzes the sector's demand for B^{*fd}_{t+1} in response to these parameters. Neither a change in the current-period discount rate, ρ_t, nor a shift in any of the sector's estimates of the positions of the market demands for currency, checkable deposits or loans or the supply of government bonds directly affects the sector's demands for D^{*fe}_{t+1}

or B^{*fd}_{t+1}. Therefore the analyses of these two functions will be confined to the effects of changes in w_{t+1}, p^n_t, ξ_f, Sf_t, B^{*f}_t and D^{*f}_t.

An increase in w_{t+1} increases the value of the marginal product of D^{*fe}_{t+1} in carrying out transactions next period that involve foreign exchange. This induces the domestic financial sector to increase its end-of-period demand for checkable deposits denominated in the foreign sector's unit of account.

An increase in p^n_t, the current-period market price of nonfinancial sector equity, raises the present value of the future net return from chckable deposits denominated in foreign exchange which the financial sector holds at time t+1. Assuming this net return is positive, i.e. that the numerator in the second term of (13.157) is positive, the rise in p^n_t causes the financial sector's demand for foreign checkable deposits to grow. An outward shift in ξ_f produces the opposite result.

An increase in Sf_t, on the other hand, reduces the net reduction in current period net dividends <u>per share</u> caused by adding to D^{*fe}_{t+1} (assuming the numerator in the first term in (13.157) is negative). This causes the sector to increase its demand for D^{*fe}_{t+1}, ceteris paribus.

An increase in B^{*f}_t, D^{*f}_t or r^{*d}_{t-1} increases the financial sector's current period net income from abroad. This in turn increases the marginal revenue to the current owners of a unit increase in the current period exchange rate since a rise in e_t means that a given amount of income denominted in the foreign unit of account represents a greater amount in terms of domestic money. Therefore, ceteris paribus, an increase in B^{*f}_t, D^{*f}_t or r^{*d}_{t-1} will induce the domestic private financial secctor to increase its demand for D^{*fe}_{t+1} since it must thereby raise the current exchange rate in order to reduce the "flow" demand for foreign exchange by the other decision-making units.

<u>Direct effects upon B^{*fd}_{t+1}</u>

An increase in w_{t+1} does not directly affect the domestic financial sector's demand for foreign bonds. An increase in Sf_t, however, reduces the marginal cost to current owners of adding one more foreign bond to the private financial sector's end-of-period portfolio, since the foregone current dividends <u>per share</u> are smaller as Sf_t rises.

An increase in p^n_t raises the present value of the anticipated future net return from foreign bonds which the financial sector plans to hold at time t, causing the sector to increase its demand for foreign bonds. An outward shift in the sector's estimate of the end-of-period demand for its own equity shares, on the other hand, reduces the anticipated future net return per share from foreign bonds, inducing the sector to buy fewer foreign bonds in the current period (and therefore distribute more dividends to its existing owners in the current period).

An increase in B^{*f}_{t}, D^{*f}_{t} or r^{*d}_{t-1} increases, ceteris paribus, the domestic financial sector's current-period income from abroad. As discussed above, this encourages the sector to raise the current-period exchange rate, which it will have to do if it increases its demand for foreign bonds, ceteris paribus. Therefore, an increase in current income from abroad induces the domestic financial sector to increase is demand for foreign bonds.

Reaction of the domestic private financial sector to changes in p^{*c}_{t} and p^{c}_{t}

Changes in p^{*c}_{t} or p^{c}_{t} affect the domestic private financial sector's choice variables at time t only through their effects on the sector's estimate of the current-period exchange rate it plans to announce at time t. Consequently, from conditions (13.152) - (13.157) it is clear that changes in p^{*c}_{t} or p^{c}_{t} directly affect only the private financial sector's end-of-period demands for foreign checkable deposits, D^{*fe}_{t+1}, and foreign bonds, B^{*fd}_{t+1}. Since an increase in e_t raises the current-period opportunity cost (in terms of forgone dividends to current owners) of adding one more unit to either D^{*fe}_{t+1} or B^{*fd}_{t+1} (expressed in terms of the foreign sector's unit of account), a change in p^{c}_{t} or p^{*c}_{t} that raises the e_t that the domestic sector anticipates it must announce for the current period causes the sector to revise downward its demands for both foreign assets. Consequently an increase in p^{c}_{t} or a reduction in p^{*c}_{t} causes the domestic private financial sector, ceteris paribus, to reduce its demands for D^{*fe}_{t+1} and B^{*fd}_{t+1} and to raise e_t.

Remaining values in the solution to (13.151)

Substituting the solution to the optimizing problem, i.e. substituting (13.159) - (13.165) back into (13.151), produces the value of the exchange rate, e_t, that the private financial sector deems optimal at time t to announce for the current period:

$$e_t = e_t(\rho_t, w_{t+1}, p^n_t, Sf_t, \xi_f, B^{*f}_t, D^{*f}_t, r^{*d}_{t-1}, r^{*d}_t, p^{*b}_t, p^c_t, p^{*c}_t) \qquad (13.166)$$

Although the amount of foreign exchange D^{*fe}_{t+1} that the private financial sector plans at time t to hold at time t+1 (as shown by (13.163) above) is consistent with its ex ante version of the "balance-of-payments" equation (13.136), the actual amount of foreign exchange that the private financial sector holds at time t+1, D^{*f}_{t+1}, is found by substituting the ex post magnitudes of the relevant variables into the right hand side of that equation.

Substitution of the solution for the above decision variables into (13.125) yields the level of dividends which the domestic private financial sector announces at time t that it will distribute to its owners during the current period. This amount corresponds to the amount that the sector deems at time t to be optimal to distribute during the current period in terms of maximizing the sector's present value:

$$\pi^f_t = \pi^f_t(\rho_t, w_{t+1}, p^n_t, Sf_t, \xi_b, \xi_c, \xi_d, \xi_f, \xi_\ell, B^{*f}_t, D^{*f}_t, r^{*d}_{t-1}, r^{*d}_t, p^{*b}_t, p^c_t, p^{*c}_t) \qquad (13.167)$$

Finally, the average number of hours of labor the sector plans to use in the current period is obtained by substituting the solution to the optimizing problem into (13.146):

$$h^f_t = h^f_t(\rho_t, w_{t+1}, p^n_t, Sf_t, \xi_b, \xi_c, \xi_d, \xi_f, \xi_\ell, B^{*f}_t, D^{*f}_t, r^{*d}_{t-1}, r^{*d}_t, p^{*b}_t, p^c_t, p^{*c}_t) \qquad (13.168)$$

while the sector's demand for workers with which to begin next period is found by substituting the solution into (13.148) to obtain

$$N^{fd}_{t+1} = N^{fd}_{t+1}(\rho_t, w_{t+1}, p^n_t, Sf_t, \xi_b, \xi_c, \xi_d, \xi_f, \xi_\ell, B^{*f}_t, D^{*f}_t, r^{*d}_{t-1}, r^{*d}_t, p^{*b}_t, p^c_t, p^{*c}_t) \qquad (13.169)$$

The Complete Model of a Large Open Economy

The preceding sections of the present chapter have respecified the optimizing behavior of the domestic government, household, nonfinancial business and private financial sectors within an open economy. A separate section has not been devoted to revising central bank behavior because the central bank's activity in this chapter remains unchanged from what was specified earlier. Just as in the closed-economy version, the central bank refrains from intervening in any market in the open economy except to announce the current-period discount rate and to lend freely to domestic private financial institutions at that rate. The only added feature in the open version insofar as the central bank is concernd is that interest rates and product prices announced by the foreign sector may affect the domestic private financial sector's demand for advances. Since the domestic central bank must estimate that demand function in order to establish the optimal discount rate, its discount rate decision may well be influenced by foreign prices and interest rates and hence by international activity.

The open model developed here contains complete domestic markets for consumption goods, capital goods, labor, equity shares of the private financial sector, equity shares of the nonfinancial business sector, personal loans, checkable deposits, government bonds, advances and foreign exchange. Taken together, these markets simultaneously constitute a market for domestic high-powered money.

The dynamic model developed here views economic agents as setting the exchange rate and all domestic wages, prices and interest rates in accordance with their attempts to optimize their respective objective functions. The prices which the various agents announce at the beginning of the period are the ones they deem to be optimal. However the price-setters base their decisions on forecasts of market demand and supply functions which are derived using imperfect information. Consequently, their forecasts may prove to be incorrect. As a result at least some markets may fail to clear by the end of the period, just as in the closed-economy version.

Basically, the present section specifies the market-trading functions for each of the markets described above and combines them with the behavioral functions derived in the preceding sections to form a complete dynamic model. Presumably the actual amounts traded in the markets for personal loans, consumption goods, capital goods and labor correspond in each case to the minimum of the price-takers' ex ante demand (or supply) of that item and the price-setter's ex ante supply (or demand) based upon its estimate of the market demand (supply) at the price it announces. In the markets for bonds, equities, advances, checkable deposits and foreign exchange, however, the amount actually traded presumably amounts to the price-takers' ex ante demand or supply.

After specifying the behavioral functions and the market-clearing equations, we will derive measures for national income and product. Then the complete model will be linearized to form a recursive system depenent upon various exogenous variables and the endogenous variables lagged one period. The exogenous variables will include the prices and interest rates announced by the foreign sector.

The government sector, in its initial phase of decision-making at time t, decides the optimal combination of labor hours, $h^g{}_t$, domestically-produced consumption goods, $c^{gd}{}_t$, and imports, $im^{*gd}{}_t$, to combine with the predetermined level of physical capital in order to produce the level of government-produced goods, g_t, that the household sector decided last period that it wanted the government to provide this period. In addition, the government prepares the menu of alternative levels of government-produced goods and taxes from which the households will select for next period. These functions were derived earlier as (13.23) - (13.37) and are repeated here as (13.170) - (13.173):

$$h^g{}_t = h^g{}_t(N^g{}_t,\ w_t,\ p^{cg}{}_t,\ e^g{}_t p^{*g}{}_t,\ D^g{}_t,\ D^{*g}{}_t,\ g_t) \tag{13.170}$$

$$c^{gd}{}_t = c^g{}_t(w_t,\ p^{cg}{}_t,\ e^g{}_t p^{*g}{}_t,\ D^g{}_t,\ D^{*g}{}_t,\ g_t) \tag{13.171}$$

$$im^{*gd}{}_t = im^g{}_t(w_t,\ p^{cg}{}_t,\ e^g{}_t p^{*g}{}_t,\ D^g{}_t,\ D{*}^g{}_t,\ g_t) \tag{13.172}$$

$$Tx_{t+1} = Tx_{t+1}(g_{t+1},\ k^*) \tag{13.173}$$

Once the government sector has announced next period's menu, the nonfinancial business sector presumably decides the optimal levels of its variable resources in the current period, the optimal levels of its current-period production of capital goods and consumption goods, the optimal money wage, the optimal prices of its products and its equity shares, the optimal levels of the various assets in its end-of-period balance sheet and current dividends to its owners. These values are given in accordance with expressions (13.107) - (13.120) above and summarized below by (13.174) - (13.186):

$$h^n_t = h^n_t(.) \qquad (13.174)$$

$$i_t = i_t(.) \qquad (13.175)$$

$$w_{t+1} = w_{t+1}(.) \qquad (13.176)$$

$$N^{nd}_{t+1} = N^{nd}_{t+1}(.) \qquad (13.177)$$

$$K^{nd}_{t+1} = K^{nd}_{t+1}(.) \qquad (13.178)$$

$$D^{nd}_{t+1} = D^{nd}_{t+1}(.) \qquad (13.179)$$

$$D^{*nd}_{t+1} = D^{*nd}_{t+1}(.) \qquad (13.180)$$

$$im^{*n}_t = im^{*n}_t(.) \qquad (13.181)$$

$$p^c_t = p^c_t(.) \qquad (13.182)$$

$$p^k_t = p^k_t(.) \qquad (13.183)$$

$$p^n_t = p^n_t(.) \qquad (13.184)$$

$$\pi^n_t = \pi^n_t(.) \qquad (13.185)$$

$$c_t = c_t(.) \qquad (13.186)$$

The central bank then announces the current discount rate and the current income to the government sector from its operations as shown by (12.15) and (12.16), repeated here as (13.187) and (13.188).

$$\rho_t = \rho_t(\xi_a) \qquad (13.187)$$

$$\pi^{cb}_t = \rho_{t-1}A_t \qquad (13.188)$$

After the domestic central bank has announced the discount rate, the domestic private financial sector announces the current interest rates on domestic checkable deposits and loans as well as the current period prices of domestic bonds and financial sector equity <u>and</u> the current exchange rate. It also decides at time t the amounts of the various assets and liabilities it plans for its end-of-period balance sheet. These plans are based in part upon the sector's estimates of the demand for domestic currency as well as of the current-period "balance of payments" with respect to those outside the domestic private financial sector. They include the sector's planned advances at time t+1, its planned holdings of foreign exchange at t+1 and its planned holdings of foreign bonds. In addition the sector announces at time t its own current-period dividends and decides the amount of labor it wants to use during the current period and the number of people it wants to employ by the beginning of next period. These decisions by the domestic private financial sector were discussed earlier as functions (13.159) - (13.165) and (13.166) - (13.169) and are restated here in summary form as (13.189) - (13.199):

$$r^d_t = r^d_t(.) \qquad (13.189) \qquad D^{*fe}_{t+1} = D^{*f}_{t+1}(.) \qquad (13.195)$$

$$r^\ell_t = r^\ell_t(.) \qquad (13.190) \qquad B^{*fd}_{t+1} = B^{*f}_{t+1}(.) \qquad (13.196)$$

$$p^b_t = p^b_t(.) \qquad (13.191) \qquad \pi^f_t = \pi^f_t(.) \qquad (13.196)$$

$$p^f_t = p^f_t(.) \qquad (13.192) \qquad h^f_t = h^f_t(.) \qquad (13.198)$$

$$e_t = e_t(.) \qquad (13.193) \qquad N^{fd}_{t+1} = N^{fd}_{t+1}(.) \qquad (13.199)$$

$$A^d_{t+1} = A^d_{t+1}(.) \qquad (13.194)$$

Next, given the array of current-period prices, wages, interest rates and exchange rates announced by the privaate nonfinancial and financial business sectors, the household sector decides the optimal levels of current purchases of domestic consumption goods, c^h_t, and imports, im^h_t, as well as the optimal values in its end-of-period balance sheet. In addition, it decides the number of people it would like to have working by the beginning of next period as well as the level of government-produced goods next period. These decisions were described above as functions (13.49) - (13.58) and are summarized here as (13.200) - (13.209):

$$c^{hd}_t = c^h_t(.) \qquad (13.200) \qquad K^{hd}_{t+1} = K^h_{t+1}(.) \qquad (13.205)$$

$$Sf^{hd}_{t+1} = Sf^h_{t+1}(.) \qquad (13.201) \qquad L^{hd}_{t+1} = L^h_{t+1}(.) \qquad (13.206)$$

$$Sn^{hd}_{t+1} = Sn^h_{t+1}(.) \qquad (13.202) \qquad N^s_{t+1} = N^s_{t+1}(.) \qquad (13.207)$$

$$Cu^{hd}_{t+1} = Cu^h_{t+1}(.) \qquad (13.203) \qquad g_{t+1} = g_{t+1}(.) \qquad (13.208)$$

$$D^{hd}_{t+1} = D^h_{t+1}(.) \qquad (13.204) \qquad im^{*hd}_t = im^h_t(.) \qquad (13.209)$$

Once the household sector has selected the optimal level of g_{t+1}, the government sector is ready to plan its end-of-period balance sheet as well as to make its employment plans for next period. These decisions were specified above by functions (13.3) and (13.24) - (13.38). They are reproduced here as (13.210) - (13.214):

$$N^{gd}_{t+1} = N^{gd}_{t+1}(.) \quad (13.210) \qquad D^{*gd}_{t+1} = D^{*gd}_{t+1}(.) \quad (13.213)$$

$$K^{gd}_{t+1} = K^{gd}_{t+1}(.) \quad (13.211) \qquad p^{bg}_{t}B^{sg}_{t+1} = B^{sg}_{t+1}(.) \quad (13.214)$$

$$D^{gd}_{t+1} = D^{gd}_{t+1}(.) \quad (13.212)$$

Next, suppose all beginning-of-period announcements as to current interest rates, wages, prices, dividends and labor hours have been made by the various price-setters. The respective current-period ex ante budget or cash-flow restrictions upon the household, government and business sectors and the central bank may then be aggregated to form a community budget restriction expressed in terms of the announced prices. This community budget constraint, in turn, implies a relationship among the "excess demands" in all markets, including the market for foreign exchange.

To derive the relevant community budget constraint, we begin by specifying the government's current period ex ante budget restriction, (13.1), in terms of the wages prices and interest rates announced for the current period:

$$\begin{aligned} Tx_t + \pi^{cb}_t + r^d_{t-1}D^g_t + e_t r^{*d}_{t-1}D^{*g}_t - B^g_t - p^c_t c^{gd}_t \\ - w_t h^g_t N^g_t - e_t p^{*c}_t im^{*gd}_t = (D^{gd}_{t+1} - D^g_t) + p^k_t(K^{gd}_{t+1} \\ - K^g_t) + (D^{*gd}_{t+1} - D^{*g}_t) - p^b_t B^{gs}_{t+1}. \end{aligned} \quad (13.215)$$

Next, from (13.39) and (13.40), the household sector's current-period budget constraint may be expressed as:

$$\begin{aligned} w_t(h^g_t N^g_t + h^n_t N^n_t + h^f_t N^f_t) + r^d_{t-1}D^h_t + \pi^n_t Sn_t + \pi^f_t Sf_t \\ - Tx_t - p^c_t c^{hd}_t - e_t p^{*c}_t im^{*hd}_t - r^1_{t-1}L_t = p^n_t(Sn^{hd}_{t+1} \\ - Sn_t) + p^f_t(Sf^{hd}_{t+1} - Sf_t) + (D^{hd}_{t+1} - D^h_t) + p^k_t(K^{hd}_{t+1} \\ - K^h_t) - (L^{hd}_{t+1} - L^h_t) + (Cu^{hd}_{t+1} - Cu_t). \end{aligned} \quad (13.216)$$

Substitution of (13.69) into (13.60) yields the following expression for the nonfinancial business sector's cash-flow constraint in ex ante terms:

$$p^{c}_{t}c^{de}_{t} + p^{k}_{t}i^{de}_{t} + r^{d}_{t-1}D^{n}_{t} + e_{t}r^{*d}_{t-1}D^{*n}_{t} - w_{t}h^{n}_{t}N^{n}_{t}$$

$$- e_{t}p^{*c}_{t}im^{*nd}_{t} - \pi^{n}_{t}Sn_{t} = (D^{nd}_{t+1} - D^{n}_{t}) + e_{t}(D^{*nd}_{t+1}$$

$$- D^{*n}_{t}) - p^{n}_{t}(Sn^{e}_{t+1} - Sn_{t}). \qquad (13.217)$$

From (13.123), the private financial business sector's cash flow constraint may be written as:

$$r^{\ell}_{t-1}L_{t} + (B^{g}_{t} - B^{r}_{t}) + e_{t}B^{*f}_{t} + e_{t}r^{*f}_{t-1}D^{*f}_{t} - r^{d}_{t-1}D_{t}$$

$$- \rho_{t-1}A_{t} - w_{t}h^{f}_{t}N^{f}_{t} - \pi^{f}_{t}Sf_{t}$$

$$= (Rs^{e}_{t+1} - Rs_{t}) + p^{b}_{t}B^{fd}_{t+1} + e_{t}p^{*b}_{t}B^{*fd}_{t+1}$$

$$+ e_{t}(D^{*fe}_{t+1} - D^{*f}_{t}) + (L^{e}_{t+1} - L_{t}) - (D^{e}_{t+1} - D_{t}) - (A^{d}_{t+1}$$

$$- A_{t}) - p^{f}_{t}(Sf^{e}_{t+1} - Sf_{t}) \qquad (13.218)$$

Note that D^{*fe}_{t+1} in (13.218) represents the amount of foreign exchange that the private financial sector plans to hold by the end of the current period. The quantity $(D^{*fe}_{t+1} - D^{*f}_{t+1})$ then represents its ex ante "flow" demand for foreign exchange (more correctly, the amount of foreign exchange it plans to acquire) during the current period. The amount of foreign exchange, $D^{*fs}_{t+1} - D^{*f}_{t+1}$, which the sectors outside the domestic private financial sector plan at the beginning of the period to bring to the private financial sector this period (i.e. the "flow" supply of foreign exchane) is found from (13.134), where the amounts on the right hand side are amounts planned by those sectors, outside the domestic depository institutions. Since the domestic private sector's demand for foreign bonds, B^{*fd}_{t+1}, also appears on the right hand side of (13.219), that side of (13.219) also contains the foreign exchange market implications of that sector's plans in the foreign bond market.

$$e_t(D^{*fs}_{t+1} - D^{*f}_t) = p^c_t ex_t - e_t p^{*c}_t(im^{*hd}_t + im^{*gd}_t + im^{*nd}_t)$$
$$+ p^b_t B^r_{t+1} - B^r_t - e_t p^{*b}_t B^{*fd}_{t+1} + e_t B^{*f}_t$$
$$+ e_t r^{d*}_{t-1}(D^{*g}_t + D^{*n}_t + D^{*f}_t) + (D^r_{t+1} - D^r_t)$$
$$- r^d_{t-1} D^r_t - e_t(D^{*gd}_{t+1} - D^{*g}_t) - e_t(D^{*nd}_{t+1} - D^{*n}_t)$$
$$- D^{*n}_t). \qquad (13.219)$$

Note that (13.219) may be viewed as defining the ex ante end-of-period supply of foreign exchange to the private financial sector, D^{*fs}_{t+1}. Finally, from (12.41), the central bank's current-period cash-flow constraint appears as follows

$$\rho_{t-1} A_t - \pi^{cb}_t = (A^e_{t+1} - A_t) - (MB^e_{t+1} - MB_t). \qquad (13.220)$$

Summing across (13.215) - (13.220) yields the following statement of Walras' law:

$$p^c_t(c^{de} - c^{hd}_t - c^g_t - ex_t) + p^k_t(i^{de}_t - (K^{hd}_{t+1} - K^h_t)$$
$$- (K^{gd}_{t+1} - K^g_t)) + p^n_t(Sn^e_{t+1} - Sn^{hd}_{t+1}) + p^f_t(Sf^e_{t+1}$$
$$- Sf^{hd}_{t+1}) + p^b_t(B^{gs}_{t+1} - B^r_{t+1} - B^{fd}_{t+1}) + (A^d_{t+1} - A^e_{t+1})$$
$$+ (L^h_{t+1} - L^e_{t+1}) + (D^e_{t+1} - D^{gd}_{t+1} - D^{hd}_{t+1} - D^{nd}_{t+1} - D^r_{t+1})$$
$$+ (MB^e_{t+1} - R^e_{t+1} - Cu^{hd}_{t+1}) + e_t(D^{*fs}_{t+1} - D^{*fe}_{t+1}) = 0 \quad (13.221)$$

According to this expression, for any given set of wages, prices and interest rates, the sum of the value of the market excess supply of domestic consumption goods <u>plus</u> the value of the market excess supply of domestic capital goods <u>plus</u> the values of the market excess supplies of business sector equity <u>plus</u> the value of the market excess supply of domestic bonds <u>plus</u> the value of the market excess supply of IOU's to the central bank ("demand for advances") <u>plus</u> the market excess supply of personal IOU's to private financial institutions ("demand for personal loans") <u>plus</u> the value of the excess supply of domestic checkable deposits <u>plus</u> the value of the excess supply of domestic high-powered money <u>plus</u> the value of the excess supply of foreign exchange must equal zero.

Actual Quantities Traded and End-of-Period Stocks

In the market for domestically-produced consumption goods, the actual amount traded during the current period presumably equals the sum of the household, government and foreign sectors' combined demand: $c^{hd}_t + c^{gd}_t + ex_t$. Presumably each component of actual purchases also corresponds to the corresponding desired amount, i.e. $c^h_t = c^{hd}_t$, etc. Assuming that the nonfinancial business sector plans at time t to hold a zero inventory of consumption goods by time t+1, its anticipated (real) sales of consumption goods equals the sum of its current production of those goods plus its initial inventory, Q_t. Consequently, the nonfinancial business sector's end-of-period inventory, Q_{t+1}, of consumption goods is given by (13.222):

$$Q_{t+1} = c_t + Q_t - c^h_t - c^g_t - ex_t. \tag{13.222}$$

As in Chapter 12, the government presumably actually purchases the number of capital goods, $K^g_{t+1} - K^g_t$, that it set out to purchase at the beginning of the period, $K^{gd}_{t+1} - K^g_t$. However, the nominal value of the physical capital that the households actually purchase during the period, $p^k_t(K^h_{t+1} - K^h_t)$, presumably equals the amount that the private financial sector lends to the households as personal loans, $L^h_{t+1} - L^h_t$, where L^h_{t+1} is given by (13.223):

$$L^h_{t+1} = \min(L^{hd}_{t+1}, L^{de}_{t+1}) \tag{13.223}$$

If $L^{hd}_{t+1} > L^{de}_{t+1}$,"credit rationing" exists, causing $K^h_{t+1} < K^{hd}_{t+1}$. But no matter whether $K^h_{t+1} < K^{hd}_{t+1}$, the amount of physical capital held by the nonfinancial business sector at the end of the period is shown by (13.224):

$$K^n_{t+1} = K^n_t + i_t - (K^h_{t+1} - K^h_t) - (K^g_{t+1} - K^g_t) \tag{13.224}$$

where i_t denotes current real production of capital goods. As in the closed-economy version, the total number of people hired by time t+1 is denoted by (13.225):

$$N_{t+1} = \min(N^s_{t+1}, N^{gd}_{t+1} + N^{nd}_{t+1} + N^{fd}_{t+1}) \tag{13.225}$$

In the remaining financial markets, the price-setters are obligated to buy, sell or issue all the bonds, equity shares, checkable deposits, or advances that the price-takers want to trade, acquire or borrow. Consequently, the volume of government bonds, B^g_{t+1}, outstanding at the end of the period corresponds to the government's ex ante supply, B^{gs}_{t+1}; the volume of shares of financial sector equity held by the households at the end of the period, Sf^h_{t+1}, corresponds to the household sector's demand for those shares, Sf^{hd}_{t+1}; the volume of shares of nonfinancial business sector equity held by the households at the end of the period, Sn^h_{t+1}, corresponds to the household sector's demand, Sn^{hd}_{t+1}; and the volume of advances outstanding at time t+1, A_{t+1}, equals the private sector's demand, A^d_{t+1}.

$$B^g_{t+1} = B^{gs}_{t+1} \tag{13.226}$$

$$Sf^h_{t+1} = Sf^{hd}_{t+1} \tag{13.227}$$

$$Sn^h_{t+1} = Sn^{hd}_{t+1} \tag{13.228}$$

$$A_{t+1} = A^d_{t+1} \tag{13.229}$$

Also, the volume of domestic bonds held by the private financial sector at time t+1 equals the number of bonds issued by the government, B^g_{t+1}, minus the number of domestic bonds held by the foreign sector, B^r_{t+1}:

$$B^f_{t+1} = B^g_{t+1} - B^r_{t+1} \tag{13.230}$$

In the foreign exchange market, all sectors outside the domestic private financial institutions presumably hold the amount of foreign exchange they planned to hold: $D^{*g}_{t+1} = D^{*gd}_{t+1}$ and $D^{*n}_{t+1} = D^{*nd}_{t+1}$. Then the amount of foreign exchange actually held by the domestic private financial institutions is determind from (13.130)

$$\begin{aligned} e_tD^{*f}_{t+1} = {} & e_tD^{*f}_t + p^c_tex_t - e_tp^{*c}_t(im^{*h}_t + im^{*g}_t + im^{*n}_t) \\ & + p^b_tB^r_{t+1} - B^r_t + e_tB^{*f}_t - e_tp^{b*}_tB^{*f}_{t+1} \\ & + e_tr^{d*}_{t-1}(D^{*g}_t + D^{*n}_t + D^{*f}_t) + (D^r_{t+1} - D^r_t) - r^d_{t-1}D^r_t \\ & - e_t(D^{*g}_{t+1} + D^{*n}_{t+1} - D^{*g}_t - D^{*n}_t) \end{aligned} \tag{13.231}$$

where

$$B^{*f}_{t+1} = B^{*fd}_{t+1} \qquad (13.232)$$

The end-of-period stocks of the various components of the domestic medium of exchange -- "checkable deposits" and "currency" for those outside the private financial sector and "bank reserves" for the private financial sector itself -- are the only values that remain unspecified. These will be considered next.

Consider, for instance, the nonfinancial business sector's end-of-period holdings of checkable deposits, D^n_t. The value of these deposits may be obtained from the ex post version of its cash-flow constraint:

$$D^n_{t+1} = D^n_t + p^n_t(Sn^h_{t+1} - Sn^h_t) + e_t r^{*d}_{t-1} D^{*n}_t - e_t p^{*c}_t im^{*n}_t$$
$$+ p^c_t c_t + p^k_t i_t + r^d_{t-1} D^n_t - w_t h^n_t N^n_t - e_t(D^{*n}_{t+1} - D^{*n}_t)$$
$$- \pi^n_t Sn^h_t. \qquad (13.233)$$

The household sector's end-of-period holdings of currency, Cu^h_{t+1} presumably equals the beginning-of-period ex ante demand Cu^{hd}_{t+1}:

$$Cu^h_{t+1} = Cu^{hd}_{t+1} \qquad (13.234)$$

Then, from the ex post version of (13.216), we obtain the following expression for the household sector's holdings of checkable deposits, D^h_{t+1}, at the end of the period:

$$D^h_{t+1} = D^h_t + w_t h_t N_t + r^d d_{t-1} D^h_t + \pi^n_t Sn^h_t$$
$$+ \pi^f_t Sf^h_t - Tx_t - p^c_t c^h_t - r^{\ell}_{t-1} L^h_t - e_t p^{*c}_t im^{*h}_t$$
$$- p^n_t(Sn^h_{t+1} - Sn^h_t) - p^f_t(Sf^h_{t+1} - Sf^h_t)$$
$$- (Cu^h_{t+1} - Cu^h_t) \qquad (13.235)$$

Since the household sector is unconstrained with respect to Sf, Sn, and Cu, this end-of-period stock also equals the beginning-of-period ex ante demand D^{hd}_{t+1}:

$$D^{h}_{t+1} = D^{hd}_{t+1}. \qquad (13.236)$$

The government's end-of-period stock of checkable deposits, D^{g}_{t+1}, may be found from the ex post version of (13.215):

$$D^{g}_{t+1} = Tx_{t} + \pi^{cb}_{t} + r^{d}_{t-1}D^{g}_{t} + e_{t}r^{*d}_{t-1}D^{*g}_{t} - B^{g}_{t} - p^{c}_{t}c^{g}_{t}$$

$$- \; w_{t}h^{g}_{t}N^{g}_{t} + D^{g}_{t} - p^{k}_{t}(K^{g}_{t+1} - K^{g}_{t}) + p^{b}_{t}B^{g}_{t+1} - e_{t}p^{*c}_{t}im^{*g}_{t}$$

$$- \; e_{t}(D^{*g}_{t+1} - D^{*g}_{t}) \qquad (13.237)$$

Since K^{g}_{t+1}, B^{g}_{t+1}, im^{*g}_{t}, D^{*g}_{t+1} and c^{g}_{t} all equal their corresponding ex ante values, it follows that

$$D^{g}_{t+1} = D^{gd}_{t+1} \qquad (13.238)$$

The volume of checkable deposits which the government holds at domestic financial institutions at the end of the period corresponds to the amount it planned to hold, given the above assumptions. Total checkable deposits at domestic depository institutions at time t+1 is denoted by

$$D_{t+1} = D^{n}_{t+1} + D^{h}_{t+1} + D^{g}_{t+1} + D^{r}_{t+1} \qquad (13.239)$$

while the stock of money held by the "nonbank public" at time t+1 corresponds to:

$$M_{t+1} = Cu^{h}_{t+1} + D^{n}_{t+1} + D^{h}_{t+1} + D^{r}_{t+1}. \qquad (13.240)$$

The actual volume of reserves, Rs_{t+1}, held by the private depository institutions at the end of the period may be obtained from the ex post version of (13.218)

$$Rs_{t+1} = r^{\ell}_{t-1}L^{h}_{t} + (B^{g}_{t} - B^{r}_{t}) + e_{t}B^{*f}_{t} + e_{t}r^{*d}_{t-1}D^{*f}_{t}$$

$$- \; r^{d}_{t-1}D_{t} - \rho_{t-1}A_{t} - w_{t}h^{f}_{t}N^{f}_{t} - \pi^{f}_{t}Sf^{h}_{t}$$

$$+ \; Rs_{t} - p^{b}_{t}B^{f}_{t+1} - (L^{h}_{t+1} - L^{h}_{t}) - e_{t}p^{*b}_{t}B^{*f}_{t+1}$$

$$- e_t(D^{*f}_{t+1} - D^{*f}_t) + (D_{t+1} - D_t) + (A_{t+1} - A_t)$$

$$+ p^f_t(Sf^h_{t+1} - Sf^h_t). \qquad (13.241)$$

The actual volume of excess reserves, X_{t+1}, at the end of the period is given by:

$$X_{t+1} = Rs_{t+1} - \hat{r}D_{t+1} \qquad (13.242)$$

where $\hat{r}$ denotes the required reserve ratio. Finally, from the central bank's end-of-period balance sheet, the actual volume of the monetary base, MB_{t+1}, outstanding at time t+1 equals the volume of advances at that time.

$$MB_{t+1} = A_{t+1}. \qquad (13.243)$$

National Income and Product

Ignoring imputed interest, the official measures of income and product originating in the nonfinancial business sector may be derived directly from (13.59), that sector's income statement (expressed here in ex post amounts):

$$p^c_tq_t + p^k_ti_t - e_tp^{*c}_tim^{*n}_t + e_tr^{*d}_{t-1}D^{*n}_t = w^n_th^n_tN^n_t + Pr^n_t - r^d_{t-1}D^n_t$$

where $p^c_tq_t$ represents the value of consumption goods produced and $p^c_tq_t + p^k_ti_t - e_tp^{*c}_tim^n_t$ represents the value added by the nonfinancial businss sector in the domestic economy during the current period. The term $e_tr^{*d}_{t-1}D^{*f}_t$ denotes the services produced abroad by the nonfinancial sector's deposits at foreign depository institutions. Consequently the left hand side of (13.248) denotes the value added by the nonfinancial business sector during the current period. The income charges against that production are depicted on the right hand side of that equation with Pr^n_t, as in Chapter 12, denoting current dividends plus additions to retained earnings.

Again ignoring imputed interest, the private financial business sector's income statement, see (13.121), in ex post form serves as a vehicle for expressing the income and product originating in that sector, except that the "financial business sector" in the national income and product accounts also includes the central bank. Consequently interest payments from the private financial business sector to the central bank, $\rho_{t-1}A_t$, cancel when the income statements of these two sectorss are combined to form (13.245):

$$e_t(1-p^{*b}{}_{t-1})B^{*f}{}_t+e_tr^{*d}{}_{t-1}D^{*f}{}_t-r^d{}_{t-1}D^r{}_t = w_th^f{}_tN^f{}_t + Pr^f{}_t + r^d{}_{t-1}(D^h{}_t + D^g{}_t + D^n{}_t) - r^d{}_{t-1}L_t - (1 - p^b{}_{t-1})B^f{}_t. \quad (13.245)$$

The first two terms on the left hand side of (13.245) denote services produced abroad by the financial sector's holdings of foreign bonds and foreign checkable deposits respectively. The term $r^d{}_{t-1}D^r{}_t$, on the other hand, denotes the services produced in the domestic private sector by the foreign sector. These services must be deducted from the first two terms to obtain the net production of the domestic financial sector. With $Pr^f{}_t$ denoting current dividends plus additions to retained earnings, the right hand side of (13.238) represents the net income generated in the domestic financial sector by its country's citizens.

As for the government sector, it presumably generates national product in the domestic economy equal to the wages it pays its employees, $w_th^g{}_tN^g{}_t$, and produces services abroad through its holdings of deposits at foreign institutions equal to the value of the interest it receives on those deposits, $e_tr^{*d}{}_{t-1}D^{*g}{}_t$. Therefore the national product generated by the government sector is given by the left hand side of (13.246). National income

$$e_tr^{*d}{}_{t-1}D^{*g}{}_t + w_th^g{}_tN^g{}_t = e_tr^{*d}{}_{t-1}D^{*g}{}_t + w_th^g{}_tN^g{}_t \quad (13.246)$$

generated in this sector presumably equals the value of the national product generated by this sector and is shown equivalently on the right hand side (13.246).

Summing equations (13.244) - (13.246) yields expression (13.247)

$$p^c{}_tq_t + p^k{}_ti_t - e_tp^c{}_tim^{*n}{}_t + e_tr^{*d}{}_{t-1}(D^{*n}{}_t + D^{*f}{}_t + D^{*g}{}_t) + e_t(1 - p^{*b}{}_{t-1})B^{*f}{}_t - r^d{}_{t-1}D^r{}_t + w_th^g{}_tN^g{}_t$$
$$= w_th_tN_t + Pr^n{}_t + Pr^f{}_t + [r^d{}_{t-1}(D^h{}_t + D^g{}_t) - r^1{}_{t-1}L_t$$

$$- (1 - p^b{}_t)(B^g{}_t - B^r{}_t) + e_t r^{*d}{}_{t-1} D^{*g}{}_t]. \qquad (13.247)$$

where $q_t = c^h{}_t + c^g{}_t + ex_t + (Q_{t+1} - Q_t)$

$$i_t = (K^g{}_{t+1} - K^g{}_t) + (K^h{}_{t+1} - K^h{}_t) + (K^n{}_{t+1} - K^n{}_t)$$

and $w_t h_t N_t = w_t(h^n{}_t N^n{}_t + h^f{}_t N^f{}_t + h^g{}_t N^g{}_t)$

Next, define personal consumption, C_t, government spending on goods and services, G_t, gross (and net) private domestic investment, I_t, exports, E, and imports, Im, respectively as:

$$C_t = p^c{}_t c^h{}_t + e_t p^{*c}{}_t im^{*h}{}_t + p^k{}_t(K^h{}_{t+1} - K^h{}_t)$$

$$G_t = p^c{}_t c^g{}_t + e_t p^{*c}{}_t im^{*g}{}_t + p^k{}_t(K^g{}_{t+1} - K^g{}_t) + w_t h^g{}_t N^g{}_t$$

$$I_t = p^c{}_t(Q_{t+1} - Q_t) + p^k{}_t(K^n{}_{t+1} - K^n{}_t)$$

$$E_t = p^c{}_t ex_t + e_t r^{*d}{}_{t-1}(D^{*n}{}_t + D^{*f}{}_t + D^{*g}{}_t) + e_t(1 - p^{*b}{}_{t-1})B^{*f}{}_t$$

$$Im_t = e_t p^{*c}{}_t(im^{*h}{}_t + im^{*n}{}_t + im^{*g}{}_t) + r^d{}_{t-1} D^r{}_t$$

Then (13.247) becomes:

$$Y_t = C_t + I_t + G_t + (E_t - Im_t) = w_t h_t N_t + Pr^n{}_t + Pr^f{}_t$$
$$+ [r^d{}_{t-1}(D^h{}_t + D^g{}_t) - r^\ell{}_{t-1} L_t$$
$$- (1 - p^b{}_t)(B^g{}_t - B^r{}_t) + e_t r^{*d}{}_{t-1} D^{*g}{}_t]. \qquad (13.248)$$

where Y_t = national product and national income. On the right hand side of (13.244), the first term denotes the general category of "compensation of employees" while the next two represent "corporate profits" plus "proprietors' income". The terms in brackets depict "net interest", as will be shown immediately.

Net interest is defined as:

interest paid by financial and nonfinancial business	$= - r^d{}_{t-1}(D^h{}_t + D^g{}_t + D^r{}_t)$

- interest received by financial and nonfinancial busisness $= - r^{\ell}_{t-1}L_t - (1-p^b_{t-1})(B^g_t - B^r t)$

$- e_t(1 - p^{b*}_{t-1})B^{*f}_t$

$- e_t r^{*d}_{t-1}(D^{*n}_t + D^{*f}_t)$

+ interest paid by foreigners to business and government $= e_t r^{*d}_{t-1}(D^{*g}_t + D^{*n}_t + D^{*f}_t)$

$+ e_t(1 - p^{*b}_t)B^{*f}_t$

- interest paid by financial and nonfinancial business to foreigners $= - r^d_{t-1}D^r_t$

= Net Interest $= r^d_{t-1}(D^h_t + D^g_t) - r^{\ell}_{t-1}L_t$

$- p^b_t(B^g_t - B^r_t) + e_t r^{*d}_{t-1}D^{*g}_t$

Finally, on the "foreign transactions account," the net payments due the domestic economy for goods and services sold abroad, i.e. "net foreign investment," I_r, is given by:

$$I_r = E_t - Im_t - (1 - p^b_{t-1})B^r_t \tag{13.249}$$

where $(1 - p^b_{t-1})B^r_t$ denotes "interest paid by government to foreigners".

Summary of the Recursive Model of a Large Open Economy

In terms of producing observed values, the model presented in this chapter may be regarded as a recursive system in the 53 endogenous variables: h^g_t, c^g_t im^{*g}_t, h^n_t, i_t, w_{t+1}, N^n_{t+1}, D^{*n}_{t+1}, im^{*n}_t, p^c_t, p^k_t, p^n_t, π^n_t, c_t, ρ_t, π^{cb}_t, r^d_t, r^1_t, p^b_t, p^f_t, e_t, A_{t+1}, B^{*f}_{t+1}, π^f_t, h^f_t, N^f_{t+1}, c^h_t, Sf_{t+1}, Sn_{t+1}, Cu_{t+1}, D^h_{t+1}, g_{t+1}, im^{*h}_t, Tx_{t+1}, N^g_{t+1}, K^g_{t+1}, D^g_{t+1}, D^{*g}_{t+1}, B^g_{t+1}, Q_{t+1}, L^h_{t+1}, K^h_{t+1}, K^n_{t+1}, N_{t+1}, B^f_{t+1}, D^{*f}_{t+1}, D^n_{t+1}, D_{t+1}, M_{t+1}, Rs_{t+1}, X_{t+1}, MB_{t+1}, and Y_t. From the assumptions presented above, equations (13.165) - (13.167) yield values for h^g_t, c^g_t and im^{*g}_t. Then, in an unemployment model with $N^s_{t+1} > N^{gd}_{t+1} + N^{nd}_{t+1} + N^{fd}_{t+1}$, equations (13.169) - (13.172) determine h^n_t, i, w_{t+1} and N^n_{t+1} while (13.175) - (13.181) yield the actual values of D^{*n}_{t+1}, im^{*n}_t, p^c_t, p^k_t, p^n_t, π^n_t and c_t respectively. Then, the central bank sets ρ_t and π^{cb}_t through expressions (13.182) - (13.183). Next, the private financial sector decides r^d_t, r^ℓ_t, p^b_t, p^f_t, e_t, A_{t+1}, B^{*f}_{t+1}, π^f_t, h^f_t and N^f_{t+1} in accordance with equations (13.184) - (13.189) and (13.191) - (13.194). The household sector then determines c^h_t, Sf_{t+1}, Sn_{t+1}, Cu_{t+1}, D^h_{t+1}, g_{t+1} and im^{*h}_t in accordance with expressions (13.195) - (13.199), (13.203) and (13.204). Once the household sector has decided the value for g_{t+1}, the government is ready to set Tx_{t+1}, N^g_{t+1}, K^g_{t+1}, D^g_{t+1}, D^{*g}_{t+1} and B^g_{t+1} using equations (13.168) and (13.205) - (13.209). Finally, Q_{t+1}, L^h_{t+1}, K^h_t, K^n_{t+1}, N_{t+1}, B^f_{t+1}, D^{*f}_{t+1}, M_{t+1}, Rs_{t+1}, X_{t+1}, MB_{t+1} and Y_t are determined from equations (13.217), (13.218), (13.41), (13.219), (13.221), (13.225), (13.227), (13.232) - (13.236) and (13.241) respectively.

Linearizing the equations just mentioned and writing them in compact form yields the system:

$$A_t y_t = B_t y_{t-1} + C_t z_t \qquad (12.250)$$

where y_t is the vector of 53 endogenous variables mentioned in the last paragraph, A_t is a lower triangular matrix and z_t is a vector of exogenous variables and shift parameters. The unique feature of (12.250) is that the system not only endogenously determines government production, taxes and the monetary base but also permits optimizing economic agents to set all domestic wages, prices and interest rates plus the exchange rate. System (12.250) views the exchange rate and all domestic quantities and prices as determined through aggragate economic choice.

Impacts of Changes in Selected Foreign Parameters upon the Domestic Economy

In Chapter 12 we examined the short-run effects upon a closed economy arising from exogenous technical advances in the household, government and nonfinancial business sectors' production functions. In the present chapter, the foreign setor provides the source for the changes in variables which the domestic sectors take as given. In particular, we consider the effects upon domestic production employment prices and interest rates due to changes in (a)the foreign-currency price of foreign-produced goods and (b)the interest rate on checkable deposits denominated in foreign currency at foreign depository institutions.

The effects of any one of these exogenous events will depend upon whether these exogenous changes occur before or after the domestic sectors formulate their current-period plans and announce their prices and interest rates. If the domestic plans are formulated and the domestic sectors announcements occur no later than the instant at which the foreign changes become visible, the effects upon the domestic economy will depend upon the extent to which the domestic sectors anticipated these changes in foreign-sector parameters when they formulated their own plans. Not surprisingly, domestic prices and interest rates will tend to adjust more quickly if the foreign-sector changes are anticipated. If these exogenous changes are not foreseen and/or are perceived as ephemeral by the domestic price setters, adjustments in prices and wages will be slower and unforseen changes in money, credit and commodity inventiories are more likely to occur. Consequently, expectations play an important role in determining the levels of output, interest, prices and employment in the model. However, rather than arbitrarily specifying "static," "rational" or "adaptive" expectations, the present model views expectations as exogenously determined, just as it views the household sector's preferences as exogenously determined.

Although not exhaustive, the following example, coupled with those at the end of Chapter 23, illustrate how a democratic economy will choose the optimal combination of household-produced, firm-produced, government-produced and foreign-produced goods as well as the optimal combination of financial assets and liabilities when (a)every wage, price, interest rate and exchange rate is explicityly announced by some optimizing economic agent and (b)the government and central bank play noninterventionist roles. In particular these examples illustrate the dynamic nature of the optimal size of government, the optimal exchange rate and the optimal level of high-powered money. They also indicate the myriad influences that a policy authority who presumes to know better than the aggregate economy what is best for it would have to identify and quantify before it could determine the "optimal" values of these variables.

An Increase in p^{*c}_t

Under the assumptions of the present model the domestic government sector decides its current-period demands for imported goods, domestically-produced consumption goods and hours of labor services before any prices are announced for the current period. It also prepares next period's menu of government-produced goods and taxes for the households before current-period prices are set. Because the present model offers no explanation as to how any sector formulates its expectations, two alternative sets of assumptions are made below as to how the government reacts at the beginning of the period to an increase in p^{*c}_t. In the first case, the government fails to foresee the price increase; in the second case, it correctly anticipates the rise in p^{*c}_t.

If the government does not forsee the rise in p^{*c}_t it will not alter the planned current-period purchases of imported goods, domestic consumption goods or labor services. Under these conditions, it also will not alter the menu it prepares for the household sector with respect to next period's taxes for each alternative level of government-produced goods. However, by the end of the period in this case, the government will find itself spending more on imported goods than it originally intended. Therefore, the government will have to issue more bonds by the end of the current period than it originally planned. Also, because the government will be spending more on imported goods, it (or those agents in the foreign sector who are selling the foreign-produced goods to the government) will demand more foreign money from the domestic financial sector by the end of the period than it would otherwise.

In this model, by the time the government is ready to decide the amount of physical capital it wants to hold by the end of the current period and the number of workers it wants to hire for next period it presumably knows about the higher price of imported goods. Given the amount of government-produced goods that the household sector has by now selected for next period, the government will not alter its end-of-period demands for these items if it anticipates that the higher current-period price of imports is ephemeral. But, if the government anticipates that this higher price will continue next period, it will be induced to substitute physical capital and labor (as well as domestically produced consumption goods) for imported goods in next-period's production of government goods. In this case, its current end-of-period demands for capital goods and labor will increase. Its end-of-period demand for deposits at domestic financial institutions will also be greater, ceteris paribus, since its anticipated expenditures next period on domestic goods and services will be higher. But its end-of-period demand for foreign money will be lower than otherwise because its presumably elastic demand for imported goods will require less foreign exchange next period.

Alternatively, suppose the governmnent sector does foresee the upcoming rise in p^{*c}_t at the beginning of the current period as it formulates its plans for producing the predetermined level of g_t and designs next period's menu for the households. In this case the government's current-period demands for domestic consumption goods and labor services will increase and its current demand for foreign-produced consumption goods will fall. If the government anticipates that the rise in p^{*c}_t will persist next period, it will revise upward the minimum level of taxes it must collect next period from the households in order to provide a given level of services to that sector. In the menu it presents to the household sector for next period, then, each alternative level of g_{t+1} will carry a larger tax bill.

Unlike the government sector, the household sector in the present study waits until all current-period prices and interests rates have been announced before it formulates its supply of labor and its demands for loans, goods and financial assets for the period. If the domestic nonfinancial business sector does not anticipate the rise in p^{*c}_t when it sets the prices of domestic goods, next period's wage rate and the price of its equity shares, then the household sector will face a higher current-period price for foreign-produced goods, but unchanged prices for domestic goods and an unchanged wage rate. If the government sector also has not anticipated the rise in p^{*c}_t in its first stage of decision-making this period, the household sector's current wage income from government-employment will also remain unchanged. In this case the rise in p^{*c}_t produces two effects upon household sector behavior. On the one hand the sector will tend to substitute domestic goods (consumption goods, capital goods and government-produced goods) for foreign-produced goods. On the other hand, the effective loss in income associated with the rise in p^{*c}_t causes the sector to reduce its demands for all goods, to reduce its demands for financial assets and to increase its supply of labor for next period.

If the substitution effects associated with a rise in p^{*c}_t

dominate the income effects with respect to domestic items and if the domestic nonfinancial business sector failed not only to foresee the rise in p^{*c}_t but also to anticipate correctly the household sector's response to this price rise, then by the end of the current period, the domestic nonfinancial business sector will find its end-of-period inventories of consumption goods and capital goods are smaller than it anticipated them to be. The sector will then have to decide whether the unforseen sales of these goods was an anomoly confined to the current period or whether they will continue at the new level.

In addition, if the substitution effects mentioned above do dominate household sector behavior, this sector will increase its current end-of-period demand for loans from private depository institutions in order to finance its increased expeditures on capital goods. If the depository institutions do not anticipate this extra loan demand or the increased demand for domestic checkable deposits by the nonfinancial sectors to finance their extra expenditures next period on domestic goods and services, then the depository institutions will not adjust the interest rates they announce at the beginning of the current period. In this case the sector may have to ration credit to the households by the end of the period. In addition, it will find its deposit liabilities are greater but that its reserves are smaller than it anticipated. (Ceteris paribus, the private financial sector's reserves will fall as the households increase their end-of-period demand for currency to aid in next period's increased purchases of domestic goods.) With a drop in total reserves and an increase in required reserves, the excess reserves of the sector will be lower than it anticipated.

Alternatively, if the substitution effects associated with the rise in p^{*c}_t dominate the household sector's behavior and if the domestic nonfinancial business sector foresees not only this price increase but also its implications for household sector behavior, then the sector will tend to raise the current period prices of both consumption goods and capital goods. It will also decide to produce more of both goods and to increase its current use of labor to produce those goods. In addition, this sector will tend to substitute current labor for imported goods in production this period. If it anticipates that the rise in p^{*c}_t will persist into next period, the sector will also increase its demand for workers for next period. This response coupled with the possibility that the sector also foresees an increase in the government's demand for workers, will induce the domestic nonfinancial business sector to raise next period's wage rate.

If the private depository institutions observe not only the household sector's response to the rise in p^{*c}_t but also the extra labor income to be received by this sector because of the actions by the domestic government and nonfinacial business sectors, then they may anticipate a greater end-of-period demand for personal loans even though the domestic sector has raised the current-period price of capital goods. In this case, the private depository institutions will increase the interest rate on personal loans. If they also foresee the increase in the government's supply of bonds, they will simultaneously reduce the market price of those bonds. And, if they correctly anticipate the increased end-of-period demand for checkable deposits, they will reduce the interest rate on those deposits.

The increased demand for checkable deposits will increase the marginal product of excess reserves held by the depository institutions by the beginning of next period. On the other hand, since the household sector's demand for currency for the end of the period rises, the depository institutions may foresee a drop in their reserves (and hence excess reserves) by the end of the period. Under these conditions, the private financial sector's end-of-period demand for advances from the central bank will increase.

If the central bank foresees this increased demand for advances, it will raise the discount rate this period. Otherwise, it will find by the end of the period that it has granted more loans to depository institutions than it anticipated. At that time, it will need to decide whether the increased demand was an anomoly or the beginning of a sustained increase in the demand for high-powered money.

The effect upon the current exchange rate will depend upon the extent to which the domestic private financial sector is able to predict the effects of the increase in p^{*c}_t upon the "current" and "capital" accounts. If the government spends more on imports because it did not anticipate the rise in p^{*c}_t, a deficit will tend to occur in the nation's balance of payments. If the domestic financial sector foresees it, it will tend to raise e_t; otherwise it will tend to lose foreign exchange to other sectors. Its end-of-period deposits at foreign depository institutions will shrink as a result.

On the other hand, if the household sector's demand for imports is elastic with respect to p^{*c}_t, its outlays for foreign goods will tend to fall. In addition, if the government and private nonfinancial business sectors reduce their respective next-period demands for imports, they will both want to accumulate fewer units of checkable deposits at foreign insitutions by the end of the current period. These responses will tend to produce a surplus in the domestic country's balance of payments. If these effects dominate, and if the private financial sector correctly anticipates these effects at the beginning of the period, it will lower e_t (revalue the nation's currency relative to foreign money).

If a change in e_t does take place, it will have repercussions on the foreign sector's current demands for domestic goods and financial assets as well as the domestic sectors' demands for foreign goods and financial assets. These effects could produce new effects that either counteract or reinforce the ones outlined above.

An Increase in r^{*d}_t

Suppose that the foreign sector at time t raises the interest rate, r^{*c}_t, that it will pay next period on checkable deposits held at foreign depository institutions by time t+1. Under the assumptions of the present model, the domestic government sector does not formulate its end-of-period demand for checkable deposits (foreign and domestic) until after the domestic and foreign depository institutions have announced r^d_t and r^{*d}_t respectively. Consequently, the government will observe the rise in r^{*d}_t in time to adjust its end-of-period balance sheet to that new information. In particular the domestic government sector will tend to increase its end-of-period demand for foreign checkable deposits and to reduce its demand for domestic deposits. The increased income from foreign deposits will tend to reduce the level of taxes the government will have to charge next period to provide a given level of goods to the households. If the government anticipated the rise in r^{*d}_t when it drew up next period's menu for the household sector, it would have incorporated the lower anticipated taxes into that menu. In any case, the government will also tend to borrow more funds in the domestic bond market in the current period, ceteris paribus, in order to purchase more foreign deposits by time t+1.

The domestic nonfinancial business sector, unlike the government sector, presumably plans its own end-of-period balance sheet before current-period interest rates are announced in either country. If the nonfinancial business sector foresees the rise in r^{*d}_t when it formulates its plans, it will tend to substitute foreign deposits for domestic deposits. This tendency to substitute one asset for the other may also affect the transactions costs associated with purchasing goods both at home and abroad. In particular, the anticipated larger volume of deposits denominated in foreign currency tends to reduce the transactions costs associated with imported goods next period while the smaller volume of domestic deposits tends to raise the transactions costs associated with payments to domestic workers next period. This may affect the factor mix the sector plans to use next period to produce consumption and capital goods. (A similar situation could also confront the government sector as it decides what factors to use in producing g_{t+1} next period.)

The household sector is not directly affected by a change in r^{*d}_t in this study since it presumably does not hold checkable deposits at foreign institutions. But the foreign sector presumably is directly affected by the change in r^{*d}_t. Assume that this sector's demand for domestic checkable deposits and domestic bonds diminishes as r^{*d}_t rises.

If the domestic depository institutions foresee the rise in r^{*d}_t they will want to hold more deposits at foreign institutions by time t+1. Since the actual volume they end up holding by time t+1 is closely related to the nation's balance of payments during the period, the domestic institutions will tend, ceteris paribus, to raise the exchange rate in order to induce a balance of payments surplus that will tend therefore to increase their own holdings of deposits at foreign institutions by time t+1. In addition, if the domestic depository instituitions also foresee the domestic government and foreign sectors' responses to the rise in r^{*d}_t, they will anticipate that unless they do raise e_t they will tend to lose their deposits at foreign institutions to these sectors. Consequently the domestic institutions have an added incentive to raise e_t.

If the domestic depository institutions also foresee the increased supply of government bonds and the reduced foreign-sector demand for them, it will tend to reduce the current period price of those bonds. Otherwise, it will find itself holding more of those bonds by the end of the period than it intended to hold. In addition, if the domestic depository institutions foresee the drop in the end-of-period demand for domestic checkable deposits, they will raise the interest rate on those deposits. By itself, the anticipated reduction in the demand for checkable deposits will reduce the marginal product of excess reserves held by time t+1. This tends to reduce the sector's demand for advances for time t+1.

Although the household sector's behavior is not directly affected by a change in r^{*d}_t, it will respond to any adjustment in the exchange rate. In particular as the private depository institutions raise e_t, the domestic households will tend to substitute domestically produced goods for foreign goods. Consequently their demand for domestic consumption goods, domestic capital goods and even government-produced goods will tend to rise. The tendency to demand more government goods is enhanced by the lower taxes the government will need to charge next period to provide a given level of g_{t+1} because of the rise in r^{*d}_t. (But if the government also incorporates a higher e_t in its estimate of next-period's menu, the menu may show that higher rather than lower taxes will be necessary next period to provide a given level of g_{t+1}.)

If the household sector's demand for domestic physical capital does rise with e_t, so will its demand for personal loans. When the private financial sector recognizes this increase in the demand for loans, it will announce a higher interest rate on those loans.

When the private nonfinancial business sector recognizes the increase in the household sector's demand for consumption and capital goods and feels the change will continue, it will raise production of those items as well as their prices. As a result it will employ its current workers longer hours and increase its demand for workers for next period. This higher labor income in turn may induce households to buy more goods next period and therefore to hold more checkable deposits and currency at the end of the period. If the depository institutions recoginize this effect and feel it will more than offset the original tendency for domestic checkable deposits to fall, they will tend to demand more high-powered money from the central bank, rather than less. If the central bank anticipates this, it will raise the discount rate. Otherwise, it will find itself issuing more advances by the end of the period than it intended at the old discount rate. Even if the central bank does not anticipate market forces, these forces will produce effects that cause the central bank to recognize later that economic conditions have changed.

Summary

The present chapter offers a dynamic disequilibruim model of a large open economy in which the behavior of all domestic sectors are based upon internally consistent microfoundations. Optimizing economic agents set all domestic wages, prices and interest rates and the domestic private financial sector sets the exchange rate between the domestic and foreign units of account. Furthermore taxes, government spending, the money supply and the monetary base all adjust endogenously in this model. The values of all these variables respond not to the dictates of an outside policy authority but to aggregate economic choices by the domestic household, government, business and central banking sectors as well as the foreign sector, with the government and central bank playing noninterventionist roles.

14. Conclusion

This study represents an attempt to construct an aggregate disequilibrium model of economic choice in which every wage, price, interest rate and even the economy's exchange rate is set by some optimizing economic agent. Because no sector possesses complete knowledge, the price-setters in this study may find that they are selling more or fewer goods, purchasing more or fewer government bonds, granting more or fewer personal loans, selling more or fewer equity shares, issuing more or fewer checkable deposits and buying more or less labor or foreign exchange than they anticipated when they set their prices.

The price-setters respond optimally in this model to unanticipated changes in their inventories or orders. Each price-setter's micro-foundations include the optimal response to existing "beginning-of-period" quantities. Over time, these beginning-of-period stocks will move in an unanticipated manner if the price-setter's actual sales differ from the anticipated amount.

This treatment is consistent with Kaldor's (1985) emphasis upon sellers as "price-makers and not price-takers." It also conforms with Weintraub's (1979) assertion that the appropriate microfoundations for macro pertain to "coordination failure" rather than to "coordination success." In addition it follows Fisher's (1983) basic notion that a proper disequilibrium theory views economic agents adjusting optimally to disequilibrium states.

The microfoundations of the optimal behavior of a given economic agent in a given market in this study are mutually consistent with the microfoundations of that agent's activities in every other market. For instance, instead of separate theories of the household sector's consumption demand, supply of labor, and demands for financial assets, a single model produces the sector's optimal behavior in every market in which it participates.

Money is a productive resource because it enables the holder to reduce the amount of time he devotes to transactions. Consequently, money releases real resources to other uses. As a result , economic agents are willing to hold money even though the market yields on other assets may be greater. This special feature of money, as well as its constant nominal value are explicitly integrated into the microfoundations of the various sectors who demand money in this study.

No economic agent directly controls the quantity of money in this model. Optimizing depository institutions instead set the interest rate on checkable deposits at the level they calculate will maximize their present value (in light of their other decisions). They then stand ready for a real length of time to accept at that rate all their customer's deposits. Their depositors include the foreign sector as well as the domestic household, government and private nonfinancial business sectors.

The central bank is prohibited from unilaterally altering the level of high-powered money in this study. It is precluded from engaging in open-market operations, adjusting the required reserve ratio or trading in the foreign-exchange market. Instead, its only activity consists of lending high-powered money to domestic private depository institutions upon demand. The central bank sets the discount rate on its advances at the level it estimates will maximize its own interest income. As we have seen through several examples, the central bank will tend to end to raise the discount rate as the demand for advances (and domestic high-powered money) grows and lower this rate as demand diminishes. As a result, central bank tends to provide new high-powered money when it is needed and to absorb it when it is in excess. But the central bank also tends to reset the discount rate to "lean against the wind" automatically.

The quantity of goods and services provided by the government sector in this study is ultimately decided by the households. The government prepares a menu for the households showing alternative levels of government-produced goods and corresponding tax burdens. The household sector, in light of its other decisions, then selects the optimal amount. The government's objective is to produce at minimum cost the level of production selected by the households.

Because of the roles assigned to the government and central bank, the present study offers no policy prescriptions for alleviating inflation or unemployment or for promoting economic growth. Neither the government nor the central bank is assumed to know better than the private sectors the optimal levels of prices, production, employment, interest rates, or exchange rates.

Instead, the objective of this study has been to understand some of the factors affecting aggregate economic choice in a democratic society whose government and central bank exist for the purpose of serving the private sector rather than controlling it. (The noninterventionist role assumed by the government in this model does not preclude society from erecting a system of transfers from those who are earning incomes to those who are not. Society may even decide to rely upon the government sector to facilitate their collection and payment.) Basically the analysis presented above indicates that the household sector will tend to demand more government-produced goods as its income and wealth grows. It will also tend to substitute government-produced goods for privately-produced goods as the prices of the latter grow. However, because the government must purchase privately-produced goods for its own production, it must usually raise the level of taxes it requires to produce a given volume of goods when the prices of privately-produced goods rise. Whether the households will select more or fewer government-goods under these conditions will depend upon the relative efficiency of the government sector (its ability to substitute factors whose prices have not risen in price) and the household sector's subjective rate of substitution between government-produced and privately-produced goods.

The models presented in this study ignore population growth, physical depreciation and endogenous technical progress. They also specify a particular sequence through which price information flows from one sector to another. The incorporation of endogenous technical progress or population growth or the specification of alternative patterns of information flows represent possible extensions of the present study.

All of the above examples pertaining to the effects of exogenous shocks (contained in Chapters 5, 6, 12 and 13), from the simplest (two-sector model) to the most complex (six-sector model), indicate that the economic effects of these shocks depend crucially upon whether they are foreseen by the various sectors and whether they are regarded as anomolies or as more permanent shifts. The planning horizons of the various sectors have not been specified in this study in terms of calendar time. Specific assumptions as to the length of "calendar" time of a price-setter's "current-period" could produce a pattern whereby interest rates and exchange rates change almost instantaneously while other prices change less rapidly and the level of government production responds very slowly. The general models presented in this study support Hahn's (1985) statement that "Although ... it is false that 'anything can be true' it is the case that a number of different things could usually be true ... The set of outcomes which are possible is simply the reflection of our lack of knowledge."

References

Fisher, F., 1983, Disequilibrium Foundations of Equilibrium Economics (Cambridge University Press, Cambridge).

Hahn, F., 1984, Equilibrium and Macroeconomics (MIT Press, Cambridge).

Kaldor, N., 1985, Economics without Equilibrium (M. E. Sharpe, Inc., Armonk).

Weintraub, E. Roy, 1979, Microfoundations, (Cambridge University Press, Cambridge).